KVO

Advancing Relational Leadership Research

A Dialogue Among Perspectives

A volume in
Leadership Horizons
Mary Uhl-Bien, *Series Editor*

Advancing Relational Leadership Research

A Dialogue Among Perspectives

edited by

Mary Uhl-Bien
University of Nebraska

Sonia M. Ospina
New York University

INFORMATION AGE PUBLISHING, INC.
Charlotte, NC • www.infoagepub.com

Library of Congress Cataloging-in-Publication Data

Advancing relational leadership research : a dialogue among perspectives /
edited by Mary Uhl-Bien, Sonia M. Ospina.
   p. cm. – (Leadership horizons)
 Includes bibliographical references.
 ISBN 978-1-61735-921-7 (pbk.) – ISBN 978-1-61735-922-4 (hardcover) –
ISBN 978-1-61735-923-1 (ebook) 1. Leadership–Research. I. Uhl-Bien,
Mary. II. Ospina, Sonia, 1955-
 HD57.7.A3178 2012
 303.3'4–dc23

                                 2012020711

Printed in the United States of America

DEDICATION

*To my husband Roger, who has taught me the true meaning
of relationality; and to my three children, for their support
when work had to come before play.*

—MUB

*To Richard Williams, husband and friend, whose brilliant mind
(and gentle soul) are a source of admiration and support; and to our son,
Ernesto, and my parents Alberto and Lola, whose interest and pride
in my work are a source of delight.*

—SMO

CONTENTS

PART II

RESEARCHING THE RELATIONAL LEADERSHIP

PART III

A CONVERSATION ACROSS PERSPECTIVES

SERIES INTRODUCTION

We continue the *Leadership Horizons* series with this sixth volume on relational leadership research, edited by Mary Uhl-Bien and Sonia M. Ospina. The purpose of this series is to challenge traditional thinking and aggressively push beyond current leadership orthodoxy to open new avenues for leadership research and practice. I believe you will find this volume fully in line with that purpose.

The volume convenes for the first time an extended discussion among entity and constructionist scholars regarding the relational nature of leadership. It also advances a much-needed discussion of paradigmatic issues in leadership research—a topic that has been overlooked in a field that may have become too paradigmatic too soon.

For those of us trained in more entitative (postpositive) perspectives, this book will challenge our thinking and assumptions about leadership on a deep level. It contains much that is unfamiliar, and some that may even be troubling, when considered relative to the assumptions in which we have been trained. For those trained in interpretivist (constructionist) perspectives, this book will raise all-too-familiar issues, but hopefully with a more open mind and dialogue than we have seen in the "paradigm wars" of the past. The express purpose is to create a space for more voices to be heard, and to challenge all of us to think more deeply about the assumptions we bring to our research.

I believe this book represents a significant advancement for the leadership field. I hope you find it enlightening, and that together we are challenged to not only continue, but to embrace, this very important dialogue at the heart of leadership research and practice.

Mary Uhl-Bien
University of Nebraska

Advancing Relational Leadership Research, page xi
Copyright © 2012 by Information Age Publishing
All rights of reproduction in any form reserved.

FOREWORD

As editors, we came to this book from very different starting points. Mary was trained in leader-member exchange (LMX) theory, and approached relational leadership from the standpoint of the leader-member (i.e., manager-subordinate) dyad. Sonia was trained in sociology and interpretive methods and approached relational leadership from the standpoint of constructionism, specifically to explore the nature of social change leadership.

Because of this, we decided to separate our voices in the Foreword so we can tell the stories of our motivations and passions behind this book. In the space below (beginning with Mary and ending with Sonia), we each share our journey leading to the production of this volume, and share our hopes and aspirations for the book and for the study of relational leadership.

Mary Uhl-Bien

One of the most common reactions to the paper I wrote for *The Leadership Quarterly* (*LQ*) in 2006 on relational leadership theory is, "I love the article, but I have no idea what to do with it." I could relate. I, too, had been struggling with the issues raised in that article, and after the 2006 piece, I still did not have clear answers. I knew we had to do something about the fact that leadership theory is missing the boat on matters of relationality. But because I was constrained by my training in LMX theory and survey methods, I could not see my way out of the dilemma.

The problem became apparent to me after George Graen and I wrote the LMX piece for the special issue on levels of analysis edited by Fred

Advancing Relational Leadership Research, pages xiii–xviii
Copyright © 2012 by Information Age Publishing
xiii

Dansereau in 1995. In commenting on our paper in the Introduction to the Special Issue (Part I, Summer 1995), Fred Dansereau, Fran Yammarino, and Steve Markham said, "Graen and Uhl-Bien suggest to us that the leader-member exchange (LMX) approach focuses solely on relationships...the leader and follower *per se* are not of interest in this approach . . . " (p. 100). I didn't understand. This certainly didn't square with the way George and I had been thinking about LMX; in fact, it was probably the complete opposite. *How could it be that we were looking at a dyad but not considering individuals?* We knew we were looking at individuals, but our theory was also clearly about the dyad. Why couldn't it be both?

For years, I pondered this question. As I began to read more broadly and better recognize the problems related to dyadic levels of analysis, the question evolved into the challenge of thinking about how to measure a relationship. It was obvious to me that a relationship was something between people—it couldn't just be an individual, because that was individual level, and not relational. But how do you get at the *relationship*, the "space between?"

It was this thinking that allowed me to so readily grasp on to complexity science, which is fundamentally about relationality. But it didn't get me out of the predicament on the LMX side, which became even worse when I "found" Dian Marie Hosking's work on relational leadership in Jerry Hunt and George Dodge's 2001 "Leadership Déjà vu" article in *LQ*. After reading Dian Marie's papers I was both *mortified* that in all my years of LMX research I had never come across her work, and *relieved* to find someone who was talking about issues of relationality. I began to see a light at the end of the tunnel.

By the time I wrote the 2006 article, I was convinced that LMX would not be able to get us to issues of relationality, and because of this, we needed work on *relational leadership theory*. I was also convinced that relational leadership theory would require methods and assumptions beyond those in which I was trained. Where to go from there, however, was still unclear. It was then that Sonia called me, not long after she saw the relational leadership article appear in press. It turned out that Sonia, too, had been thinking deeply about these issues, but she came at it from a very different place. As Sonia describes in this book, part of her frustration came from the fact that interpretivist methods had something to say about relationality, but they were being shut out of the discussion.

With Sonia, I had found someone who shared my passion for issues of relationality and my desire to strive for broader understandings of leadership. In that phone call, we decided to do this book. As it turned out, the process took much longer than anticipated . . . we had no idea what we were about to undertake. As you will see in reading the volume, these issues are not easy, and trying to engage across paradigms can feel like walking into a snake pit. It took ongoing and sustained dialogue between Sonia and me to sort through the issues, while coming to terms with our own understandings, biases, and naiveties. The real breakthrough came when the Romani, Primecz and Topcu article was published in the February 2011 issue of *Organizational Research Methods* (see the conclusion for the reference), and we were exposed to the concept of "paradigm interplay." It was at that point that we had a tool for effectively sorting through the conflicting perspectives presented in the book.

Speaking for myself, I can say that, while this project has been immensely challenging, it has also been a labor of love...and I am thoroughly enriched from the experience. I am tremendously grateful to Sonia for her intellectual engagement, passion for relationality, patience in teaching me the things I didn't understand, and tenacity in seeing this project through. Having come out of the 2006 paper feeling like I had laid out the issues but not really done much to help us get past them, I set a lofty goal: I wanted us to advance a strong multidisciplinary conversation that enhances (my own and the field's) understanding of relational leadership. It was Sonia who allowed that goal to become a reality.

I can now say that I finally get it—I understand the issue from the varied perspectives. And I have a clear understanding of the implications for us as relational leadership researchers. What I can conclude from my newfound understanding is this: The "answer" does not lie in one side or another; it requires multi-paradigmatic approaches. To advance knowledge of relational leadership, we need to engage scholars across disciplines and perspectives. This book is an attempt to do just that. And if we are successful, then this book will not be an end, but a beginning. Only time will tell...

Mary Uhl-Bien
University of Nebraska

Sonia M. Ospina

Around 2000—about midway into my career as a sociologist studying public service organizations—an exciting research opportunity about social change organizations led me to the leadership literature, and to a process that eventually shaped a new identity for me as a relational leadership scholar. I was an outsider entering unknown territory and knew I had a lot to learn; that said, I did not expect to experience such a sense of bewilderment.

That the literature privileged individuals as the source of leadership helped me understand why the topic was of little interest in contemporary sociology. Key areas of agreement among mainstream scholars seemed to be a preference for quantitative models and a misunderstanding of other methodological approaches, such as interpretivism. I also noticed that approaches and themes varied considerably by disciplinary silos (psychology, political science, management, communication, education, policy, and so on), by cultural and geographical location of scholars (the U.S., Latin America, Europe, Australasia, and so on), by sector sensibilities (research on business, government, nonprofits), and by inherited assumptions from multiple leadership schools. For the most part, people did not seem to be speaking across these silos.

The compartmentalization of ideas and lack of methodological pluralism made me see the leadership studies landscape as a "fault zone." Geologists say this is what the bare eyes can observe in the surface of a landscape as evidence of numerous internal fractures or discontinuities—*fault lines* associated with underground activity. The most ubiquitous fault line was between entity and constructionist perspectives on leadership. Work from these perspectives could have clearly belonged to different fields. But, the absence of conversation about these fractures and discontinuities—despite their glaring existence—was even more disconcerting. So was the sense that most knowledge about "leaders" seemed either incomplete or too obvious, and seemed to replicate narratives that legitimized and reproduced conditions unsupportive of human flourishing in organizations and society.

In scanning the landscape to shape our research project, I found the entity perspective's psychological lens wanting. In contrast, the then-scant work of constructionists like Drath and Hosking had resonance. Its attention to context and social embeddedness and its emphasis on the collective dimensions of leadership appealed to the sociologist in me. This refreshing approach to the study of leadership—one that punctuated so nicely the tensions between agency and structure, the individual and the collective—seemed appropriate for the multi-year research project upon which my colleagues and I were embarking.

Midcourse, however, we stumbled upon a realization that becoming interlocutors in the mainstream leadership conversation would not be easy. First, given the many conversations going on, we would have to choose *where*, in the fractured leadership landscape, we would locate our findings—at the risk of closing doors to other exchanges. We then realized that the early bet we made to use constructionism meant that we also risked our voice being dismissed in the mainstream leadership field, regardless of the project's rigor and quality.

It was in the midst of such realizations that Mary and I met in 2006. We had both published pieces that year about constructionism in leadership, but coming from such different places, we had not cited one another. I remember reading her piece and lamenting not having read before the work of this interesting entity scholar. As we talked, we realized that our conversation (across perspectives) was worth extending to others—that perhaps it could add value to the field. Thus grew the idea for doing this book.

The co-editorial process was itself a scholarly adventure and a deep developmental process, as we challenged and learned from one another and from the contributors every step of the way. It also reaffirmed the urgency of this conversation for the field. The more I understood Mary's motivations to push the boundaries of the entity side, the more I appreciated its depth and complexity with new eyes—and the more humbled I felt *vis a vis* its scholarship. I had dismissed the entity perspective too lightly, and going back to it was quite educational; I had much more to learn than I had originally thought. Our exchanges also demanded clarifying my claims about the constructionist perspective, as I had to spell out assumptions and explain taken-for-granted principles to a partner offering a critical ear.

Perhaps we were lucky to share similar sensibilities that helped us place our own perspectives at some distance and see the other's with some curiosity, even if it meant struggling with unfamiliar meanings and constructs that, when clarified, opened ever-more new vistas. This was part of the process that we later learned scholars call "paradigm interplay." It helped us go to intellectual places that I believe we would not have dared to go without each other's support.

Much has changed in the leadership field over the time that I grew into it. I would have never guessed 12 years ago that I would call myself a leadership scholar today, that leadership research could be so sociologically interesting, and that conversations with both entity and constructionist scholars would feel so stimulating. Such recognition has been a turning point for fully embracing this identity. The process had begun in collaboration with my research partners Ellen Schall, Erica Foldy and our colleagues at the Research Center for Leadership in Action, as we engaged the leaders who participated in the social change leadership research project. For all of their contributions I am grateful.

Now I've come full circle to count leadership scholars of both entity and constructionist perspectives as valuable peers in an important community of reference. The experience of co-editing this book with Mary has fully reinforced this. For her partnership and guidance in navigating the leadership landscape, I am indebted, and I particularly appreciate her relational style, inviting and inclusive, and her willingness to open her world with such generosity.

I hope that reading the chapters in this volume will stimulate provocative conversations, open intellectual doors, and build collaborative bridges for other scholars as much as working on it has done for me. I also trust that it will further clarify the meaning of the fault lines and fault zones in the field, so that we learn to make constructive sense of its fractures and discontinuities. As for the study of relational leadership, I cannot but hope that as the conversation across perspectives continues to deepen, insights will help practitioners make leadership happen more fully for the collective good, independent of their position in the web of relationships that shapes their organization.

Sonia M. Ospina
New York University

INTRODUCTION

MAPPING THE TERRAIN

Convergence and Divergence Around
Relational Leadership

Sonia M. Ospina and Mary Uhl-Bien

Relation: *an aspect or quality (as resemblance) that connects two or more things or parts as being or belonging or working.*

Relational: *characterized or constituted by* <u>*relations*</u>.

Relationality: *the state or property of having a relational force; the state or condition of being* <u>*relational*</u>.

Relationship: *the state of being* <u>*related*</u> *or interrelated; the* <u>*relation*</u> *connecting or binding participants in a relationship; a state of affairs existing between those having* <u>*relations*</u> *or dealings.*[1]

The "relational turn" has arrived to the scholarly field of leadership studies, as it arrived earlier in other fields and disciplines (Berscheid, 1999; Emirbayer, 1997; Slife, 2004). Many leadership scholars now acknowledge that both leaders and followers are "relational beings" who constitute each other as such—leader *and* follower . . . leader *or* follower—in an unfolding, dynamic relationship (Brower, Schoorman, & Tan, 2000; Crevani, Lindgren, & Packendorff, 2007; Dachler & Hosking, 1995; Ford & Seers, 2006;

Advancing Relational Leadership Research, pages xix–xlvii
Copyright © 2012 by Information Age Publishing
All rights of reproduction in any form reserved.

Ospina & Sorenson, 2006; Uhl-Bien, 2006). This powerful idea is quite consistent with the notion of "relationality," an understanding that individuals and collectives constitute *a field of relationships* (Bradbury & Lichtenstein, 2000; Carroll, Levy, & Richmond, 2008). As Gergen (2009) claims in his book *Relational Being*, "the individual represents the common intersection of myriad relationships" (p. 150). Bringing relationality to the leadership field means viewing the invisible threads that connect actors engaged in leadership processes and relationships as part of the reality to be studied. As these ideas have gained currency, the construct of *relational leadership* has emerged to convey the intellectual efforts, theoretical reflections and methodological ways of taking up relationality in leadership theorizing, research, and practice (Drath, 2001; Uhl-Bien, 2006).

As scholars participate in the relational turn, their understanding of what it means and how we ought to access the reality of leadership is challenged. Important shifts occur in their ways of seeing. Noteworthy examples include recent shifts of attention in the literature from the leader and/or the follower to the "reciprocal relationship" as a core target for conceptualizing and studying leadership (Huxham & Vangen, 2000; Shamir, Pillai, Bligh, & Uhl-Bien, 2007), and from individual to shared and distributed forms of leadership (Gronn, 2002; Mehra, Smith, Dixon, & Robertson, 2006; Pearce & Conger, 2003). Of equal interest are calls to shift attention from leadership actors to relational practices, as well as to communicative and organizing processes associated with the emergence of leadership (Drath, McCauley, Palus, Van Velsor, O'Connor & McGuire, 2008; Fairhurst, 2007; Hosking, 1988; 2007; Ospina & Foldy, 2010).

These examples from the literature reflect genuine interest in exploring relational leadership. They are leading-edge thinking, however, more so than being a broad trend in the field. The good news is that they suggest a process of convergence around greater interest in relationality among scholars who otherwise continue to have profound philosophical differences (see Chapter 1). The bad news is that there is still a long way to go. Indeed, clarifying what it means to emphasize "relationship" or to introduce the idea of "relationality" in leadership studies is still subject to considerable bemusement and debate, as the passionate conversations in this volume attest.

This is not surprising. The consequences of taking the relational turn for the field as a whole can be quite disorienting. Doing so can challenge some of our most ingrained assumptions and mental models of concepts directly associated with leadership, such as individuality, independence, rationality and agency. Slife (2004) describes the shift toward a "relational ontology" in the practice of psychology as follows:

> Suddenly, the engaged and situated character of our lives becomes clear. We are no longer primarily rational beings, with our minds and ideas as our only

or even our primary resources. We are contextual beings, with inbuilt relational resources to other contextual beings. (Slife, 2004, p. 174)

Gergen (2009) goes further in his book's conclusion: "... virtually all faculties traditionally attributed to the internal world of the agent—reason, emotion, motivation, memory, experience, and the like—are essentially performances within relationship" (p. 397). He goes on:

> ... in all that we say and do we manifest our relational existence. From this standpoint, we must abandon the view that those around us cause our actions. Others are not the causes, nor we their effects. Rather, in whatever we think, remember, create, and feel, we *participate* in relationship. (p. 397)

What would it mean for our understanding of leadership to seriously filter its current constructs through a relational lens? What would the notion of "participating in relationship" imply for our ideas of leaders and followers, for their agency, and for the leadership phenomenon as such? What would be the implications of redefining actors who are engaged in leadership processes and relationships from rational, self-contained individuals to contextual, relational beings?

While some scholars are increasingly posing these questions, they are yet to be answered for the field as a whole. Despite significant efforts to address them in the literature, relational concerns remain largely unresolved in the leadership conversation. Suffice it to say that as this challenge is taken up, new ways of tackling the field's recurrent concerns—process and context (Osborn, Hunt, & Jauch, 2002), language and discourse (Dachler, 1992; Fairhurst, 2007), time and levels of analysis (Marrone, Tesluk, & Carson, 2007; Yammarino, Dionne, Chun, & Dansereau, 2005)—have yet to emerge. After all, these issues are at the core of unpacking what it means to talk about relational leadership. We believe that the time is ripe to face them head-on. The budding convergence of interest in relational leadership across a group of diverse leadership scholars represents the perfect moment to seize the opportunity.

The field cannot afford to wait any longer. As we have entered the twenty-first century, issues of relationality have become more evident and are now paramount in the attention of those experiencing the reality (and practice) of leadership. Indeed, the incipient development of the relational turn in leadership scholarship lags behind the demand for relational solutions in the world of practice. There is a hunger to find novel ways to respond to the organizing challenges stakeholders face in our post-industrial, communication technology-driven, social media-oriented, global society. A complex social environment—characterized by conditions such as scarcity, uncertainty, interdependence, diversity, participation, and paradox—makes even more evident the relational nature of social processes like organizing and leadership (Blandin, 2007; Rost, 1993; Uhl-Bien, Marion, & McKelvey, 2007). There is increasing awareness among practitioners that today, no one single person can provide leadership acting alone (Crosby and Bryson, 2005). They recognize that complex, adaptive challenges (Heifetz, 1994) require the collective action of many people, located in different parts of interconnected networks, in *systems of systems*. Identifying the type of leadership required to successfully address the demands of this complex and nested environment is a task of utmost urgency (Heifetz & Linsky, 2002; Raelin, 2010).

The convergence around interest in the relational dimensions of leadership has great potential to help close this gap and define the future direction of the field. This, however, requires an understanding of the intersection among very different views. Studies of relational leadership today fall somewhere between two radically different perspectives, each of which speaks its own language and draws from dissimilar logics of inquiry. On the one side, an *entity* perspective on relational leadership (independent of which theoretical school it reflects) considers traits, behaviors, and actions of individuals or group members as they engage in interpersonal relationships to influence one another; on the other side, a *constructionist* perspective considers processes of social construction and emergent practices that reflect common understandings through which leadership gains legitimacy and produces outcomes.

Although these two perspectives might together add rich new understandings to relational leadership, the lack of openness to methodological pluralism and limited dialogue across perspectives have prevented them from interacting with one another in insightful and informative ways. Instead, the work of entity and constructionist scholars is occurring along parallel, and largely incommensurable, paths.

To address this problem, we suggest that *interplay* (Romani, Primecz, & Topcu, 2011) across the multiple views of relational leadership can substantially advance theoretical and empirical understanding of the processes and dynamics of leadership. Paradigm interplay can clarify the interconnections between individual and relational dimensions of leadership. It can offer insights to help practitioners face challenges with more useful conceptual handles (Vangen & Huxham, 2003) and for scholars to find ways of better understanding the intricate nature of leadership. As this book will demonstrate, this is not an easy task to undertake, but we believe it is imperative for advancing new understandings of leadership.

We strive for interplay in this book by assembling a group of forward-thinking scholars representing a broad spectrum of perspectives. We asked them to engage in multi-paradigmatic dialogue regarding the critical theoretical and research challenges in the study of relational leadership. Our original invitation to contributors stated that we hoped to develop a constructive dialogue among scholars representing the diverse perspectives constituting what Uhl-Bien (2006) coined *Relational Leadership Theory (RLT)* and Ospina and Sorenson (2006) referred to as the competing "mental models" that have defined the field. RLT suggested a vision (not yet realized) of an overarching framework for a variety of philosophical stances and methodological approaches to study *relationships* (interpersonal relationships as outcomes of, or as contexts for, interactions) and the *relational dynamics* (social interactions and social constructions) of leadership. The vision was that, independent of their emphasis on one or the other, scholars would engage in mutual learning about their ideas of *relationality* and its implications for leadership.

In our call for papers, we explicitly invited contributions from entity and constructionist scholars, calling for work that would engage the perspectives in dialogue. We also invited three pairs of leadership scholars (representing both perspectives) to read the contributions, engage in dialogue, and document their reactions and exchanges so they would become additional contributions to the book. The positive response to our call itself was evidence that the time was ripe for this conversation. The diversity of the issues raised in the contributions, the passion generated in the exchanges, and the persistent use of *the same words* to *convey different meanings and assumptions* about relational leadership also evidenced the urgency of the conversation.

These responses surface a question that is woven through the narrative of this introduction and throughout the book: Is it possible to find a space of convergence for the theorizing, research, and clinical agendas of the contributors, despite the different perspectives they bring? The answer offered by contributors is neither a unified "yes" nor a "no"; ultimately the reader must decide. We struggled with it ourselves as co-editors and learned immensely from the generative tensions that emerged from our joint efforts to produce this book given our different perspectives: Mary coming from an entity and Sonia from a constructionist tradition.

To help the reader understand the nature of the challenge, in this introductory chapter we offer a "map of the terrain" that locates the rich debates emanating throughout the chapters and dialogues in this volume. Because knowledge of the paradigmatic assumptions and assertions behind these debates is key to advancing dialogue in relational leadership, we begin by providing background in the philosophy and sociology of science to ground readers in issues of *incommensurability* and paradigm interplay (We elaborate on this in Chapter 1.) In this discussion, we contextualize leadership within the broader conversation of organization and social science research. We then present our "map" (Figure I.1) that depicts a continuum of paradigmatic perspectives brought by the authors in this book. This map helps readers to see the not-so-obvious philosophical assumptions and paradigmatic assertions implicit in the authors' theorizing. We conclude by describing the logic and structure of the book, and we provide an overview of the book's contents with a summary of the chapter contents.

THE NEED FOR INTERPLAY

This book aims to speak to leadership scholars—both those with a long trajectory in the field and those in training—who aspire to produce knowledge on leadership that is also relevant to practice. We hope the conversation resonates across perspectives regarding what constitutes legitimate research (more about this below). Because issues of legitimacy are critical to establishing the basis for an interplay among diverse scholars, we introduce below some ideas from the philosophy and the sociology of science to set the stage for the conversations that follow.

The Contested Nature of Knowledge Generation

Embedded in contemporary social science research debates are questions regarding *how can something be researched.* Answering these questions requires answering in turn questions about *how can we develop knowledge about the world* and *what is the nature of the world and of human beings.* These questions, drawn from the philosophy of science, reflect concerns of methodology (how can we capture the object of research), epistemology (how do we know what we know) and ontology (what is the nature of reality), respectively. The pragmatic methodology answer depends on responses to ontological and epistemological questions, which in turn inform the theoretical perspectives of the proposed research. This sequence of influence happens whether the researcher is aware of it or not.

Scholars who have similar perspectives on questions of ontology and epistemology will most likely agree on the best way to do research (i.e., methodology). Hatch and Yanow (2008) argue that the word "methodology" can be understood as "'applied' ontology and epistemology" (p. 3) because it "refers to the philosophical presuppositions embedded in research methods—the assumptions, often unintentionally and even unconsciously made, about the 'reality status' of the subject under study and about its 'know-ability.'" Methodologies, they argue, "provide logical structures from which to derive procedures of inquiry (methods), and they frame the ways in which we understand their products" (p. 4). Hatch and Yanow (2008) invite management and organizational researchers to be more explicitly reflective about these presuppositions and assumptions, as a way to foster scholarship in organization studies. With this book, we see this call extending to leadership, as questions of this nature pervade the discussion in a field where the tendency has been to skip the ontological and epistemological reflections and start with theoretical and methodological considerations.

With respect to the sociology of science, also embedded in contemporary theoretical and research conversations is the question of what counts as *legitimate* scientific research and what does not. Thomas Kuhn's work (1962) has strongly influenced this conversation with his book *The Nature of Scientific Revolutions*. By introducing the idea of *scientific paradigms* competing with one another for legitimacy, Kuhn ignited an exchange about how science develops and changes over time. A paradigm is "a model that governs scientific inquiry in a discipline at a given time" (Riccucci, 2010, p. 22), one to which most members of that community commit and use. Paradigms are rooted in agreements around how the three questions described above are answered. Mature science, says Kuhn (1962), develops through iterative periods of what is called "normal science," where scientists tend to agree on basic ontological and epistemological assumptions and therefore use existing paradigms to engage in puzzle solving (rather than innovation), using methodological tools appropriate to those assumptions. Transitions from one paradigm to the next happen through a transformative process (scientific revolutions) whereby old assumptions, questions, and answers are challenged and replaced by a new paradigm. Competing paradigms may coexist for a while, creating schisms in a field that reduce the potential for knowledge sharing.

Kuhn (1962) saw cyclical stages of scientific development, from pre-paradigmatic stages (with no single set of agreements or paradigm on how to do science, with lots of dynamism and creativity) to normal science (where creativity gives way to more routinized processes of scientific accumulation, often increasing productivity but also producing straight jackets that stifle innovation). Then, a new revolution would take place, when the assumptions of the unified paradigm would be challenged, and the competition among paradigms—old and new—would yield innovation, gradually giving way again to another cycle of normal science. An important characteristic of a normal science phase is the preference for a deductive (theory testing) over an inductive (theory building) mode of inquiry. Normal science motivates a preference for testing and refining hypotheses from theories previously derived from the data. An inductive mode that allows the data to speak for themselves, building theory from the ground up, is less preferred in normal science mode. This reduces the opportunity for innovation and methodological pluralism.

Much water has passed under the bridge since Kuhn (1962) introduced and later redefined these ideas (Bird, 2000). Yet, the idea that "paradigm shifts" are at the core of scientific development permeates conversations about what constitutes legitimate "knowledge generation" in the context of science and social science. With some exceptions (e.g., Walker, 2006), this conversation might be relatively new within conventional leadership studies (particularly in the context of the U.S.). Yet, it has been present in exchanges about the "scientific" identity of most disciplines (Boudon, 1988; Ritzer, 1980; Weiner & Palermo, 1973), as well as in multidisciplinary fields such as organization and management studies (Boisot & McKelvey, 2010; Daft & Lewin, 1990; Davis & Marquis, 2005; Hassard & Kelemen, 2002; Hatch & Yanow, 2003) and public administration (Ospina & Dodge, 2005; Riccucci, 2010).

From Paradigmatic Closure to Dialogue across Perspectives

Twenty years ago the first editors of the journal *Organization Science* invoked Kuhn (1962) to argue that the field seemed to have "prematurely settled into a *normal science* mindset," forcing researchers to move too soon toward few "conceptual and methodological boxes" (Daft & Lewin, 1990, p. 2). They also highlighted the dangers of a situation when "convergent thinking overtakes a field before it has matured" (p. 2). Reiterating the emergence of organization science as a new discipline, the editors made a case for taking seriously the scientific tasks associated with doing pre-normal science, rather than moving too quickly to the narrow confines of normal science that result in paradigmatic closure.

The editors observed the fact that organizational scholars spanned many disciplines and fields of inquiry, from anthropology to economics, and from organization behavior to organization theory. They argued that this made it difficult to find common ground—a single paradigm to govern scientific practice. They lamented the limited set of topics considered. They also observed barriers to publication of papers not anchored in established theories or those not using "legitimate" methods. Finally, the editors thought that the narrow focus typical of paradigmatic closure precluded dominant approaches from adequately addressing the complexity and multidimensionality of the subject of study.

These observations may very well apply to leadership studies, where the entity perspective (with its multiple theoretical manifestations and its quantitative bias) *may have become too paradigmatic too soon*. Some of the strategies that *Organization Science*'s editors proposed to loosen the existing straightjackets could not be more relevant for the dialogue needed today in the leadership field. For example, they propose focusing on equivocal problems—that is, problems whose solutions would be of interest to all scholars, independent of their stance. They also propose using "heretical" research methods—going beyond the dominant logical positivist tradition—by opening research to a new grammar, new variables, new definitions, and new logics that produce novel theoretical explanations. In addition, they suggest opening the space for creativity, innovation, and "heresy," all of which require taking a step back from a methodological to a philosophical conversation, and only then going forward to theory and methods.

These calls resonate strongly in relational leadership research today. With its variety of ontological and epistemic stances, relational leadership offers a promising entry point for such a conversation. Perhaps more importantly, relational leadership transforms the aspiration for methodological pluralism from a philosophical longing to a pragmatic concern: the need to advance more serious theoretical and practical understandings of the complex social realities of leadership.

Incommensurability of Paradigms

Achieving multi-paradigmatic theory building requires relational leadership scholars to engage one another in conversation. This, in turn, requires clarity about each other's perspectives. We cannot reach this point until we move beyond hardened positions of incommensurability toward more open (and informed) mindsets of paradigm interplay.

Entity and constructionist leadership scholars often inhabit different paradigmatic communities, and therefore do not know how to speak to one another. It is understandable that some would see their assumptions as "irreconcilable"—in Kuhn's (1962) terms "incommensurable," meaning not even comparable by the same standards or measures. Discussions about the *incommensurability of paradigms* have filled many pages of social science debate, with Kuhn himself going back and forth on the issue (Sankey, 1993). We see these issues come to life later in this book in dialogues about the extent to which entity and constructionist perspectives on leadership (and their preferred methodologies) can be integrated, reconciled, or even produce insights of common interest.

The chapters in this book are also illustrative of this debate: of the tensions it generates, and of the barriers and opportunities for authentic exchanges. The challenges tend to come more strongly from the constructionist side, which has long felt left out of the conversation by a lack of understanding (and concern) from the entity side. Drawing from Collins (1986), Deetz (1996) summarizes this problem in his description of tensions among paradigmatic stances (1996, p. 204):

> Any research group dominating over time becomes inward looking, isolated from the problems of the larger society, and filled with blinders and trained incapacities. Its acts of perpetuation exceed its attempts at social service, its prophets become priests. Similar to most societies, marginalized research groups have had to learn two systems—their own and the dominant one—and dominant groups only one. (Collins, 1986)

For this reason, efforts to generate dialogue to date have mostly occurred on the constructionist side, by scholars who have become frustrated that the "dominant group" (entity scholars) has not acknowledged or understood the issues. Their frustrations in trying to be heard have led them to make louder and stronger arguments, which in turn further aggravates the entity scholars, who do not fully grasp the problem or understand the concerns because they have not had to "learn" the other system. Entity scholars, in their own frustration, hence turn back to their own paradigmatic views and ignore the calls—which further exacerbates the problem. It is this process that gives rise to *cycles of incommensurability*.

We see the challenges of trying to break this cycle in each of the dialogues in this book. For example, in Chapter 18, Dian Marie Hosking sees these perspectives as not commensurable. The epistemic communities they represent, she argues, make "totally different assumptions" about the relationships between the self and others. They use words like relation or process to imply different meanings; and they invite different research questions and address different types of practical concerns. Therefore, she argues for "multiple thinking spaces."

An interesting impasse happens, however, when Hosking opens the dialogue organized for this book by inviting Boas Shamir to an exchange framed around the relational rules that have guided both her own scholarship and her relations (Chapter 16). This way, Hosking was inviting Shamir to dialogue while defining the terms of engagement from within her paradigmatic view. This was not comfortable for Shamir, who decided to first step back and offer ideas for the dialogue from within his own perspective (Chapter 17).

Reframing Hosking's invitation to speak from within his paradigmatic view, Shamir urges us to find common ground around some core understanding of the essence of leadership so that the conversation can take place. Unknowingly, however, in searching for a commonly accepted definition of leadership (a postpositive approach), he *de-facto* reduces the chances for a conversation with constructionists, whose "anti-essentialist" ontology would argue against researcher-imposed definitions (see Chapter 1). Consistent with his postpositive orientation, Shamir wants scholars to agree on a minimal essence (i.e., a common definition) of leadership. In inviting Hosking to agree on a definition, Shamir takes what, for Hosking, as a constructionist, is an incommensurable stance: Whereas postpositivism assumes that the essence of objects exists independently of the knower (and therefore we need to have precise definitions of our constructs), constructionist intersubjectivism assumes there is no essence in objects themselves. (Instead, meaning is given by participants as they co-construct it in context.)

The crux of the issue here is not that (as Shamir seems to conclude) there is no "agreed upon" phenomenon called *leadership*. It is that postpositivists, with their "realist" orientation, think leadership can (and must) be precisely defined by the researcher,[2] while constructionists, with their inter-subjectivist orientation, think leadership must be understood as "defined" by those who construct it in their interactions, in very particular contexts. Predictably, therefore, another impasse happens in the conversation when Hosking, consistent with her constructionist and critical orientation, resists the notion of a universal core that defines the essence of "leadership" as a fixed point of departure. Instead, she advocates for the need to explore the meaning that is given to leadership in the specific contexts in which it emerges.

We see the challenge of incommensurability again in the dialogue between Gail Fairhurst and John Antonakis (Chapter 15). Less explicit than Shamir, but equally categorical, is Antonakis—coming from an entity postpositivist perspective—in his dialogue with constructionist Fairhurst. Agreeing with Fairhurst about some of the methodological faults of leadership research, he indicates that he welcomes any kind of leadership study that builds useful theory *as long as it meets "four basic conditions of the scientific method."* When these are listed, it becomes apparent that they reflect a postpositivist approach to science—again rendering *de facto* his approach incommensurable with interpretivist scholarship.

In the dialogue between Bill Drath and David Day (Chapter 8), Day invites thinking about a continuum rather than "truly discrete ontological and epistemological classes," thus suggesting openness to commensurability. While pointing to some potential areas of convergence, he is nevertheless categorical about the primacy of agency over relationships in leadership (consistent with his entity paradigm). He recognizes the potential incommensurability of this position, asserting that perhaps this difference is at the core of the entity and constructionist impasse because it represents "a fundamental disagreement about the ontology of leadership."

Although constructionists Drath and Fairhurst, like Hosking, advocate allowing the perspectives to co-exist and inform one another and are willing to accept insights gained from postpositivist research, they also make strong paradigmatic assertions regarding the limits of postpositivism in addressing relationality. They urge entity scholars to take the notion of relationality more seriously by unpacking its more constructionist meanings. For example, in his dialogue with Day (Chapter 8), Drath, while not denying the existence of leaders or their agency, suggests these as less interesting points of entry than the question, "What's going on with leadership from a whole-system perspective?" He also questions whether only one form of influence—from leader to follower—can be defined as leadership, and invites Day and other postpositivist scholars to recognize and revisit this objectivist belief (see Chapter 1).

In her dialogue with Antonakis regarding how relationality can be researched empirically (Chapter 15), Fairhurst argues against the "heavy reliance" she sees "on the study of individuals to discern relational patterns." Highlighting potential for complementary, she points out that most leadership theorizing focuses on predicting and causally explaining leadership, when what is needed is the use of theories "more heuristically to make leadership relationships intelligible and open to insight in ways that we would not otherwise have had."

As we can see throughout these dialogues, the genuine desire for communication is as palpable as the tensions and passions that surface in the exchanges. A key issue that arises, however, is the deep challenge of being in communication with one another when the basic assumptions across the perspectives are not well understood (and are often misunderstood). The tensions between the two perspectives become evident as soon as scholars make choices on how to do research, whether they are aware of taking a paradigmatic stance or not.

In some cases, the dialogues again remind us of a degree of epistemic closure that may be indicative of a field that became too paradigmatic too soon. But is this enough of a reason to engage a conversation that will "rock the boat?" After all, leadership studies is experiencing great vitality and legitimacy as an academic field. Why not just continue to let all flowers bloom and let the quality of the products dictate their standing? We return to Deetz (1996):

> As we gradually learn socially the positive effects of diversity—beyond "separate but equal" *and* integration—organization science can also benefit from better discussions. This does not mean that we each should automatically find other groups' issues and procedures interesting or helpful, nor should we believe that all of them are. But let us make our claims and the relation between our claims and procedures clearer so objection and conflict can be on those grounds rather than impose traditional problem statements and methods on those doing something else. In doing so, the ultimate point is not in arguing it out to get it right, but to reclaim the suppressed tensions and conflicts among the many contemporary stakeholders to negotiate a life together based in appreciation of different and responsive decision making. (p. 204)

An Alternative to Incommensurability: Paradigm Interplay

Consistent with this quote from Deetz (1996), we offer in this book another approach to the issue of *incommensurability* across leadership perspectives. Our original—somewhat idealistic—motivation to produce this book was to generate dialogue that would create common ground.

We now realize that not only was this goal unattainable, it is undesirable. Rather than try to produce assimilation across assumptions, a more beneficial approach is paradigm interplay (Romani et al., 2011). Paradigm interplay recognizes the value of heterogeneous assumptions and insights from multiple perspectives for advancing understanding. The focus in paradigm interplay is on highlighting connections and distinctions among paradigms—identifying resonances *as well as* tensions—and using these to learn from one another.

There is no need to give up one's paradigm of choice. Rather, paradigm interplay represents a constructive way to develop theory when normal science reaches a point where competition for legitimacy among *incommensurable* paradigms shuts down communication. Paradigm interplay opens up a space when competition has led to a narrowing of the field, stifling our ability to develop new approaches and generate broader understandings. To illustrate the value of interplay, in our concluding chapter we present a paradigm interplay across the perspectives represented in this book in order to advance a multi-paradigmatic understanding of relational leadership.

For now, with this introductory chapter we reiterate the ideas that still hold behind our motivation to produce this book. First, neither perspective is "right"; they are just different; each is more and less helpful in illuminating various dimensions of leadership phenomena. Second, the differences do not preclude learning from the others' gained understanding of relational leadership; if anything, they promote it. Third, for genuine sharing and learning to happen, scholars in both "worlds" must be able to understand and recognize the worthiness of multiple perspectives and respect what the others are trying to do and say.

We believe that engaging this conversation around relational leadership can help address urgent concerns within each paradigm. For scholars comfortable with the entity perspective, it may open new and creative ways to tackle burning puzzles, such as how to more effectively incorporate time, context, and intersecting levels of action (e.g., levels of analysis) and their reciprocal influences. For scholars comfortable with the constructionist perspective, the conversation may open new and creative ways to theoretically translate dense ideas of relationality into usable constructs for advancing empirical research that are consistent with their postmodern ontologies. For scholars interested in either perspective, it may produce insights for developing theories with more practical implications for leadership—thus offering practitioners something more than simplistic formulas or hardly actionable and complicated propositions.

Finally, the entity and the constructionist perspectives of relational leadership represent two *ideal types*, or what Max Weber would describe as "constructs," that can be used as the reference from which to compare what we see in the world (Roth & Wittich, 1978). Despite the gap that separates scholars espousing the two perspectives, neither reflects a single unitary approach; instead, they represent clusters of "communities of inquiry" with members who approximate (in different degrees) the same ontological project and epistemic stance. These stances in turn motivate preferences for similar theoretical lenses and methodological choices. For this reason, rather than thinking of two separate "camps" we view leadership scholars within a continuum between two poles.

In Chapter 1, we *unpack* the assumptions behind the various stances associated with each pole. We also more deeply discuss the way leadership research is conceived by each perspective, and the problems these differences have created for the field. In the sections below, our focus is on locating the book contributors along the continuum to help readers better understand where the authors fall in the complex terrain of today's leadership studies. As we will see from this discussion, what our mapping reveals is that the issue is not one of dichotomies (pure entity, pure constructionist) but rather one of a range of perspectives.

MAPPING THE TERRAIN: LOCATING AND INTRODUCING CONTRIBUTORS

A key purpose of this introductory chapter is to help the reader work their way through the myriad assumptions and paradigmatic issues raised by the authors in this book. We do this with our "map of the terrain" in Figure I.1.

Figure I.1 is organized along a continuum of ontologies ranging from fully modernist to fully postmodernist (cf. Boisot & McKelvey, 2010). At the core of the modernist stance is the belief that there is a single truth about our objects of study, and that it is possible to approximate this truth with some certainty, independent of any subjectivity (i.e., objectivism). At the core of the postmodernist stance is the idea that there are multiple truths about our objects of study, and that the most we can do is attain a glimpse of these truths through interpretation of people's negotiated subjective understandings (i.e., subjectivism). (There are, of course, variations within these stances, which are further developed in Chapter 1.)

Modernist assumptions resonate with the orientation to science originally called positivism, and its contemporary version, postpositivism (or neo-positivism). Postmodernist assumptions resonate with the orientation to science called interpretivism (Hatch & Yanow, 2003; Yanow & Schwartz-Shea, 2006). Of particular interest to our discussion is one version of interpretivism, called *constructionism*.

With modernism and postmodernism as poles, the continuum ranges from soft to hard shades of gray between the poles. The most objectivist versions of postpositivism are positioned on the far left of the axis; the most

	Modernist stance: Entity perspective (Privileges individual dimensions)		Postmodernist stance: Constructionist perspective (Privileges collective dimensions)	
	From most to least objectivist →		← **From least to most subjectivist**	
	LOGICAL POSITIVISM		CONSTRUCTIVISM	
	Postpositivists -Reality is discovered-		**Interpretivist constructionists** -Reality is constructed-	
Part 1	Seers & Chopin **Day**[1]	Fletcher	Barge Kennedy et al. Alvesson & Sveningsson **Drath**	
Part 2	Ashkanasy et al. Offermann Treadway et al. Wassenaar & Pearce **Antonakis**	Fitzsimons Crosby & Bryson	Ospina et al. **Fairhurst**	
Part 3	**Shamir**	**Uhl-Bien**	Ospina **Hosking**	

Figure I.1 The contributors: A continuum from entity to constructivist stances on leadership.
[1] Names in bold indicate dialogue scholars and editors.

subjectivist versions of interpretivism are positioned on the far right of the axis. The shades in between reflect slight differences in orientation as a function of the contributors' distance from either one of the extremes.

We offer this table with two important caveats. First, the table represents our effort to make sense of the contributors' positions in a complex leadership terrain, and we alone are responsible for any misplacement; scholars themselves might not agree with their location on the continuum. Second, the one-dimensional nature of written text does not do justice to this complexity. In reality, there may have been more overlaps and slight movement to the right or the left of the continuum if we had been able to physically align the contributors in a two-, or even a three-, dimensional representation.

As the table suggests, the various book contributors who use an entity perspective fall under the broad umbrella of modernism/postpositivism; the various contributors who use a constructionist perspective fall under postmodernism/interpretivism. Some constructionists may be more postmodernist than others—just as some entity scholars may be more postpositivist than others. This may be reflected in their theoretical orientation, as well as in their applications of social science with consequent definitions of rigor. Variations among postpositivist leadership researchers are mostly a function of commitments to theoretical schools, and the consequent methodological choices in their empirical research designs. Constructionists differ according to what each scholar accentuates when looking at leadership as an emergent phenomenon, for example, language and interpersonal communication or narrative and organizational processes.

Specific contributions from each perspective approximate in different degrees the extremes to their left and right respectively, with no contributor falling on the far extremes on either side of the continuum. The arrows are intended to represent degrees of movement away from objectivism and toward subjectivism. A three-dimensional application of this model would depict this continuum as a cylinder, in which the two extremes connect according to the privileging of the individual in both perspectives of leadership. (We return to this topic in Chapter 1.)

The continuum depicted in Figure I.1, complemented with the longer discussion presented in Chapter 1, is offered to help make sense of the dense ideas and information provided in the chapters and the puzzles generated by their juxtaposition. It also offers the backdrop against which to consider the insights presented in the subsequent dialogues at the end of each part of the book. Our goal here is to offer readers material that helps them better understand the question of whether convergence is possible among the multiple perspectives, consistent with our aspiration to develop multi-paradigmatic understandings of relational leadership.

The Book's Logic and Structure

Some clarifications will help readers understand the final product they hold in their hands. The call for contributions to the volume did not specify any guidance for writing the chapter other than exploring the challenges and opportunities of relational leadership to advance the field. Once we had the contributions, we classified and clustered the pieces according to an emergent logic. We also asked the dialogue scholars to avoid doing critiques of the pieces, and instead to think about what the contributed ideas opened up for advancing the creation of the proposed space to explore relational leadership in ways that were helpful to the field as a whole.

The book is structured in three parts, bookmarked by the Introduction and Chapter 1 at the beginning, and the Conclusion at the end. In the first set of chapters, Part I: Theorizing the Practice of Relational Leadership, contributors are concerned with advancing theoretical ideas about the construct and practice of relational leadership. In the second set of chapters, Part II: Researching Relational Leadership, contributors are concerned with introducing ideas of relationality into research programs to explore either previous treatments in the literature or to identify potential ways to operationalize (entity perspective) or translate (constructionist perspective) relational assumptions in empirical research. In the final chapters of Parts I and II, "dialogue scholars" representing each perspective offer reflections triggered by reading the contributions and engaging in conversation around them. In Part III: A Conversation Across Perspectives, additional dialogue scholars and the editors engaged in a final dialogue based on reading the entire set of contributions.

Contributors' responses to the challenge posed by our invitation were not homogenous. Some authors, like Seers and Chopin (Chapter 2) and Kennedy, Carroll, Francoeur, and Jackson (Chapter 6), created an internal dialogue between the paradigms to build insights within their chapter. Similarly, Fitzsimons (Chapter 5) also compared paradigms to show how an additional relational approach rooted outside of the leadership field could bring fresh and useful perspectives to the conversation. Others, like Fletcher (Chapter 3) and Crosby and Bryson (Chapter 10), explored the complementarity of the perspectives by proposing ways to combine them with illustrations from their own work. Yet, others took up the challenge from positions firmly rooted within their own paradigms. In some cases, constructionists like Barge (Chapter 4) and Ospina, Foldy, El Hadidy, Dodge, Hofmann-Pinilla, and Su (Chapter 9) "unpacked" the logic and implications (for theory, research, or practice) of relational assumptions that they viewed as inherent to this perspective. At the extreme of this group were Alvesson & Svenningsson (Chapter 7), who complemented constructionism with critical theory to question and deconstruct the meaning of leadership. Finally, postpositivists like Ashkanasy, Tee, and Paulsen (Chapter 11), Offerman (Chapter 12), Treadway, Breland, Williams, Yang, and Williams (Chapter 13) and Wassenaar and Pearce (Chapter 14) tried to "push the envelope" of their own perspective by asking how the notion of relational leadership could advance thinking about the nature of leadership or its effective study.

Reactions to these responses and the subsequent reflections they triggered are reported in the concluding chapters for each part, where the dialogues between Day and Drath (Chapter 8), Fairhurst and Antonakis (Chapter 15) and Shamir and Hosking (Chapters 16–18) are documented.

We believe all these exercises were quite helpful in unpacking the ontological, epistemological, and methodological assumptions the contributors brought to the conversation. They also made evident the tensions and passion these assumptions generated when posed side-by-side.

In the concluding chapter of this volume, we take up some of these assumptions to advance paradigm interplay. For now, we close this introduction with a brief description of how each contributor used the idea of relational leadership to enter the conversation, followed by our closing remarks.

Overview of the Chapters

In Chapter 1, *Competing Bases of Scientific Legitimacy in Contemporary Leadership Studies*, we begin with a "primer" that helps to unpack the ontological and epistemological assumptions brought by the authors of this book. We do this by contrasting the paradigmatic assumptions of the two primary leadership perspectives that represent competing paradigms in the field: entity and constructionism. Our goal is to contextualize both the trends toward convergence within a field characterized by divergence, and the negative implications for the field as a whole of the existing gap between the two perspectives.

In Chapter 2, we begin with the first of the contributions in Part I, focused on theorizing the practice of relational leadership. With *The Social Production of Leadership: From Supervisor-Subordinate Linkages to Relational Organizing*, Anson Seers and Suzette M. Chopin engage an interplay among entity and constructionist perspectives to explore how constructionist thinking might advance entity-based views of relational leadership currently grounded in LMX theory. Arguing that present (entity-based) leadership theory focusing on "relationships" has been too static and has not adequately framed the problem of relationality, they propose instead a "relational organizing" framework that moves beyond leadership "in organizations" to a consideration of leadership *as* the organizing of behavior.

At the core of their framework is the suggestion that relational processes and social entities are mutually constitutive—that is, analysis of social entities and relational processes are "alternate manifestations of a unitary phenomenon." Focusing on role and relational identities, they consider how leaders and followers enact identities as they develop a leader-follower relationship. According to Seers and Chopin, "each relational interaction reinforces the individual actor's identity as leader or follower within that particular relationship." Hence, they argue that theoretical models in a relational, as opposed to an entity perspective, should explain both interaction processes and the levels taken on by defining attributes associated with all these entities of interest.

In Chapter 3, *The Relational Practice of Leadership,* Joyce K. Fletcher distinguishes traditional and relational/constructionist approaches to relational leadership, arguing for complementarity, rather than incommensurability, among these views. According to Fletcher, entity scholars focus on *interactional skills and competencies* that help us understand how to enact the type of relational leadership that is much needed today; constructionist scholars focus us on considering how broad systems of cognition and power co-create relational practices reflecting either leadership or non-leadership. Fletcher recognizes the value and limits of each perspective and warns readers of "the dangers of focusing on one to the exclusion of the other." Instead, she urges researchers to hold these perspectives together, even if this is "an uneasy alliance."

In her chapter, Fletcher identifies three micro-processes of relational practice that the entity perspective must address: fluid expertise, growth process beyond the dyadic, and achieving effectiveness outcomes through a relational stance. She also uncovers three relational (constructionist) processes that undermine relationality: misunderstanding motives of relational behavior, devaluing relational practice through language, and conflating relationality with femininity. Bringing personal agency back into constructionism, Fletcher's framework helps practitioners reflect on their leadership by comparing dimensions associated with entity and constructionist *relational practice, non-relational practice*, and relational *malpractice.*

In Chapter 4, *Systemic Constructionist Leadership and Working from Within the Present Moment,* J. Kevin Barge focuses on exploring the implications of social constructionist ideas for developing leadership practices, recognizing that leaders work within continually evolving and changing linguistic landscapes. According to Barge, if we take the notion of social construction seriously, leadership is about meaning work and managing contexts. Therefore, people "who wish to construct leadership positions within teams, organizations, and societies" need to learn how to operate within the flow of conversation and develop practices that allow them to "make sense of it" in ways that shape direction. Barge accomplishes this by moving from a third-person perspective focusing on "What are they doing?" and "How are they doing it?" to a first-person perspective focusing on "What am I doing here?" and "What should I do next?"

From Barge's systemic constructionist point of view, "leadership may be viewed as 'a co-created, performative, contextual, and attributional process where the ideas articulated in talk or action are recognized by others as progressing tasks that are important to them' (Barge & Fairhurst, 2008, p. 232)." This conception is relational in that it sees leadership as occurring in the joint action between or among people: It "cannot be understood in terms of the behaviors or utterances of a single individual." Barge views relationality in the contextual nature of leadership: ". . . [O]ur understanding of what counts as leadership or a leader depends on the unique combination of people, task, context, time, and place," and in its attributional processes of meaning-making that are "always performed in relation to tasks."

In Chapter 5, *The Contribution of Psychodynamic Theory to Relational Leadership*, Declan J. Fitzsimons introduces concepts from the systems psychodynamic perspective to break the polarization between entity and constructionist ontologies' focus on either the individual *or* the collective in the study of leadership. Psychodynamic Theory, he argues, embeds individuals' feelings, thoughts, behaviors, and actions within collective sources of experience (e.g., unconscious group-level processes) that go beyond the individual self. Fitzsimons proposes that psychoanalytic perspectives add considerable conceptual weight to three debates within the relational leadership conversation: how the self is theorized; the nature of relational dynamics; and how to engage process in leadership research.

In his chapter, Fitzsimons describes how psychodynamic perspectives break the polarity between entity and constructionist approaches. He also shows how Object Relations Theory, with its notion that connection drives human existence, offers a unit of analysis consistent with relational ontology: "the interactional field within which the individual arises and struggles to make contact and articulate himself." This offers a novel understanding of relational dynamics by privileging social context and recognizing the "complex field of systemic forces" in leadership that are both psychological and social. Two constructs in the psychoanalytic perspective are offered that deepen this notion: First, the relational drive originates in a fully *embodied self*; and second, *the group-as-a-whole* (not the aggregate of individual psychologies) induces behavior on individual members through collective unconscious projective processes. Fitzsimons sums this up by arguing that understanding relational leadership requires uncovering the "powerful systemic emotional dynamics unleashed" when groups work collaboratively.

In Chapter 6, *A Tale of Two Perspectives: An Account of Entity and Social Constructionist Approaches to "Conflict" in Leadership Development*, Fiona Kennedy, Brigid Carroll, Joline Francouer, and Brad Jackson tackle the issue of paradigm interplay head on. In this chapter, Kennedy et al. describe the challenges and tensions that occur when academics holding multi-paradigmatic perspectives attempt to work together in delivering leadership development programs. Using the characters of "Rachel" and "Meg," they describe the assumptions associated with differing paradigmatic views of leadership development and the tensions that arise when these assumptions come in conflict. This chapter brings to life the challenges of commensurability, even among scholars who are fully committed to working with one another.

At the core of Kennedy et al.'s chapter are issues of realism and subjectivism. Rachel, the constructivist "entity" scholar focuses on training participants in self-awareness using "objective" tools, methods, models, and technologies. Meg, the subjectivist "constructionist" scholar focuses on engaging with participants in the moment, using metaphor, imagery, and symbols to produce generative spaces in the face of unpredictability where collective learning will take place. These differences are sources of severe tension, that play out in struggles as the scholars work to maintain positions of openness, and even respect, toward one another.

In Chapter 7, *Un- and Re-Packing Leadership: Context, Relations, Constructions and Politics*, Mats Alvesson & Stefan Sveningsson use critical theory to deconstruct what they see as a naïve view of leadership: a tension-free, morally superior co-construction around shared common goals. Highlighting a social context of "politically charged co-constructions" where subjects are not equal, they explore four problematic assumptions of contemporary scholarship (leader-centrism, entitism, romanticism, and objectivism-LERO). The critique targets both entity and constructionist scholars, since the latter tend to romanticize shared meaning while neglecting the role of power and multiple voices in co-construction.

The authors argue that leader-centrism and entitism are socially invented truths that help maintain dominant discourses. According to Alvesson and Sveningsson, viewing leadership as a social phenomenon must involve consideration of how macro dynamics like "ideology, discourse, and institutionalized practices" induce the micro dynamics of local relationship. One must view the entire gestalt—not just the leadership relationship—as leadership. In other words, leadership is not an already existing entity (a given), it is "an emergent outcome of situation;" it is not an objective phenomenon, but the outcome of how people construct it as such.

Part I concludes with Chapter 8, *A Dialogue on Relational Theorizing*, where David Day and Wilfred (Bill) Drath document the conversation triggered by reading the chapters in this part of the book. In Part II, contributors answer the question of how a "relational" perspective changes the way they do their research. Independent of whether the context of the research described is nonprofit and public (Chapters 9 and 10) or private (Chapters 11 through 14), contributors discuss methodological implications of relational assumptions and constructs, as well as challenges and opportunities for advancing relational leadership by way of empirical research.

Chapter 9, *Social Change Leadership as Relational Leadership*, is the sole contribution in Part II that takes an explicit constructionist perspective. Here Sonia M. Ospina, Erica G. Foldy, Waad El Hadidy, Jennifer Dodge, Amparo Hofmann-Pinilla, and Celina Su describe a large research program focusing on leadership in community-based organizations. In this research, they explore the consequences of bringing constructionism to frame, design, choose methods, analyze and interpret the data. They describe two research decisions at the core of their commitment to relationality. First, they focus on the collective experience of leadership as manifested in group-generated narratives about how the social change work was advanced, rather than on leaders' traits, behaviors or activities. Second, they use practice theory as the anchor for interpreting the findings.

Their findings identify three leadership practices—reframing discourse, bridging difference, and unleashing human energies—as distinct types of leadership work that help the group move their own collective effort forward. Placing their findings in conversation with insights from transformational, neo-charismatic and team leadership studies, they highlight the advantages of their approach for documenting the "how" of leadership. The key achievement of this research, the authors claim, was to find practical but rigorous ways to do social-science-based empirical research that shifts attention from the individual dimensions of leadership—exhaustively documented in entity perspectives as well as in some constructionist approaches—to its collective dimensions. According to Ospina et al., exploring these dimensions will require devising more creative and innovative research methods that are consistent with relationality assumptions, rather than merely mixing methods or shifting from variance to process methods.

In Chapter 10, *Integrative Leadership and Policy Change: A Hybrid Relational View*, Barbara C. Crosby and John M. Bryson advocate the need to consider both individual and collective dimensions in understanding the role of leadership in tackling complex public problems. Building on Gidden's theory of *structuration*, the authors identify a specific set of social practices through which policy entrepreneurs contribute to successfully mobilize agendas for policy reform or social transformation (e.g., the creation and communication of shared meaning). They view these as reflecting the collective side of leadership for the common good.

Acknowledging the role of particular individuals in moving these processes, the authors then focus on the individual dimensions of leadership and identify eight leadership capabilities. Policy entrepreneurs must enact these in their leadership roles (as champions and sponsors) to successfully achieve their goals toward public problem solving. Drawing from structuration theory, the authors recognized that in shared power situations, outcomes are not achieved directly by leaders. That is, leaders do not "cause" them, but instead, outcomes are produced when formal leaders work with other actors "to shape the ideas, rules, modes, media, and methods that help determine outcomes." Through their *integrative leadership framework*, Crosby and Bryson offer a view of "relationship" in leadership that is both individual and collective. This framework is illustrated using four successful policy change efforts around the unemployment of African-American men, the isolation of elderly adults, information barriers for governmental planning, and urban traffic congestion.

While the first two chapters in this section rely on sociological and public policy frameworks, the next four are anchored within the psychology and management literatures. The reflections of the study of leadership also shift from public to private contexts. These chapters explore what it means to try to incorporate a relational perspective of leadership into an existing research agenda that highlights leader-follower exchanges within the mainstream literature. They all share a firm commitment to a postpositivist research paradigm; they differ in the emphasis given to particular constructs in making their research more relational.

In Chapter 11, *Extending Relational Leadership Theory: The Role of Affective Processes in Shaping Leader-Follower Relationships*, Neal M. Ashkanasy, Neil Paulsen, and Eugene Y.J. Tee integrate the latest developments in LMX and in emotions research to emphasize the affective dimension of leadership. They push the relational envelope by suggesting that relational approaches to leadership must conceptualize leadership processes more holistically, recognizing that organizational phenomena are produced by way of intrapersonal and interpersonal exchanges.

Ashkanasy et al. offer "a multi-level conceptualization of relational leadership processes that incorporates the influence of followers and affective processes as key determinants of the leader-follower relationship quality." Specifically, they examine affective exchanges between leaders and followers based on processes of emotional contagion, and argue for the relevance of evaluating their impact on effectiveness. To address this research program, they advocate for combined orientations and triangulated methods. They also promote multilevel quantitative methods, with a shift from a dyadic to a team context, to explore how context impacts behavior at the various levels.

In Chapter 12, *Relational Leadership: Creating Effective Leadership with Diverse Staff*, Lynn R. Offermann describes her efforts to shift from a "relationship-based" to a "relational" approach in a research project on leadership in cross-demographic organizational contexts. Offerman expands upon previous notions of relationality in postpositive research by introducing "issues of meaning" more typical of constructionist approaches. Problematizing the quality of the leadership relationship in contexts where followers are demographically different, she links constructs like social categorization from relational demography theory to constructionist assumptions of leadership to argue that leadership emerges from shared agreements, and therefore a key leadership function is that of managing meaning.

Offerman identifies "relational best practices" in leading diversity and characteristics of highly successful diversity leaders. She discusses her finding that one's mother tongue poses a "potential relational leadership obstacle" in diverse contexts, acting as a barrier for "creating a shared leadership process." She also reflects on the decision to use mixed methods, first to test the hypotheses, and second, to bring in the voices of diverse actors.

In Chapter 13, *Political Skill, Relational Control, and the Self in Relational Leadership Processes*, Darren C. Treadway, Jacob W. Breland, Laura A. Williams, Jun Yang, and Lisa Williams set out to expand the relational leadership theory framework by exploring how political communication processes impact the quality of the leadership relationship. Their comprehensive model of relational leadership integrates the concepts of influence and control to highlight political activity and behavior (such as impression management, influence tactics, and self-presentation) as a dynamic reciprocal process that constitutes the relational context, where "abilities and motivations of both the actor and the target" help to define the actual leadership relationship. The authors expand our views of relationality by introducing the idea of self as "a socially constructed relational entity."

Treadway et al. explore the role of political communication processes as relational mechanisms that moderate the leadership process, and influence the emergence and quality of the leadership relationship via individual perceptions and interpretations of self (by both leaders and followers). This attention to the emergence of self-concept within dyadic interactions highlights the role of political skillfulness of subordinates on relational control, in contrast to leader-centered models that highlight leaders' actions and motivations. To test their model, the authors propose methodologies that address network embeddedness, temporal considerations, and multi-level issues, including social network analysis, longitudinal designs, hierarchical linear modeling, and linear growth modeling.

In Chapter 14, *Shared Leadership 2.0: A Glimpse into the State of the Field*, Christina L. Wassenaar and Craig L. Pearce argue that insights from empirical research on shared leadership can shed light on relational leadership theory, given that they "occupy a similar conceptual space." They enumerate myriad antecedents and outcomes of shared leadership as documented in literature, reporting recent qualitative and quantitative studies, and drawing from a variety of organizational and cultural contexts. Among the broad range of antecedents mentioned are follower-related factors like trust in the hierarchical leader, interventions such as team training and coaching, processes (e.g., communication), and conditions (e.g., relationship longevity). Outcomes include changes in attitudes (e.g., satisfaction), cognition, behavior (e.g., constructive interaction style), employee effectiveness, and company performance.

Part II of the book concludes with a dialogue between Gail Fairhurst and John Antonakis in Chapter 15, *A Research Agenda for Relational Leadership*, which documents the conversation triggered by reading the chapters in this part of the book. This is followed by Part III, which records the dialogues and reflections about the entire set of contributions.

In Chapter 16, *On Entitative and Relational Discourses*, Dian Marie Hosking and Boas Shamir initiate their dialogue with a letter by Hosking, where she frames the invitation to Shamir within a relational discourse. Shamir responds with a request to take a step back so he can develop his ideas in an independent document, which is the content of Chapter 17, *Leadership Research or Post-Leadership Research? Advancing Leadership Theory versus Throwing the Baby Out with the Bath Water*. In Chapter 18, *Exploring the Prospects for Dialogue across Perspectives*, the two come together again, along with the editors, to engage in a spirited dialogue that draws from Parts I, II, and III of the book (including the ideas developed in Chapters 16 and 17).

We conclude in Chapter 19, *Paradigm Interplay in Relational Leadership: A Way Forward*, by returning again to the issues raised in this introduction and elaborated in the book. We draw the issues out by attempting ourselves to engage in paradigm interplay, using the guidelines laid out by Romani et al. (2011). In this chapter, we use content from the authors as the "empirical material," and present three interplays that emanated from the multi-paradigmatic discussion of relational leadership: leadership is co-constructed, leadership is a relational process, and leadership can and should be developed. Through these interplays, we were able to analyze areas of convergence and divergence, revealing new insights regarding relational leadership. We were also able to engage in the tensions, rather than get bogged down by them, to identify a way forward for relational leadership research.

CLOSING REMARKS

This book is a product of our strong and passionate beliefs that leadership research can best advance through multi-paradigmatic conversation. We are not the only ones with this belief. Like us, many scholars, independent of the stance they hold, are becoming increasingly dissatisfied with existing approaches to theorizing, researching and practicing leadership. Many of them share our concern that both entity and constructionist scholars need to take more seriously issues of relationality in leadership research.

This convergence of interest around relational leadership—despite the existing divergence in perspectives on leadership between entity and constructionist scholars—offers a rare opportunity to advance a needed conversation in the field. An important step toward engagement in productive dialogue and mutual learning consists of making visible the ontological, epistemological, and methodological scaffolding of both perspectives on leadership. We lay the ground for this work in Chapter 1, and the contributors of the book continue to deepen it in the chapters that follow.

With this book, we invite the leadership studies community to think about how we might do our research differently if we see the value of multiple stances and embrace epistemological and methodological pluralism for the field. Our motivation is to create the "thinking space" to which Hosking (Chapter 18) refers. Uhl-Bien (2006) proposed Relational Leadership Theory (RLT) as such a space, where scholars can think and talk about questions around relationality in leadership research. At the time, she believed it would lead to integration. As it turns out, in the development of this book, we now envision this as multi-paradigmatic theorizing, which requires paradigm interplay.

We see the goal of paradigm interplay as learning to share the assumptions, designs, and insights of multiple perspectives without trying to eliminate what makes each unique. It is in creating the conditions for interplay among multiple perspectives where the greatest potential lies for moving the field forward. We hope you will join the conversation.

REFERENCES

Barge, J. K., & Fairhurst, G. F. (2008). Living leadership: A systemic constructionist approach. *Leadership, 4,* 227–251.

Berscheid, E. (1999). The greening of relationship science. *American Psychologist, 54*(4), 260–266.

Bird, A. (2000). *Thomas Kuhn.* Chesham, England: Acumen, and Princeton, NJ: Princeton University Press.

Blandin, N. (2007). Leading at the edge of chaos. In R. Morse, T. Buss, & C. M. Kinghorn (Eds.), *Transforming public leadership for the 21st century* (pp. 138–153). New York, NY: M.E. Sharp.

Boisot, M., & McKelvey, B. (2010). Integrating modernist and postmodernist perspectives on organizations: A complexity science bridge. *Academy of Management Review, 35*(3), 415–433.

Boudon, R. (1988). Will sociology ever be a normal science? *Theory and Society, 17*(5), 747–771.

Bradbury, H., & Lichtenstein, B. (2000). Relationality in organizational research: Exploring the "space between." *Organization Science, 11*(5), 551–564.

Brower, H. H., Schoorman, F. D., & Tan, H. H. (2000). A model of relational leadership: the integration of trust and leader-member exchange. *Leadership Quarterly, 11*(2), 227–250.

Carroll, B., Levy, L., & Richmond, D. (2008). Leadership as practice: Challenging the competency paradigm. *Leadership, (4),* 363.

Collins, P. (1986). Learning from the outsider within. *Social Problems, 33,* S14–32.

Crevani, L., Lindgren, M., & Packendorff, J. (2007). Shared leadership: A postheroic perspective on leadership as a collective construction. *International Journal of Leadership Studies, 3*(1), 40–67.

Crosby, B. C., & Bryson, J. M. (2005). *Leadership for the common good: Tackling public problems in a shared-power world.* (2nd ed.). San Francisco, CA: Joessey-Bass.

Dachler, H. P., & Hosking, D. M. (1995). The primacy of relations in socially constructing organizational realities. In D. M. Hosking, H. P. Dachler, & K. J. Gergen (Eds.), *Management and organization relational alternatives to individualism* (pp. 1–28). Brookfield, VT: Avebury.

Dachler, H. P. (1992). Management and leadership as relational phenomena. In M. V. Cranach, W. Doise, & G. Mugny (Eds.), *Social representations and social bases of knowledge* (pp. 169–178). Lewiston, NY: Hogrefe and Huber.

Daft, R., & Lewin, A. Y. (1990). Can Organization Studies begin to break out of the normal science straight jacket? An editorial essay. *Organization Science, 1*(1), 1–10.

Davis, G. F., & Marquis, C. (2005). Prospects for organization theory in the early twenty-first century: Institutional fields and mechanisms. *Organization Science, 16*(4), 332–343.

Deetz, S. (1996). Describing differences in approaches to organization science: Rethinking Burrell and Morgan and their legacy. *Organization Science, 7*(2), 191–207.

Drath, W. (2001). *The deep blue sea: Rethinking the source of leadership.* San Francisco, CA: Jossey-Bass.

Drath, W., McCauley, C., Palus, J., Van Velsor, E., O'Connor, P., & McGuire, J. (2008). Direction, alignment, commitment: Toward a more integrative ontology of leadership. *The Leadership Quarterly, 19*(6), 635–53.

Emirbayer, M. (1997). Manifesto for a relational sociology. *American Journal of Sociology, 103(2),* 281–317.

Fairhurst, G. (2007). *Discursive leadership: In conversation with leadership psychology.* Thousand Oaks, CA: Sage Publications.

Ford, L. R., & Seers, A. (2006). Relational leadership and team climates: Pitting differentiation versus agreement. *The Leadership Quarterly, 17,* 258–270.

Gergen, K. (2009). *Relational being: Beyond self and community.* Oxford, England: Oxford University Press.

Gronn, P. (2002). Distributed leadership as a unit of analysis. *The Leadership Quarterly, 13(4),* 423–451.

Hassard, J., & Kelemen, M. (2002). Production and consumption in organizational knowledge: The case of the 'paradigms debate.' *Organization, 9,* 331–355.

Hatch, M. J., & Yanow, D. (2003). Organization theory as an interpretive science. In H. Tsoukas, & C. Knudsen (Eds.), *The Oxford handbook of organization theory* (pp. 63–87). Oxford, England: Oxford University Press.

Hatch, M. J., & Yanow, D. (2008). Methodology by metaphor: Ways of seeing in painting and research. *Organization Studies, 29*(1), 23–44.

Heifetz, R. (1994). *Leadership without easy answers*. Cambridge, MA: Harvard University Press.

Heifetz, R. A., & Linsky, M. (2002) *Leadership on the line: Staying alive through the dangers of leading*. Cambridge, MA: Harvard Business School Press.

Hosking, D. M. (2007). Not leaders, not followers: A post-modern discourse of leadership processes. In B. Shamir, R. Pillai, M. Bligh, & M. Uhl-Bien (Eds.), *Follower-centered perspectives on leadership: A tribute to the memory of James R. Meindl* (pp. 243–263). Greenwich, CT: Information Age Publishing.

Hosking, D. M. (1988). Organizing, leadership and skillful process. *Journal of Management Studies, 25,* 147–166.

Huxham, C., & Vangen, S. (2000). Leadership in the shaping and implementation of collaboration agendas: How things happen in a (not quite) joined up world. *Academy of Management Journal, 43*(6), 159–75.

Kuhn, Thomas (1962). *The structure of scientific revolutions.* (1st ed.). Chicago, IL: The University of Chicago Press.

Marrone, J. A., Tesluk, P. E., & Carson, J. B. (2007). A multilevel investigation of the antecedents and consequences to team member boundary spanning. *Academy of Management Journal, 50,* 1423–1439.

Mehra, A., Smith, B. R., Dixon, A. R., & Robertson, B. (2006). Distributed leadership in teams: The network of leadership perceptions and team performance. *Leadership Quarterly, 17*(3), 232–245.

Osborn, R. N., Hunt, J. G., & Jauch, L. R. (2002). Toward a contextual theory of leadership. *The Leadership Quarterly, 13,* 797–837.

Ospina, S., & Dodge, J. (2005). It's about time: Catching method up to meaning—The usefulness of narrative inquiry in public administration research. *Public Administration Review 65*(2): 143–58.

Ospina, S., & Sorenson, G. (2006). A constructionist lens on leadership: Charting new territory. In G. Goethals, & G. Sorenson (Eds.), *In quest of a general theory of leadership* (pp. 188–204). Cheltenham, England: Edward Elgar.

Ospina, S., & Foldy, E. (2010). Building bridges from the margins: The work of leadership in social change organizations. *The Leadership Quarterly, 21*(2), 292–307.

Pearce, C. L., & Conger, J. A. (Eds.). (2003). *Shared leadership: Reframing the hows and whys of leadership.* Thousand Oaks, CA: Sage.

Raelin, J. A. (2010). *The leaderful fieldbook: Strategies and activities for developing leadership in everyone.* Boston, MA: Bavies-Black.

Riccucci, N. M. (2010). *Public administration: Traditions of inquiry and philosophies of knowledge.* Washington, DC: Georgetown University Press.

Ritzer, G. (1980). *Sociology: A multiple paradigm science.* Boston, MA: Allyn and Bacon.

Romani, L., Primecz, H., & Topcu, K. (2011). Paradigm interplay for theory development: A methodological example with the kulturstandard method. *Organizational Research Methods, 14*(3), 432–455.

Rost, J. C. (1993). *Leadership for the twenty-first century.* Westport, CT: Praeger.

Roth, G., & Wittich, C. (Eds.). (1978). *Max Weber: Economy and society—An outline of interpretive sociology.* Vol. 1. Berkeley, CA: University of California Press.

Sankey, H. (1993). Kuhn's changing concept of incommensurability. *British Journal of the Philosophy of Science, 44,* 759–774.

Shamir, B., Pilai, M., Bligh, M., & Uhl-Bien, M. (Eds.). (2007). *Follower-centered perspectives of leadership.* Greenwich, CT: Information Age Publishing.

Slife, B.D. (2004). Taking Practice Seriously: Toward a relational ontology. *Journal of Theoretical and Philosophical Psychology, 24*(2), 157–178.

Uhl-Bien, M., Marion, R., & McKelvey, B. (2007). Complexity leadership theory: shifting leadership from the industrial age to the knowledge era. *The Leadership Quarterly, 18,* 298–318.

Uhl-Bien, M. (2006). Relational leadership theory: Exploring the social processes of leadership and organizing. *The Leadership Quarterly, 17*(6), 654–676.

Vangen, S., & Huxham, C. (2003). Enhancing leadership for collaborative advantage: Dilemmas of ideology and pragmatism in the activities of partnership managers. *British Journal of Management, 14,* S61-S76.

Walker, M. (2006). The theory and meta-theory of leadership: The important but contested nature of theory. In G. R. Goethals, & G. L. J. Sorenson (Eds.), *The quest for a general theory of leadership* (pp. 46–74). Chesterton, England: Edward Elgar Publications.

Weimer, W. B., & Palermo, D. S. (1973). Paradigms and normal science in psychology. *Science Studies, 3*(3), 211–44.

Yammarino, F. J., Dionne, S. D., Chun, J. U., & Dansereau, F. (2005). Leadership and levels of analysis: A state-of-the-science review. *The Leadership Quarterly, 16,* 879–919.

Yanow, D., & Schwartz-Shea, P. (Eds.). (2006). *Interpretation and method: Empirical research methods and the interpretive turn.* Armonk, NY: M.E. Sharpe.

NOTES

1. The first, second, and fourth definitions were retrieved from http://www.merriam-webster.com/dictionary; the third definition was retrieved from http://www.wordnik.com.

2. The challenge of definition is not lost on entity scholars, who have long struggled with the myriad definitions of the phenomenon, so much so that there are "almost as many definitions of leadership as there are leadership scholars" (Rost, 1993).

CHAPTER 1

EXPLORING THE COMPETING BASES FOR LEGITIMACY IN CONTEMPORARY LEADERSHIP STUDIES

Sonia M. Ospina and Mary Uhl-Bien[1]

*... [T]he philosophy underlying our scientific practice is a choice,
and should not simply be a default inherited without question from our teachers
and mentors. Understanding the implications of this choice... is important
for any reflective and responsible scientific inquiry.*
—Bechara & Van de Ven, 2007, p. 36)

Entity and constructionist perspectives on leadership are separated by a profound divide in philosophical understandings—in the deep meanings—regarding what constitutes the nature of leadership and the research enterprise around it. This is because they have developed from contrasting philosophies of science, that is, contrasting answers to the ontological and epistemological questions that reflect the assumptions researchers bring to their work (as reviewed in this book's Introduction). In the face of this divide, it is even more remarkable that entity and constructionist scholars have recently come together around their interest in the idea of relational

Advancing Relational Leadership Research, pages 1–40
Copyright © 2012 by Information Age Publishing
All rights of reproduction in any form reserved.

leadership; *this is a clear sign that something bigger is afoot.* As we described in our introductory chapter, we believe this something bigger is relationality.

Given the importance of relationality and the different treatments of it in both perspectives on leadership, there is a critical need in the leadership field to clarify the approaches to thinking about the relational dimensions of leadership brought by each perspective. We need to unpack entity and constructionist assumptions to leadership and point to their respective contributions for advancing knowledge in the field. Such a philosophical investigation of the roots and implications of our research choices is not so much a matter of collective choice as it is an imperative: If we are to take collective responsibility for the leadership field, we need to engage scholars who are researching leadership across perspectives in dialogue. Without this engagement, scholars from each perspective will continue to "claim" ownership of the "true" meaning of relationality, and concerns about relational leadership will become yet another object in the competition for legitimate claims of knowledge in the field, perpetuating the paradigm wars of the past.

Capitalizing on the opportunity to advance new knowledge today starts by looking at the taken-for-granted, unanalyzed presuppositions scholars from each perspective bring to their research. In doing so, we can shed light on why the divide exists and why it is felt so strongly by members of each community. This understanding will help demonstrate to the field that each perspective has its own legitimate logic, and it offers useful insights about leadership as a social reality. Scholars, independent of their research posture, can then introduce refreshing ideas to enhance scholarship in their own perspective.

In this chapter, we name and explore some of the taken-for-granted presuppositions supporting each perspective. We structure the narrative into three sections. In the first section, we acknowledge and illustrate some visible manifestations of the divide between the entity and constructionist perspectives and highlight their contrasting views on relationality. We use the next two sections to inquire into the nature of these differences, unpacking the philosophical assumptions at their root. To do this, in the second section we examine their distinct sets of assumptions about *how we know reality* and the implications for relationality in leadership research. In the third part, we show how these assumptions manifest in distinct research *postures* and *agendas for leadership research,* thus coming back full circle to the experience of scholars as they go about developing a research practice to study relationality in leadership.

Two qualifications must be offered here. First, our analytical scheme is one among other existing frameworks. Organization and management scholars interested in the research implications of the philosophy of science have developed their own versions of existing divides in the field, which include diverse classifications and labels around core assumptions.[2] These variations reflect efforts to synthesize the complex philosophical streams that feed present intellectual discussions in the philosophy of social science. They also reflect that these scholars are largely self-educated in an area not sufficiently studied in doctoral programs (Yanow & Schwartz-Shea, 2006, pp. xxiii–xxiv). Moreover, our scheme does not represent a full framework in the philosophy of science. Instead, we highlight selected elements in as much as they tell us something important about how to study relationality. Footnotes expand information and acknowledge subtleties associated with claims in the narrative.

The second qualification explains an imbalance in the chapter. Postmodernism (and the constructionist version of leadership that is derived from it) is seldom taught to leadership scholars in training (at least not in the U.S.). Therefore, we examine it in more detail in contrast to the dominant, better-understood entity postpositivist perspective. We agree with Bechara & Van de Ven (2007) that scholars must choose and synthesize the philosophy of science that fits their scholarly practice to ensure that the assumptions they use are not merely inherited or brought in by default. This requires further reflection to make informed choices about paradigmatic stances that are less familiar, or even invisible, to the interested scholar.

We hope to make the discussion as reader friendly as possible for those who are new to it. The reader versed in the philosophy of science may want to quickly scan the sections to have a sense of the building blocks for the discussion that follows in the book chapters.

ENTITY AND CONSTRUCTIONIST PERSPECTIVES OF LEADERSHIP

The divide between the entity and constructionist perspectives of leadership is not unique to the leadership field. In a recent *Academy of Management Review* article, Boisot and McKelvey (2010) pose a similar divide in the context of organization studies. Contrasting two worldviews, they argue that one is anchored in a modernist outlook, with deep roots in ideas of the Enlightenment, while the other rests on a postmodernist outlook, with deep roots in the anti-modernist period of the end of the twentieth century. Each produces a different orientation to scientific inquiry. The orientation to science originally called "positivism" (and its contemporary version, postpositivism) draws directly from modernist assumptions.[3] In contrast, the orientation to science called "interpretivism" builds from postmodern assumptions–that even challenge conventional definitions of science.[4] A postpositivist orientation to science represents the dominant tradition in disciplines like psychology (and therefore in fields like leadership and journals like *The Leadership Quarterly*).

Postpositivist and interpretivist orientations pull scholars' attention in different directions—reducing the possibility for agreements on what constitutes legitimate knowledge, and generating competing bases of legitimacy for the claims they produce. These two distinct approaches represent, in fact, competing paradigms, or to be a bit more cautious, competing *paradigmatic stances*. They mark the legitimacy of truth claims not only in the organization and leadership studies fields, but also in contemporary social science scholarship in general.

Tensions around the legitimacy of knowledge claims affect communication among entity and constructionist leadership scholars precisely because the paradigmatic stances behind their perspectives have not been acknowledged or are not sufficiently explicit. Yet, today the fundamentals of the leadership field (as in other fields of inquiry) rest on underlying assumptions that participants in each perspective simply presuppose: "Such assumptions appear so obvious that people do not know what they are assuming, because *no other way of putting things* has ever occurred to them" (Sedlacek, 2011, p. 8). Attentiveness to "*other ways of putting things*" and a degree of openness about what these may be can enhance communication among those who are part of the same field. Short of this awareness, " . . . individuals run a significant risk of talking past one another–listening without hearing and speaking without understanding" (Walker, 2006, p. 69). Leadership scholars must recognize not only what Walker calls "the meta-theoretical perspective" of their interlocutors, but also their own perspective (p. 69).

Contrasts in Published Scholarly Research on Leadership

The marked differences between the work published in the two main leadership journals, *The Leadership Quarterly* (U.S.-based) and *Leadership* (European origin), illustrate the competing paradigmatic stances in the leadership literature. Both journals have published research from the entity and the constructionist perspectives (representing the postpositivist and interpretivist orientations to science respectively). Yet, a glance at two randomly picked issues from a similar time period exemplifies their contrasting approaches to scholarly research on leadership. Distinct language and themes, as well as choices reflecting methodological commitments to a particular approach to science, illustrate these differences in the articles for the selected June 2010 issue of *The Leadership Quarterly* and May 2010 issue of *Leadership*.[5]

Considering language and themes, a sample of the featured articles of the June 2010 *LQ* issue included *The impact of positivity and transparency on trust in leaders and their perceived effectiveness; Transformational leadership and children's aggression in team settings: A short-term longitudinal study;* and *A multi-level study of transformational leadership, justice perceptions, and organizational citizenship behaviors.* Articles in *Leadership* included *Leadership as work-embed-ded influence: A micro-discursive analysis of an everyday interaction in a bank; Shaping leadership for today: Mary Parker Follett's aesthetic;* and *Spirituality at work, and its implications for leadership and followership: A post-structuralist per-spective.* The titles alone reflect quite distinct jargon and sensibilities.

The keywords accompanying the article abstracts are further illustrative. Those in the *LQ* issue referenced well-established management and leader-ship constructs (such as strategic fit, organizational citizenship behavior, leadership competencies, vision, followership, and trust). They tended to qualify a type of leadership (such as operant leadership, authentic leader-ship, and outstanding leadership) and embedded the research in formal-ized received knowledge from well-established leadership theories [e.g., so-cial learning theory, transformational theory, leader-member exchange (LMX), and dynamic network theory]. While keywords in *Leadership* also included some traditional constructs (e.g., leader-follower interactions, identity, and influence), they were complemented by terms reflecting more postmodern views of relationships and relationality (e.g., circularity, para-dox, portraiture, microdiscourse, and performances). This language wid-ened the discursive community beyond just leadership studies, with spe-cific leadership theories replaced by constructs evoking broader theoretical perspectives (i.e., post-structuralism) associated with the humanities, social theory, and critical management studies, among other fields.

These differences in language evoke distinct assumptions about the na-ture of leadership and what constitutes its legitimate study. Choices that re-flect contrasting methodological commitments also brought to the surface different approaches to science in the articles. For example, despite some variation in methods, the *LQ* articles reflected a postpositivist approach to science with a preference for quantitative studies using structural equation modeling techniques as well as experimental and historiometric studies. (There was also one qualitative study.) In contrast, methodologies in the *Leadership* articles drew more heavily from interpretivist approaches to scholarship, including choices like ethnographic methods and analytical techniques drawn from the humanities (i.e., art history).

Likewise, all *LQ* articles reported empirical research based on large samples and hypothesis testing of well-established or emergent leadership theories. In contrast, the *Leadership* issue featured both conceptual and empirical pieces and gave them equal status. Most articles tended to be embedded in broader scholarly traditions to illuminate the data, for example, a poststructuralist critique of leadership studies on spirituality at work. Finally, the *LQ* articles followed the script of deductive research reports, with the expected sequence of literature review, hypothesis formulation, methods, findings, and discussion. The *Leadership* articles were organized around unique structures and narratives, each with their own internal and distinctive logic.

This informal comparison suggests that scholars writing for these issues of *The Leadership Quarterly* and for *Leadership* tend to belong to different paradigmatic communities. The differences in each journal reflect distinct assumptions about what is theory, what is rigor, and what is legitimate scholarly research on leadership, as well as how to conceptualize and approach the notion of relationality.

Contrasts in Views of Relationality

We have characterized relationality as the understanding that individuals and collectives constitute *a field of relationships*, which in turn implies that each individual represents the intersection of multiple relationships (Bradbury & Lichtenstein, 2000; Carroll, Levy & Richmond, 2008; Gergen, 2009). (For a deeper discussion, see the Introduction of this book.) However, in the same way that the underlying entity and constructionist assumptions produce distinct decisions about how to study leadership and how to report on the findings, they also produce distinct entity and constructionist views of relationality.

Entity Views of Relationality

Most leadership theories—contingency theory, the transformational and neo-charismatic schools, LMX theory, cognitive and social identity theories, servant leadership, shared and distributed leadership, among others—can be located within the broader umbrella of postpositivism. They share a particular perspective of relational leadership that Hosking (1988, 2011) refers to as "entitative" (defined as "pure entity; abstracted from all circumstances"). Uhl-Bien (2006) in her 2006 relational leadership theory (RLT) article uses the term "entity" (defined as "something that exists independently, as a particular and discrete unit").[6]

The word *entity* reflects ontological assumptions that lead researchers to treat their objects of study—leaders and followers—as if they were independent of one another, regarding groups and organizations as a collection of individuals. The ontology associated with an entity view leads to a theorization of leaders, followers, and their surroundings as "separate units, the self and other, the person and culture, the individual and society" (Gergen, 2009, p. *xx*). Entity studies, drawing from a postpositivist epistemology, view truth as emerging from a correspondence between a claim and empirically observed facts, demanding standards of replicability as a condition of quality (Boisot & McKelvey, 2010).

The epistemic stance behind postpositivist methods leads to conceptualizing a "relationship" as something that happens when distinct entities come into contact, meaning that relations are *derivative of the independent entities*. That is, relations follow from existing entities who approach one another (Gergen, 2009). The entity perspective is concerned with identifying attributes of individuals as they engage in interpersonal relationships, characterizing the quality and antecedents of relationships, the association between relationships and outcomes, and exploring issues such as the development of the relationship (Uhl-Bien, Maslyn & Ospina, 2011).

The growing concern of entity scholars for exploring the relational dimensions of leadership stems in part from having hit the limits of postpositivist methods in the context of a heightened demand to consider issues like relationality, time, context, levels of analysis, and practical value in leadership studies (Uhl-Bien, 2006). A big challenge for entity scholars is how to tackle a construct like relationality in ways that transcend the restrictions imposed by postpositivism's tendency to partition and simplify reality.

Constructionist Views of Relationality

In contrast to the more recent attention given by entity scholars to issues of relational leadership, constructionist scholars have long been concerned with relational leadership, as relationality is inherent to the ontological and epistemological assumptions of this perspective (Ospina & Sorenson, 2006).

The constructionist perspective resonates with an interpretivist orientation to science with roots in postmodernism. It views leadership as a process of social construction produced through relationship (Fairhurst, 2007; Hosking, 2011). It is through social construction that certain understandings of leadership come about and eventually take on a life of their own, so that leadership appears "real." When enacted as if real, the consequences of thinking and doing leadership become "real." (Constructionists would say that these understandings of leadership become reified and are given ontological privilege) (Ospina & Sorenson, 2006; Uhl-Bien, 2006; Grint, 2005). Relationality is intrinsic to the constructionist view of leadership because it sees the world as constructed in and through interaction (Hosking, 2011). It is in approaching one another that individuals can define themselves socially as separate entities: relationship comes first.

This constructionist notion of "relationship" stresses the interdependent nature of those in relation. Constructionism conveys an understanding of individuals and collectives as embedded in and constituting a field of relationships, making relationality endemic to the perspective. In Gergen's (2009) words, this implies a reversal of order to consider "the individual units as *derivative of relational processes*" (p. xxi)—viewing "being" as a derivative of relating. This is exactly the opposite of an entity perspective, which views relations as derivative of individual units. In constructionist ontology, relationship comes first, and from there emerges our social world as a humanly constructed reality.

Constructionist scholars therefore enter their research on leadership in quite a different way from those doing entity research. While entity researchers privilege individual dimensions, constructionist researchers privilege the collective. The latter choose methods that are sensitive to the *apriori* relational posture of this perspective. The emphasis here is on "the rich interconnections among people acting in contexts which allow leadership to be 'co-produced' in 'the space between'" (Uhl-Bien et al., 2011, p. 307, citing Bradbury & Lichtenstein, 2000).

A big dilemma for constructionist scholars is how to clarify and translate into practical terms the research and practice implications of the fact that *individuals are derivative of relational processes* rather than the opposite and more intuitive idea that individuals create relationships. This is particularly true because, in giving priority to process, constructionist leadership researchers may easily downplay the importance of the *embodied human beings* (quite enamored with their individuality) who participate in and drive such processes.

Leadership research is caught between these two distinct understandings of relationality and their respective views of what constitutes legitimate scientific research. As we suggest in the Introduction, premature paradigmatic closure in the field has privileged the entity perspective as "the legitimate" type of leadership scholarship. Despite the inroads of constructionism in the U.S. management field (Fairhurst & Grant, 2010) this version of research has yet to gain comparable standing with the entity perspective in leadership studies. For example, *LQ* continues to give preference to a postpositive approach to science, and there are indications that it is hardening this stance. The entrance of European-based journals like *Leadership* (in response to the need for an outlet for interpretivist voices in leadership scholarship) has broadened the potential space for exposure to different interpretivist perspectives, including constructionism. Yet, learning and sharing across perspectives is still rare in the leadership field as a whole.

Mix-ups and Misunderstandings in Leadership Scholarship

The insidious consequences of this divide are quite real for the field, as suggested in the Introduction, even if entity and constructionist scholars experience them differently. The dialogues in this book between scholars representing each perspective reflect these tensions. In the broader field, they are palpable in differential access to journals for scholars in each tradition, and even in the invisibility of non-postpositivist perspectives in surveys of the field.[7] And yet, these tensions and their consequences are seldom explicitly discussed or acknowledged.

Neither are the reasons behind the differences in research practices—from framing the problems and questions to choosing specific research tools and writing reports—well understood or appreciated. The result is great potential for confusion, misunderstanding, and frustrations for scholars in the field. For example, consider the cognitive dissonance produced by differences in research reporting. Entity leadership researchers tend to start their research designs and reports at the level of theories and models, ignoring or taking for granted ontological and epistemological assumptions behind theoretical and methodological decisions. They are, on the other hand, quite meticulous about their methodological choices and (quantitative or qualitative) analyses. In contrast, constructionist scholars are very purposive about making transparent the philosophical assumptions informing their research. Yet, they tend to be less explicit, and often informal, about their methodological choices and analytical strategies.

This results in two very different types of documentation in entity and constructionist leadership research products which, in turn, represents a source of frustration for both entity and constructionist scholars. Scholars trained in the postpositivist tradition often do not know what to do with articles based on constructionist research. They may be uncomfortable with the language and approaches—often finding the narrative obscure and overly complex. More importantly, the lack of attention to methods by constructionist scholars often leads them to conclude the work is not "scientific," and therefore they do not recognize it as fully legitimate scholarship. Constructionist scholars are more familiar with the type of research published in *LQ*, but they often become impatient with what they see as too narrow a focus and a homogenous approach to research that seems to them too formulaic and reductionist. These dynamics also reflect the tension between dominant and non-dominant research perspectives described in the Introduction of this book. Recall Deetz's point (1996) that members of the dominant group tend to grow blind spots, while those in the less dominant group must learn the two systems (theirs and the dominant one) to survive.

The differences in the mode of inquiry that researchers take (as illustrated in the selected journal issues discussed above) can also generate confusion and block communication. Entity leadership scholars tend to favor the deductive phase of the cycle of theory construction. Theory is translated into a model, with established relationships between two or more constructs operationalized as variables. They thus begin with an existing theory of leadership, such as LMX or shared leadership, develop a model, and test propositions regarding the model's accuracy to validate, refine, or reject the theory. Theoretical models are built cumulatively, incrementally, and in small strands. In contrast, constructionist leadership scholars tend to enter research in the inductive phase of the theory-building cycle, letting the data illuminate the question at hand,[8] and drawing loosely from the rich heritage of broad (macro) theories associated with postmodernism (e.g., critical theory, narrativism, phenomenology, hermeneutics, social theory, feminism, queer theory, poststructuralism, and so on). They may refer to mainstream leadership theories, not so much to refine them or build on them, but to deconstruct them or challenge their logic. *The result is two relatively parallel conversations, rather than an authentic dialogue between perspectives in the field.*

Furthermore, understandings of *what is theory* or *how it is used in research* differ significantly. Entity scholars prefer to work with "theories of the middle range" (Merton, 1968): empirical, testable propositions that are positioned between all-embracing, unified theories (from which they may be derived) and descriptive empirical work, with little theoretical orientation (empiricism). New adjectives qualifying leadership give rise to new leadership theories (e.g., contingency theory, transformational leadership theory, LMX theory, relational leadership theory, complexity theory, and so on). It is from these theories that entity scholars draw their identities in the field.

In contrast, constructionist scholars do not identify with these specific leadership theories. Instead, the theories they use may reflect the "grand" theories that the sociologist Merton (1968) positioned one level of abstraction above theories of the middle range, including postmodernism as such, with its deep influence in the social sciences as a challenge to modernist assumptions at the end of the twentieth century (Hollinger, 1994). Constructionist leadership studies are highly theoretical, but not in the way that entity scholars would conceive of theory. When the entity scholar reads a research article and does not find a "theory" translated into a model with testable propositions, the inclination is to discount it as a "story" or a narrative, rather than regard it as a legitimate "scientific" research product (with numbers and hard quantitative analyses).

The potential for mix-ups and misunderstanding becomes even greater when critical theory is added to the mix.[9] Critical management and leadership researchers develop knowledge to help improve the human condition—if possible, bringing to center stage oft-silenced voices and perspectives from the margins (Collinson, 2011; Fairhurst & Grant, 2010; Ospina & Sorenson, 2006). As Alvesson and Sveningsson make clear in Chapter 7 of this book, they view the meaning of "leadership" itself with suspicion or even skepticism.

Contrary to entity leadership scholars' choice to start with a firm definition of leadership, critical leadership scholars, rather than reaffirming existing understandings, *deconstruct* these understandings (and their associated assumptions) to uncover how leadership discourses and practices contribute to reproducing power and control in organizations and society (Collinson, 2011; Fairhurst & Grant, 2010). To do so, they draw on an eclectic set of theoretical perspectives in which the line between the social sciences and the humanities is blurred, for example, "structuralism, labour process theory and critical realism . . . feminism, post-structuralism, deconstructionism, literary criticism, post-colonial theory, cultural studies, environmentalism and psychoanalysis," among others (Collison, 2011, p. 182). They apply a postmodern logic of *critical deconstruction* that is quite foreign to entity leadership scholars' modern idea of critical thinking.

It is not surprising therefore, that entity scholars find the body of constructionist and critical leadership research on leadership hard to navigate. There are no "labels" that would help them locate the perspective "theoretically," other than through the broad blanket of constructionism, or one of other multiple, associated, broad theoretical traditions. In and of themselves, these often add more confusion than insight, given the entity scholar's lack of familiarity with the perspective and its assumptions, as well as the many possible strands of social theory from which constructionists and critical scholars may draw.[10]

The dynamics of competition for legitimacy among their seemingly *incommensurable* paradigmatic stances also leads to a narrowing of the field. Yet, insights from both perspectives are needed to advance present understanding of relational leadership:

> An understanding of a complex problem or phenomenon being investigated can be enhanced by engaging the perspectives of diverse scholars. . . . Appreciating these diverse perspectives often requires communicating across different philosophical perspectives. It also requires maintaining the diverse intellectual differences that not only create an opportunity for arbitrage, but also for a productive interplay of perspectives, models and world views. (Bechara & Van de Ven, 2007, p. 37)

In the leadership field, productive interplay calls for better understanding of the modernist and postmodernist assumptions shaping the philosophies of science in the entity (postpositivist) and the constructionist (interpretivist) perspectives of leadership. We turn to the core of these distinctions in the next two sections, where we offer a simplified scheme that considers differences at three levels of the analytical ladder of abstraction. We first consider the broadest and most abstract philosophical divides suggested by Boisot and McKelvey (2010), modernism and postmodernism. At this level, the differences are about worldview. Going down one level, postpositivist and interpretivist modes of inquiry represent different approaches to science associated with the modernist and postmodernist worldviews respectively; one level below are the entity and constructionist perspectives of leadership with their distinct research agendas, linked respectively to the postpositivist and interpretivist approaches to science.[11] In the next section, we make comparisons around the first two levels of this scheme—world-views and approaches to science—leaving the third level, research agendas, to the final section of the chapter.

TRUTH AND HUMAN EFFORTS TO STUDY REALITY

The contrasts between modernist and postmodernist stances to research reflect broad historical changes in worldviews over time (Boisot & McKelvey, 2010; Hollinger, 1994). The key distinction between these two worldviews revolves around the idea of "truth" and a researcher's ability to attain it. A scholar taking a modernist stance believes that it is possible to capture truth (a unified truth) about our objects of study. This scholar also assumes the possibility of approximating truth with some certainty and with some independence from his or her own subjectivity. In contrast, a scholar taking a postmodernist stance assumes that there are multiple truths about our objects of study. This view of "truth" considers the various interpretations of those experiencing the reality studied, including that of the researcher as s/he enters their world. Postmodernist scholars do not expect to attain more than a glimpse of those multiple truths, while acknowledging their own subjectivity in doing so.

These distinctions point to different assumptions about the world ("reality"). Reflecting the assumptions and worldview of the Enlightenment, modernism offers a "realist" answer to the ontological question of *what is the nature of the world and of human beings?* They claim that reality is a concrete, objective "thing," independent of human cognition. Human beings are autonomous, relatively self-contained entities, with independent interests and desires, who respond and adapt to this external reality. This makes it possible to "see" the world as an objective reality that can be rationally manipulated and controlled to achieve social ends. These assumptions have led to a characterization of this worldview as "atomistic" and "objectivist."[12]

In contrast, to the same ontological question, postmodernists offer a *constructionist* view of the world as a *meaningful reality that is humanly constructed.* Rather than objective truth, there are "just humanly fashioned ways of seeing things whose processes we need to explore, and which we can only come to understand through a similar process of meaning making" (Crotty, 1998, p. 9). While a world may exist outside of human subjectivity, *meaningful realities* exist only through the interpretation of human relations. Moreover, these realities become "dense feedback loops" generated by intentional constructions of events, and by complex interdependencies among each other (Boisot & McKelvey, 2010, p. 420). Meaningful realities are inherently relational. Therefore, this worldview can be characterized as resting on a "connectivist" and "subjectivist" ontology (in contrast to the "atomist" and "objectivist" ontology of modernism). Objectivist and subjectivist assumptions about reality point to different assumptions about how we know and study reality (including questions about the role of the researcher).

Modernist Assumptions about How We Know Reality

To the epistemological question of *how can we develop knowledge about the world*, modernism offers the paradigmatic approaches to science of logical positivism and postpositivism. The metaphor of "a window" (Shank, 2002) illustrates the objectivist nature of the "modernist gaze" behind them, and its accompanying vision of research. The "window" can be thought of as a tool to look through, to try to get as "accurate" view as possible of what is on the other side. This is the case when using microscopes and telescopes in the natural sciences, or applying an index or a scale in a survey protocol in the behavioral sciences. Since the world behind the window is real, the goal is to "see" the world with as little distortion as possible, to capture it as best as possible. As Shank suggests, the researcher corrects for smudges in the window (bias) and tries to identify flaws in the window (error). Then s/he looks for causal relationships and trends to explain what has been observed and to predict future occurrences. This implies discovering patterns or relationships among phenomena, finding causal associations in their variation (variables), and controlling for endogenous variables and other spurious factors. Objective truth about reality can be discovered. Science offers the tools to get as close as possible to gaining truth with some degree of precision and certitude.

Variations Within the Modernist Worldview
Sharing an objectivist ontology, the approaches to science of logical positivism and postpositivism nevertheless differ in the degree to which they fully espouse pure objectivism and the consequent assumptions about the role of the researcher. Postpositivism (or neopositivism, as some prefer to call it) is a more sophisticated and more critical orientation to research, compared to logical positivism (Crotty, 1998).

Consistent with its objective ontology, logical positivism assumes that it is possible to *fully* capture a true picture of reality, that the only source of knowledge is observation, and that the researcher has *full independence* from the object of study. In contrast, postpositivism replaces "*fully*" capturing reality with "*imperfectly*," and "*full independence*" of the researcher with "*partial independence.*" In shifting from a "realist" to a "critical realist" ontology (Van de Ven, 2007; Walker, 2006), postpositivists acknowledge a limited understanding of the "real" world, and they reject the notion of a predetermined methodology to capture reality in ways that allow for the full judgment of the veracity of knowledge (Bechara & Van de Ven, 2007; Crotty, 1998).

Furthermore, some postpositivists are more "critical" than others depending on how far away they move from the original positivist realism, and the consequent implications for their understanding of the "window" metaphor. The most critical realist postpositivists assume that there is an objective world but a limited understanding of it, particularly of its emergent social processes; that the search for universal, error-free truths is merely a guiding aspiration; that all forms of inquiry are partial and value-laden rather than impartial and value-free; and finally, they see the benefit of developing models that simplify the complexity of reality, allowing for the possibility of considering multiple perspectives in the search for partial truth (Bechara & Van de Ven, 2007, p. 37).

In leadership studies, the assumptions of entity scholars vary according to where they fall within the purely realist position (of logical positivism) and the more relaxed realist position (of postpositivism). Most entity scholars who express concern with relationality tend to espouse the assumptions of critical realism. This makes it less surprising to see the convergence with constructionism around relational leadership, and this reinforces the potential for dialogue at the present time in the field. The more "critical" their realism, the easier it is for postpositivists to open up to authentic communication with constructionists, but this has yet to be realized. This possibility becomes even clearer when the assumptions of constructionist leadership scholars (and their primary postmodernist approach to scientific inquiry, interpretivism) are further unpacked.

Postmodernist Assumptions About How We Know Reality

In contrast to the metaphor of the "window" (that illustrates a positivist and postpositivist modern worldview), the metaphor of the "lantern" illustrates a way of knowing reality that reflects a postmodern worldview. The constructionist perspective of leadership falls within this paradigmatic stance. Postmodernism challenges the idea that it is at all possible to "capture reality." Instead, knowing is about understanding its meaning. A lantern helps to "shed light in dark corners" (Shank, 2002, p. 11); it illuminates patterns, relationships, gaps, discontinuities, and the underlying mechanisms that help one to *understand*. In a postmodernist worldview, inquiry is about the search for "meaning where no meaning has been clearly understood before" (p. 11). This is meaning that can be better accessed and understood in experience and through practice.[13]

In a postmodern constructionist worldview, the relationship between individuals and the world is one of reciprocal influence: The self and the world constitute one another. Human beings construct meaning, and through these constructions, they shape reality, which takes on a life of its own; then, as human beings *interpret* this reality, they are in turn shaped by it. This is why, to the question of *how can we develop knowledge about the world*, a constructionist postmodern orientation answers with an approach to research called interpretivism.[14]

Interpretivists assume that we can only access the world through that which people themselves interpret as "real," which, in turn, makes the consequences of their actions equally "real." However, one should note that this is not merely about the subjective perceptions of research subjects. Pachirat (2006) describes what it means to be an interpretivist researcher as follows: It is about "humans, making meaning out of the meaning-making of other humans" (p. 374). In this statement, the interpretivist researcher comes to understand that approaching the subjectivity of his/her subjects does not mean just reporting exclusively on their subjective perceptions. It also means that the researcher must consider their embeddedness in social and cultural contexts. This requires stepping back to make meaning of them with the use of broader social science theories and tools that, like a "lantern," help to illuminate a corner of the social world as experienced by those who inhabit it.

The answers to the ontological and epistemological questions that support the postmodernist metaphor of the "lantern" differ significantly from those that support the modernist metaphor of the "window," precisely because postmodernists challenge the modernist project. Given the gap between the entity and constructionist paradigmatic stances in leadership studies, entity scholars' strong reactions and discomfort with constructionist language might be associated with the relentless postmodernist challenge to modernist assumptions, and more specifically, to that of objectivist ontology.

Indeed, the postmodern notion that there are multiple truths represents a profound challenge to the modern aspiration to search for some degree of objective truth. This challenge may be experienced as an assault to basic beliefs underlying entity scholars' postpositivist assumptions, or to a misunderstanding of their critical realism for those postpositivists who have moved away from logical positivism's realist stance. Either reason may generate reactions like defensiveness, annoyance, or even resentment, which in turn become barriers to communication. Yet, part of the problem is that the challenge is taken as a blanket statement, when in fact, as within modernist stances to science, there are also important variations within postmodernist stances that open up opportunity for dialogue.

Variations Within the Postmodernist Worldview

If interpretivists commonly agree that realities are drawn from human meaning, they *vary in the degree to which they fully or partially embrace two postmodernist assumptions:* subjectivism (assumptions about the world), and researcher distance from the object of study (assumptions about the researcher's way of knowing).

Some postmodernist scholars embrace *a totally subjectivist ontology.* They view meaning making as a purely subjective act, essentially independent of the object. This purely subjectivist view of reality is called *constructivism* (Crotty, 1998). Other scholars view subject and object as distinguishable, *but as always united and constructed through interaction.* This *inter-subjective* view of the world is called *constructionism.* We are concerned with the second variant of postmodernism, which gives rise to the constructionist perspective of leadership.

This ontological distinction between constructivism and constructionism has important implications for the respective assumptions about ways of knowing–and their consequent approaches to research. Below, we clarify the nature of constructionism by contrasting it to its postmodern cousin, constructivism, and to the much better-understood modernist orientation of postpositivism (which underlies entity perspectives of leadership that emphasize relationality).

Constructionism: A Particular Version of Postmodernism

The labels of constructivism and constructionism are often used interchangeably, but they are not synonymous. Constructivism is the most subjectivist view of postmodernism, whereby all that counts as real is human subjectivity. The world is but projections of mental representations. In this subjectivist position, understanding the world is about understanding the *subjective interpretations of individuals* since what goes on in individuals' heads is viewed as the source of reality.[15]

In contrast to construc*tivism,* construc*tionism* is a distinct postmodernist stance that moves away from pure subjectivism. Constructionism views reality as the result of the interaction between the subjectivity of an individual and an external world (where other subjectivities also reside). However, this world only becomes a social reality (socially meaningful) when it is interpreted *in relation to other subjects.* In this ontology, the world may exist on its own, but it is, in fact, nothing more or less than an "inter-subjective reality," two subjectivities connected to "construct" a third, common—and social—reality, out of a reality that would otherwise have no meaning. At its core stands the notion of relationality: Reality is at the same time internal (subjective) and external (objective). Subjects who are engaged with one another encounter and interpret the object of attention and become co-producers of a shared, inter-subjective social world. This view is quite different from constructivism.[16]

The distinction between constructivism and constructionism suggests that three (not two) approaches to knowing have direct implications for how *relational* leadership is studied: modernist postpositivism,[17] postmodernist constructivism, and postmodernist constructionism. The constructivist subjectivist view offers a mirror image of postpositivism's objectivist view: In constructivism, reality is created through a subjective act of humans (subjectivism), while for postpositivism, objects are real and independent from subjectivity (objectivism). Despite this radical difference, they share a common feature: In both cases, it is the individual who approaches (postpositivism) or creates (constructivism) the world. Hence, constructivist and entity perspectives of leadership both emphasize individual agency as the point of entry to their study. While postpositivist entity scholars might be more inclined to attend to behaviors and relationships in addition to cognition, constructivist scholars might attend to perceptions, and mental models, as well as cognitive and affective states when studying leadership.[18]

The assumptions of both postpositivism and constructivism contrast with those of constructionism, which fits somewhere in between the two positions that prioritize agency (entity and constructivist views of leadership). Like constructivists, constructionists see meaning as the path to reality. Yet, contrary to constructivists' idealist assumption, constructionists assume the existence of a world. Human beings *construct meaning when they approach the object of study and interact with it.* This also contrasts with the objectivist assumption of postpositivism, that there is a world with *inherent meaning in its objects, independent of someone coming upon them* (Crotty, 1998). For constructionism, objects are irrelevant independent of the subject approaching them. An approaching subject makes them meaningful, thus making them real in social terms.

In sum, in contrast to constructivism, for constructionism, meaning *does not reside in the subject.* In contrast to postpositivism, meaning *does not reside in the object either.* Meaning is neither "subjective" nor "objective," it is relational: In constructionism, objectivity and subjectivity are brought together indissolubly (Crotty, 1998, p. 44). While separate, subjective reality and objective reality are inherently connected. Hence while constructivists and postpositivist scholars emphasize the individual (behavioral and cognitive) dimensions of reality, the inter-subjective, connectivist stance of constructionists leads them to emphasize the collective dimensions of reality, attending to properties and dynamics that involve *all members of a group as distinct from its individuals.* Given their postmodern, inter-subjective stance, constructionists do not see an objective reality as the locus from which to gain "objective truth." The world and truth are constructed (not discovered). And, this world is accessed through the interpretation of meaning (not through distanced observation).[19]

It follows that, rather than giving primacy to agency, constructionist perspectives of leadership attend more deliberately to its collective dimensions, and thus operate at a level of observation and analysis that is different from the individual level. From this entry point, constructionists see something collectively labeled as *leadership* emerging from the process of co-construction of meaning associated with a particular inter-subjective reality around a group's organizing and coordinating tasks. Constructionists explore the processes and the context that serve *as the raw material* for the emergence and sustenance of this something called "leadership." Constructionists privilege process and context over agency as the entry point to study leadership. They emphasize culture rather than "the unique experience of each of us" (Crotty, 1998, p. 58).

Constructivism's affinity with entity approaches to leadership lies in their similar focus on individuals as the primary source of leadership. They both differ from constructionist's focus on the collective sources of leadership. This further clarifies Kennedy, Carroll, Francoeur, and Jackson's intriguing story of leadership development in Chapter 6, where they compare the lived experience of two facilitators, viewing one account as "constructivist/entity" and the other as a "social constructionist account."

Constructionism, Critical Theory and Leadership Studies

According to constructionism, *reality is constructed when individual subjectivities meet in an inter-subjective (collective) world, and objects attain meaning.* This is a pedagogical way of describing a complex social dynamic in which many subjectivities interact to generate shared social meaning over time. The shared agreements become the basis of a potentially stable social order, one that is simultaneously tenuous and firm, flexible and resilient, changeable and enduring.

Fragile, shared meanings eventually morph into stable and long-lasting social institutions that become "real" and are treated as if they had emerged naturally—independent from human relations. Social reality is recreated over time through language and other symbolic discourses and socially accepted enactments. At some point, it appears to be natural, "independent" of its social origins. Through this process of *reification* (Berger & Luckmann, 1967), members of a society start believing that certain shared assumptions can be explained through the natural laws of the world and are therefore immutable. They then believe that these are external from the original shared agreements that gave them meaning at a given (historical) time in a given (local) context.

Some constructionist scholars add the lens of critical theory (Bohman, 2002) to this scenario.[20] For them, the relationship between the world, its actors, and the observer is also characterized by power asymmetries. Reification serves an ideological purpose for those in the dominant positions, as it makes people "forget" that recurrent agreements sustaining structures of oppression have a social, and not a natural origin, and are thus changeable. The "naturalizing" discourses that reproduce existing relations (e.g., socially constructed institutions such as slavery were presented as natural realities for a long time) serve to maintain social order as it is. Critical theorists contend, however, that social order is also tenuous because these discourses can be contested and re-constructed.

Even though not all critical theorists are constructionists, management and leadership scholars who use a critical theory lens tend to espouse a postmodern constructionist epistemic stance. Critical management and critical leadership scholars aim to uncover taken-for-granted ways in which power influences organizational outcomes. They unveil hidden mechanisms of oppression associated with management and leadership processes.

Critical management studies (CMS) draw from the critical theory tradition to explain and critique processes in organizational life and work institutions. Critical management scholars explore micro and macro processes and their interconnections. They explore how unequal power relations influence social outcomes to the advantage of some and the detriment of others (Alvesson & Sveningsson, 2003; Alvesson &Willmott, 1996; Fairhurst & Grant, 2010; Lotia & Hardy, 2008). Discourses and practices that sustain power structures and the political dynamics of systems of production and work become of paramount interest (Cunliffe, 2009). Also of concern is the unequal impact of these dynamics on various stakeholders, such as owners, shareholders, managers, and employees or workers. Leadership is one such process of organizational life that receives the same scrutiny.

Collinson (2011) points to an emergent group of critical scholars in the leadership field. He identifies them as doing studies that "share a concern to critique the power relations and identity constructions through which leadership dynamics are often reproduced, frequently rationalized, sometimes resisted and occasionally transformed" (p. 181). Key themes explored in this approach to leadership research tend to be linked to the dialectics that characterize leadership dynamics, such as control/resistance, dissent/consent, and men/women (Collinson, 2011).

To sum up, in this second section of the chapter, we clarified and contrasted the ontological and epistemological assumptions of entity and constructionist perspectives of leadership, which are respectively informed by the modernist approaches to inquiry (logical positivism and postpositivism) and the postmodernist approaches (constructionism and constructivism). We also showed the intellectual linkages between constructionism, critical management and critical leadership scholarship. Finally, we ascertained that scholars in these traditions tend to share a commitment to an interpretivist approach to inquiry, which contrasts with the commitment of entity scholars to the postpositivist approach discussed earlier. Moving one level down on the analytical ladder, we now turn to explore in the final section of this chapter how these approaches manifest differently in the way scholars do research and report their research outcomes.

METHODOLOGICAL CHOICES IN LEADERSHIP RESEARCH

Postpositivism and interpretivism offer two conflicting bases of legitimacy for the knowledge claims made about "this thing" we have agreed (or disagreed) to call "leadership." And yet, only by recognizing the legitimacy of both approaches will the conversation move in the right direction—that is, to a place where good empirical research on either perspective (i.e., research performed in a way consistent with the paradigm's definitions of *quality* and *rigor*) is viewed with equal value in the field. Having unpacked the philosophical assumptions of each, it is now time to unpack the implications for methodological choices in leadership research.

Modes of Knowing

Assumptions behind the answers to *how something can be known* manifest in research purpose and practice. Focusing on the leadership "relationship" as something between two or more relatively autonomous entities (leaders and followers), postpositivists tend to be interested in linking relational constructs, operationalized through variables, into a chain of *causal relationships* translated into linear models that explain and predict the behavior of either the leader or follower or something associated with the quality of the leadership relationship. (See, for example, Shamir, 2007, Figure 4; see also Brower, Schoorman & Tan, 2000; Tsui, Egan & O'Reilly, 1992; Wayne & Ferris, 1990). In contrast, considering *relationship* as an emergent, constructed phenomenon, interpretivist scholars tend to be interested in accessing the meaning ("discovering" is too modernist of a term) of leadership relationships in context. They want to reveal *explanatory mechanisms* that clarify how patterns and relationships associated with leadership emerge in practice, thus giving primacy to communicative and organizing processes over individual behavior (Drath, McCauley, Palus, Van Velsor, O'Connor & McGuire, 2008; Fairhurst, 2007; Grint, 2005; Hosking, 1988, 2007; Ospina & Foldy, 2010).

Causal *relationships* are about the systematic correlation of variables, one of which (everything else being equal) follows logically from the other. Explanatory *mechanisms* are about why and how phenomena are related (Lin, 1998), which involves identifying reciprocal influences and unraveling the mechanism into even finer gradations of interconnection. Patton (2002) illustrates the difference by depicting the most simple postpositivist explanation as being of the type "x caused y which in turn caused z," in contrast to the most simple interpretivist explanation as being of the type "x and y came together to create z" (or, for a critical scholar, it might be "x and y came together to cover, reproduce, or create z").[21]

At the level of methodology, it could be argued that this difference is a matter of deciding between working with numbers or words—that is, using quantitative or qualitative data. Yet, the quantitative-qualitative dichotomy is too simplistic, as it hides Hatch and Yanow's (2008) point that methodology is *the application of our ontological and epistemological presuppositions in our choices for research procedures and tools.* Despite their preference for one over the other, neither postpositivists nor interpretivists reject the possible benefits of using words or numbers; they will use them as needed, *but they will use them in ways that are consistent with their postpositivist or interpretivist approach to inquiry* (Yanow & Schwartz-Shea, 2006).

Rather, the difference between privileging causal relationships or explanatory mechanisms relates directly to differences between *modes of cognition* associated with each paradigmatic stance. Bruner (1986) describes two fundamental forms of human reasoning—the "abstract" and the "narrative" modes of knowing—that depict "distinctive ways of ordering experience, of constructing reality" (p. 11). The abstract mode privileges reason, precision, and explanation. The narrative mode privileges experience, metaphor, and interpretation.[22]

The abstract mode of knowing reflects the objectivist and realist assumptions of modernist approaches to inquiry: logical positivism and postpositivism. The narrative mode reflects the connectivist and inter-subjective assumptions of postmodernist constructionist approaches to inquiry typical of interpretivism. Bruner argues that, while "irreducible to one another," their complementarity conveys the "rich diversity of thought" that human beings can use to explore their experience (1986, pp. 11–13). The application of either mode, nevertheless, yields different stances or attitudes towards a researcher's research agenda, that is, different research postures.

Research Postures

In a classical article, Everet and Louis (1981) contrast the practices of two postures that a researcher may take—"inquiry from the outside" and "inquiry from the inside." These research postures can be associated respectively with the metaphors of the window and the lantern, the abstract and narrative modes of knowing, and with postpositivism and interpretivism. These stances, Everet and Louis argue, differ in the degree of immersion of the researcher in terms of experiential engagement, existential commitment to the subject, and physical involvement in the setting. Stemming from different modes of knowing, they produce different but equally valuable types of knowledge.

As a researcher doing inquiry from the outside (evocative of the window and of an abstract mode of knowing) one distances oneself from the subject of study and takes a detached, value-free stance, often also removing oneself from the setting. In contrast, in inquiry from the inside (evocative of the lantern and of a narrative mode of knowing), the researcher assumes that s/he can know by being immersed in the stream of events and activities, thus participating in the phenomenon studied. Hence, inquiry from the outside places the researcher as an external observer, who observes through instrumentation (window), while in inquiry from the inside, the best instrument is the researcher as actor, illuminating meaning through varying degrees of participation (lantern).

Researchers doing inquiry from the outside validate knowledge exclusively by methodological procedure and rational logic (abstract mode of knowing). In contrast, those doing inquiry from the inside assume that knowledge is validated experientially, meaning that the interpretations of the studied reality must make sense to the actors who experience it (narrative mode of knowing). (We will return to this topic in our discussion of standards of quality in interpretive research.) Consistently, in inquiry from the outside, the aim is to isolate the phenomenon and, as much as possible, reduce the level of complexity in the analysis. In contrast, inquiry from the inside aims to learn by getting a holistic picture of historically unique situations, where idiosyncrasies are important to find meaning. The goal is to disentangle elements of that complexity, rather than to ignore it, reduce it, or to hold it constant.

In terms of actual research approaches and tools, researchers doing inquiry from the outside tend to favor quantitative methods and a deductive mode of inquiry, drawing from experimental and semi-experimental methods, econometrics, survey methods, quantitative and mixed case studies, traditional ethnographies, and so on. Only when research engages in hypothesis testing is it viewed as "theory driven."

Researchers doing inquiry from the inside tend to favor qualitative research and an inductive mode of inquiry, drawing from methods that give preeminence to language and representation, such as narrative inquiry, qualitative case studies, some postmodern forms of ethnography, phenomenological studies, hermeneutics, historical analysis, participatory action research, and in the most postmodernist versions, other forms of representation like poetry, visual arts, and theater. Theory is also conceptualized differently: "for some, it is best developed inductively; for others, it is better seen as a 'resource' than as an apparatus of causal laws" (Yanow & Schwartz-Shea, 2006, p. xviii).[23]

The research practices of leadership scholars differ according to their epistemic stance (and preference for a particular mode of knowing), and the particular methodological choices associated with it. So, for example, if a researcher accepts (explicitly or implicitly) that reality exists independent of human subjectivity, s/he will naturally accept the idea that knowing the reality of leadership requires objective instruments and a distanced approach when capturing it objectively ("inquiry from the outside" type tools associated with the window and abstract knowing). It would be somewhat contradictory to then choose as the primary approach a postmodernist interpretivist method such as an auto-ethnography—i.e., an autobiographical research genre connecting the personal to the cultural (Ellis & Bochner, 2000). It would make more sense, instead, to construct instruments such as the Multifactor Leadership Questionnaire (Antonakis, Avolio & Sivasubramaniam, 2003). Likewise, if the researcher views leadership as co-constructed, data from the latter instrument would not be helpful to access, interpret, and understand the experience from which leadership constructions emerge. Instead, interpretivist methods such as narrative inquiry (Ospina & Dodge, 2005), which aim to "find meaning in the stories people use, tell, and even live" (p. 144), would offer more appropriate ways to investigate the nature of leadership.

Some degree of consistency between a research project's epistemic stance, theoretical framework, and methodological choices helps to ensure quality of the research, *independent of perspective.*[24] Acknowledging this can also help to reduce misunderstandings and judgments about the rigor of perspectives and research choices when these are different from those of the person doing the assessment. This is particularly needed because postpositivist methods have dominated leadership studies, and, given the blind spots that accompany this dominance (Deetz, 1996), their standards of rigor have become (mistakenly) the only point of reference by which to judge research quality. Below we discuss the interpretivist standards of rigor that support legitimate research choices within the logic of this mode of inquiry.

Rigor in Interpretivist Research

Interpretivists challenge the automatic translation of research methods and tools from the natural to the social and human sciences. They instead devise methodologies and techniques to ensure a degree of good fit between method and the ontological and epistemological commitments of their postmodernist stance. They derive from these the theories and methods needed to better understand the human world in all its complexity.

Interpretivists aspire to ensure rigor in their research, but it is, nevertheless, quite different from that of postpositivists (Yanow, 2006; Dodge, Ospina & Foldy, 2005).[25] Consistent with their challenge to modernist assumptions, interpretivists rethink standards like validity, reliability, and objectivity to consider instead criteria that are more appropriate to their postmodernist assumptions. Examples of the many possible standards they consider include credibility, dependability, comfirmability, and transferability of findings (Lincoln & Guba, 1985; Dodge et al., 2005; Schwartz-Shea, 2006).

In their aspirations to rigor, interpretivists start from the observation that what appears as a stable social world is, in actuality, unstable, fluid, multidimensional, and conflicting in all its messiness. Key notions of postmodernism, like "complex interdependencies" and "dense feedback loops" suggest that inter-subjectivity itself is embedded and complex. Working with these assumptions, interpretivists take quite seriously the postmodernist notion of multiple truths, and the consequent idea of "multivocality." Accessing meaningful reality therefore requires entertaining multiple voices and alternative representations—while considering each equally relevant. This means exploring how multiple perspectives contribute to producing understandings of a social phenomenon. Part of the task is to trace how this meaning emerges in action, through both communication and interaction, and how it is manifested in recurring practices over time.

For this reason, researchers must grasp two interrelated components of an "interpretive research gestalt" (Schwartz-Shea, 2006, p. 92). First, they must be attuned to the subtleties associated with the nature of meaning making—the ambiguities of human experience, the rich tacit knowledge of actors, the artifacts through which people make sense of their world (like rituals and stories), the blind spots in actors' consciousness, their taken-for-granted assumptions, and so on. Second, researchers must be sensitive to the various narrative forms that relevant data may take, from word, to imagery and sound, to space and objects, to numbers. They must collect sufficiently varied manifestations of the experiences constituting an emergent reality to ensure they are accessing multiple truths. Ensuring this gestalt yields a holistic, multi-faceted, processual understanding of human experience.

This rationale explains why the interpretive concept of inter-subjectivism replaces the postpositivist concept of methodological individualism in the theorizing and practice of interpretive research (Yanow, 2006, p. 14–15). In this view, knowledge is about mapping contexts and associated patterns of symbolic discourse (and their worldly manifestations), rather than about capturing variance to explain and predict phenomena in an objective world. The researcher aims to uncover constructed realities revealing the meaning of experience, rather than accessing reality itself. These assumptions make the postpositivist aspiration for even partial objectivity in scientific research not only impossible, but *inappropriate.*

Rigor is still demonstrated through the application of method—ensuring quality in reference to the type of criteria listed above (e.g., credibility, dependability, comfirmability, and the transferability of findings). But this is not enough. The researcher must also ensure "rigor of interpretation" (Lincoln & Guba, 1985). This means demanding from one another a systematic defense of their reasoning in regard to the process of interpretation. To guarantee both meanings of rigor, interpretivist researchers draw on practices and techniques from the interpretive research gestalt that ensures "the faithful rendering of some truth (notice the lower case t) from the perspective of socially situated actors" (Dodge et al., 2005, p. 290).

This description suggests a research posture that goes well beyond the simple act of making consistent methodological choices. The posture rests in a particular set of commitments to an epistemic community whose members agree on the meaning of what it is to do scholarly rigorous empirical research. Theoretical and methodological choices are closely connected to these commitments.

Because the difference between variance and process models has been often used to draw attention to differences in research posture, we turn to it briefly, highlighting the complexities associated with using this comparison to distinguish postpositivist and interpretivist approaches to research.

Research Models and Postures

At the level of theory, the contrast between variance and process sheds light on the distinct inquiry strategies associated with postpositivism and interpretivism. Variance theories express relationships among variations in social factors to answer "what causes what," identifying antecedents and outcomes of the studied phenomenon. Process theories express relationships among events (and actors) to answer "how did they develop and change over time" (Van de Ven, 2007).[26] Variance theories aim to make causal predictions from occurrences, while process theories aim to examine temporal sequences of unfolding events (p. 22).

Standards of rigor in exploring process and variance theories also reflect different ways to approach an object of study. Good answers to variance questions require evidence of co-variation, temporal precedence, and non-spurious associations between independent and dependent variables. Good answers to process questions require identifying "generative mechanisms" underlying the unfolding of events, and the circumstances under which these are present (Van de Ven, 2007, citing Tsoukas, 1989).

At this level of abstraction, the association to distinctive worldviews and philosophical roots works: The postmodern interpretivist researchers' assumptions offer an indication that their approach will be process oriented, and modern assumptions of postpositivists suggest that they will develop or draw from a variance theory. But at some point, the analogy between variance and process theories and postpositivist and interpretivist approaches to inquiry begins to break down.

For example, a postpositivist researcher may consider process theories, asking why something develops as it does to deepen or complement a "what" explanation. The researcher may even decide to work with a process theory alone, given the nature of the question. Yet, the opposite does not hold: It is unlikely that an interpretivist researcher would ask a "what" question alone. It is even more unlikely that s/he would consider a variance theory because interpretivist research is always process oriented. Moreover, the interpretivist might also be reluctant to organize the research around a process theory, particularly if s/he takes seriously other postmodern assumptions such as the non-linear, discontinuous nature of events, that is, the postmodernist challenge to the linear nature of change and progress (Hollinger, 1994).

The analogy "variance is to postpositivism what process is to interpretivism" is therefore limited. It breaks down even more when the researcher translates process and variance *theories* into process and variance *models* at the level of research design. The idea of a "model" itself may be problematic for interpretivist scholars. In replacing realist with "critical realist" assumptions, postpositivists propose models as ways to connect abstract theory and concrete data in the world (Van de Ven, 2007). Moving away from logical positivism, postpositivists understand that (as partial representations or maps of a theory) models are fallible and incorporate the researcher's perspective. Yet, the construct of "model" nevertheless retains a modernist flavor: Models are precisely instruments used to simplify a theory of the phenomenon so that it can be "tested" or "refined"—so that the critical realist aspiration to gain at least some partial truth can be attained.

Designed to temper the modernist expectation of an ultimate truth and to reflect only selective representations of the world, models nevertheless are generated to approach an entity that is conceived as separate from other entities and from the researcher (i.e., a separate "object"). Models are tools that aim to reduce complexity, lessen error, and minimize bias. Whether they are variance or process, models belong to the repertoire of a researcher committed to the metaphor of the "window," and to an abstract mode of knowing.

This approach to research reflects objectivist assumptions that are problematic from the postmodernist worldview underlying interpretivism. A postmodernist distrusts any encompassing attempt to "capture" even a *piece* of reality, which is what a model—variance or process—is intended to help the researcher do. Consequently, the more postmodernist an interpretivist researcher's assumptions are, the more reluctant s/he will be to use models, no matter how much they evoke the process dimensions of a phenomenon.

Even though a *process model* draws from the more relaxed objectivist assumptions of critical realism, it still echoes the language and spirit of modernism. It is therefore likely that the researcher's view of "process" will reflect this worldview and its primary research stance. A postpositivist application of a process model will most likely yield an outcome-driven explanation based on probabilistic relationships between dependent and independent variables associated with a view of change based on actions and activities (Van de Ven, 2007, p. 148).

Pushing the envelope even further, a critical realist postpositivist may shift from an outcome-driven to an event-driven explanation that aims to identify the emergent mechanisms that illuminate a temporal sequence (Van de Ven, 2007). Acknowledging greater complexity and interdependencies, the research stance of this scholar may lead him or her to incorporate the newest multilevel quantitative techniques (such as social network analysis, longitudinal designs, hierarchical linear modeling, and linear growth modeling). S/he may even decide to investigate and develop a narrative account of the mechanisms that help explain the temporal sequence.

However, the posture and product will flow from a modernist commitment to critical realism (with its objectivist ontological assumptions and its commitments to the window). The account would most likely be based on the researcher's view from outside these events, independent from the subjective experience of the event participants (despite including interviews with them). It would reflect the basic aspiration to "capture" reality as faithfully as possible from the other side of the "window," no matter how imperfectly or partially. The account would thus reflect a degree of certainty about the relatively "objective" knowledge mirroring some aspect of reality, with the truth claims guaranteed through adherence to method.

The "narrative" account of this postpositivist researcher would reflect an *abstract* mode of knowing typical of a modernist worldview, which would contrast significantly with the *narrative* mode of cognition typical of a postmodern worldview and its interpretivist approach to inquiry. The latter would assume a constructionist understanding of process and change. It would see process as contextualized and oft-discontinuous events with participating social actors embedded in webs of relationships. These would be characterized by multiple feedback loops that highlight the non-linear and complex nature of change. Interpretivist scholars would not want to simplify this complexity but would rather try to capitalize on it, reflecting this in their study design and producing quite a different research product compared to the process study of the postpositivist scholar.

The interpretivist researcher would "enter" his/her object of study through the subjective experience of the event participants, taking a posture from inside these events. The product would take the form of a rich and detailed narrative account, with a unique format and style depending on the researchers' degree of commitment to postmodernist assumptions. It could be a relatively linear, systematic account of the identified mechanisms with evidence presented in the voice of participants. Or, it could be a more creative multivocal narrative deconstructing particular beliefs and practices (and their origins) as well as uncovering their relationship to a particular regime of power (e.g., a postmodernist, Foucauldian account of a phenomenon) (Hollinger, 1994, p. 173).

No matter what format or style, the researcher would also report on his or her position *vis a vis* the subjects of study, thus acknowledging the influence of his or her own interpretations and voice in the research process and construction of meaning.[27] The narrative way of knowing would attune the interpretivist researcher to aspects of experience that emerge from unique contexts and in specific timings, and yet tell us something important about the human condition in general. The narrative account would reflect the uncertainties, blind spots, and discontinuities associated with human experience. In applying a narrative way of knowing, explanation would become interpretation, and interpretation of meaning would yield understanding.

Revisiting the Continuum

In the Introduction of this volume, we offered a "map of the terrain" (see Figure I.1) that located the book's contributors within a continuum of scholarship between a modernist "entity" perspective of relational leadership (that included logical positivism and postpositivism) and a postmodernist interpretivist perspective (that included constructionism and constructivism). Figure 1.1 in this chapter summarizes our analytical scheme, sheds light on the nature of the continuum, and further clarifies the meaning of the location of contributors in that spectrum as depicted in Figure I.1 of the Introduction to the book. For example, the left-to-right progression of ontological assumptions from objectivism to subjectivism explains why constructivism is placed to the right of constructionism, not next to postpositivism, despite the fact that it shares with entity perspectives a privileging of individual agency.

The shaded boxes in Figure 1.1 represent the competing epistemic stances underlying the perspectives in the leadership field. One level below are researchers depicted as a series of thin rectangles along the continuum. In this book, none of the contributors are located at the two extremes, or poles, of the spectrum. None of the contributors embraces the pure modernist objectivist position of logical positivism in the left pole (with its "realist," objectivist position) or the pure postmodernist subjectivist position of constructivism (with its idealist subjectivist position) in the right pole. Contributors fall somewhere between these extremes, embracing varied degrees of commitment to modernist and postmodernist worldviews and their epistemic stances, with the associated modes of knowing and research pos-

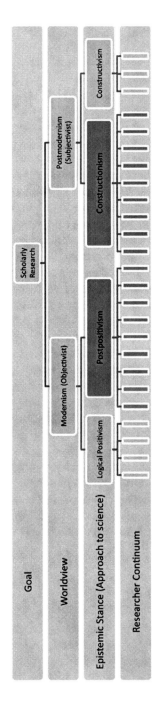

	Entity (Postpositivist)	Constructionist
Leadership Perspective		
Predominant Metaphor	Window	Lantern
Mode of Knowing	Abstract	Narrative
Research Posture	Inquiry from the outside	Inquiry from the inside

Figure 1.1 Summary of analytical scheme and key comparisons.

tures. Toward the left are various postpositivist contributors who espouse the "critical realist" position, and toward the right are various constructionist contributors who espouse the "inter-subjective" position of constructionism. A few contributors offer "hybrid" approaches connecting the two perspectives in the middle of the continuum. The closer to the right or left poles, the more likely it is that contributors find the perspectives incommensurable, even if they see room for conversation.

This chapter has also highlighted variations within each perspective other than those identified in the Introduction. For example, on the entity side, scholars vary in the extent to which they use or advocate using qualitative methods and process models to go beyond variance approaches. On the constructionist side, they vary in their commitment to critical theory and whether they commit to a full postmodernist project, or have a moderate postmodern stance. These internal differences reinforce the idea of a continuum of contributors characterized by a more or a less relaxed set of ontological and epistemological assumptions, rather than completely separate perspectives with fixed boundaries. Differences across the perspectives, however, do not disappear: The farther away from the middle of the continuum, the stronger and more distinct the assumptions are about the nature of reality and how we know, and thus how we can study leadership empirically.

Reflecting the broader trend in the field, the postpositivist and constructionist contributors find themselves converging, through different paths and for different reasons, in their interest in the relational dimensions of leadership. Even though they have agreed to join the conversation, and they may use the same words (e.g., "relations," "reciprocal influences," "process," "science," "theory," "rigor," and so forth), their words may carry different meanings depending on their epistemic stance and the consequent research posture. The farther apart from each other, and in relation to the poles of the continuum, the more different are the languages they speak. Likewise, the stronger the adherence to core modernist or postmodernist assumptions, the harder it will be for them to understand each other, unless they explicitly engage in conversation to share each others' implicit assumptions.

CONCLUSION

The comparisons presented in this chapter offer pointers to the question of *how can leadership be researched* from the two perspectives of postpositivism (with its modernist assumptions) and constructionist interpretivism (with its postmodernist assumptions). The metaphor of the window, the abstract mode of knowing, and a preference for "inquiry from the outside" evoke the assumptions of a postpositive version of research that has represented, for many years, the dominant way of doing empirical research both in the natural and the social sciences. A critical realist version of this perspective has informed mainstream leadership research in the U.S., yielding research products that have tended to dominate the management and leadership journals.

The metaphor of the lantern, the narrative mode of knowing, and a preference for "inquiry from the inside" evoke the assumptions of a constructionist version of social science—interpretivism—which has a strong following in Europe and Australia, and in some disciplines in the U.S. (such as sociology, anthropology, some branches of political science and history, and some fields in management) (Yanow & Schwartz-Shea, 2006). Constructionist leadership scholarship has flourished outside of the U.S. for quite a while; recently it has gained currency in this country, though it has still not achieved full legitimacy yet. The competition over the legitimacy for the knowledge claims that scholars in these perspectives produce is quite real, as are the tensions it raises. These tensions impact the experience of leadership scholars and affect the nature of communication across perspectives, as well as the ability to advance broader understandings in the field.

Variations *within* each perspective, nevertheless, offer opportunities for scholars to engage *across* perspectives, particularly as their postures move away from the pure objectivism or the pure subjectivism of the poles in the continuum. For example, there may be some resonance between a critical realist entity researcher and a moderate postmodernist constructionist scholar. This postpositivist's report on findings from a process model of relational leadership may not feel so far apart from the constructionist's report on the identified mechanisms underlying leadership enactments in a given context. Of course, resonance would be stronger between those two scholars than between an entity researcher using a variance model and a constructionist doing a post-structuralist analysis of a similar phenomenon.

Be that as it may, there are interesting opportunities for capitalizing on the relational leadership convergence. The space for conversation can be broadened as scholars acknowledge the reasons behind both resonant insights and incommensurable differences. For example, with respect to assumptions about the nature of the world, entity and constructionist scholars can acknowledge that both start with the notion of a reality. But the entity scholar sees it as separate from the knower, while the constructionist sees it as interdependent. With respect to assumptions about the nature of knowing, both acknowledge that the knower (researcher) *is not completely independent* of the object of study. But the entity scholar sees the lack of independence as a problem, while the constructionist sees it as an opportunity. The entity scholar strives for independence through methods that help to get as close as possible to reality, while the constructionist uses the lack of independence as the raw material from which to understand the meaning of constructed experience (what makes reality "meaningful" and thus "real").

Acknowledging that some assumptions relax as scholars move away from the extremes of the continuum opens up more space for fruitful conversation because it makes communication easier. For example, given a subjectivist epistemology (i.e., the knower's interplay with the subjective perspective of those experiencing the reality under study), a constructionist leadership scholar may be more receptive to the posture of a postpositivist entity scholar whose critical realism allows for a less objectivist and more subjectivist epistemology (i.e., the knower's perspective influences one's knowledge of reality despite any efforts to gain some distance). Likewise, drawing on objectivist ontology (reality is independent of our cognition), the entity scholar may be more open to conversation once s/he learns that the constructionist's inter-subjectivist ontology acknowledges the existence of reality (even though it only has meaning in relation).

In conclusion, entity and constructionist leadership scholars share an aspiration to advance theoretically robust and methodologically rigorous research agendas on the relational dimensions of leadership. This aspiration, however, can only be realized if scholars from both perspectives acknowledge the profound gap that exists around what it means and what it takes to produce such advancements. Indeed, while entity and constructionist scholars may converge around their interest in *relationality*, there is still much confusion, misunderstanding, and disagreement around the assumptions that help grasp its meaning for leadership from the two different but equally valuable perspectives.

Our intention has been to explore the tensions inherent in the field around the competing paradigmatic stances and the legitimacy of their knowledge claims, so that readers can explore what these mean for leadership theory, research, and practice as they engage the book chapters. We hope the ideas generated in this candid discussion will become a source of energy to identify what each perspective can bring to generate knowledge that advances the field.

We now invite readers to hear what the book's contributors have to say in the sections that follow.

REFERENCES

Abbott, A. (1988). Transcending general linear reality. *Sociological theory, 6,* 169–186.

Abell, P. (1987). *The syntax of social life: The theory and method of comparative narratives.* Oxford, England: Clarendon Press.

Alvesson, M., & Willmott, H. (1996). *Making sense of management: A critical introduction.* London, England: Sage.

Alvesson, M., & Sveningsson, S. (2003). Managers doing leadership: The extraordinization of the mundane. *Human Relations, 56*, 1435–1459.

Alvesson, M., & Karreman, D. (2011). *Qualitative research and theory development: Mystery as method*. London, England: Sage.

Antonakis, J., Avolio, B.J., & Sivasubramaniam, N. (2003). Context and leadership: An examination of the nine-factor full-range leadership theory using the Multifactor Leadership Questionnaire. *The Leadership Quarterly, 14*, 261–295.

Bechara, J.P., & Van de Ven, A.H. (2007). Philosophy of science underlying engaged scholarship. In A.H. Van de Ven (Ed.), *Engaged scholarship: A guide for organizational and social research* (pp. 36–70). Oxford, England: Oxford University Press.

Berger, P.L., & Luckmann, T. (1966). *The social construction of reality: A treatise in the sociology of knowledge*. New York, NY: Doubleday and Company.

Boisot, M., & McKelvey, B. (2010). Integrating modernist and postmodernist perspectives on organizations: A complexity science bridge. *Academy of Management Review, 35*(3), 415–433.

Bohman, J. (2002). Critical theory. In N. Smelser & P. Baltes (Eds.), *International encyclopedia of the social and behavioral sciences* (pp. 2986–2990). London, England: Elsevier Science.

Brower, H. H., Schoorman, F. D., & Tan, H. H. (2000). A model of relational leadership: The integration of trust and leader–member exchange. *The Leadership Quarterly, 11*(2), 227–250.

Burrell, G., & Morgan, G. (1979). *Sociological paradigms and organizational analysis*. London, England: Keinemann Education Books.

Bradbury, H., & Lichtenstein, B. (2000). Relationality in organizational research: Exploring the "space between." *Organization Science, 11*(5), 551–564.

Bruner, J.S. (1986). *Actual minds, possible worlds*. Cambridge, MA: Harvard University Press.

Carroll, B., Levy, L., & Richmond, D. (2008). Leadership as practice: Challenging the competency paradigm. *Leadership, 4*, 363–379.

Collinson, D. (2011). Critical leadership studies. In A. Bryman, D. Collinson, K. Grint, B. Jackson, & M. Uhl-Bien (Eds.), *The Sage handbook of leadership* (pp. 181–194). Thousand Oaks, CA: Sage Publications.

Crotty, M. (1998). *The foundations of social research: Meaning and perspective in the research process*. Thousand Oaks, CA: Sage Publications.

Cunliffe, A. L. (2009). *A very short, fairly interesting and reasonably cheap book about management*. Los Angeles, CA: Sage.

Dachler, H. P. (1988). Constraints on the emergence of new vistas in leadership and management research: An epistemological overview. In J. G. Hunt, B. R. Baliga, H. P. Dachler, & C. A. Schriesheim (Eds.), *Emerging leadership vistas* (pp. 261–285). Lexington, MA: D.C. Heath.

Deetz, S. (1996). Describing differences in approaches to organization science: Rethinking Burrell and Morgan and their legacy. *Organization Science, 7*(2), 191–207.

Denzin, N. K., & Lincoln, Y. S. (2000). Introduction: The discipline and practice of qualitative research. In N. K. Denzin, & Y. S. Lincoln (Eds.), *Handbook of qualitative research* (2nd ed.) (pp. 1–28). Thousand Oaks, CA: Sage.

Dodge J., Ospina, S. M., & Foldy, E. G. (2005). Integrating rigor and relevance in public administration scholarship: The contribution of narrative inquiry. *Public Administration Review, 65*(3), 286–302.

Drath, W., McCauley, C., Palus, J., Van Velsor, E., O'Connor, P., & McGuire, J. (2008). Direction, alignment, commitment: Toward a more integrative ontology of leadership. *The Leadership Quarterly, 19*(6), 635–53.

Ellis, C., & Bochner, A.P. (2000). Autoethnography, personal narrative and reflexivity: Researcher as subject. In N.K. Denzin & Y.S. Lincoln (Eds.), *Handbook of qualitative research* (2nd ed.) (pp. 733–768). Thousand Oaks, CA: Sage.

Everet, R., & Louis, M. R. (1981). Alternative perspectives in organizational sciences: "Inquiry from the inside" and "inquiry from the outside." *Academy of Management Review, 6*(3), 385–395.

Fairhurst, G. (2007). *Discursive leadership: In conversation with leadership psychology.* Thousand Oaks, CA: Sage.

Fairhurst, G., & Grant, D. (2010). The social construction of leadership: A sailing guide. *Management Communication Quarterly, 24*(2), 171–210.

Gaskell, G., & Bauer, M. (2000). "Towards public accountability: Beyond sampling, reliability and validity." In M. Bauer, & G. Gaskell (Eds.), *Qualitative researching with text, image and sound: A practical handbook* (pp. 336–350). London, England: Sage.

Gergen, K. (2009). *Relational being: Beyond self and community.* Oxford, England: Oxford University Press.

Glynn, M. A., & Raffaelli, R. (2010). Uncovering mechanisms of theory development in an academic field: Lessons from leadership research. *The Academy of Management Annals, 4*(1), 359–401.

Grint, K. (2005). Problems, problems, problems: The social construction of leadership. *Human Relations, 58*(11), 1467–1494.

Harrington, A. (2000). Alfred Schutz and the objectifying attitude. *Sociology, 34,* 724–740.

Herr, K., & Anderson, G. (2005). *The action research dissertation: A guide for students and faculty.* Thousand Oaks, CA: Sage.

Hollinger, R. (1994). *Postmodernism and the social sciences: A thematic approach.* Thousand Oaks, CA: Sage.

Hosking, D. (1988). Organizing, leadership and skillful process. *Journal of Management Studies, 25,* 147–166.

Hosking, D. M. (2007). Not leaders, not followers: A post-modern discourse of leadership processes. In B. Shamir, R. Pillai, M. Bligh, & M. Uhl-Bien (Eds.), *Follower-centered perspectives on leadership: A tribute to the memory of James R. Meindl* (pp. 243–263). Greenwich, CT: Information Age Publishing.

Hosking, D.M. (2011). Moving relationality: meditations on a relational approach to leadership. In A. Bryman, D. Collinson, K. Grint, B. Jackson, & M. Uhl-Bien (Eds.), *The Sage handbook of leadership* (pp. 455–467). Thousand Oaks, CA: Sage.

Kuhn, T. (1962). *The structure of scientific revolutions* (1st ed.). Chicago, IL: The University of Chicago Press.

Lakoff, G. (1992). What is metaphor? In K.J. Holyoak, & J.A. Barnden (Eds.), *Advances in connectionist and neural computational theory* (Vol. 2: *Analogical Connections*). Norwood, NJ: Ablex.

Laudan, L. (1990). *Science and relativism: Some key controversies in the philosophy of science*. Chicago, IL: University of Chicago Press.

Leonardi, P. M., & Barley, S.R. (2010). What's under construction here? Social action, materiality and power in constructivist studies of technology and organizing. *The Academy of Management Annals, 4*(1), 1–51.

Lin, A.C. (1998). Bridging positivist and interpretivist approaches to qualitative methods. *Policy Studies Journal, 26*(1), 162–180.

Lincoln, Y. S., & Guba, E. G. (1985). *Naturalistic inquiry*. Newbury Park, CA: Sage.

Lincoln, Y. S., & Guba, E. G. (2000). Paradigmatic controversies, contradictions and emerging confluences. In N. K. Denzin and Y. S. Lincoln (Eds.), *Handbook of qualitative research* (2nd ed.) (pp.163–188). Thousand Oaks, CA: Sage.

Lotia, N., & Hardy, C. (2008). Critical perspectives on collaboration. In S. Cropper, M. Ebers, C. Huxham, & P. Smith Ring (Eds.), *The Oxford Handbook of Inter-Organizational Relations* (pp. 366–385). New York, NY: Oxford University Press.

Merton, R. K. (1968). *Social theory and social structure* (Enlarged ed.). New York, NY: The Free Press.

Morgan, G., & Smircich, L. (1980). The case for qualitative research. *Academy of Management Review, 5*(4), 491–500.

Mohr, L. (1982). *Explaining organizational behavior*. San Francisco, CA: Jossey-Bass.

Naples, N. A. (2003). *Feminism and method: Ethonography, discourse analysis and activist research*. New York, NY: Routledge.

Ospina, S., & Dodge, J. (2005). It's about time: Catching method up to meaning— The usefulness of narrative inquiry in public administration research. *Public Administration Review, 65*(2), 143–58.

Ospina, S., & Sorensen, G. (2006). A constructionist lens on leadership: Charting new territory. In G. Goethals, & G. Sorenson (Eds.), *In quest of a general theory of leadership* (pp. 188–204). Cheltenham, England: Edward Elgar.

Ospina, S., Dodge, J., Foldy, E.g., & Hofmann-Pinilla, A. (2008). Taking the action turn: Lessons from bringing participation to qualitative research. In P. Reason, & H. Bradbury (Eds.), *The Sage handbook of action research participative inquiry and practice* (2nd ed.) (pp. 421–434). Los Angeles, CA: Sage.

Ospina, S., & Foldy, E. (2010). Building bridges from the margins: The work of leadership in social change organizations. *The Leadership Quarterly, 21*(2), 292–307.

Pachirat, T. (2006). We call it a grain of sand: The interpretive orientation and a human social science. In D. Yanow, & P. Schwartz-Shea (Eds.), *Interpretation and method: Empirical research methods and the interpretive turn* (pp. 373–379). Armonk, NY: M.E. Sharpe.

Patton, M. Q. (2002). *Qualitative research and evaluation methods* (3rd ed.). Thousand Oaks, CA: Sage.

Riccucci, N. M. (2010). *Public administration: Traditions of inquiry and philosophies of knowledge*. Washington, DC: Georgetown University Press.

Romani, L., Primecz, H., & Topcu, K. (2011). Paradigm interplay for theory development: A methodological example with the Kulturstandard Method. *Organizational Research Methods, 14*(3), 432–455.

Shamir, B. (2007). From passive recipients to active co-producers: Followers' roles in the leadership process. In B. Shamir, R. Pillai, M. Bligh, & M. Uhl-Bien (Eds.), *Follower-centered perspectives on leadership: A tribute to J. R. Meindl* (pp. ix-xxxix). Greenwich, CT: Information Age Publishing.

Shank, G. (2002). *Qualitative research: A personal skills approach.* Englewood Cliffs, NJ: Prentice Hall.

Schwandt, T. (2000). Three epistemological stances for qualitative inquiry. In N. Denzin and Y. Lincoln (Eds.), *Handbook of qualitative research* (2nd ed.) (pp.189–213). Thousand Oaks, CA: Sage.

Schwartz-Shea, P. (2006). Judging quality: Evaluative criteria and epistemic communities. In D. Yanow, & P. Schwartz-Shea (Eds.), *Interpretation and method: Empirical research methods and the interpretive turn* (pp. 89–113). Armonk, NY: M.E. Sharpe.

Sedlacek, T. (2011). Economics of good and evil. New York, NY: Oxford University Press.

Tsoukas, H. (1989). The validity of idiographic research explanations. *Academy of Management Review, 14*, 551–561.

Tsui, A. S., Egan, T. D., & O'Reilly, C. A. (1992). Being relationally different: Relational demography and organizational attachment. *Administrative Science Quarterly, 37*, 549–579.

Uhl-Bien, M., Maslyn, J., & Ospina, S.M. (2011). The nature of relational leadership: A multi-theoretical lens on leadership relationships and processes. In D. Day, & J. Antonakis (Eds.), *The Nature of Leadership* (2nd ed.) (pp. 289–330). London, England: Sage.

Uhl-Bien, M. (2006). Relational leadership theory: Exploring the social processes of leadership and organizing. *The Leadership Quarterly, 17*(6), 654–676.

Walker, D., Zimmerman, D. P., Cooper, J. E. (2002). The constructivist leader (2nd ed.). New York, NY: Teachers College.

Walker, M. (2006). The theory and meta-theory of leadership: The important but contested nature of theory. In G. R. Goethals, & G. L. J. Sorenson (Eds.), *The quest for a general theory of leadership* (pp. 46–74). Chesterton, England: Edward Elgar Publications.

Wayne, S. J., & Ferris, G. R. (1990). Influence tactics, affect, and exchange quality in supervisor-subordinate interactions: A laboratory experiment and field study. *Journal of Applied Psychology, 75*, 487–499.

Yanow, D. (2006). Thinking interpretively: Philosophical presuppositions and the human sciences. In D. Yanow, & P. Schwartz-Shea (Eds.), *Interpretation and method: Empirical research methods and the interpretive turn* (pp. 5–26). Armonk, NY: M.E. Sharpe.

Yanow, D., & Schwartz-Shea, P. (Eds.). (2006). *Interpretation and method: Empirical research methods and the interpretive turn.* Armonk, NY: M.E. Sharpe.

NOTES

1. The authors thank Richard Williams for reading and offering thoughtful comments on an earlier version of this chapter.
2. See Burrell & Morgan (1979) for a classic analytical scheme from organization theory, Deetz (1996) for a critique and counterproposal, and Bechara and Van de Ven (2007) for a more recent discussion in the management field. For discussions in reference to leadership, see Walker (2006) and Dachler (1988). Two relevant articles summarizing key philosophical distinctions in reference to qualitative research are Morgan and Smircich (1980) and Lincoln and Guba (2000). Riccucci (2010) offers a classification for public administration
3. Some scholars prefer the term *neopositivism* to postpositivism (see for example Alvesson and Sveningsson in Chapter 7). Postpositivism has also been used before to convey a movement *away* from positivism and *toward* postmodernism (e.g., Lincoln & Guba, 1985). We follow Crotty's (1998) nomenclature to describe *postpositivism* as the contemporary (much more sophisticated and less rigid) version of logical positivism, which espouses a philosophy of science that some scholars have called "*critical realism*" (Laudan, 1990; Van de Ven, 2007) while still maintaining its modernist roots.
4. Boisot and McKelvey do not use the term *interpretivism*. But as modernism and postmodernism represent equivalent categories, the equivalent to *postpositivism* (an approach to science reflecting modernist assumptions) is *interpretivism* (an approach to science reflecting postmodern sensitivities) (Crotty, 1998; Yanow & Schwartz-Shea, 2006). In our discussion, we have used the term *interpretivism* where Boisot and McKelvey may have used *postmodernism*, as we see appropriate.
5. *The Leadership Quarterly*, June 2010, Volume 21, Issue 3; *Leadership*, May 2010, Volume 6, Issue 2.
6. Both definitions were retrieved from the online Free Dictionary by Farlex (http://www.thefreedictionary.com), October 2011.
7. See, for example, the absence of journals favoring interpretivist research in the sampling frame of Glynn & Raffaelli's 2010 literature review.
8. Some scholars prefer to talk about *abduction* rather than *induction,* that is, a type of inference that results from engaging with the world and encountering an anomaly or inconsistency with the previous understanding or theory of the world (see Alvesson and Karreman, 2011, for a full discussion). Bechara & Van de Ven (2007) describe it as follows: "Abduction entails creative insight that resolves the anomaly if it were true. A conjecture developed through abductive inference represents a new plausible alternative to the status quo explanation of a given phenomenon in question" (p. 65).
9. Critical theory originated in the German Frankfurt School of philosophy's distinction between a traditional and a critical theory by the extent to which it sought to contribute to liberating human beings from any circumstance that obstructed their full development (Bohman, 2002). Today, there are many "broad, diverse and heterogeneous perspectives" on critical theory (Collinson, 2011, p. 181), but a common aim runs throughout: to produce scholarly

knowledge supporting thinking and actions that increase human freedom, and reduce oppression, manipulation and other forms of injustice (Bohman, 2002; Crotty, 1998).

10. The nomenclature in this book further illustrates the confusions. In our call to contributors, we proposed contrasting an "entity" and a "constructionist" perspective, thus acknowledging the presence of *relational leadership* approaches in both types of scholarship. Making labels more evocative of their ontologies would require calling them something like the "realist" and the "constructionist" perspectives, or evoking their epistemic stances, the postpositivist and interpretivist perspectives. Because the entity-constructionist distinction appears in most chapters, we have continued to use it (in the Introduction, in this chapter, and in the Conclusion) to differentiate the two paradigmatic stances that characterize the field. Furthermore, the reader should be aware that following Uhl-Bien's 2006 original distinction, some contributors use "entity" versus "relational" instead of "entity" versus "constructionist." We hope to at least clarify the reasons underlying these confusions—thus bringing further clarity to the discussion.

11. Of course, there are also many more important distinctions within these two "blocks" which are quite relevant to appreciating the choices researchers make. The extent of this complexity surfaces by studying other classifications. For example, Bechara and Van de Ven (2007) and Walker (2006) discuss four philosophical approaches to science rather than two: positivism, critical realism, and relativism. In reference to our scheme, despite subtle differences, the assumptions of the first two are more consistent with modernism and postpositivism, and those in the second two with postmodernism and interpretivism. These are indeed important differences worth exploring.

12. Deetz (1996) argues that the objective-subjective distinction proposed here and in other schemes such as Burrell and Morgan's (1979) is "misleading" because it "reproduces a neopositivist philosophy of science and obscures the nature of other research programs" (p. 194). We agree that this and other distinctions should be viewed as "a way of focusing attention rather than as a means of classification" (p. 191). At the same time, as will become clear, we find the distinction helpful to elucidate why entity and constructionist leadership scholars have had such a hard time understanding one another.

13. Walker (2006) refers to Lakoff's distinction (1992) between an objectivist view that conceives of thought as "the mechanical manipulation of abstract symbols," (p 64) and an "experientialist" view that links our experience to "thought structures," thus arguing that "thought is *embodied*" (p. 65). This dimension merits reflection for readers interested in further exploring the philosophy of science.

14. There are multiple taxonomies of the interpretivist tradition. We follow Yanow and Schwartz-Shea's (2006) view of interpretivism as an epistemic stance encompassing a spectrum of methods ranging from descriptive to critical. Often, these interpretivist methods are mixed together in empirical research, as in the case of Ospina, Foldy, El Hadidy, Dodge, Hofmann-Pinilla, and Su's chapter in this volume. Other scholars use the term "interpretivism" differently. For example, Schwandt (2000) presents interpretivism as one of three

epistemic stances for qualitative inquiry, along with hermeneutics and social constructionism. Some classifications ignore the construct of interpretivism altogether. For example, Lincoln and Guba (2000) classify non-positivist postmodernist qualitative paradigms into critical theory, constructivism (including constructionist assumptions), and participatory action research; and Boisot & McKelvey (2010) use "postmodernism" to refer to both the worldview and its manifestations in research.

15. This subjectivist position can be viewed as an "idealist" position [in contrast to the "realist" and "critical realist" (objectivist) positions of positivism and postpositivism in the modernist stance, and to the "experientialist" position of constructionism in the postmodernist stance.] (See also footnote 11.)

16. Leonardi and Barley (2010) offer a classification of five ways in which "constructivists" (their language) have contributed to advance knowledge of the social construction of technology. By failing to distinguish constructivism from constructionism they obscure important differences between the two poles of their continuum. A similar problem occurs in discussions in other fields, including leadership (e.g., see this treatment in the various classifications reported by Walker, 2006).

17. Entity scholars who fully espouse the philosophical assumptions of logical positivism are less likely to be concerned with the relational dimensions of leadership. Hence, while logical positivism represents a variation of the modernist worldview, in this discussion we consider only entity leadership scholars who espouse a postpositivist, critical realist ontology.

18. Constructivism has been systematically applied in the study of leadership in other disciplines such as education (e.g., Walker, Zimmerman & Cooper, 2002), although it is worth noting that in this field, like in others, the problem of confusing constructivism and constructionism may also be widespread.

19. There is, nevertheless, a debate among postmodern interpretivist scholars around how to address the researcher's subjectivity and his/ her distance to the "subjects" of research (e.g., Harrington, 2000). The more extreme the postmodernist stance of the researcher, the more s/he will challenge the possibility or desirability of any distance, and the more moderate the postmodern stance, the more s/he will emphasize a social science aspiration to differentiate the perspectives of the researcher and the researched. The moderate postmodern position moves closer to the modernist epistemological assumptions of postpositivism's critical realism, while maintaining a subjectivist position at the ontological level.

20. See footnote 7 in this chapter for an introduction and brief characterization of critical theory. Note that, despite the use of the same term ("critical"), "critical theory" refers to something completely different from the notion of "critical realism" discussed in reference to postpositivism's challenge of some of the assumptions of logical positivism.

21. Researchers who ascribe fully to a postmodernist project do not believe in "causality," "science," or "theory" as discussed here and below. Most constructionist leadership researchers nevertheless take a more moderate postmodernist position which aspires to produce scholarly knowledge and which takes into consideration such notions.

22. Bruner (1986) refers to the "abstract mode" as the "logico-scientific" mode of knowing, suggesting a separation between science and the humanities that is too literal. (He associates the narrative mode with "poetry, storytelling and art"). We use the distinction between the two modes as metaphor and prefer "abstract" to the "logico-scientific" label because the latter evokes a modernist, "universal" view of science associated with positivism that is too narrow. The metaphors of the window and the lantern, and abstract and narrative ways of knowing respectively are helpful to better understand the postpositivist/interpretivist distinction between *two approaches to science* and scholarly empirical research.

23. Yanow and Schwartz-Shea (2006) further describe this view as follows:

> For interpretive researchers, concepts are embedded within a literature, becoming part of the historical background that forms the context for scholarly thinking; to attempt to specify them once and for all, as universal constructs, violates interpretive presuppositions about the historical locatedness of scholars and actors. (p. xvii)

24. This is what Gaskell and Bauer (2000) call "indication of method," drawing on the analogy of medical concern with "indication of treatment": A certain medicine is well indicated for a certain condition but not for another, for which other medicines are better indicated. Some choices at the level of research methods and procedures are better indicated for particular perspectives, theories and problems and not for others (Gaskell & Bauer, 2000, p. 337). In Chapter 9 Ospina and colleagues describe their efforts to design their constructionist research around this consistency. Likewise, in Chapter 15 of this volume Fairhurst suggests checking the extent to which researchers match the ontological units (based on understandings of leadership) with the observational units and the analytical units in their study.

25. There are also variations within interpretivism. More or less adherence to a full postmodernist project influences an interpretivist's view of rigor, so that the more postmodernist the researcher, the farther away his/her practice will be from the conventional (positivist) standards of scientific rigor (Lincoln & Guba, 2000).

26. Full discussions of variance versus process theories in organization and management studies include Abbott (1988), Abell (1987), Mohr (1982), and Tsoukas (1989).

27. For a discussion of the notions of "positionality" and "reflexivity" in various traditions of interpretive research, see Herr and Anderson (2005); Naples (2003); Ospina, Dodge, Foldy, and Hofmann-Pinilla (2008); and Shea-Schwartz (2006).

PART I

THEORIZING THE PRACTICE
OF RELATIONAL LEADERSHIP

CHAPTER 2

THE SOCIAL PRODUCTION OF LEADERSHIP

From Supervisor–Subordinate Linkages to Relational Organizing

Anson Seers and Suzette M. Chopin

In academic analyses of leadership, we provide our own, indirect accounts of what transpires between the direct participants we call *leaders* and *followers*. Relational analyses provide us with the opportunity to account for what gives rise to leading and following, how leading and following may persist over time, and the role they may play in the achievement of desirable outcomes. In this chapter, we propose that an adequate account should work from the genesis of leadership, as only then will we be able to capture the whole story, from beginning to end.

A great deal of research has investigated which individual skills and abilities might best predict leadership success, but the accumulated evidence shows clearly that such attributes correlate modestly with both leader emergence and leader effectiveness. Relational leadership conceptions de-emphasize, in varying degrees, this search for the "right stuff" and its

Advancing Relational Leadership Research, pages 43–81
Copyright © 2012 by Information Age Publishing
All rights of reproduction in any form reserved.

romanticizing of leadership. Uhl-Bien's (2006) overview of relational conceptions of leadership stands as a state-of-the art summary of this domain. She argued that leadership researchers have applied the word "relation" in a variety of senses, from Likert's (1961) relationship-oriented style of leader behavior to Morley and Hosking's (2003) approach, in which intersubjective understandings are constructed in the interactions among those we come to call *leaders* and *followers.*

Among the relational conceptions inventoried in Uhl-Bien's (2006) analysis, two stand out for their particularly strong contrast. These two are the leader–member exchange (LMX) approach of Graen and his colleagues, which has been seminal within the North American tradition of largely quantitatively-oriented research, and the relational constructionism approach of Hosking and her colleagues, which grew from the European tradition of largely qualitative research. Work within each approach rarely cites developments in the other, as they operate from fundamentally different assumptions.

Uhl-Bien's (2006) analysis placed these two relational leadership conceptions on opposite sides of a distinction between entity-based versus relationality-oriented perspectives. This distinction used Bradbury and Lichtenstein's (2000) definition of a "...relationality orientation to organizational research. Such an orientation takes as primary the nexus of relations in organizations, rather than focusing on discrete, abstracted phenomena" (p. 551).

The LMX approach reflects an entity perspective in that it focuses on two individuals formally designated as subordinate and supervisor in an organizational chart. This approach considers how individuals in these roles react to each other and in doing so establish more versus less effective leadership relationships. In contrast, Hosking's work emphasizes social interaction processes as the mechanism of the relational construction of leadership. Morley and Hosking (2003) define *leadership* as "making contributions that consistently achieve acceptable influence" (p. 79) in the discursive construction of an emergent communal culture. Like most analyses that invoke the concept of social construction, its focus is on the development of shared meaning.[1] As noted by Ospina and Sorenson (2006), "Constructionism asserts that leadership is essentially about meaning making in communities of practice..." (p. 193).

Precisely because work in each of these two approaches has done so little to inform progress in the other, further analysis of their contrast may be quite fruitful. We begin by revisiting the Bradbury and Lichtenstein (2000) definition of relationality as the basis for contrasting entity versus relationality perspectives. This definition emphasizes how the former presumes an objective reality perspective, whereas the latter presumes a "multiple realities" perspective. Bradbury and Lichtenstein's (2000) description of relationality focuses on the inherent relational dynamics occasioned between researchers and their organizational subjects, eschewing any focus on modeling organizational phenomena as they might occur if researchers took no interest in them. In their view, "Taking a relational orientation means enacting a constellation of research values and interests in which organizational phenomena and the researcher's relationships with these phenomena is [sic] conceived of as interdependent and intersubjective" (p. 552). This frames the contrast between entity and relationality perspectives in terms of the intractable debate between realist versus subjectivist ontologies.

The Bradbury and Lichtenstein (2000) definition of *relationality* presumes the social constructionist perspective familiar to many from Berger and Luckman's (1966) treatise on the social construction of knowledge, which in turn drew on a long tradition of interpretive sociology. This perspective treats social reality and intersubjective knowledge as inextricably linked. There is no separation between what can be considered to be real and the act of that consideration, whether it is consideration by researchers or consideration by the interacting individuals themselves. If so, it makes no sense to contemplate any form of social reality apart from what a person can understand about that reality. The distinction between academic understandings produced through rigorous research and understandings produced through participant sense-making then reduces to the extent to which one or the other might become "privileged," and neither can be argued to be any closer to "true" reality.

The case thus far associates entity perspectives with a realist ontology, and relationality perspectives with a subjectivist ontology. In realist ontology, organizational entities exist exogenously, but in subjectivist ontology, the reality of organizational entities derives from what we know of them through our relational experience. This realist versus subjectivist divide (Burrell & Morgan, 1979; Guba, 1990) characterizes a great deal of management literature. The analysis in this paper assumes that social reality cannot be taken to be equivalent to our knowledge of it, and that neither should be presumed to be exogenous. Presenting this analysis clearly requires explicating our ontological and epistemological assumptions.

Guba's (1990) exposition makes clear that the realist versus subjectivist ontological divide is actually rooted in an epistemological divide. Positivist epistemology argues that objectively executed study allows us objective knowledge of reality, whereas a non-positivist epistemology regards completely objective analysis and knowledge as wishful thinking. The latter premise leaves only the inference that no external reality can be established independent of whatever means of inquiry we employ. Once we have assumed that no objective reality can be known, we are left with nothing other than subjective knowledge regarding reality. This epistemological inference leaves the non-positivist in an essentially agnostic stance regarding ontology. If we can know only what we think, then we have no way of knowing whether objective reality does or does not exist. Any stipulation regarding the nature of knowledge provides no logical basis for assertions either that multiple realities must therefore exist, or that one's subjective understanding, or even an intersubjectively shared understanding regarding reality therefore operates in place of a single objective reality.

The relational approach taken by the present analysis assumes a realist ontology. What is real may or may not have physical substance, but that which is real is consequential. This allows for inclusion of beliefs about reality without presuming that beliefs and reality are identical, per the classic dictum of W. I. Thomas (Thomas & Thomas, 1928) that when people define situations as real, real consequences result. Real consequences are nonetheless ubiquitous apart from our beliefs or knowledge about reality. Gravity held people to the earth long before anyone conceived of it, and it has always been impossible to sail a ship off the edge of the earth, even when no one understood it to be round.

We also reject any premise that our analysis should contrast social reality from physical reality by assuming that the essence of the former is intersubjective, whereas the essence of the latter follows the laws of physics. Such a distinction re-labels, and thus perpetuates rather than transcends, the mind versus body dualism problem of Descartes.

An alternate definition of a *relational perspective* that does not require consideration of multiple realities was set forth by Emirbayer (1997). Whereas Bradbury and Lichtenstein (2000) focus on the conduct of research, Emirbayer (1997) focuses on fundamental theoretical conception. Emirbayer (1997) drew on Dewey and Bentley's (1949) argument that substantialist thinking worked from the premise that self-subsistent entities, in the form of things, beings, or essences, constitute the fundamental units of all inquiry. Such entities might either be self-acting (under their own inherent powers) or interacting (such that particular combinations across the essential attributes of two or more pre-existing entities would cause systemic patterns of action). The contrasting relational approach rejects the notion of ultimate starting points in the guise of discrete, pre-given units such as the individual or the organization. In this relational conception, "the very terms or units involved in a transaction derive their meaning, significance, and identity from the (changing) functional roles they play within that transaction" (Emirbayer, 1997, p. 287).

Emirbayer's (1997) contrast between relational and substantialist approaches suggests that what we confront here is more familiar to us in the guise of the old chicken versus egg question. In this sense, relational processes and social entities are mutually constitutive. Rather than proposing that we treat either one as the cause and the other as the effect, we suggest analysis of social entities and relational processes as alternate manifestations of a unitary phenomenon.

We have presented our fundamental assumptions at great length because we propose that existing leadership theory has not adequately framed the problems that it has addressed. All approaches to relational leadership recognize that relationships matter greatly. Not so widely recognized is that we achieve only the labeling of an entity of interest by invoking the noun "relationship" and not a theoretically precise conceptualization. The problems that our analysis will address can be stated quite simply. In what sense do relational processes create the entities of interest with respect to leadership, and in what sense do those entities create relational processes?

LEADERSHIP: ROLES AND RELATIONS

Leader–follower relationships are clearly entities of interest. We commonly treat relationships as entities in everyday life when we refer to "my marriage." The use of the term "my marriage" is shorthand in that it evokes a communal understanding of the relationship to which we are referring. The actual details and dynamics of the marriage, however, differ greatly from unit to unit, something that is also commonly understood and accepted. The same idea is at work when LMX researchers ask respondents to report on the effectiveness of their supervisory relationship. The pronoun "we" serves as shorthand for relationships as recognized entities when the speaker personally identifies with them. Analogously, the pronoun "they" refers to such entities with which the speaker does not personally associate. Entities to which we refer with the pronouns "we" and "they" have a critically important property in that they have no existence independent of the individuals who participate in them. This recognition requires careful consideration of what it means to speak of the existence of a relationship.

When we refer to ourselves or to our relational partners individually with respect to such entities, we assume a relational role and its associated role identity, such as spouse, coworker, or leader. Relational role behavioral patterns are thus also entities of interest, as are the relational identities that attach to those roles. Stated succinctly, the entities of interest to our analysis are role and relational id*entities*, including those of a first person, one or more other salient individuals, and their joint relational identity. In colloquial terms, this reduces to "me," "you," and "we." As detailed below, the entity of primary interest within the LMX approach has been the subordinate role, conceived of as a behavior pattern, with less attention to the relationship as an entity, and even less attention to role identities. Whether supervisors and subordinates can be meaningfully identified as leaders and followers has been a concern in the individualized leadership model of

Yammarino and Dansereau (2002), even as its description of role behavior patterns has not been as elaborate as that of the LMX model.

In our conception, leader/follower relationships are both outcomes of interest and mechanisms of production for the very attributes that make leaders be leaders and followers be followers. Leaders and followers enact those identities as they develop a leader–follower relationship. Each relational interaction reinforces the individual actor's identity as leader or follower within that particular relationship. In our view, theoretical models in a relational, as opposed to an entity perspective, should explain both interaction processes and the levels taken on by defining attributes associated with entities of interest. Individual attributes remain highly relevant in our relational leadership approach because they are critical to explaining how the participants enact the context of their leader/follower relationship. Our analysis begins by reviewing how existing theory has specified entities of interest, as well as how it has specified relational processes of interest. We propose that a relational organizing approach will identify important pieces of the puzzle that have been missing in past analyses of relational leadership.

Origins of LMX in Vertical Dyad Linkage Theory

The development of LMX theory began when a master's degree student (Fred Dansereau) gained approval from his thesis advisor (George Graen) to include the Leader Behavior Description Questionnaire (Stogdill & Coons, 1957) in a larger study of managerial motivation. The focus on work motivation was an extension of Graen's dissertation research completed but a few years previously.

Results from this new study were published by Graen, Dansereau, and Minami in 1972. The investigation found marked variability in subordinate ratings of their supervisor's leadership (task and relational) style. This finding ran counter to the conventional wisdom of the time, which was that the main reason a researcher would bother obtaining responses from more than one subordinate would be to assess inter-rater reliability concerning the supervisor's true leadership style. Within specific work groups, some members rated their leader as being high on task behavior, even as others rated the same leader as being low, and the same kind of discrepancy was observed for relational behavior.

How could this be? What sense could it make to simply take the numeric average across member subordinates as a true measure of the leader's task or relational style when those subordinates gave contrasting reports? Were these questionnaires generating random numbers rather than valid measures of leadership style? Because checks for the reliability and validity of survey data looked more than satisfactory, the answer had to lie elsewhere. That answer came with the insight that the subordinates' primary source of information was their own experience, and not specifically a reflection of what the leader usually did in dealing with everyone else. What subordinates could best report on was their own individual-to-individual, or dyadic, supervisor-subordinate relationship. Ensuing studies (e.g., Graen & Cashman, 1975) used the label *vertical dyad linkage* (VDL) *theory* to refer to this one-on-one notion of leadership. As the focus of the initial research had been on the motivation of employees to develop characteristic roles (some happier and more productive than others), the overriding initial interpretation was that subordinates responded differentially to supervisory role expectations.

The Transition from VDL to LMX

As further studies proceeded to document the differentiation of these supervisor-subordinate relationships, various labels were applied to the contrasting role relationships. Dansereau, Graen, and Haga (1975) contrast leadership versus supervisory relations, Graen (1976) contrasts informal assistant roles with ordinary member roles, and Graen and Schiemann (1978) contrast high-quality versus low-quality relationships. The label "leader–member exchange" (LMX) gradually replaced the "vertical dyad linkage" label in reference to the theoretical model. A parallel evolution occurred for the central construct of the approach as well as its measure. The initial measure was called "negotiating latitude" in recognition of the premise that the in-group members had negotiated more expansive roles than had out-group members. Over time, the measure used for the central construct came to focus on asking members to report on the quality of their exchange relationship with the leader, and since the early 1980s, the name used for the construct and its measure has remained LMX.

Graen's Interpersonal Role-Making Model

Graen (1976) developed a theoretical model to integrate the still young but rapidly growing stream of VDL studies, one that grounded its view in Katz and Kahn's (1978) organizational role theory. His model proposed that in response to supervisory role expectations, some employees would seek out the minimally acceptable level of performance, whereas others would seize upon challenging and interesting tasks as growth opportunities. Because tangible compensation was generally equal, or nearly so, across employees within a work group, the inference was that any leadership-related motivational incentive to take on an enhanced role resided in the interpersonal responses of the supervisor.

Unless the supervisor showed appreciation for the extra efforts, whatever incentive the employee might have for continued extra effort would be outside the realm of leadership. It was this role-making process that would lead to the differentiation of contrasting types of subordinate roles. Graen interpreted these roles as resulting from an implicit negotiation process through which the parties tested the nature of the role reactions from each other and gradually formed expectations for the role relationship.

Dienesch and Liden (1986) pointed out that an explicit definition of the nature of the LMX relationship was conspicuous by its absence, despite its being the central concept of LMX theory. Graen and Scandura (1987) extended the focus in Graen's (1976) role-making model on the development of the follower role so as to include the development of relationship quality between the leader and a follower. Leader-member relationships were depicted as developing through three phases: an initial sampling phase, then a role-making phase, and finally a role routinization phase. As leader and follower progress through these phases, they develop a shared perception of their working relationship. This inclusion of the development of the leader–follower relationship complemented the earlier Graen (1976) model. Graen and Uhl-Bien (1995) extended conceptualization of the nature of the LMX relationship, defining it as a relationship of mutual trust, respect, obligation, learning, and accommodation. Mutuality, though, stands as an assertion rather than something established by research evidence.

Here again, we see the need for clarification of the leader–follower relationship as a naturally occurring entity, apart from any pre-existing hierarchical structure, whether formal or informal. The nature of the mutuality is asymmetric, in that what prompts us to label one participant as a "follower" and another as a "leader" are the characteristic differences between the two in both the kind and the extent of the aspects of these relationships. In none of the theoretical expositions of LMX do we see explication of leader or follower role identities, nor do we see explanation for the development of the behavioral pattern of the leader role. Attention is confined to development of follower patterned role behavior.

The Individualized Leadership Model

In the divergence of interests after the last published collaboration between Dansereau and Graen (1976), Graen pursued an approach which argued that what had become the traditional assumption that leaders should, and would, show equal treatment to all subordinates needed to be replaced by a model that assumed that different relationships must occur within supervisory groups. Dansereau continued to assume that some leadership might affect a whole unit as a group, even as some leadership differentiated among subordinates.

As described in his own (1995) retrospective, the initial curiosity that gave rise to Dansereau's interest in investigating the extent of differentiation across subordinates originated with the simple observation that, within a given work unit, some subordinates clearly were not following their supervisor as their leader, even as others were. What is of most significance for the present analysis is that Dansereau's observation called into question the very identification of the former subordinates as being followers, and the identification of their supervisor as being their leader.

Yammarino and Dansereau's (2002) model of individualized leadership depicts an instrumental exchange transaction process between an individual supervisor and an individual subordinate. Both parties are seen as making investments in each other that motivate the other party's reciprocal investments. The substance of what the partners exchange is limited to the subordinate providing work performance that is satisfying to the superior, and, in return, the superior providing support for subordinate's feelings of self-worth.

Like Graen's model, this model assumes a fixed pattern of leader role behavior, treating follower role behavior patterns and the nature of the supervisor-subordinate relationship itself as outcomes. Unlike Graen's model, it explicitly addresses subordinate self-concept. In doing so, it implicates the role identities of followers and leaders, in accord with the empirical finding of Dansereau et al., 1995) that whether a superior becomes a leader depends on the reciprocation between subordinate performance and supervisor support for self-worth.

RELATIONAL ORGANIZING

Our conception of relational organizing builds on the etymological distinction noted by Seers (2004) between the word *organization* originating in the conception of a tool, whereas the word *corporation* originated from the conception of a body. Organization is how people use each other relationally to do things that individuals cannot do alone, so we propose that analyzing the operation of this tool is prerequisite to understanding the essence of organizational entities. Like Barnard (1968), then, we see the essence of organization as being a system of cooperation, but unlike Barnard, we do not see formal organization as being essential to this tool. We do not see questions of leadership "in organizations" as especially useful, and propose that the questions we need to address involve leadership *as* the organizing of behavior.

The nature of organizational cooperation includes far more than the purposive tasks of primary interest to Barnard (1968). To explain, we invoke Wiley's (1988) mapping of four analytic levels of human experience. The first is the self or individual level, generally corresponding to how we use the pronoun "I." Our analysis will refer to this as the intra-individual level so as to minimize conflation with an individual person as a physical entity. Because of the inextricable linkage between individuals as physical individuals and the intra-personal self, this first level is fundamental to all higher levels. No form of human social action or communication is possible without the involvement of a physical person.

Wiley's (1988) second level is that of interaction, which produces a "we" and which allows us to do things beyond which the "I" is capable. For example, we can shake hands, have a conversation, or play tennis, but all such things cannot be individually accomplished, even as the specific "I" remains an essential participant. The third level is that of specific social structures, in which the "I" becomes generic and is no longer specific to the "we." At this level, the "we" gains the advantage of treating individuals as interchangeable parts in specific roles, so that when any one team member or organizational employee leaves, another can take on that role. Wiley's (1988) fourth level is that of specific cultures, in which generic selves drop out, and social structures become generic, such that social life is ordered by abstract meanings.

Viewed in this light, we can roughly describe the process of relational organizing as the process through which human behavior comes to operate simultaneously across two or more of these analytic levels. These levels remain analytic distinctions, in that they are not separable apart from observation or analysis. They do not inherently reflect properties observable in organizational charts, even as dyads, structures of generic roles, and internal cultures are all of interest to organizational research. Employees naturally continue to see themselves as unique individuals while also taking on relational role identities such as leader or follower, and collective identities such as "geek," "African American," or "senior citizen." It is by this same process that social entities themselves take definition, such that people speak not only of "my working relationship with my boss" but also of "the team" and "the organization."

We will refer to *identification* as the process through which entities get defined, and to *entitativity* as the extent to which perceptual elements actually do get commonly perceived (identified) as constituting a unit (entity). Campbell's (1958) description of entitativity[2] suggested four principles of perceptual organization that influence perception of discrete elements as parts of a whole: proximity, similarity, common fate, and perceivable form. Our definition rests on the common etymological root "ent" between the words *entity*, *identity*, and *identify*. Defined in this way, the term *entity* can be applied to functionally, temporally, or spatially associated elements. This definition allows it to apply not only to how roles and relationships get perceived systematically as entities, but also to how a supply chain, an ecosystem, a market, or an entire economy becomes perceived as a salient "thing" to us.

ACTING ORGANIZATION INTO EXISTENCE

Relational Processes

The relational processes of primary interest within constructionist analyses are those centered on understandings negotiated within relational interactions. This focus is evident in analyses such as those of Czarniawska (2008) and Hosking (1999). Hosking (1999) works from the explicit premise that relating is constructed in language and other forms of action, but the analysis has little to nothing to say about action other than language. Czarniawska's (2008) analysis begins with people constructing "action nets," such that particular collective actions tend to get repeated, but others do not. She asserts that "the reason for repetition is not important, because it can hardly be established beyond doubt; it is repetition that is important" (p. 22). Repeated actions trigger sense-making narratives, and it is the collective organizing of these narratives that is of central interest. There is no further analysis of action, apart from knowledge, narrative, or meaning.

As noted by Ospina and Dodge (2005), narrative inquiry "is about finding meaning in the stories people use, tell, and even live" (p. 144). If we have a narrative, in contrast to not having one, we have a meaningful account of what we experience. A narrative provides a representation of our experience, not the actual raw experience. Much constructionist research capitalizes on the ease of using what people say as the primary source of narrative research data. The present analysis proceeds on three key assumptions that contrast with such constructionist analyses. One of our assumptions, as stated above, is that what people understand regarding reality, whether subjectively or intersubjectively, remains a representation, or account, of reality rather than its essence. A second assumption is that an adequate understanding of relational dynamics requires understanding causes underlying the repetitive behavior patterns that trigger interpretation, meaning-making, and sense-making negotiations. The third assumption is that the sense produced as an output of relational sense-making negotiations cannot be the only cause, and may not be the major cause, that reinforces the repetition of the interactive behavior patterns. We therefore disagree with Czarniawska's argument that reasons for the repetition are irrelevant, and we argue below that they constitute the primary mechanisms of the production of leadership. Narrative provides to us a window through which action can be viewed, but it is action, not narrative, that is the primary point of leverage in social relationships.

We advance these assumptions because the accumulation of research in neuroscience and psychology (e.g., Edelman, 2006, Wilson, 2002) refutes the presumption that conscious, articulate knowledge is what controls human behavior. Conscious knowledge is our internal narrative of our experience, and not the essential cause of our behavior (Jaynes, 1976, Wegner, 2002). Conscious knowledge is nonetheless of great importance to leadership, and we will address it after outlining our perspective on the genesis of the leader–follower relationship.

We had argued above that epistemology is all too often conflated with ontology, and we extend this argument with the explicit assertion that knowledge concerning reality should not be mistaken for reality per se, based on the extensive accumulation of research in socio-cognitive psychology. This evidence (e.g., Bargh, 2007) establishes that much of our behavior occurs rather automatically, much more quickly than would be possible were our actions to result from conscious cognitive processing. We also have a great deal of research evidence (e.g., Pentland, 2008) that what we can consciously articulate regarding our interactive behavior with other individuals in face-to-face settings often systematically mis-characterizes our responses.

Although much management and organizational research does seem to conflate what organizational participants articulate with their relational interactions, there is a growing body of research bearing on social organization that cannot make such a conflation. By looking outside our own most-revered journals, we find pertinent insights in the literatures of ethology, which is the biological study of behavior, and animal cognition. Non-human animals do communicate simple meanings, but they don't elaborate and negotiate these meanings into narrative stories.

Given that we see organization as a tool and not as a body, our focus is on the functional operation of organizing, and not on the stacking of individual parts as building blocks that compose a whole. A variety of animals, other than humans, live in groups that employ coordinated activities relying on specialization and the division of labor. In doing so, they leverage each other, achieving collective results that are not possible individually. Some of these animal work teams feature as much, if not more, task interdependence than some human teams (e.g., many sales "teams"). Non-human animals working collaboratively produce relational structures with features that might often be assumed to be the products of sense-making narratives in human organizational settings.

Organization as a Tool: Examples from the Animal Kingdom

Examples abound of animals that rely on teamwork in hunting (Anderson & Franks, 2001). In the most common arrangement for team hunting, one or more individuals flush the prey from hiding, or simply chase it in the direction of others who close off escape paths. Stander (1992) showed that lion hunting teams use two general roles in a coordinated formation. Lionesses playing the "wing" role circled prey while others playing a "center" role waited for prey to move towards them. Those lionesses that occupied the center role frequently initiated an attack on the prey, while lionesses in wing roles moved relatively small distances and most often captured prey in flight from the others. Over time, each lioness in a given pride tended to occupy the same hunting formation role, and hunts enjoyed a higher probability of success when most lionesses occupied their preferred positions. Similarly, chimpanzee teams hunt a juvenile baboon by surrounding it. When the surrounded baboon climbs a tree as its avenue of escape, other chimpanzees climb up the adjacent trees to await the prey's attempt to leap to freedom.

Couzin, Krause, Franks, and Levin's (2005) analysis of effective leadership and decision-making in animal groups on the move showed that migrating and foraging groups of birds, fish, and even insects could make effective decisions collectively, and that emergent leaders were not necessarily physically larger or more dominant. Collective patterns emerged directly from behavioral reactions between adjacent individuals. These animals do not need explicit signals or complex mechanisms for information transfer, and we argue that analogous simple behavioral reactions among humans are quickly and often greatly complicated by our greater cognitive capacity. Although non-human animals produce their organizational structures without reliance on sophisticated cognition and articulate communication, it is precisely the significantly greater sophistication of human organizational structures that would be achieved through these means. We thus proceed on the assumption that our analysis must begin with reactive behavior patterns among interacting individuals, and then consider the overlying complications that we apply to our interactions.

Ways that non-human animals use organization as a tool to leverage each other's efforts have often been wrongly assumed to be uniquely human. Their ways of producing organization have more in common with human organizing than existing theory has assumed. Existing constructionist theory can inform us about aspects of organizing that are unique to the complex meanings typical of human cognitive complexity. Human organization has the overlay of Wiley's fourth analytic level, and a focus on meaning is essential to distinguishing it from the preceding levels. It is this fourth level that best distinguishes how humans complicate their social organization beyond that of other animals. Wiley's intervening second and third levels are where we should look for commonality, so a focus on meaning seems particularly ill-suited to capitalize on human and non-human similarities. A relational organizing approach attends to how interaction patterns arise and become elaborated into the constructed nature of social entities across all four of Wiley's levels. In order to more clearly distinguish a relational organizing approach from familiar constructionist theory, we prefer to speak of the social production, and not construction, of reality.

The word *production* has two particularly preferable connotations for differentiating it from existing social constructionist theory. One is that the word *construction* is often used with respect to the building of physical entities such as a house, which revisits how a corporation is designed to be a "thing" of indefinite existence apart from the individuals involved with it. Organization is a means for leveraging individual efforts to produce accomplishments beyond those achievable by individuals alone. A second is equally apt: We often refer to production with respect to theatrical plays and other artistic performances. Organization is acted into existence, and its essence can be found neither in the script written in advance of the performance, nor in reviews written as accounts of it.

RELATIONAL LEADERSHIP: A SPECIAL CASE OF RELATIONAL ORGANIZING

Both the individualized leadership model and the LMX model have assumed that the social exchange process between supervisors and subordinates revolves around transactions in which the relative contributions of subordinates to the achievement of work unit goals get reciprocated by relatively beneficial treatment by the supervisor. Several critiques (e.g., Rousseau, 1998; Schriescheim, Castro, & Cogliser, 1999; Sparrowe & Liden, 1997) of LMX theory and research have argued that it has not achieved a clear and consistent articulation of the specifics of the nature of the social exchange process within leader–member dyads. Our own observation is that work on both the individualized leadership model and the LMX model often includes no citations to seminal works in social exchange theory, and that it draws narrowly on this rich body of theoretical concepts. Work in the LMX tradition has more often referred to its other rich theoretical base, namely role theory. In our view, dyadic leadership theory has nonetheless also drawn from an overly narrow slice of role theory.

By looking at the LMX model and the individualized leadership model as alternate specifications of relational leadership theory, we highlight conceptual gaps between them. The necessary theoretical tools to fill these gaps already exist in conceptions of social exchange and role theory that the dyadic models have not put to use.

There is considerable, yet unrealized, potential in conceptions of dyadic leadership. The dyadic view has increased realization of leadership as not so much what a manager does in between reading reports and making decisions, as it is something that develops to a variable extent as supervisors interact with subordinates. In other words, as out-group members and supervisors dance through their nominally interactive motions, little if any real leadership occurs. Where leadership happens is within the substantive engagement that arises between leader and follower. By way of analogy, good leadership would be much more like the experience of an enthralling conversation than it would be like listening to a recording of an outstanding orator.

Relational leadership emerges as a naturally occurring social process. Although the leadership process is interesting in its own right, it cannot be adequately understood except as a particular instance of more general processes of social organization. In order to frame the dynamics of leadership within a general conceptual framework of relational organizing, we need to briefly outline that framework.

Before outlining our relational organizing framework, we note that the study of LMX dyads has a long history of concern with what might be called "extra-dyadic" dynamics. Examples include recent work such as that of Sparrowe and Liden (2005) as well as studies such as those of Cashman, Dansereau, Graen, and Haga (1976) and Graen, Cashman, Ginsburgh, and Schiemann (1977), which found that a leader's upward relationships affected downward relationships. Specifically, managers who have favorable relationship with their own bosses are more likely to establish favorable exchange relationships with their subordinates, fostering more favorable job outcomes across hierarchical levels. These findings were interpreted as reflecting an "organizational understructure" operating beyond the prescriptions of formal organizational structure.

This understructure of informal relationships systematically established orderly patterns of behavior that organizational participants came to see as "how things really get done around here," beyond the structure indicated by a formal organization chart. We assert, then, that how leadership "really gets done" is one particular form of how people do things relationally.

Bringing Exchange Theory Back In

Remembering that LMX theory has been criticized for presuming more about social exchange dynamics than it has explained, we'll parallel Homans' (1964) suggestion of "bringing men back in" with our interest in a fuller consideration of existing social exchange theory. The original ideas of George Homans (1958; 1961) serve as the best place to begin reassessment of social exchange in leader–follower relations.

Homans' (1961) analysis of social exchange as the most elementary form of social behavior advanced the view that all interpersonal dynamics, including influence, grew out of the development of exchange patterns between individuals. Homans endorsed the Skinnerian perspective dominant at the time, which sought no further "explanation" for the repetition of a behavior beyond evidence of an operant link to reinforcing consequences. Such reinforcing consequences were often quite subtle in their simplicity, such as an exchange of quick smiles. For Homans, individual behavior was social exchange behavior simply to the extent that it would not continue except for the reactions of other individuals. Those reactions include both understandings as well as more visceral operant consequences. Homans' view thus extends to both direct economic transactions between individuals and ongoing social exchange relationships, and excludes individual behavior that occurs apart from, and independent of, other people's behavior.

Work by Foa (1971) provides a starting point for understanding the implications of the substance and content of social exchange. Foa (1971) focused less on trying to explain observations of naturally occurring exchange relationships than on trying to refine a categorization of the social resources exchanged by people. Foa and Foa (1974) and Foa, Converse, Tornblom, and Foa (1993) report the ensuing stream of studies that generally supported Foa's (1971) proposed circumplex model, which is reproduced in Figure 2.1.

Figure 2.1 Foa's Resource Circumplex.
[a] Adapted from Foa, 1971.

The axes differentiate exchange resources along two orthogonal dimensions. The circumplex does not intersect either axis, so resources are differentiated in relative rather than absolute terms. Information and respect are the most abstract resources, whereas effort and goods are the most concrete. Money is the most universal exchange resource, whereas affect is the most particularistic, such that its value is largely determined by the identity of the exchange partner. Money is not entirely universal, as exemplified by customer loyalty to particular merchants, as well as by merchants who refused to sell based on customer skin color. Most of the research summarized in Foa and Foa (1974) and Foa et al. (1993) affirmed that people are most comfortable responding in kind, exchanging like resources (such as giving some information in exchange for receiving other information), and are most uncomfortable regarding exchanges of resources positioned in opposition by the circumplex (such as affection for money).

Some respected theorists (e.g., Coleman, 1990) distinguished social exchange from economic exchange by assuming that the latter involves money, whereas the former does not. Others cast social exchange as quasi-economic exchange, such as the contrast drawn by Clark and Mills (1979) between communal and exchange relationships, and Friedkin's (1993) expected value model of social exchange. Such views misconstrue social exchange as reflecting a cost/benefit calculus that centers on intangibles as opposed to tangible commodities. We see such distinctions as adding more confusion than clarity to the conception of social exchange.

A more useful distinction comes from Emerson's (1981) argument that social exchange and economic exchange reflect two different patterns in which exchanges may occur over time. Economic exchanges are temporally independent transactions, as in a perfectly competitive market. Social exchanges, in contrast, are serially dependent. Serial dependence, in turn, requires allegiance to particular exchange partners. This dependence may reflect either, or both, actions by each party that reciprocate past actions by the other party, and/or actions based on expectations of future reciprocation. The serial dependence of social exchange thus implies a temporal continuity of influence between exchange partners that is contradictory to principles of economic exchange. This is significant, as the continuity of reciprocal influence residing in social exchange's serial dependence gives rise to meaningful exchange *relationships* versus merely identifiable sets of exchange transactions.

We contend that the implications of Foa's differentiation of resources along his vertical and horizontal axes with respect to the distinction between social exchange and economic exchange have not been well explicated in previous research. Economic theory emphasizes the principle of market efficiency, by which economists mean the relative independence of specific exchange transactions from any and all factors that foster allegiance and thus temper or even supplant price signals (which are most clearly indicated by money.) The more particularistic are the criteria on which specific exchange transactions are based, the less those exchanges fit their ideal concept of perfect competition.

Social Exchange and Identity

The greater the particularism, then, the more that specific transactions will reflect existing social factors, and the greater the implications of such transactions for the building, maintenance, or weakening of social relationships. The serial dependence characteristic of social exchange is not possible without continuity in the identity of exchange partners. Our argument here, then, is that the role of identity has been under-appreciated in existing social exchange theory. The character of social exchange not only requires transaction partners to be identified to each other, but further serves as a mechanism for identity development, maintenance, and evolution. The natural experience of social exchange transactions prompts participants to reflect on their self-identities and their partner's identities. The discomfort, as noted above, associated with a cognition that I have just exchanged my affection for money is discomfort with the implications of such an exchange for my identity.

The symbolism inherent in more abstract resources is also important, in that the meanings they hold for us greatly affect their value. Data can be uninformative. The more particularistic and abstract resources have the most implications for identity and are the most subject to identity. The least particularistic and abstract resources (i.e., money and goods) have more to do with what we possess than with who we are. Possessions come and go, and it is the more particularistic and abstract resources to which we more often refer in speaking to the character of a person: a respectable person, a likeable person, an intelligent person, a hard worker. Our relational organizing approach proposes that social interaction patterns involving more particularistic and abstract exchange resources greatly shape identifications that attach to exchange partners and the pattern of their relationships. We label ourselves, each other, and the structural patterns associated with our exchange relations. With respect to leadership, we either become leaders or followers, but either way we build leadership relations.

We also need to recognize that the dependence of particularistic social exchange on the identity of participants is not restricted to individual or self-identity. Social exchange reciprocations are often not specific to the unique individuality of our interaction partners. Levi-Strauss (1969) noted exchange patterns in which the reciprocation was indirect but nonetheless systematic across groups of individuals, which he termed *generalized exchange.* What is generalized is group identity. Individuals are treated as representative of a category, much as in the operation of stereotyping behavior. The norms and expectations governing appropriate reciprocation behaviors apply to the categorical identity, such that patterns of exchange behavior differ more between such groups than between individual members within such groups.

Generalized exchange aids our analysis in a couple of significant ways. First, it reflects that patterns of social exchange transactions derive from, as well as reinforce, the identification and association of individuals with groups, which facilitates addressing similarities across dyads. It also provides a basis for social exchange theory to address the linkage between the individual level of analysis and the group level of analysis without reifying the group. Leaders can, and do, conduct some social exchange interactions with followers for which equal treatment is the prevailing norm. Generalized exchange analyzes interactions among individuals, but in a way that recognizes that individuals may participate in exchanges ordered by their representation of a particular group, whether this representation be of work group members, professional colleagues, neighbors, or fraternal association members.

Leadership: So Easy a Cockroach Can Do It?

Categorical identification can be minimal and yet critical to organized behavioral patterns. An illustration of just how minimal the identification can be comes from research by Halloy et al., (2007). Cockroaches congregate socially in dark places, but this behavioral norm can be modified by socially influential "leaders." Roaches have abysmal eyesight but a good sense of smell. Halloy et al. (2007) constructed robotic "roaches" identifiable to other roaches by pheromones. Researchers programmed the robots to spend extra time under bright light and less time in the dark, and the robotic leaders effectively influenced groups of real roaches to congregate in the brightly lit area. The robots succeeded as leaders because the real roaches applied to them a functional identity, rather than a technically accurate identity.

Remembering Dansereau's (1995) notion that out-group members are actually non-followers, it is important to note that the distinction is more than just a semantic one. If we define the leader/follower dyad as only one in which each accepts his or her role with apparent willingness, then the question becomes how they come to do so, when, and why. This is where the concept of relational leadership integrates previous approaches.

For true leadership to emerge, relationship development and role identity will begin and develop simultaneously. Because of the need for continuity in social exchange relationships, these two facets of relational leadership are enmeshed. As we begin to understand ourselves as leader or follower, other, specific individuals are implicated as our relational counterparts. Each partner develops expectations for the relationship, and each contributes social exchange resources based on his or her role identity.

Bringing Role Theory Back In

Just as LMX theory and individualized leadership theory have stopped short of full use of concepts from social exchange theory, existing role theory also offers untapped potential. Among organizational scholars, reference to role theory frequently evokes the structural role theory approach widely known from the seminal work of Katz and Kahn (1978). Less familiar to many organizational scholars is interactionist role theory (Stryker, 2002; Turner, 2002). Whereas the structural approach defines a role as a set of expected behaviors, the interactionist approach defines a role as "a comprehensive pattern for behavior and attitude that is linked to an identity, is socially identified more or less clearly as an entity, and is subject to being played recognizably by different individuals" (Turner, 2002, p. 234). Our notion of relational organizing builds on the premise that insights from both interactionist and structural role theory should be combined.

Interactionist theory is of use for three key reasons. First, interactionist theory focuses on the construction of identity. We argue that the only truly exogenous attribute an individual has is physical existence. Over time, personality develops through interactions with others, capitalizing on the advantages that our social existence creates for us to thrive in our physical environment. Personality is produced by social experience, within the constraints of an individual's genetic heritage. No less important is the theoretical compatibility (Emerson, 1976; McCall & Simmons, 1978) between social exchange and interactionist analyses. Although Emerson's later work did not further develop the ideas, he did (1976) suggest that self-presentations, identity negotiation, and the production of group relationships are implicit in social exchange. Finally, interactionist research has addressed how interactions among individuals can affect the very structures (Stryker, 2002; Turner, 2002) within which their behaviors continue. The structures of interest in much of this research have been personal, family, and community relationships, rather than working relationships, but the non-bureaucratic nature of such relationships befits the growing organizational fluidity of contemporary business trends.

McCall and Simmons (1978) emphasized the notion of role support, which is fundamental to a relational organizing approach. Their analysis depicts individuals as continually expressing claimed identities in their interactions. When others are responsive to these expressions and thus facilitate further expression of the claimed identity, their response is deemed to provide role support. McCall and Simmons (1978) include both extrinsic and intrinsic rewards as additional factors that can reinforce the expressed identity, but the role support from interacting others is seen as the most important determinant of which identities receive enough support to guide subsequent behavior.

This concept of role support is reinforced by the research of Swann and his colleagues (e.g., Swann, 1987; Swann, Polzer, Seyle, & Ko, 2004) on self-verification. This research has presented a major challenge to self-enhancement theory (e.g., Baumeister, 1982: Taylor & Brown, 1988) with its notion, widely accepted in psychological research, that self-esteem is the primary motivation for interpersonal feedback. The identities that people claim are less likely to be the most ideal, than they are to be identities that extrapolate from prior experience.

Our relational organizing approach proposes that, as interactions proceed, the nature of the specific social exchange resources in their transactions is a key determinant of role support. Just after individual A has contributed a suggestion about how a team should approach its work, if others reciprocate with acquiescence, thus signaling respect, individual A receives role support for a claimed identity as a group leader. Implicit in this same example is categorical role support across the participating members for the identity of group member. As we will describe below, this role support has key implications for the social "entification" of the group itself.

Our version of relational leadership assumes that the process that produces relational identities in the leadership context and the process that produces self-identities is the same. As leader/follower partners conduct transactions, they not only negotiate their roles, but also reflect on the implications of transaction patterns for their own role and relational identities as well as for their exchange partner's identity. In this process, what Aron and his colleagues (e.g., Aron, Aron, Tudor, & Nelson, 1991) describe as "inclusion of other in self" occurs naturally. Consider an example from outside the leadership realm: one's relational identity as a spouse cannot be generic; we see ourselves as the spouse of a specific significant other. Similarly, one sees oneself as a leader of specific followers or as a follower of a specific leader. These identities are person-and context-specific. This is one reason it is difficult to generalize the search for individual attributes central to entity perspectives. Whereas in one context or work group an individual assumes the leader role and in another he is the follower, how can we assume that any specific quality determined his leadership role in one situation but not another?

What is less clear from the line of research that supports Aron's concept of including the other in the self is the symmetry of that identification. Specifically, including the self in the other is integral with including the other in self. We thus incorporate ourselves in the role identity that we perceive for our spouse. Even more consequential is that the inclusion provides a source for the production of Wiley's "we," such that the word "incorporate" is quite apt here, given its etymological reference to a body. In a functionally analogous way to how the formal chartering of a business corporation creates the legal equivalent of a person, so does the "we" of a relationship become a corporate actor. This corporate actor becomes the thing that we see as our means of doing what is impossible for individual actors, which can be as simple as shaking hands, or as complex as the development of human civilization.

PRODUCING SOCIAL OBJECTS

It is a constellation of such incorporated acts that constitutes the essence of organization. McCall and Simmons (1978) applied Mead's (1934) conception of social objects for their analysis of how socially produced entities take on the character of action-orienting mechanisms. In their words:

> Let us consider one admittedly bizarre act. A rather young man, in a park in the Bronx, is standing quietly but very alertly in the afternoon sun. Suddenly he tenses and scurries a few tentative steps to his right, still rather frozen, his gaze locked on a man only a few feet away. This other man makes a sudden move with his right arm, and the first fellow breaks into sudden flight. Twenty or thirty yards away, still another fellow starts to run to cut him off, and the first man falls flat on his face, skidding and bouncing roughly along the ground as a result of his great momentum. (McCall & Simmons, 1978, p. 50)

The social entity that is created as the orienting object of this cooperative effort clearly has no substantial existence, but just as clearly, the object of this narrative can be recognized by baseball fans as a stolen base.

This example of a social entity happens to involve the inter-related action of eleven individuals playing specific roles, and its entire existence lasts for just a few seconds. All social entities are created by a "we," but the number of individuals involved can range in scope from a dyad to an entire population. All social entities must also exist over some period of time, but this can be as ephemeral as our stolen base, or as durable as the Catholic Church. The specificity of social entities can range from my personal self-identity, through my role identity (e.g., leader), on to a dyadic relational entity (e.g., my marriage), and through the scope of collective entities such as team, organization, and nation.

Weick (1979), after Simmel (1950), noted that the shift from two individuals to three has more significant implications than any other change in group size. A reason other than those emphasized by Weick and Simmel is of particular significance for our analysis. When individuals interact with only one other individual, it is natural that attributions to personal attributes of that individual remain highly salient. As described above, the inclusion of other in self tends to be specific to that individual, and the relationship thus tends to be seen in a monogamous sense. When we shift from a single dyadic partner to two or more partners, it becomes natural to think of these multiple others generically. Just as the transition between Wiley's second and third analytic levels involved shifting from a specific "I" to a generic "I," so can we shift from a singular "you" to a plural "you." Social entities larger than dyads become scalable in ways that dyads cannot.

When we generalize across alternate individual others, we can vastly simplify effective interaction patterns. Our multiple significant others can become interchangeable parts, and we can follow categorical interaction rules rather than dyad-specific rules. Leaders can display equal treatment to all subordinates, and a wide variety of interdependent activities can be approached heuristically. We can interact effectively with a range of individuals precisely because we identify them categorically rather than individually, and thus display behaviors that would be deemed appropriate for any subordinate, any coworker, or any higher manager.

Leaders and followers accept these roles through their experience of them, just as baseball players accept their roles as they enact them within a specific context. Role support from interactions with other actors both derives from the situation and creates it, whether the other actor is a pitcher or a leader. The learned patterns that underlie the role get reinforced, and, consistent with Swann's (1987) work on identity verification, do tend to extrapolate from already established identities. When the other actors expect an individual to pitch a baseball or lead a team, he or she is primed to do so. Similarly, whether the expectation is for the individual to hit the ball or to follow a leader, then that behavior—and by extension, identity—is readily enacted. These notions underscore the importance of time and context.

Revisiting Foa's (1971) circumplex, remember that the model discusses resources. The more particularistic and abstract resources are clearly different from material possessions, and do not exist apart from people. In economic terminology, they are not fungible. If I enjoy someone's affection or hold their respect, that can only have developed over time in the context of an ongoing relationship. These are the very relationships through which we come to know our own selves. So how do leader and follower role identities and their leadership relationship develop, and how does each partner contribute to the emergence of this "we"?

Our enumeration of Foa's resources emphasized that their tangible and intangible values were intertwined to varying degrees. The more abstract and particularistic resources (information, respect, affection, and effort) are the most relevant for our analysis. Individuals cannot be compelled to contribute more than a basic level of such resources—yet some do. As individuals transact these resources, they interactively enact and reinforce their complementary roles as leader and follower. These transactions invite attributions and reflections, and are thus enriched with meaning for our self-identity, for our identity in relation to our partner, and for the meaning of our relationship with that partner. When someone shares information with us, or shows us respect, we interpret why they do so, and it reflects on our role identity. In this way, we see again how the self and the other are interconnected.

We now have the necessary foundation to return to consideration of the attributes of the entities of interest for LMX and individualized leadership theory. Role identities are characterizing labels, and just as personality attributes are constructs inferred from patterns of individual behavior, role identities are attributions inferred from patterns of relational exchange transactions. A subordinate can become identified primarily as being a conscientious hard worker, or simply as an extroverted, likeable employee. Leader identities accrue naturally to well-informed and highly respectable individuals.

Another attribute of identities is their inclusion with respect to other entities. We see this in Brewer and Gardner's (1996) tripartite division of self, relational, and collective identities. Role relationships have their own associated identifiable and characteristic patterns of exchange transactions over time. For example, characteristically strong mutual efforts will define a cooperative relationship, and mutual respect will define a trusting relationship. Every relationship, though, can only be completely defined by its unique pattern across all combinations of characteristic exchange resource transactions. These defining patterns of role and relational entities thus become the social objects to which we orient a great deal of our thoughts and behavior.

As noted above, that these relationships are mutual does not mean that patterns of resource exchange are symmetric. For example, followers must contribute more effort and respect to the leader than they receive, but they will continue to do this only so long as their combined receipts across all resource categories remains sufficient. When leader and follower find the overall pattern barely sufficient, they will have what previous theory has described as a low-quality LMX relationship, and when the overall pattern approximates an optimal combination, they will have a high-quality LMX relationship.

Joint Performance: Relational Quality

So where does our conception stand with respect to the entity/constructionist divide, and where is the integration discussed in the introduction?

Whereas an entity model suggests that the formal roles of "supervisor" and "subordinate" create the relationship, and a constructionist model suggests that meanings established in the relationship create the roles, our approach suggests the simultaneous emergence of both the roles and the relationship. In a system in which one individual is formally designated as "the supervisor" and another "the subordinate," behavior will generally unfold in accord with preconceptions of these roles—much as we know how "a wife" acts in "a marriage," we similarly understand how "a subordinate" should relate to the supervisor. Unique relationships develop when we enact our version of "wife" or "subordinate" with a particular partner. The existence of a "we" relationship is thus implicit rather than explicit, but the point bears attention that this "we" gets created somehow, and we cannot take it for granted as a pre-existing state of reality. The process through which "we" develops, and then does become taken for granted by the participants, is the heart of what we call *relational organizing*.

As stated earlier, the Foa model postulates that individuals are most at ease when some sense of equivalence permeates the exchange. We agree and suggest that considerations of equity greatly affect the sense of equivalence. Supervisors have higher formal status and greater access to organizational resources. Dansereau (1995) argued that a sense of self-worth was one item in the exchange between leader and follower. Followers expect to exchange effort for information and respect from their leader. The leader expects to use information to direct the follower, and the follower expects that direction.

The asymmetry of this exchange pattern and the relative influence of the two partners is natural. Consider a follower who has more appropriate information pertaining to the direction of efforts than does the leader, or a leader who shows respect to a follower that greatly exceeds the follower's effort. Such examples feel socially inappropriate, and thus undermine leader influence. The natural ebb and flow of the relational pattern has defined to the partners who they are, an identity that is inextricably linked to who their partner is and how each should act. The leader/follower labels are continually recreated during each relational interaction. To illustrate with another example: in the case of a follower having information, the way he or she shares that information with his leader—if such an exchange occurs at all—is probably quite different from the way he or she shares it with a peer. In this way, role identities are reinforced as the leader/follower relationship develops.

Leaders and followers accept their roles as they experience them, and thus are continually re-creating and re-accepting them. Job titles and other formal organizational labels or exogenous individual attributes can only provide a point of departure for this relational process and are not integral to it. Leadership is ubiquitous, whether the participating individuals all seem to be the best and the brightest, or when none seem to be, or when the full range of the distribution is present. It is ongoing role support from interactions with other individuals for acting in line with the role of follower versus for the role of leader that reinforces the learned patterns underlying the roles.

The Leader Role

Uhl-Bien (2006) notes that LMX's emphasis on individual behaviors places it on the entity side of the entity/relational divide. Being the "superior" presumably leads to the leader acting as such. However, as we have previously discussed, LMX differs from other leadership theories because of its lack of emphasis on individual behaviors or attributes as constituting the essence of leadership. Our notion of relational leadership agrees with LMX theory's de-emphasizing of individual attributes that can be seized upon on the hallmarks of "a leader." The LMX model, however, still begins with the assumption of predefined roles and with the superior testing the limits of the member. As Graen and Scandura (1987) state, "the superior acts and the member reacts" (p. 181). It is only in the second phase, role making, that their model depicts role signaling as a two-way street.

When individuals work within a traditionally organized, stable environment, in which role identities are clearly defined, such a linear relationship model works well. But what of matrix organizations, or even those in which a traditional organizational chart exists, but is not entirely a reflection of the reality of work flow? And what of project-based teams, with leaders who aren't managers and team members who are followers on one project, but leaders on another? The complexity of how work gets done today—through an "off the books" system that nonetheless has its own leaders and followers—means that identities and relationships must be context-dependent and emerge simultaneously. Relational leadership recognizes that the labels that interaction partners create for each other are of primary relevance to their interaction as leader/follower dyads, and not simply as preexisting formal organizational labels or individual attributes. The leader in one situation may be the follower in another, and would modify his or her behavior(s) accordingly, producing the development and maintenance of different functional relationships across different contexts.

Returning to Foa's model, consider the resource allocation permitted to the leader. Leaders generally—though not always—have access to more information than followers do, and this information is used to direct the efforts of others. After information, the next greatest resource contribution of leaders is respect, or recognizing the follower's human/social/emotional needs and making some accommodation in that direction. Leaders can like followers, but as soon as getting work done takes a back seat to affect, that liking faces an upper limit that is determined by productivity. To behave otherwise detracts from the role identity of the leader. The effort that leaders need to show to followers is more political and symbolic rather than the more tangible effort that followers need to show leaders.

The role identities of leaders have an important link to the leader–follower relationship as an entity that stands in clear contrast to the linkage of follower identities to the relationship as a corporate actor. It is critical that a high proportion of the leader's exchange transactions be perceived as representative of the corporate actor, as opposed to actions associated with the "selfish" interests of the individual actor. To twist Aron et al.'s (1991) phrasing, the follower needs to include the other (i.e., the leader) in the "we" to an even greater extent than including the other individual in the self or the self in the other. Efforts I put forth on behalf of my leader need to be efforts on behalf of "the organization," and not efforts to serve the private gains that someone in a leadership position might enjoy.

Legitimizing Leadership

Our relational organizing perspective on leadership allows us to go significantly beyond the scope of both the LMX model and the individualized leadership model with consideration of leadership authority and legitimacy. In this extension, we can address the great importance of organizational narrative, to which we referred above. It is useful at the outset of this consideration to recognize the etymological heritage shared by the words "author," "authority," and "authentic." Authors construct and convey a narrative, and control of organizational stories lies at the heart of authority. When the author of narratives regarding authority is the "we," then authority will be optimal, as participants will agree to the authenticity of such narratives.

Organizational stories will be as accepted as factual (i.e., authentic) only so long as they remain reconcilable across the experiences of participating individuals. The primary source for the meanings in these stories has to be those inherent in the symbolism of social exchange transaction patterns. Individuals develop interpretations and attributions from their behavioral interactions that will be partly convergent and partly divergent. Clashing narratives between leaders and followers, or among multiple presumptive followers of the same leader, will undermine the legitimacy of leadership authority. Legitimacy reinforces inclusion between the identity of the individual acting as a leader and the collective "we." This is highly functional for leaders, as for any social object, in its reinforcement of taking that object for granted. Because actions oriented to legitimate leaders can be taken for granted, following requires little to no conscious deliberation in advance, and can proceed in the manner of a reflex reaction. There is nonetheless the risk of leaders confusing their own identity with the collective "we" such that they become prone to abusing their power.

That legitimacy and authority are matters of paramount practical concern to leaders is evidenced by the scope and elaborateness of the construction of organizational narratives. "Spin control" is practiced not only by presidents of nations, but also by leaders in small face-to-face groups. When leaders lose control of the narratives, their authority becomes increasingly contested, and an illustration of how greatly this erodes leadership effectiveness is seen when an elected president can no longer influence a legislative agenda due to low public approval.

Existing legitimacy theory provides a useful base for integrating the issues of authority and legitimacy with our relational organizing conception of leadership. Most analyses of authority and legitimacy build on the seminal ideas of Max Weber (1947). Weber's analysis worked from the observation that pure power was ultimately impotent. The stable exercise of authority requires not only that those who are subject to it cooperate willingly, but also that their willingness not be contingent on rational self-interest or simple personal preference. Barnard's theory of authority attempted to deal with this paradox by proposing that authority could operate only within an individual employee's "zone of indifference" in which neither external incentives nor internal preferences would be consequential.

The notion of a zone of indifference allowed Barnard's theory to focus exclusively on an individual level of analysis explanation, thus side-stepping the social system dynamics of legitimation. That legitimation operates systemically is clear from research in both organizational contexts (Scott, 1995) and informal group status hierarchy contexts (Branaman, 2004). The systemic nature of legitimacy derives from individuals being able to see strong social acceptance of the apparent factual nature of narratives, and not simply from internal agreement.

Johnson, Dowd, and Ridgeway (2006) review the extensive research evidence on legitimacy as a social process in both social psychology and organizational theory. Much of this research strongly supports theory originally developed by Dornbusch and Scott (1975). This theory details the weaving of a social fabric of various types of support from salient actors for the legitimacy of a social object. *Normative* legitimacy comes from support of actors whose definition of moral desirability is taken as authoritative. *Regulative* legitimacy comes from support of actors in formally authoritative roles, in which they specify procedural or legal requirements and sanctions. *Cognitive* legitimacy flows from simple consistency across other actors. When people see that "everyone else" is downloading music files without paying for them, it is cognitive legitimation that gets them thinking that it must be all right to do so.

It is the story told (the narrative) in each aspect of legitimation that is most consequential. Because earlier sections of our analysis employed examples from animals less intelligent than humans to underscore that complex human language was not the primary mechanism of organizing, we will mention briefly that non-human social animals do have at least a rudimentary form of legitimation. In their own way, animal social processes create a story that tells individuals that an individual leader is acting on behalf of the collective, such that following is simply not a matter of individual choice. Studies of leadership hierarchies among baboons (Strum, 1987), chimpanzees (de Waal, 1982) and gorillas (Harcourt & Stewart, 2007) demonstrate that lower-ranking individuals more rarely challenge higher-ranking individuals when those higher-ranking individuals have prominent alliances. Leadership succession is often triggered by the deterioration of those alliances. To paraphrase de Waal (1982), what happens in power struggles behind the closed doors of corporate board rooms has a great deal more in common with what can be seen in your local zoo than it pleases us to think.

The Follower Role

Inherent in the entity perspective is a bias against followers. After all, if certain individual attributes lead some to become leaders, there seems to be an assumption that the followers are such by default—they lack those attributes and thus are relegated to the follower role. In relational leadership, we argue, the follower is an equal partner in a social exchange process, and while much of the underlying processes does not rely on conscious choices, each interaction between partners does provide followers with the opportunity to choose to be a follower—or not.

The LMX model maintains a strong focus on the leader. But, a leader cannot be so identified if no one follows her. The question might then be asked, why do people follow? We hope the reader will see at this point that getting the right answer to this question may well be a case of getting the right answer to the wrong question. Roles and relationships evolve over time, with no specific decision point to determine whether or not to follow. As new acquaintances are made, role identities and relationships are negotiated. Individuals enact the follower role in a natural give-and-take exchange, responding to behaviors from the other that effectively fit a leader role, and the follower either falls in step as a follower, or rejects that relationship.

Followers, too, have resources at their disposal. Clearly, effort is a primary resource that can be meted out by the follower, in accord with LMX theory, but nothing precludes potentially dysfunctional relationships that the partners might subjectively describe as "high-quality" if the partners allow other resources to trump effort. Some followers can be sycophants or simply personal favorites. Such relationships will affect everything from unit output to the leader's reputation. Thus, whereas the resource contribution of the follower is different, there is still an exchange process occurring.

Each interaction with the partner is an opportunity for followers to reinforce their identity. In a sense, individuals choose how much and what kind of respect, information, and affection to exhibit toward another, and then infer the implications for their role relationship and role identity. Preferences for the type and amount of each resource spring from preexisting self-conceptions as peer, leader, or follower, and the transmission process reinforces both individuals' self-identities as well as the shared relationship. Over time, these exchanges come to follow predictable patterns, which in turn reinforce the relationship status. Time also leads to subconscious pattern repetition. The first time we meet someone, there is usually a period of feeling out an identity and status for the new person and how we identify ourselves in relation to that person, as in the forming stage of Tuckman's (1965) early model of group development. We need this to adjust our behaviors appropriately. Not having this information is disorienting because, if we don't have enough information about the other person, we don't know how to relate to them; in a sense, we don't know who we are when we are with them. This idea relates to the scalability of "we" discussed earlier, because the initial identities can be nominal. In using labels and cognitive shortcuts to identify our and others' roles, we immediately identify appropriate relational patterns.

RESEARCH METHODS AND RELATIONAL ORGANIZING

Clearly, our relational leadership approach draws on ideas established within each side of the entity versus constructionist divide among leadership theorists. Both sides offer value to organizational researchers, and we see more potential to advance our understanding of leadership by finding complementarity between the views rather than picking sides on the assumption that they are incommensurable. Our approach to bringing research evidence to bear on our conception of relational leadership analogously reaches across the methodological divide between the favored research tools of each camp. Each side's research methods reflect its contrasting assumptions, and each tool set has both limitations and advantages.

A key limitation of constructionist methods is the inherent rejection of a distinction between knowledge of reality versus objective reality. Subjectivist ontology defines testability of theory as being misguided and irrelevant.

To the extent that subjectivist ontology denies us any access to any objective reality, it precludes us from having an objective standard against which we could test our theory. Positivist ontology offers the promise of testability, but that promise has not been well fulfilled. Browsing through most any organizational behavior textbook shows that, over the past 50 years, we have accumulated a surfeit of theoretical models of leadership, as well as in other areas, such as motivation and macro-organization theory. What has not happened is the weeding out of these theoretical models by tests that refuted them.

With respect to our relational leadership approach, a key limitation of the methods favored by entity theorists is the presumption of recursive causal models. The critical assumption of recursiveness is that a theoretical model's explanation of a causal sequence begins with an exogenous variable. This is problematic because none of our important theoretical constructs can reasonably be regarded as exogenous. We don't claim that there are no exogenous variables, only that what they contribute is of minor importance.

Our conception does treat the reciprocal causation across role identities, role behavior patterns, and the nature of the leader–follower relationship as an entity as being path-dependent. Because we propose that this reciprocal causality evolves over time, what Berry (1984) describes as *block recursive* models can be used to investigate the way that leadership develops. The kind of data required for such analyses are not easy to obtain. The problem is whether to choose putatively testable models that cannot fit the phenomena of interest or those that do fit but are difficult, if not impossible, to test with conventional research methods. It is a Pyrrhic victory to achieve testability at the cost of validity.

This dilemma does not leave us helpless. Conventional ordinary least-squares statistical analysis could show that our theoretical constructs cannot be related to each other in the ways we propose, or in ways proposed in the LMX and individualized leadership models. For example, is the level of contributed effort from subordinates the best predictor of information and respect received from the supervisor? Is contributed effort actually a better predictor of the subordinate taking on an "informal lieutenant" role behavior pattern, and developing a high LMX quality relationship, than their contributions of information, respect, and liking? Such studies would help open up what Rousseau (1998) termed the "black box" of LMX theory.

A variety of pertinent alternative research methods have been developed, even if they have not commonly been applied in leadership research. Previous entity models have favored what Mohr (1982) described as variance studies, whereas previous constructionist conceptions have favored what Mohr described as process studies. Variance studies presume fixed entities with variable attributes, and investigate co-variation patterns across hypothesized cause-effect relationships among the attributes of interest. The process studies favored by constructionists have presumed that participant narratives of their experience of relationships inform us of the unfolding of co-evolving intersubjective realities.

As we suggested, variance studies can still investigate the attributes of role identities and their associated behavior patterns, and attributes of relationships as intersubjectively perceived entities, as well as process studies of relational interaction patterns. Variance studies can show the extent to which the levels of contributions and receipts of various social resources are associated with role behavior and identities. Variance studies can also inform us regarding resource combinations and contextual effects. Multiple regression models, as well as more sophisticated tools, such as structural equation modeling and hierarchical linear modeling can investigate more complex questions including interaction effects and cross-level effects. For example, do subordinate contributions of respect for the supervisor have less effect when effort contributions are relatively low? Do individual subordinate contributions of effort have less effect in work groups that have a high average level of contributed effort across subordinates?

Further, variance studies need not take the familiar form of the general linear model (GLM). Set-theoretic analysis (Fiss, 2007) offers a useful option that does not necessitate the usual GLM assumptions. The general linear model assumes that we measure variables that reflect attributes of interest along a linear continuum, and that some degree of measurement error is always involved. Central tendencies along these continua are presumed to be less subject to error, as the aggregation of observations into any type of average allows for random errors, both positive and negative, to cancel each other out. What standard correlational methods compute, for example, is the average cross-product (in standard score form) between two distributions to assess the co-variation between those distributions. When such correlations are used within a multiple regression framework, the predictor variables compete for co-variation with the criterion variable. The only combinations of predictor variables that can be investigated in general linear model analyses are central tendency-based combinations, but set-theoretic analyses could investigate any, and potentially all, possible configurations of predictive factors. If high LMX quality relationships can arise equally well from alternate configurations of resource exchange, set-theoretic analysis could document this, even as regression-based methods never could.

Process studies will nonetheless be at least as, if not more, important than variance studies because our approach treats both roles and relationships as endogenous. Set-theoretic methods could be used equally well in process studies as in variance studies. Process studies of leadership have been rare among researchers not favoring a constructionist approach, and we think that needs to change. There is no reason that process studies need to be limited to the analysis of narratives. That process studies need not even incorporate the narratives of research subjects is clear from the progress of work in animal ethology (Reznikova, 2007). Leadership researchers have our own history, albeit modest, of process research on which to draw. Early work by Bales (1950) applied interaction coding schemes in studies of emergent leadership, but it has been in organizational communication research (e.g., Fairhurst, 2007) where contemporary leadership scholars might be most likely to encounter such methods. Fairhurst (2007) cites examples such as relational control coding to illustrate how extra-verbal patterns in the process of conversational interaction might produce unambiguous directional leadership, or alternatively produce a power-struggle standoff, even with essentially the same verbal transcript. Rogers and Escudero (2004) provide an excellent guide to process studies of relational communication.

Advances in process study methods have nonetheless been made in a variety of applications in social psychology, group dynamics, and macro-organizational theory. For example, Pettigrew (1997) outlines processual analysis research on topics such as strategic management, decision-making, and organizational culture. Bakeman and Gottman (1997) provide a detailed primer on the ethological methods that they and their colleagues have applied to studies of a variety of sequential relational interactions, including children playing, married couples, and parents with children. Their system involves meticulous coding of behavioral sequences as well as of verbal interactions. It has been found to predict divorces with better than 90 percent accuracy with just a few minutes of observation.

Weingart (1997) describes techniques for analyzing sequential data, in addition to providing a thorough inventory of data collection strategies and methods for studying group process. Different types of process studies, such as lab experiments, field experiments, and field case analysis have complementary strengths and weaknesses. Combining strategies and methods offers the opportunity to gain a comprehensive understanding of group process, including actions, communications, and developmental phases.

In line with Van de Ven's (2007) recommendations, we propose that process studies of relational leadership use multiple tools in combination. This could include, for example, survey questions completed by participants as well as interviews with key managers and other participants, both at periodic intervals, along with direct observation of regularly scheduled meetings, a diary recording informal discussions with participants, and collection of pertinent organizational documents and reports. Such a comprehensive approach strikes us as the strategy most likely to produce effective advancement in our understanding of relational leadership.

CONCLUSION

In concluding, we suggest specific points of focus to address the various process research tools that we have outlined. Perhaps the most straightforward approach involves considering how the seven-item measure of LMX that has been widely used for almost 30 years represents a very generalized reflection of the dyadic exchange dynamics that we have described above. Survey measures developed by Seers, Wilkerson, and Grub (2006) separate exchange contributions versus exchange receipts for four of the resource categories for which exchange partners have the most discretion in day-to-day work activities: information, respect, liking, and effort. Such measures provide one way to investigate the complex possibilities of exchange transaction patterns. Several aspects of characteristic transaction patterns might also be measured directly, such as exchange frequency versus the symmetry of specific exchange resources, the amplitude of those resources, the range or combinations of resources, and the generalization of such patterns across specific dyadic partners within social categories that reflect groups as entities. Finally, existing measures of social identification such as those of Mael and Ashforth (1992) and Doosje, Ellemers, and Spears (1995) can be adapted so as to reflect both self-identification with relational and collective entities, as well as identification applied to exchange partners with reference to those entities.

Our relational organizing approach to leadership draws selectively from previous work in both the entity and constructionist traditions. In its view of leadership as a socially produced dynamic, it parallels constructionist thinking more than entity thinking. We nonetheless distance our view from the constructionist premise that treats narrative meaning-making as essential to leadership. Narrative elaborates, sophisticates, and complicates leadership, but leadership can be produced before it is cognitively constituted. What's essential to leadership is action—leaders leading, with followers following.

REFERENCES

Anderson, C., & Franks, N. R. (2001). Teams in animal societies. *Behavioral Ecology, 12*, 534–540.

Aron, A., Aron, E. N., Tudor, M., & Nelson, G. (1991). Close relationships as including other in self. *Journal of Personality and Social Psychology, 60*, 241–253.

Bakeman, R., & Gottman, J. M. (1997). *Observing interaction: An introduction to sequential analysis.* Cambridge, England: Cambridge University Press.

Bales, R. F. (1950). *Interaction process analysis.* Reading, MA: Addison Wesley.

Bargh, J. A. (2007). *Social psychology and the unconscious: The automaticity of higher mental processes.* New York, NY: Psychology Press.

Barnard, C. I. (1968). *The functions of the executive.* Cambridge, MA: Harvard University Press.

Baumeister, R. F. (1982). A self-presentational view of social phenomena. *Psychological Bulletin, 91,* 3–26.

Berger, P. L., & Luckman, T. (1966). *The social construction of reality: A treatise in the sociology of knowledge.* Garden City, NY: Doubleday.

Berry, W. D. (1984). *Nonrecursive causal models.* Beverly Hills, CA: Sage Publications.

Bradbury, H., & Lichtenstein, B. (2000). Relationality in organizational research: Exploring the "space between." *Organizational Science, 11,* 551–564.

Brannaman, A. 2001. Rational and irrational bases of commitment to group hierarchies. *Advances in Group Processes, 18,* 31–64.

Brewer, M. B., & Gardner, W. (1996). Who is this "we"? Levels of collective identity and self representations. *Journal of Personality and Social Psychology, 71,* 83–93.

Burrell, G., & Morgan, G. (1979). *Sociological paradigms and organizational analysis: Elements of the sociology of corporate life.* London, England: Heinemann Ltd.

Campbell, D. T. (1958). Common fate, similarity, and other indices of the status of aggregates of persons as social entities. *Behavioral Science, 3,* 14–25.

Cashman, J., Dansereau, F., Graen, G., & Haga, W. J. (1976). Organizational understructure and leadership: A longitudinal investigation of the managerial role-making process. *Organizational Behavior and Human Performance, 15,* 278–296.

Clark, M. S., & Mills, J. (1979). Interpersonal attraction in exchange and communal relationships. *Journal of Personality and Social Psychology, 37,* 12–24.

Coleman, J. S. (1990). *Foundations of social theory.* Cambridge, MA: Harvard University Press.

Couzin, I. D., Krause, J., Franks, N. R., & Levin, S. (2005). Effective leadership and decision-making in animal groups on the move. *Nature, 433,* 513–516.

Czarniawska, B. (2008). *A theory of organizing.* Cheltenham, England: Edward Elgar Publishing.

Dansereau, F. (1995). A dyadic approach to leadership: Creating and nurturing this approach under fire. *Leadership Quarterly, 6,* 479–490.

Dansereau, F., Graen, G., & Haga, W. J. (1975). A vertical dyad approach to leadership within formal organizations. *Organizational Behavior and Human Performance, 13,* 46–78.

Dansereau, F., Yammarino, F. J., Markham, S. E., Alutto, J. A., Newman, J., Dumas, M., . . . & Keller, T. (1995). Individualized leadership: A new multiple-level approach. *Leadership Quarterly, 6,* 413–450.

De Waal, F. (1982). *Chimpanzee politics.* London, England: Jonathan Cape, Ltd.

Dewey, J., & Bentley, A. F. (1949). *Knowing and the Known.* New York, NY: Beacon Press.

Dienesch, R. M., & Liden, R. C. (1986). Leader-member exchange model of leadership: A critique and further development. *Academy of Management Review, 11,* 618–634.

Doosje, B., Ellemers, N., & Spears, R. (1995). Perceived intragroup variability as a function of group status and identification. *Journal of Experimental Social Psychology, 31,* 410–436.

Dornbusch, S. M., & Scott, W. R. 1975. *Evaluation and the exercise of authority.* San Francisco, CA: Jossey-Bass.

Edelman, G. M. (2006). *Second nature: Brain science and human knowledge.* New Haven, CT: Yale University Press.

Ekman, P. (2002). *Telling lies: Clues to deceit in the marketplace, marriage, and politics.* New York, NY: W. W. Norton.

Emerson, R. M. (1976). Social exchange theory. *Annual Review of Sociology, 2,* 335–362.

Emerson, R. M. (1981). Social exchange theory. In M. Rosenberg, & R. H. Turner (Eds.), *Social Psychology: Sociological perspectives* (pp. 30–65). New York, NY: Basic Books.

Emirbayer, M. (1997). Manifesto for a relational sociology. *American Journal of Sociology, 103,* 281–317.

Erdogan, B., & Liden, R. C. (2002). Social exchange in the workplace: A review of recent developments and future research directions in leader–member exchange theory. In L. L. Neider, & C. A. Schriesheim (Eds.), *Leadership* (pp. 65–114). Greenwich, CT: Information Age Publishing.

Fairhurst, G. T. (2007). *Discursive leadership: In conversation with leadership psychology.* Thousand Oaks, CA: Sage Publications.

Fiss, P. (2007). A set-theoretic approach to organizational configurations. *Academy of Management Review, 32,* 1180–1198.

Foa, U. G. (1971). Interpersonal and economic resources. *Science, 171,* 345–351.

Foa, U. G., & Foa, E. B. (1974). *Societal structures of the mind.* Springfield, IL: Charles C. Thomas.

Foa, U. G., Converse, J., Tornblom, K. Y., & Foa, E. B. (1993). *Resource theory: Explorations and applications.* San Diego, CA: Academic Press.

Friedkin, N. E. (1993). An expected value model of social exchange outcomes. *Advances in Group Processes, 10,* 163–193.

Graen, G. B. (1976). Role-making processes within complex organizations. In M. D. Dunnette (Ed.), *Handbook of industrial and organizational psychology* (pp. 1201–1245). Chicago, IL: Rand-McNally.

Graen, G., & Cashman, J. F. (1975). A role-making model of leadership in formal organizations: A developmental approach. In J. G. Hunt, & L. L. Larson (Eds.), *Leadership frontiers* (pp. 143–165). Kent, OH: Kent State University Press.

Graen, G., Cashman, J. F., Ginsburg, S., & Schiemann, W. (1977). Effects of linking-pin quality on the quality of working life of lower participants. *Administrative Science Quarterly, 22,* 491–504.

Graen, G., Dansereau, F., & Minami, T. (1972). Dysfunctional leadership styles. *Organizational Behavior and Human Performance, 7,* 216–236.

Graen G. B., & Scandura, T. A. (1987). Toward a psychology of dyadic organizing. In L. L. Cummings, & B. M. Staw (Eds.), *Research in organizational behavior* (pp. 175–208). Greenwich, CT: JAI Press.

Graen, G., & Schiemann, W. (1978). Leader-member agreement: A vertical dyad linkage approach. *Journal of Applied Psychology, 63,* 206–212.

Graen, G. B., & Uhl-Bien, M. (1995). Relationship-based approach to leadership: Development of leader–member exchange (LMX) theory of leadership over 25 years: Applying a multi-level multi-domain perspective. *Leadership Quarterly, 6,* 219–247.

Guba, E. G. (1990). *The paradigm dialog.* Newbury Park, CA: Sage Publications.

Halloy, J., Sempo, G., Capari, G., Rivault, C., Asadpour, M., Tache, F., ... & Deneubourg, J. L. (2007). Social integration of robots into groups of cockroaches to control self-organized choices. *Science, 318,* 1155–1158.

Harcourt, A. H., & Stewart, K. J. (2007). Gorilla society: Conflict, compromise, and cooperation between the sexes. Chicago, IL: University of Chicago Press.

Hedstrom, P., & Swedburg, R. (1998). *Social mechanisms: An analytic approach to social theory.* Cambridge, England: Cambridge University Press.

Homans, G. C. (1958). Social behavior as exchange. *American Journal of Sociology, 63,* 597–606.

Homans, G. C. (1961). *Social behavior: Its elementary forms.* New York, NY: Harcourt Brace and World.

Homans, G. C. (1964). Bringing men back in. *American Sociological Review, 29,* 809–818.

Hosking, D. M. (1999). Social construction as process: Some new possibilities for research and development. *Concepts and Transformation, 4,* 117–132.

Jaynes, J. (1976). *The origin of consciousness in the breakdown of the bicameral mind.* Boston, MA: Houghton Mifflin.

Johnson, C., Dowd, T. J., & Ridgeway, C. L. (2006). Legitimacy as a social process. *Annual Review of Sociology, 32,* 53–78.

Katz, D., & Kahn, R. L. (1978). *The social psychology of organizations.* (2nd ed.). New York, NY: Wiley.

Kotter, J. P. (1990). *A force for change: How leadership differs from management.* New York, NY: Wiley.

Langley, A. (1999). Strategies for theorizing from process data. *Academy of Management Review, 24,* 691–710.

Levi-Strauss, C. (1969). *The elementary structures of kinship.* Boston, MA: Beacon Press.

Likert, R. (1961). *New patterns of management.* New York, NY: McGraw-Hill.

Mael, F., & Ashforth, B. E. (1992). Alumni and their alma mater: A partial test of the reformulated model of organizational identification. *Journal of Organizational Behavior, 13,* 103–123.

McCall, G. J., & Simmons, J. L. (1978). *Identities and interactions: An examination of human associations in everyday life.* (2nd ed.). New York, NY: The Free Press.

Mead, G. H. (1934). *Mind, self, and society.* Chicago, IL: University of Chicago Press.

Mohr, L. B. (1982). *Explaining organizational behavior.* San Francisco, CA: Jossey-Bass.

Morley, I., & Hosking, D. M. (2003). Leadership, learning, and negotiation in a social psychology of organizing. In N. Bennett, & L. Anderson (Eds.), *Rethinking educational leadership: Challenging the conventions* (pp. 43–60). London, England: Sage Publications.

Ospina, S. M., & Dodge, J. (2005). It's about time: Catching method up to meaning—The usefulness of narrative inquiry in public administration research. *Public Administrative Review, 65,* 143–157.

Ospina, S., & Sorenson, G. (2006). A constructionist lens on leadership: Charting new territory. In G. R. Goethals, & G. L. J. Sorenson (Eds.), *The quest for a general theory of leadership* (pp. 188–204). Cheltenham, England: Edward Elgar.

Pentland, A. (2008). *Honest signals: How they shape our world.* Cambridge, MA: MIT Press.

Pettigrew, A. M. (1997). What is a processual analysis? *Scandinavian Journal of Management, 13,* 337–348.

Reznikova, Z. (2007). *Animal intelligence: From individual to social cognition.* New York, NY: Cambridge University Press.

Rogers, L. E., & Escudero, V. (2004). *Relational communication: An interactional perspective to the study of process and form.* Mahwah, NJ: Lawrence Erlbaum Associates.

Rousseau, D. M. (1998). LMX meets the psychological contract: Looking inside the black box of leader–member exchange. In F. Dansereau, & F. J. Yammarino (Eds.), *Leadership: The multiple-level approaches* (pp. 149–154). Stamford, CT: JAI Press.

Schriesheim, C. A., Castro, S. L., & Cogliser, C. C. (1999). Leader-member exchange (LMX) research: A comprehensive review of theory, measurement, and data-analytic practices. *Leadership Quarterly, 10,* 63–110.

Scott, W. R. (1995). *Institutions and organizations.* Thousand Oaks, CA: Sage Publications.

Seers, A. (2004). Leadership and flexible organization structures. In G. B. Graen (Ed.), *New frontiers of leadership, Vol. 2.* (pp. 1–31). Greenwich, CT: Information Age Publishing.

Seers, A., Wilkerson, J. M., & Grubb, W. L. (2006). Social resources in leader–member exchange relationships: Reciprocal contributions and receipts. *Psychological Reports, 98,* 508–510.

Simmel, G. (1950). *The sociology of Georg Simmel.* (K. H. Wolf, Trans.). New York, NY: The Free Press.

Sparrowe, R., & Liden, R. C. (1997). Process and structure in leader–member exchange. *Academy of Management Review, 22,* 522–552.

Sparrowe, R. T., & Liden, R. C. (2005). Two routes to influence: Integrating leader–member exchange and social network perspectives. *Administrative Science Quarterly, 50,* 505–535.

Stogdill, R. M., & Coons, A. E. (1957). *Leader behavior: Its description and measurement.* Columbus, OH: Bureau of Business Research, Ohio State University.

Stander, P. E. (1992). Cooperative hunting in lions: The role of the individual. *Behavioral Ecology and Sociobiology, 29,* 445–454.

Strum, S. (1987). *Almost human: A journey into the world of baboons.* New York, NY: Random House.

Stryker, S. (2002). Traditional symbolic interactionism, role theory, and structural symbolic interactionism: The road to identity theory. In J. H. Turner (Ed.), *Handbook of sociological theory* (pp. 211–231). New York, NY: Plenum Publishers.

Swann, W. B. (1987). Identity negotiation: Where two roads meet. *Journal of Personality and Social Psychology, 53,* 1038–1051.

Swann, W. B., Polzer, J. T., Seyle, D. C., & Ko, S. J. (2004). Finding value in diversity: Verification of personal and social self-views in diverse groups. *Academy of Management Review, 29,* 9–27.

Taylor, S. E., & Brown, J. D. (1988). Illusion and well-being: A social psychological perspective on mental health. *Psychological Bulletin, 103,* 193–210.

Thomas, W. I., & Thomas, D. S. (1928). *The child in America: Behavior problems and programs.* New York, NY: Alfred A. Knopf.

Tuckman, B. W. (1965). Developmental sequences in small groups. *Psychological Bulletin, 63,* 384–389.

Turner, R. (2002). Role theory. In J. H. Turner (Ed.), *Handbook of social theory* (pp. 233–254). New York, NY: Kluwer Academic/Plenum Publishers.

Uhl-Bien, M. (2006). Relational leadership theory: Exploring the social processes of leadership and organizing. *Leadership Quarterly, 17,* 654–676.

Van de Ven, A. H. (2007). *Engaged scholarship: A guide for organizational and social research.* Oxford, England: Oxford University Press.

Weber, M. (1947). *Max Weber: The theory of social and economic organization.* (A. M. Henderson, & T. Parsons, Trans.). New York, NY: Oxford University Press.

Wegner, D. M. (2002). *The illusion of conscious will.* Cambridge, MA: MIT Press.

Weick, K. (1979). *The social psychology of organizing.* Reading, MA: Addison-Wesley.

Weingart, L. R. (1997). How did they do that? The ways and means of studying group process. *Research in Organizational Behavior, 19,* 189–239.

Wiley, N. (1988). The micro-macro problem in social theory. *Sociological Theory, 6,* 254–261.

Wilson, T. D. (2002). *Strangers to ourselves: Discovering the adaptive unconscious.* Cambridge, MA: Harvard University Press.

Yammmarino, F. J., & Dansereau, F. (2002). Individualized leadership. *Journal of Leadership and Organizational Studies, 9,* 90–99.

Zaleznik, A. (1977). Managers and leaders: Are they different? *Harvard Business Review, 55*(5), 67–78.

NOTES

1. Morley and Hosking (2003) also discuss organizing as a sense-making process. This chapter will also address organizing, but instead of analyzing sense-making as the essence of the process, our approach reaches back to what Weick (1979) described as "pure organizing" as the essential antecedent to sense-making.

2. Hosking's (1999) approach also addresses the problems inherent in treating both individual and organization as exogenous entities. We suggest that such problems are intractable with the terminology currently conventional among students of human organization. The present space doesn't allow full elaboration, but we would propose using the terms "individual" and "corporation" to refer to entities appropriately treated as exogenous in behavioral research, and "person" and "organization" to refer to the associated endogenous entities.

CHAPTER 3

THE RELATIONAL PRACTICE OF LEADERSHIP

Joyce K. Fletcher

The goal of this chapter is to explore the construct of leadership as relational practice and delineate a particular way of thinking about the connection between entity and constructionist dimensions of that construct. First, I discuss the entity/constructionist dimensions of leadership and where the trajectory of my own research places me on this continuum. Second, I summarize the characteristics of emerging models of leadership that highlight its relationality. Third, I summarize my work on relational practice and place it on the entity/constructionist continuum drawing heavily on Stone Center Relational Cultural Theory (RCT). Last, I offer a framework for operationalizing a particular connection between entity and constructionist approaches to leadership and the implication of that connection.

ENTITY AND CONSTRUCTIONIST PERSPECTIVES

I write this chapter from a particular standpoint. The passion and energy that has fueled my own work on the relationality of leadership is normative and my early stance was one of critique. In my early work (Fletcher,

Advancing Relational Leadership Research, pages 83–106
Copyright © 2012 by Information Age Publishing
All rights of reproduction in any form reserved.

1994; 1999), I focused on work practice and used a particular theoretical framework, Stone Center Relational Cultural Theory (RCT), from which to critique and "unpack" the discourse of good work, competence, and leadership to reveal, as organizational poststructuralists do (Calas & Smircich, 1993; Flax, 1990; Jacobsen & Jacques, 1997; Martin & Knopoff, 1995; Mumby & Putnam, 1992), what is absent, ignored, devalued or marginalized in that discourse. This early work revealed relational dimensions of good work and competence that I argued had been ignored and devalued in mainstream understandings of how to achieve good organizational outcomes because of their association with the feminine (Fletcher 1994; 1999). The constructionist dimension of leadership in this approach was captured by the articulation of the largely subconscious, meaning-making processes that acted on the practice of leadership to construct it such that some practices were held to be leadership and some, arguably as important to organizational ends, were not. Applying the entity/constructionist distinction to my own work yields the following definitions:

> **Entity:** As I understand the term, entity perspectives on leadership are positivist in that they treat leadership as a set of skills, attributes, and practices that, when enacted through individual agency, will produce an entity that can be labeled "leadership." The list of characteristics and practices will differ depending on the leadership theory, but the constant is that leadership is treated as a construct that can be abstracted from the larger societal context and presented as an entity that can be enacted and understood at the micro level of individual analysis. An entity perspective on *relational* leadership focuses on a particular set of leadership skills and competencies that are relational and interactional in nature and are thought of as key to implementing a particular type of leadership with particular organizational outcomes.

> **Constructionist:** Constructionist dimensions of leadership focus on understanding macro level contextual forces that operate on micro level interactions in which actors wittingly or unwittingly enact or "do" leadership. Constructionist dimensions of leadership are inherently relational in that they highlight the interactional processes through which leadership is socially constructed. However, as I use the terms, constructionist dimensions of *relational* leadership highlight the way a particular set of (relational) leadership practices is perceived, co-created, and "acted upon" by larger organizational and societal systems, including systems of sense-making and cognition, as well as systems of power and privilege.

In this chapter, I respond to the challenge presented by Ospina and Uhl-Bien to explicate entity and constructionist dimensions of relational leadership and explore how they can be theorized together such that the dangers of focusing on one to the exclusion of the other are avoided, and the advantages of holding them together, even in an uneasy alliance, can be realized.

LEADERSHIP AS A RELATIONAL CONSTRUCT

The relationship between leader and followers has always been at the heart of leadership theory and practice. In the last decade, as the nature of work has changed, the concept of relationality has deepened, become more explicit, and expanded beyond positional leadership to a concept that emphasizes personal leadership regardless of position or organizational role.

There are many reasons why the changing nature of work has precipitated an effort to incorporate deeper dimensions of relationality into models of leadership more explicitly. The complexity of knowledge work, for example, means that it is unlikely that any one person will have all the necessary capability and competence to achieve effective outcomes. Instead, it is recognized that positional leaders must be learners, open to influence from multiple sources, able to empower and inspire others (Bryman, 1996; Manz & Sims, 2001) as well as foster organizational learning, adaptability, and innovation (Heifetz & Laurie, 1999; Senge, 1990b). Thus, the practice of good leadership is increasingly conceptualized as the ability to work in and through relationships (Lipman Blumen, 1996; Luthans & Avolio, 2003). Applied (e.g., Kouzes & Posner, 2003; Wheatley, 2001) as well as scholarly approaches (e.g., Graen & Uhl-Bien, 1995; Graen & Scandura, 1987; Pearce & Conger, 2003b; Uhl-Bien, 2006) increasingly define leadership itself as a relationship and leadership practices as occurring in the context of interactions among organizational members.

RELATIONAL LEADERSHIP AS ENTITY

From an entity perspective, I would argue that there are three characteristics that distinguish new, more explicitly relational models of leadership from more traditional conceptualizations: leadership skills, leadership processes, and leadership outcomes.

Leadership Skills: As the requirements of good leadership practice have shifted, so too has the discourse around what skills, competencies and attributes are needed to enact this practice. Relational and emotional intelligence are now considered key to effective leadership and the skills required include things such as empathy, vulnerability, self-awareness, self-regulation, humility, resilience, and resolve (Badarraco, 2002; Collins, 2001; Cox, Pearce, & Sims, 2003; Goleman, 1998; Goleman, Boyatzis, & McKee, 2002; Luthans & Avolio, 2003; Sutcliffe & Vogus, 2003; Vera & Rodriguez-Lopez, 2004).

Leadership Processes: Relational models of leadership emphasize the role of social interactions in the process of enacting leadership. The practice of leadership is portrayed as a dynamic, multi-direction activity that, like all human action and cognitive sense-making, is embedded in the social context in which it occurs (Lave & Wenger, 1991; Suchman, 1987). The micro-processes of leadership are conceptualized as occurring in and through the relational interactions that make up these relationships and networks of influence (Fletcher & Kaeufer, 2003; Gardner, 1990; Hosking, Dachler, & Gergen, 1995; Kahane, 2004; Mayo, Meindl, & Pastor, 2003; McNamee & Gergen, 1999). In particular, the relational interactions that typify good leadership are characterized as egalitarian, mutual, collaborative, and two-directional, with followers playing an integral, agentic role in the leadership process (Aaltio-Marjosola, 2001; Harrington, 2000).

Leadership Outcomes: Relational models of leadership recognize that effectiveness in a knowledge intensive workplace depends less on the individual, heroic efforts of a few, and more on the degree to which an organization has constellations of positive collaborative working relationships throughout (Badarraco, 2002; Bass, 1998; Beer, 1999; Conger, Spreitzer, & Lawler, 1999; Drath, 2001; Hargadon, 2003; Heifetz & Laurie, 1999; Pearce & Sims, 2000; Senge & Kaeufer, 2001; Yukl, 1998). Thus, the practice of good leadership is increasingly conceptualized as the ability to create conditions under which co-constructed outcomes, such as coordinated action, collective achievement, and shared accountability can be achieved (Conger, 1989; Gittell, 2003; Hosking, Dachler, & Gergen, 1995; Kanter, 2001; Lipnack & Stamps, 2000; Seely Brown & Dugid, 2000; Thompson, 2004; Wheatley, 2001; Yukl, 1998). Multi-level learning is the key organizational outcome of good leadership: dyadic learning when the relationship is between individuals, group learning in teams and communities of practice, and ultimately organizational learning that results in positive action (Agashae & Bratton, 2001; Heifetz & Laurie, 1999; Kim, 1993; Senge, 1990a). Thus, the conventional distinction that managers "do things right" and leaders "do the right thing" (Zaleznik, 1992) is increasingly blurred as the knowledge of the "right thing" is conceptualized as something that is co-created and emergent from positive, learning relationships distributed throughout an organization (Day, Gronn, & Salas, 2004; Hill, 2004; Kayes, 2004; Kim,1993; Vera & Crossan, 2004; Watkins & Cervero, 2000), and the leadership task is conceptualized as creating organizational conditions in which all relational interactions at work are "high quality connections" (Dutton, 2003) that enhance organizational learning, innovation, and adaptation.

Despite the increasing acceptance of the relationality of leadership, there are a number of gaps in the development of the construct. In earlier research, I have identified gaps in both entity and constructionist dimensions of the construct, without naming them as such. In this chapter, I will summarize my earlier work to place it on the entity/constructionist continuum and explore its potential to respond to the challenge issued by Uhl-

Bien and Ospina that theorists be mindful of these dimensions and how they connect and interact.

ENTITY PERSPECTIVES

Gap 1: Micro-Processes

Entity perspectives on relational leadership typically contrast it with traditional conceptualizations and focus on the way it is more egalitarian, two-directional, and collaborative than top-down leadership perspectives. This is not a trivial shift. Because of its significance, I believe entity perspectives need to explicate the characteristics and micro-processes of this shift in three specific ways. First, there is a need to unpack and identify specific micro-processes between actors that would operationalize two-directional concepts such as egalitarianism or mutuality in a leadership context, where there are status differences due to position or organizational level. Second, there is a need to explicate or give a theoretical frame for understanding the process by which outcomes achieved at the dyadic level link to broader leadership goals such as organizational learning and adaptability. Third, while the skills necessary to enact relational leadership are aligned with tenets of emotional and social intelligence (Cherniss, 2009; Goleman, 2006; Goleman et al., 2002), there is a need to understand the motivating set of beliefs or "logic of effectiveness" (Fletcher, 1999; 2004) that would prompt someone to use these skills to enact mutuality and two-directionality in a context that traditionally has been neither.

In my work, I have drawn heavily on tenets from Stone Center Relational Cultural theory to address these gaps. Stone Center Relational Cultural Theory (RCT) is a model of human growth developed by feminist psychologists and psychiatrists at the Stone Center for Developmental Services and Studies at Wellesley College. Its tenets detail a process of human development the authors call growth-in-connection (Jordan 1986; 1991; Jordan, Kaplan, Miller, Stiver, & Surrey, 1991; Miller, 1976; Miller & Stiver, 1997; Surrey, 1985). The theory's hallmark is that it privileges connection as the primary site of human growth. Rather than simply adding relationality to existing models of human development, RCT offers a set of principles, guidelines, and definitions of what it means to grow, develop, and achieve. It has a unique ability to inform the micro-processes of relational interactions because it details the critical relational skills, processes, and attributes that are needed to engage growth-in-connection at the level of one relational interaction or "relational episode." Although RCT was developed in a clinical context, there is a growing body of work that applies its tenets to work relationships, such as the field of positive relationships at work (Cameron,

Dutton, & Quinn, 2003; Cross, Baker, & Parker, 2003; Dutton & Heaphy, 2003; Dutton & Ragins, 2006) and the field of relational practice (Fletcher & Jacques, 2000; Gittell, 2003; Jacques, 1993; Jordan, 1999; Walker, 2002).

Elsewhere (Fletcher & Kauefer, 2003; Fletcher, 2006) my colleagues and I have applied the tenets of RCT to the construct of relational leadership and offered several ways entity perspectives could be further theorized and understood using this theoretical perspective. For purposes of this chapter, I will summarize briefly three constructs identified in this earlier work that I believe need to be further developed in entity perspectives on relational leadership.

Fluid Expertise. The first has to do with operationalizing egalitarianism through a construct I call "fluid expertise" (Fletcher, 1999). According to the tenets of RCT, a positive relational interaction is one in which "five good things" are mutually achieved (Miller & Stiver, 1997). These five things include zest, empowered action, increased sense of worth, new knowledge, and a desire for more connection. The requirement that these outcomes must be mutually achieved for an interaction to be characterized as "positive" is a way to operationalize the egalitarianism implicit in entity perspectives on relational leadership. Using this framework to study relational practice at work, I found that it is the presence of "fluid expertise" in the process of co-creation of new knowledge that is key to the behavioral outcomes associated with relational leadership. Fluid expertise is defined as a process in which:

> ... power and/or expertise shifts from one party to the other, not only over time but in the course of one interaction. This requires two skills. One is a skill in empowering others: an ability to share—in some instances even customizing—one's own reality, skill, knowledge, etc. in ways that made it accessible to others. The other is skill in *being* empowered: an ability and willingness to step away from the expert role in order to learn from or be influenced by the other. Expecting mutuality in this type of interaction implies an expectation that others will have both sets of skills and will be motivated to use them, regardless of the individual status of the parties involved. (Fletcher, 1999, p. 64)

I believe that entity perspectives on relational leadership could benefit from a deeper explication of this construct to understand the inner workings of the co-creation process, the particular skills it requires, and how, specifically, it is enacted in relational interactions in which there are power differences.

Relational Processes. The second construct I suggest be used to further the understanding of entity perspectives on relational leadership has to do with the process by which instrumental outcomes are achieved through relational processes. The "five good things" identified in RCT as outcomes of positive relational interactions hold particular value for theories of positional leadership because they integrate commonly identified affective outcomes, such as caring and increased energy (Carmeli, Ben-Hador, Waldman, & Rupp, 2009; Cross, Baker, & Parker, 2003) with outcomes more directly associated with organizational goals such as learning and empowered action. In addition, the last of the five outcomes, a desire for more connection, offers a process by which individual level outcomes can spiral outward to affect the larger organizational community. In other words, while most entity perspectives on relational leadership assume that relational leaders will have an effect on organizational goals, the process by which this would happen is not always clear. Most focus on the individual level dynamics between a positional leader and his or her follower(s). Documenting in organizational settings the existence of the spiral of growth suggested by RCT affords theorists a chance to identify specific ways in which relational expertise exemplified by positional leaders can affect the organization beyond the leader-follower dyadic.

Relational Stance. The third construct I believe needs to be more fully developed in entity perspectives on relational leadership is the notion of relational stance. In earlier work, I identified what I called a relational "logic of effectiveness" or set of beliefs about human growth and achievement (Fletcher, 1999) that appeared to motivate relational behavior in the workplace. The emerging field of positive work relationships has furthered this concept in non-leadership contexts to explicate several important dimensions of the motivation to engage in mutually growth fostering interactions (Dutton, 2003; Dutton, Debebe, & Wrzesniewski, 1998; Vera & Rodriguez-Lopez, 2004).

I believe this construct of relational stance is key to understanding relational leadership and deserves more attention. Entity perspectives on relational leadership tend to characterize it as a set of behaviors or practices that, when enacted, can lead to positive organizational outcomes. I believe it is not so simple. The behaviors and practices underlying these theories are motivated by a relational belief system, or logic, about how growth, achievement, collective outcomes, and ultimately effective business practice is achieved. This logic runs counter to traditional assumptions about paths to organizational achievement. The more traditional logic of effectiveness ingrained in leadership lore and narrative is one that tends to privilege individual action and independence as the path to effective action. Merely suggesting or even exhorting positional leaders to enact an alternative, more relational set of practices will have little effect on overall leadership behavior unless the difference between these two logics of effectiveness are clearly articulated and examined.

Once again, RCT has an important contribution to make in this regard. RCT is a relational ideology that challenges prevailing theories of human development on which most of our institutions are built (Miller, 1976).

Rather than simply adding relationality to existing models of human development, RCT explicates an alternative path to achievement and offers a set of principles, guidelines, and definitions of what it means to grow, develop, and achieve that have relationality at the core (Miller, 1976; Miller & Stiver, 1997; Fletcher, 1999). Exploring RCT from a leadership perspective has the potential to enhance entity perspectives on relational leadership in several important ways, many of which I have articulated in earlier work (Fletcher, 2007). I believe further refining and bringing into conscious awareness what it means to have a "relational stance" in one's leadership would advance the theory and practice of relational leadership in important ways.

In summary, I believe that entity perspectives on relational leadership have much to offer to traditional theories of leadership and have the potential to influence leadership practice in significant ways. As a theorist and leadership development professional, an important part of my work stands firmly in the entity perspective of relational leadership that Ospina and Uhl-Bien describe as a being a real phenomenon, with attributes, characteristics, skills, and practices that not only can be studied but influenced, learned, and developed in practitioners.

Gap 2: Social Context

Despite my stance and previous work on entity perspectives, I have also worked to identify a serious gap in these perspectives, which is that they too often ignore what Uhl-Bien and Ospina call constructionist dimensions of leadership. That is, while entity perspectives on relational leadership do a good job of articulating a new paradigm for leadership and the attributes of an ideal leader, they often fail to identify or theorize the implications of the social processes through which a leadership narrative is created and maintained. Instead entity perspectives are typically abstracted or lifted from the larger organizational and societal context and presented as context-neutral concepts.

For example, it has long been recognized that relational interactions are occasions in which we enact our social identities (Goffman, 1959), a good part of which are our gender identities, such that when we interact with others we "do gender" (West & Zimmerman, 1991). A related body of work details the way in which displays of good work often get conflated with displays of masculinity (assertiveness, strength, invulnerability, heroic individualism, etc.), such that doing gender at work has traditionally meant, for both women and men, "doing masculinity" (Ely & Meyerson, 2009; Martin, 1996; Martin & Collinson, 1998). Despite this association of traditional notions of leadership and competence with masculinity, and the suggestion that more relational models rely on traditionally feminine attributes such as collaboration, caring, and connection (Calvert & Ramsey, 1994; Fletcher, 1994; Fondas, 1997), entity perspectives on relational leadership rarely include a strong gender analysis. Thus, although the emotional and relational skills needed to enact a more relational model of leadership are identified, entity perspectives are largely silent on how individual level social identity characteristics such as race, class, or gender might influence one's ability to enact these more relational skills and still be perceived as a strong leader.

In my early work on the disappearing of relational practice, I drew on concepts from feminist poststructuralist perspectives (cf. Fletcher, 1999) to study this issue. My research explored a specific set of social processes— or what I called "disappearing acts"—that acted on relational constructs to render them invisible, largely through their association with femininity. Again, I drew heavily on Stone Center Relational Cultural Theory to inform this perspective. Unlike many relational ideologies, Stone Center Relational Theory does not abstract relationality from its broader social context. Rather, its tenets of growth-in-connection and its alternative view of the path to human growth and development are explicitly located within the social context of patriarchy and other power dynamics in which they occur and address two important questions that most entity perspectives on relationality ignore: Why, if connection is a basic site of growth and human development, have conventional models of development so emphasized separation, independence, and individuation? And why, if relational skills and attributes are key to the growth fostering process for all humans, have they been historically associated with femininity and the private sphere of life and so devalued in the public realm?

Jean Baker Miller (1976) offers a gender and power analysis to explain these contradictions. She notes that in Western society, men are socialized to devalue and deny in themselves the relational skills needed to survive psychologically. Instead, they are socialized to rely on women to provide these attributes. Women, on the other hand are socialized to provide these skills, usually invisibly and without acknowledgment that the provision of these attributes is needed or that something valuable has in fact been done. In this way, women become the "carriers" of relational strengths in Western society, responsible for creating relational connections for others and meeting basic relational needs without calling attention to the needs themselves. Rather than strengths, these relational attributes have traditionally been surrounded by what Miller (1976) calls a "language of deficiency" (e.g., emotionally needy, co-dependent, or overly dependent on relationships, low ego strength, etc.) and in the psychological domain, often characterized as the source of psychological problems rather than psychological strength. Miller (1976) observes that the invisibility and devaluing of relational activity allows society to perpetuate a myth of self-reliance and independence, even though most people have a network of people supporting their "individual" achievement.

Miller asserts that the belief that independence is a state that can be achieved belies the essentially interdependent nature of the human condition. Moreover, she asserts that the myth of individual achievement is actually a discursive exercise of power whereby some in society are expected to provide the collaborative subtext of life invisibly so others can enact the "myth of individual achievement" without acknowledging that this collaborative subtext of support is needed and important. Growth-in-connection depends on a belief in the essentially human nature of *inter*dependence, but the myth of individual achievement that permeates Western society precludes that belief and makes growth-in-connection difficult to achieve. The theory points out that both a gender power dynamic associated with patriarchy and a more general power dynamic are involved in sustaining these so called myths of independence and individual achievement.

Gender. RCT places the construct of relationality squarely within the discourse on the social construction of gender (West & Zimmerman, 1991), highlighting the fact that relationality is not a gender-neutral concept. Gender socialization, especially in Western society, assigns to women the task of creating the relational conditions under which human growth- in-connection can occur (Chodorow, 1978; Fairbairn, 1952; Miller, 1976; Miller & Stiver, 1997; Winnicott, 1958) especially as it relates to the private sphere of family and motherhood. The result is that enacting relational skills and adopting a relational stance is one way in which women "do gender" (West & Zimmerman, 1991) in Western society. The fact that, at a societal level, women are the carriers of relationality and expected to provide conditions of growth invisibly may inappropriately associate the stance, and the relational skills it takes to engage it, with *femininity.*

Power. In addition to this gender power dynamic, there is a more general power dynamic influencing relationality. In systems of unequal power (e.g., inequities based on race, class, organizational level, sex), it behooves those with less power to be ultra-sensitive and attuned to the needs, desires, and implicit requests of the more powerful (Jost, 1997; Miller, 1976). In other words, in systems of unequal power, what marks you as more powerful is the entitlement of having others anticipate your needs and respond to them without being asked; what marks you as less powerful is being required to do the anticipating and accommodating without any expectation of reciprocity. The fact that those with less power need to develop a distorted, non-mutual relation stance toward others in order to survive may inappropriately associate the stance, and the relational skills it takes to engage it, with *powerlessness and vulnerability* (Bartolome & Laurent 1988; Miller, 1976).

This analysis of gender and power dynamics underpinned my original study of relational practice in the workplace (Fletcher, 1999). I studied software engineers in an engineering firm and identified three specific ways gender and power dynamics inherent in the organizational discourse about competence and good work acted on relationality to render it invisible as effective or strategic action. Put in an entity/constructionist framework, my findings can be framed as an identification of the inner workings of the social (i.e., relational and interactional) processes through which an organizational narrative about competence is constructed. More specifically, I identified three such processes that had the effect of marginalizing displays of relationality in the workplace: misunderstanding of motive, the limits of language, and the conflation of relational practice with idealized motherhood and femininity. These three processes, or disappearing acts, are summarized below.

Misunderstanding the Motive: The first disappearing act is to misinterpret why someone would be enacting relational practice. My research found that others often attributed the motivation to engage in relational behaviors as an issue of personality and style rather than strategic intervention (Fletcher, 1999). That is, although relational practice is done in the service of good work, it can be (mis)understood as a personal idiosyncrasy or trait. These traits sometimes have a negative connotation, such as naiveté, powerlessness, weakness, or emotional need. But they may also be more positive, as when relational practice is seen as an expression of thoughtfulness, personal style, or being nice.

The Limits of Language: The second disappearing act has to do with language. Because of its traditional association with the private sphere, language used to describe relational behavior (e.g., nurture, care, empathy, listen, etc.) often evokes family rather than work relationships, thereby subtly associating relationality with something inappropriate to the workplace. In addition, using soft, feminine language to describe relational skills can evoke more general gendered dichotomies (such as strong/weak, work/family, rational/emotional) that underlie organizational discourse, thereby reinforcing these dichotomies even when they are not explicitly mentioned (Calas & Smircich, 1993; Flax, 1990; Jacobsen & Jacques, 1997). Using such language, then, is not only limited in its ability to capture the strategic intention and effectiveness dimension of relational practice, it actually serves to maintain the dichotomous thinking in which relational practice is devalued or perceived as inappropriate in organizational settings.

Confusing Relational Practice with Femininity: The third disappearing act I found in my data—how relational practice gets confused with femininity—is a phenomenon with special implications for women (Fletcher, 1999; Eagly & Carli, 2007). When men do relational practice, the first two disappearing acts might render their relational competence invisible. That is, they might be misinterpreted as weak, and they might have trouble finding language that adequately describes the power and contribution of their behavior. But for women, something additional happens. When they do relational practice, it often gets confused with their social roles in society as nurturing wives and mothers. When they engage relational practice, women are likely to be seen as "mothering" rather than leading, as selflessly giving (expecting nothing in return) rather than modeling a new, more relational way of working. This confusion is problematic. Selfless giving is, by definition, non-mutual. And effective relational practice, whether practiced by men or women, depends on conditions of mutuality and reciprocal influence (Zaccaro, Rittman, & Marks, 2001). People who put relational leadership into practice have every right to expect that this stance of mutuality will be met and matched by others—that others will join them in co-creating the kind of environment where these conditions can prevail, such that someone else will head up the next time-consuming initiative. Indeed, early research on the construct of mutuality (Jordan, 1986) would suggest that the promised outcomes of newer models of leadership such as collective learning, mutual engagement, learning across difference, and mutual empowerment cannot occur under conditions of non-mutuality. On the contrary, for relational practice to be widely adopted, it must have embedded within it an invitation to reciprocate in kind. But gender expectations constrain this possibility for women. When a woman's attempt to use relational practice to work more effectively is misunderstood as "doing mothering," the expectation of reciprocity embedded in the practice is rendered invisible. Thus, women may find they are expected and even relied on to practice many of the relational aspects of leadership but to do it without a recognition that this is strategic behavior and without expecting similar behavior from others.

Summary

I have used research findings about relational practice in the workplace to identify and begin to address two gaps in entity perspectives on relational leadership. Based on research findings that identified micro-processes of relational practice as enacted by software engineers, I have identified three constructs, fluid expertise, growth process beyond the dyadic, and the notion of relational stance that I believe need to be further developed to explicate the specific processes by which relational leadership can achieve the organizational effectiveness outcomes generally attributed to its practice. Secondly, I have identified and applied to leadership, three social or relational processes through which the organizational narrative on competence is socially constructed in ways that can undermine relationality: misunderstanding motive, use of language, and conflation with femininity.

CONSTRUCTIONIST PERSPECTIVES

Unlike entity perspectives that treat relational leadership as a particular type of intentionally enacted practice, constructionist perspectives view all forms of leadership (with or without the descriptor relational) not as an entity in and of itself, but as a process of social construction that is continually being negotiated in relational interactions. My efforts to apply relational practice to the construct of leadership have embraced both these perspectives. That is, it uses constructionist ideology to suggest that traditional entity perspectives on leadership are constructed through a hegemonic leadership narrative that devalues certain (relational) characteristics, skills, and beliefs about ways to accomplish good work. In this way, it treats leadership as an entity made up of a body of knowledge that can and should be expanded to include formerly marginalized voices, thereby creating a new, potentially transformative model of leadership practice. It further uses constructionist principles to caution against abstracting this practice from the societal context in which it is occurs. That is, I have used constructionist principles to suggest that simply identifying relational constructs and adding them to traditional leadership criteria uncritically is problematic. I argue that to do so could lead to the new entity being co-opted by the status quo and stripped it of its value and transformational capacity by three specific processes or "disappearing acts."

Constructionist perspectives on relational leadership often take some aspects of this hegemonic context into account but fail to offer help or guidance on how flesh-and-blood leaders can navigate that context or influence the ways in which a narrative of leadership gets constructed in the "spaces between" (Bradbury & Lichtenstein, 2000). I believe that while constructionist perspectives do a great service to leadership theorists by calling attention to social and relational processes by which leadership narratives are constructed, they do little to identify the practical implications of these processes or help practitioners strategize ways to influence them. Thus, I believe constructionist perspectives could benefit from exploring the entity dimensions of the social construction of leadership to identify how actors in the discourse can exercise individual level agency to resist and even influence these powerful forces.

Gap: Practical Implications of Constructionist Perspectives

My stance in studying the construct of relational leadership is to accept that there is an entity, or new set of relational practices, that could transform the traditional practice of leadership. I have sought to explicate the particulars of this entity as well as identify certain social processes that act to "disappear" these particulars to render them "not leadership." One of the critiques of critical management studies and other perspectives that focus on the social construction of reality is that they so often leave practitioners feeling powerless, with few options to engage personal agency. Indeed, I have found that discussions of the constructionist dimensions of my work have sometimes had the effect of making practitioners feel powerless, as if these social processes are beyond the reach of individuals to influence. Practitioners who are faced on the one hand with entity perspectives of relational leadership that tout it as a new model more appropriate to today's global context and on the other with constructionist perspectives that detail the social processes by which leadership is constructed, need help in reconciling these two perspectives at the level of individual action. Over the years, I have worked with practitioners in workshops, seminars, and leadership development courses to understand the dilemmas they face and help strategize ways to interrupt and influence the social construction of leadership such that their relational practices get constructed as leadership, rather than as "not leadership."

Through this work I have concluded that one of the key challenges of constructionist perspectives is that they do not do a good job of helping individuals understand and reflect on opportunities to resist these social processes or on the way in which we ourselves are actors in the discourse, perhaps unwittingly reinforcing the very dynamic we seek to interrupt. For example, one of the practical realities that surfaces is the difficulty of differentiating relational practice from something I have come to call relational *mal*practice. Relational practice is the use of relational principles in the service of doing excellent work. Yet, because relational principles have so long been associated with the realm of family life and personal relationships, practitioners often engage in behaviors that are not so much in the service of the work as they are in the service of the relationship itself. Thus, in the name of caring, leaders may engage in a type of pseudo-relationality or relational malpractice. This includes things like not giving colleagues accurate feedback, suppressing rather than airing conflicts or contradictions, and retaining or protecting incompetence rather than confronting it. Often this behavior is undertaken in the mistaken belief that avoiding difficulties will enhance the relationship and create a better work environment when in fact it does just the opposite (Perlow, 2003). In a similar vein, trivial relational activities intended to show caring—things like remembering birthdays or arranging for pizza parties to celebrate organizational events—can divert the focus from more organizationally significant relational activities such as listening, mutual learning, transparency, and the accurate communication of important organizational realities. Using the word *trivial* to describe some of these activities may be unfair. Certainly, celebrating together can have a beneficial effect on the overall atmosphere and in some instances might even be critical to the work. But by and large, in terms of cost to benefit, it is far more important for leaders to focus energy and time on more central relational activities that facilitate the kind of open, transparent, egalitarian connections that lead to organizational learning and collective achievement.

In working with executives on these issues, I have found that leaders have difficulty reflecting critically on their own practice, partly because they have internalized stereotypical (gender-linked) notions of caring behavior (and what that looks like in practice) that have little to do with creating high quality, growth-in-connection relational interactions in the service of the work. Over the years I have developed a rubric (see Table 3.1) that I believe can help practitioners reflect on their own behavior, not only to distinguish between relational practice and relational malpractice, but also to map the terrain of perception and practice. This rubric, which has been published elsewhere for a different audience (Fletcher, 2010) is reprinted below.

Column 1 represents older, more traditional entity perspectives on leadership that are typically used as a contrast to relational approaches. For the sake of this contrast, Column 1 focuses on the dysfunctional, non-relational aspects of traditional images of leadership such as "command and control" behavior or hyper individualism exemplified by lack of consultation and unwillingness to admit mistakes. Column 2 represents the best characteristics of a relational practitioner. I have used principles of relational competence identified in my own explication of relational leadership as an entity (i.e., a leader who thinks more fluidly about self and other, focuses on

TABLE 3.1 Relational Practice Versus Non-relational Practice and Relational Malpractice

1 Non-relational Practice	2 Relational Practice	3 Relational Malpractice
Dysfunctionally command and control	Relationally intelligent	Dysfunctionally relational
Self	Self-in-relation	Other
Task	Create conditions where task can get done (process and task)	Process
Knows everything (never get input)	Fluid expertise (nature of task decides)	Knows nothing (always get input)
Authoritarian	Authoritative	Authority-less
Good for my career?	Is it good for the work?	Will they like me?
Concerned with enacting masculine gender identity	Concerned with doing good work	Concerned with enacting feminine gender identity

process as well as task, lets the nature of the work determine when to get input, and thinks about the needs of the work rather than career or self in determining what action to take), but characteristics detailed in any entity perspective on relational leadership could be listed in this column. Column 3 represents a phenomenon that did not emerge in my original research on relational practice but emerged later in discussions about strategies for implementation. This column represents what can be thought of as a leader who is *dysfunctionally* relational. That is, someone who exhibits relational malpractice, focusing exclusively on others and their needs, afraid to move ahead with decisions, and focused on meeting others' expectations in order to be liked and accepted.

I have used this rubric with different audiences for different purposes, most often with senior executives who want to reflect on their own leadership behavior and strategize ways to be more effective. For this chapter, I suggest that it can be seen as a way leaders can integrate entity and constructionist perspectives on leadership at the level of practice. That is, it is a framework that can help relational leaders take into account—and resist—some of the social forces that may be operating on their practice of leadership while at the same time, help them reflect on how they are prey to these same forces. There are three points of reflection with practical implications for leaders.

First, the rubric can be used to help leaders reflect on the extent to which they are confusing gender-linked images of relationality with relational leadership such that they—whether men or women—are "doing femininity" or "doing mothering" rather than "doing leadership." That is, leaders may believe they are operating in Column 2 and enacting a set of principles described in entity perspectives as relational leadership. On reflection, however, they may recognize that they are actually operating in Column 3 and are enacting a type of pseudo-relationality based on images of relationality garnered from (gender-linked) stereotypes of what it means to be caring or thoughtful. Examples of pseudo-relationality abound, such as meetings that go on endlessly with a leader unwilling to make a decision or take strong action or leaders who avoid the tough work of giving negative feedback or addressing an underlying conflict in a misguided attempt to foster harmony, feelings of closeness, and a "caring" environment. In most of these cases, the issue is that the relational practitioner has confused true growth-in-connection with non-mutual acts of deference or selflessness in the mistaken belief that it will enhance the relationship and lead to positive organizational outcomes. The relational practice of leadership is not about creating a culture of closeness or intimacy, although affective outcomes such as these might be a by-product of it (Fletcher, 2006). The primary goal and intention of relational leadership is to enact effective working relationships characterized by mutuality and authenticity, where the goal is learning, effectiveness, and mutual growth-in-connection. Mutuality and authenticity mean tackling the tough issues, putting one's own needs and positional requirements in the mix and giving primacy to the needs of the work. These principles are not in opposition to accountability, responsibility, and effectiveness, but are prerequisites to it.

The second way in which the rubric can help practitioners integrate entity and constructionist perspectives in their practice is to help them reflect on the social processes that might be acting on their relational leadership such that it is not constructed as leadership in the perceptions of others or in the broader organizational narrative. That is, leaders can reflect on the principles in Column 2, either the ones I have listed or those from other entity perspectives, and determine if they are truly applying these principles in their leadership practice. If the answer is "yes" and they fear their actions are being misunderstood as being guided by principles in Column 3, then they may be victims of the "disappearing dynamic." That is, they may be enacting relational competence, but social processes such as the three disappearing acts may be acting on their relational leadership to socially construct it not as leadership but as evidence of personal inadequacy, weakness, or powerlessness. If leaders believe this is happening, it is important to recapture the leadership and effectiveness dimensions of the behaviors that have gotten disappeared by addressing each of the three "disappearing acts" described in the previous section. Being clear about the intention of the relational practice and connecting it clearly to the quality and effectiveness of the work can establish a strong link between relational practice and doing good work, interrupting the meaning-making process in which intention is (mis)understood. Stating intention while being mindful of the language used to describe one's behavior and making sure the words and descriptors are organizationally strong can interrupt the conflation of relationality with femininity and powerlessness. Pushing back on these three disappearing acts can rescue the behavior from being devalued or unrecognized and help leaders remove themselves from potentially exploitive situations.

The third way the rubric can help practitioners integrate entity and constructionist perspectives is that it can help surface instances in which leaders are operating according to the entity principles of Column 2 (relational practice) but are subject to social processes that construct and understand them as enacting principles from Column 1 (command and control). Because of gender stereotypes, this is a dynamic more likely to be experienced by women. When women are authoritative, focus on task as well as process, or make unilateral decisions when the situation calls for that, they can be perceived as bossy, bully broads, or worse (Eagly & Carli, 2007; Kristof, 2008). It is one-half of the double bind in which women can find themselves. Not all women are naturally relational, but because of gender stereotypes, most are expected to be. The result is that gendered expectations of women can make even simple behavior, like acting with authority or being brief and direct in communication, seem inappropriately assertive or authoritarian.

Female leaders who work in nonprofits note that this dynamic is especially relevant for them. People who have chosen to work in the nonprofit world because they want a different work environment may themselves confuse relational practice with relational malpractice, holding leaders (especially female leaders) to misguided norms of caring, compassion, and process that can spiral into dysfunction. Efforts to stay firmly in relational practice by, for example, engaging fluid expertise or making sure conflicts and contradictions are addressed and not avoided, can be challenging.

Summary

Constructionist perspectives on relational leadership offer a window on the social processes through which a leadership narrative is constructed. I believe that adding the element of personal agency to these perspectives can strengthen both theory and practice. My work has focused on gendered processes of construction and the rubric I offer is especially relevant for uncovering the specific gendered dynamics I have studied. It is important, I believe, because the gender dynamics underlying the practice of relational leadership are significant and affect both women and men and, more important, the practice of good leadership. Robin Ely and Deborah Meyerson (2009) in their study of work on oil rigs note that the conflation of "doing masculinity" and doing work has led to many ineffective, unsafe work practices, such as not admitting mistakes or not asking for help. Interestingly, they note that when leaders in an organization focus on work outcomes and clearly articulate the connection between enacting behaviors typically thought of as *not* leadership (admitting mistakes, asking for help) and organizational effectiveness, it is possible to disrupt the conflation of "doing gender" with "doing work." Using the three-column rubric, this would mean focusing on staying in the middle column, not because one is trying to balance competing demands but because the middle column is a way of asking ourselves about the work and making sure that the requirements of the task at hand are the guide for leadership behavior, rather than expectations, gendered or otherwise, about how to be perceived as a good leader.

CONCLUSION

There is great benefit in meeting the challenge offered to theorists in this book to integrate entity and constructionist perspectives on relational leadership so they can inform each other and move our theoretical understanding of this construct forward. Entity perspectives can benefit greatly from an awareness of the social processes, especially the hegemonic processes in the dominant discourse that work to maintain the status quo and resist change. The notion of transformation implicit in new models of leadership, especially those that tout skills and behavior that traditionally have been antithetical to organizational effectiveness, cannot live up to their transformational potential without such an analysis. By the same token, constructionist perspectives can benefit greatly from an exploration and explication of the specific, micro-processes through which the social construction of leadership occurs. This is important not only because it helps identify opportunities for resistance, but also because it has the potential to advance entity dimensions by explicating the specific behaviors needed to enact relational leadership as well as the language needed to describe it and connect it to strategic intention.

REFERENCES

Aaltio-Marjosola, I. (2001, June). *Charismatic Leadership, Manipulation and the Complexity of Organizational Life.* Paper presented at the MIT Sloan School of Management Organizational Studies Seminar Series, Cambridge, MA.

Agashae, Z., & Bratton, J. (2001). Leader-follower dynamics: Developing a learning environment. *Journal of Workplace Learning, 13*(3/4), 89–103.

Badaracco, J. (2002). *Leading quietly.* Cambridge, MA: Harvard Business School Press.

Bartolome, F., & Laurent, A. (1988). Managers: Torn between two roles. *Personnel Journal, 67*(10), 72–83.

Bass, B. M. (1998). *Transformational leadership.* London, England: Lawrence Erlbaum Associates.

Beer, M. (1999). Leading, learning and learning to lead. In J. Conger, G. Spreitzer, & E. Lawler (Eds.), *The leader's change handbook* (pp. 127–161). San Francisco, CA: Jossey Bass.

Bradbury, H. & Lichtenstein, B. (2000). Relationality in organizational research: Exploring the space between. *Organization Science, 11*(5), 551–566.

Bryman, A. (1996) Leadership in organizations. In S. Clegg, C. Hardy, & W. Nord (Eds.), *Handbook of organization studies* (pp. 276–292). London, England: Sage.

Calàs, M. B., & Smircich, L. (1993). Dangerous liaisons: The "feminine-in-management" meets "globalization." *Business Horizons, 36,* 73-83.

Calvert, L., & Ramsey, V. J. (1992). Bringing women's voice to research on women in management: A feminist perspective. *Journal of Management Inquiry, 1*(1), 79–88.

Cameron, K., Dutton, J., & Quinn, R. (Eds.). (2003). *Positive organizational scholarship.* San Francisco, CA: Berrett-Koehler.

Carmeli A., Ben-Hador, B., Waldman, D. A., & Rupp, D. E. (2009). How leaders cultivate social capital and nurture employee vigor: Implications for job performance. *Journal of Applied Psychology, 94* (6), 1553–1561.

Chodorow, N. (1978). *The reproduction of mothering.* Berkeley, CA: University of California Press.

Collins, J. (2001). *Good to great.* New York, NY: Harper Business.

Conger, J. (1989). Leadership: The art of empowering others. *Academy of Management Executive, 3,* 17–24.

Conger, J., Spreitzer, G., & Lawler, E., (Eds.). (1999). *The leader's change handbook.* San Francisco, CA: Jossey Bass.

Cox, J., Pearce, C., & Sims, H. P. (2003). Toward a broader leadership development agenda: Extending the traditional transactional-transformation duality by developing directive, empowering and shared leadership skills. In S. Murphy, & R. Riggio (Eds.), *The future of leadership development.* Mahwah, NJ: Lawrence Erlbaum.

Cross, R., Baker, W., & Parker, A. (2003). What creates energy in organizations. *MIT Sloan Management Review, 44*(4), 51–56.

Day, D., Gronn, P., & Salas, E. (2004). Leadership capacity in teams. *The Leadership Quarterly, 15* (6), 857–868.

Drath, W. (2001). *The deep blue sea. Rethinking the source of leadership.* San Francisco, CA: Jossey Bass.

Dutton, J. (2003). *Energize your workplace: How to create and sustain high quality connections at work.* San Francisco, CA: Jossey Bass.

Dutton, J. & Heaphy, E. (2003). The power of high-quality connections. In K. Cameron, J. Dutton & R. Quinn, (Eds.), *Positive organizational scholarship,* (pp 263–278). San Francisco, CA: Berrett-Koehler.

Dutton, J. E., & Ragins, B. R. (Eds.). (2007). *Exploring positive relationships at work: Building a theoretical and research foundation.* Mahwah, NJ: Lawrence Erlbaum.

Dutton, J., Debebe, G., & Wrzesniewski, A. (1998, January). *Being valued and devalued at work.* Paper presented at ICOS Seminar, University of Michigan, Ann Arbor, MI.

Eagly, A., & Carli, L. (2007). *Through the labyrinth.* Cambridge, MA: Harvard Business School Press.

Ely, R., & Meyerson, D. (2009). Undoing Gender in a Traditionally Male Workplace. Working paper, Cambridge, MA: Harvard Business School.

Fairbairn, W. D. R. (1952). *An object relations theory of personality.* New York, NY: Basic Books.

Flax, J. (1990). *Thinking fragments.* Berkeley, CA: University of California Press.

Fletcher, J. K. (1994). Castrating the female advantage. *Journal of Management Inquiry, 3*(1), 74–82.

Fletcher, J. K. (1999). *Disappearing acts: Gender, power and relational practice at work.* Cambridge, MA: MIT Press.

Fletcher, J. K. (2004). The paradox of post heroic leadership: An essay on gender, power and transformational change. *The Leadership Quarterly, 15,* 647–661.

Fletcher, J. K. (2006). Leadership, power and positive relationships at work. In J. Dutton, & B. R. Ragins (Eds.), *Exploring positive relationships at work: Building a theoretical and research foundation.* NJ: Lawrence Erlbaum Press.

Fletcher, J. K. (2010). Leadership as relational practice. In K. Bunker, K. Kram, & D. T. Hall (Eds.), *Extraordinary leadership: Addressing the gaps in senior executive development.* San Francisco, CA: Jossey Bass.

Fletcher, J. K., & Jacques, R. (2000). Relational practice: An emerging stream of theorizing and its significance for organizational studies. CGO Working Paper. Center for Gender in Organizations. Simmons School of Management. Boston, MA. Retrieved from www.simmons.edu/som/cgo.

Fletcher, J. K., & Kaeufer, K. (2003). Shared leadership: Paradox and possibility. In C. Pearce, & J. Conger (Eds.), *Shared leadership: Reframing the hows and whys of leadership* (pp. 21–47). London, England: Sage.

Fondas, N. (1997). Feminization unveiled: Management qualities in contemporary writings. *Academy of Management Review, 22*: 257–282.

Gardener, H. (1990). *On leadership.* New York, NY: The Free Press.

Gittell, J. (2003). A theory of relational coordination. In K. Cameron, J. Dutton, & R. Quinn, (Eds.), *Positive organizational scholarship* (pp. 279–295). San Francisco, CA: Berrett-Koehler.

Goffman, E. (1959). *The presentation of self in everyday life.* New York, NY: Doubleday.

Goleman, D. (1998). *Working with emotional intelligence.* New York, NY: Bantam Books.

Goleman, D. (2006). *Social intelligence,* New York, NY: Bantam Books.

Goleman, D., Boyatzis, R., & McKee, A. (2002). *Primal leadership.* Cambridge, MA: Harvard Business School Press.

Graen, G. B., & Scandura, T. A. (1987). Toward a psychology of dyadic organizing. In L. L. Cummings, & B. M. Staw (Eds.), *Research in organizational behavior* (pp. 175–208). Greenwich, CT: JAI Press.

Graen, G., & Uhl-Bien, M. (1995). Relationship-based approach to leadership: Development of leader-member exchange (LMX) theory of leadership over 25 years: Applying a multi-level multi-domain perspective. *The Leadership Quarterly, 6*(2), 219–247.

Hargadon, A. (2003). *How breakthroughs happen.* Cambridge, MA: Harvard Business School Press.

Harrington, M. (2000). *Care and equality.* New York, NY: Routledge.

Heifetz, R., & Laurie, D. (1999). Mobilizing adaptive work: Beyond visionary leadership. In J. Conger, G. Spreitzer, & E. Lawler (Eds.), *The leader's change handbook.* San Francisco, CA: Jossey Bass.

Hill, L. (2004). New manager development for the 21st Century. *The Academy of Management Executive, 18*(3), 121–126.

Hosking, D., Dachler, H. P., & Gergen, K. J. (Eds.). (1995). *Management and organization: Relational alternative to individualism.* Aldershot, England: Ashgate Publishing.

Jacobsen, S., & Jacques, R. (1997). Destabilizing the field. *Journal of Management Inquiry, 6*(1), 42–59.

Jacques, R. (1993). Untheorized dimensions of caring work: Caring as a structural practice and caring as a way of seeing. *Nursing Administration Quarterly, 17*(2), 1–10.

Jordan, J. (1986). *The meaning of mutuality.* Working Paper #23. Centers for Women, Wellesley, MA. Retrieved from http://www.wcwonline.org.

Jordan, J. V. (1991). *The movement of mutuality and power.* Working Paper # 53. Wellesley College Centers for Women, Wellesley MA. Retrieved from http://www.wcwonline.org.

Jordan, J. (1999). *Toward connection and competence.* Working Paper #83. Centers for Women, Wellesley, MA. Retrieved from http://www.wcwonline.org.

Jordan, J., Kaplan, A., Miller, J. B., Stiver, I., & Surrey, J. (Eds.). (1991). *Women's growth in connection.* New York, NY: Guilford Press.

Jost, J. (1997). An experimental replication of the depressed entitlement effect among women. *Psychology of Women Quarterly 21,* 387–393.

Kahane, A. (2004). *Solving tough problems.* Berkeley, CA: Berrett-Koehler.

Kahn, W. (1998). "Relational systems at work." In B. M. Staw, & L. L. Cummings, (Eds.), *Research in organizational behavior, 20* (pp. 39–76). Greenwich, CT: JAI Press.

Kanter, R. M. (2001). *E-volve!* Cambridge, MA: Harvard Business School Press.

Kayes, D. C. (2004). The 1996 Mount Everest climbing disaster: The breakdown of learning in teams. *Human Relations, 57*(10), 1263–1285.

Kim, D. H. (1993). The link between individual and organizational learning. *Sloan Management Review, 34,* 37–50.

Kouzes, J., & Posner, B. (2003). *The leadership challenge.* (3rd ed.). San Francisco, CA: Jossey Bass.

Kristof, N. D. (2008, June 12). The sex speech. *The New York Times,* pp. .

Lave, J., & Wenger, E. (1991). *Situated learning: Legitimate peripheral participation.* New York, NY: Cambridge University Press.

Lipman Blumen, J. (1996). *The connective edge.* San Francisco, CA: Jossey Bass.

Lipnack, J., & Stamps, J. (2000). *Virtual teams.* New York, NY: Wiley.

Luthans, F., & Avolio, B. (2003). Authentic leadership development. In K. Cameron, J. Dutton, & R. Quinn (Eds.), *Positive organizational scholarship* (pp 241–258). San Francisco, CA: Berrett-Koehler.

Manz. C. C., & Sims, H. P., Jr. (2001). *The new superleadership: Leading others to lead themselves.* San Francisco, CA: Berrett-Koehler.

Martin, J., & Knopoff, K. (1995). The gendered implications of apparently gender-neutral theory: Re-reading Weber. In E. Freeman and A. Larson (Eds.), *Ruffin Lecture Series, Vol. 3: Business Ethics and Women's Studies.* Oxford, England: Oxford University Press.

Martin, P. Y., & Collinson, D. L. (1998). Gender and sexuality in organizations. In M. M. Ferree, J. Lorder, & B. Hess (Eds.), *Revisioning gender.* London, England: Sage.

Martin, P. Y. (1996). Gendering and evaluating dynamics: Men, masculinities and managements. In D. Collinson, & J. Hearn (Eds.), *Men as managers, managers as men* (186–209). London, England: Sage.

Mayo, M., Meindl, & Pastor, J. (2003). Shared leadership in work teams: A social network approach. In C. Pearce, & J. Conger (Eds.), *Shared leadership: Reframing the hows and whys of leadership* (pp. 21–47). London, England: Sage.

McNamee, S., & Gergen, K. J. (1999). *Relational responsibility: Resources for sustainable dialogue.* Thousand Oaks, CA: Sage.

Miller, J. B. (1976). *Toward a new psychology of women.* Boston, MA: Beacon Press.

Miller, J. B., & Stiver, I. (1997). *The healing connection.* Boston, MA: Beacon Press.

Mumby, D. K., & Putnam, L. (1992). The politics of emotion: A feminist reading of bounded rationality. *Academy of Management Review, 17*(3), 465–486.

Pearce, C., & Conger, J. (2003a). All those years ago: The historical underpinnings of shared leadership. In C. Pearce, & J. Conger (Eds.), *Shared leadership: Reframing the hows and whys of leadership* (pp. 3–13). London, England: Sage.

Pearce, C., & Conger, J. (2003b). A landscape of opportunities: Future research on shared leadership. In C. Pearce, & J. Conger (Eds.), *Shared leadership: Reframing the hows and whys of leadership* (pp 285–304). London, England: Sage.

Pearce, C., & Sims, H. (2000). Shared leadership: Toward a multi-level theory of leadership. In M. Beyerlein, D. Johnson, & S. Beyerlein (Eds.), *Advances in the interdisciplinary studies of work teams* (Vol. 7). New York, NY: JAI.

Perlow, L. (2003). *When you say yes but mean no: How silencing conflict wrecks relationships and companies . . . and what you can do about it.* New York, NY: Crown Publishing.

Seely Brown, J., & Duguid, P. (2000). *The social life of information.* Cambridge, MA: Harvard Business School Press.

Senge, P. (1990a). *The fifth discipline.* New York, NY: Doubleday.

Senge, P. (1990b). The leader's new work: Building learning organizations. *Sloan Management Review, 32* (1), 7–23.

Senge, P., & Kaeufer, K. (2001). Communities of leaders or no leadership at all. In S. Chowdhury (Ed.), *Management 21C,* (pp. 186–204). New York, NY: Prentice Hall.

Suchman, L. (1987). *Plans and situated actions: The problem of human-machine communication.* New York, NY: Cambridge University Press.

Surrey, J. (1985). *The Self in relation.* Working paper #13, Centers for Women, Wellesley College, Wellesley, MA. Retrieved from http://www.wcwonline.org.

Sutcliffe, K., & Vogus, T. (2003). Organizing for resilience. In K. Cameron, J. Dutton, & R. Quinn (Eds.), *Positive organizational scholarship,* (pp. 94- 110). San Francisco, CA: Berrett-Koehler.

Thompson, L. (2004). *Making the team.* (2nd ed.). Upper Saddle River, NJ: Prentice Hall.

Uhl-Bien, M. (2006). Relationship leadership theory: Exploring the social processes of leadership and organizing. *The Leadership Quarterly, 17*(6), 654–676.

Vera, D., & Crossan, M. (2004). Strategic leadership and organizational learning. *Academy of Management Review, 29*(2), 222–240.

Vera, D. & Rodriguez-Lopez, A. (2004). Strategic virtues: Humility as a source of competitive advantage. *Organizational Dynamics, 33*(4), 393–408.

Walker, M. (2002). *Power and effectiveness: Envisioning an alternative paradigm.* Working Paper #94. Centers for Women, Wellesley College, Wellesley, MA. Retrieved from http://www.wcwonline.org.

Watkins, K. E., & Cervero, R. M. (2000). Organizations as contexts for learning: A case study in certified accountancy. *Journal of Workplace Learning, 12*(5–6), 187–194.

West, C., & Zimmerman, D. (1991). Doing gender. In J. Lorber, & S. Farrell (Eds.), *The social construction of gender,* (pp. 13–37). Newbury Park, CA: Sage.

Wheatley, M. (2001). *Leadership and the new science: Discovering order in a chaotic world.* London, England: Sage.

Winnicott , D. (1958). *The maturational process and the facilitating environment.* New York, NY: International Universities Press.

Yukl, G. P. (1998). *Leadership in organizations.* (4th ed.). Englewood Cliffs, NJ: Prentice Hall.

Zaccaro, S. Rittman, A. L., & Marks, M. A. (2001). Team leadership. *The Leadership Quarterly, 12*(4), 451.

Zaleznik, A. (1992). Managers and leaders: Are they different? *Harvard Business Review, 70*(2), 126–136.

CHAPTER 4

SYSTEMIC CONSTRUCTIONIST LEADERSHIP AND WORKING FROM WITHIN THE PRESENT MOMENT

J. Kevin Barge

One perspective toward relational leadership that has emerged in recent years has been grounded in social constructionist theory and research (Uhl-Bien, 2006). While several different social constructionist approaches to leadership exist (Ospina & Sorensen, 2006), one important thread within social constructionism is the role that language plays in building, maintaining, and elaborating our social worlds. This strand of social constructionism adopts a constitutive approach to language, maintaining that our understandings of leadership are made, not found, which means that the way people use language creates our understanding of leadership as well as our social arrangements with others in terms of our identities, relationships, and cultures. It therefore becomes important for scholars to explore how particular understandings of leadership are linguistically constructed and made ontologically real. Social constructions of leadership are local, as the unique configuration of people, time, and place may move individuals to

Advancing Relational Leadership Research, pages 107–142
Copyright © 2012 by Information Age Publishing
All rights of reproduction in any form reserved.

construct leadership in particular ways but not others. Moreover, our social constructions of leadership are also fluid and dynamic as shifts in language create fresh understandings for leadership as well as new patterns of social arrangements.

Such social constructionist approaches tend to document that language and discourse construct the way leadership is practiced (e.g., Galanes, 2009). They adopt a third-person perspective toward communication that focuses on describing the rules, moral orders, vocabularies, and grammars that inform the performance of leadership, that investigates how actors construct leadership through the sequence of jointly performed communicative acts, and that explores how the pattern fits with other practices and conversations in the larger organizational and cultural context (Pearce, 1994). From a third-person perspective, the burning analytical questions are, "What are they doing?" and "How are they doing it?" The burning questions regarding leadership change, however, if we adopt a first-person perspective. A first-person perspective centers on questions such as, "What am I doing here?" and "What should I do next?" These are questions of orientation and judgment that emerge within the flow of conversation. These questions focus on the ways individuals consciously or unconsciously respond to others from within the flow of communication and the associated working definition of the situation that they have co-created with others.

My interest is in exploring the implications of social constructionist ideas for developing leadership practices that individuals may appropriate as they work within a continually evolving and changing linguistic landscape. If we take the notion of social construction seriously, leadership is about meaning work and managing contexts. People who wish to construct lead positions within teams, organizations, and societies need to learn how to work within the flow of conversation and develop practices that allow them to make sense of it and create new potentials for meaning making and action that can shape its direction. As the ancient Greek philosopher Heraclitis said, "You can never step in the same river twice," which is also *apropos* of leadership from a social constructionist perspective. The unfolding conversation and conversational moments have the quality of being for the first time, something that has never been experienced before in quite this way. To be sure, there are regularities in communication patterns and frameworks for sense-making and action within any human system, but the unique combination of people, topic, time, place, and context gives the conversations and conversational moments a unique flavor. Though it may be tempting for leaders to feel, "I've heard this all before," to paraphrase Heraclitus, "You can never enter into the same conversation twice."

In a series of essays, I have begun outlining how a systemic constructionist framework could be used as a theoretical and research lens for articulating leadership (Barge, 2004a, 2004b, 2007; Barge & Fairhurst, 2008; Barge

& Little, 2002, 2008). My interest in this chapter is to shift the focus from the ways that a systemic constructionist approach may be used to further theory and research, to exploring the implications of this approach for the kinds of discursive practices that help individuals make sense of situations and facilitate constructive patterns of joint activity that co-create leadership.

If conversations and conversational moments are dynamic, continually unfolding as new linguistic material enters in, what suggestions can this approach offer leaders for helping them orient themselves from within the flow of conversation as they manage communication, meaning, actions, and relationships? The key interactional challenge is one of orientation, how to make sense of the emerging conversation, and how to help others make sense of the conversation in ways that generate productive patterns of coordination and moving social arrangements. I begin by outlining some of the basic ideas associated with a systemic constructionist approach to leadership and then present a preliminary set of discursive practices that enable individuals to co-create leadership with others.

A SYSTEMIC CONSTRUCTIONIST APPROACH TO LEADERSHIP

There has been a tendency to treat social constructionist approaches to leadership as if they were monolithic and singular. Despite sharing a common interest in the connections among language use, the social features of human activity, and the construction of reality, leadership scholars connect these elements differently, creating a multi-verse of social constructionist leadership approaches. While various approaches may share a family resemblance to each other, they simultaneously make important theoretical and practical decisions that make them unique. Fairhurst and Grant (2010) suggest that social constructionist approaches to leadership can be distinguished by their emphasis on theory or praxis, whether the aim of leadership is critical emancipatory or pragmatic-interventionist, whether the approach emphasizes the social construction of reality or the construction of social reality, and whether researchers pay attention only to the way language creates meaning in organizations (mono-modal) or whether other modes of communication can affect the meaning making process (multi-modal).

A systemic constructionist approach is a particular approach within the family of social constructionist leadership perspectives that is based on systemic thinking and social constructionism. Systemic thinking emerges from a European tradition of therapy and consultancy that emphasizes the importance of developing tools that allow practitioners such as family therapists and organizational consultants to observe and work with the connectedness of people, patterns of interaction, meaning making, and context

(Campbell, 2000; Dallos & Draper, 2000). Systemic thinking can be traced back to Bateson's (1972) ecological perspective toward human systems. He argued that understanding a human system requires us to focus on the patterns that connect, the reciprocal or mutually causal patterns of communication among people. From his perspective, we cannot reduce our explanations of human behavior to simple linear-cause effect explanations where we attribute someone's behavior to psychological mechanisms such as personality traits, motives, or drives. Rather, we need to create systemic descriptions of joint human activity, which provide us the means to explain how any individual's behavior is the product of the interactional system jointly created by people.

Bateson's (1972) original explanation of human systems was grounded in cybernetic theory and emphasized the importance of feedback loops and how feedback created and sustained certain patterns of interaction within human systems. Contemporary systemic approaches have built on the contribution of second-order cybernetics focusing on the way that meaning making occurs within human systems (Campbell, 2000; Hedges, 2005; Oliver, 2005). The shift from feedback to meaning making has led systemic approaches to incorporate social constructionism into their frameworks.

While several different approaches to social constructionism exist, most share an allegiance to three key assumptions: (1) our sense of who we are, or our identity, as well as other social arrangements, such as relationships, organizations, and cultures, are reflected in and shaped by our language use; (2) our explanations of social phenomena are grounded in the interaction patterns and social practices of persons; and (3) our knowledge and understanding of social phenomena are historically and culturally bound (Burr, 2003). The result is that social constructionism moves us to explore how individuals draw on historical and cultural knowledge to co-create particular patterns of coordination and meaning making with other people in conversation by using linguistic material such as words, metaphors, stories, and narratives as well as nonlinguistic forms of representation such as nonverbal communication and the way space and time are managed during interaction.

I use the term systemic constructionism to emphasize the important contributions systemic thinking and social constructionism jointly make to our understanding of leadership theory and practice. Campbell (2000) suggests that systemic thinking has been concerned traditionally with describing patterns of interaction within a system and focusing attention on "what is happening." Social constructionism, on the other hand, moves us from description to explanation, as it addresses how people construct linguistic accounts of their social experience and how this creates certain identities, subjectivities, and relationships. When we connect these two theoretical tributaries, it becomes important for leadership theory and practice to generate systemic insight.

This means leadership scholars become concerned with creating interpretations and analyses that: (a) focus on the patterns of connections comprising human systems rather than on their individual elements; (b) treat aspects of the human system as "made" versus "found;" (c) view relationships as contextually embedded within other relationships as opposed to being decontextualized; and (d) recognize how the joint interplay of all participants within a particular human system works to co-create leadership (Pearce, Villar, & McAdam, 1992). Systemic constructionism focuses our attention on articulating leadership theories and analyses that help us describe and explain the coordination of meaning and action within human systems and how language invites, creates, and sustains particular patterns of coordination and discourages others.

Situating Leadership

What counts as leadership? This is a difficult question to answer from a systemic constructionist perspective because the meaning of any social practice is viewed as co-created, contextual, and contestable. What counts as leadership depends on the resources that people draw on in the conversational moment to perform utterances, how they construct leadership in their talk, and whether they share a common understanding regarding the situation. From a systemic constructionist perspective, a discursive context exists that sets up our understanding of what counts as leadership. A discursive context is made up of a wide variety of linguistic bits and pieces such as the big-"D" Discourses—ideologies and worldviews—that are widely shared in an organization or culture (Alvesson & Karremann, 2000), the conversations that have already taken place about the current conversation, as well as the stories that are circulating about the conversational participants, their identities, and their relationships. What counts as leadership in a particular conversational moment depends on how these various linguistic elements cohere into discursive context that qualifies certain forms of talk as leadership but not others.

Determining what counts as leadership is made even more difficult and vexing when we consider that situations are dynamic. While leadership actors act from context, they also act into context which means new contexts may be created through their talk that legitimate different understandings of leadership. For example, Grint (2005) observes that when individuals are able to use language in a way that shapes other people's view of a situation as a crisis, they create a discursive context that legitimates exercising command forms of leadership. On the other hand, when situations are framed as being "wicked," consisting of numerous interlocking sets of problems, a more inquiry-based form of leadership that emphasizes questioning becomes appropriate. This suggests that determining what counts as leadership can only be accomplished by exploring how people negotiate a working definition of a situation. The working definition of a situation is constructed by the way already existing macro-narratives, conversations, and stories are talked about and invoked in the current conversation. The way that already existing linguistic and nonlinguistic resources are brought into the conversation creates the discursive context that people must respond to, which offers opportunities and constraints for people to make meaning and take action in particular ways but not others.

What counts as leadership? While it may be tempting to answer the question saying, "It depends" or "I don't know," such answers are incredibly unsatisfying for individuals who wish to work from a systemic constructionist perspective. It is possible, however, to offer a conception of leadership that highlights what facets of leadership are important to focus on from a systemic constructionist perspective. The following conception is offered in the spirit of a sensitizing concept which directs our attention to the important processes and activities constituting leadership; not as a definition or categorizing tool which moves us to classify actions and behaviors as being or not being leadership (e.g., Deetz, 1992).

Leadership, from a systemic constructionist point of view, may be viewed as "a co-created, performative, contextual, and attributional process where the ideas articulated in talk or action are recognized by others as progressing tasks that are important to them" (Barge & Fairhurst, 2008, p. 232). This conception focuses on several important features and processes associated with leadership:

1. Leadership occurs in the joint action between or among people and cannot be understood in terms of the behaviors or utterances of a single individual.
2. Leadership is performative and is shown and constructed through the overt conversational behavior of participants.
3. Leadership is contextual as our understanding of what counts as leadership or a leader depends on the unique combination of people, task, context, time, and place.
4. Leadership, as well as the idea that someone acts as a leader, is an attribution process engaged in by self and others.
5. Leadership involves meaning making and creating contexts such that ideas expressed in talk or action connect with people's interests and stakes in the unfolding conversation.

6. Leadership is always performed in relation to tasks and involves creating patterns of meaning making and action that move them forward.

While we cannot offer a universal definition of what counts as leadership for every situation, we can offer a concept of leadership that focuses attention on the crucial features and processes that help construct our understanding of leadership within local conversations.

Developing Systemic Constructionist Leadership Theory and Research

Any conceptualization of leadership is grounded explicitly or implicitly in a set of value commitments that inform what scholars should take into account as they develop their theoretical and research accounts. For example, trait theories of leadership place value on the individual as the unit of analysis and, as a result, explore how particular combinations of personality, physical, cognitive, or social traits enable leadership. The value commitments that are embedded within a particular approach also influence what practices become important for scholars to focus on and include as they theorize and research leadership. For example, charismatic approaches to leadership place value on the way that leaders develop and communicate their visions for societies, organizations, and groups. As a result, many analyses of charismatic leadership focus on the rhetorical practices that are used by leaders, such as framing, language, and imagery to articulate and communicate their visions (Seyranian & Bligh, 2008). A systemic constructionist approach carries with it a particular set of value commitments and associated practices that inform how leadership scholars may develop theory and conduct research.

Value Commitments

In an earlier set of essays (Barge, 2007; Barge & Fairhurst, 2008), I have argued that there are at least five important values that inform a systemic constructionist approach to leadership. They include:

1. *Communication:* Leadership actors co-create identities, relationships, and cultures through linguistic performances. This means leaders need to take into account the way that language creates the social worlds they inhabit.
2. *Connection:* Understanding leadership within a human system depends on articulating the connections among persons-in-conversation, action, meaning, and context. This means that leaders need to

think systemically and work with the ecology of relationships that are created and sustained through talk and action.

3. *Uniqueness:* Leadership actors operate within unique contexts defined by time, place, people, and topic. Leaders need to talk and act in ways that appreciate the novel complexity of the way the distinctive qualities of situations, events, and people connect within conversation at a particular moment.

4. *Emergence:* Leaders need to focus attention on the possibilities for new patterns of meaning making and action that emerge within the unfolding conversation. Leaders should develop ways of working that give attention to the openings and conversational moments that are created through talk and action which are ripe for developing new meaning making and action potentials.

5. *Affirmation:* Leadership actors are encouraged to connect with each other's moral orders and grammars in order to affirm other's lived experiences. Leaders need to find ways through their talk and action to connect with what is good, valuable, and excellent in order to elaborate it further in the conversation.

What these values set up is a framework for assessing the quality of scholar's efforts at theorizing and researching from within a systemic constructionist perspective. The quality of systemic constructionist theory and research may be judged by its ability: (a) to account for the way language generates particular constructions of identity, relationships, events, and situations; (b) to articulate the systemic interplay among people, communication, action, meaning, and situation; (c) to capture the unique qualities of situations, events, and people; (d) to track the way possibilities for new meaning making and action emerge, fade, and become closed; and (e) to recognize what works well in situations and to elaborate the positive values and meanings that people employ during conversation.

Many of these values and standards are self-explanatory. However, one that is particularly novel to a systemic constructionist perspective and worthy of further explanation is the importance of affirmation. The value of affirmation is partially inspired by the literature on Appreciative Inquiry which emphasizes the importance of identifying what gives life to people's activity in organizations—typically in the form of core values, best practices, strengths, assets, and other positive elements of people's experience (Cooperrider &Whitney, 2000). Working appreciatively means that leaders affirm some element of another's experience as valued, which "requires connecting with what others value in the moment and coordinating aims and purposes in ways that enhance organizational life" (Barge & Oliver, 2003, p. 130). The process of affirmation involves giving attention to the life-generating properties that are co-created by leaders and others in the emerging conversation.

The ability to coordinate aims and purposes within conversation depends on an individual's ability to pick up on particular linguistic elements within the conversation and respond to another person's utterances in a way that simultaneously affirms and challenges what is said by introducing a "difference that connects" (Barge, 2004a). For example, imagine an organizational member said, "I think we've got to find a strategy for minimizing costs if our unit is going to survive." Within this utterance, there are several key words a leader might pick up and respond to such as "thinking," "strategy," "costs," "unit," or "survive." A leader could respond in any number of ways to this utterance. A leader could respond and negate the meaning of the other's utterance saying, "That way of thinking is just stupid." By responding this way, the leader destroys the meaning making potential of the organizational member's contribution, thus limiting the leader's ability to connect with the organizational member's way of making sense and curtailing the establishment of a shared focus or topic to orient the conversation around. On the other hand, a simple agreement such as, "I agree with your line of thinking," simply duplicates what has been said before and does not significantly extend the meaning potential of the utterance. However, if a leader said, "I agree that we need to think about minimizing costs, but I think we need to consider other possibilities as well," the leader affirms what the organizational member has said while simultaneously challenging it a bit by introducing the notion that it is important to explore other alternatives.

Coordinating aims and purposes in a way that creates life, energy, and development within a conversation requires keeping the processes of affirmation and challenge in a useful tension. Cunliffe (2002) observes that too much affirmation in response to conversation simply duplicates what has been said and minimizes learning. However, if too much challenge is given, the ability to establish a common focus for organizing the conversation is not established and people may feel threatened and defensive. As a result, scholars operating from a systemic constructionist perspective need to give attention in their research accounts to the way that affirmation and challenge are managed within the process of meaning making.

Discursive Practices

Any number of discursive practices may be used to characterize a systemic constructionist approach to leadership and serve as the basis for creating research accounts of leadership (Barge & Fairhurst, 2008). A practice is a set of activities that are commonly engaged in, and meaningful in particular ways, among people familiar with a certain culture or operating from a particular worldview, in this case, a systemic constructionist perspective (Craig, 2006). My interest is in articulating *discursive* practices because they explicitly focus on the activities that are associated with working with language, meaning making, and the social construction of identities, relationships, and organizations. An analysis of how leadership is understood and practiced from a systemic constructionist perspective focuses on three discursive practices: (1) sense-making—how individuals and larger collectivities, such as teams and organizations, develop resources to make sense of the system they participate in; (2) positioning—how individuals use language, stories, narratives, and other linguistic and non-linguistic devices to create social arrangements; and (3) play—how a sense of discursive openness is sustained in human systems through the management of differences in meaning making activities and how this is connected with creating and generating energy during organizing.

How might one use these discursive practices to approach leadership from a research position? Consider the following example provided by a leader of a team of architects:

> To maintain working relationships, I positively connoted the client's antagonism as a challenge to my team to demonstrate their abilities....Subsequently, I started potentially heated meetings by seeking agreement to concentrate initially on exploring problems....Later, we could argue about solutions....That was not usually necessary. So long as people felt that others were trying to take aboard their concerns, there was a willingness to be creative and flexible....By establishing agreement about the form and purpose of the meeting at the outset and by reframing or re-contextualizing critical or dismissive remarks, it was possible to create an atmosphere in which people felt safe to speak freely. From this sense of safety flowed not only enthusiasm and friendliness, but imaginative and practical solutions. Because these solutions took account of the concerns of all, rather than just those of dominant individuals or groups, their implementation was not resisted or sabotaged. (Barge, 2004a, p. 88)

There are several elements within this example that a researcher working from a systemic constructionist perspective might focus on using the discursive practices of sense-making, positioning, and play. The researcher may notice that the leader made a choice to make sense of this situation using an inclusive frame ("took account of the concerns of all"), which suggested that the needs of both the architects and clients should be respected. This way of sense-making led him to create "an atmosphere in which people felt safe to speak freely" which positioned them to be enthusiastic, friendly, and imaginative participants. The ability of the leader to position the other architects turns on his ability to play with meaning by "reframing or re-contextualizing critical or dismissive remarks." Such an analysis moves the researcher to look at the consequences of the way that sense-making, positioning, and play cohere to transform an antagonistic and hostile meeting into a friendly and imaginative one.

LEADERSHIP AS CO-AUTHORSHIP WITHIN THE FLOW OF CONVERSATION

What I want to do now is give attention to the way systemic constructionist ideas and practices can be used to help individuals co-create constructive forms of leadership. I want to shift from viewing leadership from a 3rd-person perspective where scholars and researchers use systemic constructionist ideas to describe the performance of leadership to a 1st-person perspective that engages the lived dynamic experience of individuals wishing to create leadership positions. A 1st-person perspective focuses our attention on articulating the ideas and practices associated with helping people orient themselves to the emerging conversation and making judgments about what to do next as they participate within the flow of conversation. My hope is to articulate an evolving set of discursive practices that enable leadership actors to work with meaning making to foster productive patterns of coordination. In doing so, I want to draw on a growing body of practice-oriented work that explores how systemic constructionist ideas and practices can be woven into the daily working lives of leadership actors (e.g., Campbell & Groenbeck, 2006; Campbell & Huffington, 2008; McCaughan & Palmer, 1994; Oliver, 2004). A shift from a 3rd- to 1st-person perspective carries with it two important implications regarding the position of leaders within the conversation and the role of values in making decisions about one's practice.

First, leadership actors are viewed as acting from within the flow of conversational activity, not outside it. Relatively little research has explored how leaders create a sense of orientation from within the flow of conversation. Perhaps the closest is the work by Morgan (1999) and Bolman and Deal (2008) who emphasize that leaders can use multiple metaphors to help them read situations. The idea of reading treats situations as ontologically real and positions the leader to generate numerous interpretations in order to arrive at the most accurate or useful portrayal of the situation. Situations exist and are out there, consisting of numerous individual, organizational, and cultural variables, such as the nature of the task, power, and maturity of the followers that open up and constrain possibilities for leadership. Leaders are encouraged to develop multiple ways to read situations and relationships in order to develop rich ways of understanding situations.

Shotter (1993) challenges the notion that leaders are simply readers of situations who *construct interpretations of social reality*. He argues that individuals, such as leaders, are authors of situation who *construct the social reality* that they participate in:

... when faced with ... un-chosen conditions, [individuals] can, by producing an appropriate *formulation* of them, create (a) a 'landscape of enabling—constraints (Giddens, 1979) relevant for a range of next possible actions; (b) a network of 'moral positions' or 'commitments' (understood in terms of the rights and duties of the 'players' on that landscape); and (c) are able to argue persuasively and authoritatively for this 'landscape' amongst those who must work within it. (Shotter, 1993, p. 149, emphasis original)

He calls this approach practical authorship, whereby individuals such as leaders are viewed as authoring and writing the conversation from within, as they participate in constructing the conversation. As Cronen (2001) observes, "the logic of system functioning evolves inside the system as conjointly created understandings about how to act and respond to others so that coherent action can go on" (p. 19). Practical authors literally make the conversational road as they walk it from within the emerging linguistic landscape.

Practical authors attempt to create a surveyable landscape that enables others to act in ways that follow by inviting them to participate in the linguistic formulations they offer. Practical authorship focuses on "*formative* power: the ability of people in otherwise vague, or only partially specified, incomplete situations ... to 'give' or to 'lend' to such situations a more determinate linguistic formulation" (Shotter, 1993, pp. 149–150, emphasis original). What is important to remember, however, is that conversations are always co-authored: the other participants are also practical authors who may offer similar or different formulations of the linguistic landscape, as well as sometimes contest the formulations offered by others. The intersection of multiple practical authors, entering and leaving the conversation at different times, and making different bids for creating the landscape in particular ways, creates an emergent changing linguistic landscape that individuals must manage as it is being constructed. The notion of situations as being dynamic and co-authored by multiple practical authors has significant implications for leadership and leaders.

Second, the value commitments associated with a systemic constructionist approach to leadership create a normative framework for practice. Value commitments provide a sense of orientation to individuals desiring to create lead positions in human systems and enable them to develop a sense of coherency in their practice. The meaning of particular forms of talk and action are highly contingent on the emerging situation, which suggests that a particular utterance in one situation might count as an act of leadership, but not in another. While the performance of leadership is highly dynamic and fluid, the values that inform leadership practice are relatively stable. This means that leadership actors can create a sense of coherency in their practice by working in ways that fit their values or ideals concerning leadership with the concrete particulars of the situation. This process of acting from a relatively stable value set while fitting talk and action to the concrete particulars of the situation has been called by a variety of names including phronesis (Grint, 2007), wisdom in action (Raelin, 2009), and sensibility (Barge & Little, 2008). Similar to explorers using the North Star to help them navigate their way about the physical terrain, values are like guide stars that help orient individuals to an emerging linguistic landscape.

Values also provide a set of living standards for individuals to judge the effectiveness and appropriateness of their talk and action. The ability to live out one's values provides a living standard for leaders to evaluate their practice as it unfolds in conversation. Whitehead and McNiff (2006) equate good practice with the alignment between the values that individuals espouse and the way they live them out in practice, "Making judgments about the quality of practice means making value judgments in terms of what you find valuable in the practices. Value judgments then become standards of judgment. You judge things in terms of what you think is good" (p. 71). Values provide leadership actors the ability to assess the quality of their practice as it unfolds within emerging conversations and to make judgments about the degree to which their actions are virtuous, that is, the degree to which they live out their values in practice.

LEADERSHIP AND DISCURSIVE PRACTICE

Leaders operating within a systemic constructionist framework need to develop ways of working that facilitate patterns of meaning making that enable forward movement on tasks by engaging the dynamics of the unfolding conversation and the linguistic and nonlinguistic material that constitutes those conversations. Using the framework of sense-making, positioning, and play, it is possible to articulate a preliminary set of discursive practices that facilitate ways of working with meaning making and developing contexts. As discussed earlier, discursive practices center on those activities that are associated with working with language, meaning making, and the construction of social arrangements, such as identities and relationships.

To be included in this framework, a discursive practice needs to meet the following criteria. First, the discursive practice has to develop people's ability to be sensitive to the aims and purposes of self and other. If working systemically involves engaging all parts of a human system, then discursive practices must develop a sense of awareness or way to engage with the complexity of conversation. Second, discursive practices must be grounded in the doing. A discursive practice must have some kind of action referent; you must be able to point to some concrete activity or action that a leader performs. Third, the discursive practice must be teachable. Discursive practices should be able to be learned and developed; therefore, a discursive practice needs to be heuristic enabling the construction of various concepts, practice models, and exercises that can inspire individuals to learn how to perform the practice. Fourth, the discursive practice needs to be able to be used by individuals in their internal and external conversations. Internal conversations refer to the conversations people have in their own head about what is going on in the situation, while external conversations are what overtly transpires between people as they talk. Internal and external conversations are intertwined, and discursive practices need to enable people to make sense of the conversations that are occurring within themselves and between people, in order to take action that develops the meaning potential of the situation. Fifth, discursive practices need to enable leaders to develop a sense of anticipation for, presence in, and reflection about the conversation.

If we think of conversations as unfolding, then leaders need to be able to position themselves in three ways: (a) they need to be able to develop anticipations of what might happen that help guide their subsequent actions; (b) they need to be present in the situation connecting to what is unfolding in the here and now; and (c) they need to develop the ability to look back on the conversation and reflect on what has transpired and what they have learned from the process. Rather than attempt to articulate separate sets of discursive practices for these three processes, it makes more sense to articulate a set of discursive practices that thread themselves through the temporal flow of conversation and are equally applicable in anticipating, being present, and reflecting back on leadership conversations.

The following set of discursive practices are offered as one take on the kinds of skills and abilities that leaders might need to develop in order to create a sense of orientation from within the flow of conversation. They draw on the wealth of material that has already been generated by systemic constructionist practitioners, such as process consultation professionals (e.g., Campbell & Huffington, 2008), but they place this material in the framework of sense-making, positioning, and play. The discursive practices that are identified are not exhaustive or definitive, and it is my hope that additional concepts and practice models will be elaborated in the future. Moreover, many of the specific practices that are discussed below perform many activities simultaneously, meaning that a particular process may facilitate concurrently sense-making, positioning, and play. The practices are grouped to present the material more easily and clearly, but the reader needs to keep in mind that these practices are closely connected and intertwined fulfilling multiple functions at the same time.

Sense-Making

Sense-making is an activity leaders may engage in both at a preconscious intuitive and reflective conscious level. The former shows itself when people have a sense of how to go on intuitively, spontaneously, without having to put their experience into words. The latter shows itself when leaders deliberately step back from the situation and reflect on their conversational experience. The former reflects the notion of working with the "present moment" within living conversations, where leaders have an intuitive sense of how to go and do so without great forethought, feeling their way into the moment. The latter set of experiences may be characterized as "now moments" or bifurcation points where leaders step back and feel that there is an important choice to be made around alternative meanings and consciously engage in a process of reflection to make that choice (Pearce, 2007; Stern, 2004). Our living conversational experience may be thought of as a series of fleeting "present moments," typically consisting of just a few seconds (Stern, 2004), that are punctuated by "now moments," where leaders' experiences are disturbed, which moves them to reflect on what's happening.

The systemic practitioner literature points to the importance of using stories as tools for leaders to make sense of their unfolding experience (Lang & McAdam, 1995). The following practices highlight the way that leaders work with stories in their practice to make sense of situations. The performance of these practices may be preconscious or intuitive as well as being quite conscious and intentional. The preconscious and conscious are not separate threads of practice, but are intertwined and build off each other. As leaders consciously work within a tradition of practice such as systemic constructionist leadership, they develop certain habits of working, or what Bourdieu (1977) would call a *habitus* that provides them with a framework for their practice. As leaders become more skilled at working with stories as tools for sense-making, these practices become natural, a key part of their identity, which become a normalized practice for leading others, that may be used quite intuitively and spontaneously. On the other hand, when leaders become disturbed in their practice, they shift from working at the preconscious level and become aware of something in the situation, working with stories consciously in order to determine what is going on and to make a wise choice about what to do. Therefore, the following discursive practices are particularly useful tools for working with stories—either at a conscious reflective or preconscious intuitive manner.

Punctuating Stories

The discursive practice of punctuating stories involves creating a rich description of the sequence of utterances and how they cohere to create the beginning, middle, and end of a story. When we punctuate stories, we ask the question, "What is going on here?" To answer this question we need to focus on the temporal dimension of stories asking when "what" began, how "what" developed, and where "what" is now. Pearce (2007) highlights that there are many ways to punctuate the beginning, middle, and end of stories concerning an issue or event.

Consider the current spate of businesses that are declaring bankruptcy in the United States due to poor financial performance. One way to tell the story is to begin the story from the point when the national economy fell dramatically, how this caused upper management to take drastic action such as downsizing, and how this downsizing failed to meet the demands of the market, leading to bankruptcy. Another starting place for the story could be at an earlier point, such as the deregulation of the financial markets. From this starting point, one could punctuate the story as beginning with deregulation, how the deregulation of financial markets moved upper management to make risky financial decisions, which positioned them poorly to cope with a tight economy, which led to financial ruin. Furthermore, one could start the story much earlier beginning with the shift of hiring CEOs and upper management from within a particular industry to the current practice of hiring upper management talent from outside the industry, particularly people with legal and financial backgrounds. From this starting point, the story might be one of how U.S. business leadership has been taken over by lawyers and accountants, not the people who know the product or service intimately, which leads them to make decisions based on short-term financial issues.

The point is that punctuating stories—their beginnings, middles, and endings—have important implications for how leaders make sense of their situation and subsequently respond to it. The way a story is punctuated influences who is included as important characters, the relationships among characters, the challenges they face, the way they resolved these challenges, and the state of play at the ending. The way that stories are punctuated creates a particular take toward the situation in view (Cronen, 2001). Leaders need to develop discursive practices that allow them to work with punctuating the flow of experience in different ways and realize how alternative punctuations influence the way they story the situation and make sense of it.

Multiplying Stories

Punctuating stories focuses on the way temporality influences how stories are created and their subsequent influence on sense-making. The practice of multiplying stories shifts the focus from articulating when the story begins and when it ends, to the way the multiple meanings for a single storyline can be created by using different perspectives. Chatman (1978) observes that all stories have a set of common elements including the content and chain of actions, characters, and setting, and challenge. However, these basic elements can be connected in various ways generating different kinds of stories such as comedies, dramas, adventures, fantasies, and tragedies. Connecting the same elements in a story in different ways generates a divergent set of meanings and interpretations regarding what the story is about. For example, how can one tell the story of giving large bonuses to financial services executives who have managed their companies so badly that the government has to give financial assistance? From the position of the financial services industry, one can create a story where bonuses are treated as key to retaining highly qualified personnel. From the position of the citizen, a story of corporate greed where individuals are handsomely rewarded for extremely poor performance may be generated.

Discursive practices associated with multiplying stories, therefore, aim to generate numerous divergent alternative stories of people, situations, and events. The systemic practice literature suggests a large number of possible methods for generating multiple stories including exploring stories from various stakeholder positions, investigating stories according to the domains model, which focuses attention on the domains of production, explanation, and aesthetics (Lang, Little, & Cronen, 1990), the LUUTT model which highlights our attention to the stories that are told (or not) about situation and what stories may be as of yet unheard (Pearce & Pearce, 1998), and back-casting, where individuals think about the event sometime in the future, and reflect back on the present from the future position, which generates stories about what that event might mean.

There are numerous ways to tell a story, and leaders need to develop discursive practices that allow them to explore the divergence among stories and how the telling of a story from a particular position enables particular lines of sense-making but precludes or discourages others. By being able to narrate different stories from various positions, leaders can begin to grasp the complexity of the system they are engaging, and subsequently create another story that takes into account the divergent stories. By creating a story that takes into account multiple perspectives, a leader is better positioned to make a move that will connect with the various stakeholders or participations in the conversation. The way leaders punctuate and multiply stories to generate a single story that accounts for the various perspectives of participants within the conversation and enables action is captured in the notion of systemic story making.

Systemic Story Making

Systemic story making represents a particular kind of story telling that values the alternative meanings which can be generated by divergent stories about a situation and attempts to integrate them into a unified story that respects the various positions. It gives attention to the unique details of a situation from the various perspectives of the members involved and moves the leader to articulate possible connections among communication, context, and meaning while keeping a sense of curiosity about the situation (Barge, 2004b; Lang & McAdam, 1995).

Systemic stories have a different flavor from other kinds of stories as they try to account for the detailed complexity of the situation in an affirmative way. Consider the following example from a leader in a psychological unit in a hospital:

> Over a period of 24 hours three nurses came to see me about what they viewed as "serious problem with the management of one of their patients." ... All of the nurses told similar stories about how a young male patient and his girl-friend were "withdrawn" and "very private" and appeared "not to be coping to what was happening." They all said they could not get through to either of them. They all felt "stressed" about this and also felt "helpless." They felt they did not have anything to offer. They wondered if I could help... I was asked if I would go and see the patient and his family. I declined to go and see the patient or his family and chose to see the clinical ward sister who had been one of the nurses who had come to see me. I hypothesized that if I could enable her to consider the situation from more of "a meta position," this could enable her in turn to help her staff. I hypothesized that if I got involved in this situation one possible "reflexive effect" would be that the story told could be "this situation really is a problem, Shirley has got involved!" I therefore considered "the art of the nudge," "What is the smallest thing that I can do that will make a difference?" (Barge, 2004b, p. 118)

What makes this a systemic story? First, the leader values the different perspectives of participants in the story. The story from the nurse's position would construct good leadership as being associated with the leader complying with the request. The leader constructed leadership as developing the capacity of the nurses to manage workplace challenges. The leader began the process of systemic story making by acknowledging and valuing these two different stories regarding leadership. Second, the systemic story she created incorporated elements from different parties' stories. The systemic story she created regarding the "art of the nudge" reflects the nurses' desire to receive guidance from their leader while at the same time reflects the leader's desire to create a situation where the capacity of the nurse is elaborated. Third, systemic stories enable action by introducing differences to create change. By making sense of the situation in this way, the "nudge" is generated, which is a concrete action that is taken to help change the system. Systemic stories, therefore, value the perspectives of multiple participants in the system and try to connect them in a way that respects their differences but enables action.

The process of systemic story making involves two key activities: (1) exploring multiple stories; and (2) creating stories of fit. The former is facilitated by punctuating and multiplying stories. The latter is facilitated by creating systemic stories that provide a specific accounting of the details of the situation, respect and appreciate the behaviors of the participants in the story, and enable managerial action. Systemic story making can be an individual activity as leaders may engage in this discursive practice to help them make sense of situations. It can also be a collective process as leaders may design meeting practices for organizational teams and groups to explore multiple stories and create stories of fit.

Positioning

Positioning theory refers to the process of how utterances within conversations construct positions that influence how people act. Harre and van Langenhove (1999) define a position as, "a complex cluster of generic personal attributes, structured in various ways, which impinges on the possibilities of interpersonal, intergroup and even intrapersonal action through some assignment of such rights, duties and obligations to an individual as are sustained by the cluster" (p. 2). Positions are moral, specifying what people can and can't do, and they generate a set of understandings regarding the rights and duties of persons as they make sense of situations and act. For example, if leaders are positioned by the organization as being knowledgeable, they will be accorded the right to participate in discussions and have the duty or obligation to give their opinion and share their knowledge in a variety of meetings and conversations. Positioning theory focuses on the dynamics of conversational episodes by focusing on the way utterances generate fluid parts and roles that people take up during conversation. Positioning theory allows us to focus on the dance of positions, how leaders position others through their talk, as well as how leaders are positioned by others.

Positions are different than roles in the sense that they are more temporary, fluid, and dynamic. Roles tend to be associated with stable, temporally durative responsibilities, duties, and functions that people perform. The shift from role to position directs our attention to the way that positions are created, unfold, and change within conversation. Position in this sense also differs from the widely held definition in the conflict management literature, which equates position with a fixed and rigid perspective that states the want or need rather than the reason or logic for it (Fisher & Ury, 1990).

Harre and van Langenhove (1999) emphasize the importance of the position/act-action/storyline triad. They argue that acts or actions create positions for self and other and that the act/actions and positions that are created in conversational episodes contribute to creating, sustaining, and developing storylines. The notions of act/actions, positions, and storylines form a mutually determining triad whereby: (a) acts/actions can sustain existing positions and storylines within conversations as well as invoke and call forth new ones; (b) the storylines that individuals bring into the conversation that are part of their personal and professional identities influence the kinds of positions they take up during conversation and what they feel permitted, obligated, and prohibited from saying; and (c) the positions they create, in the form of moral obligations, which influence what they can say in conversation as well as the kinds of storylines they may create and invite others to participate.

Positioning theory focuses leaders on engaging in what Pearce (2008) calls episode work, focusing on the way discourse and language evokes different kinds of identities, relationships, organizations, and cultures. As Harre and van Langehove (1999) explain:

> It is our belief that if one looks to three basic features of interactions, one is indeed able to understand and explain much of what is going on and how social and psychic phenomena are "constructed." These three basic features are: i. the moral positions of the participants and the rights and duties they have to say certain things, ii. the conversational history and the sequence of things already being said, iii. The actual sayings with their power to shape certain aspects of the social world. (p. 6)

This suggests that leaders need to develop their abilities to position themselves and others in ways that foster productive forms of meaning making and coordination. There are at least three discursive practices that leaders may develop to help them position themselves and others: (1) making positions; (2) taking positions; and (3) changing positions.

Making Positions

The practice of making positions is aimed at heightening leaders' awareness of the reflexive interplay among messages, utterances, and speech acts within conversation and the social arrangements they create. One approach that captures this dynamic quite well is a communication theory called the Coordinated Management of Meaning theory or CMM (Pearce & Cronen, 1980; Pearce, 1994, 2007). From the perspective of CMM, one way to approach the positioning triad is to focus on the sequence of turns within a conversation and explore what they create. This is a type of episode work where a leader begins to work with the unfolding sequence of turns in the conversation, becoming mindful of the episodes that are invited by sequencing utterances in particular ways (Pearce, 2008). Based in part on Weick's (1979) notion of double interact, what becomes important is to focus on what Pearce (2008) calls the conversational triplet. This means that the meaning of any utterance is partially determined by the preceding move in the conversation, how what has transpired in the preceding move positions the leader to respond in a particular way. However, the meaning of the leader's utterance is also determined by how the other person in the conversation responds to the leader's utterance. The notion of the conversational triplet can be captured like this:

$$Utterance_1 \rightarrow Leader's\ Utterance_2 \leftrightarrow Utterance_3$$

What this means is that leaders need to recognize that their actions are not the first turn in the conversation; they are always the second turn. This makes it important for individuals wishing to take a lead position to develop sensitivity to the way that a linguistic utterance (utterance$_1$) positions them to respond (utterance$_2$). Leaders can develop their practice by developing the ability to anticipate others' responses (the arrow moving from utterance$_3$ to utterance$_2$) as well as reflecting on what their utterance means after someone has responded (the arrow moving from utterance$_2$ to utterance$_3$). For example, poor performance by an employee may move a leader to offer assistance; what the leader anticipates will be viewed as a supportive act by the leader. However, if the employee then rejects it saying the leader is "feeling sorry for the employee," the meaning of offering assistance changes from an act of assistance to one of offering pity. By following the sequence of utterances, we can begin to explore how particular patterns of conversational triplets create different positions in the conversations.

CMM can also be used to explore how storylines can invite or discourage the performance of particular utterances as well as position people. CMM suggests that meaning systems are hierarchically organized and can consist of many levels. Pearce and Cronen (1980) developed a hierarchical model of meaning that looks like this:

As we have discussed previously, the utterances, or what they call *speech acts*, can position people to create different social arrangements in terms of the kind of episode they perform (i.e., appraisal, coaching, advice, etc.), the kinds of identities they adopt (i.e., I am a manager, a good friend, supportive, competent, etc.), the relationships among the participants (i.e., we are friends, co-workers, antagonists, etc.), the organizational culture (i.e., what people like us to do in this organization), and the cultural identity (i.e., how persons in the United States act). When one moves from the bottom of the hierarchy toward the top, one can explore how speech acts invoke different kinds of social arrangements. However, when you move from the top to the bottom, you can begin to see how these various contexts or stories contextualize the speech acts and create a sense of obligations, permissions, and prohibitions for how to act. For example, the stories that inform the organizational culture may generate expectations for how individuals should construct leadership in their everyday lives.

This model is heuristic in nature as people may use many more (or fewer) as well as the same (or different) levels of hierarchy to make sense of and act in situations. However, it points to two important discursive activities that leaders must engage and provides a practice model of how to do it. First, leaders can build their capacity for working with the dynamic flavor of conversational activity by developing sensitivity to the act-by-act unfolding of messages and what they invite. Second, leaders may need to develop sensitivity to the way various storylines in terms of episodes, relationships, identities and the like influence their actions.

Taking Positions

Leaders often need to take a position in the conversation by making arguments, challenging people's behaviors, correcting mistakes, issuing commands or otherwise taking an expert position where they assert direction and control over people's activity. From a systemic constructionist perspective, the issue is not whether leaders should or should not forcefully articulate their position, assert control in a conversation, or adopt an expert position. There will be times in their practice that they are positioned in such as way that they must do these things or that the context demands it. However, they must perform these acts in ways that continue to allow meaning making to emerge, versus freezing the process of meaning making, and to facilitate the coordination of the varied expertise that each conversational participant brings to the interaction. Puutio (2009) provides a useful example from process consulting to organizational leaders that highlights the dilemmas associated with creating expert position. He observes that the process of giving expert advice can harm or jeopardize the chance for reflection or learning by leaders. By creating the role of expert, the consultant shuts down the opportunity for leaders to learn because the consultant position is privileged, positioning the leader to follow the consultant's advice and not question it. The contribution of the leader is dismissed and the possibility for co-creating new understanding, meaning, and action is actively discouraged.

The issue is how to develop discursive practices that support learning and the ongoing elaboration of meaning making and action potentials when taking positions where you argue for your viewpoint or adopt an expert position. There at least three discursive practices that leaders may develop to help them work with taking positions that facilitate the co-creation of meaning and action.

Invitational Practices. Leaders may work with discursive practices that are invitational. The notion of invitation carries with it the idea that we need to invite people into our way of thinking, which acknowledges that our perspective is partial and may be enriched by others contributing their views (Foss & Foss, 2003). For example, Puutio (2009) identified a number of ways that advice can be given, such as using the client's invitation to offer expert reflections on what is going on, giving advice that builds on positive managerial responses, offering challenges by softening the style by offering it as personal opinion, using "we" language then transitioning into "you" language, and using language that softens the forcefulness rhetoric or qualifies it (i.e., sort of, probably, etc.). Such discursive moves create the space for other conversational participants to play with the argument and position of the other and offer the possibility of creating something new.

Collaborative Practices. Leaders can work with developing discursive practices that encourage collaborative argument. Much of the work on dialogical approaches to leadership tend to characterize argument and debate as bad, portraying it as an adversarial process where individuals fight to the death over their positions (i.e., Isaacs, 1999). While this is true of polarized debate (see Chasin et al., 1996), argumentation and debate theory have always been accompanied by a more dialogical thread, where arguments are viewed as a cooperative, collaborative process, where arguers are partners in a problem-solving process (Mallin & Anderson, 2000). This is consistent with work in the team learning literature where advocacy of one's position must be brought into close contact with inquiry (Senge, 1999). When leaders attempt to position themselves in ways that constructively juxtapose advocacy with inquiry, then a space for co-creation among people is fashioned as various perspectives are acknowledged and valued. Leaders may develop their ability to work with dialogical forms of argumentation, such as tag-team arguments where people work collectively to generate the argument (e.g., Meyers, 1997).

Framing Practices. Leaders need to develop framing skills. Framing refers to creating a context for people to make sense of and interpret events, situations, and people in particular ways (Fairhurst & Sarr, 1996). In the context of having to take a position and perhaps act in ways that create an expert position which could minimize the contribution of others to meaning making, leaders need to develop the ability to frame their activity in ways that keep the meaning making process fluid and dynamic. For example, there will be moments when leaders need to take unilateral action in conversations, such as termination episodes where an employee is dismissed from the organization due to violation of company policies. In this context, there is little choice for what the leader must do. However, such situations are quite difficult because leaders are usually prohibited legally from discussing personnel matters, and yet other people will witness this termination within the organization.

The concern is not with what is done, but how it is done. How does the leader create a context where it is permissible to take these kinds of actions? It becomes important for leaders to develop a repertoire of framing practices, such as metaphors, jargon, spin, contrast, and stories (Fairhurst & Sarr, 1996), that allows them to shape contexts. However, the ways these practices are enacted within conversation are less concerned with persuading others to follow the lead of the individuals but to create a context that facilitates the co-creation of meaning. Framing practices may be used to create the space for leaders to make arguments and create expert positions in ways that keep the co-creation of meaning making alive such that people feel they are being "done with" versus "done to." As Holman (2000) points out, it becomes important to articulate a formulation of the linguistic context that legitimates the individual's actions.

Changing Positions

An implicit thread that weaves its way through this portrayal of discursive practices is that leaders will need to make situated judgments regarding when and how to punctuate stories, multiply stories, engage in systemic story making, how they make positions, and take positions. The kinds of decisions they make can alter or change the positions that they prefer and invite the other into. Changing positions involves articulating a set of discursive practices that allow leaders to consciously or pre-consciously make choices about how to act from within the flow of conversation. In a sense, the practices associated with changing positions involve articulating a meta-position that explains how leaders might go about improving their ability to discern situations and make wise judgments.

The leadership literature tends to equate change in positions with consciousness (e.g., Schon 1983). For example, within the reflective practice literature, the importance of consciously stepping back and taking an observer position to reflect on one's own experience is quite important. Taking a *reflective position* within the flow of communication means that leadership actors shift positions from being a participant to being an observer to their experience whereby they treat themselves, others, and situations as objects for reflection (Heifetz, 1994). By reflecting on their actions and the situation, people can begin to order their experience and reflect on the way that different orderings facilitate their ability to move forward in the conversation and solve problems or accomplish goals.

Barge (2004a) highlights that the idea of using conscious reflection to order one's experience and assess the utility of using one frame over another is at the heart of reflective practice as it emphasizes individuals "learning to experiment with naming and framing situations in different ways and to assess the pragmatic utility these frames and names held for achieving desired ends" (p. 72). Creating a reflective position involves the creation of an explanation: how did a certain phenomenon come to be, why does it operate the way it does, what kinds of consequences does it produce and why. Within the reflective practice literature, a number of theoretical tools, such Morgan's (1999) metaphors of organization, causal maps (Argyris, 1993), "getting on the balcony" (Heiftez, 1994), and the left-hand column exercise (Senge, Kleiner, Roberts, Ross, Roth, & Smith, 1999) have been created that can be applied by practitioners to the situations they face.

Leaders may also engage in *reflexive positioning*, which is a form of self-awareness regarding how the moves they make in conversation help create the very conversation in which they find themselves having to respond. Reflexive practice typically opens up a conversation with oneself regarding the assumptions one makes about practice, "Whereas reflective analysis is concerned with a systematic searching for patterns, logic, and order, critically reflexive questioning opens up our own practices and assumptions as a basis for working toward more critical, responsive, and ethical action" (Cunliffe, 2004, p. 415). Reflexive practice emphasizes becoming aware of how our language and actions invite responses from others and how our assumptions inform the kinds of language and actions we perform in interaction.

While reflective and reflexive positioning are different, they share a common assumption that conscious reflection using language is an important process to help us make sense of a situation and make choices of how to influence the conversation. Reflective and reflexive positioning involve what Shotter (2007) calls "aboutness thinking." This is a form of thinking that tends to use pre-existing ideas, concepts, and frameworks for creating explanations of situations.

On the other hand, Shotter (2007) suggests that challenges of contemporary organizational life are not rooted in problem solving, but in what Shotter (2007) refers to as "difficulties of orientation." From Shotter's (2007) perspective, the starting point for creating a sense of orientation is for people to be relationally sensitive and adaptive to their surroundings, to be spontaneous in their connecting with others as opposed to executing pre-established plans. Shotter emphasizes the importance of "withness thinking," a style of thinking and connecting that keeps individuals in close contact with others, open to the influences of the situation, and responsive to the dynamic flow of communication. He stresses that learning occurs through feeling our way forward in situations versus applying a pre-existing theoretical schema to an already defined problem:

> To repeat, like someone walking alone and in the dark, our task is that of learning how to proceed step by step, feeling around in the course of each step, to gain an awareness of the guidance available to us from "being in touch with" our immediate local circumstances. But it is only "from within" our continued movement that we can learn our way forward. (Shotter, 2007, p. 7)

Shotter (2005) argues that "withness" thinking is pre-cognitive and pre-linguistic, "It is the character of our thinking and acting while 'in motion,' before we 'stop to think' reflectively about such thinking and acting" (Shotter, 2007, p. 2). "Withness thinking" is rooted in a language of spontaneity and feeling. Individuals are viewed as being continually "in motion" where they constantly are being called on to address their utterances to others. The character of this way of thinking and connecting with others is grounded in people's bodies, the way they use their bodies to experience what is happening and how they use their bodies to respond:

> ...we think along with a subsidiary awareness of certain felt experiences as they occur to us from within our engaged involvement in a particular unfolding process, and that these inner feelings play a guiding role in guiding our actions. It is this 'action guiding' function of subsidiary awareness in providing us with an anticipatory sense of at least the style of what is to come next that is crucial. (Shotter, 2006, p. 586)

This suggests that leadership actors also need to develop their ability to work with *resonant positioning*. Resonant positioning focuses on articulating the way people make connections spontaneously and intuitively prior to the moment of thinking or reflecting from within the flow of conversation. Cunliffe (2004) calls this style of communicating *reflex interaction* where, "We respond to other people on the basis of instinct, habit, and/or memory (reflex), and in doing so, we draw intuitively on our tacit knowing (Polanyi, 1966) and on who we are" (p. 412).

While the concept of reflex interaction captures the notion of our actions being habitual, involuntary, and immediate, it does not highlight the sense of being moved, of feeling that something is important, or being struck with the power of a particular emotion. Yet, the idea of being "struck by" something or being "arrested in the moment" is imbued with the idea that some type of strong meaningful emotional association is present. This is why I prefer to use the term "resonant positioning" to fully capture the role that feeling and emotion play in the construction of leadership because the meaning of *resonance* emphasizes the richness or significance connected with an association or strong emotion. When something "resonates" with us, we make a strong emotional connection with it, feeling there is something there that is worth exploring. (See Burns, 2007, for a discussion of resonance.)

While it may seem counterintuitive, I would suggest that people can develop practices that help them give orientation to the conversation that can lead to subsequent linguistic reflection. For example, Shotter (2007) suggests that practitioners such as leaders can focus on the way individuals use words, utterances, and gestures to trace what people give attention to in the unfolding conversation and what they do not. We must focus on those "striking moments" (Katz & Shotter, 2004), "arresting moments" (Katz & Shotter, 1996), and "connective triggers" (Cunliffe, 2001) that capture our attention and explore how they are used as a resource for orienting ourselves to the flow of communication.

We must explore the stances that people can take from within conversation that allow them to connect fully to the emerging set of relationships among themselves, others, and the situation they jointly construct. For example, Katz and Shotter (2004) suggest that a "conversational-poetic" stance keeps individuals attuned to the "striking moments" and the changing dynamics of the evolving situation. Lowe (2005) suggests that the "conversational-poetic" stance is less about prose, with an emphasis on the linear progression of a narrative, and more about the fleeting images of poetry that enter our imagination, "The elaboration of striking moments occurs 'poetically' through association of images, rhythms, and themes, rather than through narrative progression" (p. 73).

The ideas of reflective, reflexive, and resonant positioning provide leaders a set of practices that can help them make choices, consciously or pre-consciously, of how to move in the conversation. They honor both knowing that emphasizes linguistic reflection as well as bodily knowing that pays attention to feeling, movement, and emotion.

Play

The notion of play refers to the process of trying out alternative forms of meaning making and action to see what it creates within the system. The purpose of play is to help leaders and other conversational participants retain a sense of discursive openness in their practice, where they are open to new forms of meaning making and action as opposed to discursive closure, where the meaning of an event is fixed and cannot be challenged (Deetz, 1996). Central to the notion of play is working with differences in language and meaning within human systems. Derrida (1988) observes that discursive openness is kept alive through the play of differences within symbolic action because it acts to defer the meaning, keeping the dynamic evolution of meaning alive versus finalizing it. Discursive leadership practice involves "flirting with meaning" and engaging in pragmatic experimentation where linguistic differences are introduced into the conversation in an attempt to foster new patterns of meaning making and action (Eisenberg, 1998; Wicks & Freeman, 1998). This is not light-hearted or frivolous play; it is serious play because playing with meaning by introducing new elements into the conversation has real consequences in terms of the identities and relationships that are created.

Playing with meaning is intended to be life generating. Systems theory has always stressed that a system can only avoid decay and entropy by importing energy. In linguistic systems, energy takes the form of the linguistic differences that are introduced into the conversation as they give the participants new material to play with, to work with, and develop. A systemic constructionist perspective toward leadership, with its emphasis on affirmation, would suggest that constructive play involves discursive practices that affirm elements of an other's experience, while challenging it, keeping the play of meaning alive.

Affirmative Noticing, Naming, and Connecting

The affirmative value of systemic constructionist leadership emphasizes respecting other peoples' positions and interests, focusing on the life generating elements of organizational experience, and connecting them from within the flow of conversation in ways that keep the meaning making process alive. The notion of affirmative noticing means that leaders work at developing their capacity for spotting what is working well in the organization or in the situation, or what a person is doing well. Rather than focussing on the deficits and problems that organizations and individuals have, leaders need to focus on the strengths, resources, and assets that can be used as the basis for organizing.

Affirmative naming involves positively connoting an activity or placing it in a more positive frame. For example, many times leaders are criticized for being inconsistent in their behavior, and this puts a set of negative stories into motion that can hamper the leader's ability to manage within the organization. However, inconsistency can also be reframed as being responsive to a changing set of circumstances. In the case of an individual who has just been promoted to a leadership position, the inconsistency could be attributed to his or her "learning the ropes" which requires a bit of time and patience. Affirmative naming involves focusing on some positive element within the experience and being generous in the way that it is named. Affirmative noticing and naming heightens feelings of support by inviting, not commanding, others to act in the frame which then provides a sense of control. Rather than be locked into a language of problem and blame, which can foster negativity and resistance (Barge & Oliver, 2003), affirmative noticing focuses the conversation on strengths, contributions, and assets of individuals and teams which reaffirm their value and worth.

Systemic Reflecting and Questioning

Playing with meaning involves creating different punctuations and stories about situations in order to foster alternative meanings. In the discussion of sense-making, punctuating and multiplying stories were offered as a set of practices that can help leaders generate multiple reflections regarding the unfolding conversation. As these practices of reflecting have already been discussed, I will not cover them here and instead focus on the role of systemic questioning in playing with meaning.

Systemic questioning is a form of questioning that emphasizes the Socratic method (Boscolo, Cecchin, Hoffman, & Penn, 1985). It treats the act of asking questions as a form of inquiry that elaborates new meaning. Traditional forms of questions, rooted in the information transmission model, assume that the purpose of questions is to either access people's mental models and cognitive structures, in terms of the beliefs, attitudes, or values, and unlock their mind to create an accurate picture of the person's mind, or to ask questions in ways that create accurate details portraying people and situations.

Systemic questioning operates from a different set of assumptions. First, systemic questioning assumes an inclusive orientation toward the relationship between the leader and others. This means that each party influences the other through the questions they ask and the responses they provide. Second, questions create new possibilities for making distinctions in the flow of experience and creating new connections. Questions do more than simply obtain information; they introduce new distinctions and connections into the conversation which shape the pattern of meaning making and the kinds of social arrangements that are invited. Third, the act of questioning is interventive; that is, change within a human system begins at the moment of asking a question. Traditional models of change within organizations tend to treat the process of inquiry or asking questions as distinct from intervention and implementation. However, inquiry and change simultaneously occur within a human system when a question is asked (Cooperrider & Whitney, 2000); the act of inquiry creates change and is not a precursor to implementing change.

Take the following example of a senior-level manager whose unit was in chaos, in part due to his actions, and who has decided to postpone leaving the unit for a new job until he has stabilized his unit. One of his middle managers sees this "generous offer" as having the potential to create more turmoil, and through systemic questioning plays with the meaning of his offer to stay with the unit:

How can I tell this man that his generous offer is not going to be helpful without negatively connoting him and further disempowering him through what was left of his stay? . . . I found that this format of [systemic] questioning rescued him from the potential chaos of overwhelming information and enabled him to make decisions and act. The following are some of the questions I asked: Who would miss you most if you left? What differences will there be after you leave? Who would be the least/most likely to gain from your staying? Which people in your new team are most/least likely to be upset if you delay arriving?

The manager began to see more clearly his position in the organization and with it the responsibilities he needed to exercise (i.e., I should not create extra anxiety for those who live and work in the unit by being unable to fix a leaving date). He began to consider future possibilities as opposed to present restrictions (how can I leave with the unit in such turmoil). He began to see that the unit turmoil was to some extent mirrored by his own position and that future uncertainty (even if it was his leaving) was likely to create more stability than the present confusion. (Barge, 2004b, p. 120)

This example shows the power of systemic questioning to create new understandings of the situation. The middle manager asks questions that ask for comparisons, such as who would least/most likely to gain from the manager staying, which positions the manager to consider how different elements of the situation might fit together. The middle manager opens up new ways of making sense of the situation by engaging in inquiry and playing with meaning by asking questions that connect elements of the situation in different ways.

A number of essays have been written that highlight a variety of systemic questions (Cecchin, 1987; Krause, 2003). One important model for systemic questioning is provided by Tomm's (1988) interventive questioning model. Working from a systemic family therapy tradition, Tomm (1988) suggests there are a number of questions that can help individuals make sense of situations and their experiences. They include:

1. *Lineal questions:* Questions that clarify the sequence of events over time.
2. *Circular questions:* Questions that clarify the here and now of the situation by articulating that the patterns of interaction that occur and the connections among people.
3. *Reflexive questions:* Questions that enable a reflexive understanding of the situation by offering new alternative meanings, often by asking questions in ways that pick up on the other's understanding and mobilize new patterns.
4. *Strategic questions:* Questions that help formulate actions and are designed to influence clients in particular ways.

Questions such as these are intended to help inquire into various elements of the situation. Using these different questions helps establish new connections within the linguistic material.

Systemic questioning models are intended to help clinicians and therapists become more aware of the various types of questions they can ask and develop judgment of when to ask them. The hope is for individuals to become aware of the differential effects of their questioning. Similarly, when leaders learn how to ask questions in different ways, they invite different forms of social arrangements and create new understandings of the situation. Therefore, the act of questioning is not a benign activity aimed at eliciting information; the way that leaders play with their questions invokes new connections for meaning making.

Setting Context

Setting the context, or creating a frame for conversation, becomes important because it creates the space for play, inviting certain forms of conversations but not others. This highlights the importance of creating a discursive context for leaders and others to play on as they progress their tasks. In an earlier essay, I have argued that setting context involves meeting three important criteria: (1) it is important to set contexts that invite the co-creation or joint activity of individuals in the meaning making process; (2) setting contexts should enable co-creation by introducing a "difference that connects," that moves things forward by connecting with participants' rules for meaning and action while simultaneously introducing a difference; and (3) conversational frameworks should establish a safe space for conversation (Barge, 2004a). As a result, setting context involves the activity of designing a conversational architecture that inspires and guides the interaction.

There are numerous ways to set up conversational contexts. For example, a leader might say at the beginning of a meeting, "The reason for the meeting today is . . ." which establishes a focus for the meeting and positions the leader and others to act in particular ways. Alternatively, a context might be set by creating a detailed conversational architecture that is designed to call for a certain type of conversation in order to obtain a particular aim and purpose. There are a number of possible meeting formats that can be used to shape the discursive activity of individuals, such as Appreciative Inquiry Summits (Powley, Fry, Barrett, & Bright, 2004), Open Space (Owen, 2008), and Future Search (Weisbord & Janoff, 2000), as well as strategies for establishing safe space (Chasin et al., 1996). From a systemic constructionist perspective, it becomes important for leaders to develop skills at setting context, which includes the ability to design meeting formats that enable co-creation.

A NEW CANON FOR LEADERSHIP
COMMUNICATION SKILLS?

A relational approach to leadership grounded in social constructionism offers great potential for highlighting new ways of approaching the complex interplay among communication, meaning, action, and relationships. It offers a set of conceptual and analytic tools that can help scholars grapple with the social construction of leadership within human systems. Moreover, it offers new possibilities for rethinking the kinds of skills and abilities that leadership actors may need to develop if they take social constructionist ideas and practice seriously and wish to work with them.

In this chapter, I have taken one social constructionist approach to leadership, a systemic constructionist approach, and have begun to articulate the discursive practices that may be associated if an individual chooses to work from this perspective. These discursive practices emphasize the ability to work with meaning making and context in ways that further learning, cocreation, and development. The discursive practices of sense-making, positioning, and play represent a preliminary set of practices that individuals aspiring to leadership positions can develop and be taught. These practices are not exhaustive, as there are other possibilities for doing meaning and context work that either exist currently or have yet to be developed.

My hope by offering this chapter is that it will move other leadership scholars to place attention on how leadership might be constructed from a first-person position, from within the unfolding flow of conversation. The implications for rethinking the kinds of skills and abilities that are associated with leadership are great and the potential impact on how we think about and construct leadership education programs has yet to be fully explored. But it seems to me that this is relational leadership's next great challenge.

The challenge is to shift from talking about the way that leadership is constructed, to developing practices that help leaders to anticipate how they might act within an unfolding situation and to be present in the situation. Moreover, the task ahead is also to articulate practices than enhance a leader's ability to sense what is unfolding and take action that leads toward progressing the task, and to reflect on what they have done and how they might do it differently the next time. If we can develop ways of working that assist leaders in developing their linguistic capacity to anticipate, to be present, and to reflect on their conversational experience, then we will have begun to fulfill the promise of relational leadership.

REFERENCES

Alvesson, M., & Karreman, D. (2000). Taking the linguistic turn in organizational research. *The Journal of Applied Behavioral Science, 36,* 136–158.

Argyris, C. (1993). *Knowledge for action: A guide to overcoming barriers to organizational change.* San Francisco, CA: Jossey-Bass.

Barge, J. K. (2004a). Reflexivity and managerial practice. *Communication Monographs, 71,* 70–96.

Barge, J. K. (2004b). Antenarrative and managerial practice. *Communication Studies, 55,* 106–127.

Barge, J. K. (2007). The practice of systemic leadership: Lessons from the Kensington Consultation Centre Foundation. *OD Practitioner, 39,* 10–14.

Barge, J. K., & Fairhurst, G. F. (2008). Living leadership: A systemic constructionist approach. *Leadership, 4,* 227–251.

Barge, J. K., & Little, M. (2002). Dialogical wisdom, communicative practice, and organizational life. *Communication Theory, 12,* 365–397.

Barge, J. K., & Little, M. (2008). A discursive approach to skilful activity. *Communication Theory, 18,* 505–534.

Barge, J. K., & Oliver, C. (2003). Working with appreciation in managerial practice. *Academy of Management Review, 28,* 124–142.

Bateson, G. (1972). *Steps to an ecology of mind.* Chicago, IL: University of Chicago Press.

Bolman, L. G., & Deal, T. E. (2008). *Reframing organizations: Artistry, choice and leadership* (4th ed.). San Francisco, CA: Jossey-Bass.

Boscolo, L., Cecchin, G., Hoffman, L., & Penn, P. (1985). *Milan systemic family therapy.* New York, NY: Basic Books.

Bourdieu, P. (1977). *Outline of a theory of practice.* Cambridge, England: Cambridge University Press.

Burns, D. (2007). *Systemic action research.* Bristol, England: Polity Press.

Burr, V. (2003). *Social constructionism* (2nd ed.). London, England: Routledge.

Campbell, D. (2000). *The socially constructed organization.* London, England: Karnac.

Campbell, D., & Groenbeck, M. (2006). *Taking positions in organizations.* London, England: Karnac.

Campbell, D., & Huffington, C. (2008). *Organizations connected: A handbook of systemic consultation.* London, England: Karnac.

Cecchin, G. (1987). Hypothesizing, circularity and neutrality revisited: An invitation to curiosity. *Family Process, 26,* 405–413.

Chasin, R., Herzig, M., Roth, S., Chasin, L., Becker, C., & Stains, R. R., Jr. (1996). From diatribe to dialogue on divisive public issues: Approaches drawn from family therapy. *Mediation Quarterly, 13,* 323–344.

Chatman, S. (1978). *Story and discourse: Narrative structure in fiction and film.* Ithaca, NY: Cornell University Press.

Cooperrider, D. L., & Whitney, D. (2000). A positive revolution in change: Appreciative inquiry. In D. L. Cooperrider, P. F. Sorensen, Jr., D.Whitney, & T. F. Yaeger (Eds.), *Appreciative inquiry: Rethinking human organization toward a positive theory of change* (pp. 3–28). Champaign, IL: Stipes Publishing.

Craig, R. T. (2006). A practice. In G. J. Shepherd, J. St. John, & T. Striphas (Eds.), *Communication as . . . perspectives on theory* (pp. 38–48). Thousand Oaks, CA: Sage.

Cronen, V. E. (2001). Practical theory, practical art, and the pragmatic-systemic account of inquiry. *Communication Theory, 11,* 14–35.

Cunliffe, A. L. (2001). Managers as practical authors: Reconstructing our understanding of management practices. *Journal of Management Studies, 38,* 351–371.

Cunliffe, A. L. (2002). Reflexive dialogical practice in management learning. *Management Learning, 33,* 35–61.

Cunliffe, A. L. (2004). On becoming a critically reflexive practitioner. *Journal of Management Education, 28,* 407–426.

Dallos, R., & Draper, R. (2000). *An introduction to family therapy: Systemic theory and practice.* Buckingham, England: Open University Press.

Deetz, S. (1996). Describing differences in approaches to organization science: Rethinking Burrell and Morgan and their legacy. *Organization Science, 7,* 191–207.

Derrida, J. (1988). *Limited Inc.* Evanston, IL: Northwestern University Press.

Eisenberg, E. M. (1998). Flirting with meaning. *Journal of Language and Social Psychology, 17,* 97–108.

Fairhurst, G. T. (2007). *Discursive leadership.* Thousand Oaks, CA: Sage.

Fairhurst, G., & Grant, D. (2010). The social construction of leadership: A sailing guide. *Management Communication Quarterly, 24*(2), 171–210.

Fairhurst, G. T., & Sarr, R. A. (1996). *The art of framing: Managing the language of leadership.* San Francisco, CA: Jossey-Bass.

Foss, S. K., & Foss, K. A. (2003). *Inviting transformation* (2nd ed.). Prospect Heights, IL: Waveland Press.

Galanes, G. J. (2009). Dialectical tensions of small group leadership. *Communication Studies, 60,* 409–425.

Gergen, K. J., Gergen, M. M., & Barrett, F. J. (2004). Dialogue: Life and death of the organization. In D. Grant, C. Hardy, C. Oswick, N. Phillips, & L. L. Putnam (Eds.), *Handbook of organizational discourse* (pp. 39–60). Thousand Oaks, CA: Sage.

Grint, K. (2005). Problems, problems, problems: The social construction of "leadership." *Human Relations, 58,* 1467–1494.

Grint, K. (2007). Learning to lead: Can Aristotle help us find the road to wisdom? *Leadership, 3,* 231–246.

Harre, R. & van Langenhove, L. (1999). *Positioning theory.* Oxford, England: Blackwell Publishing.

Hedges, F. (2005). *An introduction to systemic therapy with individuals: A social constructionist approach.* London, England: Palgrave Macmillan.

Holman, D. (2000). A dialogical approach to skill and skilled activity. *Human Relations, 53,* 957–980.

Isaacs, W. (1999). *Dialogue and the art of thinking together.* New York, NY: Currency.

Katz, A. M., & Shotter, J. (1996). Hearing the patient's "voice": Toward a social poetics in diagnostic interviews. *Social Science and Medicine, 43,* 919–931.

Katz, A. M., & Shotter, J. (2004). On the way to "prescence": Methods of a "social poetics." In D. A. Pare & G. Larner (Eds.), *Collaborative practice in psychology and therapy* (pp. 69–82). New York, NY: Haworth Clinical Practice Press.

Krause, I. B. (2003). Learning how to ask in ethnography and psychotherapy. *Anthropology and Medicine, 10,* 3–21.

Lang, P., Little, M., & Cronen, V. (1990). The systemic professional: Domains of action and the question of neutrality. *Human Systems, 1,* 39–56.

Lang, P., & McAdam, E. (1995). Stories, giving accounts, and systemic descriptions. *Human Systems, 6,* 71–103.

Lowe, R. (2005). Structured methods and striking moments: Using question sequences in "living" ways. *Family Process, 44,* 65–75.

Mallin, I., & Anderson, K. V. (2000). Inviting constructive argument. *Argumentation and Advocacy, 36,* 120–133.

McCaughan, N., & Palmer, B. (1994). *Systems thinking for harassed managers.* London, England: Karnac.

Meyers, R. A. (1997). Social influence and group argumentation. In L. R. Frey & J. K. Barge (Eds.), *Managing the tensions of group life: Communication in decision-making groups* (pp. 183–201). Burlington, ME: Houghton Miflin.

Morgan, G. (1999). *Images of organization* (2nd ed.). Thousand Oaks, CA: Sage.

Oliver, C. (2004). Reflexive inquiry and the strange loop tool. *Human Systems, 2,* 127–140.

Oliver, C. (2005). *Reflexive inquiry: A framework for consultancy practice.* London, England: Karnac.

Ospina, S., & Sorenson, G. L. J. (2006). A constructionist lens on leadership: Charting new territory. In G. R. Goethals and G. L. J. Sorenson (Eds.), *The quest for a general theory of leadership* (pp. 188–204). Cheltenham, England: Edward Elgar.

Owen, H. (2008). *Open space technology: A user's guide* (3rd ed.). San Francisco, CA: Berrett-Koehler.

Pearce, W. B. (1994). *Interpersonal communication: Making social worlds.* New York, NY: HarperCollins.

Pearce, W. B. (2007). *Making social worlds: A communication perspective.* Malden, MA: Blackwell Publishing.

Pearce, W. B. (2008). Toward a new repertoire for skills for leaders and managers. *The Quality Management Forum, 34,* 4–7.

Pearce, W. B., & Cronen, V. E. (1980). *Communication, action, and meaning.* New York, NY: Praeger.

Pearce, W. B., & Pearce, K. A. (1998). Transcendent storytelling: Abilities for systemic practitioners and their clients. *Human Systems, 9,* 167–184.

Pearce, W. B., Villar, E., & McAdam, E. (1992). "Not sufficiently systemic"—An exercise in curiosity. *Human Systems, 3,* 75–87.

Powley, E. H., Fry, R. E., Barrett, F. J., & Bright, D. S. (2004). Dialogic democracy meets command and control: Transformation through the appreciative inquiry summit. *Academy of Management Executive, 18,* 67–80.

Puutio, R. (2009). *Hidden agendas: Situational tasks, discursive strategies, and institutional practices in process consultation.* Jyvaskyla, Finland: University of Jyvaskyla.

Raelin, J. A. (2007). Toward an epistemology of practice. *Academy of Management Learning & Education, 6,* 495–519.

Senge, P. M. (1999). *The fifth discipline: The art and practice of the learning organization.* New York, NY: Doubleday.

Senge, P. M., Kleiner, A., Roberts, C., Ross, R. B., & Smith B. J. (1994). *The fifth discipline fieldbook.* New York, NY: Currency Doubleday.

Seyranian, V., & Bligh, M. C. (2008). Presidential charismatic leadership: Exploring the rhetoric of social change. *The Leadership Quarterly, 19,* 54–76.

Shotter, J. (1993). *Conversational realities: Constructing life through language.* London, England: Sage.

Shotter, J. (2005). 'Inside the moment of managing': Wittgenstein and everyday dynamics of our expressive-responsive activities. *Organization Studies, 26,* 113–135.

Shotter, J. (2006). Understanding process from within: An argument for 'withness'-thinking. *Organization Studies, 27,* 585–604.

Shotter, J. (2007). Getting *it—Withness thinking and the dialogical. . . in practice.* Unpublished manuscript.

Stern, D. M. (2004). *The present moment in psychotherapy and everyday life.* New York, NY: W. W. Norton & Company.

Tomm, K. (1988). Interventive interviewing part 3: Intending to ask lineal, circular, strategic, or reflexive questions. *Family Process, 27,* 1–15.

Uhl-Bien, M. (2006). Relational leadership theory: Exploring the social processes of leadership and organizing. *The Leadership Quarterly, 17,* 654–676.

Weick, K. E. (1979). *The social psychology of organizing* (2nd ed.). New York, NY: McGraw-Hill.

Weisbord, M. R., & Janoff, S. (2000). *Future search.* San Francisco, CA: Berrett-Koehler.

Whitehead, J., & McNiff, J. (2006). *Action research, living theory.* London, England: Sage.

Wicks, A. C., & Freeman, R.E. (1998). Organization studies and the new pragmatism: Positivism, anti-positivism and the search for ethics. *Organization Science, 9,* 123–140.

CHAPTER 5

THE CONTRIBUTION OF PSYCHODYNAMIC THEORY TO RELATIONAL LEADERSHIP

Declan J. Fitzsimons

*Psychodynamic theory provides social science depth by drawing attention to the
sources of energy and motivational forces being experienced within individuals, small
groups, their leaders, and the linkages between them. The operable psychological
word for psychodynamic is "within." Social scientists working with psychodynamics
represent a subset of the broad field of psychology. They study the activity of and the
interrelation between various parts of an individual's personality or psyche.*

—Neumann & Hirschhorn, 1999

This chapter identifies three fundamental debates within Relational Leadership Theory (RLT) (Uhl-Bien, 2006) and looks at ways in which concepts from a systems psychodynamic perspective can contribute to these issues. These debates are: how the self is theorized; the nature of relational dynamics in social systems; and how process can be engaged within organizational settings. These three debates have been addressed within RLT, and important distinctions have been made between relational theories that take an entity-based perspective and those that reflect a constructionist perspective.

To come to grips with these debates, we must explore the ontological and epistemological assumptions that underpin them. An ontological

Advancing Relational Leadership Research, pages 143–174
Copyright © 2012 by Information Age Publishing
All rights of reproduction in any form reserved.

stance on social reality that claims that underlying regularities (causal relationships between social phenomena) can be reliably identified differs in important ways from an ontological stance that construes social reality, not as something "out there"—external to individuals—but constructed within the on-going flow and flux of social interactions between individuals. The latter stance regards social reality as embedded within highly contextualized social, cultural, and political processes. These two ontological stances are associated with contrasting epistemologies or theories of what constitutes knowledge. A view of social reality as external to individuals tends to see the world as populated by discrete entities with stable properties, which can be reliably identified, measured, and generalized to wider populations in unproblematic ways. Knowledge consists of identifying and measuring these discrete variables using quantitative survey methods and establishing correlations between them. Such an epistemological stance and its attendant research methodologies are problematic within a constructionist paradigm. Both approaches are concerned with objectivity but have powerfully contrasting means for achieving it. One attempts to remove the subjectivity of the researcher by using research designs that simulate laboratory conditions or adopt survey methods, while the other demands a disciplined examination of subjectivity as one enters a system for the purpose of exploring how social reality emerges from human relations.

Thus, contrasting accounts of the ontological and epistemological assumptions that underpin entity and constructionist approaches within the RLT model potentially represent quite polarized perspectives on relational leadership based on strongly contrasting ways of construing the individual in relation to others and their contexts. A systems psychodynamic perspective on leadership presents useful paradoxes which we can use to explore this polarized space within relational leadership: It focuses on individuals as finite, but emphasizes the ways in which unconscious group-level processes influence individual behavior. An individual's feelings, thoughts, and actions are not seen as a function of individual psychologies but of systemic group processes that are often unconscious. Thus, while individual experience is acknowledged within a systems psychodynamic perspective, this experience is defined in terms that identify the sources of this experience as being beyond the individual. This, as we shall see, contrasts strongly with a view of the individual from within both entity and constructionist perspectives with concomitant implications for how relationships are understood.

This chapter addresses the ways in which a systems psychodynamic perspective contributes theoretical depth and breadth to three important debates central to RLT. Although, as we shall see, a systems psychodynamic perspective has obvious implications for practice, that is not the primary focus of this chapter. This application to practice reflects a research stance rooted in action research methods that contrast strongly and often appear irreconcilable with methodologies familiar to scholars whose worldview is entity-based. Although to constructionist scholars these differences are perhaps less problematic, the contrasting view of the ontological status of the self and the ways in which the intrapsychic world of individuals is theorized from a systems psychodynamic perspective make for noteworthy differences. A systems psychodynamic perspective is not presented as a better alternative to either entity or constructionist approaches, but it can, it is argued, add considerable conceptual weight to areas that are of central concern to RLT. In addition, while there are obvious implications in this discussion for research methodologies, contrasting social research methods is again not the primary focus of this chapter.

Such an approach is consistent with the expressed aims of the RLT model—to provide a framework in which relational approaches to leadership with widely differing ontological and epistemological assumptions can be considered. The Relational Leadership Theory framework is not intended as a way to unify theories, but to provide a means whereby differing perspectives can engage with one another (Uhl-Bien, 2006, p. 222) and achieve some measure of integration.

Because the psychodynamic perspective is a broad field, I do not claim to offer either an exhaustive review of the vast literature on theories of the self, or a complete survey of systems psychodynamic approaches. It would also be misleading to present a systems psychodynamic perspective as if it is a coherent body of theory about which all scholars in the field agree. Let us begin by considering the historical roots of the term "systems psychodynamic."

THE HISTORICAL ROOTS OF THE SYSTEMS PSYCHODYNAMIC PERSPECTIVE

The systems psychodynamic model emerged from work at the Tavistock Institute of Human Relations in London, founded in 1946 by members of the Tavistock Clinic with a grant from the Rockefeller Foundation. During the Second World War, members of the Tavistock Clinic had done pioneering work in preventative social psychiatry, working with officer-troop relations and officer selection. The intention was to establish a means of extending this work into the task of peacetime social and economic re-construction, and the Institute was established to do that.

From its inception, the pioneering work of Kurt Lewin had a profound and lasting impact on both the formation and the professional identity of the Institute (Neumann, 2005). Lewin's emphasis on what he termed *action research*, based on his idea that the best way to understand an organization was to try to change it, was congruent with the new Institute's mandate to not only study social problems but to attempt to resolve them. It reflected a concern that traditional forms of scientific research might not help to elucidate the complexities of human collectives. This led to an emphasis on pragmatic applied social science that attempted to integrate theories across the social sciences with an application research model within organizations. The journal *Human Relations*, established in 1947 jointly by the Tavistock Institute and MIT where Lewin was based, was dedicated to this ethos of integration.

Over the next 20 to 30 years, a conceptual framework and an applied action research model emerged into a body of pragmatic theory underpinned by what has broadly come to be termed as a *systems psychodynamics model.* *Systems psychodynamics* refers to a broad range of concepts with a multi-disciplinary source stemming from the social systems theories of Lewin (1946, 1947, 1950) and relational forms of psychoanalysis, particularly the work of Melanie Klein (1946, 1952, 1959). The *systems* part thus refers to the influence of Lewin, who first drew attention to the "Gestalt" properties of groups and the integration of his thinking with the open systems theory of the biologist Bertalanffy (1950). A gestalt perspective on groups refers to Lewin's insistence on studying groups as wholes rather than the sum of the individual behaviors of group members:

> . . . there is no more magic behind the fact that groups have properties of their own, which are different from the properties of their sub-groups or their individual members, than behind the fact that molecules have properties which are different from the properties of the atom or ions of which they are composed. (Lewin, 1947, p. 8)

This notion of group properties was integrated with an open systems perspective that viewed a human system as dependent for its survival, rather like a biological organism, on the continuous exchange of materials, resources, information, and ideas across the boundaries between the system and its environment, and between sub-systems within the organization. The behavior of individuals is asserted to be a function of powerful systemic dynamics in which they participate consciously and unconsciously. Insight on the potential unconscious processes within groups seen as open systems and activated by group level processes was developed through the work of Wilfred Bion (1961), whose theory of group processes integrated systems thinking with psychoanalytic theory for the first time.

Based on his clinical work with groups, Bion postulated that, at any one time, a group is working on two levels. On one level, a group can be working on its assigned task, to which extent Bion suggested it is a "sophisticated" or work group, while on another level and at the same time, the group can be mobilized by unconscious irrational processes. When caught up in these irrational processes, a group works as if any one of three assumptions (i.e., fight/flight; pairing; dependency) were true. These "basic assumption" groups work as if the group were facing an external or internal threat (e.g., a fight/flight response), as if the creation of a pair could save the group (e.g., pairing), or as if a group can be caught in a dynamic of dependency on a particular individual or idea (i.e., dependency). Bion suggested that individuals contributed to these dynamics unconsciously. The purpose of basic assumption behavior is to provide some defense against emotional turbulence engendered by the demands of the task. Thus, for example, a project group tasked with formulating new approaches to the market may find itself overwhelmed by anxieties relating to that task and unconsciously retreat into a view of reality in which certain senior figures are trying to undermine their work. By integrating a range of concepts from the fields of systems thinking, open systems and psychoanalysis, a systems psychodynamic framework allows for the exploration and illumination of such processes.

The psychodynamic part of the term *systems psychodynamic* refers to the influence of relational forms of psychoanalytic thinking, particularly Object Relations (Gomez, 1997) and the work of Melanie Klein (1959). Originally a British development of Freudian psychoanalytic theory, "rather than seeing the human being as a system of biological drives, Object Relations places relationship at the heart of what it is to be human" (Gomez, 1997, p.1). Our need for others is central to how we come to know ourselves. By placing the longing for human relationship so centrally, Object Relations brings to RLT a perspective on relating that highlights the risks individuals face when reaching for, developing, and sustaining human relationships. It highlights relational processes that are not only about social interactions and meaning-making, but about the ever-present anxieties of acceptance and rejection that are entailed when we try to form relationships. A systems psychodynamics perspective ensures that these relational dynamics are not read as interpersonal phenomena but instead explores how they can be understood at a group, intergroup, and system levels. If the head of finance and the head of marketing are in conflict, this can potentially be as much an expression of interdepartmental tensions as individual differences.

In the sections below, I discuss three main debates as they apply to Relational Leadership Theory. The first and second debates address entity and constructionism with respect to psychodynamic perspectives. The third debate focuses on the ways in which process can be viewed from a systems psychodynamic perspective. To ease presentation, for the rest of this chapter I will use the terms *systems psychodynamic* and *psychodynamic* interchangeably.

THE WAY THE SELF IS THEORIZED

Yes! In the sea of life enisled, With echoing straits between us thrown,
Dotting the shoreless watery wild, We mortal millions live alone. The islands feel
the enclasping flow, And then their endless bounds they know.
—Matthew Arnold, "To Marguerite" (1852)

Perhaps the most central debate the RLT model elicits, and one reflected in the opening stanza of Arnold's hauntingly evocative poem alluding to the new subjectivity that the dawning of the Modern industrial age engendered, is how the self is construed. From this stems all subsequent theorizing about the nature of relationship and relational dynamics with respect to the link between individuals, the collectives to which they belong, and their wider social, political, and cultural contexts.

An Entity Perspective on the Self

Entity approaches to relational leadership focus on individual agency as the main constituting element of organizational life. Individuals are assumed to be ontologically complete entities to the extent that there is a clear separation between mind and nature. In other words, individuals are in possession of a "knowing mind" and have access to the knowledge within those minds.

Such a view is "consistent with an epistemology of objective truth and a Cartesian dogma of a clear separation between mind and nature" (Uhl-Bien, 2006, p. 655). The pervasive influence of the Cartesian "split," separating cognitive from the corporeal, the mind from the body, has far-reaching consequences for theory development and research methodologies. It is not only that the mind and body are separate, but as Descartes describes, "the natures of the mind and body are not only different, but in some way opposite." The notion, "I am" because "I think" carries with it implications for how we build theories. Standards for what constitutes valid, reliable, and generalizable knowledge are built on an approach to social inquiry that considers that which can be experienced by the body, particularly emotion, as not only irrelevant, but as a source of contamination. An epistemological stance that limits what can be known to what can be thought by individual minds theorizes leaders as heads without bodies.

Construing leadership in this way is a consequence of an epistemological stance that considers the only form of valid and reliable knowledge as that produced by methods emulating the natural sciences. In other words, the requirement to produce a form of knowledge that can be formulated and codified in ways generalizable to bigger populations, and later disseminated widely in the form of universal statements, requires research methodologies that focus on individuals as disembodied mind-entities.

The entity perspective represents the dominant paradigm in leadership research. As Drath and colleagues have recently pointed out (Drath, McCauley, Palus, Van Velsor, O'Connor, & McGuire, 2008), despite the apparent diversity of leadership theories, there is an underlying ontological framework that provides a unifying philosophical base on which much of the literature stands. This implicit framework sees leadership as being enacted by three interlocking elements—leaders, followers, and mutual goals. Within this framework, these three elements are construed as ontologically complete "entities." This entity perspective constitutes a founding ontological framework of leadership that "is virtually beyond question within the literature" (Drath et al., 2008, p. 635). It permeates all aspects of the research process, and constitutes the dominant paradigm within the social sciences. The focus is on discerning the intentions, attributes, characteristics, perceptions, and behaviors of individual mind-entities in relation to other individual entities and the goals to which they aspire.

A Constructionist Perspective on the Self

The contrast between entity and constructionist approaches to the self is considerable. Within an entity perspective, the *self* is defined as a discrete mind entity; from a constructionist perspective, the existence of an inner psychological core to which agency is ascribed is considered highly suspect.

The constructionist perspective on the self is rooted in social constructionist thinking, a signature element of which is postmodernism with intellectual roots in early Greek philosophy (Chia, 2003). Postmodern theorists assert the importance of examining the underlying assumptions—the implicit social, political, and cultural values on which knowledge claims of any kind are based.

The briefest of sketches of the history of social constructionism's influence on how we think of the self would have to include the writings of social theorists such as William James (1890), Charles Horton Cooley (1902), and later, George Herbert Mead (1934). These writers challenged the idea of the self as a separate entity by showing how an individual's sense of self was bound up with how others viewed them. Notions such as the social self and symbolic interaction (Blumer, 1969) which emerged from this early thinking emphasized the primacy of interpretive processes constructed in social interactions, and spurred the development of qualitative research methodologies that sought to inquire into how social actors constructed their worlds through social interactions in particular settings.

More recently in his book *Relational Being: Beyond Self and Community*, Gergen (2009), a leading social constructionist thinker, advocates a significant shift from an entity perspective of what he calls "bounded being" toward one in which it is possible "to eliminate the very distinction between outer and inner, and to replace it with a view of relationally embodied action" (p. xx). In Gergen's theory, there is no isolated self or fully private experience. He wishes to assert a world in which what we construe as individual self-entities are "derivative of relational process."

That Gergen's views are recognizable within the description of the constructionist perspective within RLT is not a surprise since he has written collaboratively with Dachler and Hosking, whose work is widely cited within the RLT model. The self is considered as a construction arising out of social processes. The emphasis is therefore not on identifying the attributes of already complete knowing minds, but on the processes through which meaning and understandings of what constitutes leadership come to be attributed within a social system.

In the same way, knowledge is not assumed to be the property of individual minds but is embedded within shifting social and cultural contexts. Organizational phenomena are held in interdependent relationships; they are created and constantly shift and are negotiated in the flux of intersubjective meaning-making. Knowing is thus always a process of relating—an on-going process of creating meaning through language limited by different socio-cultural contexts (Uhl-Bien, 2006).

It is typically part of the agenda of social constructionist thinking to reveal multiple realities, and by so doing, undermine any claims that a particular form of knowledge—especially scientific knowledge—might have to value neutrality. From the point of view of the way the self is theorized, the social constructionist perspective on the self is concerned with exploring the values embedded within the dominant objectivist paradigm of the social sciences and how this leads us to conceptualize the self as a discrete mind object. A social constructionist approach would also scrutinize the knowledge claims of the systems psychodynamic perspective in the same way. For example, a social constructionist critique of psychoanalytic approaches to emotion in organizational settings points out that psychodynamic writers don't pay enough attention to the emotions which derive from a particular organizational or cultural context and instead tend to emphasize the ubiquity of anxiety (Fineman, 1996).

In a similar fashion, social constructionism can be used to explore the values underlying the early focus in psychology on explicating constructs such as self-awareness, self-autonomy, and self-efficacy. This is very important for the purpose of this chapter, since how the self is theorized strongly influences the way we think about relationships and relational dynamics, which are central to any theory of relational leadership. One possible "reading" of psychology's historical and current preoccupation with the self reflects the central role that Western, and in particular American, individualism plays in the development of psychological theories (Josselson, 1996). It is probably not a co-incidence that this reification of the self plays down our need to belong and how we come to think of our relationships with others. Postmodern, social constructionist thinking, suspect of how psychology has come to reflect, but not reflect *on*, some basic cultural assumptions that reify the individual self, has contributed to the emergence of alternative developmental theories.

Feminist writers at the Stone Center and the Jean Baker Miller Training Institute at Wellesley College have posited an alternative approach to development based on the capacity, not for autonomy, but for relating to others (Jordan, 1986; Jordan, Kaplan, Miller, Stiver, & Surrey, 1991; Miller, 1984,). They argue that, reflecting the values of individualism, mainstream developmental theories have emphasized autonomy and independence as hallmarks of the mature adult and by so doing, deny our dependence on one another. The researchers at Wellesley College have been influenced by the Object Relations school of psychoanalysis. This perspective, to which we will now turn our attention, is central to the systems psychodynamic perspective.

A Systems Psychodynamic Perspective on the Self

The self, theorized within a systems psychodynamic perspective, reflects the influence of relational psychoanalytic theories. The emergence of these relational theories contrasted strongly with Freud's earlier drive theories. Drive theories refer to Freud's belief in a mind driven by largely biologically determined instincts. Thus, in classical Freudian theory, other people are of interest only as objects for the satisfaction of instinctual drives. In contrast to this instrumental view of relationship, early relational theorists within the psychoanalytic world, particularly the British Object Relations theorists, placed more emphasis on *relatedness*, proposing that the object of human drives is connection with others (Gomez, 1997). From this more relational perspective, the basic unit of study is not the individual entity, but the "interactional field within which the individual arises and struggles to make contact and articulate himself" (Mitchell, 1988, p. 3). Of the relational theories within psychoanalysis, the Object Relations school has most influenced the development of the systems psychodynamic perspective. The name most associated with Object Relations theory is Melanie Klein (1946, 1952, 1959). Her theories of infant development and the patterns of anxiety attendant with this development and their influence in adult life have been widely influential (Klein, 1952).

Based on her pioneering clinical methods of child observation and psychotherapy, Melanie Klein developed a theory of infant development in which young infants polarize their world between pleasurable and comforting experiences and experiences that may be distressful and painful. Klein claimed that an infant experiences intolerable anxieties on discovering that the source of these contrasting experiences is the one and same mother. This realization represents the sundering of the more manageable polarized world in which the mother could be split into bad and good aspects, rather than embodying both good and bad experiences. What was a simplified world, with separate senses of good and bad experience, now becomes a more complex and distressing world in which "good" and "bad" have an integrated source. Resulting patterns of defense against such anxieties become a permanent part of our psychic life into adulthood, where we unconsciously recruit from our external world a cast of characters who ensure that a particular pattern of defenses are sustained (Josselson, 2007).

Thus, when we as adults experience conflict and turmoil internally, we manage our inner worlds by projecting our conflicts onto the outside world, finding enemies and friends, and manifold imagined "others" that are distorted to serve the purpose of reducing internal anxieties (Neumann & Hirschhorn, 1999). In this way, the self within Object Relations theory is paradoxical since, as Gomez (1997) explains, it "focuses its attention on individual experience while defining the essence of this experience as beyond the individual" (p. 212).

The resolution of anxiety within the infant depends to a large degree on the "containment" provided by what Winnicott (1965, 1971) described as the "good enough" mother—that is, a relationship in which the anxieties of the infant can be sufficiently understood and tolerated without retaliation. This psychoanalytic concept of containment has been applied in the work of Heifetz (1994) and Heifetz & Laurie (1997, 1999), in which they suggest that in the face of adaptive challenges, leaders must, by their behavior and their design of organizational structures, create a "holding environment" which provides sufficient containment of the systemic emotional dynamics engendered by the learning required to face adaptive challenges.

Klein's (1946, 1952, 1959) theories of splitting and projection reflect a fundamental assumption within psychodynamic theory that sources of energy and motivational forces are often not available to the conscious mind of individuals, even though behavior and emotion are being affected (Neumann & Hirschhorn, 1999). Hence, in order to explore the relational dynamics between individuals, we must pay attention to unconscious relational dynamics *within* individuals—that is, between different aspects of the psyche of individuals. Furthermore, the idea that the infant's capacity to manage anxiety is a function of how it is received, how its distress is interpreted by the containing mother, emphasizes the relational nature of these psychoanalytic concepts. What is formative is not the anxiety per se, but the way it is met (Phillips, 2007).

In terms of relational leadership, at the heart of a psychodynamic theory of the self is a process of self-management, often under the influence of unconscious forces that regulate disturbing affect (Miller, 1993b). The self in Object Relations theory comes to understand itself only in relation to other people; in other words, to manage our internal worlds is to manage our experience of others. If we consider such dynamics in organizational settings, then mechanisms such as splitting and projection that occur within and between individuals can become collectively held perceptions, values, and beliefs which are likely to represent a distortion or oversimplification of the external world in some way. Aspects of the external world most likely to be constructed in this way are our experiences of those immediately around us (e.g., other team members) and aspects of our environment, including the rest of the organization, customers, and other stakeholders. The familiar dynamic of scapegoating is instantly recognizable to managers from their experience of organizational life. It is not unusual for middle managers to perceive the senior team as aloof and divisive. It is not unusual for one department in an organization to have idealized or contemptuous feelings toward other departments.

To write of splitting and projection and the dynamics of how individuals and groups within organizations, society, and even internationally, can come to regard each other and how such relationships are sustained, is to begin to extend our analysis beyond the way the self is theorized and to touch on the nature of relational dynamics. As we consider accounts of relational dynamics within these three perspectives, we encounter strongly contrasting ways of construing relationship. The various ways in which the self is theorized lead to very different conceptions of human relating with considerable consequences for relational leadership theory.

THE NATURE OF RELATIONAL DYNAMICS

Relational Leadership Theory is concerned with understanding more about the "relational dynamics by which leadership is developed throughout the workplace" (Uhl-Bien, 2006, p. 672). New forms of leadership, such as shared (Pearce & Conger, 2003), distributed (Spillane, 2006), and complexity leadership (Marion & Uhl-Bien, 2001), are inherently relational to the extent that they emphasize leadership as something which is not associated with a formal role, but which can occur at all levels of an organization. This shift of focus from formally appointed leaders to leadership coming from any or all group members enhances the importance of relational dynamics within leadership studies. Shifting from studying uni-directional influence to a shared influence process requires new ways to study the complex nature of leadership processes in reciprocal and recursive social systems (Yukl, 1998). The notion of relational dynamics, as we shall now explore, varies considerably between entity and constructionist approaches. A systems psychodynamic perspective both highlights these differences and offers potentially useful conceptual depth to the discussion.

An Entity Perspective on Relational Dynamics

Consideration of relational dynamics from an entity perspective is inextricably bound up with research methodology since relating and relationships are construed in ways amenable to the forms of inquiry considered legitimate within this paradigm. Within the entity-based and objectivist paradigm that has dominated leadership, to talk of leadership is to focus on the ways leaders influence followers. Effective leadership consists of strategies for getting other people to do things that ultimately the leader wants. The focus of research is on identifying the behaviors, traits, or characteristics of leaders that can be shown to influence followers in pursuit of organizational outcomes.

These discrete entities, leaders, and followers, interact with other discrete entities, establishing relationships for the purpose of exchange, influence, and goal achievement. The focus in such models is therefore on these individuals as architects of an interpersonal relational web designed for their own purposes. In this sense, relationships are formed by entities and do not exist *a priori* to those individuals. Theories of relational leadership from an entity perspective thus focus on the minds of individuals to determine their perceptions and cognitions in the context of interpersonal relationships in which influence and exchange are the main features. This has often led to a focus on modes and styles of influence that can be operationalized and measured in systematic ways. Determining how these measures are related to desired organizational outcomes is a key aim of such theories. These variables are themselves considered to be stable entities within individuals, and their effects are not only measurable but also generalizable to larger populations in unproblematic ways.

Based on an atomistic ontology of discrete and complete mind entities, relational dynamics are understood to be constant enough over time to be measured and statistically analyzed. Reality is seen to consist of entities that are related causally and stably, requiring us to discover those causal relationships by deploying quantitative techniques, which often involve survey methods and questionnaires. Obviously, these approaches do not easily lend themselves to inquiry into on-going, unfolding dynamics as they occur within organizational settings. There is little means or cause to conceptualize such dynamics, since they would be considered outside the limits of social inquiry as defined within this perspective.

As an example that demonstrates the usefulness and the limitations of entity approaches, we can look at the most often cited empirical study within the shared leadership literature, the 2006 study by Avolio and his colleagues (Avolio, Jung, Murry, & Sivasubramaniam, 2006). Using groups of undergraduate students engaged in community volunteer projects, the study showed shared leadership to be positively correlated with self-reported ratings of effectiveness. Such studies, since replicated in various settings and industries, legitimize further inquiry into shared and distributed leadership. More detailed accounts of the actual relational dynamics within the groups, between groups, and the dynamics between the researchers and the institution could not be explored using these research methods. For example, group process was measured by items such as collective efficacy: "when we set goals, I'm sure we will achieve them'; potency: "our group expects to be known as a high performance team; cohesion: "members of our team have established a close working relationship'; and trust: "I mistrust members of my team." Measures were taken after one month and repeated toward the end of the semester. While these approaches allow for the aggregation of data and measurement of co-variance, they do not allow for any fine-grained description of the actual group processes occurring between the two time periods.

A Constructionist Perspective on Relational Dynamics

From a constructionist perspective, relationships are not conduits for the transportation of knowledge or influencing strategies between entities. Rather, they are processes in which individuals come to experience themselves, others, and other organizational phenomena through the on-going flow of intersubjective meaning-making in different cultural and social contexts. This view is central to the social constructionist focus on the dynamic processual nature of social organization (Hosking & Fineman, 1990). The focus is not on organization as a fixed entity of external administrative arrangements, but on organizing as an on-going emergent process embedded within on-going relational dynamics out of which co-ordination and change may evolve. The focus is not on leaders but on leadership processes in which coordination and change are constructed and produced. So, in this perspective, relational dynamics are central to the emergence and maintenance of leadership processes, which in turn are constitutive of and constituted by relational dynamics.

According to Hosking (1988), leadership processes are those in which:

> influential "acts of organizing" contribute to the structuring of interactions
> and relationships, activities and sentiments; processes in which definitions
> of social order are negotiated, found acceptable, implemented and re-nego-
> tiated; processes in which interdependencies are organized in ways which,
> to a greater or lesser degree, promote the values and interests of the social
> order. (p. 147)

Fletcher (2004) illustrates how this valuing process can influence what
may be recognized as leadership and what may not. She suggests that by
not paying attention to the gender and power dynamics implicit within new
forms of "post-heroic" leadership (such as shared and distributed leadership), there is a danger that such forms of leadership will either "disappear" because they are simply not recognized as leadership, or be co-opted by the mainstream managerial discourse in ways that neutralize their
radical challenge to existing practices. One of Fletcher's key points is that
certain behaviors encouraging more distributed forms of leadership are
often culturally associated with the "feminine" (e.g., empathy, community,
vulnerability, and skills of inquiry and collaboration), whereas behaviors associated with traditional "heroic" leadership (e.g., advocacy, individualism,
assertiveness, and control) are culturally associated with the "masculine."
Thus, a manager displaying behaviors that encourage the development of
distributed or shared leadership practices may not be recognized as taking
up leadership at all. This constructionist analysis reveals the value-laden
structures that underpin what may otherwise be presented as value-neutral
in social science.

Drath (2001) similarly emphasizes a constructionist perspective on relational leadership and elaborates some of the points made by Fletcher. For
Drath, thoughts, words, and actions play a central role in understanding
leadership. The question of how we know leadership when we see it—how
certain words, thoughts, and actions come to be known as leadership—
is central. Leadership is not something that exists out in the world and
impresses itself on our senses. Instead, it is leadership if we say it is, or if
certain actions come to be spoken of and commonly understood as leadership. Drath distinguishes three different principles—personal dominance,
interpersonal influence, and relational dialogue—which represent possible
ways in which leadership can be recognized.

These principles represent shared achievements because they are general knowledge principles that allow people in a particular context to organize reality, to see meaning in such a way as to label something "leadership." They are not definitions of *leadership*, but a set of taken-for-granted
rules on which people agree.

Implicit in both Fletcher and Drath's work is the assumption that, within relational dynamics, cognition is necessarily a process of valuing. Some people will perceive change positively because it supports their interests, while others will resist it. Some people will construe a facilitative approach as leadership while others will see it as weakness. Thus, "organizing processes have an intrinsically *emotional or affective texture which may be positive or negative*" (Hosking & Fineman, 1990, p. 586). The organizational literature pays little attention to these emotional processes: "What little interest there is seems largely to concentrate on 'negative' aspects such as the stressful consequences of particular organizational forms, or neurotic organizations" (Hosking & Fineman, 1990, p. 586).

Relational dynamics from a social constructionist perspective theorize affective elements in important ways. Social constructionist thinking emphasizes how context influences "emotional rules"– individuals in organizational settings will enact a set of explicit and implicit rules about what is acceptable and not in terms of the expression and experience of emotions in that context. The exclusively cognitive approach to theorizing emotion in organizations has also been supplemented by an acknowledgment that the childhood roots of adult emotional expression may influence the way emotion manifests in organizational life: "It is plausible that organizational executives will design work structures that mirror their own biographies in some way, thereby setting the basic parameters or feeling rules, for emotional expression in the organization" (Hosking & Fineman, 1990, p. 602). Thus, a systems psychodynamic perspective on relational dynamics can add considerable conceptual depth to such processes—to the ways in which the intrapsychic world of individuals manifests within group and organizational life, and vice versa.

A Systems Psychodynamic Perspective on Relational Dynamics

Like constructionism, a psychodynamic approach is concerned with the social, political, and cultural context in which organizational phenomena, such as leadership, take place. However, these links are understood as the result of a complex field of systemic forces that are psychological as well as social in origin. A systemic view requires us to pay attention to how the emotional needs of individuals and groups influence the processes, structures, and cultures which emerge and are sustained in organizations, and how these processes, structures, and cultures in turn shape the emotional experiences of individuals and groups (Petriglieri & Petriglieri, 2010) without privileging one above the other.

A psychodynamic perspective offers a counterbalance to the dominance of the entity perspective on human relating. This dominance has led to a paucity of concepts with which to describe this relational terrain. As Josselson (1996) points out, "because our speech in this realm is so restricted, we end up with a cultural mythology of human intercourse that overemphasizes the easily described phenomena of individuality and ignores or distorts interpersonal bonding" (p. 2).

A psychodynamic perspective offers depth and a means to link individuals to collectives, to address central questions within RLT, such as how leadership is produced by social interactions. As Uhl-Bien (2006) explains:

> As an outcome, the focus of investigation is on how leadership relationships are produced by social interactions. For example, relationships involve some type of connection or bond between an individual and another (a person, group, collectivity, organization, etc.). In some cases, social interactions produce these bonds, and in other cases they do not. However, we do not know why relational bonds form in some instances but not in others, or what factors contribute to formation of relational bonds. (p. 669)

Concepts such as Bion's theory of groups (1961), the theory of social defences (Jacques, 1955; Menzies, 1960), and Melanie Klein's concept of projective identification (1946) can help us see how these processes work. Therefore, I turn to these topics next. I start, however, with a discussion of the body and the idea of the individual as fully embodied. This notion links to the previous section on the contrasting ways the self is theorized and is the basis on which all subsequent theory about relational dynamics can be built.

Relational Dynamics and the Fully Embodied Individual

In contrast to entity perspectives, in which the body is problematic from a theoretical point of view, the self within a systems psychodynamic perspective is fully embodied. Phillips (1995) eloquently articulates the issues this raises for relational leadership:

> ... the mind-object is that figure in the internal world that has to believe—and go on proving, usually by seeking accomplices—that there is no such thing as a body with needs. It is a fiction invented to solve the problem of wanting, to make the turbulence disappear. The body is misleading because it leads one into relationship, and so toward the perils and ecstasies of dependence and risk; it reminds us of the existence of other people. (p. 93)

While constructionist views usefully highlight the social construction of the body in different cultural settings, a systems psychodynamic perspective highlights the ubiquity of a deeply held ambivalence to the body. Acknowledging the body reminds us of the existence of others, leads us into relationship, and exposes us to the risks entailed. Being in relation to others is potentially problematic, and in order to deal with the potential risks involved, for example rejection, acceptance, abandonment, or being overwhelmed, we as individuals might unconsciously develop strategies to reduce, avoid or defend against the possibility of such distressing affect. The work of Melanie Klein suggests that patterns of anxiety and defense in adulthood have origins in earlier phases of development. How these defenses can influence our patterns of relating in adult life is shown by the work of Ruthellen Josselson in her book *Playing Pygmalion* (2007), in which she shows how relationships within a psychodynamic perspective can exist *a priori*: "We create ourselves and our relationships in interaction with one another. We recruit people to be characters in dramas that we are enacting even as they recruit us to be characters in theirs" (p. 2).

Within the interior worlds of individuals, certain relationships, or "object-relations," still play an active dynamic role in an inner theater of characters, some of whom will be recruited in the external environment to fulfill certain roles. The implications of a relational self dictate that there is an interior drama or relational schema that exist *a priori* to current relationships. By recruiting and being recruited, we are not necessarily who we say we are, but partly what others need us to be for them, and others in turn may have aspects of themselves called forth to fulfill some of our unconscious needs. This applies in organizations, too, in which formally appointed leaders may find themselves subject to powerful projective dynamics (Hirschhorn, 1999). Managers, who have found themselves either formally or informally in a particular organizational role, are able to link early roles within the relational matrix of their families to the relational dynamics of their current roles. For instance, a child who took up a mediating role between divorcing parents might grow up to find him or herself working as a trouble-shooting expatriate in an international company called in to mediate cross-functional disputes. Hundreds of role analysis groups, including individuals sharing aspects of their personal life histories, show that correlations between formative experiences and later organizational roles are commonplace (Triest, 1999). They are also often revelatory to the individual.

The "Group as a Whole"

An important development in the systems psychodynamic understanding of relational dynamics was the elaboration of the dynamics of projection and splitting to explain group level phenomena—the concept of the group-as-a-whole (Wells, 1985). One key contributor to this development was Wilfred Bion (1961), one of the founders of the Tavistock Institute.

A key insight from Bion's work is that anxiety provoked by group membership arises from the tension between the need for autonomy and the need for belonging. To be fully ourselves, we need others, but this needing of others exposes us, as Phillips (1995) explains, to the risks that relating entails: acceptance, rejection, misunderstanding, and so forth. This suggests that group membership *per se* is problematic and exposes us to a range of dilemmas (Smith & Berg, 1987). As Bion (1961), explains: "The individual is a group animal at war, not simply with the group, but with himself for being a group animal and with those aspects of his personality that constitute his 'groupishness'" (p. 131).

Bion (1961) went on to elaborate a theory of relational dynamics within groups that has been widely influential. In a series of seven papers published between 1948 and 1951 in *Human Relations* and his book *Experiences in Groups* (1961), Bion laid out his key postulate based on the tension engendered by group membership and the external group task: that at any one time, a group could be working simultaneously at two levels. A group is a "sophisticated" or "work" group to the extent that it is working rationally on the overt task for which it was formed; at the same time, it is a "basic" group or "basic assumption" group to the extent that it is acting on one of three basic primitive unconscious assumptions (i.e., fight/flight; pairing; dependency) to which individual members contribute without awareness. In other words, the group is acting *as if* (hence the word "assumption') one of the three assumptions were true: fight/flight, in which the group members act as if there is an external enemy; pairing, in which the group acts as if something can be produced which will "save" the group; and dependency, in which the group becomes dependent on an apparently omniscient leader or idea. All of these dynamics have the potential to work in favor of task performance, for example when fight/flight dynamic encourages a group to focus its competitive energies against a competing company. However, for the most part, there is a danger that these dynamics become inimical to task performance, suggesting that attention should be paid during task performance to the extent to which a group may be "on task" and to the extent that irrational unconscious "basic assumption" group processes may hold sway.

Bion (1961) identified group level phenomena that are not simply the aggregate of individual psychologies. An individual may experience sadness, joy, or aggression, but these say as much about the group as about the individual. Two individuals apparently locked in conflict may in fact be representatives of two sub-groups, the other members of which remain silent. An individual can be induced through group processes to express anger, for example, on behalf of others, that is, to "do" the anger for the group. An individual's propensity to experience and enact certain emotions and behaviors is considered a function of the individual's "valency" to do so. The group's capacity to induce members to experience and act out something on its behalf is explained through processes such as projective identification, first elaborated by Melanie Klein in 1946.

The work of Elliot Jacques (1955) further elaborated thinking about relational dynamics by suggesting that organizations can become places where individuals seek to have their defenses maintained or contained. Certain kinds of organizational arrangements, structures, cultures, norms, and narratives can serve to protect individuals from disturbing affect. Menzies (1960) observed in her pioneering study of nursing practices that forms of work procedure protected nurses from the understandable distress evoked by work with patients. These procedures, processes, norms, or cultural inflections particular to a work context serve as what became known as "social defenses," which form a central part of the systems psychodynamic perspective. The function of leadership in this case is to ascertain to what extent these unconscious social defenses are at play and to what extent they serve or are inimical to learning and task performance. The work of Jacques suggests that individuals may seek out organizations in order to contain their defenses, while Menzies highlights the ways in which the tasks with which organizational members are engaged can in themselves be anxiety inducing. This idea has been developed further in Heifetz's description of technical and adaptive challenges and the ways in which leaders should respond (Heifetz, 1994).

An Application of Systems Psychodynamic Analysis to a Sales Organization

An example from the author's own experience can serve to illustrate some of these points. Although this description clearly pertains to practice, the purpose is the further exposition of the theoretical material presented so far.

The four business directors of a sales organization, all with profit and loss responsibility for their regions, agreed to set up a small internal recruitment department responsible for the selection of new sales people for the organization. Since the turnover of sales people was high (over 40%), this issue was a cause for concern among the directors, who competed for the limited pool of talented sales people. A shortage of sales people adversely affected revenue and profits, and directly impacted the directors' bonuses. Moreover, even though no other organization in the industry had a similar structure, this internal recruitment department (consisting of four individuals) was maintained over a number of years.

On entering the organization as a consultant-researcher, it was quickly apparent to me that there were serious concerns about the quality of the internal recruitment team. The frequency of these comments, the surprising degree of anger expressed, and the apparent unanimity of opinion, coupled with a limited scope for nuanced reflection in relation to the issue suggested, and which was later confirmed, that some form of scapegoating was present. It was hypothesized that this small department had been created for the purposes of distancing the conflict that might otherwise occur between the sales directors in competition for sales people, and it was a convenient location for projections of concerns about poor performance. Directors avoided conflict among themselves, and they projected their own anxieties about poor performance onto the four members of the team and, in particular, the manager.

It is important to note that, within a systems psychodynamic perspective, through a process of projective identification, those individuals on the receiving end of projective processes can actually begin to exhibit the very behavior that is being attributed to them. Thus, competence cannot be considered an attribute of an individual, but it is a relational concept. Just as one person may perform badly if the projections and concomitant but very subtle behaviors are sufficient to induce incompetence—what Klein called projective identification—so individuals may perform well partly because they have successfully projected their own anxieties onto someone else. Another notable feature of such dynamics is their rigidity. It took over a year of continued consultation before the senior team of this company, and in particular the sales directors, were able to let go of the need to hold the internal recruitment department in contempt.

If relational dynamics are so central to our understanding of the nature of relational forms of leadership, and they occur in the context of on-going organizational social processes (i.e., the actual day-to-day social interactions that constitute the experience of organizational members), then the question arises: What are the ways of engaging with process in order to explicate the nature of and a way of working with relational dynamics from which leadership emerges?

The following section concentrates on a description of how this might be done using a systems psychodynamic perspective. It is not intended as a description of how leaders can effectively work with relational dynamics in practice, but rather as a description of the theoretical basis of process as seen from a systems psychodynamic perspective. For this, we will keep in mind the general definition of relational leadership from the RLT model: that *relational leadership* is a social influence process through which emergent coordination (i.e., evolving social order) and change (i.e., new values, attitudes, approaches, behaviors, ideologies, etc.) are constructed and produced (Uhl-Bien, 2006). The only caveat is that we will not be applying a social constructionist lens and, hence, rather than "are constructed and produced," we will consider how social structure and change *emerge.*

HOW PROCESS IS UNDERSTOOD AND WORKED WITH

Let us start this section with a statement about the importance of a focus on process within Relational Leadership Theory (Uhl-Bien, 2006):

> The objective of RLT is to enhance our understanding of the relational dynamics—the social processes—that comprise leadership and organizing. The key question asked by RLT is: What are the relational (social) processes by which leadership emerges and operates? I contend that we have little understanding currently of these relational dynamics because the vast majority of our existing studies of leadership have neglected to focus on process (Hosking, 1988; Hunt & Dodge, 2000; Hunt & Ropo, 1998; Ropo & Hunt, 2000). Therefore, RLT is, at its core, a process theory of leadership. (p. 666)

Since process is so central to RLT, this section will focus on how a systems psychodynamic perspective can be used to engage with organizational processes leading to the emergence of both social structure and change. For example, if we set aside for a moment the key ontological and epistemological differences between entity and constructionist perspectives (e.g., whether reality lies in an individual or in a socially constructed reality) and focus on an objective of enhancing understanding about relational leadership, we can see that the biggest practical difference between the two perspectives is in how they approach, or operationalize, process. Entity perspectives, although they refer to process (e.g., social exchange, role-making), never really examine it. Approaches to study to date have been static, in the sense that, if they do address process (which is rare), these examinations are limited "snapshots" of relational realities as viewed through the perceptions and reported behaviors of respondents (most often using a few variables operationalized with survey questions) (e.g., Uhl-Bien & Maslyn, 2003). Even with a greater number and more in-depth snapshots (e.g., longitudinal study), entity methodologies are limited in their ability to capture process, which requires a more dynamic examination of relational interactions as events emerge and unfold. Probably because of this, entity perspectives have done little to highlight the processes by which relationships develop to produce effective leadership.

Hence, we now bring together previous analysis and add concepts to outline how relational processes that lead to the emergence of structure or change can be engaged with by using a systems psychodynamic perspective. The point has already been made, and is here repeated, that the ontological and epistemological assumptions of entity approaches make it hard to address process. Rather than highlighting effective methods for engaging organizational processes to enhance practice from a systems psychodynamic perspective, I outline the conceptual framework that action researchers use to address issues of practice. This approach to theory development contrasts strongly with research methods familiar to entity-based researchers for whom organizations are sites for research rather than settings for intervention.

Because of the Tavistock Institute's historical commitment to pragmatic theory (Miller & Rice, 1967) and its applied action research methodology (Miller, 1993a), research there is carried out in the context of consulting to organizations. Thus, in the text that follows, I refer to the "consultant-researcher," rather than to the "researcher." The purpose of this section is to outline the application to working with process of the various theoretical concepts from this perspective that we have discussed so far.

Working with Process in an Organizational Setting

Let us start with a statement by Miller (1989), a central figure in the development of the psychodynamic framework, that "in the field of human behavior no conceptual framework is complete without a statement of the role of the observer and his/her relation to the observed" (p. 8). Referring to the Heisenberg principle in sub-atomic physics in which electrons are perceived as either waves or particles depending on the frame of reference, Miller suggests that, in a similar fashion, researchers, consultants, and all organizational members should consider the ways in which the system influences their thoughts, feelings, and behavior and how, in turn, we might influence the system of which we are a part. For researchers hoping to explore relational dynamics in an organization, therefore, there is a requirement to pay close attention to their personal experience in role when entering and working within a system. While such requirements are not new for those familiar with qualitative research methods, the application of the psychodynamic perspective provides a rich conceptual framework from which to gather data and on the basis of which to develop theory. The use of the self as an instrument has a long tradition within psychotherapy in terms of transference and counter-transference, but this principle can be applied more widely when working in organizational contexts.

The psychodynamic perspective on the self that we described in the opening sections and the relational dynamics operating at group and organizational levels apply as much to the researcher-consultant as to organizational members. These dynamics thus inform the methods by which organizational process can be engaged with. The internal world of a social actor registers a wide range of affective data in any organizational context. What is required, if we are to make sense of our experience in a particular setting, is to be able to discern intrapsychic boundaries between feelings and thoughts, which may tell us something about the system we are part of, and feelings and thoughts which are more likely to have their genesis elsewhere. In other words, we must be able to discern what we may be "carrying" from the system and be able to distinguish it from more personal material. A researcher engaged in working with organizational process in this way will spend many years developing the skills necessary to work effectively in such settings.

To help managers and others working with organizations to do just this, the Tavistock Institute developed the group relations model. This consists of the creation of temporary institutions over several days in which individuals, members, and staff can work together to learn about the unconscious processes in groups and organizations and how these influence and are influenced by the way individuals take up their authority within their institutional roles. As Miller (1989) outlines in his description of the purpose of the Tavistock Institute, the founding of the *Human Relations* journal, and group relations "conferences," as these temporary institutions were called:

> Our central theoretical and practical interest was and remains what we later came to term "relatedness": the processes of mutual influence between individual and group, group and group, and group and organization, and, beyond that, the relatedness of organization and community to wider social systems, to society itself. (p. 7)

Objectivity within such a perspective can only be achieved by the skills of engaging with one's own subjectivity. This is only possible if the individual remains linked to the context through a focus on his/her role. It is not the experience of the particular individual, whether external consultant-researcher or the individual employee, but the experience of the individual within the organizational role that matters. If one is a tall, well-built, 50-year-old white European male entering an organization, this will attract different projections than if one is a tall, slim, 30-year-old Asian woman entering the same organization. It is critical that the consultant-researcher develops over a number of years a familiarity with the way their own personal history may be influenced by and influence the organizational dynamics of which they are a part. If the consultant-researcher is a younger brother from a family of six, then the role he comes to take up within the client system may at certain times reflect this. It is at the same time important to be aware of what projections the role of external consultant-researcher may attract. For organizational members, the role he/she occupies will be subject to a whole range of expectations and evaluations.

Being able to reliably identify the projections one is receiving within a system is only the first part of what is required. Since projection is a form of communication, the question then becomes how one reacts to them. This is why it is essential to have done what can be described as "personal" work to be aware of the types of projections one might get and our own typical reactions to these projections. It is then essential to be able to make sense of these projective dynamics in terms of the organizational challenges and to be able to develop some theory that not only explains, or describes, but provides interpretive hypotheses about the unconscious enactment of broader system wide dynamics which is manifest. To illustrate the application of these concepts, the following is a simplified example from the author's own experience.

Having spent a year working on strategic projects with a client, a new marketing director was recruited. All other team members, with the exception of the HR director, had grown up in the firm—they had never worked anywhere else. In addition, this was the first marketing director the firm had ever had. Over time, it became apparent that the HR director, also an "outsider," and the marketing director were struggling in their roles. Both support functions had to work across the territories of the sales directors, who were accustomed to having a full say in all aspects of the running of their areas. In the course of the next 6 months, the narrative around the projects changed from one of appreciation to hostility.

The data to support this came from interactions in meetings, decisions, formal, and informal statements from individuals "off-line," and in a range of emotional responses that I experienced in my role working with the senior team and working with the strategic projects. The data included interactions between senior team members, each of whom sponsored one project, and the project teams. I had access to all senior team meetings and was part of several smaller groups that met to discuss strategic issues. Extensive written notes, formal minutes, and other documentation were collected. While this process is not dissimilar to other phenomenological studies, the psychodynamic stance provides a rich conceptual framework from which to generate theory in order to produce interpretations that can then be brought back to the organization to be worked on.

Over the course of several months, it became apparent that the senior team had become frustrated with its own abilities to function effectively as a decision-making body. The projects came to be a convenient place to project the anxiety about not being able to function as a team. I also had the experience of being "set up" to fight with the marketing director, who was the most vociferous of all team members in opposition to the strategic projects. This experience provided important additional data to support a number of emerging hypotheses that linked the fine-grained dynamics I was observing to aspects of the wider organization and beyond.

Some months later at a team debriefing session, team members acknowledged that the projects, and the work I was conducting, were being scapegoated and that the marketing director was leading this attack. The aggression focused on the projects and the consultants was typical of basic assumption fight/flight dynamics and inimical to effective teamwork, since the projects were sponsored by team members in the room and yet were being spoken of as if they had an independent life. Furthermore, team members were not addressing their own concerns about their own competence in the face of a challenging business environment and the increased organizational complexity represented by the new functional heads, the HR director and the marketing director.

This account represents only a fraction of the complexity of group process encountered during this consultation process, but it gives an indication of the way a systems psychodynamic conceptual framework can be used to explore relational dynamics. From the point of view of Relational Leadership Theory, these dynamics gave rise both to social structure and to change, and can be considered relevant to the study of relational leadership.

CONCLUSIONS

A number of conclusions can be drawn from our examination based on a systems psychodynamic perspective. These address the way the self is theorized, the nature of relational dynamics in social systems, and the way process can be engaged within organizational settings.

The Way the Self Is Theorized

First, *with respect to the way the self is theorized,* a systems psychodynamic perspective provides a rich conceptual framework that can populate the theoretical landscape between the two poles of the entity and constructionist perspectives. The former limits definitions of the *self* to the thinking mind, to the contents of which the individual is assumed to have access. The latter tries to reveal the ways in which this view of the self is rooted in the aspiration to mimic the objectivism of the natural sciences and the developmental discourse of Western individualism. A systems psychodynamic perspective contributes to this debate in the following ways:

1. By bringing the body to leadership, a psychodynamic view highlights the ways in which an entity perspective abstracts out the mind as a discrete object, leaving out the aspects of the individual most likely to play a central role in relational dynamics. It is the body with its longings and desires that leads us into the fraught world of relationships, and to admit it into the scope of social science inquiry is to restore a central aspect of what it is to be human. Entity approaches, by focusing on the individual as a disembodied mind, are in danger of paying too little attention to relational processes that could provide a rich source of data on the nature of human relating. Although

social constructionist accounts contribute to RLT by revealing the relative ontological and epistemological stance of entity perspectives, a systems psychodynamic perspective adds a focus on the limitations of relational leadership theories that avoid central aspects of how and why humans relate.

2. The assumption that individuals are constantly engaged, often unconsciously, in attempts to regulate distressful affect by exporting chaos and importing order through projective processes, provides a conceptual richness for exploring the "what" and the "how" of links between individuals and their contexts which is central to RLT. Implicit within psychological processes, such as splitting and projecting, is an on-going process of self-management, implying in part that our relationships "without" are part of a process of managing difficult affect "within."

3. This way of theorizing the self—a relational self that can only know itself in relation to others—provides a powerful language for exploring the nature of shared reciprocal influence in relating. Rather than a function of personality, individual behavior can be understood as a recursive process in which behavior is induced by others and in others. Such descriptions address the demand for new conceptual frameworks that can address the nature of relational dynamics within social systems characterized by the flow and flux of on-going mutual and reciprocal influence (Yukl, 1998). Relational leadership theories require new methodologies—a systems psychodynamic perspective on the self provides the basis of one such methodology.

Relational Dynamics within a Social System

Second, with respect to *the nature of relational dynamics within a social system,* a systems psychodynamic view of relational dynamics provides the following contributions to RLT:

1. The work of Bion (1961) links relational dynamics to task complexity in important and innovative ways. While much of the narrative that surrounds new forms of relational leadership (such as shared, distributed, and complexity leadership) relates to increased complexity and ambiguity in the workplace, few theories can offer the conceptual richness and face validity of psychodynamic descriptions of how relational dynamics in a group shift in response to task related anxiety.

2. Systems psychodynamic theory provides a conceptual framework for linking individuals to group-level phenomena in ways which supplement and augment entity and constructionist perspectives. Entity-based perspectives capture group level phenomena by altering line items on survey questionnaires to take into account the group rather

than an individual manager or team member. Such approaches, however, fail to pick up the constant shifting of relational dynamics within a group, particularly in situations where the task environment is complex and challenging. Constructionist approaches to relational dynamics, while paying close attention to the meaning-making aspect of social interactions in different contexts, pay little attention to the powerful systemic emotional dynamics unleashed as groups work collaboratively on challenges requiring adaptive learning. Deploying a systems psychodynamic conceptual framework can both capture the shifting nature of relational group-level dynamics and provide the means to articulate and hypothesize the nature of systemic affect in organizations. Group level phenomena within a systems-psychodynamic perspective refers to the ways in which, for example, a group induces behavior in individual members through collective unconscious projective processes.

3. Finally, a major contribution to RLT from a systems psychodynamic perspective on relational dynamics is the notion of *a priori* patterns of relationship. Stemming from the idea that selfhood emerges from on-going patterns of relating during developmental stages, the assumption of *a priori* patterns of relationships dramatically shifts the landscape of relational dynamics. It suggests that, rather than a web of relations being entered into instrumentally for our own purposes—relationships seen as objects manipulated by the self-directed agency of self-entities—we must consider that relationships may come looking for us (and vice versa). In other words, patterns of relating within organizational settings may reflect the enactment of unconscious patterns of relating designed to defend against distress and unsettling affect. Since RLT seeks to explore the ways in which structure and change emerge in organizational settings, a systems psychodynamic framework provides rich concepts for exploring the nature of relational dynamics in complex work environments.

Engaging with Group Processes

Third is the issue of *how group process might be engaged within organizational settings*. After describing the way in which the division of labor has shifted in the workplace and the difficulty of disaggregating organizational results to specific individuals, Gronn (2003) suggests that, "In order to get to the bottom of the division of labor and what managers and leaders do, and how they accomplish it, researchers need to understand organizations in process terms, rather than as entities" (p. 30). Constructionist approaches to process within RLT focus strongly on the on-going nature of *social* processes and the unfolding meaning-making embedded within interactions in different contexts. Powerful though these approaches are for elucidating the ways in which culture, organizing, and leading, as well as organizational structure, are on-going achievements rather than static entities, a systems psychodynamic conceptual framework can add considerable insight to the study of process. It does this by theorizing a plural self with intrapsychic dynamics and thus focusing on *psychological* as well as social processes. Such an approach provides two contributions:

1. As Gronn (2003) points out, "arguably more than writers from any other theoretical standpoint, psychodynamic theorists have provided powerful explanations for how and why organization members devise elaborate patterns of defensive and resistant emotional behavior" (p. 113). As a result, psychodynamic theory of process provides a set of concepts for identifying emerging and on-going social and psychological dynamics and the defensive routines that may underpin relational dynamics of leadership.
2. Psychodynamic theory provides a set of methods for how such processes can be investigated.

The implications for taking a psychodynamic stance on process for researchers, in terms of methodology and research methods, are far-reaching. Instead of achieving objectivity through carefully designed survey methods designed to explore co-variance, objectivity is achieved by the systematic examination of one's own subjectivity within the system or context in which the study is taken. Rigor is achieved not by the degree of fidelity to statistical procedures but by testing hypotheses with those about whom theory is being developed. In the same way that entity approaches to relational leadership are limited in their capacity to capture some of the central elements of the phenomena of human relating, so, too, are research methods that stem from an entity perspective limited if they are confined by standards of what constitutes valid knowledge from the natural sciences. The implication here is that relational leadership theories such as complexity, shared, and distributed leadership may require relational research methodologies which are inclusive of those that are studied rather than rendering them as objects of study. At the heart of RLT is a relational agenda to create an "overarching framework for a variety of methods, approaches and even ontologies that explore the relational dynamics of leadership and organizing" (Uhl-Bien, 2006, p. 668). RLT highlights the central need to address issues of ontology and epistemology that underpin theories using the term *relational*, but which have very different ideas about what that word means. At the heart of those differences are debates about the nature of the self, relational dynamics, and how process can be engaged with. Adding a systems psychodynamic perspective to these debates deepens and broadens them, illuminating potential areas for future theoretical development, and raising further questions of methodology.

To conclude, a relational perspective on leadership has the potential to revolutionize leadership studies. Leadership from a psychodynamic perspective sees individuals not as entities, but as relational beings whose emergence into selfhood is mediated by relationships with others. We live and act within a complex relational field consisting of intrapsychic, interpersonal, group and intergroup level phenomena. When humans work on tasks together, the emerging patterns that inhibit or augment task performance is the "stuff" of leadership. Thus, what is often taken for leadership—the actions of individual leaders—is nothing more than the *appearance* of leadership, the surface phenomenon that constitutes smoke and mirrors to the more complex and multi-faceted relational and highly contextualized leadership phenomenon that manifests, above, below, and around the actions of individual leaders.

What this means for Relational Leadership Theory is that it must continue to provide a space in which methodologies that take account of these complex relational dynamics can be developed and legitimized. For this to happen, all researchers, whether drawing mainly on entity, social constructionist, or systems psychodynamic approaches, must be willing to explore the limits as well as the possibilities these perspectives provide. But, perhaps the real potential of relational leadership theories is best expressed through analogy. While the author doesn't make any claims to any specialized knowledge within the field of astronomy, the ways in which the development of infrared astronomical telescopes revealed for the first time the importance of the hitherto invisible dust clouds of interstellar material could have no less exciting parallels within leadership studies. Our old picture of the universe as consisting of planets and stars surrounded by empty space suddenly gave way to a view of the universe in which planetary formation and collapse could be better understood. Rather than these dust clouds being irrelevant, they held the key to understanding the dynamics of the universe. For those who have seen the photographs of deep space taken through infrared telescopes, it is hard to dispute that the universe seen that way, as well as being rendered more comprehensible, is also extraordinarily beautiful.

REFERENCES

Avolio, B. J., Jung, D.I., Murry, W., & Sivasubramaniam, N. (1996). Building highly developed teams: Focusing on shared leadership processes, efficacy, trust, and performance. In M. M. Beyerlein, D. A. Johnson, & S. T. Beyerlein (Eds.), *Advances in interdisciplinary study of work teams: Team leadership* (Vol. 3, pp. 173–209). Greenwich, CT: JAI Press.

Bertalanffy, L.V. (1950). The theory of open systems in physics and biology. *Science, 3,* 23–29.

Bion, W. R. (1961). *Experiences in groups and other papers.* New York, NY: Routledge.

Blumer, H. (1969). *Symbolic interactionism: Perspective and method.* New York, NY: Prentice Hall.

Chia, R. (2003). Organization theory as a postmodern science. In H. Tsoukas, & C. Knudsen (Eds.), *The Oxford handbook of organization theory: Meta-theoretical perspectives* (pp. 113–140). New York, NY: Oxford University Press.

Cooley, C. H. (1902). *Human nature and the social order.* New York, NY: Charles Scribner.

Drath, W. H. (2001). *The deep blue sea: Rethinking the source of leadership.* San Francisco, CA: Jossey-Bass.

Drath, W. H., McCauley, C. J., Palus, C. J., Van Velsor, E., O'Connor, M. G., & McGuire, J. B. (2008). Direction, alignment, commitment: Toward a more integrative ontology of leadership. *The Leadership Quarterly, 19,* 635–653.

Fineman, S. (1996). Emotion and organizing. In S. Clegg, C. Hardy, & W.R. Nord (Eds.), *Handbook of organization studies* (pp. 543–564). London, England: Sage Publications.

Fletcher, J. K. (2004). The paradox of post-heroic leadership: An essay on gender, power, and transformational change. *The Leadership Quarterly, 15,* 647–661.

Gergen, K. J. (1999). *An invitation to social construction.* Thousand Oaks, CA: Sage Publications.

Gergen, K. J. (2009). *Relational being: Beyond self and community.* New York, NY: Oxford University Press.

Gomez, L. (1997). *An introduction to object relations.* London, England: Free Association Books Ltd.

Gronn, P. (2003). *The New work of educational leaders: Changing leadership practice in an era of school reform.* Thousand Oaks, CA: Sage Publications.

Heifetz, R. (1994). *Leadership without easy answers.* Cambridge, MA: Harvard University Press.

Heifetz, R. A., & Laurie, D. L. (1997). The work of leadership. *Harvard Business Review,* January 1997. Reprinted in *The Best of HBR: Breakthrough Leadership,* Spring 2001, (p. 6). Cambridge, MA: Harvard Business Press.

Heifetz, R. A., & Laurie, D. L. (1999). Mobilizing adaptive work: Beyond visionary leadership. In J. A. Conger, G. M. Spreitzer, & E. E. Lawler (Eds.), *The Leaders Change Handbook* (pp. 55–86). San Francisco, CA: Jossey-Bass.

Hirschhorn, L. (1999). *The workplace within.* Cambridge, MA: The MIT Press.

Hosking, D. M. (1988). Organizing, leadership, and skilful process. *Journal of Management Studies, 25*(2), 147–166.

Hosking, D., & Fineman, S. (1990). Organizing processes. *Journal of Management Studies, 27*(6), 583–604.

Jacques, E. (1955). Social systems as a defence against persecutory and depressive anxiety. In M. Klein, P. Heimann, S. Isaacs, & R. E. Money-Kyrl (Eds.), *New directions in psychoanalysis* (pp. 478–98). London, England: Tavistock Publications.

James, W. (1890). *Principles of psychology.* New York, NY: Henry Holt.

Jordan, J. (1986). *The meaning of mutuality.* (Working Paper 23). Wellesley, MA: Wellesley College Center for Women.

Jordan, J., Kaplan, A., Miller, J. B., Stiver, I., & Surrey, J. (1991). *Women's growth in connection.* New York, NY: Guildford.

Josselson, R. (1996). *The space between us: Exploring the dimensions of human relationships.* Thousand Oaks, CA: Sage Publications.

Josselson, R. (2007). *Playing Pygmalion: How people create one another.* New York, NY: Jason Aronson.

Klein, M. (1946). Notes on some schizoid mechanisms. *International Journal of Psychoanalysis, 27,* 99–110.

Klein, M. (1952). Some theoretical conclusions regarding the emotional life of the infant. In M.

Klein, P. Heimann, S. Isaacs, & J. Riviere (Eds.), *Developments in psychoanalysis* (pp. 198–236). London, England: Hogarth Press.

Klein, M. (1959). Our adult world and its roots in infancy. *Human Relations, 12,* 291–303.

Lewin, K. (1946). Action research and minority problems. *Journal of Social Issues, 2,* 34–46.

Lewin, K. (1947). Frontiers in group dynamics: I. Concept, method and reality in social sciences; social equilibria and social change. *Human Relations, 1,* 5–41.

Lewin, K. (1950). *Field theory in social science.* New York, NY: Harper Bros.

Marion, R., & Uhl-Bien, M. (2001). Leadership in complex organizations. *The Leadership Quarterly, 12,* 389–418.

Mead, G. H. (1934). *Mind, self and society.* Chicago, IL: University of Chicago Press.

Menzies, I. E. P. (1960). A case study in the functioning of social systems as a defence against anxiety. *Human Relations, 13,* 95–121. (Reprinted as Tavistock pamphlet. Vol 3., London: England: The Tavistock Institute (1961), and in Menzies Lyth (1988), 43–85.

Miller, E. J. (1989). The 'Leicester' model: Experiential study of group and organizational processes. (Occasional paper No. 10.) London, England: The Tavistock Institute.

Miller, E. J. (1993a). *From dependency to autonomy: Studies in organization and change.* London, England: Free Association Books.

Miller, E. J. (1993b). The Human dynamic. In R. Stacey (Ed.), *Strategic thinking and the management of change: International perspectives on organizational dynamics* (pp. 98–116). London, England: Kogan Page.

Miller, E. J., & Rice, A. K. (1967). *Systems of organization: Task and sentient systems and their boundary control.* London, England: Tavistock Publications.

Miller, J. B. (1984). *The development of women's sense of self.* (Working Paper No. 12). Wellesley, MA: Wellesley College Centers for Women.

Mitchell, S. A. (1988). *Relational concepts in psychoanalysis: An integration.* Cambridge, MA: Harvard University Press.

Neumann, J. E. (2005). Kurt Lewin at the Tavistock Institute. *Educational Action Research, 13* (1), 119–135.

Neumann, J. E., & Hirschhorn, L. (1999). The challenge of integrating psychodynamic and organizational theory. *Human Relations, 19*(6), 683–695.

Pearce, C.L., & Conger, J. (2003). All those years ago: The historical underpinnings of shared leadership. In C. L. Pearce, & J. Conger (Eds.), *Shared leadership:*

Reframing the hows and whys of leadership (pp. 1–18). Thousand Oaks, CA: Sage Publications.

Petriglieri, G., & Petriglieri, J. L. (2010). Identity workspaces: The case of business schools. *Academy of Management Learning & Education, 9*(1), 44–60.

Phillips, A. (1995). *Terrors and experts*. London, England: Faber and Faber.

Phillips, A. (2007). *Winnicott*. London, England: Penguin.

Spillane, J. D. (2006). *Distributed leadership*. San Francisco, CA: Jossey-Bass.

Smith, K., & Berg, D. (1987). *Paradoxes of group life*. San Francisco, CA: Jossey-Bass.

Triest, J. (1999). The inner drama of role taking in an organization. In R. French, & R.Vince (Eds.), *Group relations, management, and organization* (pp. 209–223). New York, NY: Oxford University Press.

Uhl-Bien, M. (2006). Relational leadership theory: Exploring the social processes of leadership and organizing. *The Leadership Quarterly, 17,* 654–676.

Uhl-Bien, M., & Maslyn, J. M. (2003). Reciprocity in manager-subordinate relationship: Components, configurations, and outcomes. *Journal of Management, 29*(4), 511–532.

Wells, L., Jr. (1985). The group-as-a-whole perspective and its theoretical roots. In A. D. Colman, & M. H. Geller (Eds.), *Group relations reader* (pp. 109–126). New York, NY: A. K. Rice Institute.

Winnicott, D. (1965). *The maturational process and the facilitating environment*. New York, NY: International Universities Press.

Winnicott, D. (1971). *Playing and reality*. London, England: Brunner Routledge.

Yukl, C. A. (1998). *Leadership in organizations (4th Ed.)*. Englewood Cliffs, NJ: Prentice Hall.

CHAPTER 6

A TALE OF TWO PERSPECTIVES

An Account of Entity and Social Constructionist Approaches to "Conflict" in Leadership Development

Fiona Kennedy, Brigid Carroll, Joline Francoeur, and Brad Jackson[1]

This chapter's intention is to speak to the experience of developing a relationally orientated leadership. In so doing, we map the journey (still ongoing) towards a critical social constructionist practice among our facilitation team at Compass. This journey has involved marked shifts, debates, swings, arguments, conflict, and discoveries focusing on the differences between social constructionist and constructivist perspectives. Many of the pinch points on that journey have been created by the association between constructivist ideas and an entity perspective. That being the case, we begin by defining these terms as we have used them here. We elaborate on the implications for a conversation between the different perspectives throughout this chapter.

Advancing Relational Leadership Research, pages 175–201
Copyright © 2012 by Information Age Publishing
All rights of reproduction in any form reserved.

Both constructivism and social constructionism are concerned with meaning-making but locate this activity quite differently. Constructivism is concerned with the sense-making activity of individuals. The location of sense-making then is *within individual minds* and is concerned with an individual's perceptions and cognition. For example, one of the earliest constructivists, George Kelly (1995), developed personal construct theory that was specifically concerned with how individuals construe a unique world of experience. Social constructionism locates meaning-making in the spaces between people. Ideas, concepts, and memories are seen as arising out of social interchange and mediated through language. "All knowledge... evolves in the space between people, in the realm of the common world or the common dance" (Hoffman, 1992, p. 6). Thus, both constructivism and social constructionism take issue with the "modernist idea that a real world exists and can be known with objective certainty" (Hoffman, 1992, p. 6). However, the differences in where meaning-making are located are consequential. Accordingly, constructivism has been associated with an "entity" perspective and social constructionism with a relational perspective (Uhl-Bien, 2006). The former perspective is associated with a realist ontology viewing "individuals as separate, independent bounded entities" (p. 665). This chapter is, in part, a reminder that a realist ontology is not inherent to constructivism, and we draw attention to the difficulties of holding that distinction in the field of leadership development.

We have used the term *constructivist/entity* when a constructivist perspective seems to tilt toward a realist ontology. Indeed, we note that movement from constructivist to entity can be very hard to catch and that pinpointing the exact places where constructivism "crosses over" is not always possible. Therefore, we use the term *constructivism/entity* when elements of both perspectives are present and/or when the distinctions between them are elided.

Broadly speaking, we have discovered more of a capacity for dialogue between constructivist and social constructionist perspectives than we expected, but less of a platform for shared design, development, and practice than we might have hoped for. We use this chapter to consider why this might be the case. We will argue that the strength of the relational theory construct will lie in how it theorizes, characterizes, and delineates the "relational" (defined by us as "the space between people"), particularly in relation to more individually orientated approaches. We have made choices in how we have constructed this chapter that are important to address up front. The first is that we have assumed that it is impossible to separate epistemology from perspective, something which umbrella or parent theories such as relational leadership theory may find particularly problematic to honor. We contend that leadership development practices feed decisive epistemological directions just as much as epistemologies shape practice. With Robert Unger (2001), we argue that:

We cannot sharply distinguish the method of our ideas from their content. We cannot hold a framework of thought constant as our beliefs about the world change. Everything is on the line to the extent that anything is—only some things are more directly on the line than others. (p. 655)

This is where practice can help challenge and inform theory, for much of the "lived" difference between entity/constructivist and social constructionist perspective concerns what constitutes, privileges, and counts as knowledge.

The second choice that has affected the authors of this chapter is our strong social constructionist assumption that knowledge is inextricably embedded within situated, embodied, and contextual processes. As such, we have tried to be open about our own situated, embodied ways of working: These include the gradual awareness of epistemological differences between members of our team, our different orientations to particular relational ways of knowing, and the problems in understanding that are created when constructivist assumptions become entangled with an entity perspective. This ongoing conversation sometimes articulates new spaces and at other times conceals space, leaving us fractious and uncertain. It is fair to say that, at times, we have found ourselves "mis-hearing, misunderstanding and mis-shaping new possibilities by forcing them into already molded forms" (Bouwen & Hosking, 2000, p. 21) that are often taken for granted in the development terrain.

Finally (with another strong social construction assumption), the writers pay attention to the "storying" of the representation of our thinking and experience. We've chosen the topic of "conflict" (in quotation marks) because even the language of this is in dispute between constructivist/ entity and social constructionist perspectives. "Conflict" has been chosen because, firstly, it would be one of the staples of any type of leadership development experience; secondly, because it is a dimension of everyday relating where the construction of meaning is "very obviously in the making" (Boewen & Hosking, 2000, p. 269); and lastly, in a spirit of reflexivity, because it mirrors what we are talking about in this chapter. Additionally, we use stories as a vital part of the construction of this chapter with an account of our own Institute "story." That is, within our story, we have two separate facilitator accounts of approaching "conflict," first from a constructivist/entity perspective and then from a social construction perspective. This is followed by fragments of the stories that our program participants constructed from their participation in either developmental experience. Moreover, we are conscious of our wish to disentangle ourselves from entity perspectives which we feel have reined dominant in the leadership development field. At the same time, we welcome the voices of our constructivist colleagues in this exploration and conversation and have worked to protect the strength and authenticity of these voices in this chapter.

This chapter is divided into three parts. We start with Compass and facilitator stories in order to give a rich, thick context for our subsequent discussion, but also to bring visibility to our own understanding of constructivist/entity and social construction perspectives. Then, we compare the facilitator accounts and discuss the construction of "conflict" from each of these perspectives. Lastly, we track the implications of these differences for leadership development theory and design and the impact we see this having on leadership program developers and participants.

DEVELOPMENT OR FACILITATOR EXPERIENCE OF CONSTRUCTIVIST/ENTITY AND SOCIAL CONSTRUCTIONIST PERSPECTIVES

Our experience of growing into an institute committed to the research and development of leadership from a social construction perspective is an important context for this chapter. This, of course, intimates that our social construction orientation has been definitive and purposeful, but this is not the case. Compass started just over 5 years ago with a mandate and dedicated support from the private sector and University of Auckland to grow national and international leadership understanding and practice. From the outset, Compass's purpose included pushing the boundaries and inhabiting the cusp of the leadership research and development field. Being a university-affiliated research and development center is a critical part of Compass's identity, challenging researchers and practitioners to shape a distinctive research voice and development pedagogy. It is the development voice and pedagogy we focus on in this chapter, as relative to that, the research voice and philosophy has been more organic and less structured. There are a number of factors that account for that.

Research is done by a far smaller team (4 people) as opposed to the much larger facilitation team (approximately 10 people). While those 4 people have collaborated in different and fluid ways across time, research has been conducted in singles, pairs, or threes, either with internal or external co-authors. Different research projects and inquiries, therefore, are shaped more by smaller combinations of voices at different times and in different locations. There have been fewer opportunities amidst this different tempo, rhythm, and trajectory to be in the same room engaging with the same topic with the same urgency that is demanded by a team of facilitators sharing the responsibility for one program or workshop. Since research tends to work towards longer time frames than development deliverables, a shared commitment to social constructionism has unfolded more subtly and gradually and from far less diverse foundations.

While over time our development voice and pedagogy has become increasingly critical and social constructionist in purpose, tone and approach, it has done so through more direct talk, interaction, and more embodied encounters. Such a voice has grown from within a mixed group of academics, researchers, developers, and practitioners who could be considered as spanning the paradigmatic spectrum from positivism, through entity/constructivism, to critical social construction. This chapter is the result of numerous research, design, and planning conversations which sought to build shared thinking with respect to leadership development and how to "know" and explore the leadership terrain. Many of those conversations have not been entirely comfortable. They have often been contentious and contested and have always (ultimately) led to surprises in insight, connection, and action.

The following two accounts have been written by two of the facilitators at Compass. While those facilitators did work together in design and planning, their facilitation chiefly occurred in different programs. Consequently, they represent quite different trajectories and interventions in the name of "conflict." (Compass primarily offers 18-month programs of leadership development which encompass residential and virtual modules. Programs in the first 5 years of Compass's existence were completed for a wide range of in-house corporate, community, and open groups.) Twelve such 18-month programs were completed in that period and involved diverse sectors, such as financial services, science, sport and infrastructure, cross- sectorial programs for senior managers, CEOs, and youth, and regional programs for geographical communities. Compass works predominantly with adaptive leadership (Heifetz, 1994) for contexts of complexity (Grint, 2005) and understands leadership to be inherently relational and contextual. This has resulted in a strong emphasis on leadership as practice (Carroll, Levy, & David, 2008), leadership as identity work (Caroll & Levy, 2009), and leadership as an alternative rationality to management (Carroll et al., 2008). While programs always have their customised story and structure, they would share a commitment to fostering the reflective, creative, and strategic practices of participants in order to build a leadership that is connected and collaborative. The following two facilitator accounts give an idea of how differently it is possible to do that with respect to just one of the components, "conflict," which constitutes a vital "part" (or ongoing thread) for any Compass program.

Rachel: A Constructivist/Entity Account

Rachel is one of the facilitators who work with the cross-sectorial, open programs. Her conflict session is usually done half-way though a program and is often linked to conversation and relationship work. The rationale for linking conversation, relationship, and conflict is that first, the quality of relationships and conversations are predicated on the capability of those in leadership to shape and sustain them, and second, the quality of those conversations and relationships determine the leadership that results. In order to understand this account, picture a traditional off-site format with approximately 30 senior managers out of their offices for 3 days, doing a variety of activities and sessions in the area of conflict and conversation. Six weeks before this workshop, they filled out a conflict assessment (the TKI) and they have been promised their 'results' at this session. This is normally a 3-hour session that involves a power-point presentation, whole group discussion, and individual reflection.

While Rachel prepared each of the TKI reports for the upcoming workshop, she thought about the individuals who had completed the assessment. She wondered how many of them had found it difficult. The forced choice nature of the assessment often created a sense of frustration...one of the feelings underpinning conflict. She also wondered how many of them had discovered they were unable to follow her recommendation, creating another "pinch point" in the process. Rachel had recommended that when completing the assessment, each person reflect on their behavior across contexts and to choose responses that reflected their preferences, in general. She knew that individuals often behaved differently across contexts–especially when one context was "home" where love relationships are central. She was thinking that the discovery of how our significant relationships impact our behavioral choices around interpersonal conflict would be transparent in the workshop...and, vice versa, that our choosing to minimize relationships, allows us to behave in ways that threaten our connections to others.

As she read each report, she wondered how clearly individuals could "see themselves." She wondered if some of the assessment choices appeared culturally "taboo" or "preferred" to them. Rachel's experience in using the TKI across cultures had shown her that to effectively interpret the results, a local norm group was required. She had learned that some of the words could carry negative or positive connotations despite their being emotionally neutral.

Just prior to the workshop, Rachel reflected on her own issues regarding conflict and talked through her views and recent experiences with a trusted colleague. She wanted to "hold" a workshop space that was reflective of the participants' results and potential learning and not one that was skewed by her personal issues. Rachel expected the workshop would be seen as engaging and interesting to the participants with some "aha" moments...she expected that some of the results of the assessments would be less than "frank"... and would still provide insight to the participants. As with any self assessment, her only worry was that some participants might want to "wear" their results as a "badge"... something "set" or "immovable"... a remnant of psychological or educational assessments of the past. Sometimes participants' desires to be seen in a particular way exceeded their desire to see themselves "in a moment"... with the responsibility or burden of choice ever-present going forward...

Rachel's feelings in the workshop moved with the feelings she saw displayed on the participants' faces... she loved when they reflected curiosity and a genuine playfulness with the concepts. Although the topic of conflict often brought concern or even fear into the room, she was hopeful that looking purposefully together at conflict, in a reasonably safe environment, would generally minimize anxiety. She enjoyed the participants questioning the theory and thinking out loud about whether the simple model had something to offer them. Playing with the concepts and having the participants choose to stand in a particular part of the room to represent what they thought they would do, generally sparked a bit of fun and friendly banter amongst everyone. When it came time for the assessments to be handed out, the feelings usually changed... often, way too much like they were getting the results from a medical exam from Rachel's perspective.

As the participants read through their personal results, Rachel listened and watched intently while wandering amongst them answering individual questions. She knew from her previous interactions with the group, that some were likely to be unsettled... this seemed to be triggered around the preferred, self-selected strategy to avoid conflict. The word "avoid" seemed to be contaminated, somehow... making the strategy "unpopular" in word but not in action. She watched and waited to see what would "pop"... the "pop"or pushing back generally came from those participants who perceived their results were not representative of the way they see themselves. They would "push back" at the assessment, questioning the theory and the process, denying that the results had captured their preferences. Rachel accepted their push back and asked if the group could explore what conflicts they had reflected upon when they completed the assessment. Exploring what they had in their heads about a particular conflict situation and then, looking at the assessment results, often showed an alignment. In this conversation, Rachel tried to provide enough space for individuals who completed the inventory according to how they would like to see themselves responding to conflict but not as they actually did. She tried to help them own their attempt at self-deception and to go beyond it.

We present Rachel's story as indicative of, not only what a session on conflict and by extrapolation leadership development, looks and feels like, but also as indicative of how assumptions that underpin thinking and working from a constructivist perspective move, almost "naturally," into an entity perspective. Accordingly, we want to talk to meaning-making, the importance of the self or individual, the use of models, tools, and technologies, and the capture of knowledge as core tenets of the perspective that constitutes Rachel's account.

As we have noted earlier, a concern with the particular ways that individuals construe experience is at the heart of the constructivist perspective. Constructivist psychologist Dorothy Rowe suggests that the privilege of dominant social groups is challenged by the assumption that truth is only known through our interpretations. For example, in her address to the 10th International Congress on Personal Construct Psychology, Rowe (1996) reminded her colleagues of the historic fate of those who construe meaning in ways that challenge prevailing social beliefs. She drew attention to "...the history of the persecution of men and women who questioned the existence of absolute truths, or who wished to impose a different absolute truth from the one currently imposed by those in power" (p. 11). Thus, the constructivist argument—that realities are produced and confirmed in minds as individuals engage with the world—can be seen as a challenge to a realist ontology. However, in the practice of leadership and organizational development, constructivist ideas invariably move in a realistic direction, raising influential ideas about individuals and their autonomy to act. To the extent that "entities can be distinguished from other entities (i.e., people) and the environment," one can contemplate a spectator-like relationship to the social world (Sampson, 1998; Steier, 1991). Relating is viewed as an individual act (Uhl-Bien, 2006, p. 665), and therefore leadership development involves the development of individual *selves*. Self-examination (or what we might more commonly call self-development) then becomes the foundation for developing leadership. Further, the language of self-examination locates this work as internal to individuals. As Rachel puts it, participants in leadership development are "exploring what they had in their heads."

As we noted in the introduction to this chapter, a realist ontology is not at all consistent with constructivist assumptions. Further, holding a space where constructivism is not automatically linked to mainstream ontological assumptions has been vital for our facilitation team because seeing one another in terms of finite categories that don't quite fit produces a sense of disrespect in our conversation. We would like to continue holding that space quite strongly because we suspect that there is much more fertile conversation to be had between constructivist-oriented and social constructionist-oriented researchers and practitioners.

Having said that, we find that the tools and methods associated with a constructivist perspective, and that are used in leadership development, move things straight to the middle of the realist camp. In order to get at what is in people's heads, entity/constructivist approaches tend to use models, tools, and technologies. Thus, when Rachel "does" conflict, she uses the Thomas Killman Inventory (TKI) to help participants access their "pre-ferred behaviour in interpersonal conflict situations–that is, situations in which the concerns of two people appear to be incompatible." The TKI considers behavior along the dimensions of assertiveness and cooperative-ness in order to define five specific methods or strategies (avoiding, ac-commodating, compromising, competing, and collaborating) for dealing with conflict. Thus, the TKI could be seen as a constructivist tool because the feedback is based entirely on an individual's self- ratings. Tools such as this are congruent with constructivist assumptions because they set out to surface and make sense of individual "contents of mind." Rachel's account includes the notion of "effectively interpret[ing] the *results*...," suggesting that such knowledge can be clearly identified and codified. She also uses the language of "denial" and "self-deception," suggesting that "truth" and "reality" are unproblematic and attainable.

Methods such as the TKI contribute to ideas that leadership is a "well delineated, static and in many cases, universal set of dimensions" (Conger & Toegal as cited in Ford & Harding, 2008, p. 483). Indeed, Rachel draws attention to the propensity for participants to assume that the categories for understanding conflict are permanently fastened to themselves:

> As with any self assessment, her only worry was that some participants might want to "wear" their results as a "badge"...something "set" or "immov-able"...a remnant of psychological or educational assessments of the past.

Accordingly methods that promote the development of *self* through ad-vancing the Socratic quest to "know thyself" become the tools of leader-ship development practice. "Seeing" the contents of mind, and activities such as changing mental models, shifting perceptions, changing "systems of belief," the development of emotional intelligence and reflective prac-tices capture the "know thyself/construct thyself" mood of constructivist thought in popular leadership development. Thus, as Rachel prepares for the workshop, she wonders "how *clearly* individuals could 'see themselves,'" and about the "negative or positive connotations" in the wording of the TKI. Her commentary suggests that a "true," "emotionally neutral" view of self is both desirable and possible.

These ideas are built on a separation between self and environment, sup-porting the possibility that individuals can step *outside* their environment in order to first know it and then act upon it. That is why Rachel's preparation for the workshop includes developing a context where her biases are mini-mized and controlled. She visits a trusted colleague in preparation for the workshop in order to foster a state of emotional neutrality. Her professional responsibility is associated with making space for a conversation that is not "skewed" or tainted by her own needs or judgment of good or bad, and holding her own unique history separate from those of her participants. Managing this separation is understood to contribute to leadership development experience that is more effective than would be possible without this preparatory work.

Meg: A Social Constructionist Account

Meg is a facilitator who primarily works on the organizational, as opposed to cross-sectorial, programs. She also has a research role and consciously tries to integrate her design, development, and research thinking and practice. This session would again be likely to occur at the mid-way point of a program. It would not be entitled "conflict" at all and would likely be part of an adaptive leadership process experience aiming to build the leadership required for contexts of complexity and innovation. Most often, this session is designed from something experiential where program participants have begun a leadership initiative in their organizational context and need new ways of thinking and working adaptively beyond the conventional norms of organizational life. This work unfolds over a day, where parts of the material are presented, discussed, and then tested out by participants to construct a very fluid, experiential, and connected process.

> Meg had been working with her participants in their online environment. She was part of their journey and felt both the thrill of fostering energy alongside the disappointment of seeing momentum die. The residential coming up was going to look at adaptive leadership and how leadership needed to hold and shape spaces with others. She was playing with a whole set of words in her mind that once she might have collected under the umbrella of conflict, but now she wanted to make room for their nuances so she thought of them as disequilibrium, disruption, unsettling, tension, and doubt. She prepared for the residential by collecting and building metaphors through pictures. She knew she couldn't make assumptions about how the group would arrive, what would spark, and what they would take to work with, so she aimed to work with broad and evocative continuums. The metaphors this time were around different states of clay and heat and the leadership energy that could create newness. This part of design was always intense for her. She would find an edge not knowing how a group would work with concepts or where they would take the metaphors and pictures and how they would adapt them. She would have to trust in what happened in the moment as context, participants, facilitation, words, and images came together. She had learned to trust that whatever happened would provide more than enough depth and richness to work with.
>
> The day began in an exploratory way. Each member of a group had to assess how far their group had got with their work using a series of pictures representing different constructs of clay. Some groups hadn't got their clay out of the packet and others felt ready to fire an already completed "object." They

were working with the metaphor very readily and happily but no surprises yet. Then, a group disagreed... some had thought they were well on the way to producing something and one thought they hadn't touched the real guts of their work... all at once tension was in the room. Other groups began to feel they could risk divergence of opinions and what looked like homogenous and compliant groups begin to articulate and even embody difference. Then the temperature series of pictures was introduced... the importance of unsettling too easy and automatic ways of being and "warming" things up enough so that the energy of what was latent... frustration, withdrawal, passion... could be worked with. Groups were talking differently, participants were risking new ways of being with each other, emotion was present in all sorts of ways. Conflict was present and participants weren't learning about it, they were learning through it. That continued through the day and would flow through to the improvisation, experimentation and action parts of adaptive leadership work.

Meg had to be as adaptive as the material she was working with. She could only do this work by being interdependent with the rest of the facilitation team around her (as they saw things she didn't and brought their own difference into the room in vital ways) and participants who after all were their own experts on themselves, their contexts and the difference they wanted to bring to their leadership. She found it exhausting as sometimes inevitably she would make the "wrong" intervention, mis-read a moment or get stuck and she had to live with those like anyone. She was always on an edge... of both adrenalin and fear... as the energy in this kind of process was a problematic, shifting and critical kind of energy. People would leave with questions and not answers and there were always different capacities in this. People would feel a whole lot of things that would take time to make sense of. It felt like lifting the lid on things, making things messy and complicated, and inviting different selves and "realities" out of hidden places. But at the same time it felt undeniably "real." Like catching the feel and tempo of real leadership work in that very room and stretching and growing people to find extra resources and capacity and strength to do this work.

Since Meg's account follows Rachel's, we are in a position to juxtapose the social constructionist assumptions and facilitator practices of Meg with those Rachel identified and discussed in the previous entity/constructivist section. We identify the power of the "social," the assumption that the "self" is always in relationship to others, the embedding of knowledge in discourse and power, and the use of disruption and edges to challenge and extend existing and accepted "realities," as core to social construction thinking and practice.

While constructivism focuses on the intentionality of individual minds, social constructionism focuses on the shaping of our minds by culture (Crotty, 1998). Social constructionism moves away from the individual as the site of attention, arguing that meaning-making occurs *between*–rather than *within*–individuals. *Social constructionism* can be differentiated from the more general term *constructionism* because of its attention to the social nature of construction. Lynn Hoffmann (1992) addresses where meaning-making is assumed to occur when she describes social constructionist approaches:

> Social construction theorists see ideas, concepts and memories arising from social interchange and mediated through language. All knowledge...evolves in the spaces between people, in the realm of the "common world" or the "common dance." (p. 8)

Social constructionist accounts are important to leadership development because they deliver necessary reminders that the self-contained and -centered individual is a fiction, that we are always embedded in interactions, that others enable and constrain us, and that we cannot live our lives apart "from such an ongoing stream of engagements" (Shotter & Lannamann, 2002, p. 601). *Critical* social constructionism takes up social constructionist assumptions but is particularly attuned to power relations. Here, attention is paid to the silent power of practices that shape contemporary culture and the "necessity" and "rightness" attributed to routines that we anticipate and know (Ospina & Sorenson, 2006; Unger, 2001).

From a critical social constructionist perspective, the practices by which we customarily know about our social world are immediately called into question. While our work in this area feels new and experimental we can identify ways of focusing attention that help to develop a social constructionist practice and that can be contrasted with a constructivist approach. Ruffling things up and going against the grain is one such practice. Thus, Meg is described as wanting to find an edge. One of her intentions is to warm things up in order to unsettle "too easy and automatic ways of being." One of the implications of disturbing the taken-for- granted is that Meg is faced with the knowledge that she "cannot know how a group would work with concepts..." Therefore her work involves engaging with others in the face of unpredictability, managing the "paradoxical 'knowing and not knowing,' and being in control and not being in control at the same time" (Christensen as cited in Stacey & Griffin, 2005, p. 302). Meg and the participants must work with the edges of fear and adrenaline that are produced by the uncertainties of holding an emergent view of leadership development. Thus, while Rachel's work involves cooling things down and mitigating or at least smoothing the potential edges, Meg's work involves moving into unpredictable terrain.

Second, Meg is looking for cracks or spaces that can enrich, disrupt, and complicate meaning. Instead of more tangible and rational models, tools, and technologies, she uses conceptual and discursive ways of knowing such as metaphor, imagery, and symbols to stimulate and construct meaning in a development context. Her preparatory work involves finding ways to disturb the solidarity of taken-for-granted language, such as the term "conflict" and the expectations that are "naturally" called up by this term. So, she resists gathering up diverse facets of human experience under a single unifying concept such as "conflict," and she "makes room for nuances" that have been partially concealed by "umbrella" language by building a rich and diverse store of language terms such as disequilibrium, unsettling, disruption, and doubt. Through this activity, she widens and complicates the conflict terrain. Thus, she is concerned with *"inviting different selves and realities out of hidden places"* through a wide array of discursive resources.

Her involvement is focused in the present moment and with dynamics that are between people rather than within individuals, reflecting a different understanding of what constitutes knowledge and where to find it. The most critical dimensions of her facilitation cannot be planned out ahead of time. As the narrative suggests, Meg engages with design work *"not knowing how a group would work with concepts or where they would take the metaphors and pictures and how they would adapt them."* While Rachel can be reassured by her wealth of knowledge 'about' conflict styles, Meg is working with local conditions in the present. A social constructionist practice asks facilitators to work without templates that bring a sense of order and predictability to their development work. This practice reflects the assumption that "reality" is constructed between people in the present. The premise of development includes making those processes visible. As this occurs, those who share an interaction can begin to recognize their existing practices and then experiment and adapt, making room for something new.

Different notions of *inside* and *outside* structure this account. In social constructionism, there is a presumption of interdependence, with no one standing outside the interaction of which they are a part (Stacey, 2001). So, in contrast to Rachel, who purposefully separates her own issues in order to be available for participants, Meg assumes a position of "interdependen[ce] with the rest of the facilitation team . . . and participants . . . " Meg is 'in there' just like everybody else, discovering and complicating things, making mistakes as she goes along. Such an assumption equally applies to the focus of this work (in this case conflict). Conflict is framed as being constructed through an interdependent interaction or process and not, as in Rachel's account, with respect to a pre-existing preference that a self brings into a group. Consequently, as Meg states, participants aren't "learning about it [conflict] . . . .but learning through it." Meg, then, is as "inside" the process as anyone else and any perceived facilitator detachment might be seen as a fiction produced by dominant theories about the individual in social life.

COMPARING ENTITY AND SOCIAL CONSTRUCTIONIST LEADERSHIP DEVELOPMENT PRACTICE

For simplicity of discussion at this point, we have constructed Table 6.1 to highlight the key elements of the entity/constructivist and social construction perspectives from a design and facilitation viewpoint. Many of these points have been discussed in the previous section, but we wanted to make some further broad comparisons. These comparisons will be important as we discuss the implications of these differences for leadership, leadership development and relational leadership theory specifically.

TABLE 6.1   A Comparison of the Constructivist/Entity and Social Constructionist Accounts

Dimension	Constructivist (Rachel)	Social Constructionist (Meg)
development material	• self-assessment conflict inventory (TKI) • theory • personalized data report	• metaphors • discourse • interaction
location of conflict	in completing the inventory, the data, and participants	in the room, in the moment, and in the facilitators
temporality	past personal history across contexts with interpersonal conflict	conflict in the present
facilitator role	• exploration guide • holder of development space • participant care	• designer of conceptual material • holder of development space • catalyst
facilitator voice	• experienced user of inventory • neutral, calm, encouraging, responsive	• embedded in group as much as is possible • source of energy, power, and disruption • precipitating reactions
facilitator preparation	• external "supervision" prior to session—"grounding" • linking to ongoing development trajectory • identifying those who may be unsettled by their results	• linking to ongoing development trajectory • checking in with fellow facilitators • searching for edges in language, metaphors, and concepts • focus on "in the moment" reflexivity
facilitator assumptions	• self-assessments carry results that often reflect how participants wish to be seen by others • working "inside-out" or working with internal assumptions/ perceptions and self limiting	• facilitator as disruptor • working "outside in" or seeing/ naming what is in room to enable wider choices

(continued)

TABLE 6.1 A Comparison of the Constructivist/Entity and Social Constructionist Accounts (continued)

Dimension	Constructivist (Rachel)	Social Constructionist (Meg)
underlying metaphor	Interpersonal conflict as a vehicle for extending a leader's personal options and improving relationship experiences	conflict as a vehicle for facilitating leadership work/ action
risks (as perceived by each facilitator)	• some ways of behaving when experiencing conflict remain less desirable and less positive • participants like their results so much that they take them as being "given"—"badges" • anxiety prevents personal exploration	• participants will learn radically different things from same experience • the discomfort of conflict carries forward into wider development process • the unpredictability of working adaptively
under-developed	• the collective/group • what's in the moment	• the "I" story • past personal histories
purpose	"using TKI self-perceptions for participants to see themselves, others and conflict differently"	"keeping things in motion for participants to experience being in leadership differently"

Placed side by side, these two perspectives can be seen as quite radically distinctive approaches. This is most strongly highlighted with respect to the underlying metaphors. The entity/constructivist column positions itself as primarily personal development, whereas the corresponding social constructionist column understands itself in terms of fostering a collective, adaptive process. Another way of saying this is that entity/constructivist approaches are orientated at building the individual capability of *leaders*, while social construction is engaged in building the collective capacity for leadership (Van & McCauley, 2004). The above proposition gives us some insight into what presents as a cohesive and interlinked series of dimensions through each column.

If a personal development imperative sits at the heart of entity/constructivist approaches then providing self-assessment material, examining one's self history with conflict, and facilitating greater awareness of personal triggers, motivations, and preferences would seem like the place for new learning. Similarly, facilitators who boundary their own selves in this work, to better focus on and work with the unfolding stories of their participants, as Rachel does, act in ways that are highly congruent with this imperative. The purpose descriptors at the end of the table indicate that the power of this approach lies in a greater "seeing" of self in order to differently enter relationships with others. If that were successful, then one might imagine someone in a leader position who was sensitized to his/her own drivers of conflict, able to utilize a range of conflict modes, and confident in engaging with conflict, as well as structuring or regulating conflict for others.

However, if building collective and adaptive capacity characterizes the social construction process, then the emphasis on creating and sustaining powerful collective interaction, bringing disruption and energy and being prepared to be a catalyst equally addresses social construction assumptions about where the leadership and learning can occur. In such a case, bringing disruption and energy into the present creates the opportunity for groups/collectives to capture the choices, decisions and dynamics that have constituted (or not) the conflict required to shift patterns of thinking and doing. The need for a facilitator like Meg to be ready to be some kind of catalyst in such work also makes sense. The language of movement in the social construction purpose row reflects the assumption that each new moment brings the potential to enact existing patterns or improvise differently, and that leadership (or not) is created by a sequence of such choices.

LEADERSHIP DEVELOPMENT PARTICIPANTS TALK OF THEIR CONFLICT WORK

For the most part, we would argue that participants in our programs are largely unaware of the different perspectives that inform and delineate their development space. The programs from which the following data comes involved either a constructivist or social constructionist approach to conflict in leadership development. Consequently, participants aren't in a position to compare one with another. Having said that, participant conversations directly after these workshops do indicate something of the immediate impact of this work on their language and thinking and the very different nuances entailed in constructivist and social constructionist approaches. We are not drawing on an extensive and completed data project and analysis here, but rather are indicating the general nature of the response to the accounts narrated earlier. This data comes from the online learning platforms which support each of Compass's programs. The bulk of the conversation here was initiated by participants as they made sense of what conflict work had meant to them.

Talk from Rachel's Conflict Session

The general discourse of participants responding to Rachel's session is focused most strongly on the use of the tool (TKI). Some use the freighted language of *"results," "outcomes," "assessment," "test,"* and *"measurement".* Thus, they breathe life into the language of science and instrumental rationality which remains dominant in both education and organizations.

> At first the biggest impact was talking through the results of the TKI assessment. I realized why I was getting certain outcomes at work and why I felt like I was not adding value, and also I understood better the feedback I had received from supervisors in the past about trying to be more assertive.

> The TKI model was interesting but to me does not go far enough. If we could I would love to do a **test** that **measures** my adaptability... When entering into a conflict situation you may have days to think about it or you may have to make the above assessment in a split second. So I would rather **know** how well I can make that assessment under pressure and then how well I can actually adopt the strategy.

So, while the TKI is based on constructivist assumptions, the *method* sounds out the "big round shining truths" and "little tick-tock-tick-tock truths [of objectivist science] that keep repeating themselves in the corner" (Kelly, 1977, p. 227). Indeed, in the second quote, the desire for scientific and objective truth grows louder as seen with the participant who proposes "the TKI... does not go far enough... I would *love* to do a *test* that *measures* my adaptability." She anticipates instruments and expertise that *goes further,* delivering up more objective knowledge, giving her an even more detailed set of information about what is possible for her –and what is not– as she moves into the future. The use of the tool seems to reaffirm the hope of "so-called unbiased analysis of data" (Bradbury and Lichtenstein, 2000. p. 555) that can reveal herself to herself in ways that presumably have some real authority. That is, the tool, rather than providing insight into how one is constructing one's experience (with all the nuance and contextuality that this implies) instead surreptitiously instills the notion that there is an objective set of options that can be categorized and assessed with an accuracy that is worthy of special attention.

Paradoxically, while the intent may be to create options for individuals, a constructivist orientation may have the effect of constraining options they see for themselves because it focuses them on only their role in a situation of conflict. The following data suggest that participants are inclined to treat the five specific methods or strategies for dealing with conflict as a set of static behaviors that don't have relational or contextual dimensions. All possibilities are presumed to be accounted for. Accordingly some of our participants consider the scope of possibilities for themselves with respect to the limited set of pre-determined categories used in the TKI:

> I'm trying to operate more in collaboration and compromise and less in avoidance and accommodate.

> I find myself thinking about the diagram, and trying to work out whether I am compromising (lose/lose) or collaborating or accommodating or avoiding or competing and making an active decision to move into another zone depending on how I feel about a situation.

> I saw in the post a bit of solution-giving (assertive-competing) and collaboration (asking questions).

> Assertiveness is important...for me, I've found it's about changing the assertiveness from competitive to collaborative...I see this as important for you too Rupert—highly assertive but presently operating in competing.

While this could be interpreted as constraining choice over conflict options, equally we could interpret the knowledge of five conflict styles as concrete and manageable enough for most of the participants to realize that they could be different in how they approached this thing called *conflict.* Most of the above statements indicate that participants feel they have some new options for responding in conflict situations.

Earlier, we introduced the separation of self and other, self and environment as an assumption that underpins constructivist epistemology. This separation implies that one can stand "outside" interactions in order to manage or shift realities in an intentional and designed way. Hayek (1982) uses the term "constructivist rationalism" (p. 6) to describe the familiar relationship where constructivist assumptions are bound up with concepts related to intentionality and "deliberate human design" (p. 501). He has drawn attention to the tight relationship between constructivist epistemology and rationalist approaches to the future. Participants' comments speak to this relationship, suggesting that their responses to conflict situations are "thought first" in order to influence a desired outcome. They suggest that responses are selected before they happen, from a range of possible options:

> ...so there's a time to bring assertiveness into the mix and close the loop...I've been trying to strike a balance between compete, compromise, accommodate and collaborate...it's picking when to be in each of the zones...

> ...as you say it's picking when to be in each of the zones, picking battles? As silly as it sounds, it is situational leadership...

Again this could be interpreted two ways: as inviting individuals to "fix" their options before they are even in a grounded relational context, or as inviting them to work consciously and intentionally in preparing themselves to be different. Regardless of which interpretation is favored, participants seem willing and prepared to undertake such work.

Talk from Meg's Conflict Experience

Not surprisingly, online comments from participants in Meg's conflict workshops reflect some of the themes that we have connected with social constructionist assumptions. For example, some comments draw attention to unsettling fixed categories and making space for dimensions of experience that might otherwise be concealed. The participant below says that his expectations for a conflict-oriented workshop were disturbed. He says that his predictions about the sort of conversation and activity that would take place were thwarted:

> Big shifts in my understanding, but not related to the things I thought were on the agenda (e.g., voice/conflict). Rather in relation to the group dynamics, the exertion of influence, collective mood, stuff like that.

Indeed, he has remembered the collective dynamics in the moment, an experience that does not sit easily with the chunking of time and material that is traditionally associated with a learning agenda.

The visibility of language and its power to constitute a new reality caught the attention of another participant:

> The thing I mostly enjoyed was learning new languaging. This has really helped me as now I can actually name it whereas before you know what it is but don't know what it's called.

The "languaging" she is referring to is not preset or standardized categories but imagery and metaphor. In this case, imagery and metaphor have given existence and form to what this participant has previously known but has been unable to articulate. Thus, she addresses the constitutive view of language and its capacity to speak things into existence.

While participants who have worked with the TKI deal in the solidarity of the constructs associated with that instrument, some participants in the social constructionist workshop can be "heard" unsettling fixed categories and seemingly robust truths. For example, both of the participants speaking below are engaged in processes of reflection and sense-making in how to work with these concepts. The work of sense-making has not been structured for them:

> It's left me doing lots of thinking ... I have been particularly thinking about the concept of disequilibrium and my reaction/responses to that 'heat.' Lots more to think about ...

> The perspective of conflict as creative and the double dichotomy of emotion and analysis to define dialogue, debate, relationship, ritual. I am not sure where I will take this but it is a new way of seeing for me.

While this could also be interpreted as not being able to translate the experience and thinking into new practice, the statements do indicate a mindset that is more open to new possibilities and therefore likely to lead to new forms of leadership action.

Another participant reflects on the same workshop. She tells a story to capture the notion of the movement and shift of disruption/disequilibrium:

> A week ago I had a conversation with a colleague at work. It started off when they emailed me an article about business (pretty dry, self-evident, do-it-yourself type thing). I read, said "ho- hum," and mailed back a few things that I thought gave interesting points of view on the matter. Back came a totally dismissive reply: Well, totally instructive on how not to have a conversation (all sorts of excuses possible), but anyway decided to revisit this with this person today... We each spoke about what was really sitting behind our words —about other conversations that preceded this lot involving judgements of coping and busyness, about resentments of being told what to do all the time by everyone, and so on for a couple of hours. But in the end it was like that Woody Allen skit where two people are having a conversation in bed and then suddenly in there also are the mothers and fathers and grand-fathers and everyone else whose voices are impacting on the present moment...

Her story appears to start with what once was existing and fixed practice (*"I read, said 'ho-hum'"*) to elicit what was an expected and predictable reply conversation (*"all sorts of excuses possible"*). What brings in the unpredictable is a choice to *"revisit"* the conversation and embark on it differently. The "differently" is about speaking what sounds like difficult truth telling (*"what was really sitting behind our words"*). That kind of speaking precipitates a shared history (*"other conversations that preceded this lot"*), a sense-making of choices already made (*"judgements of coping and busyness"*), and a connection to an embodied response (*"resentments of being told what to do all the time by everyone"*) that sounds a lot like conflict. The ending (*"like that Woody Allen skit"*) is a discovery that different "selves and realities" were somehow invited in and contributed to the sense of shifting what was possible in that relationship and in that conversation.

Neither selection of data can validate or legitimize one perspective over the other. What they can do, however, is attest to the capacity of each approach to foster a different kind of conversation, elicit a different kind of cognitive and embodied response, and in effect do a very different kind of work. They confirm that choices of epistemology and perspective are not just games that researchers play, but are decisions that set possible futures in motion. It is those alternative trajectories and possibilities that we wish to engage within the following section.

Implications

A number of implications for the theory, design, and facilitation of leadership development programs and for the relational theory of leadership are suggested by this discussion. We would like to use this section to engage with those implications for theory and practice, and we address each in turn. Our intention in this section is to firstly open up further choice and possibilities in how leadership development is understood and practiced, secondly to make our contribution to the robustness of relational leadership theory, and thirdly to defend and extend its capacity to challenge more individualist notions of leadership.

Implications for Leadership Development Theory and Practice

One hope we would have for people reading this chapter is that they become more aware of the pervasiveness of entity thinking. While constructivist and social constructionist perspectives potentially disrupt totalizing ideas, developing a conversation between these perspectives has shown the extent to which entity thinking creeps into development practice and is driven into the basic structures of such work. This chapter is designed to show that our encounter with the manifestations of these ideas is an emergent, stumbling, back and forth story. For example, no one on our team is exempt from "finding" themselves using static dimensions to describe the work of leadership. Each of us continues to use constructs that perpetuate objectivism, not seeing through them until we bang up against them, suddenly catching sight of implications that had been invisible, only moments before. Further, it is easy for those of us who identify strongly with social constructionism to "miss" our constructivist colleagues, focusing on the presence of entity thinking so that we don't see where we can think and work together.

In quite radical contrast, social constructionist practice is showing that story-lines bring a certain magic into the development process. Stories build in conversations and offer detours into unexpected terrain. Through these detours, new possibilities are sometimes encountered and worlds have become enriched and expanded. However, we are also learning that entity thinking is inhospitable to this process, that the legacy of entity thinking lives on in the very structure of development programmes and that the potential in constructivist perspectives seem to be closed out by the methods of mainstream leadership development. Beyond methods such as the TKI, it is common for leadership development to 'do' particular content by way of time-bound modules, lead by particular subject experts who may come and leave when their bit is 'done.' These familiar practices construe a world of bounded, finite concepts where knowledge is something that can be stored or transferred, moved from one place to another like a parcel.

These practices interrupt the build of story-lines and infer a mechanistic metaphor for the processes of change and development.

Social constructionism invites facilitators to increasingly address questions of continuity, movement and flow in the design of their programs and to make such issues visible for participants. For example, in our own practice we use the language of 'joined-up-action' to describe leadership practice, in order to suggest the links between the individual and the social, and one piece of story with another. That means facilitation practices include listening for threads that might connect one conversation with another, asking questions that might help enliven those connections and engaging with those threads over long periods of time. This also involves paying more attention than ever to shaping a larger story for workshops and for designing workshops that are not social constructionist 'for a bit' or 'just a bit,' but that hold constant, pervasive social constructionist attention.

When difference is recognized and held between entity/constructivist and social constructionist leadership development and practice, then what is held as established practice is quite markedly unsettled on a number of dimensions. In our own development practice for instance, the gradual elimination of topics, skills, and tools (the building blocks of entity perspectives) with story, metaphor, and experience present new issues of communication and translation. While participants in programs can be initially mystified and baffled by shifting attention from what is more concrete and familiar (entities such as selves), then equally they can be surprised and entranced by the capacity to see what is more intangible (conversation, relationship, interaction). While the lessening of reliance on order, linearity, and rationality in the learning process can be challenging, it nonetheless can deliver a taste of a genuine alternative to mainstream organizational functioning that rewards participants' involvement. However, for those outside of the program but connected to participants (such as sponsors of development programs, work teams, those who participants report to, and their colleagues), it can be ambiguous and exceedingly complex to understand the trajectory of a program and to gain access to what is being experienced.

Moreover leadership development from a social construction perspective can't easily (and wouldn't want to) use the same reporting, measurement, and evaluation tools that are readily linked with development for an entity/constructivist perspective. Such tools don't relate to the spaces in between people where collective leadership builds. Thus, our facilitation team has moved from questionnaires to interviews and observations, from rankings to stories, and from competency-type frameworks to accounts and descriptions of interactions. Indeed, participants are not asked for numbers but metaphors to capture their developmental understanding. We find then that epistemology and theory eventually play out far beyond the participant development space into how program proposals, updates, and assessments are constructed.

Social constructionist ways of working tend to speak an unfamiliar language and follow a logic that disturbs the expectations of partners and participating organizations. We have experienced advantages and disadvantages to this. Anxiety and confusion about what we are doing and why can make it difficult for program champions who are working inside participating organizations to sustain confidence and support. However the development often spills out beyond participants, contributing to the development of other organizational members and stimulating an interest in further programs, thereby increasing collective learning and capacity. With this in mind, we are about to bring together program sponsors from different organizations who have completed social-constructionist oriented leadership programs. For the first time, we will embark on conversations about the experience and meaning-making from the various perspectives of some quite different stakeholders.

This takes us to the issue of how social constructionist facilitators and practitioners need to be supported in their facilitation practice. Returning to our narratives helps give us insight here. The narrative accounts suggest that Rachel supports herself through a friendship that is loosely akin to a supervisory relationship—a relational practice that is grounded in long-standing therapeutic traditions. While our narratives do not address what happens 'after' a session for Rachel, one assumes that she will continue to use some sort of loose supervisory process as a way of debriefing, refocusing and thinking about 'what next.' Meg, on the other hand, starts out in conversation with herself and then with her co-facilitators. She is immersed in the possibilities of a story-line "playing with a whole set of words in her mind." As we have noted earlier, from a social constructionist perspective, there is no 'outside of interaction,' and therefore Meg cannot return to some 'outside' or 'neutral' space after the workshop. She is *in* the work and touched by it. She cannot just step 'outside' in the same way that Rachel can, to make sense of her experience as a single episode. We do not have answers for Meg, but we would like to suggest that just as some of the root structures of a development program must be reconsidered in light of social constructionist ideas, so too might our ideas about how to develop and support social constructionist practitioners.

Implications for Relational Leadership Theory

We began this chapter by suggesting that constructivist and social constructionist oriented practitioners could engage in productive dialogue but that this called for rhetorical skills and commitment. However we have also drawn on empirical material to suggest that the TKI, while constructivist in orientation, quite actively draws objectivist talk into the conversation. While drawing attention to some forms of meaning-making, tools such as this can rule out possibility, ultimately contributing to "a way of not seeing" as Ann Oakley (1974) has advised (p. 27). Indeed, we question whether such tools have any place in constructionist-oriented leadership development programs, for it seems to us that tools close off the potential in constructivist thought, calling objectivist assumptions into the conversation, and limiting what is possible for our participants.

Indeed, whether—and how much—constructivism is a departure from objectivism is a contested issue. For example, Bradbury and Lichtenstein (2000) have argued that constructivism is "...consistent with an epistemology of an objective truth and a Cartesian dogma of a clear separation between mind and nature" (as cited in Uhl-Bien, 2006, p. 655). As we have noted earlier, constructivism often becomes associated with an "entity" perspective:

> which considers relationships from the standpoint of individuals as independent, discrete entities i.e., individual agency...It assumes that a) individuals have a knowing mind, b) individuals have access to the contents of their mind and c) these entities can be distinguished form other entities (i.e., people) and the environment. (Uhl- Bien, 2006, p. 655)

We have been brought up close to these different opinions by stint of the implications for practice. From a practice perspective, we have noticed that the relationship between constructivism and objectivism can be stimulated by the tools that advance constructivist ideas. Thus, while constructivist assumptions may challenge objectivism, the related tools and practices may stimulate the imaginative framework of absolute truths. And once this framework is introduced, multiple knock-on effects are likely to be produced. As Unger (1987) writes:

> the institutional and imaginative frameworks of social life are the hardest of social facts, not because they are easy to measure but in the sense that they are both the most resistant to transformation and the richest in the range of their effects. (p. 60)

Some of the ways that an objectivist framework is stimulated by the TKI as a tool for working with conflict include eliciting the language of objectivism; advancing a view of leadership as compromising known, static dimensions; and, in the field of leadership and organizational development, through inviting a discourse that might be described as constructivist rationalism (Hayek, 1982).

However as we have already argued, these remnants of the past are likely to be stimulated and carried forward in ways that go well beyond what is already *"inside"* the minds of individual participants. Thus, as a facilitation team, we struggle with our different responses to the question of whether in using the TKI and other similar tools, we become co-constructors of limited, or possibly even fixed "leadership realities for participants in these programmes" (Ford & Harding, 2008, p. 486).

CONCLUSION

The different empirical material drawn on over this chapter should help us direct attention to the different implications of relational leadership theory. The accounts of Rachel and Meg offer very distinctive ways of constructing "conflict" in a leadership development process. We have proposed that the former account focuses on individual leader capability (entity/constructivist perspective) and the latter on collective leadership capacity (social constructionist perspective). Yet, the separation between leader and leadership development is certainly not as clear-cut and simple as that, and Day (2001) reminds us that most programs would seek to create some combination of leader and leadership development. The comparative table perhaps challenges us even further along this thinking, particularly through the "underdeveloped" row, where what is underdeveloped in the entity/constructivist perspective, ("the collective group," "what's in the moment') is precisely what is strongest in the social construction perspective. Of course, the reverse is equally true, and what is underdeveloped in terms of social construction (the "I" story, "past personal history") is precisely what an entity/constructivist perspective brings to the development picture.

Clearly, at least on paper, there is some "perfect" combination of the two where each perspective complements and fills the gaps of the other, in order to construct robust leaders to take their place in a broader collective leadership terrain. Relational leadership theory, in bringing the two perspectives into one broad umbrella theory, could be credited with making such a prospect seem more imaginable and possible. However the theoretical and developmental journey represented in this chapter makes us cautious and doubtful about this prospect. Participant comments hold a clue as to why, in that their lived experience, as opposed to the neat theoretical picture on paper, where the tools, models and instruments favoured by entity/constructivist perspectives frame the perspective in decidedly objectivist and instrumental tones. We propose that such objectivism and instrumentalism challenge the relationality so core to relational leadership theory to the extent that entity/constructivism and social construction struggle to even be in dialogue together.

Through these stories, we suggest that a "broad church" that is home to both constructivist *and* social constructionist assumptions presents problems for the design and facilitation of leadership programs. While an overarching framework of Relational Leadership Theory (Uhl- Bien, 2006, p. 1) is a useful construct, we suggest that in practice, working with fundamentally different orientations to relationships is a very tall order. At the very least, it requires a community of practice where differences and their implications can be articulated and where members have the rhetorical skills (Bouwen & Hosking, 2000) and commitments to address these differences. The sense of an overarching framework that is shared has given our team the courage to keep pushing questions about where we are different and what it means for our relationships, our leadership development practice, and our research. Indeed, we have been reassured by the proposition of a common framework when our differences have felt particularly threatening. Beyond this, we need a discipline to address the creeping objectivism that can beset both the construction and ongoing development of theories, such as this, that seek to bring perspectives into what is both a greatly needed but undeniably uncomfortable dialogue.

REFERENCES

Bouwen, R., & Hosking, D. M. (2000). Reflections on relational readings of organizational learning. *European Journal of Work and Organizational Psychology, 9*(2), 267–274.

Caroll, B., & Levy, L. (2009). Leadership development as identity construction. *Management Communication Quarterly, Special issue on Communication and the Social Construction of leadership.*

Carroll, B., Levy, L., & David, R. (2008). Leadership as practice: Challenging the competency paradigm. *Leadership, 4*(4), 363–379.

Crotty, M. (1998). Constructionism: The making of meaning. In (Eds.), *The foundations of social research* (pp. 42–65). Sydney, Australia: Allen & Unwin.

Ford, J., & Harding, N. (2008). Move over management, We are all leaders now. *Management Learning, 38*(5), 475–493.

Grint, K. (2005). *Leadership, limits and possibilities.* New York, NY: Palgrave Macmillan.

Hayek, F. A. (1982). *Law, legislation and liberty.* London, England: Routledge & Kegan Paul.

Heifetz, R. A. (1994). *Leadership without easy answers.* Harvard, MA: Belknap.

Hoffman, L. (1992). A reflexive stance for family therapy. In S. McNamee & K. J. Gergen (Eds.), *Therapy as social construction* (pp. 7–25). London, England: Sage Publications.

Kelly, G. (1955). The nature of personal constructs. In *The psychology of personal constructs. Vol. 1: A theory of personality.* New York, NY: W.W.Norton and Company.

Kelly, G. (1977). Confusion and the clock. In F. Fransella (Ed.), *Personal construct psychology, 1977* (pp. 209–232). London, England: Academic Press.

Oakley, A. (1974). *The sociology of housework.* London, England: Martin Robinson.

Ospina, S., & Sorenson, G. (2006). A constructionist lens on leadership: Charting new territory. In G. Goethals, & G. Sorenson (Eds.), *The quest for a general theory of leadership,* (pp. 188–204). , MA: Edward Elgar.

Rowe, D. (1996). The importance of personal construct psychology. In B. Walker, J. Costigan, L. Viney, & B. Warren (Eds.), *Personal construct theory: A psychology for the future* (pp. 9–24). , Australia: The Australian Psychological Society Ltd.

Sampson, E. E. (1998). Life as embodied art: The second stage—Beyond constructionism. In B. M. Bayer, & J. Shotter (Eds.), *Reconstructing the psychological subject- bodies, practices and technologies* (pp. 21–32). London, England: Sage Publications.

Shotter, J., & Lannamann, J. W. (2002). The situation of social constructionism. *Theory & Psychology, 12*(5), 577–609.

Stacey, R. (2001). *Complex responsive processes in organizations—Learning and knowledge creation.* London, England: Routledge.

Stacey, R., & Griffin, D. (2005). Experience and method: A complex responsive processes perspective on research in organizations. In R. Stacey, & D. Griffin (Eds.), *A complexity perspective on researching organizations: Taking experience seriously* (pp. 13–38). London, England: Routledge.

Steier, F. (1991). Reflexivity and methodology: An ecological construction. In F. Steier (Ed.), *Research and reflexivity* (pp. 163–185). London, England: Sage Publications.

Uhl- Bien, M. (2006). Relationship leadership theory: Exploring the social processes of leadership and organizing. *The Leadership Quarterly, 17,* 654–676.

Unger, R. M. (1987). The making of society through politics: Routine without reason. In *False necessity: Anti-necessitarian social theory in the service of radical democracy.* Part 1 of *Politics, A work in constructive social theory* (Vol. 1, pp. 41–115). Cambridge, England: Press Syndicate—University of Cambridge.

Unger, R. M. (2001). *False necessity: Anti-necessitarian social theory in the service of radical democracy.* (New ed.). London, England: Verso.

Van, Velsor, E., & McCauley, C. D. (2004). Afterword. In C. D. McCauley, & E. Van Velsor (Eds.), *The Center for Creative Leadership: Handbook of leadership development* (2nd ed.). pp. 465–473). San Francisco, CA: Jossey- Bass.

NOTE

1. With acknowledgments to Compass, particularly the remainder of its facilitator team (Peter Blyde, Regena Mitchell, Sarah Bowman, and Terry Kayes), who supported the conversations and writing that resulted in this chapter.

CHAPTER 7

UN- AND RE-PACKING LEADERSHIP

Context, Relations, Constructions, and Politics

Mats Alvesson and Stefan Sveningsson

Contemporary talk and writing on managerial leadership covers broad terrain indeed, and there are no limits to what leadership is supposed to accomplish in terms of improving the feelings, thinking, values, ethics, change-mindedness, satisfaction, and performance of followers (subordinates). Much of this interest in leadership revolves around change and development and the ability of leaders to make people engaged and committed to opportunities beyond everyday realities. Followers are thought to be inspired and influenced by leaders overcoming uncertainty, narrow-mindedness, and low motivation.

In organizations, we usually expect managers to practice these activities; it is managers whom we expect to formulate the visions, initiate change, and motivate subordinates. It is as leaders we nowadays often evaluate managerial efforts. Leaders are often portrayed as being strong, directive, and

Advancing Relational Leadership Research, pages 203–225
Copyright © 2012 by Information Age Publishing
All rights of reproduction in any form reserved.

persuasive with abilities to engage and commit others to follow visions and missions in voluntary and non-coercive manners (Barker, 2001). It is popular to regard the leader as someone who initiates and communicates transformation in a convincing manner, partly by use of charismatic abilities and compelling visions about the future (Conger & Kanungo, 1998; Rost, 1992). Leaders have robust characteristics with stable traits and abilities. The transformational leader capable of transforming followers—rather than negotiating with subordinates about rewards for contributions—is the ideal, and various versions of this ideal circulate frequently in the enormous amount of literature and research on leadership. There is often a heroic luster in many of these portraits of the charismatic and visionary leaders. Successful organizational outcomes, turnarounds, mergers, and acquisitions are routinely attributed to the extraordinary traits, heroic abilities, and skills of the leader (Meindl, Ehrlich, & Dukerich, 1985). This suggests a narrow, leader-centric view on leadership.

There is, of course, an expanding skeptical literature on leadership, questioning a range of dominant assumptions, including ideas on leadership having a strong significance for results (Pfeffer, 1977), the sole leader (Gronn, 2002), the passive follower (Collinson, 2006), the coherence and "realness" of leadership (Alvesson & Sveningsson, 2003b), the ideological celebration of the positive, indeed heroic leader (Yukl, 1999), the monologic (as opposed to dialogic) character of leadership (Fairhurst, 2001; Ladkin, 2010) and idealized notions of the moral superiority of the good or authentic leader (Alvesson, 2011b). Critics draw attention to the masculine nature of conceptualization of the leader and leadership (Alvesson & Billing, 2009), leadership as involving social domination (Knights & Willmott, 1992), and the very notion of leaders doing leadership encouraging elitism and legitimizing managerial privilege and power. There is a body of studies emphasizing the constructions or attributions of leadership, seeing it mainly as an invention of followers and others (Meindl, 1995; Pfeffer, 1978). Some authors also question "entity" thinking (rigid categories of "leaders" and "followers") in favor of taking relations seriously (Uhl-Bien, 2006). And, there are authors eager to emphasize the complexities involved and pay attention to both positive and negative aspects (Alvesson & Spicer 2011; Grint, 2009; Western, 2008).

The field(s) of leadership has (have) thus received some degree of skeptical attention, but there is still a dominant mainstream built on a set of problematic and constraining assumptions. This chapter will emphasize four key basic assumptions, leader-centrism, entitism, romanticism, and objectivism, discuss these, and suggest some alternative point of departures in leadership and, perhaps, post-leadership research.

FOUR BASIC PROBLEMS IN LEADERSHIP STUDIES

Conventional leadership research requires critical attention to a variety of problematic areas. We will below zoom in on four problems inherent in dominating view(s) on leadership. In addition to critically scrutinizing these, we will also put forward alternative ways of conceptualizing these areas of leadership.

Leader-Centricism

A central problem in conventional leadership research is an overemphasis on the leader and the impact of his/her traits, style, and/or behavior on the response of followers. The division between leader and follower is usually taken for granted, and the former is believed to be the key agent, while the latter is seen as a more or less passive receiver of influence. There is limited recognition that social relations may look quite differently than captured by the idea that leaders lead followers. The so-called leader may not be the key driver of social relations and, in those cases, somebody being a central subject in leadership this is still very much a matter of relations and interactions and the broader set of institutional, ideological, and cultural ideas and arrangements regulating what people in managerial and authority positions do and how interactions take place.

Entitism

There is a strong tendency to view the so-called leaders, but also others (followers, subordinates), as robust and integrated units with fixed boundaries. A dominant idea is that there are fixed traits and characteristics that can be studied in isolation, "outside" discourses, situations, and relations. When relations are considered, they are often seen as between "fixed" subjects, with their respective set of characteristics (e.g., leadership or follower styles or values, attitudes, skills, or other dispositions). This means that the idea of subjects as relational beings is being neglected.

Romanticism

In contrast to the romance of leadership as related to leader-centrism, we here refer to romanticism as an idea of leadership as being about conflict-free, positive relations involving authentic individuals interacting positively and productively. It includes assumptions about coherence of meaning and a harmonious integration of experiences based on consensus-based mutual interaction and the creation of positive relationships based on and leading to "good" will, qualities, and outcomes. A significant problem in leadership theory is the strong ideological under- and often over-tone. Leaders and leadership are to be celebrated. Whatever the problem, there is always a positively formulated form of leadership that will offer a solution—practically or theoretically. And, when the ideological value of a theory or an expression is high, then it is easier to get away with rather crude and un-nuanced thinking.

Objectivism

Partly as a consequence of the strong influence from academic psychology, natural science ideals such as finding law-like patterns, correlations between variables, and measuring leadership dominate the field. One could challenge this by arguing that leadership is inherently subjective; it is about appealing and influencing people through triggering cognitions and emotions, values, fantasies, and influencing identities. Efforts to use abstract definitions and turn leadership phenomena into variables, objects for the control and dissection of neo-positivism, means that rather poor and abstract knowledge is being produced. There is very little feeling for what goes on, including an appreciation of how subjects involved construct their realities in social interaction.

* * *

These four assumptions arguably form the essence of much conventional leadership thinking. We can refer to this as LERO (leader-centric, entitistic, romantic, objectivistic). These four notions of the idea of leaders being coherent, integrated subjects, originators of leadership exercised over others (recipients) in a positive, need-fulfilling way that is possible to study objectively can be challenged. An alternative view, building but going somewhat further than current relational and constructionist ideas (e.g., Ospina & Sorensen 2006; Uhl-Bien 2006), takes issue with these notions and pays attention to the complexity of workplace conditions and positions, emphasizing relationships as crucial for not only the influencing but also the being of subjects at work. Attention is also drawn to how issues around "leadership" need to be seen as constructions, in which cultural definitions of *meaning-making, communication,* and *language* use are crucial. Here, the often messy—ambiguous and political—nature of organizations needs to be appreciated. Let us look more closely at how one can move from dominating assumptions to proceed from an alternative set of ideas.

BEYOND LEADER-CENTRICISM: FROM THE LEADER
TO THE SOCIAL AND CULTURAL CONTEXT

One of the many peculiar and problematic features of leadership research is its leader-centric focus. Leadership is typically defined as some sort of an influence process where one person (the leader) leads other people (followers). It is the leader who is the central character, whose dispositions and acts create effects. Followers are then mainly responses to this influence. A lot of research assumes that by focusing on the manager (labeled a leader) or—in rare cases, the informal leader—you then study leadership. There are ideological overtones in this reasoning that stress managers as superior, uni-directionally acting on—rather than interacting with—subordinates, and that neglect that most managers are also subordinates and thus have a hierarchy above themselves (Laurent, 1978). In general, people are inclined to ascribe strong impact to leaders, reflecting a want to see somebody as responsible for different outcomes, good or bad (Meindl, 1995; Pfeffer, 1977). This fits the self-image of many managers and reinforces their status and claims for high wages, prestige and authority in companies and society. Management writers, teachers, and consultants would perhaps find that their market would be smaller and less sympathetic if they should argue for the significance of factors other than management and leaders, as well as the complexity and ambiguity of how to account for performance. The strong faith in leadership, the attribution of causal powers to it, and the heroization of leaders may be seen as interesting cultural manifestations—reflecting socially invented "truths."

It is, of course, possible to study how managers think about or do leadership—or at least how do they like to talk about this topic in interviews and educational settings, but the relevance of this for their practices is doubtful (Alvesson & Sveningsson, 2003a; 2003b). And even if this talk is stretched a bit and seen as indicating some information about leadership practices (managerial/leader behavior), how followers may perceive and attribute meaning to these practices of leadership are unknown.

There has been some work done on followership, including on the attribution of leadership (Meindl, 1995), the various constructions of "follower" positions (Uhl-Bien & Pillai, 2007), and there are calls for studies of the imaginative consumption of culture (how people sometimes creatively respond to and use cultural ideas), including ideas on leadership in circulation (Linstead & Grafton-Small, 1992). To study the attribution/construction/consumption processes of leadership disconnected from the leader's intentions and acts is interesting and important work, but a sole follower focus appears as one-sided as leader-centric work.

Studying both sides of the relationship and process appear as equally, if not more, important. Some recent work on shared or distributed leadership broadens the spectrum of those leading and loosens the distinction between leader and follower (Gronn 2002; Pearce & Conger, 2003). Work on the dialectics of leadership upgrade the role of followers and suggest attention to "the complex, interactional relationship between leaders and followers" (Collinson, 2005, p. 1425) and point to "leadership as a more relational process, a shared or distributed phenomenon occurring at different levels and dependent on social interactions and networks of influence" (Fletcher & Käufer, 2003, p. 21). But, much work aiming to redirect attention from the leader and broaden the approach to include followers and relations still sticks to the dyad or the small group.

In studies taking groups seriously, these are often seen as existing more or less in social isolation from a broader context. For example, in work on social identity and leadership, the relationship between leader and follower is sometimes abstracted from the social context, and issues around prototypicality and in/out-group saliency are disconnected from an organizational and broader cultural context (e.g., Hogg & Van Knippenberg, 2003). Yukl (1999) argues that the emphasis on the dyadic perspective in, for example, theories of charismatic and transformational leadership, should be "replaced by a systems perspective that describes leadership in terms of several distinct but inter-related influence processes at the dyadic, group, and organizational level" (p 301). Fairhurst (2001) believes that "...although an individualistic orientation has been the heavy favorite in leadership research, pressures are building to consider wider systems dynamics" (p. 383). But, this systems dynamic is seen as including everything from dyads to broad collectives (like an industry) and the emphasis, when researchers move away from a myopic focus on the leader, still seems almost exclusively to be in the micro end of the "systems" spectrum. More recent post-heroic and relational approaches that encourage a break away from the individual leader also tend to stay on the level of interpersonal relations and the interplay, and possibly position-switching, between various subjects leading/following (Gronn, 2002; Uhl-Bien, 2006). Also, critical approaches sometimes limit the perspective to deal with the identities of people involved in the leader-follower relationships (e.g., Collinson, 2006). Leader-centric assumptions are replaced by slightly broader but still narrow localist ideas, including those directly interacting.

One could, however, argue that leadership—as ideology, discourse, and institutionalized practice—is very much a societal phenomenon. Viewed as a discourse we understand leadership as verbal and textual ways of reasoning about a phenomenon that also produces certain truth effects about it. Leadership is here regarded as anchored in a specific vocabulary—that is, a division between leaders and followers— that can be said to produce certain versions of the social world. In contemporary discourse on leadership, there is a strong individualization of leadership: The leader (often the manager) is the main actor and the underlings follow. Strictly speaking, the manager is the only actor, while the followers are objects of leadership turned into some kind of tools to be used as an extension of the manager. Considering the present popularity of contemporary discourse on leadership as forming a regulative ideal for people in business and working life and producing subjects eager to constitute themselves as "leaders" doing "leadership" (Foucault, 1976; 1980; see also Alvesson & Sveningsson, 2003a), we could frame this as a very powerful discourse or Discourse with big "D" (Alvesson & Kärreman, 2000). Taking this seriously would mean that a much less myopic view would be emphasized. If this is considered, meanings, understandings, ideals, and norms on the organizational level appear not as something at the margins of leadership but rather as something intimately intertwined with it. Also, organizational culture frames and guides leadership; the cultural context is crucial for what is viewed as "leadership"—how people in formal and informal capacities relate to this (or pay little attention to it), ideals and norms for its practices and receptions, and so forth.

Culture thus forms leadership rather than the other way around (Alvesson, 2011a). Such is the case for at least the large majority of all people designated as or emerging as leaders. As Biggart and Hamilton (1987) put it: "All actors, but perhaps leaders especially, must embody the norms of their positions and persuade others in ways consistent with their normative obligations" (p. 435).

The "culture- and Discourse-driven" nature of leadership is neglected in most of the literature and in talk by management gurus and practitioners. Without denying the importance of considering the person(s) supposed to do the leadership, one can accordingly see leadership as multi-level phenomena, where societal and organizational cultures and discourses are key elements, produce regulatory ideals for doing leadership—as leaders and followers—to which individuals and groups adapt, vary, and improvise. This means that a key source of leadership is the cultural context (a blend of societal, professional/industrial, and group/organizational level assumptions, templates, and norms). This does not necessarily imply a strong societal or organizational level focus of study, as one can look at the local adaptations and variations of leadership discourses translated and put into operation. The level of leadership practice needs, of course, to be studied at the local level. But, the origin and framing of leadership is viewed as macro-induced more than coming from the leader or even leader-follower (or leadership co-construction people) interacting.

One way of formulating this would be to stop seeing leadership primarily as a trait or even a small group relational issue, but a broader Discourse and/or cultural phenomenon associated with society and/or organization (cf. Foucault, 1980). As such, it works as an ideal, exercising normative pressure on people supposed to do leadership. The contemporary dominant Discourse means that managers and others are called upon to work with values, manage meanings, and make people comply in a voluntary way, forming positive relations in which conflicts are to be smoothed over. Particularly relevant is transformative leadership where leaders are called upon to rely on their personal abilities and exercise leadership from a position of authority and work through overt, although non-coercive, strategic and visionary means in order to influence people's feelings and thinking directly (Zaleznik, 1977). Increasingly, those in management are supposed to act as leaders in facilitating change, and indeed, the capacity to act in this way is often what is deemed to separate leadership from management (Barker, 1997; Carroll & Levy, 2008).

Leadership is here addressed as a societal and organizational normative ideal that regulates and frames the ordering and doing of leadership (Alvesson & Willmott, 2002). The latter is seen as interpretation—adaption, improvising, fine-tuning—of this regulatory ideal. The ideal puts certain pressure and provides courses of action—that is, formulating visions and managing with values and meanings—for those involved, and this is typically a blend between broader societal ideals, contemporary dominating Discourses (like transformational leadership and managerialism in general), and local, organizational cultural meanings. This regulatory ideal would be the key driver of leadership, setting the scene and framework, and we can study the local actions, meaning-making, and joint performances living up to the ideal. Leaders and followers—if/when these terms seem to make sense to use—are then consumers, interpreters, and adapters of this regulatory ideal, not originators of leadership.

BEYOND ENTITISM: FROM INDIVIDUALS AND OTHER SEPARATE ENTITIES TO SOCIAL RELATIONS

Common sense invites us to think about individuals as fairly fixed entities. There are different people in groups and organizations, with selves, traits, values, skills, and so on, and these relate "externally," through exchanges, negotiations, or in various steps influencing each other, either—common in leader-centric work—in a mainly one-sided way or—in more novel approaches—in more distributed, mutual ways.

However, rather than foregrounding individuals and seeing them as robust and integrated subjects connecting in various ways, one can see relational aspects as central and view individuals as secondary to these. Leadership is intrinsically social and relational, an on-going process of shared making of meaning. Some authors see "the basic unit of analysis in leadership research as relationships, not individuals" (Uhl-Bien, 2006, p. 662).

This highlights the need to look at relations, interactions, and the mutuality of influencing in the leader/follower dyad and also to go beyond that level and consider systemic aspects (Fairhurst, 2001) and "to a consideration of how leadership arises through the interactions and negotiations of social order among organizational members" (Uhl-Bien, 2006, p. 672).

The overall idea of a relational approach is to try to go beyond "conventional" or entity-based views on relations. Uhl-Bien (2006) compares scholars from entity and relational perspectives. When the former takes relations seriously, they assume that robust and distinct individuals exist and that these produce connections. Leaders and followers are separate units related to, or having connections with, each other. Their properties and behaviors as individuals are central. This means that relational processes are trivialized and marginalized. In contrast, a more ambitious relational perspective downplays individuals as entities and sees the relationship as the fundamental aspect (Uhl-Bien, 2006). Individuals are here being constructed in the relational context rather than being treated as distinct and separate entities. The situation and the interaction will make the subjects. We are, as teachers in classes, researchers among peers in a conference, parents with small children, children to our parents, employees/subordinates in relationship to the dean and consultants in relationship to well-paying and demanding clients, quite different persons, in terms of how we and others agree or disagree upon the construction of the situation and making efforts to adapt to it. Also, in various situations—with different constellations of co-workers, relations, and negotiations around authority—consensus and (a)symmetries of definitions of reality and paths forward vary a lot, making selves outside the relational context less central for understanding leadership.

As leadership always involves not a person doing something in splendid social isolation but people acting together, it makes sense to see how people construct issues around authority, direction, support, and agreement together as crucial. It is within relationships that leadership is created: "leadership is relational and systematic. It emerges and manifests itself through relations and in relationships, and it cannot exist outside of these relations. These relationships, in turn, are grounded in wider systems of interdependence and constrained by social structure" (Ospina & Sorensen 2005, p. 193). The last sentence reflects our first theme above, although we think it should be emphasized even more strongly by relationally oriented scholars.

Uhl-Bien (2006) observes that, while many new ideas on leadership emphasize relationships, for example, distributed (Gronn 2002) or shared (Pearce & Conger, 2003) leadership, we know relatively little about how relations are formed, developed, and changed. A large amount of work looks at specific verbal interactions between managers and others in workplaces based on conversation and discourse analysis (see Fairhurst 2001, 2007 for overviews), but this tends to sidestep the richness of relational qualities that are only partly manifest in verbal interactions. Arguably, our relations are much more than the details of our conversations—history, memory, fantasies, unconscious process, meaning-making, and feelings that people keep for themselves are key ingredients in relations. On the whole, there is not much work taking the relational aspects seriously, at least not using a more ambitious or advanced relational understanding: "investigation into the relational dynamics of leadership as a process of organizing has been severely overlooked in leadership research" (Uhl-Bien, 2006, p. 672; see also Hosking, 1988).

Uhl-Bien (2006) defines "relational leadership as a social influence process through which emergent coordination (i.e., evolving social order) and change (i.e., new values, attitudes, approaches, behaviors, ideologies, etc.) are constructed and produced" (p. 668). Based on this, a question of how we can know what "really" is leadership enters the discussion. Possible criteria could be that some social order is created and there is recognition within a group that an actor (or a constellation/group) contribute to such ordering and therefore is given a particular (higher) status. Participants can be seen as leaders when they "1. Consistently make effective contributions to social order and 2. Are both expected and perceived to do so by fellow participants" (Hosking & Morley, 1988, as cited in Uhl-Bien 2006, p. 667). Leadership is thus not given (as contingent upon a managerial position), but rather it is a process outcome. It is not what shapes the outcome of situations; it is shaped by and can better be seen as an emergent outcome of situations.

To link up with the first point of moving beyond a narrow focus, relations are not just issues of micro level relations. Processes are framed and guided by a cultural context and norms for identities and how people relate to each other. Age, gender, race, ethnicity, expertise, authority, formal structures, corporate ideologies all frame and guide the ways relational work is being done. These cultural framing ingredients are never given, but are played into and negotiated in specific situations, where institutionalized ideas around leadership as related to formal managerial positions and "management" put their imprints on actors. These macro- and meso-level framing forces guide and constrain the relational work being conducted and often give it a hierarchical form where managerial positions and managerial leadership often play a larger role than purely emergent or informal or bottom-up forms of leadership although, in certain contexts, cultural orientations work against forms of managerialism and thus constrain leadership strongly in line with formal positions. This is often the case in professional and other knowledge-intensive organizations.

Leadership must be understood as a relation, and in relations, subjects are formed in specific ways. We are different in different relations. It is therefore not subjects producing relations as much as relations—producing dialectics—producing subjects, that is, the individual as being formed in the specific context. But relations and relational work bears the imprints of all the social selves and variety of relations (aged, gendered, professional, intra-organizational) of which we are a part and through which we carry various community orientations (cultures).

FROM ROMANTICISM TO THE IMPERFECT ORGANIZATIONAL WORLD: ACKNOWLEDGING POWER AND POLITICS

Ideas around leadership being a purely positive quality associated with what is socially shared in terms of meanings and interests is common in much conventional leadership, reflecting a rather romantic view of organizational reality. Romanticism as a concept is used in different ways in social science. Within leadership studies the attribution theory approach refers to dominating views of the leader being the key driver behind all sorts of outcomes as a romantic view (Meindl, 1995). Here we use the term to refer to assumptions and portrayals of leadership as (normally) building on and producing consensus and harmony. In leadership, all good things tend to be combined: good intentions, good outcomes, and shared interests and meanings around the situation. A strong belief in leadership as a (tension-free) co-construction indicates such a view.

Romanticist assumptions inform most leader-centric views of leadership. Integrity and high ethical standards are often viewed as characteristics of a good leader. Sometimes authors claim that, when the leader is not of the right moral caliber, it is not a case of leadership, but something less noble. For instance, some researchers claim that transformational leaders "must incorporate a central core of moral values" (Bass & Steidlmeier, 1999, p. 210) to be assessed as "authentic." In the crudest form, many assume that a real leader is good. If he or she is bad, then he or she is not a leader, (e.g., Hitler was not a leader but a tyrant) (Jackson & Parry, 2008). This seems to indicate that people are eager to preserve some purist and idealized notion of the leader, possibly blocking this category from critical reflection (Harter, 2006).

A problem is of course, that the enthusiasm of devoted followers may have little to do with Bass and Steidlmeier's idea of what is authentic and not. As stated by Grint (2009), there is "preciously little evidence that admiring followers of Mao, Stalin, Hitler or Osama bin Laden followed their leaders because they were psychopaths... and much more evidence that they followed them because these followers assumed they were ethical" (p 13).

There are strong efforts in leader-centric writings to boost moral qualities of leadership. One example is "Superleadership," which involves leading followers to lead themselves through empowerment and the development of self-leadership skills. The Superleader is a morally superior person who:

> ...focuses primarily on the empowering roles of helping, encouraging and supporting followers in the development of personal responsibility, individual initiative, self-confidence, self-goal setting, self-problem solving, opportunity thinking, self-leadership, and psychological ownership over their tasks and duties. (Houghton, Neck, & Manz, 2003, p. 133)

The Superleader expresses a range of orientations and behavior, all of which echo positive moral ideals, such as encouraging learning from mistakes, avoiding punishment, listening more, talking less, and creating independence and interdependence.

Literature on "servant leadership" also scores high on assumptions of the excessive goodness of leaders of the true grit. Ideas include that "servant leadership requires that leaders lead followers for the followers' own ultimate good" (Sendjaya, Sarros, & Santora, 2008, p. 403). Servant leaders are said to put "followers first, organizations second, their own needs last" (p. 403). Servant leaders are authentic, altruistic, humble, and create "an intensely personal bond marked by shared values, open-ended commitment, mutual trust, and concern for the welfare of the other party" (p. 407). Those served by the servant leaders "are positively transformed in multiple dimensions, e.g., emotionally, intellectually, socially, and spiritually" (p. 408). The good leader then appears a saintly figure capable of producing moral peak performance and avoiding the vulnerabilities that characterize the large majority of the population (Alvesson, 2011a).

Much of this research originates from the U.S. and bears strong imprints of North American ideologies, sometimes with religious under- or overtones. They often stand in strong opposition to most studies of organizational life, seldom being free from conflicts of interest and power dynamics (Jackall, 1988). As indicated above, issues of power only marginally enter the picture of leadership, when it does, leaders are using power only when circumstances force them to do so (Bass & Steidlmeier, 1999) or do use power for the benefit of the organization they work for and/or the subordinates (McClelland & Burnham, 1976). However, one does not have to be a cynic to assume that almost all people have some self-interest and may not be willing to subordinate their interests to those of everybody else.

Also researchers with "post-leader-centric" lenses tend to share romantic ideas portraying leadership in pink colors. There is, for example, an interest in "the collaborative subtext of life, the numerous acts of enabling, supporting, facilitating, and creating conditions" (Fletcher & Käufer, 2003, p. 23). Such acts dominate in settings characterized by "shared leadership." This is about "a dynamic, interactive influence process among individuals in groups for which the objective is to lead one another to the achievement of group or organizational goals or both" (Pearce & Conger, 2003, p. 1). In shared leadership, the "influencing process involves more than just downward influence on subordinates by an appointed or elected leader" (p. 1). Leadership is viewed as a "relational dialogue, the source of leadership is not a person or a role, but a system, as leadership emerges by way of dialogue and collaborative learning to achieve a shared sense of the demands of collective work" (Ospina & Sorensen, 2006, p. 195). In all these quotes, we find a view of leadership as circling around harmony, where people support, facilitate, share, and collaborate for the common goal.

However, cleansing leadership from communication problems, goal diversity, power, coercion, compliance, and interest differences, is not necessarily a good move. To assume that "leadership" transforms potential divergence of views and interest variation into harmony and consensus appears naïve. Leadership in organizations is typically intertwined with political organizational reality, and the use of power in various forms is not outside this. The idea that when "true" leadership occurs (or is accomplished), less positive forces and ingredients simply vanish, are marginalized, or are productively dealt with (e.g., through dialogue-based compromises) may be of greater ideological than theoretical value.

The idea here is not to replace consensus, harmony, and "real"-leadership-means-good-doing ideas with opposite assumptions about organizations being populated by individuals driven solely by sectional interests, and engaged in more or less strong struggles for realizing their own egotistical subgoals, prepared to fight off those with competing agendas. We do not have to choose between leadership being exercised in the happy family or the ruthless corporate jungle. It seems reasonable to assume that people to some degree are guided by their own interests and logics, and are only partly driven by an idea of what may be the best for other constituents (i.e., top management, shareholders, community, or subordinates/colleagues). Many managers delving into "servant leadership," putting their followers first, may find that their own senior managers may pursue another agenda. Varieties of interests and divergence of worldviews lead to most leadership contexts including degrees of power and politics.

Leadership then "exists" in contexts where the people involved do struggle to get a say and get their interests secured (maximized or at least satisfied). Autonomy, status, privilege, and getting things done as one sees as the "best" way (also for the common good) means politically charged co-constructions, where the impact on organizing acts reflect the strengths and fortunes of different subjects. People typically need to do some fighting to get voice and responsiveness, and if and when there is a more or less collectively supported choice of direction, then the compliance may not be a matter solely of shared meanings but also of the exercise of power. This power may be about some actors holding others responsible, through persuasion, appeal to loyalty, reference to legitimate authority (manager priority, participatory agreement), but also involve themes and feelings like fear, shame, and self-doubt. Leadership certainly involves guiding, supporting, inspiring, facilitating and organizing; but it also means dealing with the other side of the coin—for example, commanding, sanctioning, and encouraging group pressures.

Acknowledging leadership as a political process means there will be acts, arrangements, and agreements involving people not spontaneously or voluntarily adapting to prescribed positions of "leaders," "followers," or "team members," or even alternative ideals and collective forms of leadership. This is independent of whether we assume more leader-centered or collective forms of leadership.

Here it should be added that this is not just a matter of senior people exercising power over subordinates, but also the latter using power and politics over the former, encouraging or forcing managers/leaders into a specific leadership mode, such as being more autocratic, democratic, putting the followers first, or whatever. Also, in more dialogue-based joint constructions of leadership, the constructions—consensual or conflictual—may more or less bear imprints of certain actors using power of various forms (coercive, agenda-setting, symbolic), acting relationally, but not necessarily in a symmetrical way.

Leadership can't be liberated from power. Also, under favorable conditions (growing market, no shortage of resources, etc.), not everything is pure harmony. Leadership—individual and collective—means typically a blend of dialogue and free consensus-seeking and the use of means involving a mix of positive and negative elements. Tensions and conflicts are associated with intolerance for people seen as pushing self-interest or defining means, goals and rules different from others and in particular from those having access to resources of power. Leadership—as opposed to pure management—often blends positive and less clearly rosy forms of persuasion. Leadership blind to power and political issues may have limited space in most organizations—in direct opposition to leadership publications where such blindness occupies most of the space.

BEYOND OBJECTIVISM: VIEWING LEADERSHIP AS CONSTRUCTION AND RE-CONSTRUCTION PROCESS

Conventionally, social reality has been viewed as made up of objective phenomena waiting for the scientific study to be measured and analyzed. Law-like patterns have been searched for and the ideal has been abstract theories proven to be valid across situations and domains. It is increasingly common to assume that reality is a social construction, and this insight is slowly working itself into also the rather conservative field of leadership studies. The process of sense-making and meaning development is central to human life, including to leadership being anchored in and producing shared agreement. It is "a process of meaning-making" and "a dynamic and on-going undertaking" (Ospina & Sorensen, 2006, p. 191).

Leadership is, then, not just an objective phenomenon, but an outcome of people constructing this as such. Whether people in managerial positions or positions of authority are viewed as "leaders" or something else (administrators, managers, bosses, senior colleagues) is a matter of constructions. Whether people position themselves or are positioned as "followers" is also a construction (Uhl-Bien & Pillai 2007).

Many people advocating a social construction view put a rather strong emphasis on what is shared. Attention is shifted from the individual leader to the work of leadership; from leadership qualities, to collective agreements and the actions that embody them. Less important than behavior are social practices and experiences, and these need to be related to the community. Based on the idea that "reality is a shared construction" (Ospina & Sorensen, 2006, p. 193), leadership is viewed as a "relational dialogue, the source of leadership is not a person or a role, but a system, as leadership emerges by way of dialogue and collaborative learning to achieve a shared sense of the demands of collective work" (p. 195).

This approach does not rule out the possibility of individual persons being important although the social process involving several actors is viewed as typically crucial. If a single actor becomes central, then one should not just see this as self-evident, normal, and given, but ask "how and why does this happen?" and consider "what role individuals and groups play in bringing leadership into being, and how contexts affect the actual work of leadership in communities" (Ospina & Sorensen, 2006, p. 197).

Researchers suggest that the co-construction of reality through on-going interactions should focus on how people construct together (Dachler & Hosking, 1995). Communication is here central. Leadership is not a matter of personal dominance or one-sided influence, but a process of relational dialogue. One could talk of a monologic or dialogic framing of the process; the former implies a leader-driven dialogue (like participative leadership) while the latter suggests that the definitions of the situation are less one-sidedly defined by the leader and a result of negotiations and mutual influence by those involved (Fairhurst, 2001, 2009; Ladkin, 2010). Alignment of meaning is then not a result of the leader's efforts but an outcome of collective work. Self and other are not separable, but coevolving in interactions. The distinction between leader and follower is loosened up or even breaks down, and people involved are seen as participants creating leadership through interactive process work.

There is, however, a tendency to overestimate the sharedness of the constructions around leadership. Leadership is often defined as the management of meaning, as emphasized by researchers on symbolic and transformational leadership (Smircich & Morgan, 1982, Fairhurst, 2005; Ladkin, 2010; Sandberg & Targama, 2007) or what some authors refer to as "new leadership" (Parry & Bryman, 2006). Here, the idea is that the leader's talk or action tends to be accepted by subordinates broadly adapting and aligning their understanding to those of the leader.

However, parts of social science argue that the complexity and dynamics of the social world means that ambiguity, differentiated worldviews, varied values, different individual needs, expectations, and cognitive processing lead to variation in meaning and interpretation. Against integration paradigms in organizations—assuming shared meanings—one can put differentiation, ambiguity and fragmentation perspectives (e.g., Meyerson & Martin, 1987; see also Alvesson, 2012, Martin, 2002) in organizational culture studies, and postmodernists and conflict theorists have done so more broadly (Alvesson & Deetz, 2000; Cooper & Burrell, 1988). Parry & Bryman (2006) briefly refer to this variation, but leadership research does not seem to take seriously the idea that there may be considerable discrepancy between the leader and those supposed to follow in terms of their view of leadership behavior/acts and the relationship. In many cases, whether the supposed "leader" is seen as such by others who see themselves as "followers" is an open question. Various self- and other-constructions may be varied, inconsistent, and lead to friction (Alvesson, 2010c). Or, in cases of (perspectives emphasizing) shared leadership, people involved may have different and not necessarily highly responsive understandings and interests. Group efforts may trigger or increase dissensus rather than consensus.

Consequently, a high level of shared, consensual meanings may be accomplished less frequently and less strongly than assumed in the leadership literature (Alvesson, 2011c). Even roughly or partly shared meanings may be hard to accomplish in turbulent times and where people involved have different backgrounds (ethnic, gendered, professional) or personal characteristics and individualized expectations or experiences. Leadership may be accomplished through the use of a much more varied set of means (resources) than only or mainly shared meanings, for example, repressing non-wanted meanings. Social constructions may therefore often be more "a-social" than is commonly believed. Careful attention is needed to explore how people involved in leadership processes and relationships must consider ambiguities, frictions, and fragmentations, as well as the power elements, as often being key elements in social relations.

One part of this difficulty in producing social constructions is that individuals may not always construct their own coherent realities. One may talk of construction deficits or cracks. Efforts to produce and maintain a strong sense of identity and practice in a leadership context may be unsuccessful. A study of middle and senior managers indicated that while they said they were working with strategic issues, developing cultures, working with visions and values and other slightly grandiose and important things, administrative, operative and technical issues were actually dominating their work (Alvesson & Sveningsson, 2003a). Carroll and Levy (2008) point to the uncertainty and ambivalence managers express about the meaning of leadership. We can thus doubt the degree of alignment within specific individuals; they may be much more varied, contingent, fragmented, and fluid than conventional wisdom which presses people into types or styles of leadership, often relying on rigid dualisms (Fairhurst, 2001). This is often missed by the pattern- and coherence-seeking mainstream research, which disregards ambiguity and fragmentation (Alvesson, 2002).

Although it makes sense to replace assumptions of an objective reality and move toward constructionism, we suggest that the latter is better seen as characterized by a *multitude of construction efforts and breakdowns in these.* Complex topics such as leadership often lead to a multitude of diverse, shiftin,g and incoherent meanings, not only between but also *within* subjects. The constructions are still social in the sense that they draw upon cultural ideas and norms, but they are not necessarily socially shared in the sense of various subjects producing the same meaning of a specific topic. The idea of a harmonious co-construction in which subjects create a shared social universe may underestimate the difficulties with the production and re-production of shared meanings. Leadership may thus be viewed as a highly ambiguous organizing or influencing effort/attribution (Alvesson & Sveningsson, 2003a). Leadership is a source of diverse constructions and incoherence of meaning as much as it is a key driver behind socially shared meanings.

Thus, rather than to assume leadership being an organizing force—the solution or productive response to ambiguity or disorder—it may be part of divergent construction work involving disorganization. Leadership research should therefore not equate the subject matter with integration or accomplishment of shared meanings, but rather see leadership as a complex set of construction processes, sometimes coalescing, sometimes diverging, and leading to ambiguity and confusion or reinforcement of divergence of meanings around the goal, means, and relations typically characterizing leadership processes. Perhaps a common key quality would be frictional and fragile co-constructions; that is, there are ingredients of shared, but mainly temporal shared meanings providing some direction, but also covering/marginalizing diversities and ambiguities.

UNPACKING LEADERSHIP

Most definitions of leadership include leaders doing something and follow-ers responding to that, thereby shaping some form of influencing process. According to Antonakis, Cianciolo, and Sternberg (2004):

> Most leadership scholars would agree, in principle, that leadership can be de-fined as the nature of the influencing process—and its resultant outcomes—that occurs between a leader and followers and how this influencing process is explained by the leader's dispositional characteristics and behaviours, fol-lower perceptions and attributions of the leader, and the context in which the influencing process occurs. (p. 5)

This would imply a strong interest in both what the leader brings in and does *and* how followers perceive and attribute meaning to (reason about) these inputs and acts. But, these two elements are often conflated in lead-ership research and seldom targeted for careful scrutiny. When the con-cept of leadership includes both the influencing process and the resultant outcome (as in the definition just cited), a common, cardinal error is ac-complished. The act and the outcome should not be seen as more or less per definition the same. An effort to influence is not necessarily leading to an aimed-for outcome. So, when leadership is focused, the intention, the act, and the outcome are often coupled and placed in the same box. This kind of reasoning is common in organization studies (Sandelands & Drazin, 1989) and also within, for example, research on transformational leadership (Yukl, 1999).

This seems to be accepted, but it encourages research with a tendency to in-built results and insensitivity to process and relational issues. When con-struction-oriented researchers do this, relational issues tend to be viewed as fuelling positively into the process so that the outcome becomes also positive. When authors, for example, talk about "the collaborative subtext of life, the numerous acts of enabling, supporting, facilitating, and creating conditions..." (Fletcher & Käufer 2003, p. 23), we get a wealth of acts pack-ing together intention, process and outcome.

It is important to open up and study what is happening—and not over-pack leadership with a set of possibly quite diverse elements, from intentions, to behavior, and to responses and feedback. The elements in Antonakis et al.'s (2004) definition above—leader's dispositional characteristics and be-haviors, follower perceptions and attributions of the leader, and the con-text—should be considered separately, if taken seriously, and relations inves-tigated. The leader's behaviors may not be a direct offspring of dispositional characteristics; follower's perceptions of behavior may deviate from the lead-er's intention and meaning of behavior; and attribution processes may go beyond and not be the same as the perceptions of specific behaviors, but may reflect "background constructions" guided by a variety of discourses and ideologies. And the context is not just given but presumably interpreted by those involved—and possibly in different ways (e.g., issues around customer demands, crises, and moves of competitors may lead to varied readings). Although being a counterpoint to functionalist literature on leadership, this point is not radically challenging the dominant assumptions of entitism and objectivism. We think that we need to go much further than that.

Taken together, the four major points above— cultural context, relations, workplace politics, and (a)social constructions—make a case for the need to unpack what, according to the quotation of Antonakis et al., "most leadership scholars agree" upon. The leader's dispositional characteristics may matter little and be of moderate importance given the significance of people's constructions in a relational dynamic. This occurs in cultural and political contexts that impact on the constructions made. Behaviors are not produced as an offspring of the leader as the prime mover, but created and constructed in the relation, strongly shaped by cultural rules and dominant Discourses. Followers do not just perceive and attribute passively and reactively, and they may not construct themselves as followers (or they may do so in different and varied ways, e.g., selective or reluctant). They also actively construct what the person assumed by researchers to be the leader does. The behaviors may also be an outcome of the constructions of the others—whether seen as "followers," "professional," or whatever—and the "leader's" anticipation, interpretation, and reinterpretations of their responses, including feedback, resistance, initiative, and so on. The context not only forms an outside scene for the influencing process, but guides, frames, and actually produces the dispositions, attributions, and so forth. Actors involved draw upon constructions already there when they do the local work of who and what is a leader and a follower (and if there are such characters/positions), what dispositions do I/the other have (identity construction work rather than traits), and what forms of relationality and dissociations from such are being aimed for. Here the interest and action space for various actors to influence, be influenced, and sometimes minimize being influenced (maximizing autonomy) are key ingredients, making the influencing process less linear and more of a battleground where power and politics are important ingredients, whether played out more openly and directly or in more subtle and concealed ways.

CONCLUSION: AN ALTERNATIVE DEFINITION OF LEADERSHIP

We see it as crucial to take relations seriously and understand that organizing processes, including leadership, are about the constructions people make about themselves and their relations, tasks, and objectives. We also argue that it is misleading to view leadership exclusively or mainly as a local phenomenon involving the leader and/or people constructing leadership, the latter best understood as a regulatory ideal anchored in organizational and societal phenomena. Local actors are informed and constrained by organizational/societal cultural meanings and dominating Discourses. Finally, in organizations but also in other domains where leadership is supposed to take place, power and politics are crucial to consider as core aspects of leadership relations.

Based on these suggested alternative starting points for understanding leadership, the topic calls for a redefinition. It is time to move beyond LERO (leader-centric, entitistic, romantic, objectivistic thinking). An alternative formulation would be to see leadership as a local variation of the organizational and cultural frameworks and templates for structuring and producing meaning around authority and to some extent systematic relations between actors or groups involved in and/or producing a-symmetrical relations. These constructions are to various degrees broadly shared, diverse, fragmented, and conflictual, making any agreement (co-construction) of the leader(ship) relation potentially fragile and contested. The actors and groups are typically trying to produce some degree of consensus and compromise around authority and influencing around work—means, relations, and objectives—while driven by sectional interests around rewards (broadly defined) and increasing autonomy (implying a degree of control over others, minimally reducing their impact), thereby acting in politically conscious ways. These actor interests contribute to diversity of constructions. Effective political action involves the use of power, best accomplished through making sectional interests appear as the shared interest of the group and organization (Alvesson & Deetz, 2000). Both people emerging as leaders (active/dominant subjects) and as non-leaders (or less salient in leadership) may be involved here, busy constructing relations around leadership in (for them) not too unfavorable ways. These would always be framed and constrained by ideologies, discourses, and institutions putting structuring imprints on local interactions. Efforts in a more or less contested setting to make one's own construction influential and stick in formation and revisions of the self-, other-, and relation-construction work would be a key element in leadership, then seen as an expression of, as well as driver of power relations.

In this chapter, we have offered a fairly broad critique of dominant assumptions and starting points for leadership studies. We have drawn upon recent developments in constructionist and relational thinking, but gone broader and somewhat further in an effort to formulate alternative sets of point of departures for "post-leader-centric" and "post-leadership-idyllic" leadership studies. In short, we make a case for post-LERO understandings.

Do we need yet another framework for, and definition of, leadership, the (over)saturated reader of texts on leadership may ask? There is no shortage of numbers, but if relations, constructions, cultural context, and workplace interest variety are seen as key ingredients in how leadership—to the extent that the label/phenomenon captures well the constructions and relations involved—takes place, then the conceptualization suggested here adds important aspects to the picture.

REFERENCES

Alvesson, M. (2002). *Postmodernism and social research*. Buckingham, England: Open University Press.

Alvesson, M. (2011a). Leadership and organizational culture. In Collinson, D. et al. (Eds.), *Handbook of leadership studies*. London, England: Sage. (forthcoming)

Alvesson, M. (2011b). The leader as saint. In M. Alvesson, & A. Spicer (Eds.), *Metaphors we lead by: Understanding leadership in the real world*. London: Routledge.

Alvesson, M. (2011c). *Leadership—Alignment and misfit of images in leadership relations*. WP: Lund University.

Alvesson, M. (2012). *Understanding organizational culture*. London, England: Sage.

Alvesson, M., & Billing, Y. (2009). *Understanding gender and organization*. London, England: Sage.

Alvesson, M., & Deetz, S. (2000). *Doing critical management research*. London, England: Sage.

Alvesson, M., & Spicer, A. (2011). (Eds.) *Metaphors we lead by: Understanding leadership in the real world*. London: Routledge

Alvesson, M., & Sveningsson, S. (2003a). The great disappearance act: Difficulties in doing "leadership." *Leadership Quarterly, 14*, 359–381.

Alvesson, M., & Sveningsson, S. (2003b). The good visions, the bad micro-management and the ugly ambiguity: Contradictions of (non-)leadership in a knowledge-intensive company. *Organization Studies, 24*(6), 961–988.

Antonakis, J., Cianciolo, A., & Sternberg, R. (Eds.). (2004). *The nature of leadership*. Thousand Oaks, CA: Sage.

Barker, R. (2001). The nature of leadership. *Human Relations, 54*, 469–493.

Bass, B. M., & Avolio, B.J. (1993). Transformational leadership: A response to critiques. In J. G. Hunt, B. R. Baliga, H. P. Dachler, & C. A. Schriesheim, (Eds.), *Emerging leadership vistas* (pp. 29–40). Lexington, MA: D. C. Health.

Bass, B. M., & Steidlmeier, P. (1999). Ethics, character, and authentic transformational leadership behavior. *Leadership Quarterly, 10*, 181–217.

Biggart, N., & Hamilton, B. (1987). An institutional theory of leadership. *The Journal of Applied Behavioral Science, 23*(4), 429–441.

Carroll, B., & Levy, L. (2008) Defaulting to management: Leadership defined by what it is not. *Organization, 15*(1), 75–96.

Collinson, D. (2005). Dialectics of leadership. *Human Relations, 58*, 1419–1442.

Collinson, D. (2006). Rethinking followership: A post-structural analysis of follower identities. *Leadership Quarterly, 17*, 179–189.

Conger, J. A. (1999). Charismatic and transformational leadership in organizations: An insider's perspective on these developing streams of research. *Leadership Quarterly, 10*(2), 145–179.

Conger, J. A., & Kanungo, R. N. (1998). *Charismatic leadership in organizations.* Thousand Oaks, CA: Sage.

Cooper, R., & Burrell, G. (1988). Modernism, postmodernism and organizational analysis: An introduction. *Organization Studies, 9,* 91–112.

Dachler, H. P., & Hosking, D. M. (1995). The primacy of relations in the social construction of organisational realities. In D. M. Hosking, H. P. Dachler, & K. Gergen (Eds.), *Management and organization: Relational alternatives to individualism,* Aldershot, England: Avebury.

Fairhurst, G. (2001). Dualisms in leadership research. In F. Jablin, (Eds.), *Handbook of organizational communication.* Thousand Oaks, CA: Sage.

Fairhurst, G. (2005). Reframing *The art of framing:* Problems and prospects for leadership, *Leadership, 1,* 165–185.

Fairhurst, G. (2007). *Discursive leadership.* Thousand Oaks, CA: Sage.

Fletcher, J. K., & Käufer, K. (2003). Shared leadership: Paradoxes and possibility. In C. I. Pearce, & J. A. Conger (Eds.), *Shared leadership: Reforming the hows and whys of leadership* (pp. 21–47). Thousand Oaks, CA: Sage.

Foucault, M. (1976). *Discipline and punish: The birth of the prison.* London, England: Penguin.

Foucault, M. (1980). *The history of sexuality. Vol. 1: The will to knowledge.* New York, NY: Vintage Books.

Foucault, M. (1982). The subject and power. In H. L. Dreyfus, & P. Rabinow (Eds.), *Michel Foucault. Beyond structuralism and hermeneutics.* London, England: Harvester Wheatsheaf.

Grint, K. (2009) The sacred in leadership: Separation, sacrifice and silence. Paper.

Gronn, P. (2002). Distributed leadership as the unit of analysis. *Leadership Quarterly, 13,* 423–451.

Harter, N. (2006). *Clearings in the forest: On the study of leadership.* West Lafayette, IN: Purdue University Press.

Hogg, M. A., & van Knippenberg, D. (2003). Social identity and leadership processes in groups. In M. P. Zanna (Ed.), *Advances in experimental social psychology.* (Vol. 35, pp. 1–52). San Diego, CA: Academic Press.

Hosking, D. M. (1988). Organising, leadership and skillful process. *Journal of Management Studies, 25*(2), 147–166.

Hosking, D. M. (2007). Not leaders, not followers: A post-modern discourse of leadership processes. In B. Shamir, R. Pillai, M. Bligh, & M. Uhl-Bien (Eds.), *Follower-centered perspectives on leadership: A tribute to the memory of James R. Meindl* (pp. 243–264). Greenwich, CT: Information Age Publishing.

Houghton, J. D., Neck, C. P., & Manz, C. C. (2003). Self-leadership and super-leadership: The heart and art of creating shared leadership in teams. In C. L. Pearce, & J. A. Conger, J. A. (Eds.), *Shared leadership: Reframing the hows and whys of leadership* (pp. 123–140). Thousand Oaks, CA: Sage.

Jackall, R. (1988). *Moral mazes.* Oxford, England: Oxford University Press.

Jackson, B., & Parry, K. (2008). *A very short, fairly interesting and reasonably cheap book about studying leadership.* London, England: Sage.

Knights, D., & Willmott, H. (1992). Conceptualizing leadership processes: A study of senior managers in a financial services company. *Journal of Management Studies, 29,* 761–782.

Ladkin, D. (2010). *Rethinking leadership: A new look at old leadership questions.* Cheltenham, England: Edward Elgar.

Laurent, A. (1978). Managerial subordinacy: A neglected aspects of organizational hierarchy. *Academy of Management Review, 3,* 220–230.

Linstead. S., & Grafton-Small, R. (1992). On reading organizational culture. *Organization Studies, 13*(3), 331–355.

Martin, J. (2002) *Organizational culture.* Thousand Oaks, CA: Sage.

Meindl, J. M. (1995). The romance of leadership as a follower-centric theory: Social-constructionist approach. *The Leadership Quarterly, 6,* 329–341.

Meindl, J., Ehrlich, S., & Dukerich, J. (1985). The romance of leadership. *Administrative Science Quarterly, 30,* 78–102.

Meyerson, D., & Martin, J. (1987). Culture change: An integration of three different views. *Journal of Management Studies, 24,* 623–647.

Ospina, S., & Sorenson, G. (2006). A constructionist lens on leadership: Charting new territory. In Goethals, George, & Sorenson (Eds.), *The quest for a general theory of leadership* (pp. 188–204). Cheltenham, England: Edward Elgar.

Parry, K., & Bryman, A. (2006). Leadership in organizations. In S. Clegg, C. Hardy, T. Lawrence, & W. Nord (Eds.), *The Sage handbook of organization studies.* (2nd ed. pp. 447–468). London, England: Sage.

Pearce, C., & Conger, J. (2003). All those years ago: the historical underpinnings of shared leadership. In C. L. Pearce, & J. A. & Conger (Eds.), *Shared leadership: Reframing the hows and whys of leadership* (pp. 1- 18). Thousand Oaks, CA: Sage.

Pfeffer, J. (1977). The ambiguity of leadership. *Academy of Management Review, 2*(1), 104–112.

Rost, J. (1992). Leadership: A postindustrial approach. *European Management Journal, 10*(2), 193–202.

Sandberg, J., & Targama, A. (2007). *Managing understanding in organizations.* London, England: Sage.

Sandelands, L., & Drazin, R. (1989). On the language of organization theory. *Organization Studies, 10,* 457–478.

Sendjaya, S., Sarros, J. C., & Santora, J. C. (2008). Defining and measuring servant leadership behaviour in organizations. *Journal of Management Studies, 45*(2), 402–424.

Uhl-Bien, M. (2006). Relational leadership theory: Exploring the social processes of leadership and organizing. *The Leadership Quarterly, 17*(6), 654–676.

Uhl-Bien, M., & Pillai, R. (2007). The romance of leadership and the social construction of followership. In B. Shamir, R. Pillai, M. Bligh, & M. Uhl-Bien (Eds.), *Follower-centered perspectives on leadership: A tribute to the memory of James R. Meindl* (pp. 187–209). Greenwich, CT: Information Age Publishing.

Western, S. (2008). *Leadership: A critical text.* Thousand Oaks, CA: Sage.

Yukl, G. (1999). An evaluation of conceptual weaknesses in transformational and charismatic leadership theories. *Leadership Quarterly, 10,* 285–305.

CHAPTER 8

DIALOGUE

A Dialogue on Theorizing Relational Leadership

David V. Day and Wilfred (Bill) Drath

DAY'S FIRST LETTER TO DRATH

Dear Bill,

I wanted to start off our dialogue about "Theorizing Relational Leadership" with some brief personal reactions, observations, and questions that perhaps you could help clarify, illuminate, or just plain discuss. After reading through our set of papers, I think my general reaction was "pizzled." I know it's not a word, but I heard it used in a TED talk and thought it captured my reaction quite well: simultaneously pissed off and puzzled.

Now, that may seem a little harsh, so let me elaborate. The p.o.'d part of my reaction, I think, stems from the postmodern tone in several of the chapters. To me, much of postmodernism, including deconstruction, smacks of modern-day Sophistry—and I do mean that in a pejorative sense. The focus is on argument and not on trying to measure, predict, and understand empirically what is the essence of, in the present case, "relational-

Advancing Relational Leadership Research, pages 227–251
Copyright © 2012 by Information Age Publishing
All rights of reproduction in any form reserved.

ity," which is perhaps why I'm puzzled as well. How can I engage in a dialogue in which my values are so misaligned with the topic? My training is in industrial-organizational (IO) psychology, which is hardly the bastion of postmodernism in the academy! Nonetheless, it does highlight my unease (or I could be cute and say *dis-ease*) with some of the underlying assumptions and values reflected in the chapters. Specifically, that postpositive—or what I would call scientific—approaches to theorizing about relationship leadership (RLT) need to be chucked. I think the approaches also overly simplify things into and Entity versus a Constructivist approach. Is there not a continuum there?

So Bill: HELP ME UNDERSTAND why I'm pizzled.

Sincerely,

Dave

DRATH'S FIRST LETTER TO DAY

Dear Dave,

I think you're pizzled because it's a pizzling time we live in.

Let's say the key dividing line between "modernism" and "postmodernism" is a disagreement over whether truth is "found" or "made."

The modernist, an advocate for science as the pre-eminent tool for revealing the nature of the world, tends to believe that there are big important truths out there waiting to be found. Not all truths; there are, say, personal truths in which what is true for me may not be true for you (like the way we can disagree about God). But, for the empirical truths about the way things really are, science is capable of (eventually) finding them out.

For the postmodernist, truths are sentences (strings of sounds), and sentences are human artifacts. As artifacts, they are constructed when people talk. Some truths—like many of the ones about physics and biology—tend to work better than others for some purposes, like smashing atoms or curing psoriasis. Others, like the varying truths told within differing cultures, are incommensurable. But, all truths are thought to be constructs, artifacts of human interaction through language.

Both of these positions have their flaws. For the modernist, for whom truth is correspondence to the way things really are, the challenge is to say how she would ever tell "the way things really are." She cannot put "things as they really are" in one column on a chart and truths about those things in another column to show how the truths correspond to the "reality." Both columns would be representations; comparing one representation to another is not what the modernist means by the truth corresponding to the way things really are. The difficulty in meeting this challenge leads the modernist to accuse the postmodernist of splitting hairs and acting silly.

For the postmodernist, for whom truth is a social agreement, or the end of ideal discourse, the challenge is to say how he can explain the way some things are true even when no one is talking about them, or when people are saying the wrong things about them. There was nuclear energy before anyone even dreamed of it; the continents drifted even when geologists agreed 100% that they didn't. This challenge leads many postmodernists to discount truth itself. Everything seems up for grabs in a great big language game.

So, it seems best not to insist too strongly on either one of these views. It seems more useful not to speak of truth on the basis of whether it is found or made. It's more productive to adopt a position that humans construct truth under pressure from causal forces. Of course, truth consists of sentences, and sentences are human-made, but some sentences work (or not) within limits and constraints imposed by forces humans do not control.

So, there are two important questions about the empirical versus constructionist approach to leadership, the entity versus the relational approach: (1) What are the sentences that make the most difference to our understanding of leadership? (2) Under what limits and constraints are those sentences useful in making leadership more effective?

What if we approached our conversation about these papers using these two questions?

Sincerely,

Bill

DAY'S SECOND LETTER TO DRATH

Dear Bill,

That was well-put. I appreciate your patience in helping me better understand social construction and postmodernism. So, OK, I'm game for what you have proposed—although I'm not sure what I'm getting myself into here!

I get the point that social construction is about how "truths" are created or co-created through social interaction. The notion that leaders as well as leadership are at least partly a function of how others think about those constructs is something that makes a good deal of sense. My graduate advisor was Bob Lord, who was instrumental in advancing what we know about leadership perceptions and implicit leadership theories. But, this knowledge was constructed from a modern or entity-based perspective. That is why I don't see the two approaches as necessarily at odds or relegated to an either/or proposition. Although having said that, I can see how something like a cognitive categorization approach to leadership (Lord, Foti, & De Vader, 1984) puts most of the impetus for "meaning-making" on the individual perceiver rather than on a social process in which meaning is co-created.

Something that I think is at the root of my "pizzlement" (!) is the notion that it is solely through social interaction that truths are constructed. In terms of taking up your offer to identify what are the sentences that make the most difference to our understanding of leadership, I went to the chapters that we read as background for our dialogue to find an exemplar that we might use to begin framing our thinking around entity and constructionist perspectives. This particular statement stood out:

> If we take the notion of social construction seriously, leadership is about meaning work and managing contexts. People who wish to construct lead positions within teams, organizations, and societies need to learn how to work within the flow of conversation and develop practices that allow them to make sense of it and create new potentials for meaning-making and action that can shape its direction (Barge, Ch. 4)

This seems to jump to a pretty sophisticated or complex way of thinking about leadership (e.g., meaning-making). Where I struggle to see this as making leadership particularly more effective is that it is likely to be at odds with how most individuals perceive or construct leadership. We know from the research conducted on implicit leadership theories (Eden & Leviathan, 1975; Epitropaki & Martin, 2004; Rush, Thomas, & Lord, 1977) that individuals hold particular notions of what constitutes effective leadership, and these implicit theories generally do not include things like working within the flow of conversation to create new potentials for meaning-making.

So, the risk is that if we attempt to put this social construction perspective into practice, there may be the real possibility that it creates a mismatch between what an aspiring leader is actually doing and what others in the situation expect him/her to do. If direction is needed in a team, then most would expect the leader to focus on providing that direction rather than create new potentials for meaning-making. You articulated this dilemma quite well in your book *The deep blue sea* (Drath, 2001) with the difficulties that Elena experienced being seen as an effective leader among employees of the Zoffner Piano Company. More complex leadership principles were being called forth, yet those engaged in the social construction of Elena's leadership were not prepared to see leadership in those terms. That story had a happy ending, but I'm not at all convinced that it would end so well in other contexts.

In more practical terms, if the first step in developing an effective team—something that many consider to be essential to effective leadership—then it is recommended that a leader first establish his or her competence. Without that perceived competence, there is little reason to trust that the leader has what it takes to actually lead the team. I can't tell whether this is the same as "meaning work and managing contexts." Maybe it is, but if so, then why is all the jargon about social construction even needed?

I'm getting pizzleder and pizzleder....

Sincerely,

Dave

DRATH'S SECOND LETTER TO DAY

Dear Dave,

If we make no other contribution in this exchange of views, we will at least have tried out a useful new word and put it through its paces (pizzled, pizzlement, pizzleder—pizzledest!) Is pizzlement a new emotion or a new word for an old emotion? Does it matter?

Back to leadership. You say that at the root of your pizzlement is "the notion that it is solely through social interaction that truths are constructed." I assume this means you think there are some truths about leadership that fall outside the sphere of human talk, such as: Leadership is a natural, biological fact about humans (and other creatures as well). A natural leader can just show up. No one has to "construct" such a person.

OK, but someone (other than the natural leader herself) has to believe that (and respond as if) what the leader is doing is, for want of a better term, *leadership*. Who's to say that the behavior of the natural leader is not taken to be offensive butting in, inappropriate egotistical preening, or even wimpy persuasion where force is needed? The basic relational point is that whatever is *given* (a leader, a rock, a fact) must be *taken* before it's anything at all. Relations precede entities because relations (the given *plus* the taken) pick out some things and not others as entities.

Having harangued you about this, I must say that relationalism is not an idea that, on its own, necessarily makes for good leadership practice. It's a useful idea for understanding what's going on with leadership from a whole-system perspective. But—and maybe this helps your pizzlement—understanding leadership that way may or may not (and perhaps more often may not) help a person become what others take to be a leader. (Of course, being taken to be a leader does not exhaust what leadership is or may become.)

The sentence you cite can sound like a prescription for how to "do" leadership when everyone "takes the notion of social construction seriously." Needless to say, everyone doesn't; in fact, only a few do. But, I read the sentence another way.

First, I take your point that there are many contexts in which people do in fact believe in natural leaders (and not in, say, leadership as dialogue). In such a context, natural leaders are looked for and looked to. When they show up, they are welcomed as special people who can take charge and get things done. In such a context, therefore, it might be more than a stretch to describe the leader as working "within the flow of conversation." Unless! Unless working within the flow of conversation refers not to some particular way of talking and instead refers to playing the culturally meaningful role of take-charge leader. I don't see anything in Barge's sentence that rules that out. In fact, "meaning work and managing contexts" seems to refer directly to how an effective leader has to make sense within a given culture. Where the sentence goes astray, if it does, is in its implication that a leader on her own can do meaning work and manage contexts. From a constructionist and relational perspective, she is always a participant with others in doing that. If this is true, then great leaders might be those folks who find themselves in a great-leader culture and figure out how to play the part. This seems like a relational take on what your teacher was saying long ago, eh?

Sincerely,

Bill

DAY'S THIRD LETTER TO DRATH

Dear Bill,

Whoa there—the sound you hear is that of my eyeballs spinning around in my head. OK, I got 'em focused.

I am with you, up to a point.

Working backwards from your previous statements, I agree wholeheartedly that it takes more than a solitary leader for leadership to happen. It is embedded in interactions and social relations. But, at some point, the leader has to offer something of value, no? For example, a compelling vision of the future is often highlighted as important for attracting followers and enacting successful change (Kotter, 2007). In more everyday kinds of contexts, leaders (and, yes, followers, too) make decisions. There is something tangible there. The relational piece comes into play in terms of how others receive the proposed vision or react to the leader's decisions, also acknowledging that who is exercising leadership in the form of decisions, influence, or whatnot can change dynamically. If others reject those overtures, then perhaps it is fair to say that effective leadership has failed. But, there is something offered initially—the vision does not always emerge through a co-creative process. Does it? It is more than merely figuring out how to play the part of a "great leader" in the appropriate culture. It is bringing something of substance to bear in a particular context.

So, if there is an objective truth in all this, it is that individuals vary in terms of how effective they are as leaders. Sure, some of this has to do with others granting them leadership space for lack of a better term. But, the reasons why individuals vary in their leadership effectiveness goes to some concrete basis in expertise, creativity, inspiration, or other individual difference factors that have at their core a quantifiable skill. Relational processes play a role in crafting what becomes or does not become "leadership" in a given context, including how the purported leader, as well as his or her vision (decision, behavior, or other action), are constructed by others. But, at the essence of that social construction process, something tangible has happened. A simple test of that is whether or not others agree on the meaning of that action (Bliese, 2000). If there is evidence of agreement, would that not suggest that there is something substantively behind that agreement? Or, are people agreeing on what has been *taken* irrespective of what has been *given?* To me, the alternative would be that "there is no there there," to quote Gertrude Stein about Oakland, California. Perhaps that is the point of the social constructionists, *which neatly dispenses with any sense of individual merit or differential human abilities.*

"Oh, I'm sorry," he says, dripping with sarcasm. "It must be my creeping objectivism rearing its ugly head again." Not to get off on a tangent, but what is all that about? There appears to be entity thinking and objectivism creeping all over the place (see Kennedy, Carroll, Francoeur, & Jackson, Chapter 6) despoiling the virginal social construction ideas that a "certain magic" (this volume) comes about when story-lines are brought into development practice. This is not only ridiculous, it is offensive. Talk about marginalization!

Ok, now I am pizzled again with a capital P.

Help me, Bill, help me! I know you to be a reasonable person. . . .

Sincerely,

Dave

DRATH'S THIRD LETTER TO DAY

Dear Dave,

Chill, my friend. Reasonableness on the way. By my lights, anyway.

You say, "The relational piece comes into play in terms of how others receive the proposed vision or react to the leader's decisions." But, the relational piece must also come into play in the very idea of the leader. I don't assume that the leader is a pre-existing given that is prior to the relations in which leaders and followers find themselves. If it's important for a leader to have leadership effectiveness with "some concrete basis in expertise, creativity, inspiration, or other individual difference factors," it's because there is some need for a leader and for leadership effectiveness at all. Once people agree that a leader is needed, and what a leader is like, and what constitutes leadership effectiveness, and so forth, then what you say is more than likely true. But, all that social stage-setting counts for a lot in my book and is often ignored in the literature where (priorly-existing) leaders usually just show up ready to enter into relations with (priorly-existing) followers.

Once people agree that part of leader effectiveness is supplying a vision, then, and only then, does it make sense for the leader to create a vision. But, without that initial construction of "leader-as-vision-giver," or "vision-as-effective leadership," an individual offering a vision might be taken as a poet, or a dreamer, or a scamp.

However, I do share some of your frustration with the relational talk in some of these papers. Relational thinking (constructionism especially) is about as user-friendly as a PC. There are a lot of menus, sub-menus, shortcuts, and code needed to talk about everything one is accustomed to explaining relatively simply in terms of essence, character, personality, and substance (those things we Westerners have assumed for so long that a person simply *possesses* as a distinct individual) which must now be explained in terms of a "space between" where there doesn't seem to be any there there.

For example, I think it's a mistake to say (see Kennedy et al., Chapter 6) that the traditional tools used to measure and evaluate leadership development "don't relate to the spaces in between people where collective leadership builds." But, of course they do! If a relational approach to leadership development is worth anything, we don't need to change the rules about what is important to measure. We should be able to deliver on the old measures and *some new ones as well* that have never been contemplated from the entity perspective!

The point is not to make entity thinking the "bad old way," but to recognize its limitations. For example, taking an entity approach to understanding leadership has not been particularly helpful in trying to understand how to make shared leadership or leadership across significant differences more effective. I think a relational perspective can help with these needs for leadership by pointing to the generative capacity of the spaces in between, where people share or where they meet difference. Those spaces aren't just barriers; they can be productive of new ideas that integrate old ideas. But, only if the people doing shared leadership or leadership across boundaries see leadership in new ways that go beyond concepts of leadership effectiveness based on leader behavior.

Sincerely,

Bill

DAY'S FOURTH LETTER TO DRATH

Dear Bill,

You are such the voice of reason—thanks for that! But, despite your reasonableness, I am still having some difficulty with what I see as the strong relational approach. To paraphrase the old Zen joke (oxymoron?), it sounds like it is relationships all the way down. To me, this sounds as potentially limiting as the LERO (leader-centric, entitism, romanticism, and objectivism) approach that has been heavily criticized (see Alvesson & Sveningsson, Chapter 7). Let me try and explain.

You propose that leadership cannot be called forth until people agree that leadership is needed and what form of leadership effectiveness is required. I can see this, at least in certain situations. This goes to my earlier comment about others recognizing and allowing for a leadership space. But, my concern is that, if the focus is on what you call the *social stage setting*—regardless of how important it might be and how overlooked it has been—that it risks allowing the pendulum to swing too far in the direction of social construction in ignoring the potential skills required to participate effectively in leadership. From what you are saying, it sounds that if a group must first decide what a leader is like and what constitutes leadership effectiveness (although the research on leadership prototypes and implicit leadership theories would suggest that there is some general agreement on these expectations even across cultures) that it is pretty much pot luck in terms of the quality of leadership it will get. To me, it goes directly to the issue of whether or not leadership can be considered as a type of skilled performance. Can individuals be prepared to participate more effectively in leadership roles and processes, or is the leadership that evolves or emerges in a collective dependent on something other than individual capabilities?

I am sure that you will likely say yes, it depends on more than individual capabilities. It also depends on the quality of the social interactions and relationships that ultimately define leadership (Uhl-Bien, 2006). Fair enough. But, here then is the burning question at hand: *Does it then make any sense to invest in leader development?* As you well know, because this description comes from the Center for Creative Leadership, *leader development* has been defined as "those efforts targeted at increasing the capabilities of individuals to effectively participate in leadership roles and processes" (McCauley, Van Velsor, & Ruderman, 2010). This definition is very entity-oriented and also has its roots solidly in objectivism; however, it also recognizes the multi-level nature of leadership. Individuals form the essential building blocks of dyadic interactions, which are then part of the broader collectives that are formed in terms of teams and organizations. I agree that a sole focus on individuals is LERO-limited (now there's a pizzler), but ignoring the individual completely risks having leadership processes completely untethered to any knowledge, skills, and abilities that might help make these relationships and other interactions that compose leadership operate more effectively.

I will be forthcoming in my biases that I consider leader development from an expert performance model (Day, Harrison, & Halpin, 2009). Similar to domains such as music, sport, and other fields (e.g., medical diagnoses), becoming an expert in a particular domain requires not just training and development but also practice (Ericsson & Charness, 1994; Ericsson, Krampe, & Tesch-Römer, 1993). There are some individuals who need less training and practice due to their natural gifts, but an assumption in this approach is that anyone can become a better leader, and if properly prepared and *when called to do so*, will likely contribute more effectively to relevant leadership outcomes than those who are unprepared.

To be clear on my thinking, social construction is important. Relationships are important. But, individuals and their differential levels of knowledge, skills, and abilities are important, too. It is not relations all the way down in my book. At the foundation of all of this are individuals, which is why their individual development is so important.

But, perhaps I'm missing something here.

Tell me, Bill, from a non-entivist perspective, does leader development matter?

Sincerely,

Dave

DRATH'S FOURTH LETTER TO DAY

Dear Dave,

To answer your last question, yes leader development usually matters (see below for exceptions). But, leadership development *always* matters, and I believe we'd be better off if we didn't think these were the same thing. Leadership development is the development of the collective capacity to produce leadership outcomes (such as direction, alignment, and commitment). To conflate *leader* with *leadership* development is to identify leadership outcomes solely with leaders, as if such outcomes were not a collective product. Follower development, peer development, colleague development, professional development, and organization development (to name a few) are also called for. To make leadership better, all of these "entities" require development in addition to leaders.

Surely, there are collectives in which leader development is not needed to develop leadership, simply because leadership happens without leaders. Think of a workgroup comprising professional peers who each studiously *avoid* taking on a leader role, and insist on creating a vision, organizing themselves, and generating commitment to their shared task through consensus and dialogue. They may even want to improve their ability to do this, and so they may seek leadership development and not need leader development. This is when leader development doesn't matter and is not worth investing in. Current providers of leader development better gear up their developmental curricula to include development of leadership, which means developing the beliefs and practices by which the whole of a collective produces leadership, even when those beliefs and practices do not include individuals known as leaders.

Is leadership a skilled performance? Yes, of course, but not of the leader alone. The performance of leadership is the achievement of everyone who participates. If the approach to leadership being taken in a collective—say aboard a Royal Navy frigate in the Napoleonic Wars—is one of total dominance and command of the leader, and the leader is unskilled, you have a disaster. But, in that same condition, if the followers are not right seamen and lack the skill of bending to command with just the proper amount of give and not too much, you have other varieties of disaster: mindless obedience or mutiny. These interact: The skilled captain calls forth the right seaman, and vice versa. Total dominance and command is a cultural achievement within which the personal skills are integrated.

Yes, my friend, if pushed to the wall on this, I would say that it is relations all the way down. I must put the term "entity" in quotes to express the way in which I see "entity" as an outcome of relations. Everything stands in relation to something else. Even such seemingly absolute entities as the hardness of a stone stand in relation to that which strikes it and finds it hard. The ability of a pianist to play perfect trills stands in relation to the ability of a listener to detect such perfection (even if the listener is the pianist herself); without the proper detection, the perfect trill might become a spasmodic rattle; my imperfect trills can at times sound perfect to me. I think "entity" is a way of thinking about relations that simplifies the product by unifying it under a self-contained description. It's easier to think of a rock as being inherently hard or a leader as being inherently skilled. This simplification will continue to serve a purpose in everyday life probably forever. But, in certain professional endeavors such as leadership development, I believe this simplification is a ladder we have climbed up which we need to think about how to throw away because creating leadership in our ever more interconnected world requires us to think of things as relations.

Sincerely,

Bill

DAY'S FIFTH LETTER TO DRATH

Dear Bill,

Well Bill, I hope you know that you are "preaching to the choir" about the need to distinguish between leader development and leadership development. I argued for this distinction in the research literature over a decade ago (Day, 2000), and I completely agree with your point that failing to do so runs the risk of attributing all leadership outcomes to leaders. There is also an important distinction in terms of intervention focus with regard to leader and leadership development. With the former, I see the focus as being on developing individual *human capital* skills, and more specifically, enhancing one's intrapersonal competence base through self-awareness, self-regulation, and self-motivation. In terms of leadership development, the focus is more on developing interpersonal relations in the form of *social capital* skills, which involve building and accessing social resources embedded in work relationships. The underlying leadership model is inherently relational, based on commitments, trust, and mutual respect. In comparison (or should I say relationally??), the leader development model is grounded more in individual power and influence, knowledge (i.e., expertise), and personal trustworthiness. So to summarize, I think we are pretty much on the same page about leader development and leadership development. But, I also see some potential points of difference in our relative perspectives.

You say that leadership development *always* matters (your emphasis). I am not so sure. I think there is a real risk in jumping to leadership development before individuals have had the opportunity to develop individual competence to participate effectively in leadership roles and processes. Just as differentiation always precedes integration (Gharajedaghi, 1999), I think that leader development must always precede leadership development. If it doesn't, it would be like dumping all the individual ingredients in a mixing bowl and popping it into an oven in hopes that a cake will eventually materialize. Those various ingredients need to be first carefully prepared and then combined in a prescribed manner in order to get the desired result. Similarly, putting unprepared people into situations in which leadership needs to be developed is asking for frustration and futility—what Kegan (1994) would term putting people "in over their heads" to the extreme extent that they are paralyzed and unable to learn. This is why I believe that leader development should *always* precede leadership development. Intrapersonal competence is needed as a foundation on which interpersonal competence and social capital can develop. The more pressing concern is with how to best connect leader development with leadership development in a systematic manner. Maybe that is where our biggest differences reside in the whole entity/relational debate about the nature of leadership.

Along these lines, you mentioned that a group might want to create a vision, organize, and generate commitment to shared work through consensus and dialogue. But, is it a reasonable expectation that a group could effectively use a more complex leadership principle in the form of dialogue without a firm grounding in the more basic principles of personal dominance and interpersonal influence? According to a very wise sage (Drath, 2001), a complex leadership principle such as dialogue is needed mostly when the limits of the other less complex principles are experienced. My interpretation of this is that trying to engage in something like relational dialogue without the proper foundation in more basic leadership principles (and having experienced their respective limits) is unlikely to bring about the desired leadership. I see this as a very important point in helping me better understand how we might be able to throw away the ladder of leader development as you suggest, without leaving us up a tree without the requisite skills to either climb higher or descend to a more appropriate level for the particular collective at hand.

Speaking of dialogue, I'm not sure whether what we have been engaged in here can be characterized as such, but I have enjoyed and learned much from it just the same. It is interesting how the topic morphed into a discussion of development rather than leadership, *per se*. But, given our respective interests, it probably comes as no surprise. Where I leave this conversation is with a bit of a better understanding about Relational Leadership and the role that social construction processes play in that form of leadership. Alas, I am not convinced that it is "relations all the way down" as you suggest. To me, effective leadership has at the bottom of all those relations an individual skilled component that enhances the likelihood that effective relations will be developed when called upon.

In any event, thanks for sharing your insight and wisdom, It has helped me come to what I think is a deeper appreciation for these kinds of relational perspectives on leadership and its development.

Sincerely,

Dave

DRATH'S FIFTH LETTER TO DAY

Dear Dave,

Of course, we are in the main in full-throated, choir-singing harmony. I expect we could put our heads together to come up with a way to connect leader with leadership development in a systematic way, throw the ladder away, and declare victory over the forces of disorganization.

But, first . . .

First, I'm going to push out a bit of "strong" relational theory, which I'm sure will be familiar to you (if a bit over the top), then back off, and offer what I hope is a pragmatic alternative to the whole entity/relational distinction.

You say, "effective leadership has at the bottom of all those relations an individual skilled component that enhances the likelihood that effective relations will be developed when called upon." From the admittedly minority perspective of a strong relational theory, as I know you know, there is no individual component (skilled or not) at the bottom of all those relations. Individual skill (as well as individual beliefs, attitudes, values—up to and including individual psychology overall) is *constituted by* the relations in which the human creature is embedded. (I must say something like "human creature," since "person" or "individual" assumes the priority of the very feature I am trying to relationalize.) Before, or without, relations with other humans and the culture overall, you got *nada*: a bundle of nerves and tissue with a grey blob on top. It is participation with other humans who are already in relations with other humans who are all connected up into human cultures that brings about "the individual." Strong relational theory denies that there is *any* aspect of a human being beyond its physical existence that exists prior to its relations. There is no such thing as a private, self-generated psychological being who goes out into the world to find relations to enter into. So, there is no way that some prior "individual skilled component" can enhance the "likelihood that effective relations will be developed when called upon." From a strong relational perspective, that idea gets everything backwards. The "individual skilled component" is itself already relational, so it can't be something essentially non-relational waiting at the bottom to make relations more effective.

I am inserting a moment here for your eyeballs to stop spinning.

OK, so the strong theory is a bit much to swallow. However, I do believe the strong version of relational theory is important as a counter-weight to the individualism juggernaut that Western culture has created. It is important to offer an alternative to the idea that, "at bottom," human beings are essentially separate, independent, and capable of private self-generation. Considering the extent to which we humans are social creatures, depending for our very survival on our ability to create sustaining cultures, this individualist view seems a bit romantic, even nostalgic. The strong theory is just another way to point out that there isn't anything "essential" about human beings since we are products of ongoing and ever-changing relations; we are embedded social creatures who transform as societies and cultures transform.

But, I would rather be pragmatic about all of this. What difference does it make if we leadership theorists and professionals think of the individual as an entity or as a relationality? Seems like we can disagree about that while agreeing that leadership does not spring newborn from the mind of the leader, that it is not a protean force of the leader's personality, that followers are not passive receivers of the leader's thoughts, that it is, one way or another, the product of people working, thinking, talking, and acting *together*. This is the important bit of constructionism: Leadership in the sense we mean it (that is, as a non-coercive process) is not a naturally occurring biological fact, but a human-made, social artifact.

If we were to shift our focus from the actors (leaders and followers) to the outcomes (direction, alignment, commitment) we would get two benefits: (1) All of the research on the actors would become an available resource to help us figure out how to make leadership as a system work better (instead of settling for how to make leaders better); and (2) we could learn how to support the emergence and skilled practice of new forms of leadership, including various kinds of shared leadership, leadership across cultural and valuational differences, leadership as a complex system, and who knows what else around the corner (Drath, McCauley, Palus, Van Velsor, O'Connor, & McGuire, 2008). This is a project that can be carried out by leadership constructionists of every stripe.

A final note regarding individual skill and your point that individual development must precede development of social systems. This makes sense, and it may be true (because it is assumed to be true) in many, if not most, cases. Yet, maybe this is because we don't know how to support the development of individuals while they develop leadership. I have worked with a number of action learning teams who invariably construct some version of shared leadership and accomplish their work as peers and colleagues. From a traditional perspective, this may not look like either leader or leadership development, but if we see leadership wherever and whenever we see its outcomes, peers can and do create leadership without leaders. Surely, this calls forth developmental growth simultaneously at both the individual and systemic levels.

Thanks, David, for your patience and openness in this conversation. Your thoughtful questions and critique have given me a chance to practice speaking a relational language of leadership. I appreciate your willingness to let me try it out on you.

Sincerely,

Bill

CONCLUSION[1]

Reflection on "Advancing Relational Leadership" Dialogue by David V. Day

In reading the papers for the first section of this book, as well as in corresponding with Bill Drath during our electronic "dialogue" process, a number of issues bothered me (hence, my "pizzlement"). On reflection, these bothersome issues were based, to some degree, on tone, but more centrally on the content of the various relational perspectives. The issues of tone are less substantive so I will highlight those quickly and move on to the more weighty issues of content. But, as will be discussed, there is a connection between tone and content because, if scholars interested in relational leadership cannot recognize that entity and constructionist perspectives are equally worthy, then there is no possibility of dialogue occurring. And, ongoing dialogue is necessary and needed if the leadership field is going to move forward. Also, I will try to not repeat points raised by Boas Shamir (Chapter 17) in his eloquent critique of the social constructionist approaches presented in this book, but I will begin with reiterating his general theme.

Throwing Out the Baby

As noted in my correspondence with Bill, I took exception to certain tones perceived to be dismissive of an entity approach to leadership. In some cases, there were references to "creeping objectivism" as compared with the introduction of social constructionist story-lines that were heralded as bringing "certain magic" into the development process (Kennedy,

Carroll, Francoeur, & Jackson, Chapter 6). There was also what I read as a flippant comment (apologies if that was not the intent) that leadership development from a social constructionist perspective cannot easily use— *and would not want to* (my italics)—the same reporting, measurement, and evaluation tools linked with the entity perspective. Why wouldn't they want to use such methods? Are these methods inherently flawed? If so, then how are they flawed? Without greater justification as to the purported limits of traditional research methods, this is not very constructive (pun intended) or helpful. There is a related comment by Kennedy et al. that "it is impossible to separate epistemology from perspective." This appears to mean that, if one wants to study something relational, then only certain theoretical perspectives and corresponding types of methods are appropriate. I am concerned that these kinds of proposals will only serve to enhance exclusivity over inclusiveness when it comes to how to best conceptualize and study relational leadership. It is important to remember that "a way of seeing is a way of not seeing" (Poggi, 1965, p. 284).

A similar but less pejorative perspective can be found in Uhl-Bien (2006) in which it is stated that relational perspectives "require new standards of validity, reliability, and trustworthiness that are often uncomfortable to entity researchers" (p. 666). Perhaps entity researchers are uncomfortable with such statements because no suggestions are offered as to what might be these new standards of reliability, validity, and trustworthiness. I am not sure that constructionist, poststructuralist, and postmodernist approaches would even acknowledge such concepts as reliability and validity. But, the deeper issue is that there seems to be this nagging assumption that traditional tools of measurement and analyses are hopelessly inadequate or otherwise inappropriate to use in studying aspects of relational leadership. Whereas the focus of entity research might have missed important aspects of relational processes, it does not necessarily mean that the traditional research tools are so inherently flawed that they cannot be used in better understanding process issues. As Bill Drath noted in our dialogue, we do not need to completely change the rules about what is important to measure or how to measure. New tools would be welcome additions to the traditional ones, but the latter do not need to be completely discarded in order to study relational leadership appropriately and comprehensively.

The point has been made by others (e.g., Drath, 2001) that social constructionist approaches to fostering relational dialogue are most appropriate when the limits of more basic (i.e., entity-based) approaches are reached. Thus, there should be a place at the relational leadership table for both kinds of approaches. Research that is inclusive in terms of epistemology is surely likely to yield greater insights into relational leadership than those perspectives that operate from a platform of exclusivity. As expressed by Shamir (Chapter 17) there is a difference between advancing Relational Leadership Theory and "throwing the baby out with the bathwater."

Definition and Terminology

The content issues are more interesting from a scholarship perspective, so I will spend the remainder of this brief reflection piece highlighting the issues that surprised, interested, and/or bothered me, starting with definitional and terminology issues. Returning to the foundational work of Uhl-Bien (2006), relational leadership was defined as a *social influence process* in which emergent coordination and change are constructed and produced (italics added). This seems like a reasonable operational definition, but it hardly is paradigm breaking. Most of the traditional definitions of leadership refer to some sort of social influence process. What is surprising and conspicuous in its absence across the chapters is any discussion of social influence processes as part of relational leadership. Based on this definition, relational leadership could be studied from either an entity (i.e., constructivist) or relational (i.e., constructionist) perspective. In other words, when one closely examines what is actually being proposed with regard to relational leadership, it is a less radical departure from traditional leadership approaches than some of its proponents let on.

There are some issues of terminology that are bothersome. Uhl-Bien (2006) differentiates between *relational constructionist* and *cognitive constructivist* approaches. The former is purportedly steeped in relational ontology (i.e., all social realities are interdependent or co-dependent constructions) in which the primacy of relations is assumed, whereas the latter is grounded in an entity perspective in which the basic unit of analysis is the individual. The terminology of *constructionist* versus *constructivist* is quite important but probably not readily apparent to those outside this field of study. More pointedly, some further discussion and dialogue is needed as to whether these can be conceptualized along a continuum of entity to relational, or are these truly discrete ontological and epistemological classes. The assumption reflected across a number of these chapters suggests—or overtly states—that it is the latter. Alternative ways to think about these possibilities might be one particular way of engaging constructively in advancing relational leadership.

Another point of clarification needs to be made regarding whether relational leadership is based mainly in relationships or in relational ontology. There is a difference. Bill Drath clearly articulated what he called "strong relational theory" that "denies that there is *any* aspect of human being beyond its physical existence that exists prior to its relations" (italics in original). In other words, it is relations all the way down. But, even Drath acknowledges that strong relational theory is a bit hard to swallow and is not very helpful practically. He suggests that it is perhaps most useful as a philosophical foil to strong individualism and the entity approach, which has dominated scholarly fields such as leadership. But, again, this is not the same as studying relationships. Those working in the field of relational leadership need to clarify the primary focus of study and whether a strong relational ontology is truly being embraced if the focus of study is purely on interpersonal relationships.

The Nature of Leadership

The question of "what is leadership" has been debated for ages and will not be resolved here; however, and more troubling, I am skeptical that what are proclaimed as advances in relational leadership will bring any greater clarity to the debate. In an early piece that might be considered foundational to Relational Leadership Theory, Hosking (1988) argued that it is not enough to understand what leaders do in advancing a better understanding of leadership. What matters from her perspective (and presumably those promoting relational leadership) is to go beyond the entitative approaches to focus on leadership processes. This so-called "processual approach" has its basis in what Hosking calls "skillful" organizing. It is beyond the scope of this brief reflection to expand on what "skillful organizing" means, but suffice it to say that it is not what you think—especially if you endorse an entity perspective.

The point about the need to focus on process in order to understand leadership in going beyond understanding leaders is well-taken, but there are also potential limits in just focusing on processes and the "space between." This issue probably goes to the heart of where Bill and I disagree most vigorously. This disagreement clearly reveals my entitative biases because I believe that individuals can and do develop leadership-related skills. These skills can be in relevant areas, such as self-awareness, communication, decision-making, social influence, and ethics, among a whole host of other intrapersonal and interpersonal competencies. But, as already noted in this reflection, Bill sees it truly as relations all the way down. In his words, individual skill is *constituted by* the relations in which the person (or "human creature" in his words) is embedded (italics in original). Without relations, there is nothing (i.e., *nada*). I can appreciate his point, but I disagree with it. This is the entity and relational standoff in a nutshell.

This standoff reflects a fundamental disagreement about the ontology of leadership. I see leadership as grounded in individual knowledge, skills, and abilities, which is why I have argued that leader development must precede leadership development to be effective (Day, 2000; Day, Harrison, & Halpin, 2009). Bill believes that leadership development—defined in terms of a broader, collective capacity to produce leadership outcomes such as direction, alignment, and commitment (McCauley, Van Velsor, & Ruderman, 2010)—can be sought without preliminary development of individual leaders. Unfortunately, I fear there might be some misunderstanding in how I conceptualize leader development, which is reflected in Bill's priority of leadership development over leader development. I agree completely with Bill that leadership outcomes can be realized without the efforts of any single leader. But, another possibility is that everyone in the collective participates in leadership processes; thus, the effectiveness of that process can be enhanced by first developing the leadership-related skills of those individuals.

Everyone can become a better leader, but that does not necessarily make any of them *the* leader. Also, becoming a better leader means being better prepared to participate more effectively in leadership roles and processes, which includes such things as followership. A simple example of this is in understanding when to talk and when to listen in enhancing leadership and accomplishing its underlying tasks of direction, alignment, and commitment (Drath et al., 2008). In this way, individual leaders (who could be anyone) are connected to broader leadership processes. From my perspective, and in this way, the entity and the relational are inherently connected in enhancing effective leadership processes.

To reiterate (because I think this is key to our respective philosophical differences), at the core of effective leadership processes are competent individuals, and this competence can be developed initially in an intrapersonal manner and applied interpersonally. My take on Bill's thinking is that there is no individual competence—just as there is no independent entity—devoid of relations. To put a finer point on the distinction, I believe in individual agency, but Bill apparently does not. So, how might this standoff ever be sorted out? This might turn out to be pretty difficult, especially if entity and relational perspectives continue to disagree so strenuously on what constitutes sound research.

This actually helps me to better understand my rather visceral reaction (read: rant) about what I took to be dismissive comments about more traditional research approaches. If the entity tradition continues to be based in what some consider as obsolete approaches (i.e., the scientific method) whereas the relational perspective rejects those approaches in favor of constructionist, interpretive, poststructuralist (i.e., postmodernist) paradigms, then the standoff will never be resolved, and rapprochement will not occur. I am not smart enough to know the way forward on this dilemma, but it certainly seems that this is an ideal opportunity to walk our talk as a scholarly community with regard to dialogue. Collectively, we have to transcend dominance and influence approaches in this philosophical and scientific turf battle. It is not a matter of which approach is better. The limits of those leadership principles in this debate have been reached. Transcending these limits would help facilitate constructive scholarly dialogue on a variety of approaches to studying relational leadership. But, to do so, the first step is to acknowledge that we all have a stake in this dialogue (i.e., there is shared work), and second and more important, *our differing worldviews about the nature of leadership are equally worthy* (Drath, 2001, italics added). It does not help advance relational leadership to marginalize either set of epistemological and ontological assumptions. Without this recognition of the inherent worth of our very different worldviews and corresponding tools as a foundation from which to work in terms of enhancing dialogue, the real risk is in deepening the fractures among leadership scholars from entity and constructionist approaches. This would not only be unhelpful, it could further serve to slow the progress in developing broader, more integrative approaches to leadership.

Reflection: "Relational Leadership for the Future" by Wilfred (Bill) Drath

Imagine a group of managers from a large healthcare company coming together from a variety of functions to create an action team. Their goal is to formulate a vision along with a prototype test-of-concept for how their organization can make the transition away from a primary orientation on critical care (ERs and hospitals) to chronic illnesses such as diabetes, obesity, and cardio-pulmonary disorders (helping patients manage their health). They have been empowered by the executive committee not just to make a recommendation, but actually to make something happen, to run an experiment, to try out new approaches. None of them is an expert in chronic care. Although they come to this task from different levels in the organization, they come together as peers.

My experience working with such teams as this tells me that this group will function, and function well—although not without struggles—without a leader and therefore without followers. They will make decisions by consensus—and they will have to figure out how to do that; they will each propose ideas and guiding frameworks, and they will each take on implementation work; each will function in a variety of roles. Leadership will emerge not in the form of a leader or leaders, but in the form of certain outcomes, such as shared direction, alignment of work, and mutual commitment to the team and the work.

I am not alone in thinking that this is a microcosm of how work will be done in the future, as is plain from the chapters in this book. I believe an overall constructionist approach to leadership will be a key to helping people understand and develop this kind of leadership without leaders. A constructionist approach is needed if people are to understand leadership as something that is socially created, not leader-created.

I also believe that a relational approach will be needed if individuals are to actually *practice* leadership as a social achievement. The idea that *leaders* are socially constructed only goes halfway: Social construction gets you leaders, and then you're back to leader-created leadership. The idea that leader*ship* is socially constructed is a relational idea.

The key to a relational understanding of leadership is this: All leadership is shared leadership. From the highly charismatic leadership of an inspirational individual, to garden-variety leadership in a hierarchy, to messy political leadership in government, to joint leadership in an emergency room, to consensus on a project team, all leadership is shared leadership. What is usually called "shared leadership," referring to individuals taking turns being in charge, is just one point on a continuum of social practices by which people produce direction, alignment, and commitment.

To avoid confusing this continuum of leadership practices with the term shared leadership in its commonly-accepted usage, I refer to the continuum as relational leadership, because it is only by adopting a relational perspective on leadership that the full continuum of leadership practice comes into view, as shown in Figure 8.1.

Here are a few points on this relational leadership continuum: (Forms of leadership practice toward the left end are more individually-based, while forms toward the right end are more collectively-based; all of them are conceived as relational.)

All of these practices are shared social achievements; they are all produced by people working together. The thrust of this point is to de-center the leader-follower dynamic as the *sine qua non* of leadership. With a relational understanding of leadership, the leader-follower distinction and the dynamics based on it come into play in the forms of leadership practice toward the left of the continuum, but leadership practice continues with full force all the way to the right side, where the leader-follower dynamic disappears. In effect, a relational view of leadership diminishes the role of the word *leader* as the cognate of the word *leadership: Leadership* is not *leader-ship* (the act of the leader) but is a shared social activity (the act of a collective) that can be freed from a dependence on leaders. Leaders (and their followers) are not the only agents of leadership. Under some conditions—such as on the project team described above—people can achieve vital leadership outcomes as peers without leaders.

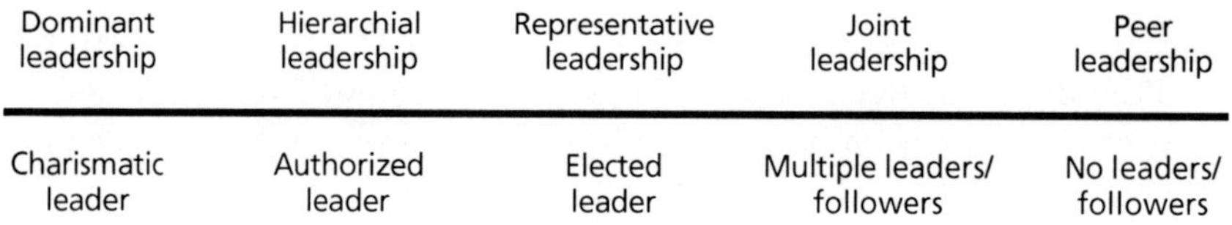

Dominant leadership	Hierarchial leadership	Representative leadership	Joint leadership	Peer leadership
Charismatic leader	Authorized leader	Elected leader	Multiple leaders/ followers	No leaders/ followers

Figure 8.1 Leadership Practices Continuum.

To de-center the role of the leader in leadership, one replaces the leader-follower dynamic as the heart of leadership with a set of socially desirable outcomes supporting cooperation (Drath et al., 2008). Leadership is then no longer essentially about leaders and followers, but about producing a set of outcomes (such as direction, alignment, and commitment) that support cooperation. This is just as true for leadership practices toward the left end of the continuum as it is for those toward the right end.

To see the force of this counter-intuitive conclusion, consider a highly dominant and charismatic figure, such as a naval commander in the British Navy during the Napoleonic Wars. Lord Nelson is just one example of an individual from that era who could lead a band of rough-and-ready seamen, many of whom were outright criminals, unite them into a formidable fighting force, inspire them to die for a cause remote to many of them, and, through the force of his personality, bring about victory. But, these charismatic abilities are not one-way; seeing them as the galvanizing acts of the leader that affect relatively passive followers is a blinkered view. The followers, the seamen, that Nelson led, like followers everywhere, are active agents. Followers participate directly in the production of leadership outcomes: There can be no direction if followers do not understand and accept; no alignment if followers do not coordinate; no commitment if followers do not put the shared work above their own interests. This is why followers must influence the leader if leadership is to happen.

This is no more radical than saying that in the leader-follower dynamic, the role and influence of the leader cannot be teased out from the role(s) and influence of the followers where the production of outcomes is concerned. (When leadership is framed in terms of the leader's action and the followers' more or less passive response, the leader is naturally understood to be predominant; but when considering outcomes, who is to say that the leader's initiative is more constitutive than the followers' response?)

From a relational perspective, even the highly charismatic leadership of Lord Nelson was a form of shared leadership practice. What connects this form of practice to what would appear to be its complete opposite (peer leadership without leaders or followers) is the production of outcomes supporting cooperation.

The left half of this continuum is well-developed in our Western world. Most leadership theory and leadership development practice is concerned with the left half. But, it is the right half of this continuum that will be important in the future, and it is therefore the right half that should be a central concern for leadership theorists and development practitioners. How can joint leadership and peer leadership be developed? What skills and abilities are required of individuals to achieve these leadership kinds? What factors in the culture of an organization need to be created or nurtured to support the creation or emergence of leaderless leadership? What revisions need to be made to our understanding of such ideas as the individual, individual skills, and individual responsibility?

The need to develop robust theory and practice for conceptualizing and developing leadership practices on the right side of the continuum should be a key driver behind the relational leadership conversation. We have developed impressive theories and have put into place effective developmental practices centered on the leader-follower dynamic. I believe we need to do the same for relational leadership. The chapters in this book represent a beginning for this agenda.

REFERENCES

Bliese, P. D. (2000). Within-group agreement, non-independence, and reliability: Implications for data aggregation and analysis. In K. J. Klein, & S. W. J. Kozlowski (Eds.), *Multilevel theory, research, and methods in organizations: Foundations, extensions, and new directions* (pp. 349–381). San Francisco, CA: Jossey-Bass.

Day, D. V. (2000). Leadership development: A review in context. *The Leadership Quarterly, 11,* 581–613.

Day, D. V., Harrison, M. M., & Halpin, S. M. (2009). *An integrative approach to leader development: Connecting adult development, identity, and expertise.* New York, NY: Routledge.

Drath, W. H. (2001). *The deep blue sea: Rethinking the source of leadership.* San Francisco, CA: Jossey-Bass.

Drath, W. H., McCauley, C. D., Palus, C. J., Van Velsor, E., O'Connor, P. M. G., & McGuire, J. B. (2008). Direction, alignment, commitment: Toward a more integrative ontology of leadership. *The Leadership Quarterly, 19,* 635–653.

Eden, D., & Leviathan, U. (1975). Implicit leadership theory as a determinant of the factor structure underlying supervisory behavior scales. *Journal of Applied Psychology, 60,* 736–741.

Epitropaki, O., & Martin, R. (2004). Implicit leadership theories in applied settings: Factor structure, generalizability, and stability over time. *Journal of Applied Psychology, 89,* 293–310.

Ericsson, K. A., & Charness, N. (1994). Expert performance: Its structure and acquisition. *American Psychologist, 49*(8), 725–747.

Ericsson, K. A., Krampe, R. T., & Tesch-Römer, C. (1993). The role of deliberate practice in the acquisition of expert performance. *Psychological Review, 100*(3), 363–406.

Gharajedaghi, J. (1999). *Systems thinking: Managing chaos and complexity.* Boston, MA: Butterworth Heinemann.

Hosking, D. M. (1988). Organizing, leadership and skilful process. *Journal of Management Studies, 25,* 147–166.

Kegan, R. (1994). *In over our heads: The mental demands of modern life.* Cambridge, MA: Harvard University.

Kotter, J. P. (2007). Leading change: Why transformation efforts fail. *Harvard Business Review, 85*(1), 96–103.

Lord, R., G., Foti, R. J., & De Vader, C. L. (1984). A test of leadership categorization theory: Internal structure, information processing, and leadership perceptions. *Organizational Behavior and Human Performance, 34,* 343–378.

McCauley, C. D., Van Velsor, E., & Ruderman, M. N. (2010). Introduction: Our view of leadership development. In E. Van Velsor, C. D. McCauley, & M. N. Ruderman (Eds.), *The Center for Creative Leadership handbook of leadership development.* 3rd ed. (pp. 1–26). San Francisco, CA: Jossey-Bass.

Poggi, G. (1965). A main theme of contemporary sociological analysis: Its achievements and limitations. *British Journal of Sociology, 16,* 283–294.

Rush, M. C., Thomas, J. C., & Lord, R. G. (1977). Implicit leadership theory: A potential threat to the internal validity of leader behavior questionnaires. *Organizational Behavior and Human Performance, 20,* 756–765.

Uhl-Bien, M. (2006). Relational leadership theory: Exploring the social processes of leadership and organizing. *The Leadership Quarterly, 17,* 654–676.

NOTE

1. Editors' Note: For this dialogue, the conclusion takes the form of individual reflections on the exchange. These reflections follow.

PART II

RESEARCHING THE RELATIONAL LEADERSHIP

CHAPTER 9

SOCIAL CHANGE LEADERSHIP AS RELATIONAL LEADERSHIP

**Sonia M. Ospina, Erica Gabrielle Foldy, Waad El Hadidy,
Jennifer Dodge, Amparo Hofmann-Pinilla,
and Celina Su**

This chapter offers a theoretical framework of social change leadership derived from a 7-year, multimodal empirical study of nonprofit social change organizations in the United States.[1] A constructionist/relational lens to leadership research (see Uhl-Bien, 2006, and the introductory chapter of this volume) informed the research program's data gathering, analysis, and interpretation. Our goal was to illuminate participants' meaning-making process in co-construction the leadership necessary to create social change.[2] Findings from the study revealed key elements that constitute the theoretical basis for understanding how leadership happens in social change organizations.

Social change organizations go beyond simply serving the disadvantaged to the harnessing of their power so that they can participate in actions that alter their constituents' material circumstances. Our framework (see Figure 9.1) has at its foundation the assumptions and values that give meaning to work and interaction, as participants in these organizations—leaders and followers alike—create a shared vision of the possible. This vision then

Advancing Relational Leadership Research, pages 255–302
Copyright © 2012 by Information Age Publishing
All rights of reproduction in any form reserved.

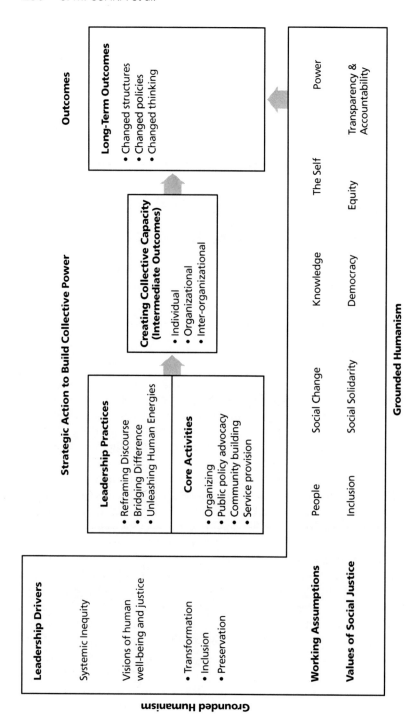

Figure 9.1 Theorizing social change leadership: A framework.

drives the practices and organizing activities to generate collective capacity. Finally, this capacity is leveraged as power in order to influence key external decision-makers who have authority to address problems affecting the organizations' constituents. We refer to this framework throughout this chapter.

Our approach contrasts with traditional or entity research in several critical ways. First, we do not draw from or aim to produce a testable causal model with propositions about antecedents or outcomes of leadership. Rather, consistent with interpretive epistemologies, we theorize social change leadership in ways that underscore the interconnections between various dimensions of leadership (i.e., its values, practices, and outcomes) and various levels of action (individual, organizational, and societal). These have largely been treated in isolation in the leadership literature, despite calls to find linkages (Yammarino, Dionne, Chun, & Dansereau, 2005). Second, rather than focusing on the variables found in traditional research, such as individual traits or behaviors, we highlight collective phenomena that are forged through mutual sense-making and action, such as values and practices (Drath, McCauley, Palus, Van Velsor, O'Connor, & McGuire, 2008; Foldy, Goldman, & Ospina, 2008; Hiller, Day, & Vance, 2006). Third, because we are interested in social change, our examination of individual and organizational levels is located within a broader societal context. We agree with scholars who argue that all leadership—including organizational leadership—is foundationally shaped by its social context (Bryman, Stephens, & à Campo, 1996; Osborn, Hunt, & Jauch, 2002; Ospina & Hittleman, forthcoming; Porter & McLaughlin, 2006).

Constructionist approaches have gained considerable theoretical traction in the leadership literature by highlighting the collective, generally tacit, agreements necessary for any type of leadership to emerge, from dictatorial, to hierarchical, to collaborative (Drath, 2001; Hosking, 2007; Ospina & Sorenson, 2006; Smircich & Morgan, 1982). Yet, to gain equal standing with entity-based research, constructionist scholarship must explicitly unpack the theoretical and methodological decisions associated with specific empirical findings.

By offering insights from our research program, this chapter contributes to advancing leadership knowledge in three ways. First, by presenting a framework that documents social change leadership, the chapter brings attention to an organizational context—social change organizations—that remains underexplored in the field. While this context may appear somewhat narrow, in fact it holds relevance for many types of organizations. Social change organizations (SCOs) explicitly attempt to re-shape society, yet many other kinds of organizations—from public agencies, to consumer product corporations, to communications firms—may implicitly do so as well. Moreover, SCOs are exemplars of how to strive for ambitious goals within turbulent environments with few material resources.

Second, the chapter offers a key tool for operationalizing construction-ist leadership research: "leadership practices." These collectively created, purposive bundles of activities that build leadership capacity represent a useful entry point to meaning-making and an appropriate unit of analysis. The construct draws on practice theory developed over the last several decades by sociologists and anthropologists (Bourdieu, 1998; Reckwitz, 2002; Schatzki, Cetina, & Von Savigny, 2001; Swidler, 2001) and more recently introduced in the leadership literature (Drath et al., 2008).

Third, lessons drawn from implementing this approach allow us to further explore the feasibility of a relational theory of leadership that bridges what today are two separate streams of research, the entity and the constructionist approaches (Uhl-Bien, 2006). The chapter illustrates these potential areas of convergence and the limits of this aspiration.

We have structured the chapter to reflect these three contributions. We begin by tracing the theoretical roots of our research in transformational, collective, and constructionist approaches to leadership, linking key concepts to practice theory, and showing the intrinsic connections between theoretical assumptions and methodological choices. In the second section, we illustrate the implications of the fit between theory, methods, and empirical work by describing the overall findings of our research through the introduction of our framework. We include the logic and key dimensions of our research with illustrations from our dataset. This allows us to offer empirically grounded insights about the relational nature of leadership that can enter into conversation with existing theory. In the third section, we identify lessons that can contribute to the dialogue between the entity and the constructionist perspectives, which Uhl-Bien (2006) proposes to unify into Relational Leadership Theory.

FROM THEORETICAL LENS TO RESEARCH PRACTICE: OPERATIONALIZING RELATIONALITY TO STUDY LEADERSHIP

Our research program is anchored in three interrelated leadership traditions—transformational leadership, collective leadership, and constructed leadership. We also integrate insights from the scarce research on social change leadership.

Transformational Leadership

Transformational leadership theory (Burns, 1978) dramatically changed the field's understanding of the leader-follower relationship and the leadership influence process (Bass & Avolio, 1993; Bryman, 1996; Conger, 1999; Hunt, 1999; Kark & Shamir, 2002; Parry & Bryman, 2006; Shamir, House, & Arthur, 1993; Shamir, Zakay, Breine, & Popper, 1998). In this view, leadership as a long-term relationship raises both leaders and followers to higher levels of motivation and morality, and encourages followers to assume leadership roles. According to Burns' (1978) original thinking, transformational leadership is characterized by the reciprocal learning relationship that produces the paradoxical idea that leaders best lead by being led (Preskill & Brookfield, 2009).

Follower-centered perspectives address the school's psychological and leader-centered approach, broadening the focus and highlighting the reciprocal influences between followers and leaders (Beyer, 1999; Jackson & Parry, 2008; Shamir, Pillai, Bligh, & Uhl-Bien, 2007). Shamir (2007) urges the field to "correct the overemphasis on leaders" so as to "include the many ways in which followers influence the leadership process" (p. *x*). This follower-centered perspective starts to reveal leaders and followers as interdependent, rather than autonomous, entities. Uhl-Bien and Pillai (2007), for example, suggest that implicit theories about followership are formed from shared images of leadership and followership. They invite research on how emergent norms among followers influence these constructions *at the group level*. This agenda illustrates a growing interest in the relational and collective dimensions of leadership.

Collective Leadership

Some scholars who acknowledge both individual and collective dimensions of leadership share a renewed interest in investigating the latter, empirically and theoretically (Drath et al., 2008; Gronn, 2002; Hiller et al., 2006; Ospina & Foldy, 2010; Ospina & Su, 2009; Pearce & Conger, 2003; Seers, Keller, & Wilkerson, 2003). Challenging traditional views of leadership, they shift attention from formal leaders and their influence on followers, to the relational processes that produce leadership in a group, organization, or system. Three clusters of research are of particular interest for our framework.

First, some scholars of leader-member exchange theory (LMX) have become interested in multi-level models of leadership (Graen & Uhl-Bien, 1995). Narrow attention to the leadership dyad has broadened to consider group and collective levels of action, and to investigate potential effects of individuals and teams on one another (Ford & Seers, 2006; Tse, Dasborough, & Ashkanasy, 2008). Second, work on shared and distributed leadership has started to explore the nature of leadership that emerges from members of a group, rather than an appointed leader (Gronn, 2002; Hauschildt

& Kirchmann, 2001; Howell & Boies, 2004; Pearce & Conger, 2003; Pearce & Sims, 2002). This research also investigates the impact of shared forms of leadership on performance and effectiveness, suggesting that shared leadership is more appropriate for contemporary organizations (Pearce & Sims, 2002). Third, research on team leadership has generated interest in collective processes at the group level of analysis. Researchers have examined, for example, the relationship between peer leadership and group process (Gerstner & Tesluk, 2005), the impact of the collective leadership roles on team effectiveness (Hiller et al., 2006), and the impact of teamwork and team learning on team capacity (Day, Gronn, & Salas, 2004). Recent studies shift attention to group processes and outcomes (thus emphasizing the collective dimensions of leadership) as they explore "ways that leadership is drawn from—instead of only added to—teams" as a means to accomplish shared work (Day et al., 2004, p. 858).

Constructed Leadership

A constructionist approach to leadership pushes relationality past the limits of the entity perspective by attending to the adaptive, organizing, meaning-making and communicative processes that constitute the substance of leadership (Dachler & Hosking, 1995; Drath, 2001; Fairhurst, 2007; Hosking, 2007; Ospina & Sorenson, 2006; Uhl-Bien & Marion, 2008; see also the introduction to this volume). Some leadership scholars have drawn from constructionist theories such as complexity theory (Uhl-Bien & Marion, 2008) and Relational-Cultural Theory (Fletcher, 2002; Fletcher & Kaufer, 2003; Jordan & Hartling, 2002). Our work intends to take a constructionist perspective to implement research on leadership.

Constructionism invites the scholar to amplify the relational and constructed dimensions of leadership by viewing leadership as the outcome of shared sense-making emerging from the rich interdependencies of organizations and their members (Drath, 2001; Hosking, 2007; Ospina & Sorensen, 2006; Uhl-Bien, 2006). In this view, persons and organizations are themselves constructed in process, rather than treated as discrete subjects that construct processes (Fairhurst, 2007; Hosking, 2007). Constructionist approaches thus give attention not only to the relationship between individual leaders and followers, but to their embeddedness in a broader system of relationships and to the meaning-making, communicative, and organizing processes that help to define and constitute such relationships. Hence, leadership is always a collective phenomenon, with individual, group, or collective manifestations. This constructionist lens shifts the appropriate focus of leadership research from individual relationships to meaning-making processes and their physical manifestation in practices.

While management scholars have long pointed out the potential advantages of a constructionist perspective to leadership (Meindl, 1995; Pfeffer, 1997; Smircich & Morgan, 1982; Tierney, 1987), there is still scant empirical work (e.g., Dachler, 1992; Fiol, Harris, & House, 1999; Gronn, 1999; Pastor, 1998). Our main contribution is to implement constructionist empirical research, using social change leadership as an important domain from which to theorize about the nature of leadership (Foldy, Goldman, & Ospina, 2004; Ospina, Dodge, Godsoe, Mineri, Rez, & Schall, 2002; Ospina & Saz-Carranza, 2010; Ospina & Su, 2009; Schall, Ospina, Godsoe, & Dodge, 2004).

Constructed Leadership in Social Change Organizations

Social change organizations (SCOs) are a type of nonprofit characterized by their members' commitment to addressing "systemic problems in a way that will increase the power of marginalized groups, communities or interests" (Chetkovich & Kunreuther, 2006, p. 14). Some are linked to broader social movements, but many work independently and for a community, combining activities such as service delivery, organizing, advocacy, and community building to address selected dimensions of social and economic injustice. They work in areas as varied as the environment, social exclusion (i.e., sexism, racism, homophobia), immigration, labor rights, predatory lending, homelessness, poverty, and so on. SCOs tend to be small (in size and budget) but formal (i.e., legally incorporated and structured around roles and accountability relations). They work directly with a particular community, be it defined geographically (like a neighborhood) or identity-based (like the immigrant community, women in prison, or families in poverty).

Drath (Drath, 2001; Drath et al., 2008; Drath & Palus, 1994) argues that the basic tasks that call forth leadership are direction, commitment, and adaptation. Leaders and followers in social change organizations engage these tasks in order to create meaningful changes in the lives of the marginalized. They do so under conditions of uncertainty, complexity, and even hostility from their environment. They also aspire to embody democratic values, pursue human dignity and citizenship, and work for the common good—even if in practice they often fall short (Bryson & Crosby, 1992; Chetkovich & Kunreuther, 2006; Evans & Boyte, 1986; Terry, 1993). Given the complexity of this ambitious agenda, their work is characterized by adaptive challenges (Heifetz & Laurie, 1997), and it takes place in a shared-power world where no one single actor has the capacity to address any given social problem (Crosby & Bryson, 2005). Responding to adaptive challenges in a shared-power world requires embedding the responsibility of the few within the broader context, where power and other resources are distributed. The challenges associated with the decentered, collective, everyday dimensions of social change leadership point to the advantages of viewing it as "the work of leadership" (Heifetz & Laurie, 1997). Drawing on these ideas, we explore how organizational actors in social change organizations work together to find the direction, ensure the commitment, and adapt to new challenges to advance their goal. That is, how they take up the work required to address the tasks through which leadership emerges as a collective achievement (Drath, 2001), or what Hosking (1988) calls the organizing demands of collective action.

Allen (1990) argues that traditional leadership research in the U.S. has limited its theoretical insights by focusing mostly on Anglo-Saxon male leaders in large corporations, thus overlooking more diverse forms of leadership. She invites scholars to look "where we have not looked before" (p. 8). This call implies studying different kinds of people, organizations, and domains, and paying greater attention to the nature of the work in these contexts (Allen, 1990; Ospina, 2004). Transformational and collective leadership traditions have broadened the scope of study to include different kinds of leaders, such as world class and historical leaders and low- to mid-level managers, in addition to those in a corporate context. But, this widening has largely excluded leaders in community-based organizations doing social change work (Selsky & Smith, 1994). Our focus on social change organizations (SCOs) addresses both these omissions. These small, grassroots, nonprofit organizations are often led by people of color, and are distinct from both corporate organizations and from other nonprofit contexts where leadership has been studied, such as large professionalized nonprofits working in service delivery, mainstream politics, or social movement organizations.

Public leadership scholars who highlight social change stress the interconnections between organizational dynamics and broader societal contexts (Chrislip & Larson, 1994; Crosby, 1999; Crosby & Bryson, 2005; Huxham & Vangen, 2000, 2004; Selsky & Smith, 1994).[3] Selsky and Smith (1994) developed a social change leadership framework from their study of an interorganizational community setting in Philadelphia. They embed social problems (and thus of the type of leadership needed to address them) within "the structural and normative relationships among a large number of organizations, and with the wider institutional setting" (p. 278). Bryson and Crosby (1992; Crosby & Bryson, 2005) also proposed a public leadership framework that highlights "shared power problems" requiring interorganizational leadership. Their framework considers the interconnections between individual leadership and policy levels of action, and between personal, interpersonal, group, and organizational dynamics.

These frameworks broaden the focus of study from the leader to a set of tasks, activities, and functions embedded in power dynamics. They also consider several levels of action, from individual acts to organizational factors and societal forces. Yet, they continue to give priority to the capacity of visible leaders rather than exploring how leadership is constructed at the organizational level to produce collective achievements. This is the goal of our research. To achieve it, we draw on Practice Theory, an analytic construct that matches our lens. Practice is a collective construct. It is the outcome of collective meaning-making, and rests upon shared knowledge that is largely tacit and embodied, historically and culturally specific, and transcends the innate mental faculty of individuals (Orlikowski, 2002; Wenger, 1998). A focus on practice helps us to tap into the construction of leadership by helping identify the recurrent assumptions, actions, and interactions that document how leadership emerges as a collective achievement from the organizing demands of social change. Further, it helps us break down this process into component parts to make empirical study easier (Schatzki et al., 2001).

As Bourdieu (1998), DeCerteau, Giard, and Mayol (1998), and Giddens (1984) contend, social action is neither an unmediated response to social factors (as in the objectivist tradition), nor an outgrowth of pure human will and consciousness (as in the subjectivist tradition). Rather, social action is the product of a dialectical relationship between humans and their world. A recent group of practice theorists have argued that "practice" should be a basic unit of social analysis (Reckwitz, 2002; Schwartz, 2006; Swidler, 2001).

Positivist approaches to social inquiry that draw heavily on the scientific method developed in the natural sciences are not useful to implement this approach, which requires instead interpretive, qualitative research (Crotty, 1998; Ospina & Dodge, 2005; Schall et al., 2004). This type of research has a distinct notion of rigor. While rigor in positivist studies often demands deductive reasoning and unambiguously establishing causal relationships, interpretive research draws from "philosophical rigor" (Yanow & Schwartz-Shea, 2006, p. *xvi*), which requires documenting the logical choices made through the research—such as decisions about case selection, interview subjects, observations, and interviews—in relation to the research context, its purposes, and theoretical assumptions.

UNPACKING THE LOGIC OF OUR METHODOLOGICAL CHOICES

Given our social constructionist approach to leadership, we developed a design that would allow us to understand how research participants made sense of leadership work from their own perspectives and experiences (Evered & Louis, 1981; Schall et al., 2004). Our research question was: In what ways do communities making social change engage in the work of leadership? Below, we describe our key methodological choices and their relationship to our constructionist lens.

Selection: Studying Leadership Exemplars

Research participants were award recipients in a leadership recognition program.[4] For 5 years, a tiered selection committee picked 17 to 20 leaders or leadership teams from among 1,000–3,000 nominations.[5] They were affiliated with nonprofit organizations developing systemic solutions to address critical social problems. The high nominee to awardee ratio (at least 50:1) and the rigor of the selection process made these organizations leadership exemplars and suitable subjects for leadership research.

Given the nature of the program, only progressive organizations were selected, excluding conservative social change organizations. Furthermore, the sample did not include examples of "bad leadership," and therefore we cannot make assertions about the key factors that "make the difference" between effective and ineffective leadership. Rather, our inquiries focused on how positional "leaders," "followers," allies, board members, constituents, and other organizational affiliates performed their work and struggled to achieve collective goals within and across organizations. Even though the program gave awards to individuals, our research focused on the work they did in their organizations. As described earlier, "leadership practices" became our organizing construct, analogous to a unit of analysis, for exploring the work that produced leadership in the organization.

Given our interest in the intersubjective meaning-making of those engaged in social change leadership, we were compelled to invite the people engaged in the work to inquire about its meaning with us, thus studying leadership from the inside out (Evered & Louis, 1981). We chose a stance of co-inquiry, where we conducted research *with* leaders *on* leadership (Clandinin & Connelly, 2000).

In the end, the program recognized 150 leaders, some in teams, from 92 organizations. Because research participation was voluntary, and because some research tapered off in later years, 83 out of the 92 organizations were included in the full sample. We included research findings from the 60 organizations for which we had the most complete data in the development of our framework.[6]

A Multi-Modal Methodology

Aiming for multiple perspectives to capture the intersubjective nature of experience, we integrated three methodologies consistent with constructionism: narrative inquiry, ethnography, and cooperative inquiry. Each motivated participants to share individual and collective narratives of their experience of leadership.[7] As Clandinin and Connelly put it (2000), practice is composed narratively. Narratives contain important knowledge about practice. Narratives help individuals make sense of experience and re-present meanings to others (Bruner, 1986; Clandinin & Connelly, 2000; Czarniawska & Gagliardi, 2003; Riessman, 2002). While each method is grounded in narrative theory, each also has a unique contribution to make to our understanding of relational leadership.

Narrative Inquiry

While narrative inquiry can take on a variety of forms, at its heart, it illuminates social meaning through the collection and analysis of stories (Bruner, 1986; Clandinin & Connelly, 2000; Czarniawska & Gagliardi, 2003; Feldman & Skoberg, 2002; Gardner, 1995; Mischler, 1987; Ospina & Dodge, 2005; Riessman, 2002). Our narrative inquiry stream included site visits with the first 40 organizations recognized by the program, centered around in-depth interviews with leaders, staff and board members, constituents, funders, and allies. It also included surveys and phone interviews with leaders and other informants from an additional 20 organizations who joined the program in subsequent years.

For the site visits, researchers designed interview protocols that elicited stories about the organization's work (not about leaders, leadership, or relationships) when it was happening at its best. Interviews were framed around dimensions that participants identified as critical to their leadership work in a prior conversation. Two members of the research team developed "analytic memos" (roughly equivalent to a case in case study research) that described each organization, its work, and central leadership practices. These memos represent first-order analysis of the data. Researchers then used these memos, as well as the original transcripts, to develop second-order interpretations of leadership practices across cases.

The surveys and phone interviews with the 20 additional organizations were more targeted since, by the time they were conducted, we had identified key themes that required further exploration in the cross-case comparisons. The survey interviews lasted approximately 3 hours. Each focused on the nature of the organization's work, its strategies, approaches, challenges, and context. We created a summary of the data for each organization, again similar to a case, and then used those summaries to deepen our already-existing investigations into specific leadership practices.

Participatory Ethnography

While narrative inquiry allowed us to examine the practice of leadership from participants' points of view, ethnography helped us view leadership in context over time. Characterized by a long history in organizational and leadership studies (Ashcraft, 1999; Perlow, 1998; Pratt, 2000), ethnography gives "explicit interpretations of the meanings and functions of human actions" in context (Hammersley & Atkinson, 1995, p. 248), and it draws on "unstructured" data that do not necessarily conform to pre-set analytic categories.

A key paradox in ethnography lies in the ethnographer's simultaneous status as insider and outsider. Ethnographers spend considerable time in the field with subjects, but are never able to escape the researcher's privilege and ethnographer's gaze. As Clifford Geertz (1973) put it, "We are not... seeking either to become natives (a compromised word in any case) or to mimic them....We are seeking... to converse with them, a matter a great deal more difficult... than is commonly recognized" (p. 13). Participatory ethnography responds to this paradox by highlighting multiple voices in the final text, not just the researcher's, and including researchers' reflections about their participation throughout. Although the insider-outsider paradox is never fully resolved, participant-researcher collaboration (Amabile et al., 2001)—to develop questions, methods, and products — provides a way to address it.

Our research supported a total of 12 ethnographies spanning the 5 years of the program. (See Appendix 9.3 for topics.) Ethnographers spent 3 to 6 months in the field documenting leadership through interviews, informal conversations, and participation in organizational events and activities. Local ethnographers and participants co-designed the research so that it made a contribution both to leadership research and to the participants' organizational objectives, focusing on different aspects of leadership relevant to each case. The ethnographies provided detailed information about selected organizations' history, leadership dynamics, collaborations, and development; and some incorporated photography and video.

While each ethnography was unique in its focus, method, and writing style, each also drew conclusions that had broader relevance for understanding leadership. For example, one ethnography examined how two very different organizations—one largely white group dedicated to ending discrimination against gays and lesbians, and the other largely composed of Latino workers and immigrants—were able to create common cause, thus making an important contribution to understanding leadership that brings together unlikely allies. We also reviewed the ethnographies in order to identify common insights across organizations.

Cooperative Inquiry

Both narrative research and ethnography helped in studying leadership qualitatively and from the inside out. Despite the effort to capture the leaders' perspective, the separation between the researcher and the researched was integral to both methods. The epistemology of practice theory suggested the benefits of triangulating the two chosen forms of traditional qualitative research with a third method that challenges this separation in its definition of rigor. This method would capture the experience of practice without the intermediation of a researcher. Participants in the leadership program were thus invited to participate in cooperative inquiries.

Cooperative inquiry is a form of action research "in which participants work together in an inquiry group as co-researchers and as co-subjects developing an 'extended epistemology' that includes experiential, presentational, propositional, and practical ways of knowing" (Heron & Reason, 2001, p. 366). The cooperative inquiry group defines a research question that arises from participants' practices in their work, and creates new knowledge based on collective interpretations through cycles of action and reflection around members' personal experience, which becomes the main source of "data." Co-researchers—which may include both academics and practitioners—collect data on their own practice and bring it to the group to make collective sense of its meaning. Because each inquirer participates fully in all decisions that affect the process, there is co-ownership of the process and the knowledge produced (Bray, Lee, Smith, & Yorks, 2000; Ospina, El Hadidy, & Hofmann-Pinilla, 2008).

The research supported a total of 10 cooperative inquiries. (See Appendix 9.3 for topics.) Participants organized themselves into groups based on a shared interest around a pressing leadership challenge. For example, one group explored the role of the arts in social change, while another investigated the practice of leadership development. Groups usually included 8 to 10 members, plus two facilitators from the research team. The groups met about five times over the course of 2 years, with each meeting lasting about 2 days. Through the systematic and rigorous process of action and reflection—of asking questions, exploring them in the real world of practice, and coming together to develop answers—the groups produced practitioner-based knowledge. The group findings were captured in final reports, which became additional "data" for our theory building, complementing the findings from the parallel narrative and ethnographic research.

Integration Across Organizations and Research Streams

Throughout the research program, the team engaged in comparative analyses, integrating insights across organizations and research streams over time. The analysis slowly yielded a variety of leadership practices including, for example, "reframing how external audiences perceived the organization's work." Subsets of researchers investigated these specific practices by going back to the data set and creating appropriate coding schemes to systematically analyze it in search of patterns within and across organizations, and writing papers about individual practices (Dodge, 2009; Foldy et al.,

2008; Hoffman-Pinilla, Olavarria, & Ospina, 2005; Ospina & Foldy, 2010; Ospina & Saz-Carranza, 2010; Ospina & Su, 2009; Su, 2009).

The theoretical framework we present here was developed from material from the first 40 organizations in the program (Ospina & Foldy, 2005). This was then refined over time with additional information from the next 20 organizations. While the research team did much of the integrative work, program participants were engaged at key moments (Ospina et al., 2002) to ensure that there was resonance around the key findings (Gibbons, 2001; Mohrman, Gibson & Mohrman, 2001). For example, in 2003, we held an "integration event" with the first cohort of participants to share early findings, get feedback, and deepen our learning. In December 2005, we held a small conference for participants in the ethnography projects to discuss their insights. In 2006, we convened a conversation among participants from the cooperative inquiry groups and the broader leadership program community. The insights gained from these conversations generated additional material that was incorporated into subsequent iterations of the framework.

THE RESEARCH FINDINGS: A FRAMEWORK OF SOCIAL CHANGE LEADERSHIP

The framework we describe in this section represents an integrative effort that brings together the findings of this inductive research program. The research was designed to implement a constructionist lens and to build theory from the data. Rather than emulating a research report that displays detailed narratives that "show" in the qualitative tradition, this section presents general descriptions that "tell" about our key findings and offers some illustrations.[8]

At the core of social change organizations are leadership practices that represent distinct leadership work. They are enacted both internally and externally, and support the collaborative sense-making that moves collective efforts forward. Our framework poses that these practices, along with organizing activities, build collective capacity to leverage power for social change. In this sense, the work of leadership in SCOs is geared less to create an effective organization and more to create the collective capacity to generate effective change outside the organization. Together, we call the dimensions that constitute this work "strategic action." In turn, strategic action is supported by an integrated philosophy or worldview—which we call "grounded humanism"—that provides a powerful source of meaning to participants in social change organizations. This worldview includes leadership drivers anchored in a set of assumptions about social change and core values of social justice. Ultimately, both the worldview and the strategic action are harnessed to create real outcomes such as a change in policy or a change in how people think about an issue.

Figure 9.1 offers a visual representation of our theoretical framework and its constitutive elements. These apply variably depending on the context and strategic choices of any particular organization. Therefore, we theorize that the nature of the leadership that emerges within a group engaged in social change work is the result of the emphasis its members give to various elements in the framework, given the opportunities and challenges found in their particular environment. We first discuss grounded humanism, then strategic action, and finally long-term outcomes, describing each element and its interrelationships with other elements.

Grounded Humanism: A Worldview That Supports the Work

Our research identified a set of leadership drivers, assumptions, and values of social justice that ground the work of social change organizations. Together, these elements produce a coherent and encompassing worldview we call "grounded humanism." Humanism reflects an appreciation of the humanity of all individuals and a faith in their potential to contribute to the work required to transform society. It is grounded because an understanding of how society operates supports this faith, which includes an awareness that shifting power is central to social change.

Leadership Drivers

The work of social change leadership is driven by images of both the present and the future. Individuals identify a current, pressing systemic inequity and name it. They also envision a world without that inequity; they create a picture of a just and fair future. These depictions motivate action.

Images of the Present: Systemic Inequities.   At the core of social change organizations is a motivation to redress identified systemic inequities, that is, injustice that is based not on idiosyncratic or arbitrary considerations, but is built into the implicit rules that govern our society. To address these rules in ways that produce tangible, enduring results for those facing the inequity, organizations must confront immediate problems, identify their underlying causes, and marshal resources. Systemic inequities trigger action when a group agrees they have a problem to be redressed. For example, the New Road Community Development Group in Virginia was formed when residents of a largely African-American neighborhood identified the lack of indoor plumbing in their rented houses as a problem that should not exist in 1990s America. In 1993, they came together to do something about it. Over the following years, the organization also managed to increase home ownership among the neighborhood's families and engage in a long—term community building program to address issues of employability.

Visions of the Future.   The decision to redress inequities drives the work in SCOs toward creating new visions for the future. One cooperative inquiry group of leaders in eight organizations articulated "a common vision for health and life for all people" (Asis et al., 2002, p. 10) and invited their constituents "to dare to dream" that this vision could actually come to pass (p. 5). Visions of the future also link immediate action with the ultimate goal of eliminating a systemic inequity. For example, the New Road Group ultimately developed a much more far-reaching vision of the future than simply getting indoor plumbing, one that extended to home ownership and greater community control.

While visions for the future share common features, we found distinctions that reflect variations in the underlying theories of change in SCOs. The extent of systemic change being demanded may range from "inclusion" to "transformation," or the group may also articulate a parallel need for "preservation." When the underlying theory of change is *transformation*, systemic change means replacing the current system with another one. This view sees "the system" as the source of the identified problem. The Burlington Community Land Trust (BCLT), for example, works for land reform, which for them means changing the fundamental nature of land ownership in the United States. The group's leaders disagree with the basic notion of private ownership of the land. "People should not think that they can own a piece of land and do whatever they want with it. They can't own water. They can't own air," said one member. The group wants a change from individual to communal ownership of land: "That is the essential element of land reform: that land is owned in common. And individuals make use of the land as they need it. . . . But the land is ultimately owned by the community. . . ."

When the underlying theory of change is *inclusion*, systemic change means altering the current system so that its benefits reach everyone equally. SCOs holding this view recognize that some groups are systematically excluded from benefits such as adequate housing, clean air and water, and educational opportunities. New Road again provides a useful illustration. It does not envision a fundamental change like BCLT, but is simply interested in gaining access for its community to the same resources and privileges held by other communities, like appropriate housing and home ownership. When the underlying theory of change is *preservation*, systemic change means stopping the destruction of traditional cultures by the great maw of American life. This view focuses on making room in the system for an independent cultural heritage that has been undermined or nearly eradicated.

While preservation is an end in itself, it generally accompanies an inclusive or transformational view of change. Groups can fight to preserve their way of life while also demanding the same benefits as other Americans. Or, they can advocate for the wholesale replacement of particular systems, even as they struggle to preserve their own. The Gwich'in Nation, a native tribe in the northern reaches of North America with members in both the United States and Canada, has seen massive changes over the decades that threaten their traditions and customs. To preserve their way of life, they are battling against opening the Arctic National Wildlife Refuge to oil and gas development. This organization does not advocate for a whole new system, but that the current system should protect their human rights as it protects others', seeking inclusive rather than transformational change.

These visions of present and future are the most immediate motivators of action. However, they are rooted in even more fundamental assumptions and values that also motivate action.

Working Assumptions and Beliefs. Underlying, shared assumptions about the nature of people, social change, knowledge, the self, and power motivate the work participants in the SCO do to seek social change. By definition, members of SCOs see social change as institutional and systemic, as truly "social." Social inequities are viewed as rooted in power imbalances. Change requires amassing power in some form and leveraging it to influence external actors with the capacity to support transformation, and is driven by the understanding of individual problems as manifestations of broader social problems. Social problems are seen as interconnected and based in broadly inequitable structures and institutions. Social change leaders believe in the power of knowledge as a key resource to make decisions, recognizing many ways of knowing and paths to knowledge, giving primacy to local knowledge based on personal experience. They underscore the humanity of individuals and promote faith in the potential contribution of anyone who is, or can become, involved in the work.

Core Values of Social Justice. Anchoring the implicit leadership drivers and working assumptions of social change leadership is a shared set of explicit core values that inspire, awaken, fuel and direct the passion of those engaged in the work. In a group conversation, a leader from one of the SCOs studied defined the work of leadership as connecting values to actions: "There are a wide variety of strategies that allow effective social change leadership to happen. What seems to be constant is a strong commitment to core values as the 'bottom line' to guide decisions about the work" (field notes). The overarching value is social justice—a call for fairness and equality of opportunity for all human beings. It encompasses particular values of inclusion, social solidarity, transparency and accountability, democracy, and equity.

The leadership drivers, working assumptions and beliefs, and the values of social justice constitute the worldview we have called *grounded humanism*. This worldview becomes a moral compass to ground and guide the leadership work in social change organizations. It helps to establish parameters about appropriate strategic action to build collective power.

Strategic Action to Build Collective Power

SCOs engage in a variety of integrated practices and activities geared toward *strategic action.* Their action is strategic because it is outcome-oriented and attends to the particular challenges and opportunities in the environment. It is also built on the recognition that power is central to making change, and a key goal is to build and leverage the power necessary to achieve long-term outcomes. But, action is also expressive, not just instrumental: it is infused with a set of beliefs that demand expression in the work of building community and creating a better world.

Leadership practices

Leadership practices that make up the day-to-day work of the organization cluster around three distinct types of leadership work. Together they help SCOs build collective power by helping to frame and reframe their issues, building meaningful connections with others, and creating the environments that allow people to flourish and be prepared to take action.

Reframing Discourse. Leaders in social change organizations realize they cannot advance their mission by relying on the same language, images, or cognitive models that dis-empower and alienate their communities (Teske & Tetreault, 2000). SCOs work to disrupt established frames, while forming new ones congruent with their vision for the future. We identified reframing as leadership work that articulates practices to challenge and dispel existing cognitive models that create or reinforce injustices (Bartunek & Moch, 1987; Walsh, 1995).

Because reframing discourse is not as simple as presenting counterfactuals, it is adaptive leadership work (Heifetz, Grashow & Linsky, 2009). Reframing practices rely on understanding dominant frames and their permeability, and crafting new repertoires, language, and narratives, and living them through action. It requires using frames that are recognizable, so that they resonate with people, while rejecting dimensions of them that reinforce the status quo and dehumanize experience.

For example, the Gwich'in Nation (described above) reframes its issue. They subsist on a caribou herd that is threatened by oil drilling. While many outside the community may view the issue as environmental, the Gwich'in reframe it as one of human rights. This frame evokes a life-and-death struggle, and reaches an audience who might not be moved by an environmental frame. SCOs may also use constituency-related reframing to interrupt the ways a community sees itself, or others see a community. CASA of Maryland, which fights for equal treatment and full access to resources and opportunities for low-income Latino immigrants, infuses its narratives with signifiers of power. Rather than describing their constituents as victims, they refer to them as "makers of history" and "co-authors of justice."

Social change organizations also reframe relational dynamics, enacting the egalitarian frame they wish to invoke. Many have explicit procedures for meetings and decision-making to ensure equitable relations and voice. Others imbue their work with cultural or identity-based rituals that assert their ways of being. PODER—People Organized in Defense of Earth and her Resources—based in a low-income community in East Austin, fights encroaching industry. Reaffirming their indigenous roots, the co-leaders of the organization begin public appearances, including public hearings and other formal meetings, with a statement from their ancestors: "There was a time that we were all sisters and brothers; the night sky, our ceiling; the earth our mother; the sun our father; our parents were leaders and justice our guide." When done consistently, this act reminds others of the legitimacy of the community claims, validates the community's ways, and positions their voice differently.

Bridging Difference. Bridging difference entails practices that create the conditions to bring diverse actors together and facilitate their joint work while maintaining and appreciating their differences (Ansell & Gash, 2008; Crosby & Bryson, 2005; Gasson & Elrod, 2006; Huxham & Vangen, 2000; O'Leary, Gerard & Bingham, 2006; Ospina & Foldy, 2010). Some practices operate at the intraorganizational level, building connections across diverse affiliates or potential supporters in one organization, while others are interorganizational, creating alliances among organizations. However, all bridging work develops interdependencies within which collective action becomes obvious and collective achievements natural (Ospina & Foldy, 2010).

Weaving relationships among people from different worldviews builds community and ends the isolation and fragmentation that many individuals experience as a consequence of poverty and marginalization. For example, the Brotherhood/Sister Sol (Bro/Sis) aims to provide Black and Latino youth in Harlem with mentoring and peer support to cope with adversity. To bridge Blacks and Latinos, Bro/Sis builds an elastic sense of community where there is no "us" and "them." It implements an intensive curriculum to incite reflective, critical, and emotional analyses among young people, who spend over a year together discussing what connects them and writing a manifesto and mission statement for their cohort. Bridging difference is also adaptive leadership work because it is fraught with paradox, and thus requires finding new ways of being in connection and responding to challenges by reinventing available problem-solving formulas (Heifetz et al., 2009). Bridging work entails building connections without suppressing difference or ignoring its value, as well as cultivating difference that does not turn into disunity. A key leadership goal is not to reify a community as monolithic, but to find ways to draw unity from diversity (Ospina & Saz-Carranza, 2010; Saz-Carranza & Ospina, 2011).

Bridging difference can also happen at the organizational level to leverage resources and advance missions. The director of the New York Immigration Coalition describes that "we've been able . . . to bring so many different groups to the table that don't normally advocate together. . . ." She explains that when the coalition speaks "with this very diverse voice . . . ," decision-makers take notice of unity among groups with different ideologies and roles in immigrant communities, and who come from different parts of the city. "That's when they realize that they have to pay closer attention." Ensuring this type of unity in diversity requires leadership work across organizations to address leadership challenges of the network as a *whole*, something that in itself demands a different mindset (Saz-Carranza & Ospina, 2011).

Unleashing Human Energies. Practices to unleash human energies stem from the assumption that knowledge is power and the fundamental source of power comes from within the community, despite its perceived scarcity. Yet, this instrumental approach is influenced by the expressive commitment to support human development, not just as a means but as an end, in the spirit of authentic transformational leadership (Bass & Steidlmeier, 1999; Belenky, Bond, & Weinstock, 1997; Burns, 1978; Preskill & Brookfield, 2009). Unleashing practices create conditions for transformational learning, which allow every member of the group to reclaim their full humanity and, in the process, recognize their inherent power to direct their lives. One of the leaders of Junebug Productions, an organization based in New Orleans which draws on the transformative power of the arts, describes: "...it's about recognizing wisdom. It's about bringing the genius that's there up and out."

The point of departure for this work is the belief that people already come with a certain mastery over the problem, which is derived from their own lives. Lived experience is regarded as a legitimate source of expertise, equally valued as other forms of expertise recognized by society: science, legal discourse, technical knowledge, and so forth. Sylvia Herrera of PODER describes the challenge of validating the community's expertise with government:

> You would go with a problem to them, an issue. And well, they would have to say, "Which book is that in?" Well, we know the issues, listen to me, don't read those books, listen to us, we live it everyday. You know, so they can't tell us, "Well, this is not what's going on" we know because we live it everyday, we live these issues that they're still trying to read about.

One way to tap into knowledge of the quotidian experience is storytelling, which links one's personal experience to that of others and helps people realize that what they experience is connected to larger systemic forces. This practice helps people to address internalized oppression, while recognizing the power of their own agency and humanity.

Unleashing human energies can be facilitated through formal educational mechanisms, such as language classes, trainings, and leadership development. It also happens through dialogic interaction that enables people to reflect on the structural causes of their situation, their roles in both the current and envisioned societies, and the solutions that will transform society (Freire, 1970). The National Day Labor Organizing Network (NDLON) is a network that coordinates day laborer organizations across the country and opposes discriminatory, anti-immigrant and anti-day laborer policies. Rather than telling day laborers they are powerful and capable, NDLON organizers unleash human energies by facilitating a power analysis in which day laborers identify different actors who have influenced their lives. Organizers also ask day laborers to question their idea of "a leader" when they give this title to politicians but not their peers. The idea is to facilitate a conversation through which day laborers come to realize they can be leaders.

Practices that produce these three types of leadership work—reframing discourse, bridging difference, and unleashing human energies—help these organizations accomplish their mission. They ensure the conditions that make it possible to engage in the core activities that are strategically undertaken to reach the organization's social change goals (Chetkovich & Kunreuther, 2006).

Core Activities and the Work of Leadership

Core activities are modes of engagement that reflect the group's overall approach to achieving change and are manifested in specific influence strategies (Chetkovich & Kunreuther, 2006). The four modes of engagement identified in the framework have been consistently documented in the social change literature (Smock, 2004; Su, 2009; Wood, 2002). While these are highly codified modes of action, leadership practices infuse them with particular character. An organization's choice of activities and the strategies deployed reflect what they believe is the most effective and most legitimate way to leverage power, given their visions, values, assumptions, and the pressing demands and challenges they face.

Organizing—recruiting, educating and mobilizing a base of members directly affected by the organization's issues to reach their long-term goals.

Public Policy Advocacy—getting involved in the legislative process on the local, state, or federal level and working with elected officials and policymakers to change policies affecting the organization's constituency.

Community Building—developing social capital and collective efficacy to act on behalf of a group with a common identity.

Direct Service Provision—meeting immediate and long-term needs of individuals or groups by providing goods, such as food or clothing, and services, such as job training, health care or counseling.

While SCOs may adopt a single strategy, it is more common for them to integrate two or more in order to keep pace with increasing demands and uncertain conditions, and to fit their model of social change (Chetkovich & Kunreuther, 2006). CASA of Maryland integrates all four. As the primary representative for immigrant Latinos in Maryland, it provides services such as English language instruction; it lobbies on issues such as domestic trafficking; it supports tenants organizing in public housing; and it has established an employment and training center for day laborers, a contribution to community economic development.

The combination of activities and leadership practices builds power by creating collective capacity. This capacity is then leveraged to bring about long-term changes in policy, social structures, and thinking. In the following sections, we describe collective capacity and long-term outcomes and link them to different notions of power because social change organizations view outcomes as things that are won, not granted. While power has been an important dimension of leadership in entity perspectives (Ammeter, Douglas, Gardner, Hochwarter, & Ferris, 2002; Bedell-Avers, Hunter, Angie, Eubanks, & Mumford, 2009; Harvey, 2006; House & Howell, 1992; McClelland, 1985; Sosik & Dinger, 2007), it is often associated with the individual leader and his or her capacity to influence followers. Our framework suggests that the role of power in social change leadership is different, in that it is a collective capacity to influence forces that are external to the organization. In this sense, this perspective on power draws more closely from the social movements, social change, and organizational theory literatures (Brass, 2005; Foldy, 2002; Gaventa, 2000; Teske & Tétreault, 2000).

Our distinction between building power and leveraging power, for example, parallels Gamson's work on "power in repose" and "power in use" in his study of social movements (1968, 1990). Power in repose is potential power manifested in various kinds of resources and assets, both material and discursive. It conceptualizes individual, organizational and interorganizational strength. In our framework, power in repose is called "building power." It involves identifying and marshalling the financial, political, human, and symbolic resources necessary to attain organizational goals. Power in use includes two ways in which real outcomes are manifest: gaining new advantage and gaining new acceptance. An organization gains new advantages by bringing about specific outcomes (such as passing legislation, building housing, or changing the way people think). New acceptance means having a seat at the table, being included in decision-making, or being consulted before a step is taken. We call this "leveraging power." It is about helping to attain tangible and enduring benefits for communities. In practice, organizations build and leverage power simultaneously. There is also a virtuous cycle: leveraging power successfully helps the organization attract resources, thus building greater power, and enabling more powerful leverage in the future.

Creating Collective Capacity—Means and Intermediate Outcomes

Collective capacity is power in repose; it is capability waiting to happen. When it is leveraged as a means toward achieving long-term outcomes, power in repose becomes power in use. But collective capacity is also an outcome in itself: Achieving individual, organizational and interorganizational capacity—even without gaining concrete social changes—builds confidence, strengthens commitment, and cultivates hope.

> *Individual Capacity*—At one level, individual capacity is realized in SCOs when people recognize their self-worth and understand that their disadvantages are linked to systemic structural conditions, and not to personal shortcomings. It holds potential for growth the moment individuals recognize that leadership is not something external to them and that anyone is capable of being a leader. Self-efficacy, the belief in one's capabilities to perform at the level needed to exercise influence over events that affect one's life (Bandura, 1997; 2000; Hannah, Avolio, Luthans, & Harms, 2008), is another manifestation of individual capacity fostered by SCOs.

> *Organizational Capacity*—When organizations can influence the contexts in which they work to further their agenda, they can identify and marshal the financial, material, symbolic, and relational resources needed to deploy the work. Collective efficacy, a group's belief in its capacity for effective action, stems from a collective sense of trust and cohesion and a willingness to intervene for the common good of the group (Bachrach & Abeles, 2004; Hannah et al., 2008; Sampson, Raudenbush, & Earls, 1997).

> *Interorganizational Capacity*—Interorganizational capacity is realized in connections with like-minded and "unlikely" allies in various sectors that strengthen the SCO's work. Interorganizational capacity is at its best when the work gains depth and momentum because it connects and is channeled within a broader collective effort. This effort can be a social movement or organizational relationship such as a partnership, alliance, or collaboration. In "Building Alliances: An Ethnography of Collaboration between Rural Organizing Project (ROP) and CAUSA in Oregon" (Stephen, Lanier, Ramírez, & Westerling, 2005), two organizations from our study document their collaboration: One is primarily white, the other is of people of color. They developed a working relationship over 10 years that built capacity that contributed to numerous victories for immigrant and farm worker rights, and greater consciousness among white, rural activists who supported anti-racist work.

As an intermediate outcome, creating collective capacity could be depicted as the construction of a lived social space that is full of leadership (Raelin, 2003; 2005). It is a space characterized by a sense of abundance and possibility in the midst of scarcity, a space that offers an experience that is counterfactual for people who experience marginalization, powerlessness and inequality on a daily basis.

Long Term Outcomes: Leveraging Power

Actual social change achievements produced by participants in social change organizations bring the future into the present and represent the coming together of grounded humanism and strategic action, the two described components of the framework. We identified three categories of change that SCO's efforts are meant to produce. *Changed policies* are manifested in changes in some kind of rule, law, or regulation at the local, state, federal, or even global level. *Changed structures* are represented in longer-term, more systemic change, and could refer to changes in particular systems, altered governance structures, or changes in patterns of relations. *Changed thinking* is about a transformation in the language and mental models that sustain existing structures of power. It is reflected in changes in the collective imagination, or interruptions in harmful myths, mental models, or actions about the way things are and what people believe is possible.

Justice Now, an organization that focuses on women's prisons in California, works toward all three outcomes. For example, it participated in legislative hearings and lobbied for passage of a bill to change prison health care policy after nine women prisoners unnecessarily died in an 8-week period. It also focuses on broader structural change by arguing for the abolition of the prison system, because it sees prisons as the problem, not the solution. Finally, to advance such a fundamental shift, it has had to change popular thinking. To do so, it even used music and storytelling to demonstrate that prisons are inherently toxic for prisoners, their families, and their communities.

In sum, the social change leadership framework we have presented here integrates and summarizes findings from empirical, multi-method, inductive research done over the course of a 7-year research program. The framework offers a holistic answer to our original research question about the ways in which communities doing social change engage in the work of leadership. It represents our effort to theorize about the work of leadership in social change organizations using a constructionist lens. At the core of the framework, we find three bundles of relational practices that represent leadership work constructed collectively. This work is driven by a worldview grounded in social justice values and anchored in collective meaning-making around a vision that brings a different future into the present in response to an identified social problem affecting the community. The practices suggest that social change leaders seem to give explicit attention to relational interactions as a means to advance their work and as an end that expresses a worldview that values connection. At the same time, the work is strategic because it is oriented to cultivating and leveraging the power that will allow organizational members to influence those with capacity to transform policies, structures, and thinking in ways that consider the communities' best interests.

REFLECTIONS AND CONTRIBUTIONS TO THE RELATIONALITY DIALOGUE

By drawing on a social constructionist lens on leadership and drawing from an under-explored context where leadership takes place, our framework contributes in two significant ways to the dialogue on relational leadership. First, leadership practice understood within a constructionist perspective becomes key for understanding and analyzing relational leadership. Second, our framework illustrates opportunities for the convergence of different approaches to understanding relational leadership (Uhl-Bien, 2006) and also points to areas of divergence that give pause to the idea of a single relational leadership theory.

Introducing Practice as the Focus of Leadership Research

Our framework advances leadership practice as a foundational construct that helps to grasp and interpret the work of leadership as a relational phenomenon. According to practice theorists (Bourdieu, 1998; de Certeau et al., 1998; Giddens, 1984), social action is the product of a dialectical relationship between humans and their world. Because the individual does not act alone on his/her world but in fellowship with others, practice as a social construct emerges from the relational nature of social interaction (Barnes, 2001). It incorporates both the individual and the collective: When individuals engage in a practice, they join an epistemic community which ultimately "owns" the practice.

Leadership practices are purposive interventions (Polkinghorne, 2004) that contribute to accomplishing leadership. This definition is similar to that offered in Drath et al. (2008) whereby "a leadership practice is a pattern of behavior of a collective aimed at producing" the achievements of direction, alignment, and commitment (p. 645). Rather than being mechanistic sequences of behaviors or tasks, these contingent patterns of behavior (Hellstrom, 2004; Latour, 1987; Reckwitz, 2002) emerge organically through experimentation, and as such, are situation- and time-sensitive. They are co-constructed in every purposeful interaction, in every exchange that is geared toward finding common ground to pursue collective work. This is also consistent with Heifetz's argument (1997) that intractable challenges require leadership that adapts to challenge and context, as opposed to technical solutions.

Attention to practices has important implications for developing Relational Leadership Theory because the construct can help integrate what previously have been treated as separate ways to capture the reality of leadership. Using practice as the entry point helps to operationalize recent calls in the literature to go beyond the obvious when defining the locus of leadership research, particularly going beyond what traditionally has counted as quantifiable. A focus on practices invites attention to the underlying assumptions and shared agreements that reveal the logic behind participants' appreciation of given leadership traits, or their choice of particular leadership behaviors and tasks, emphasizing sensitivity to issues like time, power, and context (Bluedorn & Jaussi, 2008; Bryman, Stephens, & à Campo, 1996; Osborn, Hunt, & Jauch, 2002; Osborn & Marion, 2009; Ospina & Hittleman, forthcoming; Porter & McLaughlin, 2006).

A focus on practice thus helps to broaden the scope of the scholar's vision. The leadership literature has traditionally tried to understand leadership by inquiring into how leaders address the codified management activities intended to keep organizations going. These include strategic planning, financial and human resources management, and, in the case of nonprofits, board and staff development and fund-raising (Herman & Associates, 2005)—what we call the technologies of management. Scholars studying social change organizations have broadened the focus to include the core activities of social change, like organizing, advocacy and service delivery—that is, efforts that influence the environment and produce social transformation (Chetkovich & Kunreuther, 2006; Smock, 2004; Su, 2009; Wood, 2002). A constructionist lens motivates the scholar to zero in on what takes place in what Bradbury and Lichtenstein (2000) would call "the space between" the technologies of management and social change strategies. The goal is to unveil the essence that gives character to the way actions are taken to ensure organizational mission.

Other Areas of Convergence and Their Limits

We find interesting points of convergence shared by our constructionist approach to relational leadership and the work of entity scholars who explore the collective dimensions of leadership. To contribute to the dialogue fostered in this book, we describe three points of convergence and highlight their limits.

Recapturing the Transformational Legacy

Our findings are quite consistent with the tenets of transformational leadership that emphasize collective leadership, values, and behaviors (Pearce & Sims, 2002). Transformational scholars emphasize values as a way for leaders and followers to transform and elevate each other to produce collective change (Burns 1978; Conger, 1999). In our framework, we also articulate what we call "grounded humanism," a secular worldview that anchors leadership work in social justice values and that highlights the relevance of "inner meanings" behind the work of leadership (Kriger & Seng, 2005).

The key leadership behaviors in the transformational tradition (Bass & Steidlmeier, 1999; Burns, 1978), as Pearce and Sims' summarize them (2003), are congruent with our framework. Behaviors like providing vision and expressing idealism are implicit in our "visions of the future." Others, like having high performance expectations, are parallel to the assumption that constituents are experts and can lead the process of social change. The behaviors of challenging the status-quo and using inspirational communication relate to the work associated with reframing discourse and bridging differences; providing intellectual stimulation similarly relates to unleashing human energies.

Yet, we suggest that these behaviors do not illuminate much if considered as independent behaviors that can be translated into formulas leaders can use in any context. The emphasis cannot remain on the assumptions or behaviors *per se,* or on who is enacting them—leaders or followers. More interesting is to explore how assumptions and behaviors work together to help the group move the work forward, given context-specific drivers, values, and desired outcomes that trigger collective work. This represents a shift to exploring shared assumptions and images at a collective rather than individual level (Uhl-Bien & Pillai, 2007). In our framework, focus on leadership practices replaces narrow attention on the giving or receiving of influence among leaders and followers, with a holistic approach that prioritizes the interrelationships among the components of the work of leadership and considers capacity at the individual, organizational, and interorganizational levels. This approach, we believe, is more attuned to the original assumptions of transformational leadership theory (Burns, 1978).

Complementing Entity Perspectives of Collective Leadership

We find many points of convergence with the emphasis entity scholars give to collective leadership. First, Uhl-Bien (2006) contrasts entity scholars' emphasis on outcomes with relational scholars' emphasis on process. Our relational framework converges with entity perspectives in that it considers both process and outcomes. From the beginning, we were interested in how both process—what Hosking (1988) calls "collective organizing"—and outcomes—what Drath (2001) calls "collective achievement"—helped us to understand how people make collective meaning to advance social change work.

Yet, our emphasis on outcomes has a different character than that of entity scholars. We examine outcomes from the inside out, from the perspective of those engaged in the collective work of leadership. We found that participants in social change organizations constructed the work of leadership around expected outcomes. They focused particularly on enhancing internal collective efficacy and capacity, and through this, influencing those with power and authority to change thinking, structures, and systems in ways that would redress communities' disadvantages.

We found that the work of leadership in SCOs is geared less to create an effective organization and more to create the collective capacity to generate effective change outside the organization. This is consistent with results from a recent study of larger nonprofit organizations that focused on organizational performance rather than leadership *per se* (Grant & Crutchfield, 2007). While larger, richer, and much more structured than the SCOs we studied, the organizations Grant and Crutchfield studied also had at the core of their mission to become "forces for good," that is, to address problems through the transformation of the environment in which they occur. Grant and Crutchfield argue that the organizations' success was based on working outside their boundaries rather than managing their internal operations. Focusing on leadership, the authors find that these organizations also used more distributed models of leadership, sharing leadership within and outside the organization, and empowering others to lead, in addition to cultivating strong seconds-in-command, stable and committed executive teams, and large, powerful boards.

We also differ in that our study did not document a causal link between leadership work and outcomes, as entity scholars would expect. Rather, because these organizations had been recognized as leaders of social change, we started with the assumption that they were successful and then worked backward to see how they made sense of what they did. Investigating the causal relationship between practices and outcomes would require broadening the sample to include organizations that were not exemplars of effective organizations. Consistent with the epistemological base of our interpretive research, and in ways similar to those described in a grounded theory approach, our theoretical framework emerged inductively from the data through the analysis of stories and reports from leaders' meaning-making activities (Strauss & Corbin, 1998). The knowledge and experience of the participants in our research program were reflected both in the dimensions of the work of leadership and its impact on expected outcomes.

Second, findings from our framework also speak to the recent interest in the nature of shared and distributed leadership that seeks to link organizational form to outcomes (Gronn, 2002; Howell & Boies, 2004; Pearce & Conger, 2003; Pearce & Sims, 2002). We did not study this link (even though our sample of organizations ranged from traditional to horizontal structures, and from individual executive directors, to co-directors and leadership teams). Yet, we documented a general trend toward internal and external democratization, and explicit efforts to develop leaders *and* leadership that would generate collective capacity throughout the organization. These findings suggest that these organizations practice distributed leadership, and that shared and vertical leadership can coexist (Pearce & Sims, 2002).

Third, we also find an interesting convergence with entity scholars who distinguish individual from collective levels of analysis and their interconnections (Ford & Seers, 2006; Graen & Uhl-Bien, 1995; Tse et al., 2008). For example, Tse et al. (2008) argue that studying interpersonal relationships between leaders, subordinates, and coworkers requires a level of analysis beyond the leadership dyad and should consider "an interconnected social system that operates in teams and organizations" (p. 196). In this tradition, quantitative analysis isolates group- and collective-level effects beyond individual and dyadic ones and tests interaction effects, while holding context constant. Despite important insights, this represents only one possible way to address interaction between levels.

Interpretivist methodologies bring context center-stage as the raw material within which organizational actors interpret, negotiate and co-construct their experience. Our framework is built on findings derived from applying these methodologies. Because actors make meaning within networks of relationships with unique structural features and cultural meanings, attention to the interconnections among various levels of social experience becomes an inherent part of the analysis.

Rethinking Treatment of Context and Levels of Analysis

Likewise, we find high convergence with entity research on leadership in team contexts, particularly the approach that emphasizes its systemic nature. For example, Day et al. (2004) define team leadership as a shared, distributed process that creates team capacity by providing "resources for better team adaptation and performance in subsequent performance cycles" (p. 858). They argue that this focus shifts attention from leadership as an input to team performance (that is, the leader does something that helps the team perform) to leadership as an outcome of team processes like team learning (that is, group members enact leadership to achieve team performance).

Our approach to leadership as collective achievement is similar. However, while the team leadership literature focuses on self-managed and work teams, our boundary was the social change organization, a meso-level of action. Similar to what Day et al. propose, the various components of our framework reflect the notion of leadership as a shared, distributed process. But, the leadership practices we document cut across organizational sub-units and teams to address the demands of organizing which occur both at the intimate level of microinteraction and at a broader system level, the organization, in relation to the external environment where powerful others are to be influenced. While we did not test it empirically, our framework would suggest that leadership practices encompass information about the interrelations between individual behavior, dyadic and group interactions, and broader intra- and interorganizational dynamics.

That our findings come from an organizational context that remains relatively underexplored in the leadership field—i.e., social change organizations—and from actors who previously have been relatively invisible in the literature, is relevant to the discussion. As Selsky and Smith (1994) argue, these organizations represent very different contexts for exercising leadership compared to traditional organizational settings: Participants are more diverse, agreed-upon decision-making processes are less codified and tend to be more horizontal, and given, the sensitivity to political changes, the level of environmental turbulence is extreme. These conditions may now resemble new forces affecting organizations in other sectors, a trend reflected in the recent research interest in more collective and distributed forms of leadership (Conger & Pearce, 2003). Documenting how leadership happens through the organizational experience of social actors who seem to prioritize relational practices could potentially enrich the received knowledge about organizational leadership considerably.

Within the transformational leadership tradition, for example, our findings reiterate a core message of Burn's argument (1978) that has been misplaced in the efforts to test the theory: Leadership is moral work around the construction of shared identities, and this work is always collective and historically grounded. This underscores the importance of analytically embedding the leader-follower relationship within the broader social context. It means consideration of the historical conditions and local circumstances that influence a group's experience of the present and its vision of the future, as well as the drivers and core assumptions its participants use to make sense of their individual and collective experience.

In our framework, context explains the way each element relates to the others. To understand why practices geared toward reframing discourse, bridging difference, and unleashing human energies are so relevant to the pursuit of social change goals, the framework must be viewed as a whole. Context is not a separate variable to be taken into account or to control for, and it is not the background environment within which leaders relate to followers, enact their behaviors and make decisions. It is instead the raw material within which leadership emerges (Ospina & Hittleman, 2011). As Hosking argues, "leadership cannot be abstracted from the organizational processes of which it is a part," it requires instead a focus on "the process in which flexible social order is negotiated and practiced so as to protect and promote the values and interests in which it is grounded" (Hosking, 1997, p. 315). This means considering various levels of action in an interconnected way.

Like us, other scholars of leadership in public settings have had to embed leaders within a broader social context that highlights various levels of action and the complex interconnections of leadership work. For example, Crosby and Bryson's framework (2005) encompasses a broad scope of action, as they consider eight capabilities that span all possible levels of change.[9] They argue that work is needed at each level to achieve a "regime of mutual gain," that is, a system yielding "widespread benefits at reasonable costs" and tapping "peoples' deepest interest in their own well-being and that of others" (p. 360). This regime is certainly a collective phenomenon that reflects shared agreements at each level of action. Understanding the type of leadership work needed to attain it requires exploring the way intrapersonal, interpersonal, intraorganizational and interorganizational dynamics interact to produce specific leadership work.

Recognizing the embeddedness of experience in context, and the reciprocal impact of levels of action, can change the quality of research on collective leadership. Many scholars recognize the need to broaden methods to incorporate qualitative and mixed modes of inquiry (Alvesson, 1996; Bryman, Bresnen, Beardsworth, & Keil, 1988; Bryman et al., 1996; Conger, 1999; House & Aditya, 1997; Ospina, 2004; Parry, 1998; Tierney, 1996).Yet, the solution of simply replicating logics of quantitative research in qualitative or mixed designs is too narrow. Designs that control for context or that try to isolate individual, organizational, and environmental contextual factors with sophisticated multi-level analysis techniques will not illuminate the underlying meanings that shape the dynamics, antecedents, and outcomes of collective leadership.

Merely switching to process models without questioning the underlying assumptions of the entity approach will not do the trick either (Langley, 1999; Van de Ven & Huber, 1990). What is needed instead is nothing less than a cognitive shift that allows scholars to simultaneously broaden and sharpen the scope of vision. This will reframe the relationship between leadership and context, not as foreground and background, but as phenomena that constitute each other. This shift will drive leadership scholars to explore how different types of methods can be used—or not—and perhaps even generate motivation to invent other methods more appropriate to the task.

CONCLUSION

In this chapter, we presented an emergent theoretical framework that captures the various elements of social change leadership found from a multimethod multi-year interpretive research project. The framework is our attempt to unpack how these organizations, along with their communities and through their collective leadership, are able to affect change and alter the status quo. We have argued that understanding leadership requires attention both to the parts—context, values, practices and activities—and the whole—how these parts interact to create something greater than their sum. The notion that the whole is greater than the sum of its parts is emblematic of leadership at its best.

The framework consists of two main elements: a worldview, entailing a set of leadership drivers which are anchored in assumptions and core values of social justice; and strategic action, which consists of leadership practices and primary social change activities. The worldview and strategic action inform and reinforce each other in building collective power, which is then leveraged to produce long-term social change outcomes. The framework poses that the work of leadership emerges in a complex and co-constructed context where various dimensions of leadership—assumptions, values, practices and outcomes—interact. Context thus becomes the vantage point from which collective achievements emerge, based on the combined effect of values, practices, and activities. Pertinent to the calls from recent scholarship on collective leadership (Ford & Seers, 2006; Hiller et al., 2006; Pearce & Sims, 2002), the framework also considers individual, organizational, and societal levels of action in an integrated manner, while still giving primacy to intraorganizational dynamics.

This framework builds on received knowledge from theories of transformational leadership (Bass & Steidlmeier, 1999), collective leadership (Hiller et al., 2006), constructionist leadership (Hosking, 2007), and practice theory (Schwartz, 2006). However, the framework adds a layer of nuance to the traditions that have informed our thinking. While we acknowledge that the entity perspective has informed much of our thinking, we argue that the constructionist approach allows us to see something bigger that integrates elements of the entity perspective into a whole system, giving us a much richer, more complex understanding.

Finally, we make an additional contribution to the conversation by offering insights about a particular organizational context that has been seldom considered in the study of leadership and which, we argue, has great promise as a locus to theorize about leadership. Chetkovich and Kunreuther (2006) claim that while the label of "social change organizations" has great meaning for practitioners and activists in the U.S., it is relatively absent from the academic literature, in part because these organizations tend to be lumped together with social movement organizations into a very broad category. In fact, they argue that while ignored in the literature, and despite their smaller size, SCOs represent a key feature of today's socio-political environment in the U.S., and a "potentially significant force for change" (p. 2). Indeed social change organizations present a fertile opportunity to study leadership that can be especially effective in illuminating transformational and collective leadership processes.

APPENDIX 9.1 Research Participants from LCW by Issues Area, City, and State

Organization	Primary Issue	City/State
American Friends Committee Wabanaki Youth Program	Economic/Community Development	Perry, ME
AIDS Housing of Washington	Economic/Community Development	Seattle, WA
Aid to Children with Imprisoned Mothers	Human Development	Atlanta, GA
Appalachian Sustainable Development	Economic/Community Development	Abington, WV
Boys, Girls, Adults Community Development Center	Economic/Community Development	Marvell, AR
Black AIDS Institute	Sexual & Reproductive Health	Los Angeles, CA
The Brotherhood/Sister Sol	Human Rights	New York, NY
Burlington Community Land Trust	Economic/Community Development	Burlington, VT
Coalition of African, Asian, European, and Latino Immigrants of Illinois	Human Development	Chicago, IL
CASA of Maryland	Economic/Community Development	Silver Spring, MD
Campaign to End the Death Penalty	Human Rights	Chicago, IL
Colorado Coalition for the Homeless	Human Development	Denver, CO
Colorado River Intertribal Fish Commission	Economic/Community Development	Portland, OR
Community Voices Heard	Economic/Community Development	New York, NY
Cornerstone Theater Company	Arts	Los Angeles, CA
Center for Young Women's Development	Economic/Community Development	San Francisco, CA
EVS Communications	Economic/Community Development	Washington, DC
Families Against Mandatory Minimums	Human Rights	Washington, DC
Fanm Ayisyen Nan Miyami, Inc.	Human Rights	Miami, FL
Fifth Avenue Committee	Economic/Community Development	New York, NY
Great Leap Inc.	Economic/Community Development	Santa Monica, CA
Gwich'in Steering Committee	Human Rights	Fairbanks, AK
Hazard Perry County Community Ministries	Economic/Community Development	Hazard, KY
Iowa Citizens for Community Improvement	Economic/Community Development	Des Moines, IA

(continued)

Social Change Leadership as Relational Leadership ▪ **289**

APPENDIX 9.1 Research Participants from LCW by Issues Area, City, and State (continued)

Organization	Primary Issue	City/ State
Jewish Community Action	Economic/Community Development	St. Paul, MN
Junebug Productions	Arts	New Orleans, LA
Justice Now	Human Rights	Oakland, CA
Laotian Organizing Project	Environment	Richmond, CA
Líderes Campesinas	Human Rights, Economic/Community Development	Oxnard, CA
Misión Industrial de Puerto Rico	Environment	San Juan, PR
Metropolitan Organizing Strategy Enabling Strength	Economic/Community Development	Detroit, MI
National Day Laborer Organizing Network	Economic/Community Development	Los Angeles, CA
Nebraska Appleseed Center for Law in the Public Interest	Human Rights	Lincoln, NE
Neighborhood Economic Development Advocacy Project	Economic/Community Development	New York, NY
New Road Community Development Group of Exmore	Economic/Community Development	Exmore, VA
Northwest Federation of Community Organizations	Economic/Community Development	Seattle, WA
New York Immigration Coalition	Human Rights	New York, NY
Oaxaca Binational Indigenous Coalition	Human Rights, Economic/Community Development	Fresno, CA
Ohio Valley Environmental Coalition	Environment	Huntington, WV
Piñeros y Campesinos Unidos de Noroeste	Human Rights, Economic/Community Development	Woodburn, OR
People Organized in Defense of Earth and Her Resources	Human Rights, Environment	Austin, TX
Project H.O.M.E	Economic/Community Development	Philadelphia, PA
Powder River Basin Resources Council	Environment	Sheridan, WY
Parents United for Responsible Education	Economic/Community Development	Chicago, IL
Regional Aids Interfaith Network	Sexual & Reproductive Health	Charlotte, NC
The Rebecca Project for Human Rights	Human Rights	Washington, DC
ReGenesis	Human Development	Spartanburg, SC
Rural Organizing Project	Economic/Community Development	Scappoose, OR

(continued)

APPENDIX 9.1 Research Participants from LCW by Issues Area, City, and State (continued)

Organization	Primary Issue	City/State
Sacramento Valley Organizing Community	Economic/Community Development	Sacramento, CA
Southeast Asia Resource Action Center	Economic/Community Development	Washington, D.C.
Service Employees International Union-Justice for Janitors	Human Rights, Economic/Community Development	Portland, OR
Sapelo Island Cultural and Revitalization Committee	Economic/Community Development	Sapelo Island, GA
Silver Valley People's Action Coalition	Economic/Community Development	Kellogg, ID
SisterLove	Education, Sexual & Reproductive Health	Atlanta, GA
Southwest Network for Environmental and Economic Justice	Human Rights	Albuquerque, NM
Teamsters for a Democratic Union	Human Rights	Detroit, MI
Tonatierra Community Development Institute	Human Rights	Phoenix, AZ
Triangle Residential Options for Substance Users	Human Development	Durham, NC
The Village of Arts and Humanities	Economic/Community Development	Philadelphia, PA
Wing Luke Asian Museum	Arts, Education	Seattle, WA

APPENDIX 9.2 LCW Research Design

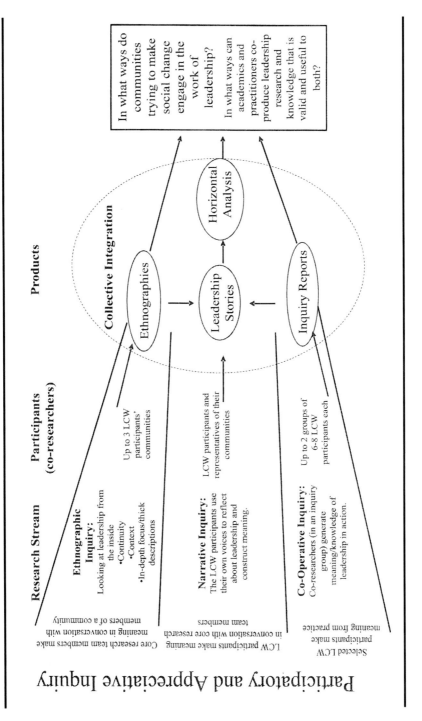

APPENDIX 9.3   Cooperative Inquiry and Ethnography Questions by Program Cohort

	Cooperative Inquiry	Ethnography
Cohort 1	How can we create the space/opportunities for individuals to recognize themselves as leaders and develop leadership?	How does an organization build political relationships that are spiritual and communication that is democratic? How does an organization overcome the divisions of the everyday?
	How do grassroots community organizers keep their organizational autonomy and build a wider movement to bring justice to our communities?	How does an organization practice leadership as part of everyday life?
Cohort 2	How can we be more effective in helping others become more strategic, conceptual, and creative in their thinking?	What is the very personal process by which people begin to act and self-identify as leaders?
	What makes social change leadership successful, and what values are held in common across such diverse leaders and organizations?	How does leadership emerge through struggle so that it results in transformations, individual as well as social, in the context of personal struggles for recovery and family reunification, collective struggles for fair housing and equality, and administrative struggles to stay true to the vision and pursue appropriate avenues for organizational growth?
Cohort 3	How do we engage and sustain a social justice movement that seizes power?	What challenges do two organizations face in their collaborations based on the social, cultural, and economic differences of their constituents and the way they frame and conceptualize each other's struggles?
	What is the transformative power of the arts in fostering and sustaining social change?	How can a community organization engage the community and develop leadership from the ground up as an ongoing, emergent process in the neighborhoods of North Philadelphia?
Cohort 4	How do we raise money to develop sustainable social change organizations?	What were the successes and challenges faced by Aid to Children of Imprisoned Mothers (AIM) in transitioning youth to leadership?

(continued)

APPENDIX 9.3   Cooperative Inquiry and Ethnography Questions by Program Cohort (continued)

	Cooperative Inquiry	Ethnography
	How can we Integrate Human Rights, Social Justice, and Sustainability?	How can a network of organizations that safeguard workers' and immigrants' rights engage in collective action to build and maintain leadership, develop a critical consciousness among the day labor workforce, and unite day laborers as a force for social change? What does a leadership development model look like when it is based on the principles and techniques of Popular Education—a pedagogical theory and practice designed to raise the consciousness of its participants and enable them to become more aware of how an individual's experiences are connected to broader socio-political forces?
Cohort 5	How do we build and empower grassroots organizations led by people of color to contribute to a movement that is both about domestic and global democracy and justice? How can we as leaders help cultivate in ourselves and in others change from within that inspires individual liberation and seeks/builds/sustains a movement for social justice?	

REFERENCES

Allen, K. (1990). *Diverse voices of leadership: Different rhythms and emerging harmonies.* Ann Arbor, MI: University of Michigan.

Alvesson, M. (1996). Leadership studies: From procedure and abstraction to reflexivity and situation. *The Leadership Quarterly, 7*(4), 469–485.

Amabile, T. M., Patterson, C., Mueller, J., Wojcik, T., Odomirok, P. W., Marsh, M., & Kramer,. (2001). Academic-practitioner collaboration in management research: A case of cross profession collaboration. *Academy of Management Journal, 44*(2), 418–431.

Ammeter, A. P., Douglas, C., Gardner, W. L., Hochwarter, W. A., & Ferris, G. R. (2002). Toward a political theory of leadership. *The Leadership Quarterly, 13,* 751–796.

Ansell, C., & Gash, A. (2008). Collaborative governance in theory and practice. *Journal of Public Administration Research and Theory, 18*(4), 543–571.

Ashcraft, K. L. (1999). Managing maternity leave: A qualitative analysis of temporary executive succession. *Administrative Science Quarterly, 44*(2), 240–280.

Asis, D., Dominguez, R., Fout, J., Herrera, S., James, S., Jordan, L., ... & Wise. (2003). *Social justice leadership and movement building.* Cooperative Inquiry Report. New York, NY: Research Center for Leadership in Action.

Bachrach, C. A., & Abeles, R. P. (2004). Social science and health research: Growth at the National Institutes of Health. *American Journal of Public Health, 94*(1), 22–28.

Bandura, A. (2000). Exercise of human agency through collective efficacy. *Current Directions in Psychological Science, 9*(3), 75–78.

Bandura, A. (1997). *Self-efficacy: The exercise of control.* New York, NY: Freeman.

Barnes, B. (2001). Practices as collective action. In T. R. Schatzki, K. K. Cetina, & E. Von Savigny (Eds.), *The practice turn in contemporary theory* (pp. 25–37). London, England: Routledge.

Bartunek, J. M., & Moch, M. K. (1987). First-order, second-order, and third-order change and organization development interventions: A cognitive approach. *Journal of Applied Behavior Science, 23*(4), 483–500.

Bass, B. M., & Avolio, B. J. (1993). Transformational leadership: A response to critiques. In J. G. Hunt, B. R. Baliga, H. P. Dachler, & C. A. Schriesheim (Eds.), *Emerging leadership vistas* (pp. 29–40). Lexington, MA: D. C. Health.

Bass, B. M., & Steidlmeier, P. (1999). Ethics, character, and authentic transformational leadership behavior. *The Leadership Quarterly, 10*(2), 181–217.

Bedell-Avers, K., Hunter, S. T., Angie, A. D., Eubanks, D. L., & Mumford, M. D. (2009). Charismatic, ideological, and pragmatic leaders: An examination of leader-leader interactions. *The Leadership Quarterly, 20*(3), 299–315.

Belenky, M. F., Bond, L. A., & Weinstock, J. S. (1997). *A tradition that has no name: Nurturing the development of people, families and communities.* New York, NY: Basic Books.

Beyer, J. M. (1999). Taming and promoting charisma to change organizations. *The Leadership Quarterly, 10*(2), 307–330.

Bluedorn, A. C., & Jaussi, K. S. (2008). Leaders, followers and time. *The Leadership Quarterly, 19*(6), 654–668.

Bourdieu, P. (1998). *Practical reason: On the theory of action.* Palo Alto, CA: Stanford University Press.

Bradbury, H., & Lichtenstein, B. (2000). Relationality in organizational research: Exploring the "space between." *Organization Science, 11*(5), 551–564.

Brass, D. J. (2005). Intraorganizational power and dependence. In J. Baum (Ed.), *The Blackwell companion to organizations* (pp. 992). Malden, MA: Blackwell.

Bray, J. N., Lee, J., Smith, L. L., & Yorks, L. (2000). *Collaborative inquiry in practice: Action, reflection, and meaning making.* Thousand Oaks, CA: Sage Publications.

Bruner, J. S. (1986). *Actual minds, possible worlds.* Cambridge, MA: Harvard University Press.

Bryman, A. (1996). Leadership in organizations. In S. Cleegg, C. Hardy, & W. Nord (Eds.), *Handbook of organization studies* (1st ed., pp. 276–292). Thousand Oaks, CA: Sage.

Bryman, A., Bresnen, M., Beardsworth, A., & Keil, T. (1988). Qualitative research and the study of leadership. *Human Relations, 41,* 13–30.

Bryman, A., Stephens, M., & à Campo, C. (1996). The importance of context: Qualitative research and the study of leadership. *The Leadership Quarterly, 7*(3), 353–370.

Bryson, J. M., & Crosby, B. C. (1992). *Leadership for the common good: Tackling public problems in a shared-power world.* San Francisco, CA: Jossey-Bass.

Burns, J. M. (1978). *Leadership.* New York, NY: Harper and Row.

Chetkovich, C., & Kunreuther, F. (2006). *From the ground up: Grassroots organizations making social change.* Ithaca, NY: Cornell University Press.

Chrislip, D., & Larson, C. (1994). *Collaborative leadership: How citizens and civic leaders can make a difference.* San Francisco, CA: Jossey-Bass.

Clandinin, D., & Connelly, F. (2000). *Narrative inquiry: Experience and story in qualitative research.* San Francisco, CA: Jossey-Bass.

Conger, J. A. (1999). Charismatic and transformational leadership in organizations: An insider's perspective on these developing streams of research. *The Leadership Quarterly, 10,* 145–180.

Conger, J. A., & Pearce, C. L. (2003). A landscape of opportunities: Future research on shared leadership. In C. L. Pearce, & J. A. Conger (Eds.), *Shared leadership: Reframing the hows and whys of leadership* (pp. 285–303). Thousand Oaks, CA: Sage.

Crosby, B. (1999). *Leadership for global citizenship.* Thousand Oaks, CA: Sage Publications.

Crosby, B., & Bryson, J. (2005). *New leadership for the common good.* San Francisco, CA: Jossey-Bass.

Crotty, M. (Ed.). (1998). *The foundations of social research: Meaning and perspective in the research process.* St. Leonards, Australia: Allen & Unwin.

Czarniawska, B., & Gagliardi, P. (2003). *Narratives we organize by.* Philadelphia, PA: John Benjamins.

Dachler, H. P. (1992). Management and leadership as relational phenomena. In M. V. Cranach, W. Doise, & G. Mugny (Eds.), *Social representations and social bases of knowledge* (pp. 169–178). Lewiston, NY: Hogrefe and Huber.

Dachler, H. P., & Hosking, D. M. (1995). The primacy of relations in socially constructing organizational realities. In D. M. Hosking, H. P. Dachler, & K. J. Gergen (Eds.), *Management and organization relational alternatives to individualism* (pp. 1–28). Brookfield, VT: Avebury.

Day, D. V., Gronn, P., & Salas, E. (2004). Leadership capacity in teams. *The Leadership Quarterly, 15,* 857–880.

deCerteau, M., Giard, L., & Mayol, P. (1998). *The practice of everyday life.* Minneapolis, MN: University of Minnesota Press.

Dodge, J. (2009). Environmental justice and deliberative democracy: How social change organizations respond to power in the deliberative system. *Policy and Society, 28*(3), 225- 239.

Drath, W. (2001). *The deep blue sea: Rethinking the source of leadership.* San Francisco, CA: Jossey-Bass.

Drath, W. H., McCauley, C. D., Palus, C. J., Van Velsor, E., O'Connor, P. M. G., & McGuire, J. B. (2008). Direction, alignment, commitment: Toward a more integrative ontology of leadership. *The Leadership Quarterly, 19*(6), 635–653.

Drath, W. H., & Palus, C. J. (1994). *Making common sense: Leadership as meaning-making in a community of practice.* Greensboro, NC: Center for Creative Leadership.

Evans, S. M., & Boyte, H. C. (1986). *Free spaces: The sources of democratic change in America.* New York, NY: Harper and Row.

Evered, R., & Louis, M. R. (1981). Alternative perspectives in organizational sciences: 'Inquiry from the inside' and 'inquiry from the outside'. *Academy of Management Review, 6*(3), 385–395.

Fairhurst, G. (2007). *Discursive leadership: In conversation with leadership psychology.* Thousand Oaks, CA: Sage.

Feldman, M., & Skoldberg, K. (2002). Stories and the rhetoric of contrariety: Subtexts of organizing change. *Culture and Organization, 8*(4), 275–292.

Fiol, C. M., Harris, D., & House, R. (1999). Charismatic leadership: Strategies for effecting social change. *The Leadership Quarterly, 10*(3), 449–482.

Foldy, E. (2002). 'Managing' diversity: Power and identity in organizations. In I. Aaltio-Marjosola, & A. Mills (Eds.), *Gender, identities and the cultures of organizations* (pp. 92–112). London, England: Routledge.

Foldy, E., Goldman, L., & Ospina, L. (2004). Shaping policy, making history: The role of cognitive shifts in social change leadership. *Association for Public Policy Analysis and Management 26th Annual Research Conference,* Atlanta, GA.

Foldy, E., Goldman, L., & Ospina, S. (2008). Sensegiving and the role of cognitive shifts in the work of leadership. *The Leadership Quarterly, 19,* 514–529.

Ford, L. R., & Seers, A. (2006). Relational leadership and team climates: Pitting differentiation versus agreement. *The Leadership Quarterly, 17,* 258–270.

Gardner, H. E. (1995). *Leading minds: An anatomy of leadership.* New York, NY: Basic Books.

Gasson, S., & Elrod, E. M. (2006). Distributed knowledge coordination across virtual organization boundaries. *Proceedings of the 2006 International Conference on Information Systems.* Milwaukee, WI. 947–966.

Gaventa, J. (2000). Towards participatory governance: Assessing the transformative possibilities. In S. Hickey, & G. Mohan (Eds.), *Participation : From tyranny to transformation?: Exploring new approaches to participation in development* (pp. 25–41). London, England: Zed Books.

Geertz, C. (1973). *The interpretation of cultures: Selected essays.* New York, NY: Basic Books.

Gerstner, C., & Tesluk, P. (2005). Peer leadership in self-managing teams: Examining team leadership through a social network analytic approach. In G. Graen (Ed.), *LMX leadership: The series* (pp. 131–151). Greenwich, CT: Information Age Publishing.

Gibbons, M. (2001). Mode 2 society and the emergence of context-sensitive science. *Science and Public Policy, 27*(3), 159–163.

Giddens, A. (1984). *The constitution of society: Outline of the theory of structuration.* Berkeley, CA: University of California Press.

Graen, G. B., & Uhl-Bien, M. (1995). Relationship-based approach to leadership: Development of leader-member-exchange (LMX) theory over 25 years: Applying a multi-level multi-domain perspective. *The Leadership Quarterly, 6,* 219–247.

Grant, H. M., & Crutchfield, L. R. (2007). Creating high-impact nonprofits. *Stanford Social Innovation Review, Fall,* 32–41.

Gronn, P. (2002). Distributed leadership as a unit of analysis. *The Leadership Quarterly, 13*(4), 423–451.

Gronn, P. (1999). Substituting for leadership: The neglected role of the leadership couple. *The Leadership Quarterly, 10,* 41–62.

Hammersley, M., & Atkinson, P. (1995). *Ethnography: Principles in practice.* (2nd ed.). New York, NY: Routledge.

Hannah, S., Avoglio, B., Luthans, F., & Harms, P. D. (2008). Leadership efficacy: Review and future directions. *The Leadership Quarterly, 19*(6), 669–692.

Harvey, M. (2006). Power. In G. J. Sorenson, & G. R. Goethals (Eds.), *The quest for a general theory of leadership* (pp. 74). Cheltenham, England: Edward Elgar.

Hauschildt, J., & Kirchmann, E. (2001). Teamwork for innovation—the troika of promoters. *R & D Management, 31*(1), 44–49.

Heifetz, R. A., Grashow, A., & Linsky, M. (2009). Leadership in a (permanent) crisis. *Harvard Business Review, 87*(July/August), 62–69.

Heifetz, R., & Laurie, D. (1997). The work of leadership. *Harvard Business Review, 75,* 124–134.

Hellström, T. (2004). Innovation as social action. *Organization, 11*(5), 631–649.

Herman, R. and Associates. (2005). *The Jossey-Bass handbook of nonprofit leadership and management* (2nd ed.). San Francisco, CA: Jossey-Bass.

Heron, J., & Reason, P. (2001). The practice of co-operative inquiry: Research "with" rather than "on" people. In P. Reason, & D. Bradbury (Eds.), *Handbook of action research: Participative inquiry and practice* (pp. 179–188). London, England: Sage.

Hiller, N. J., Day, D. V., & Vance, R. J. (2006). Collective enactment of leadership roles and team effectiveness: A field study. *The Leadership Quarterly, 17,* 387–397.

Hofmann-Pinilla, A., Olavarria, M., & Ospina, S. (2005). Collective narrative, identity and leadership: A comparative analysis of migrant worker, environmental and indigenous grassroots groups. *Association for Research on Nonprofit Organizations and Voluntary Action Annual Conference,* Washington, DC.

Hosking, D. (2007). Not leaders, not followers: A post-modern discourse of leadership processes. In B. Shamir, R. Pilai, M. Bligh, & M. Uhl-Bien (Eds.), *Follower-*

centered perspectives of leadership (pp. 167–186). Greenwich, CT: Information Age.

Hosking, D. (1988). Organizing, leadership and skillful process. *Journal of Management Studies, 25*, 147–166.

Hosking, D. M. (1997). Organizing, leadership and skillful processes. In K. Grint (Ed.), *Leadership: Classical, contemporary and critical approaches* (pp. 293–318). Oxford: Oxford University Press.

House, R. J., & Aditya, R. N. (1997). The social scientific study of leadership: Quo vadis? *Journal of Management, 23*, 3409–3473.

House, R. J., & Howell, J. M. (1992). Personality and charismatic leadership. *The Leadership Quarterly, 3*, 81–108.

Howell, J. M., & Boies, K. (2004). Champions of technological innovation: The influences of contextual knowledge, role orientation, idea generation, and idea promotion on champion emergence. *The Leadership Quarterly, 15*, 130–144.

Hunt, J. (1999). Transformational /charismatic leadership's transformation of the field: An historical essay. *The Leadership Quarterly, 10*(2), 129–144.

Huxham, C., & Vangen, S. (2000). Leadership in the shaping and implementation of collaboration agendas: How things happen in a (not quite) joined up world. *Academy of Management Journal, 43*(6), 159–175.

Huxham, C., & Vangen, S. (2004). *Managing to collaborate: The theory and practice of collaborative advantage.* New York, NY: Routledge.

Jackson, B., & Parry, K. (2008). *A very short, faintly interesting, and reasonably cheap book about leadership.* London, England: Sage Publications.

Kark, R., & Shamir, B. (2002). The dual effect of transformational leadership: Priming relational and collective selves and further effects on followers. In B. J. Avolio, & F. Yammarino (Eds.), *Transformational and charismatic leadership: The road ahead* (pp. 67–91). Stamford, CT: JAI Press.

Komives, S. R., & Wagner, W., & Associates. (2009). *Leadership for a better world: Understanding the social change model of leadership development.* San Francisco, CA: Jossey-Bass.

Kriger, M., & Seng, Y. (2005). Leadership with inner meaning: A contingency theory of leadership based on the worldviews of five religions. *The Leadership Quarterly, 16*(5), 771–806.

Langley, A. (1999). Strategies for theorizing from process data. *Academy of Management Review, 24*(4), 691–710.

Latour, B. (1987). *Science in action: How to follow scientists and engineers through society.* Cambridge, MA: Harvard University Press.

McClelland, D. C. (1985). *Human motivation.* Glenview, IL: Scott, Foresman.

Meindl, J. (1995). The romance of leadership as a follower-centric theory: A social constructionist approach. *The Leadership Quarterly, 6*(3), 329–341.

Mischler, E. G. (1987). *Research interviewing: Context and narrative.* Cambridge, MA: Harvard University.

Mohrman, S. A., Gibson, C. B., & Mohrman, A. M., Jr. (2001). Doing research that is useful to practice: A model and empirical exploration. *Academy of Management Journal, 44*(2), 357–374.

O'Leary, R., Gerard, C., & Bingham, L. B. (2006). Introduction to the symposium on collaborative public management. *Public Administration Review, 66*(s1), 6–9.

Orlikowski, W. J. (2002). Knowing in practice: Enacting a collective capability in distributed organizing. *Organization Science, 13*(4), 249–273.

Osborn, R. N., & Marion, R. (2009). Contextual leadership, transformational leadership and the performance of international innovation seeking alliances. *The Leadership Quarterly, 20*(27), 191–206.

Osborn, R., Hunt, J. G., & Jauch, L. R. (2002). Toward a contextual theory of leadership. *The Leadership Quarterly, 13*, 797–837.

Ospina, S. (2004). Qualitative research. In G. R. Goethals, G. J. Sorenson, & J. MacGregor Burns (Eds.), *Encyclopedia of leadership* (pp. 1279–1284). London, England: Sage.

Ospina, S., & Dodge, J. (2005). It's about time: Catching method up to meaning—The usefulness of narrative inquiry in public administration research. *Public Administration Review, 65*(2), 143–158.

Ospina, S., Dodge, J., Godsoe, B., Mineri, J., Reza, S., & Schall, E. (2002). From consent to mutual inquiry: Balancing democracy and authority in action research. *Action Research, 2*(1), 47–69.

Ospina, S., El Hadidy, W., & Hofmann-Pinilla, A. (2008). Cooperative inquiry for learning and connectedness. *Action Learning: Research and Practice, 5*(2), 131–147.

Ospina, S., & Foldy, E. (2005). *Toward a framework of social change leadership.* Unpublished manuscript.

Ospina, S., & Foldy, E. (2010). Building bridges from the margins: The work of leadership in social change organizations. *The Leadership Quarterly, 21*(2), 292–307.

Ospina, S., & Hittleman, M. (2011). Thinking sociologically about leadership. In M. Harvey, & R. Riggio (Eds.), *Research companion to leadership studies: The dialogue of disciplines* (pp. 89–100). Cheltenham, England: Edward Elgar.

Ospina, S., & Saz-Carranza, A. (2010). Leadership and collaboration in coalition work. In Z. van Zwanenberg (Ed.), *Leadership in social care* (pp. 103–128). London, England: Jessica Kingsley, Publishers.

Ospina, S., & Sorensen, G. (2006). A constructionist lens on leadership: Charting new territory. In G. Goethals, & G. Sorenson (Eds.), *In quest of a general theory of leadership* (pp. 188–204). Cheltenham, England: Edward Elgar Publishers.

Ospina, S., & Su, C. (2009). Weaving color lines: Race, ethnicity, and the work of leadership in social change organizations. *Leadership, 5*(2), 131–170.

Parry, K. (1998). Grounded theory and social process: A new direction for leadership research. *The Leadership Quarterly, 9*(1), 85–105.

Parry, K., & Bryman, A. (2006). Leadership in organizations. In S. C. Clegg, T. Hardy, T. Lawrence, & W. Nord (Eds.), *The Sage handbook of organization studies* (2nd ed., pp. 448–468). Thousand Oaks, CA: Sage Publications.

Pastor, J. C. (1998). *The social construction of leadership: A semantic and social network analysis of social representations of leadership.* Ann Arbor, MI: University of Michigan.

Pearce, C. L., & Conger, J. A. (Eds.). (2003). *Shared leadership: Reframing the hows and whys of leadership.* Thousand Oaks, CA: Sage Publications.

Pearce, C. L., & Sims, J. P. (2002). Vertical versus shared leadership as predictors of the effectiveness of change management teams: An examination of aversive, directive, transactional, transformational, and empowering leader behaviors. *Group Dynamics: Theory, Research, and Practice, 6,* 172–197.

Perlow, L. A. (1998). Boundary control: The social ordering of work and family time in a high-tech corporation. *Administrative Science Quarterly, 43*(27), 328–357.

Pfeffer, J. (1997). The ambiguity of leadership. *Academy of Management Review, 2,* 104–112.

Polkinghorne, D. (2004). *Practice and the human sciences: The case for a judgment-based practice of care.* Albany, NY: State University of New York.

Porter, L. W., & McLaughlin, G. B. (2006). Leadership and the organizational context: Like the weather? *The Leadership Quarterly, 17,* 559–576.

Pratt, M. G. (2000). The good, the bad and the ambivalent: Managing identification among Amway distributors. *Administrative Science Quarterly, 45*(3), 456–493.

Preskill, S., & Brookfield, S. D. (2009). *Learning as a way of leading: Lessons from the struggle for social justice.* San Francisco, CA: Jossey-Bass.

Raelin, J. A. (2003). *Creating leaderful organizations: How to bring out leadership in everyone.* San Francisco, CA: Berrett- Koehler.

Raelin, J. (2005). "We the leaders: In order to form a leaderful organization". *Journal of Leadership and Organizational Studies, 12*(2), 18–30.

Reckwitz, A. (2002). Toward a theory of social practices: A development in culturalist theorizing. *European Journal of Social Theory, 5*(2), 243–263.

Reissman, C. K. (2002). Narrative analysis. In A. M. Huberman, & M. B. Miles (Eds.), *The qualitative researcher's companion* (pp. 217–270). Thousand Oaks, CA: Sage Publications.

Sampson, R. J., Raudenbush, S. W., & Earls, F. (1997). Neighborhoods and violent crime: A multilevel study of collective efficacy. *Science, 277*(5328), 918–924.

Saz-Carranza, A., & S. Ospina. (2011). The behavioral dimension of governing interorganizational goal-directed networks: Managing the unity/diversity tension. *Journal of Public Administration Research and Theory, 21*(2): 327–365.

Schall, E., Ospina, S., Godsoe, B., & Dodge, J. (2004). Appreciative narratives as leadership research: Matching method to lens. In D. L. Cooperrider, & M. Avital (Eds.), *Advances in appreciative inquiry* (pp. 147–170). Oxford, England: Elsevier Science.

Schatzki, T., Cetina, K. K., & Von Savigny, E. (Eds.). (2001). *The practice turn in contemporary theory.* London, England: Routledge.

Schwartz, D. L. (2006). Pierre Bourdieu and North American political sociology: Why he doesn't fit in but should. *French Politics, 4*(84), 99.

Seers, A., Keller, T., & Wilkerson, J. M. (2003). Can team members share leadership? Foundations in research and theory. In C. L. Pearce, & J. A. Conger (Eds.), *Shared leadership: Reframing the how's and whys of leadership* ( ). London, England: Sage.

Selsky, J. W., & Smith, A. (1994). Community entrepreneurship: A framework for social change leadership. *The Leadership Quarterly, 5*(3/4), 277–296.

Shamir, B. (2007). From passive recipients to active co-producers. In B. Shamir, M. Pilai, M. Bligh, & M. Uhl-Bien (Eds.), *Follower-centered perspectives on leadership* (pp. *ix-xxxix*). Greenwich CT: Information Age Publishing.

Shamir, B., House, R., & Arthur, M. B. (1993). The motivational effects of charismatic leadership: A self-concept based theory. *Organization Science, 4*(4), 577–594.

Shamir, B., Pilai, M., Bligh, M., & Uhl-Bien, M. (Eds.). (2007). *Follower-centered perspectives of leadership.* Greenwich CT: Information Age Publishing.

Shamir, B., Zakay, E., Breine, E., & Popper, M. (1998). Correlates of charismatic leader behavior in military units. *Academy of Management Journal, 41*(3), 387–409.

Smircich, L., & Morgan, G. (1982). Leadership: The management of meaning. *Journal of Applied Behavioral Science, 18,* 257–273.

Smock, K. (2004). *Democracy in action: Community organizing and urban change.* New York, NY: Columbia University Press.

Sosik, J. J., & Dinger, S. (2007). Relationships between leadership style and vision content: The moderating role of need for social approval, self-monitoring, and need for social power. *The Leadership Quarterly, 18*(2), 134–153.

Stephen, L., Lanier, J., Ramírez, R., & Westerling, M. (2006). *Building alliances: Collaboration between CAUSA and the rural organizing project (ROP) in Oregon.* New York, NY: Research Center for Leadership in Action.

Strauss, A. L., & Corbin, J. (1998). *Basics of qualitative research; Techniques and procedures for developing grounded theory.* Thousand Oaks, CA: Sage.

Su, C. (2010). We call ourselves by many names: Story telling and inter-minority coalition building. *Community Development Journal, 45*(4), 439–445.

Swidler, A. (2001). What anchors cultural practices. In T. Schatzki, K. K. Cetina, & E. Von Savigny (Eds.), *The practice turn in contemporary theory* (pp. 74–93). London, England: Routledge.

Terry, R. W. (1993). *Authentic leadership: Courage in action.* San Francisco, CA: Jossey-Bass.

Teske, R., & Tetreault, M. A. (2000). *Conscious acts and the politics of social change: Feminist approaches to social movements, community and power.* Columbia, SC: University of South Carolina Press.

Tierney, W. (1987). The semiotic aspects of leadership: An ethnographic perspective. *American Journal of Semiotics, 5,* 223–250.

Tierney, W. (1996). Leadership and postmodernism: On voice and the qualitative method. *The Leadership Quarterly,* (7), 3–371.

Tse, H. M., Dasborough, M. T., & Ashkanasy, N. M. (2008). A multilevel analysis of team climate and interpersonal exchange relationships at work. *The Leadership Quarterly, 19*(195), 211.

Uhl-Bien, M. (2006). Relational leadership theory: Exploring the social processes of leadership and organizing. *The Leadership Quarterly, 17*(6), 654–676.

Uhl-Bien, M., & Pillai, R. (2007). The romance of leadership and the social construction of followership. In B. Shamir, R. Pillai, M. Bligh, & M. Uhl-Bien (Eds.), *Follower-centered perspectives of leadership* (pp. 187–210). Greenwich, CT: Information Age.

Van de Ven, A. H., & Huber, G. P. (1990). Longitudinal field research methods for studying processes of organizational change. *Organization Science, 1*(3), 213–219.

Wenger, E. (1998). *Communities of practice: Learning, meaning, and identity.* Cambridge, England: Cambridge University Press.

Wood, R. (2002). *Faith in action: Religion, race and democratic organizing in america.* Chicago, IL: University of Chicago Press.

Yammarino, F. J., Dionne, S. D., Chun, J. U., & Dansereau, F. (2005). Leadership and levels of analysis: A state-of-the-science review. *The Leadership Quarterly, 16*, 879–919.

Yanow, D., & Schwartz-Shea, P. (2006). What's 'interpretive' about interpretive methods? In D. Yanow, & P. Schwartz-Shea (Eds.), *Interpretation and method: Empirical research methods and the interpretive turn* (pp. xi–xxvii). Armonk, NY: M.E. Sharpe.

NOTES

1. The authors acknowledge the contribution of social change leaders as active participants in the project, and thank the Ford Foundation for its generous support.
2. "We" refers to the authors of this chapter and the members of our research team which, over time, included faculty, doctoral students, master's students, and administrative and research staff.
3. Komives, Wagner, and Associates (2009) propose a framework of leadership development that emphasizes elements of leadership similar to our model, including interconnectedness and values. However, it was derived from their cumulative knowledge of leadership programs and interventions rather than from empirical research.
4. Leadership for a Changing World (LCW), a program of the Ford Foundation.
5. The annual selection process began when supporters nominated individuals and teams. A national committee selected about 250 top candidates who moved on to regional selection committees. The regional committees, using new essays from each nominee, selected 5 primary and 4 secondary regional finalists per cohort. These were cut down to 36 semi-finalists who hosted site visits. A national selection committee reviewed all their materials, and by consensus recommended 24 finalists, 17 to 20 of whom made the final cut each year. Members of the research team did not participate in selection.
6. See Appendix 9.1 for list of the 60 organizations in this analysis, organized by issue area and geographic location.
7. See Appendix 9.2 for a visual representation of our overall research design.
8. For standard articles that report on our detailed findings, see Foldy et al., 2008; Ospina & Foldy, 2010; Ospina & Saz-Carranza, 2010; Ospina & Su, 2009; Saz-Carranza & Ospina, 2011.
9. The proposed leadership capabilities, ordered from lower to higher levels of action, include: understanding leadership in context; understanding self and others as leadership actors; building productive work groups; nurturing effective and humane organizations; creating and communicating shared meaning in the appropriate forums; making policy decisions in arenas; sanctioning conduct and resolving conflicts; and coordinating leadership tasks over the course of the policy change cycle.

CHAPTER 10

INTEGRATIVE LEADERSHIP AND POLICY CHANGE

A Hybrid Relational View

Barbara C. Crosby and John M. Bryson

We have long been interested in how leaders and followers (or constituents, citizens, collaborators) successfully work together to tackle complex public problems, needs, and opportunities (Bryson & Crosby, 1992; Crosby, 1999; Crosby & Bryson, 2005). Along the way, we came to define *leadership* as the inspiration and mobilization of others to undertake collective action in pursuit of the common good. Over the last three decades, we have researched numerous cases of policy change efforts in order to ground our theory building and offer practical advice and tools for aspiring leaders.

Our research reinforces the view that many determined leaders (in formal and informal roles), along with numerous committed followers, are required if complex problems like AIDS, environmental degradation, or poverty are to be remedied effectively and if new institutions or promising technologies like computer-assisted social networking are to be developed for the benefit of all. We follow in the tradition of scholars like James MacGregor Burns (1978) and Joseph Rost (1991) who saw leadership as

Advancing Relational Leadership Research, pages 303–333
Copyright © 2012 by Information Age Publishing

a relationship between leaders and followers or constituents, focusing on their shared purposes. We also see leader and follower roles as shifting over the course of an effort to reform or transform existing policy regimes—for example, an individual may move in and out of a role as team leader as her team takes on different tasks or enters a new phase.

Leadership aimed at tackling complex public challenges is necessarily a shared and collective phenomenon. At the same time, we have found that the characteristics, strengths, and weaknesses of particular individuals who act as formal and informal leaders significantly affect the outcome of this leadership work. Thus, we are among scholars who view leadership as replete with polarities and paradoxes (Terry, 2001).

Two leadership roles—champions and sponsors—seem to be especially important in bringing diverse stakeholder groups together to tackle complex public challenges (Crosby & Bryson, 2005). Champions are people who work hard, often over many years, to initiate and sustain change processes; frequently, they draw mainly on informal authority to gain support for the initiative. Sponsors are people (usually with substantial formal authority) who can supply legitimacy, resources, and supportive policy decisions that are vital to supporting the change process.

Recently, we have worked with colleagues at the University of Minnesota's Center for Integrative Leadership to understand how policy entrepreneurs (especially sponsors and champions) develop sustainable cross-sector collaborations to remedy complex public problems. In the course of our earlier work, we became convinced that all major sectors (government, business, nonprofits, media, and community) were implicated in complex public challenges and therefore ideally would be involved in tackling the challenges (Bryson & Crosby, 2008). Along with Melissa Stone, we developed a set of propositions about the key factors affecting the success of cross-sector collaboration (Bryson, Crosby, & Stone, 2006). In this chapter, we present an integrative leadership framework that relates leadership to the literature on cross-sector collaboration. We discuss the relational nature of integrative leadership. We then introduce four cases in which policy entrepreneurs have brought diverse stakeholders together across sectoral and other boundaries to tackle public challenges. Most of the chapter describes categories of leadership practices that seem to be most important for initiating and sustaining cross-sector collaboration.

INTEGRATIVE LEADERSHIP FRAMEWORK

Integrative leadership refers to the work of linking and integrating diverse constituencies—along with resources, processes, and structures—in sustainable arrangements for remedying a public problem or responding to a public challenge. The integrative leadership framework ties together key elements of cross-sector collaboration, leadership capabilities, and leadership practices.

Five inter-related elements appear to be crucial for the success of cross-sector collaborations. Shown in Figure 10.1, they are: initial conditions; process, structure and governance; constraints and contingencies; and accountabilities and outcomes (Bryson, Crosby, & Stone, 2006; Crosby & Bryson, 2010). Champions and sponsors striving to initiate and sustain such collaborations face the challenge of "aligning initial conditions, processes, structures, governance, contingencies and constraints, outcomes and accountabilities such that... public value can be created" (Bryson, Crosby, & Stone, 2006, p. 52). Our research indicates that champions, sponsors, and their colleagues need to exhibit and foster a comprehensive set of leadership capabilities if complex public problems occurring in a shared-power world are to be remedied.

The key leadership capabilities for public problem solving—including in cross-sector collaborations—are presented in full detail in *Leadership for the Common Good* (Crosby & Bryson, 2005). They are:

- *Leadership in context*—understanding the social, political, economic, technological, and ecological 'givens' as well as potentialities,
- *Personal leadership*—understanding and deploying personal assets on behalf of beneficial change,
- *Team leadership*—building effective work groups,
- *Organizational leadership*—nurturing humane and effective organizations,
- *Visionary leadership*—creating and communicating shared meaning in forums,
- *Political leadership*—making and implementing decisions in legislative, executive, and administrative arenas,
- *Ethical leadership*—sanctioning conduct and adjudicating disputes in courts, and
- *Policy entrepreneurship*—coordinating leadership tasks over the course of policy change cycles.

The integrative leadership framework connects those capabilities to the elements of cross-sector collaboration and highlights categories, or sets of practices, that appear to be vital for achieving public value through cross-sector collaboration. (See Table 10.1.) The practices will be explained later in the chapter as we examine four cases of policy change.

This framework has emerged from our engagement in a protracted dialogue between leadership theory and practice. For nearly three decades, our basic research question has been "How do leaders and followers work

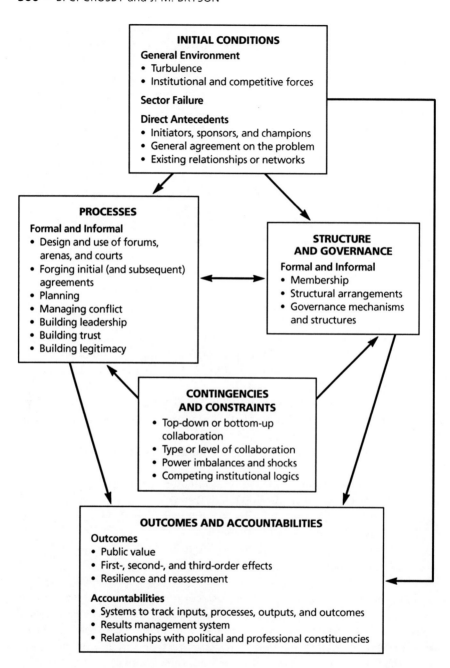

Figure 10.1 A Framework for Understanding Leadership and the Creation and Maintenance of Cross-Sector Collaborations (adapted from Bryson, Crosby, & Stone, 2006, p. 45; Crosby & Bryson, 2010).

TABLE 10.1 Integrative Leadership Framework

Aspect of Cross-Sector Collaboration	Practice Focus	Leadership Capabilities
Initial Conditions	Diagnosis • windows of opportunity • stakeholder identification • stakeholder views and connections	Leadership in context Personal leadership
Integrative Process	Design and use of forums Design and use of arenas Design and use of courts Navigation of policy change cycle	Visionary leadership Political leadership Ethical leadership Policy entrepreneurship
Structure and Governance	Management of structural ambidexterity Formation and maintenance of boundary groups	Organizational leadership Team leadership
Contingencies and Constraints	Management of transaction costs and production of desirable outcomes Balancing power Anticipation of change Management of competing logics	Policy entrepreneurship Policy entrepreneurship Policy entrepreneurship Visionary leadership
Outcomes and Accountabilities	Identification of 1st-, 2nd-, and 3rd-order effects Construction of accountability and results management systems Demonstration of resilience, reassessment	Policy entrepreneurship Policy entrepreneurship Personal leadership Visionary leadership

together successfully (and unsuccessfully) to remedy public problems or build more humane communities?" In structuration theory (especially Giddens, 1979/1984), we found a guide to understanding the broad social practices that both alter and reinforce existing ways of responding to collective problems. Building on structuration theory, we developed a multi-dimensional view of power linking agency and structure and comprising three basic social practices: the creation and communication of shared meaning, policy making and implementation, and the management of residual conflict and enforcement of underlying norms (Crosby & Bryson, 2005, pp. 401–426). We related that view of power to the comprehensive set of leadership capabilities listed above and derived from studies of leadership from the team to interorganizational and interinstitutional levels. A central conclusion of our application of structuration theory to leadership has been that leaders in shared-power situations do not achieve outcomes directly, but rather through indirection—they work with constituents to shape the ideas, rules, modes, media, and methods that help determine outcomes, but do not directly cause them. (The ideas, rules, modes, media, and methods in turn are shaped by "deep structures" of meaning, resource asymmetry, and legitimacy.) The common good is thus an emergent phenomenon resulting from the engagement of diverse stakeholders in mutual problem solving.

Because of our interest in power and development of shared understanding of public problems, we also have drawn substantially on five additional literatures: neo-institutional theory, in which human agency is vital to changing organizational and institutional structures (e.g., Scott, 1987; Selznick, 1957, 1996); stakeholder theory (Bryson, 2004; Freeman, 1984); organizational sense-making (e.g., Smircich & Morgan, 1982; Weick, 1995); agenda-setting (e.g., Baumgartner & Jones, 1993; Kingdon, 1995); and coalition building (e.g., Sabatier & Jenkins-Smith, 1993). Recently, we have added insights from the emerging literature on collaborative public management (see Bingham & O'Leary, 2008; Huxham & Vangen, 2005), as well as on actor network theory (Bryson, Crosby, & Bryson, 2009; Latour, 2005), and on theories of social learning in communities of practice (especially Wenger, 1998). These recent explorations have helped us deepen our understanding of how leaders develop shared meanings and enduring commitments across sectoral, cultural, and geographic divisions (see Bryson 2010; Bryson, Crosby, & Stone, 2006; Crosby & Bryson, 2010). Attention to communities of practice is especially helpful because communities of practice will have formed around "old solutions" to old or ongoing problems. These communities have previously negotiated and over time crafted behaviors that have become taken for granted and are now effectively practices, what Reckwitz (2002) calls "a routinized way in which bodies are moved, objects are handled, subjects are treated, things are described and the world is understood" (p. 250). Wenger provides insights into how communities of practice resist change, but also how they can innovate as they connect with new or existing communities of practice.

In addition to drawing on these literatures, we have compiled numerous case studies of leadership in relatively successful policy change campaigns. These studies, four of which are described in this chapter, have informed our theoretical framework as well as the guidance we offer practitioners. The integrative leadership framework thus draws on numerous theories of leadership, social interaction, public policy, and management, and bridges theory and practice.

RELATIONAL NATURE OF INTEGRATIVE LEADERSHIP

Our view of integrative leadership combines aspects of the "relationship as entity" and "relationship as lens" approaches described in Mary Uhl-Bien's

(2006) review of relational leadership theory. In keeping with the entity approach, we highlight the importance of qualities, characteristics, attributes, and skills of numerous individual leaders, and we argue that shared, or collective, leadership is increasingly required to engage in effective public problem solving to achieve the common good. We emphasize leaders' social ties as a source of personal power (Balkundi & Kilduff, 2005). At the same time, we agree with theorists applying the relationality lens to leadership, who see leadership practices as mutually constructed by leaders and followers, as well as participating organizations and institutions. We certainly also agree that individual qualities, characteristics, attributes, skills, and interpersonal relations are shaped (though, we emphasize, *not determined*) by the organizational, institutional, and physical environment. We see individuals and groups leading through structures and processes that they affect, and are affected by, as they move through time and particular spaces. Individuals engaged in tackling public problems are necessarily in dynamic relations with each other and with tangible and virtual groups and objects (Emirbayer, 1997; Kellogg, Orlikowski, & Yates, 2006; Latour, 2005; Wenger, 1998).

From a structurational perspective, problems and solutions are socially constructed. Communities of practice are central to this activity. In such communities, particular individuals and groups possess and use competencies associated with problem formulation, solution development, and solution implementation; the competencies may be embedded in the relationships among members of a community of practice (Eden & Ackermann, 2001). Processes and practices are made possible by an underlying set of generative rules and resources (including interpretive schemes available to individuals); in turn, processes and practices create and recreate the rules and resources. This generativity, however, is not without limits since, in any situation, some things must be taken as given—at least temporarily—or nothing would get done.

The distinctive contributions of the integrative leadership framework to relational leadership theory are its wide-ranging consideration of leadership and public problem solving; its multi-dimensional and contextual view of power; its attention to constructing shared meaning and enduring commitments across organizational, sectoral, cultural, and geographic divides; its attention to public value and the common good; and its insistence on lengthy time frames. The framework also alerts leaders, followers, and scholars to their embeddedness in communities of practice, and it structures narratives of actual cases of integrative leadership that highlight the work of specific sponsors and champions.

Elements of Cross-Sector Collaboration and Associated Leadership Practices

In preparing this chapter, we reviewed our previous case analyses and publications, synthesized prior work, and searched in a disciplined way for leadership practices across the cases. The resulting catalogue of practices described in this chapter has emerged from our analyses of four particular cases of integrative leadership that we and our colleagues have followed over a number of years. (Among all the cases we have studied, these are the ones we have explored in the most depth.) The cases focus on very different policy areas, but all are strongly connected to Minnesota and began within the last 15 years. The sponsors and champions of policy change are mainly from the government and nonprofit sectors, but all the initiatives have involved business-sector people and organizations, as well as community groups, and to a lesser extent mass media. The cases are:

- The African American Men Project (AAMP), an ambitious effort, begun in 1999, to improve the lives of African American men in Hennepin County, Minnesota, which contains Minneapolis, the state's largest city. (The case is described in more detail in Crosby & Bryson [2005] and at http://www.northpointhealth.org/African AmericanMenProject/tabid/85/Default.aspx.)
- The Vital Aging Network (VAN), formed in 2000, to improve opportunities for older adults to lead productive lives. (The case is described in more detail in Crosby & Bryson [2005] and at http://www.vital-aging-network.org.)
- MetroGIS, a geospatial information system (GIS) that, since its beginning in 1995, has dramatically improved the ability of governments and other organizations in the Minneapolis-St. Paul region to make accurate predictions and better informed decisions about population trends, economic development, and services. (The case is described in more detail in Bryson, Crosby, & Bryson [2009].)
- The Minnesota Urban Partnership Agreement (UPA), part of a national path-breaking multi-modal transportation project launched in 2006 to fight urban traffic congestion. (The case is described in more detail in Crosby & Bryson [2010].)

Each of the cases has produced significant and broadly beneficial change in how a public problem is defined and remedied. The African American Men Project, which continues today, has created public value by treating African American men between the ages of 18 and 30 not as program recipients, not as victims, and not as representatives of particular problems like the educational achievement gap, but rather as full human beings who have tremendous potential for exerting personal responsibility for their lives if supported by community organizations and institutions. The program has discovered and implemented a variety of solutions that have far better cost-benefit ratios than existing solutions. As a result, a number of African American men and boys are more fully included in the Minneapolis community, and the project has led to related initiatives around the U.S.

The Vital Aging Network has helped empower older adults to contribute to their communities and care for themselves. It continues as part of a transnational "vital aging movement" that is changing how societies view citizens over 60 and the aging process.

MetroGIS has improved the availability, accuracy, timeliness, and comparability of geospatial data for planning, decision-making, and policy evaluation in the Minneapolis–St. Paul region. It continues to help many policy makers think geospatially about policy as a matter of course.

Minnesota's Urban Partnership Agreement has fostered more holistic transportation planning and system management and innovative uses of technology. It is expected to reduce traffic congestion significantly in major corridors linking Minneapolis and southern suburbs.

All of the cases were researched via engaged scholarship (Van de Ven, 2007). In three of them—the African American Men Project, the Vital Aging Network, and MetroGIS—we assisted policy entrepreneurs with various problem-framing and problem-solving tasks as they sought to build coalitions, launch projects and programs, reform and transform policies, and radically alter ways of thinking and behaving among a broad array of stakeholders. Research on the fourth case—Minnesota's Urban Partnership Agreement—was conducted with colleague Melissa Stone and research associates, Clare Mortenson and Emily Saunoi-Sandgren. In this case, the researchers had more limited roles in advising practitioners and engaging stakeholders, but practitioners have helped shape the research design, provided feedback on reports, and used our findings.

In all the studies, we used traditional tools of case study development (Yin, 2009)—structured and open-ended interviews with key participants, analysis of documents and news reports, and observation of events (sometimes as participants ourselves). In the UPA case, we used NVivo coding to identify and explore themes across interviews.

Any detailed consideration of the cases highlighted here would reveal a host of champions and sponsors. Only a few will be introduced, however, in order to illustrate the identified types of leadership practices.

In the VAN case, Jan Hively, Darlene Schroeder and Hal Freshley were concerned about the "graying" of Minnesota communities as the twentieth century concluded. They invited others who shared their concern to join a "vital aging" initiative that especially would help individuals and communities respond to challenges and opportunities associated with imminent retirement of the first ranks of the U.S. baby boom generation. At the time Hively, was Director of Community Outreach for the College of Education and Human Development at the University of Minnesota; Schroeder directed the Elder Advocacy Network, which was sponsored by the Minnesota Department of Human Services; and Freshley coordinated planning and policy for the Minnesota Board on Aging.

In the African American men case, a conservative Hennepin County commissioner, Mark Stenglein, and the county's planning director, Gary Cunningham, combined forces to secure county endorsement of an in-depth study that would engage African American men and other experts in studying causes and consequences of multiple problems—such as high unemployment rates—affecting these men.

In the MetroGIS case, regional government employee and former city planner Randall Johnson was supported by regional administrator Richard Johnson in convening diverse government, business, and academic stakeholders to consider how to improve production and sharing of geospatial information in the Minneapolis-St. Paul region.

In the UPA case, officials such as Bernie Arseneau from the Minnesota Department of Transportation (MnDOT) and Arlene McCarthy from the Metropolitan Council, the regional government for the Minneapolis-St. Paul metropolitan area, worked with John Doan from the SRF consulting firm and congestion pricing advocates from the University of Minnesota and elsewhere to compete for one of the innovative federal Urban Partnership grants. The U.S. Department of Transportation (USDOT) initiated the grants to foster large-scale multimodal attacks on urban traffic congestion.

The remainder of this section considers key leadership capabilities and practices associated with each of the five main elements of cross-sector collaboration. Illustrative examples are drawn from the cases.

Initial Conditions

Deciding where and when a change process begins (and thus what to consider as initial conditions) can be difficult. There may be no real beginning and end, only middles. Recall Latour's (2005) notion that "context" is what we call a network of actors we don't understand. Still, we can locate a time in all of the cases that policy entrepreneurs decided to undertake an ambitious change effort involving multiple stakeholders. At this point (and leading up to it), they needed skills of *leadership in context*, since the contours and dynamics of the political, social, economic, technological, and ecological environment strongly affect whether a cross-sector collaboration aimed at solving public problems will get off the ground and show early promise (Bryson, Crosby, & Stone, 2006).

Our cases indicate that, at the outset of a change effort, policy entrepreneurs would be wise to engage in a diagnostic practice (or set of practices) that focuses on three aspects of the environment:

- How shifts in politics, demographics, culture, the economy, and the physical world are (or are not) opening what Kingdon (1995) calls "windows of opportunity" for policy change
- Which stakeholders (individuals, groups, and organizations) are most affected by the problem (or challenge) of concern, have responsibility for doing something about it, and have critical resources, and
- How existing and potential connections among the stakeholders are fostering the status quo or offering opportunities for improvement.

Windows of Opportunity. In all of these cases, pressures had mounted to do something about a public problem that already was full-blown or threatened to be so soon. The sectors (government, business, nonprofit, or community) that would normally be expected to remedy the problem were failing to do so. Additionally, a political, demographic, economic, or technological shift or trend provided more favorable conditions for acting on the urgency of the problem.

In the case of the African American Men Project, outcomes for African American men aged 18–30 in Hennepin County were terrible when compared to those for white men in same age range. In the mid-1990s, many African American men were doing quite well, but their educational achievement and employment rates were well below those of their white counterparts, and their incarceration rates were significantly higher. One cause, and a significant initial condition, was a history of racism and failed interventions in the United States as a whole. "Blame the victim" was all too often an underlying assumption of government programs serving these men. Some analysts had concluded that categorical federal programs and their local implementation were counter-productive and agreed that a more holistic approach was needed. In particular, critics of government programs pointed to disincentives for these men to be active parents, though such a focus threatened to stir up old disagreements and resentments about the plight of black families.

The economy was in good shape at the time, and this highlighted the paradox of African American males' unemployment (though the trend toward full employment offered promise for putting these men to work). In effect, all sectors were failing these men: Government programs had spent lots of money with disappointing results; businesses weren't hiring them; nonprofit programs that served them were underfunded and not coordinated; and their communities were unable to muster adequate informal supports; the mass media were more likely to portray them as people with problems than as diverse citizens.

In the case of the Vital Aging Network, the aging of communities and workforces was a phenomenon in post-industrial societies generally by the 1990s. At the same time in the U.S., ageism was prevalent since the youth-oriented society tended to view aging as something to be avoided. Images of elderly people as frail and dependent evoked a policy mindset that focused on caretaking, while ignoring the likelihood that many, if not most, older adults can lead independent, productive lives well into their eighties. Social institutions were unprepared for the coming wave of older adults on the verge of retiring from full-time employment. Some government programs such as Medicare existed, but most were not well-designed to help older adults remain independent and productive. Moreover, shortages in Medicare funding were predicted in the not-so-distant future. Few businesses had set up programs to retain older workers with flexible and part-time arrangements; many failed to prepare older workers for productive retirement and to protect their pensions. The growth of the Internet was a technological development that offered promise for developing educational programs and networks for older adults.

In MetroGIS, the Metropolitan Council (the regional government) had provided needed regional planning and other services for the Minneapolis-St. Paul area since its creation in 1967. Yet, its relations with local governments were sometimes tense and conflict-ridden. One source of friction was the questionable accuracy of the data that council staff used to project regional trends and set policies affecting local development. By the mid-1990s, increasingly sophisticated geospatial information systems (GISs) offered potential remedies, but only if local governments could agree to share information and if some entity could be created to develop a regional GIS.

In UPA, by the end of the 1990s, the sheer number of government agencies involved in transportation at the federal to local levels had resulted in competing agendas and programs that were uncoordinated at best and working at cross purposes at worst. Significant tensions existed inside US-DOT and MnDOT, between MnDOT and local governments, between US-DOT's national and regional offices, and between residents, business owners, and their representatives in one corridor and those in another corridor. The conflicts between highway versus transit supporters was long-standing and played out within government agencies and the state legislature.

Government and market failures have both contributed to making urban traffic congestion—with its economic and environmental toll—a tough and urgent public problem. The market for transit is underdeveloped, and business adoption of telecommuting is still quite limited. Government decision-makers have encouraged dependence on automobiles and highway building, developed transportation programs that focus on single modes (e.g., highways or rail) rather than multimodal systems, and subsidized commercial and residential sprawl. A crucial political shift in this case provided an important window of opportunity for reformers, and that was the decision by the U.S. Secretary of Transportation in 2006 to promote congestion pricing, along with a congressional stalemate that resulted in the temporary suspension of the practice of earmarking a substantial portion of transportation funding, thus giving the secretary discretionary authority over a much larger pot of money than normal. Meanwhile, transponder technology had made it possible to eliminate cumbersome toll plazas and vary lane pricing depending on levels of congestion.

In all the cases, policy entrepreneurs took advantage of the windows of opportunity resulting from the problem's urgency and from environmental shifts or trends. In some, policy entrepreneurs helped create or expand the window.

Stakeholders and Their Connections

Stakeholders are essentially people with a "relationship" to the problem, either because it affects them directly, they have some responsibility to do something about it, or they have expertise or other resources that can help remedy the problem. Each of the sponsors and champions we have introduced was a stakeholder in the public challenge at the heart of the case in which he or she was involved and brought qualities, expertise, and authority that helped them to credibly promote a collaborative effort to tackle the challenge. Champions like Jan Hively, as a professional woman in her late 60s, and Gary Cunningham, as an African American man, actually were exemplars of the most affected stakeholders in their cases. Together, champions and sponsors had considerable, though incomplete, knowledge about the problems that concerned them, as well as a belief in the possibility of solutions. They had the wisdom to recognize the limitations of their own knowledge. Most importantly they were able to draw on a wealth of personal relationships with other stakeholders to initiate a change effort that would require enrolling even more stakeholders, researching the problem, and searching for solutions. In other words, sponsors and champions were skilled in *personal leadership*, understanding, and deploying personal assets on behalf of beneficial change.

Since policy entrepreneurs seek to develop new policy regimes, they will also need to understand the way formal and informal stakeholder relationships (or lack thereof) sustain existing problematic policy regimes. For example, in the UPA case, the federal agencies handling transit and highways were disconnected from each other, and regional offices of these agencies were the intermediaries with direct links to state, regional, and local transportation agencies. To implement a multimodal congestion reduction strategy in metro areas, policy entrepreneurs would need to build or strengthen connections between people working on transit and highways at the different levels.

Finally, our cases indicate that policy entrepreneurs are well advised to be aware that different stakeholders will have different understandings of who leaders are and how leadership is or should be practiced (see Drath, 2001; Calás & Smircich, 1997). That is, in keeping with the relationality lens, both leaders and leadership are socially constructed, and different individuals and groups will construct these concepts differently. (Drath suggests three main ways in which leadership is constructed: personal dominance, interpersonal influence, and participatory or generative relationship.) Some individual and organizational stakeholders are likely to view leaders as those with formal titles (such as director, commissioner, board chair, or project manager) that carry positional authority in hierarchies (analogous to Drath's dominance category); others may view leaders as those who use informal authority in networks to bring diverse groups of people together to seek the common good (analogous to Drath's interpersonal influence category). Viewing leaders and followers as mutually defining and engaged in the construction of communities of practice (analogous to Drath's relational category) is also possible and evident in the social change organizations studied by Ospina and her colleagues (Ospina, & Sorensen, 2006; Ospina & Foldy, 2010).

Take an example from just one of our cases, the Urban Partnership Agreement. Champions of an integrated approach to reducing traffic congestion lobbied positional leaders—especially the governor and state legislators—to participate in the Urban Partnership program. These champions, from a nonprofit citizen group and from a University of Minnesota policy program, played a delicate game as they sought to "inspire and mobilize" people who saw themselves (and were seen by many others) as the *real* responsible leaders in transportation policy. They faced criticism from some observers who felt they were "interfering" with the policy-making hierarchy. Ultimately, however, the champions succeeded in securing desired commitments from positional leaders. They used their own interpersonal influence, based in part on their organizational and network positions, but they also engaged in joint meaning construction with the positional leaders as they negotiated the meaning of what constituted "congestion pricing." An alliance of champions and sponsors appears to be one way of overcoming the tensions between hierarchical, network, and generative views of leadership.

Integrative Process

Cross-sector collaborations seem to be more likely to succeed if organizers use processes to bridge differences, build inclusive and functional structures, plan effectively, and manage power imbalances (Bryson, Crosby,

& Stone, 2006). (Managing power imbalances will be discussed later under "contingencies and constraints.") Of particular importance is the creation of "boundary experiences," "boundary objects," and "boundary groups" (Carlile, 2002, 2004; Feldman, Khademian, Ingram, & Schneider, 2006; Kellogg, Orlikowski, & Yates, 2006). These allow diverse stakeholders to articulate and bridge different understandings of a public problem and potential solutions. Boundary experiences, objects, and groups will be discussed more specifically below in connection with designing and using forums.

The four cases offer evidence that four interconnected types of leadership practices are at the heart of this work:

- Wisely designing and using forums, the settings in which shared meaning is created and communicated;
- Wisely designing and using arenas, the settings in which policy decisions are made and implemented;
- Wisely designing and using courts, the settings in which conduct is sanctioned and residual conflicts are resolved; and
- Navigating the policy change cycle.

These practices are explored in depth in *Leadership for the Common Good* (Crosby & Bryson, 2005). In this chapter, we devote most attention to the wise design and use of forums because this practice determines what is even considered a public problem, what solutions are viable, and what public programs, projects, and policies are discussed by policy makers (Crosby & Bryson, 2005).

The wise design and use of forums is at the core of *visionary leadership*, which we view as a shared process of meaning-making. Visionary leaders design forums to engage stakeholders in framing and reframing complex public problems, deciding what to do about them, and developing a shared vision for moving toward a desired future. As scholars like Burns (1978, 2003) and Gardner (1995) have suggested, the most compelling visions will speak to leaders' and followers' needs and aspirations and allow them to see themselves as part of a hopeful narrative that is also likely to include some elements of potential danger (Crosby & Bryson, 2005). In sync with relationality theorists, we see visioning as principally about meaning-making, which may involve an explicit statement of vision, but not necessarily. It does involve the creation of a shared view that allows people to say, "I see what we are trying to do." Our view of visionary leadership resonates somewhat with the four-fold view of transformational leadership identified by Bass & Avolio (1998). The four dimensions are idealized influence, inspirational motivation, individualized consideration, and intellectual stimulation. The first two dimensions are especially associated with personality-based charismatic leadership. Our emphasis, however, is on the mutual problem-solving work of leaders and followers, and not on the charismatic allure and sway of an individual. Like Heifetz and his colleagues (Heifetz, 1994; Heifetz, Grashow, & Linsky, 2009), we see attributions of charismatic leadership as one of the ways groups have of avoiding work on complex problems. Leaders (and followers) who take what might be called a post-charismatic view of leadership (Jackson & Parry, 2008; Parry & Bryman, 2006) recognize that any leader has limitations and weaknesses and that a grandiose image of that person's power and status is a social construction rather than an accurate reflection of the person's special prowess.

Probably the most helpful set of tools for designing and using forums focuses on stakeholder analysis and involvement (Bryson, 2004a, 2004b; Bryson, Cunningham, & Lokkesmoe, 2002). Identifying stakeholders and analyzing their interests, expectations, and influence is vital for putting together forums that offer boundary-crossing experiences for boundary groups—that is "collections of actors who are drawn together from different ways of knowing or bases of experience for the purpose of coproducing [cross-]boundary actions" (Feldman et al., 2006, p. 95). Examples include networks, task forces, and teams; coordinating committees; and representative policy-making bodies. Boundary objects are "physical objects that enable people to understand other perspectives" (Feldman et al., 2006, p. 95) and thus are important in helping people create shared meaning (Carlile, 2002, 2004; Star & Griesemer, 1989). Examples include stakeholder maps (Bryson, Cunningham, & Lokkesmoe, 2002), strategy maps (Bryson, Ackermann, Eden, & Finn, 2004), reports, mission statements, and GIS maps.

Attention to boundary experiences, boundary objects, and boundary groups is crucial because of the practice-based view that meaning is negotiated jointly through participation and reification (i.e., treating as concrete, material objects things that are not properly concrete, material objects). Every practice produces abstractions, tools, symbols, stories, terms, and concepts that reify something in a congealed form (Wenger, 1998, pp. 58–59). Participation and reification are both needed to make up for the shortcomings of the other. In other words, "things" are meaningless in and of themselves. Think about the last time you had to use a map to get somewhere. Without your active engagement with the map—meaning your efforts to understand it and its relation to what it is supposed to represent—the map would be useless. In parallel fashion, participation without a focus on "some thing" is pointless.

To be effective, the work of forums must be linked to work in arenas (where *political leadership* is crucial) and courts (where *ethical leadership* is crucial). The proposed policy changes developed in forums ultimately must be adopted and implemented by decision makers in executive, legislative, and administrative arenas, so visionary leaders should ensure that key stakeholders in those settings are considered and sometimes involved in the forums developing proposals for new laws and policies. Once adopted in arenas, new policies and laws must be enforced by formal and informal courts, so visionary leaders also should help their groups design enforcement mechanisms able to withstand court challenges.

Finally, policy entrepreneurs seeking to use forums, arenas, and courts to produce sustainable solutions to public problems may think of them in terms of a purposeful approach to the policy change, such as the "policy change cycle" (Crosby & Bryson, 2005). The cycle includes the following interconnected and iterative phases: initial agreement; problem formulation; search for solutions; proposal formulation; proposal review and adoption; implementation and evaluation; and continuation, modification, or termination. In general, forums are most significant in the first three phases, arenas come more strongly into play during proposal formulation and dominate during proposal review and adoption and implementation and evaluation phases; courts also are highly important in the implementation and evaluation phase.

In the four cases, policy champions organized numerous cross-boundary forums that allowed diverse stakeholders to hammer out agreements for working together, and to develop shared understanding of the problem that concerned them, as well as solutions worth pursuing. All used facilitated conversations and planning sessions; the second author of this chapter was one of the facilitators involved in the African American Men Project and MetroGIS.

In the African American Men Project, Gary Cunningham assembled a Steering Committee that included a diverse array of African American men who were business professionals, academics, and organizers of nonprofit organizations. Under the auspices of the committee, he and his associates organized multiple forums focusing on multiple aspects of African American men's lives. The forums brought together people with different kinds of expertise—including on fathering and on the psychology of being a black male. The forums focused on the men and gave them voice, rather than focusing on services or government programs. Participants spent a long time trying to understand and agree upon what the problem was. Ultimately, they engaged in reframing by declaring, "What's good for African American men is good for all Hennepin County residents." They moved away from social service and social justice frames to a civic action frame, in which everyone has partial responsibility to build a community that benefits all. They emphatically rejected the notion that African American men were the problem. The stakeholder analysis diagrams developed in some of the forums were crucial in this reframing process and provided the basis for a potent coalition across the political spectrum. Interim and final reports were boundary objects that conveyed African American men's voices across numerous boundaries and provided a new vision that could inspire diverse constituencies. The report's recommendations were specifically aimed at an important policy-setting arena—the Hennepin County Board of Commissioners.

Champions in the vital aging case convened monthly meetings focusing on topics of interest to network members and organized two Summits on Aging to attract a broader range of participants into shaping an agenda for vital aging in Minnesota. The forums helped participants reframe the conversation on aging: Older adults were consistently viewed as productive workers and citizens (aging vitally) rather than as frail dependents. A few years after its founding, network members undertook strategic planning partly to obtain a grant from Atlantic Philanthropies, a foundation focusing on vital aging. Consultants tied to VAN facilitated the process, which led to important boundary objects: the plan itself and the grant application to the foundation. The VAN website might also be considered a virtual boundary object that allowed users to encounter VAN's conceptualization of the challenges facing older adults and find educational and networking opportunities. Because VAN sought institutional support from the University of Minnesota, Hively in particular made sure that university faculty and staff were part of VAN and its forums, and she helped VAN secure approvals from the university president and other administrators to provide needed funding or staff.

In the MetroGIS case, Randall Johnson and his small staff organized multiple forums that were boundary experiences leading to a major reframing of the purpose of local government data—from a quasi-proprietary possession of each government, to a shared resource that could be vastly improved if data were pooled and organized through geospatial technology. In some ways, this visionary work was a continuation of a reframing underway in the Twin Cities since 1950s, in which area citizens and elected officials increasingly saw public problems and solutions in regional terms.

Strategic planning forums produced strategy maps and other boundary objects that captured shared understandings and commitments and laid the foundation for creation of boundary groups such as the MetroGIS Policy Board. The forums created a mandate for action by government legislative arenas, specifically the Metropolitan Council and county boards. Johnson made sure that county commissioners were involved in the forums; they also comprised the membership of the MetroGIS Policy Board.

In the UPA case, policy entrepreneurs put together multiple forums that informed local governments, legislators, and transportation-related nonprofits about the Urban Partnership process and began gathering ideas for what projects would be included in the Minnesota application for an Urban Partnership grant. The biggest conflicts were over which major transportation corridors would be included in the final proposal. Ultimately, facilitators secured consensus for emphasizing Cedar Avenue and I-35W, the two corridors linking downtown Minneapolis and southern suburbs, in part because some projects in the corridors were "shovel ready" and could be incorporated, and partly because a coalition of local governments had already come together and developed a shared agenda for transportation improvements in the 35W corridor. The idea-gathering and consensus-building processes used in the forums added to earlier starts at reframing the problem of traffic congestion and debates over possible solutions. The problem came to be viewed as less about inadequate highways and more about poor management and pricing of highway use; tolling shifted from being viewed as a cumbersome surcharge on a "free" good to a flexible mechanism that helped all traffic flow more smoothly and let some drivers pay for faster lanes. Instead of focusing on road management, UPA partners focused on corridor management. In the UPA, champions like consultant John Doan and MnDOT's Nick Thompson, who was appointed to oversee the Minnesota project after the grant was awarded, needed superb project management skills—the ability to work with multiple players, staying mindful of timing and due dates, ensuring that information flows were adequate, and resolving glitches and conflicts.

Structure and Governance

The work of cross-sector collaborations is facilitated by structures that include diverse stakeholders, provide governance for the collaboration, and help the collaboration implement its decisions. These structures have varying degrees of hierarchy and from the relationality perspective may be seen as "relational networks of changing persons moving together through space and time" (Uhl-Bien, 2006, p. 661). Putting together, maintaining, and revising these structures appropriately is an important *organizational leadership* skill. The cases indicate that two key practices for champions and sponsors are:

- Managing structural ambidexterity—that is, finding workable blends of hierarchical and participatory network structures that typically vary over time; and
- Forming and sustaining boundary groups.

Managing Structural Ambidexterity. The very nature of cross-sector collaboration requires that many stakeholders be included in governance—that is, setting policies, coordinating activities, and monitoring outcomes. The challenge for policy entrepreneurs is creating governance structures that are inclusive yet actually carry out these functions. In the cases, policy entrepreneurs designed governing structures such as steering committees, policy boards, or leadership groups to perform this function as well as make necessary interfaces with more hierarchical organizations that were existing or potential collaboration partners. They often used other types of committees and working groups in order to include people and organizations that did not directly participate in the governing group, especially when those stakeholders had needed expertise for some part of the collaboration's work.

Initially, the African American Men Project was staffed and managed in the county planning department, directed by Gary Cunningham. The steering committee oversaw the completion of initial research, the planning forums, and development of the report to the county board. After the county board adopted the report's recommendations it established a highly inclusive African American Men Commission (included in the recommendations). The commission, in turn, set up several committees to carry out further planning and implementation.

At the same time that AAMP got underway, Hennepin County was reorganizing along business lines, seeking to integrate or align program and funding streams, which was complementary to the AAMP vision. Gary Cunningham was a driver behind both initiatives. The ongoing challenge for AAMP would be managing the tension between achieving independence from county government and needing it as a funding and implementation vehicle for number of AAMP goals.

The Vital Aging Network was established as a voluntary network of individuals who had ties to organizations representing or serving older adults, though the organizations were not members. For a time, the group had no formal governance structure, but they eventually decided to elect a small Leadership Group that could represent VAN to outside organizations that needed reassurance that one person or a few people could be held accountable for the network's actions and resource use.

MetroGIS's initial strategic planning process resulted in the creation of several boundary groups: the Policy Board, the Coordinating Committee, and the Technical Advisory Group. Putting supportive county officials on the Policy Board meant that the endeavor had powerful sponsors in county boards that had ultimate decision-making authority over counties' participation in MetroGIS. Randall Johnson and other advocates made a point of not challenging local and regional and state governmental structures. Location of the network management in the Metropolitan Council offered legitimacy and dedicated staff time for the whole endeavor.

In the UPA case, policy entrepreneurs in USDOT altered traditional federal program structures in that regional offices were bypassed during proposal development stage and traditional separations between highway and transit programs, in particular, were overridden. At the state level, this meant that state highway officials and regional transit officials had to cooperate much more directly and thoroughly than ever before. In Minnesota, the Steering Committee formed to oversee the grant proposal, and post-award planning process included representatives of state and regional agencies, transit authorities, and local governments, along with academic experts, and congestion pricing advocates. However, once implementation got underway, the collaborative Steering Committee became less prominent, and hierarchical government structures had more sway over the various sub-projects that made up the larger Minnesota UPA project. MnDOT and Met Transit remained dominant transportation players throughout, but the structuring of the Steering Committee and of implementation task forces allowed many other partners to play important roles and established significant changes in ways of thinking and working on transportation problems that many participants expect to persist, at least in part.

Initiating and Sustaining Boundary Groups

In none of the cases did policy entrepreneurs attempt thorough transformation of existing structures, but they did undertake significant transformation of work, policies, and practices. In order to do this, they established alternative structures (boundary groups) to make excluded stakeholders more visible and able to affect and sometimes implement policies. These structures gave voice to people who had not had a forum that allowed them to be heard across boundaries. In the Vital Aging Network, these stakeholders were older adults; in the African American Men Project, they were African American men. (As an example of using boundary groups to include less powerful stakeholders, Gary Cunningham violated convention by persuading the county commissioners to accept everyone who applied to be a member of the African American Men Commission.) In the UPA case, groups of cities and suburbs received stronger-than-normal positions in transportation planning—that is, they gained power *vis à vis* the state transportation department and the regional office of the Federal Highway Administration. MetroGIS raised the visibility and impact of data users and of GIS experts.

As boundary groups take on specific assignments, they are expected to become productive work groups, the aim of *team leadership* (Crosby & Bryson, 2005). Leaders can foster a number of practices—such as active listening and dialogue, managing conflict, clarifying mission and roles, and fostering resilience—that sustain such groups.

Contingencies and Constraints

The contingencies and constraints that appear to have most influence on the success of cross-sector collaboration are top-down versus bottom-up collaboration, type or level of collaboration, power imbalances, and competing institutional logics (Bryson, Crosby, & Stone, 2006). Another important contingency is environmental shifts that may help or hinder the collaboration.

The cases indicate that important leadership practices include:

- Keeping transaction costs manageable while producing desirable outcomes,
- Balancing power,
- Preparing for changes in the external environment and among partners, and
- Managing competing institutional logics.

Keeping Transaction Costs Manageable. Regardless of whether a collaboration is initially top-down or bottom-up, policy entrepreneurs will confront significant transaction costs or overhead costs resulting from major investment in the inclusive processes described above. If a collaboration is initiated and possibly mandated from the top of organizational hierarchies, as in the African American Men Project, UPA, and MetroGIS cases, the sponsors will certainly need to also act as, or recruit, champions who can organize needed forums and engage in extensive efforts to get participation from those outside the hierarchies. If collaboration is initiated from people acting without organizational authority, these champions will also have to spend time developing agreements with collaborators, but they will need to devote energy and effort to recruiting sponsors, as was case with the Vital Aging Network.

Different types of collaboration require different amounts of negotiation between stakeholder interests and modes of operating (Bryson, Crosby, & Stone, 2006). All of these cases were aimed mainly at systems change rather than administration or service delivery and thus required comparatively high levels of negotiation. The work of inclusion and negotiation, and then coordinating multiple activities results in high transaction costs. Some of these can be absorbed by policy entrepreneurs who simply donate a lot of their time to a cause they believe in. In all the cases, policy entrepreneurs recruited consultants with strategic planning, facilitation, or design skills to ensure processes worked well. Policy entrepreneurs, especially sponsors, may also be able to use incentives and staff resources that they control to facilitate stakeholder participation and to coordinate the work. In the African American Men Project and MetroGIS, for example, Gary Cunningham and Randall Johnson respectively provided staff to help manage the collaboration. USDOT used two main incentives—very large grants and short timelines—to attract partners and ensure that the collaboration produced fairly quick results. Sometimes, lesser priorities will simply need to be ignored or minimized, as occurred in the UPA case, when transportation agency staff gave less attention to normal duties or when planned transit "park and ride" facilities were postponed because they weren't part of the time- and money-consuming UPA project. MetroGIS partners adopted the philosophy "build once, then share with others" to maximize the impact of technological innovation and minimize the network's need to reinvent the wheel.

Balancing Power. Policy entrepreneurs in these cases used several methods of increasing the power of stakeholders that were disadvantaged by the existing policy system. Securing the right allies was important as was helping powerful players see that their interests were tied to those of the less powerful. The inclusive processes described earlier were also helpful.

In the African American Men Project, Gary Cunningham sought the support of African Americans who had overcome the odds to win political office or rise to the top of corporations; they in turn could exert influence across racial lines because of the organizations and groups to which they belonged. Reframing the problem was also crucial: The argument that the entire community's fate was wrapped up with that of African American men offered the potential for a very broad coalition for change. Both conservative and liberal county commissioners threw their support behind the project. The project sponsored numerous public events and documentaries, which highlighted young African American men and their successes; the project also developed specific programs that provided tools these young men needed to succeed.

The Vital Aging Network held public events and offered tools and a certificate program to increase the visibility and clout of older adults. Yet, the network struggled to deal with requirements imposed by the University of Minnesota, a powerful partner. Ultimately, network members found new sponsors and spun off from the university.

In MetroGIS, the most powerful players were the Metropolitan Council and county boards. A set of guiding principles adopted early on was basically a power- balancing mechanism. The policy entrepreneurs reminded powerful players that they had more to gain by joining the endeavor than by going it alone. The MetroGIS governance structures—Policy Board, Coordinating Committee, Technical Advisory Committee, and task forces—provided ways for people to exercise their expertise and political connections. Peer pressure kept people working together.

In the UPA case, the structure of the grants competition forced a flattening of transportation agency hierarchies. Potential collaborators could see what the collaborative advantage of participating would be, and that network power was the only way to obtain it. Many participants—local governments (cities and counties), Metropolitan Council, USDOT, MnDOT—had veto power but no group of decision makers wanted to be the ones to scuttle the project, so they compromised. The I-35W Solutions coalition maximized the power of local governments in the corridor. Existing hierarchies became more dominant in the implementation phase, but many stakeholders said they were permanently altered in favor of more lateral work among stakeholder organizations. Participants have seen the benefits that a collaborative, multimodal, coordinated, and quicker approach brings.

Preparing for Changes in the External Environment and Among Partners.
The collaboration cases presented here have all experienced major shifts in leadership or in political economic conditions. In the case of AAMP, Gary Cunningham moved on from Hennepin County to become vice president of a major foundation, but the project had become part of a county health and wellness center and has continued with a committed executive director, in the midst of an economic downturn that affects African American men more adversely than most. One way that the project has survived is to focus on a few initiatives, such as assisting ex-offenders with re-entry into their communities.

Jan Hively, who was the central champion for VAN, also moved on, but the Leadership Group provided a mechanism for sustaining the network and attracting several network members to leadership responsibilities. The demographic changes that prompted VAN's formations are becoming even more pronounced and thus provide some additional impetus for its continued existence.

Seventeen years after it began, MetroGIS is only now facing the prospect of losing a sizable number of its initial sponsors and champions to retirement and other opportunities. The most recent strategic planning process is part of the preparation for this transition.

The UPA has survived a change in presidential administrations, though many still raise some questions about its Republican, market-oriented provenance. The fact that it is pouring money into tangible highway and bus improvements, however, has tended to make Minnesotans supportive across partisan lines, and if congestion does markedly improve, the use of pricing and collaborative planning will likely continue despite political shifts.

Managing Competing Institutional Logics. The logic of collaborations resides in the intangible benefits of relationship building and the tangible benefits collaborators can gain together that would not happen otherwise, but partners within the collaboration are likely to operate with competing logics. Business partners and increasingly governments and even philanthropic funders are operating with a "bottom-line, return-on-investment" mentality. They want evidence of tangible, quantifiable, often monetized results. Our cases indicate that policy entrepreneurs usually will need to produce evidence of some tangible results before these partners become too impatient. They also may introduce those partners to research that shows that complex collaborations usually take at least a couple of years to be able to engage in full implementation of proposed projects and programs. In the MetroGIS case, for example, the Metropolitan Council authorized an audit of the project several years after it began. The upshot was evidence of substantial return on investment, a finding that actually strengthened the project against critics who favored turning its functions over to businesses. Policy entrepreneurs also may highlight the creation of "social capital" by tracing new networks and surveying participants about what the network has enabled them to do differently.

The logic of networks, which emphasizes lateral cooperation and coordination, also competes with the logic of hierarchies, which emphasize top-down control and compliance. Policy entrepreneurs in our cases had to balance these two competing logics as they tried to foster the innovation and creativity that networks allow while meeting reporting requirements imposed by hierarchical partners. The UPA case is a prime example, in which USDOT waived a number of rules and regulations at the outset, but during the implementation phase, project leaders found they still had to file the usual reports with the Federal Transit Authority, for example. Meanwhile, a host of waivers from Metropolitan Council regulations were required, and Nick Thompson devoted a lot of his time during the planning phase to obtaining those.

Finally, when partners from the government, nonprofit, or community sectors dominate a network, they may question, in effect, whether business partners will have the same commitment to obtaining public value that they do. Many participants in VAN are eager to work with businesses in preparing employees for retirement, but some have been skeptical about admitting business people to the network itself. Similarly, MetroGIS government representatives have been reluctant to give businesses the same access to GIS databases that the governments have. In terms of competing organizational logics, the lesson we draw from these cases is that entrepreneurs should find ways to build on individuals' and organizations' self-interests along with each sector's characteristic strengths, while finding ways to minimize, overcome, or compensate for each sector's characteristic weaknesses.

Outcomes and Accountabilities

The outcomes of collaboration may be categorized as immediate, mid-term, and long-term (or as first-, second- and third-order effects; see Innes & Booher [1999]).

First-order effects of successful collaborations include the creation of social, intellectual, and political capital; high-quality agreements; and innovative strategies. Second-order effects, likely to occur when collaboration is well underway, might include: new partnerships, coordination and joint action, joint learning that extends beyond the collaborative, implementation of agreements, changes in practices, and changes in perceptions. Third-order effects might include new collaborations; more co-evolution and less destructive conflict between partners; adaptations of services, resources, cities, and regions; new institutions; new norms and approaches to addressing public problems; and new modes of discourse (Lawrence, Hardy, & Phillips,

2002). Together, these outcomes constitute significant public value, or regimes of mutual gain. Our research on cross-sector collaboration (Bryson, Crosby, & Stone, 2006) and analysis of the cases point to three main sets of practices through which policy entrepreneurs can help collaborations create significant public value:

- Explicitly identifying and seeking first-, second-, and third-order effects;
- Building an accountability system that tracks inputs, processes, and outcomes; uses a variety of methods for gathering, interpreting, and using data; and uses a results management system built on strong relationships with key political and professional constituencies; and
- Demonstrating resilience and engaging in regular reassessments.

Seeking First-order, Second-order, and Third-order Effects.   In the African American Men Project, first-order effects included the engagement of African American men in the project, the commitment of the county board, and systematic planning. Second-order effects were successful initiatives, like the Day of Reconciliation (in which people with minor offenses could have them expunged in return for community service). Third-order effects included the institutionalization of Days of Reconciliation within the Hennepin County court system and Gary Cunningham's convening of forums under the auspices of the Northwest Area Foundation throughout the northwestern United States to build African American leadership.

In VAN, first-order effects were a network of people interested in vital aging; second-order effects included visible events like the summits on aging, the website, the Advocacy Leadership in Vital Aging (ALVA) program; third-order effects included a multitude of initiatives (some with Jan Hively as a central figure and some instigated by other VAN and ALVA participants) focusing on older workers, retirees, and post-80 seniors—for example, a training program that helps workers nearing retirement age to plan multiple aspects of their lives in addition to the financial aspects that normally receive attention in retirement planning.

In MetroGIS, first-order effects were building a new network and settling on mission, goals, and strategic initiatives. Second-order effects included completing and furthering the initiatives and creating the DataFinder search technology and other applications. Third-order effects included developing a new, expanded mission that focuses on helping stakeholders do their work better and getting elected officials to routinely use geospatial data for decision-making.

In UPA, first-order effects were a completed and successful grant proposal and stronger relationships among metro area stakeholders. The most obvious second-order effects are new park and ride facilities, lanes and shoulders subject to dynamic pricing, continually updated signage, and faster bus commute times. Third-order effects will be changed ways of thinking about transportation planning and management.

Building an Accountability System

Policy entrepreneurs can employ various methods and levels of accountability and assessment. Peer pressure among partners helps maintain responsibility for contributing to outcomes, but since each partner is often accountable to the partner's own organizations or constituencies, policy entrepreneurs have an incentive to collect and organize evidence in ways that appeal to diverse constituencies. Thus, the entrepreneurs can have multiple ways of showing support for the value proposition that infuses the collaboration: That is, the results of our work are deeply and broadly beneficial for the cost, and the results won't happen without the collaboration.

USDOT built in very systematic evaluation into the Urban Partnership program and has contracted with Battelle Corporation to collect information independent of that provided directly by the recipients of UPA grants. MetroGIS has had very open participative process of developing and assessing projects; the awards it has received constitute external assessments. Its value was also revealed by an internal Metropolitan Council audit (prompted by an oppositional council member). The African American Men Project has demonstrated its value in part through tracking tax dollars saved by its initiatives. VAN used a grant from Atlantic Philanthropies to engage in a systematic assessment of its ALVA program.

Policy entrepreneurship may be seen as identifying in a general way at the outset of a policy change effort the desired first-, second-, and third-order effects and pursuing and refining them through the various phases of the policy change cycle while matching appropriate leadership capabilities and practices to the phases. Our research indicates that, at least by the proposal formulation phase, policy entrepreneurs should help their constituents develop an accountability system to track outcomes and facilitate needed revisions of new policies, projects, and programs during implementation.

Demonstrating Resilience and Reassessing

In part because of their complexity, efforts to build sustainable collaborations across sectoral, cultural, and geographic divides are likely to produce undesired outcomes, otherwise known as setbacks and failures. Ultimately, successful collaborations often take a long time, and when their history is written, it is replete with difficulties and defeats. When champions and sponsors help themselves and their constituents learn from failure, take the long view, and bounce back from defeat, they are exercising *personal leadership* to foster the resilience that itself is a desired (and usually necessary) outcome of collaboration. In the final phase of the policy change cycle (continuation, modification, or termination), champions and sponsors who want to ensure that a new policy regime actually is remedying the problems or needs for which it was designed are likely to need *visionary leadership* skills once again as they help constituents look anew at the policy regime and raise fundamental questions about its meaning, purpose, and effectiveness. This reassessment helps the collaborating partners decide whether the regime should be continued with minor tweaks, significantly modified, or terminated.

The MetroGIS case provides an especially strong example of champions and sponsors fostering resilience and reassessment. Randall Johnson (and other champions) along with county commissioners who were on the Policy Board remained focused on achieving the wins that were possible over many years and refused to let unresolved issues and disputes unravel the enterprise. In 2007, having reached the continuation, modification, or termination phase of the policy change cycle, they organized a Strategic Directions Workshop for an array of the system's stakeholders to assess its future. The outcome was planning for significant modification of the system, including an expanded mission statement and new goals and strategies.

CONCLUSION

This chapter has presented an integrative leadership framework focusing on how policy entrepreneurs can build cross-sector collaborations to tackle complex public problems and achieve the common good or public value. The framework integrates numerous theoretical strands and ties together key elements of cross-sector collaboration, types of leadership practices, and leadership capabilities.

The framework has been illustrated with examples from four quite different cases of public problem solving efforts. We have introduced a few of the policy entrepreneurs who have played important leadership roles in initiating and sustaining these collaborations and the relationships that constitute them. Only novels could do justice to the full cast of characters in each case—all the key sponsors, champions, and supporters, some of whom switched roles as projects proceeded.

The framework is infused with a hybrid relational understanding of leadership that blends attention to the qualities, characteristics, attributes, skills and interpersonal relations of particular policy entrepreneurs, on the one hand, with consideration of leadership and public problem solving as a highly dynamic, socially constructed, contextually based activity, on the other. We propose the framework as a possible template for policy entrepreneurs who seek to develop and enact leadership capabilities that foster sustainable, cross-sector collaborations that achieve broadly beneficial policy change.

REFERENCES

Balkundi, P., & Kilduff, M. (2005). The ties that lead: A social network approach to leadership. *The Leadership Quarterly, 16*(6), 941–961.

Bass, B. M., & Avolio, B. J. (1998). *Manual for the multifactor leadership questionnaire.* Redwood, CA: Mindgarden.

Baumgartner, F. R., & Jones, B. D. (1993). *Agendas and instability in American politics.* Chicago, IL: University of Chicago Press.

Bingham, L. B., & O'Leary, R. (2008). *Big ideas in collaborative public management.* Armonk, NY: M.E. Sharpe.

Bryson, J. M. (2004a). *Strategic planning for public and nonprofit organizations: A guide to strengthening and sustaining organizational achievement* (3rd ed.). San Francisco, CA: Jossey-Bass.

Bryson, J. M. (2004b). What to do when stakeholders matter: Stakeholder identification and analysis techniques. *Public Management Review, 6*(1), 21–53.

Bryson, J. M. (2010). The future of strategic planning. *Public Administration Review,*

Bryson, J. M., Ackermann, F., Eden, C., & Finn, C. (2004). *Visible thinking: Unlocking causal mapping for practical business results.* New York, NY: Wiley.

Bryson, J. M., & Crosby, B. C. (1992). *Leadership for the common good: Tackling public problems in a shared power world.* San Francisco, CA: Jossey-Bass.

Bryson, J. M., & Crosby, B. C. (2008). Failing into cross-sector collaboration successfully. In L. B. Bingham, & R. O'Leary (Eds.), *Big ideas in collaborative public management.* Armonk, NY: M.E. Sharpe.

Bryson, J. M., Crosby, B. C., & Bryson, J. K. (2009). Understanding strategic planning and the formulation and implementation of strategic plans as a way of knowing: The contributions of actor-network theory. *International Public Management Journal, 12*(2), 172–207.

Bryson, J. M., Crosby, B. C., & Stone, M. M. (2006). The design and implementation of cross-sector collaborations: Propositions from the literature. *Public Administration Review, 66*(1), 44–55.

Bryson, J. M., Cunningham, G. L., & Lokkesmoe, K. J. (2002). What to do when stakeholders matter: The case of problem formulation for the African American Men Project of Hennepin County, Minnesota. *Public Administration Review, 62*(5), 568–584.

Burns, J. M. (1978). *Leadership.* New York, NY: Harper Collins.

Burns, J. M. (2003). *Transforming leadership: The pursuit of happiness.* New York, NY: Atlantic Monthly Press.

Calás, M., & Smircich, L. (1997). Voicing seduction to silence leadership In K. Grint (Ed.), *Leadership: Classical, contemporary and critical approaches* (pp. 338–376). Oxford, England: Oxford University Press.

Carlile, P. R. (2002). A pragmatic view of knowledge and boundaries: Boundary objects in new product development. *Organization Science, 13*(4), 442–455.

Carlile, P. R. (2004). Transferring, translating, and transforming: An integrative framework for managing knowledge across boundaries. *Organization Science, 15*(5), 555–568.

Crosby, B. C. (1999). *Leadership for global citizenship: Building transnational community.* Thousand Oaks, CA: SAGE.

Crosby, B. C., & Bryson, J. M. (2005). *Leadership for the common good: Tackling public problems in a shared-power world.* San Francisco, CA: Jossey-Bass.

Crosby, B. C., & Bryson, J. M. (2010). Integrative leadership and the creation and maintenance of cross-sector collaborations. *The Leadership Quarterly, 21*(2), 211–230.

Drath, W. H. (2001). *The deep blue sea: Rethinking the source of leadership.* San Francisco, CA: Jossey-Bass.

Eden, C., & Ackermann, F. (2001). Mapping distinctive competencies: A systematic approach. *Journal of the Operational Research Society, 51,* 12–20.

Emirbayer, M. (1997). Manifesto for a relational sociology. *American Journal of Sociology, 103*(2), 281–317.

Feldman, M. S., Khademian, A. M., Ingram, H., & Schneider, A. S. (2006). Ways of knowing and inclusive management practices. *Public Administration Review, 66,* 89–99.

Freeman, R. E. (1984). *Strategic management: A stakeholder approach.* Boston, MA: Pitman.

Gardner, H. (1995). *Leading minds.* New York, NY: Basic Books.

Giddens, A. (1979/1984). *Central problems in social theory: Action, structure and contradiction in social analysis.* Berkeley, CA: University of California Press.

Heifetz, R. A., Grashow, A., & Linsky, M. (2009). *The practice of adaptive leadership.* Boston, MA: Cambridge Leadership Associates.

Heifetz, R. A. (1994). *Leadership without easy answers.* Boston, MA: Belknap.

Huxham, C., & Vangen, S. (2005). *Managing to collaborate: The theory and practice of collaborative advantage.* New York, NY: Routledge.

Innes, J. E., & Booher, D. E. (1999). Consensus building and complex adaptive systems: A framework for evaluating collaborative planning. *Journal of the American Planning Association, 65*(4), 412–423.

Jackson, B., & Parry, K. (2008). *A very short, fairly interesting and reasonably cheap book about studying leadership.* London, England: SAGE.

Kellogg, K. C., Orlikowski, W. J., & Yates, J. (2006). Life in the trading zone: Structuring coordination across boundaries in postbureaucratic organizations. *Organization Science, 17*(1), 22–44.

Kingdon, J. W. (1995). *Agendas, alternatives, and public policies* (2nd ed.). New York, NY: Harper Collins.

Latour, B. (2005). *Reassembling the social.* New York, NY: Oxford University Press.

Lawrence, T. B., Hardy, C., & Phillips, N. (2002). Institutional effects of interorganizational collaboration: The emergence of proto-institutions. *Academy of Management Journal, 45*(1), 281–290.

Ospina, S., & Foldy, E. (2010). Building bridges from the margins: The work of leadership in social change organizations. *The Leadership Quarterly. 21*(2): 292–307.

Ospina, S., & Sorenson, G. (2006). A constructionist lens on leadership: Charting new territory. In G. Goethals, & G. Sorenson (Eds.), *In quest of a general theory of leadership* (pp. 188–204). Cheltenham, England: Edward Elgar.

Parry, K. W., & Bryman, A. (2006). Leadership in organizations. In S. Clegg, C. Hardy, & W. Nord (Eds.), *Handbook of organization studies* (2nd ed., pp. 447–468). London, England: SAGE.

Reckwitz, A. (2002). The status of the "material" in theories of culture: From "social structure" to "artefacts." *Journal for the Theory of Social Behaviour, 32*(2), 195–217.

Rost, J. C. (1991). *Leadership for the twenty-first century.* New York, NY: Praeger.

Sabatier, P. A., & Jenkins-Smith, H. C. (1993). *Policy change and learning: An advocacy coalition approach.* Boulder, CO: Westview.

Scott, W. R. (1987). *Organizations: Rational, natural and open systems* (2nd ed.). Englewood Cliffs, NJ: Prentice-Hall.

Selznick, P. (1957). *Leadership in administration: A sociological interpretation.* Berkeley, CA: University of California Press.

Selznick, P. (1996). Institutionalism "old" and "new." *Administrative Science Quarterly, 41*(2), 270–277.

Smircich, L., & Morgan, G. (1982). Leadership: The management of meaning. *The Journal of Applied Behaviorial Science, 18*(3),

Star, S. L., & Griesemer, J. R. (1989). Institutional ecology, 'translations' and boundary objects: Amateurs and professionals in Berkeley's museum of vertebrate zoology, 1907–39. *Social Studies of Science, 19*(3), 387–420.

Terry, R. W. (2001). *Seven zones for leadership: Acting authentically in stability and chaos.* Palo Alto, CA: Davies-Black Publishing.

Uhl-Bien, M. (2006). Relational leadership theory: Exploring the social processes of leadership and organizing. *The Leadership Quarterly, 17*(6), 654–676.

Van de Ven, A. H. (2007). *Engaged scholarship: A guide for organizational and social research.* New York, NY: Oxford University Press.

Weick, K. E. (1995). *Sensemaking in organizations.* Thousand Oaks, CA: SAGE.

Wenger, E. (1998). *Communities of practice: Learning, meaning, and identity.* Cambridge, England: Cambridge University Press.

Yin, R. K. (2009). *Case study research: Design and methods.* Thousand Oaks, CA: SAGE.

CHAPTER 11

EXTENDING RELATIONAL LEADERSHIP THEORY

The Role of Affective Processes in Shaping Leader–Follower Relationships

Neal M. Ashkanasy, Neil Paulsen, and Eugene Y. J. Tee

Leadership, defined by Yukl (2006) as a social interaction process in which an individual (the leader) attempts to influence the behaviors of another (the follower), continues to be an area of intense research in organizational behavior. Moreover, research on organizational leadership tends to revolve around individual-level elements, as evidenced by the distinct foci placed on leader traits, behaviors, contingencies, and situational factors. Chemers (2000), however, notes that focusing on these aspects of leadership often produces overly-simplified and unrealistic theories of leadership effectiveness. In Chemers' words, "leadership theory and empirical research have been regarded as a fractured and confusing set of contradictory findings and assertions without coherence of interpretability" (p. 27). Yukl agrees with this, arguing that extant leadership theory disregards the social nature of the leadership process and how interactions between leaders and followers shape leadership effectiveness.

Advancing Relational Leadership Research, pages 335–359
Copyright © 2012 by Information Age Publishing
All rights of reproduction in any form reserved.

Among the early attempts to address these limitations, leader–member exchange (LMX) stands out. LMX theorists, such as Graen and Uhl-Bien (1995), argue in particular that leadership effectiveness depends on the *quality of the relationship* between leaders and followers. In contrast to earlier leadership theories, LMX theory constituted an advance insofar as it conceptualized dyadic leader–follower relationships as the key unit of analysis and antecedent of leadership effectiveness. Thus, leadership outcomes are seen not to be solely reliant on leader-related elements, but also depend on the interplay of leader and follower cognitions, behaviors, and affect. As can be seen in the more recent literature on this topic (e.g., see Chen et al., 2007; Tangirala, Green, & Ramanujam, 2007; Tse, Dasborough, & Ashkanasy, 2008), LMX theory continues to be an important framework for understanding leader–follower interactions and processes and, subsequently, its implications for leadership effectiveness.

The more recent developments in relational leadership theory extend further in this direction by detailing the leader–member exchange dynamics of reciprocity and perceptions, and by clarifying the distinctions between constructs relevant in leader–member exchanges (e.g., see Brower, Schoorman, & Tan, 2000). For example, Uhl-Bien (2006) recently pointed out that relational leadership theory has potential to serve as a robust framework from which to understand the deeper relational dynamics of leadership. Uhl-Bien, however, also concluded that we still know little about how relationships form and develop in the workplace. Likewise, Bradbury and Lichtenstein (2000) argue that organizational processes and dynamics should not be conceptualized as independent of each other. Rather, these authors suggest that organizational phenomena are essentially created via intrapersonal and interpersonal exchanges.

In this chapter, therefore, we seek to advance the research frontiers for relational leadership theory from both a conceptual and methodological point of view. Central to our position is that our understanding of relational leadership processes can be further developed by recognizing the importance and implications of affective processes and how these processes shape effective leader–follower relationships. We argue that studies of relational leadership to date have largely overlooked the affective dynamics that exist among team members and leaders, particularly how affect influences relationship quality among team members and, in particular, between team members and their leaders. To this effect, we focus especially upon the social phenomenon of emotional contagion, which involves the tacit expression and mimicry of affective states, and underscores the influence of emotional contagion processes in relational leadership theory (Hatfield, Cacioppo, & Rapson, 1994). In the following section, therefore, we briefly review current issues in relational leadership research, incorporating a discussion on the influence of affect in relational leadership dynamics.

EMOTIONS AT MULTIPLE LEVELS
AND FOLLOWERS' EMOTIONS

Prior to our discussion on the role of emotional contagion in relational leadership theory, we first argue for the relevance of emotions in relational leadership research. We focus on how emotions at various levels, and followers' emotions in particular, influence relational leadership.

Multi-level modeling implies a statistical analysis technique that allows researchers to account properly for the means by which elements at different levels of analysis interact to influence outcomes. In the context of relational leadership research, multi-level modeling allows for researchers to consider how varying levels of behavioral processes (i.e., differentiation of leader's treatment of different team members) may impact overall leader–follower relationship quality. In this respect, calls for multi-level research on leadership by Yammarino and Dansereau (2008) have been heeded and are evidenced in recent studies of relational leadership processes that account for multiple levels of analyses (e.g., see Ashkanasy, 2003; Chen et al., 2007; Tangirala et al., 2007; Tse et al., 2008). Yet, these researchers also acknowledge that, while multi-level research accounts for leaders' differentiation between high and low LMX team members, little attention to date has been paid to understanding of how this differentiation is manifested in the affective reactions that leaders portray towards group members. Thus, we agree that researchers should continue employing multi-level research methods and analysis, but we recommend, in line with Ashkanasy (2003), that future research must also consider the different affective processes and states that inherently exist in leader–follower relationships. To this effect, new and interesting questions can be asked, for example: What are the affective outcomes for relational processes in a group where some followers share a positive, high-quality affective relationship with their leader and others do not? What broader, macro-level factors influence the quality of relational leadership processes at the micro-levels of analysis?

A second, possibly more important area for further conceptual advancement in relational leadership theory revolves around the roles of followers. As Weierter (1997) observed, researchers have largely focused on leader-centric elements as the key antecedents to effective leadership processes, but little attention has been given to the roles of followers in influencing leadership outcomes. LMX research is essentially leader-focused, with an emphasis on the means by which leaders form relationships with, and subsequently manage, followers depending on their LMX quality. By focusing exclusively on the leader's role, however, scholars have neglected the influence that followers might have on the emergence and creation of truly effective leaders. This view is consistent with Lord and Hall (1992), Hollander (1992), and Lord, Brown, and Freiberg (1999), who suggest that the social nature of leadership will be better appreciated if the roles and qualities of followers are considered in greater detail.

One reason the role of leaders takes precedence over followers may derive from the emphasis and interest among practitioners, whose primary focus is on how to develop more effective leaders from a top-down perspective. We argue, however, that this is inherently an overly narrow focus, and that the social and, hence, relational nature of leadership processes can be appreciated only if the role of followers is considered in greater detail. We do not discount the value of the leader-focused approach to the study of relational leadership, but instead encourage researchers and practitioners to give greater consideration to how followers may influence the leader–follower relationship, and subsequently, leadership outcomes. In effect, we encourage a more follower-centric approach in both relational and general leadership theory in order to balance out the current over-dominant emphasis on leader-centric elements (Hollander, 1992; Meindl, 1995; Shamir et al., 2007).

So the question then arises: What can followers do to influence leadership effectiveness? One such mechanism of influence may be the attributions that followers make towards their leaders. As Dasborough and Ashkanasy (2002) have shown, followers' attributions of their leaders may influence their perceptions, and subsequently, their behaviors towards their leaders (see also Dasborough & Ashkanasy, 2005). We propose, however, that followers' ability to influence leaders may not necessarily stem from cognitive, but perhaps also from affect-based, processes. We suggest that followers' emotions need to be considered in greater detail in the study of relational leadership. In short, we argue that followers' expressions of emotions towards other team members, and towards leaders themselves, will have implications for relational leadership processes. Hence, while the focus of relational leadership theory is on social exchanges between the leader and the follower, we advocate here a focus specifically on the roles of followers, and how their emotions shape the quality of the leader–follower relationship.

In summary, our position is that the largely leader-centric perspective on leadership that has tended to dominate the leadership landscape to date has resulted in a lack of understanding about how followers' perceptions and behaviors impact the leader–follower relationship. Clearly, therefore, there is a need for researchers to give greater consideration to how followers' affect might shape relational leadership processes.

EMOTION AND AFFECT IN RELATIONAL
LEADERSHIP THEORY

The role of emotions and affect in organizational behavior research has traditionally been understated by the assumption that logic and rationality underlie human behavior (Albrow, 1992; George, 2000). Beginning with Ashforth and Humphrey (1993), however, scholars have taken an increasing interest in affect in organizations (see also Ashkanasy & Ashton-James, 2005; Ashkanasy & Humphrey, 2011; Ashkanasy & Tse, 2000; Humphrey, 2002). To date, research on emotions within the organizational behavior domain is notable in studies of group-level affective climate (Bartel & Saavedra, 2000; Totterdell, 2000), emotional labor and regulation processes (Brotheridge & Grandey, 2002; Grandey, Dickter, & Sin, 2004; Totterdell & Holman, 2003), and emotional intelligence (Wolff, Pescosolido, & Druskat, 2002; Wong & Law, 2002).

Within the organizational leadership domain, research incorporating affective processes is evident in studies of charismatic leadership (Ashkanasy & Tse, 2000; Bass, 1985; Bono & Ilies, 2006; Conger & Kanungo, 1998; Erez et al., 2008), particularly affective processes involving the transfer of affect between leaders and followers (e.g., see Sy, Côté, & Saavedra, 2005). The role of affect in workplace exchange relationships is also garnering attention. For example, Tse and colleagues (2008), in a study of workplace friendship and affective processes in teams, found that team affective climate moderated the quality of team members' workplace relationships. Glasø and Einarsen (2006) also concluded from their study that leader–member relationships are inherently emotion-laden, impacting both parties' judgments and perceptions in the workplace.

The role of affect in leader–member exchange relationships, however, is only just beginning to receive attention. Indeed, this has been a somewhat surprising omission from scholarly research on relational leadership, given that effective leaders lead not just by appealing to their followers' cognition, but also to their emotions in order to achieve desired organizational outcomes (Ashkanasy, Härtel, & Daus, 2002).

Researchers' attention to affect in relational leadership is, however, starting to grow. For example, Brower and colleagues (2000) suggested that affective influence processes impact the cognitive processes inherent in leader–follower relationships; including followers' perceptions of their leader's trustworthiness and the formation and maintenance of trust with their leaders. Ballinger, Schoorman, and Lehman (2009) recently tested this idea. These authors examined the impact of affect on the formation of followers' trust towards new leaders, and concluded that affective states heavily influence followers' motivation to trust their leaders, as well as their judgments of their leaders. Clearly then, relational leadership theory and research can be further extended by giving greater consideration to how affective processes influence leader–follower relationships.

Nonetheless, while scholars have a developed good understanding of the cognitive processes involved in leaders' perceptions of in-groups and out-groups, less is known about the role of affective processes that influence the creation of these two distinct groups of followers. Research might also examine how leaders may tacitly make use of affective processes to facilitate and/or to maintain the distinction between high and low LMX team members. In this respect, Glasø and Einarsen (2006) suggest that leaders may maintain an emotional distance from specific subordinates in an attempt to prevent development of privileged relationships with certain followers. Hence, it seems probable that leaders will react and portray different types and levels of affect towards different followers, depending on the quality of their relationships with their team members. The affective exchanges between the leaders and their followers will therefore likely differ depending on LMX quality. For example, positive affective exchanges are more likely to exist in high-quality leader–follower relationships, characterized by social attraction, affiliation, and liking for the leader. Conversely, negative affective exchanges would be likely to exist in low-quality leader–follower relationships, resulting in feelings of alienation, disaffection, and perhaps even result in followers' resistance of the leader's influence attempts.

Following on the discussion of the role of followers in relational leadership theory, recent studies have also suggested the importance of considering how followers' affect influences the quality of relational leadership processes. As Dasborough et al., (2009) argue, followers' experience and expressions of negative affect are likely to impact followers' attitudes towards leaders. In line with this idea, Tee and Ashkanasy (2007; 2008) conducted laboratory studies to test the hypothesis that followers' expressed affect would influence leaders' affect and behavior; they found that followers' expressions of affect, and the resulting emotional contagion processes, impacted leaders' affect and cognitive performance. These theoretical and empirical results have implications for future research on relational leadership processes, suggesting that followers and their expressed affect appear to be notable influences in shaping the quality of leader–follower relationships. Moreover, and consistent with the aim of relational leadership theory to conceptualize leadership processes more holistically, these studies provide evidence that effective, high-quality, leader–follower relationship outcomes go beyond leader-centric, cognitive-based processes.

In summary, while extant relational leadership theory has tended to emphasize the cognitive processes involved in the creation of in- and outgroup followers, less attention has been given to the affective processes inherent in both the creation and division of LMX quality. With growing interest in how affective processes influence organizational behavior, the study of relational leadership can also benefit from a greater understanding of how affect moderates the quality of leader–follower relationships. A more in-depth appreciation of these affective processes will allow researchers not only to understand better how LMX quality is created, but also to understand how this quality is maintained. Practically, this also suggests that the challenges in effectively managing low-quality LMX members lie not only in changing followers' cognitions, but also in appealing to their emotions. In line with this idea, we encourage researchers to consider the role of affective processes in addition to the cognitive processes that exist in relational leadership processes.

Following on from our arguments in the preceding sections, we discuss the implications of affective exchanges, driven by emotional contagion processes, on relational leadership dynamics. We refer, in particular, to recent work by Hareli and Rafaeli (2008) and Dasborough et al. (2009), and suggest a multi-level conceptualization of relational leadership processes that incorporates the influence of followers and affective processes as key determinants of leader–follower relationship quality. As Dasborough and her colleagues suggest, followers' experience and expressions of negative affect can consequently impact followers' attitudes towards leaders. Drawing on attribution theory, these authors theorized that negative perceptions of followers form the basis for their experience and expressions of negative emotions towards other organizational members, including both team members and leaders. These negative emotions may then become manifest in negative behavioral outcomes, permeating multiple levels within the organization, and impacting individual, group, and organizational-level affect (see also Mumford, Dansereau, & Yammarino, 2000).

Dasborough and her associates (2009) argue in particular that emotional contagion processes play a central role. In the following section therefore, we elaborate on this emerging area of research and discuss how emotional contagion might ultimately impact leader–follower interactions and relationship quality across multiple levels of organization. We build on our discussion of how emotional contagion among followers (lateral contagion), and between followers and leaders (upward and downward contagion) ultimately impact relational leadership outcomes across multiple levels of analysis.

EMOTIONAL CONTAGION IN RELATIONAL LEADERSHIP

Hatfield et al. (1994) define *emotional contagion* as "the tendency to automatically mimic and synchronize facial expressions, vocalizations, postures and movements with those of another person, and consequently, to converge emotionally" (p. 5). Emotional contagion is thus conceptualized as a subconscious and tacit process by which affective states are transferred and/or shared among individuals. According to emotional contagion theory, an individual's affective state is linked to her or his own verbal and nonverbal expressions of emotions, so that a change in either will automatically trigger a congruent response in the other. The contagion effect therefore occurs when a second individual or party "catches" the portrayed affective state of the conveyor and, subsequently, converges on the affective state of the conveyor.

Hareli and Rafaeli (2008) argue further that emotional contagion processes result in "emotion cycles" (p. 35) that can permeate and transcend formal hierarchical boundaries, impacting the experience of emotions at the various levels of an organization. In the following discussion, therefore, we treat emotional contagion as it occurs among team members (lateral contagion), from leaders to followers (downward contagion) and from followers to leaders (upward contagion), and argue how each of these three types of emotional contagion processes might impact the leader–follower relationship.

Lateral Emotional Contagion

Emotional contagion processes have been examined within the context of both formal and informal groups. Totterdell et al. (1998) posit that emotional contagion may explain how an individual's mood becomes linked with that of a group. Results from these authors' study indicate that individuals tend to mimic fellow group members' affective displays automatically and subconsciously, and consequently to converge on the overall group-level affect. In a subsequent study, Totterdell (2000) found that the collective mood of a group was related to the mood of individuals in the group, and that the emotional contagion effect impacts individual-level perceptions of group achievement. In support of this idea, Bartel and Saavedra (2000), in an observational study, reported that work group members do indeed tend to converge on a collective group-level mood, and that each group's dispositional mood is constructed by team members' observable facial, vocal, and postural cues via emotional contagion. More recently, in a series of quasi-experimental studies, Anderson, Keltner, and John (2003) reported that participants in close relationships converged emotionally over time, and that the resulting intertwining of affective states was partially attributable to emotional contagion.

The studies above share a common finding, in that emotional contagion occurs at the group-level, and can affect individual-level moods and emotions. Totterdell (2000), however, asked if individuals themselves may influence group-level affect. Similarly, Kelly and Barsade (2001) theorized that individual team members bring their own moods, emotions, and sentiments to groups; so, it is plausible that group-level affect may be built from these multiple individual-level team members' feelings. Barsade (2002) has since conducted an experimental study to test this hypothesis, examining emotional contagion processes occurring from the individual- to the group-level, and found that individual-level affective displays influenced group-level affect via emotional contagion. Barsade's results also illustrated the implications of emotional contagion on group dynamics. Positive-mood contagion, relative to negative-mood contagion, led the groups in her study to experience better levels of cooperation, lower levels of conflict, and more favorable perceptions of the group's task performance. Taken together, this research tells us that group-level affect can influence and, in turn, be influenced by, individual-level affect so that, in effect, emotional contagion operates reciprocally.

In view of the foregoing findings, we believe it is plausible to argue that emotional contagion among team members, and the resulting lateral contagion effect, is likely also to have implications for relational leadership processes. Since groups consist of multiple individuals with varying ranges of felt emotions, we argue that it follows that emotional contagion processes that occur among team members are likely to be shaped by the emotions at both the individual- and group-level, and further that this will present important considerations for the leadership of these groups. Researchers examining collective action in the social identity literature (e.g., Butz & Plant, 2006; Cottrell & Neuberg, 2005) suggest in particular that in-group members may experience and portray negative emotions towards out-group members, and that this may also encourage in-group members to take action against out-group members in order to preserve their group identities. Studies of collective action towards out-groups also show that anger and hostility are the emotions most associated with intentions to take action towards out-group members. More generally, these studies concur with Smith and Crandell's (1984) suggestions that group-level emotions serve to provide emotional support, thereby reducing subjective uncertainty caused by situational stressors.

It may therefore be plausible that out-group members' perceptions of the leaders' treatment of in-group (high LMX) members may also serve to incite negative emotions among out-group (low LMX) members. In line with recent discussions on how followers' attributions translate into expressions of affect (Dasborough et al., 2009), out-group members may thus display negative emotions towards in-group members in order to balance out what they perceive to be unwarranted treatments of favoritism rendered by leaders towards in-group members. The implications of followers experiencing these feelings may then translate into behavioral reactions that go beyond the group context.

In this respect, Mumford and colleagues (2000) found that followers' evaluations and assessments of their status in comparison with their peers may also motivate their intentions to perform in groups and thence to comply with or to resist their leader's influence. The consequences of followers' perceptions of being an out-group member also have implications that resonate beyond that of their own personal satisfaction and or well-being. Similarly, Stamper and Masterson (2002) found that subordinates who perceived themselves as being out-group members were more likely to engage in acts of deviant behaviors.

Such expressions of negative emotions towards in-group members may be one way in which out-group members cope with their status as out-group members: serving firstly to reduce feelings of uncertainty, ostracism, and unpleasantness associated with poor quality relationships between themselves and their leaders; and secondly to express negative feelings tacitly towards in-group members on the basis that they are receiving unjustified special treatments by leaders. The lateral contagion effect that results from these expressed negative emotions may subsequently impact the affective climate and performance of the group (see also Barsade, 2002; Totterdell, 2000). These, in turn, are likely to present challenges to the leaders of these groups, especially as to how they might manage the different perceptions and felt emotions that exist within any one team.

Downward Emotional Contagion

Researchers have recently shown interest in how emotional contagion impacts upon leadership specifically. For example, Sy and his colleagues (2005) examined emotional contagion from leaders to followers in an experimental study and found that contagion influenced followers' collective mood and performance. Leaders in a positive mood expressed a positive mood that was subsequently caught on by followers, resulting in followers experiencing positive mood and exhibiting elevated group coordination. When the leader was in a negative mood, on the other hand, the followers caught on to the leader's expressed negative mood and were less coordinated than teams that were led by a positive-mood leader.

Bono and Ilies (2006) and Erez and colleagues (2008) subsequently extended on Sy and colleagues' (2005) study, and found evidence that charismatic leaders' displays of positive affect are linked with followers' own experience of positive mood. They also reported that charismatic leaders' displays of positive mood were associated with followers' perceptions of effectiveness and attractiveness towards the leader. These findings are congruent with results of survey research by Johnson (2008), who studied emotional contagion processes in educational leadership. Johnson found that emotional contagion explained the relationship between leaders' and followers' experienced affect and that positive affect contagion caused followers to perceive their leaders as being more charismatic and also to engage in more organizational citizenship behaviors.

In sum, these studies suggest interesting implications for relational leadership theory. Beyond impacting followers' experience of affect and task performance, downward contagion may have long-term implications for followers' perceptions of a leader's fairness, and the extent of followers' trust towards their leader. Ballinger et al. (2009), for example, found that followers' felt affect played a significant role in determining how group members formed perceptions of their judgments and trust towards newly-appointed leaders. In these authors' field study of veterinary hospital employees, followers' affect was found to influence the degree of trust towards newly-appointed leaders. Ballinger and associates in effect demonstrated that the formation of high-quality leader–follower relationships, particularly during the initial formation stages, may be strongly dependent on how these new leaders make their followers feel. Hence, beyond proving their technical competence, leaders need to be aware that they need to appeal to their followers' emotions in order to facilitate the creation of long-term, high-quality, leader–follower relationships. Positive downward contagion, in this regard, may help leaders create a warm relationship with their newly-acquainted followers and assist in the formation of trust in the leader, at least within the initial stages of the relationship.

The relevance of downward contagion, however, may differ in more established leader–follower relationships. As initially discussed, leaders' expressions of emotions towards their followers may be one way leaders create and maintain distinctions between in-group (high-quality LMX) and out-group (low-quality LMX) members (Glasø & Einarsen, 2006). Building on this point, we suggest further that leaders' expressions of emotion towards their followers will also shape followers' perceptions of leader fairness and attraction towards their leaders. Out-group members, who are share a more distant relationship with the leaders, are more likely to have their leaders express negative affect towards them, in contrast with in-group members. Consequently, such expressions of leader negative affect may impact followers' perceptions of how fairly they treat their followers, their attraction towards their leaders, and the overall leader–follower relationship.

Upward Emotional Contagion

Existing research on emotional contagion processes in leadership is often framed under the assumption that emotional contagion in leadership settings occurs exclusively from leaders to followers. As Sy and colleagues (2005) note, positional power infers a leader with additional control and hence more opportunities to express and to transmit affect to followers. The possibility of followers (or individuals with comparatively less power) influencing leaders, however, should not be overlooked. Consistent with our suggestions that emotions can permeate formal organizational boundaries, we suggest that followers themselves can influence leaders and the leader–follower relationship via emotional contagion processes. In this respect, an experimental study by Hsee et al. (1990) provided initial evidence for the possibility that followers influence their leaders through emotional contagion processes. Hsee and colleagues hypothesized that emotional contagion was more likely to occur from powerful to powerless (or less powerful) individuals but found, contrary to their predictions, that individuals with greater, rather than lesser, power were more susceptible to emotional contagion. These findings suggest an interesting consideration for further follower-centric studies on leadership and the role of affect in leader–follower relationships.

More recently, Tee and Ashkanasy (2007; 2008), conducted laboratory studies to test the hypothesis that followers' expressed affect can influence leaders. They found that followers' expressions of affect, and the resulting emotional contagion processes, did indeed impact leaders' own affect and cognitive performance. Results from these studies have implications for future research on relational leadership processes. Consistent with arguments that relational leadership theory should be viewed from a more holistic perspective, upward contagion processes may be one way in which followers impact the leader–follower relationship. We thus suggest that followers' experience and expression of emotion can also be directed upwards—towards the leaders themselves.

In this regard, expressions of positive affect towards leaders (positive upward contagion) may serve to encourage and communicate acceptance and approval of a leader. Conversely, expressions of negative affect (and resulting negative upward contagion) may instead be seen as a way in which followers convey disapproval of a leader's actions. For instance, followers who perceive their leaders to be displaying unwarranted favoritism towards specific in-group members may tend to express more negative affect towards their leaders (see Dasborough et al., 2009). The resulting upward contagion impact may then impact a leader's own perceptions of how much followers trust them and, ultimately, the quality of the working relationship between the leader and the follower. Collectively, these propositions are in line with both our initial discussions of how relational leadership theory and research can be enhanced by considering more follower-centric perspectives, along with the impact of emotions in leader–follower relationships.

Summary

In this section of our chapter, we introduced the notion of emotion and affect as core drivers of relational leadership. More particularly, we discussed how the process of emotional contagion underlies the conveyance and experience of emotions at multiple levels of the organization. We built on recent work by Hareli and Rafaeli (2008) and Dasborough and colleagues (2009) and suggested how emotional contagion processes that occur among team members (lateral contagion), from leaders to followers (downward contagion) and from followers to leaders (upward contagion) can impact relational leadership processes. Consistent with relational leadership theory's aims of conceptualizing leadership processes more holistically, we also suggested that high-quality leader–follower relationship outcomes go beyond leader-centric, cognitive-based processes. On this basis, it is clear that future research should consider how the quality of leader–follower relationships is also influenced by followers, and affective exchanges between leaders and followers.

In the following section, we discuss ideas for methodological advancement that may help researchers to understand further the implications of affect and emotional contagion processes in relational leadership interactions.

IDEAS FOR METHODOLOGICAL ADVANCEMENT

Mixed Methods in Relational Leadership Research

Owing to the inherent complexity of leadership (Uhl-Bien, Marion, & McKelvey, 2007), researchers will need sophisticated and nuanced approaches if they are to understand the nature of relational leadership. One approach lies in the use of mixed methods, or research designs that utilize both quantitative and qualitative methods to provide a holistic interpretation and representation of the phenomena of research interest. Studies that integrate perspectives from both a positivist/empiricist paradigm and a constructivist/phenomenological orientation are, however, rare and under-applied in organizational research (Tashakorri, 1998). Qualitative researchers take the view that the persistence of employing quantitative research methods is one reason why findings from leadership research are often conflicting, and explain only small amounts of variance (Prasad & Prasad, 2002; van Maanen, Dabbs, & Faulkner, 1982). Despite this criticism, leadership has traditionally been examined from an objectivist, empirical perspective. Consequently, the presuppositions imposed by such quantitatively-driven paradigms orientate the organizational researcher towards survey-based and experimental research designs. Bolden and Gosling (2006), on the other hand, argue that the concept of an effective leader may not simply stem from one specific leader or follower-related element, but rather as a result of multiple, interrelated components that cannot be captured via a single research paradigm.

The use of mixed methods in the study of leadership processes may thus be particularly beneficial for advancing current understandings and uncovering additional dynamics in leader–follower relationships. For example, Tashakkori (1998) noted the dialogue between quantitatively and qualitatively oriented researchers, and concluded that these diverging orientations to social science research are not incompatible, and that both paradigms can be used to complement the quality and depth of research (see also Cresswell & Plano-Clark, 2007). We believe that this pragmatic perspective in social science research is promising (e.g., the pragmatic critical realism of Johnson and Duberley, 2000), and may ultimately benefit organizational and leadership research, a social research domain traditionally characterized by clear-cut distinctions between research conducted from different paradigms. Of course, effectively integrating these two research paradigms in the study of relational leadership processes is a challenge in itself, but researchers stand to be rewarded with a more holistic understanding of relational leadership.

We also point out that employing multiple methods in relational leadership research is likely to yield two particular advantages: triangulation and refinement of theory. Triangulation refers to the use of other data sources, research designs, or measurement scales in order to circumvent biases inherent in relying on any one single data source (Creswell, 1994). We suggest that one form of triangulation is to utilize methods from different research paradigms to augment the findings from any one study. Thus, relational leadership theory research could benefit substantially from the complementary use of quantitative (e.g., survey-based) methods and qualitative research methods, such as interviews and focus groups. In particular, some aspects of relational leadership theory, such as follower-centered models, are not currently well enough informed by a strong research tradition. In this respect, we lack a firm understanding of the impact of the follower (e.g., follower perceptions and affect as discussed in the preceding section) on leadership effectiveness. These processes can be explored in rich contextual detail via qualitative and ethnographic methods (e.g., see Pratt, 2000).

The value of employing mixed methods is evidenced in our own research. In one recent study, for example we (Tee, Ashkanasy, & Paulsen, 2009) employed interviews and focus group methods to uncover the different emotions felt and expressed by followers towards their leaders in the workplace. Building on the laboratory studies we mentioned earlier (Tee & Ashkanasy, 2007, 2008), this approach provided rich, first-hand accounts from organizational members as to how emotions affected the quality of interactions between leaders and followers, confirming that relational leadership processes in organizations are indeed impacted by the affective exchanges between leaders and followers.

Our qualitative study also built upon earlier findings that a leader's personality traits may result in their elevated susceptibility to followers' affect. Thus, while Tee and Ashkanasy (2008) reported that that neurotic leaders were more susceptible to followers' negative affect, Tee and colleagues' (2009) found in their qualitative study that empathy also inclined leaders to be more receptive of their followers' emotions. In this regard, the qualitative study not only added to, but also refined, theory by uncovering additional affect-based factors (in this case the leader's empathy and reactivity towards emotions) as key determinants of leader's overall effectiveness.

In line with Tashakkori's (1998) suggestions, the above studies illustrate that studies of relational leadership processes from both quantitative and qualitative perspectives are not incompatible. Rather, mixed research methods can be used in a complementary manner, ultimately contributing towards a more refined understanding of relational leadership. As such, we recommend that researchers make use of mixed methods designs in order to develop data sets that allow complementary analyses of leadership phenomena. Given that studies incorporating such traditionally distinct research paradigms are limited, we hope that our discussion in this chapter will serve to encourage researchers to tap into the strengths of both quantitative and qualitative methods to expand and refine relational leadership theory.

Studying Emotions in Relational Leadership

Despite the late entry of emotional dimensions into the organizational research domain, we believe that considerable progress has now been achieved. Positive outcomes include the qualitative and ethnographic approaches that we discussed above (see also Fineman, 2005; Maitlis & Özçelik, 2005), as well as survey methods (Dasborough, Sinclair, Russell-Bennett, & Tombs, 2008), laboratory methods (e.g., Barsade, 2002; Sy et al., 2005; Tee & Ashkanasy, 2007, 2008), and field research (e.g., Totterdell, 2000).

One of the characteristics of emotion that would seem to present a complication is that it tends to be transient. Moreover, as Robinson and Clore (2002) point out, relying on individual's recollections of emotional events is inherently problematic because respondents tend to state their *beliefs* about emotional experiences, rather than report accurately the experiences themselves. The solution to this is to collect emotion data in real time. This can be done using diary studies (e.g., see Weiss, Nicholas, & Daus, 1999) or what is termed the Experience Sampling Method (ESM) (Larson & Csikszentmihalyi, 1983), where respondents enter data in real time (see also Amabile, Barsade, Mueller, & Staw, 2005; Fisher, 2008).

Finally, we acknowledge that there still exists a level of uncertainty about the nature of emotional phenomena. For example, Gooty, Gavin, and Ashkanasy (2009) recently outlined four particular challenges that confront today's emotion researchers. These are that (1) definitions of emotions are often inconsistent; (2) researchers need to study discrete emotions (rather than positive versus negative affect); (3) emotions need to be studied as dynamic phenomena; and (4) emotions need to be studied in context. Clearly, these represent challenges for researchers in this field. Despite these issues, however, and like Ashkanasy and Ashton-James (2005), we see a bright future for the study of emotions in organizational settings. Moreover, based on our earlier arguments of the central role played by emotion in relational leadership, we believe that untapped opportunities exist to research the role emotions play in this field.

Multi-level Methods in Relational Leadership Research

Our final point, consistent with our earlier theorizing, is that multi-level organizational research designs that seek to account for relationships and interactions between individual-, group-, and organizational-level variables (Ashkanasy, 2003; Hofmann, Griffin, & Gavin, 2000; Raudenbush & Bryk, 2002) are crucial for understanding relational leadership, and especially to study the role of emotions and affect in these processes. Multi-level models in leadership research imply that individual-level leader and follower variables will influence, and will in turn be influenced by higher-level, group-related variables. Multi-level research is fundamentally distinct from traditional organizational research that simply aggregates scores across various respondents as a mean score of a variable of interest. Instead, studies that account for the different levels of analysis acknowledge that meaningful variances exist at both the individual and group-levels, and should be properly accounted for in data analysis. Multi-level models are a quantitative attempt to circumvent the "ecological fallacy" problem inherent in simply aggregating survey scores (i.e., averaging) across different raters and groups (Hofmann, 1997; Hox, 2002; Luke, 2004; Nezlek, 2002).

Consistent with this argument, Klein and Kozlowski (2000) note that inferences and conclusions drawn from aggregated data make the unjustified assumption that phenomena occurring at the group level can be assumed to hold for individuals. Yammarino and Dansereau (2008) advocate the use of multi-level approaches, particularly within the study of leadership, and their suggestion is also consistent with calls for more integrative studies of organizational behavior (House, Rousseau, & Thomas-Hunt, 1995). More specifically, Schriesheim, Castro, and Cogliser (1999) recommend that researchers employ appropriate analytic techniques to account for the effects of leader–follower exchanges at different levels of analysis. These authors also note that, unless researchers address this limitation in LMX research, subsequent research findings may not provide further understandings of relational leadership processes beyond what leadership scholars already know. In this respect, Henderson et al., (2009) note that the limited number of research designs that incorporate different levels of analysis in LMX research is surprising, given that LMX research essentially revolves around how multiple subordinates collectively influence group-level outcomes.

In line with our earlier discussion of conceptual issues, and extending on our suggestions for researchers to reconceptualize leader–follower relationships in the context of teams (as opposed to dyads), we advocate the development of models that appropriately account for the leader's relationships with multiple followers. Reconceptualizing relational leadership theory and research in this manner necessitates the need for methods and analytical techniques that appropriately account for both within-group and between-group differences of followers' relationships with their leaders. In the context of our discussion, followers' perceptions, and subsequent felt and expressed affect towards their leaders may depend on their status as either in-group or out-group members, and hence, these within-group variations may impact leaders' relationships with their groups as a whole. Could a few out-group members significantly impact the leader's overall relationship quality with his/her team?

Finally, and consistent with Johns' (2006) suggestions that researchers should consider the contextual influences that impact organizational behavior, multi-level research in relational leadership can account for the ways in which group-level, between-group differences may impact on leader–follower relationships. Tse and colleagues (2008), for example, found that team affective climate moderates team member relationships. Tangirala and associates (2007) likewise found that LMX quality was partly moderated by the leaders' relationship with their own supervisors, while Harris, Wheeler, and Kacmar (2009) found that the relationship between LMX quality and followers' perceptions of job satisfaction and turnover intentions were moderated by their perceptions of empowerment. These studies illustrate that contextual and higher-level factors have implications for individual-level, leader–follower relationships. Further research can examine whether team affective climate (i.e., a group-level factor) influences leader–member relationships. Henderson and his associates (2009) suggested that researchers consider organizational-level factors such as organizational culture, structure, and human resource practices as potential factors that may impact leader–follower relationships and differentiation. James et al. (2008), likewise, argue for the importance of organizational-level climate as a determinant of group and individual-level satisfaction and well-being in organizations. More recently, Ashkanasy and Humphrey (2011) presented a multi-level model of leadership and emotions (see also Ashkanasy, 2003).

In summary, it is clear that theory, measurement, and research design require a more realistic conceptualization of these multi-level factors, and researchers need to consider that leaders are embedded within the context of multiple groups. We also need to understand how group-level factors impact on relational leadership processes. Our suggestion is for researchers to account appropriately for these meaningful individual-level and group-level differences in further research, thereby circumventing potentially inaccurate inferences made via aggregation of individual-level variables.

CONCLUSIONS

In this chapter, we have highlighted avenues for advancement in relational leadership theory, both conceptually and methodologically. We focused specifically on the affective dimensions of relational leadership theory, and we suggest the means by which followers and leaders collectively shape leadership outcomes through emotional contagion processes. Following this, we discussed ideas for methodological advancement and how researchers can effectively capture the affective elements of interest in leader–follower relationships.

We suggested first that researchers consider the affective exchanges between leaders and followers as a key determinant in shaping relational leadership outcomes. We also pointed out that further research on relational leadership processes should distinguish between multiple levels of analysis, and we added that the multi-level conceptualization of relational leadership should also capture the different affective elements that exist at both the individual- and group-level of any one team. Additional research on other contextual, higher levels, such as organizational culture and climate (see James et al., 2008), can also shed further light on how leader–follower relationship quality may be moderated by affective elements that exist at the macro-level.

Second, we suggested that researchers more carefully consider the role that followers play in the relational leadership processes. Our current understanding of leader–follower relationships from extant research focuses heavily on leader-centric elements, driven by the assumption that followers are compliant and reactive towards the leader's influence attempts. We propose instead that followers themselves can act collectively in their own interests (or in the interest of their teams) and effectively convey support or disapproval of their leaders, subsequently impacting their leader's overall effectiveness. While we do not understate the importance of leader-centric perspectives in relational leadership theory, we also argue that our understanding of relational leadership processes can be enhanced by studying high-quality leader–follower interactions from the followers' point of view.

Building on our emphasis on the affective aspects of relational leadership processes, we also highlighted the importance of understanding how the followers' affect (not just the leader's affect) influences relational leadership outcomes.

Following this, we discussed the role of emotions, focusing on how affect is conveyed in leader–follower interactions. Additional research on the means by which affect enhances or inhibits the development of high- and low-quality leader–follower relationships can complement our understanding of cognition in relational leadership processes. The growing interest in the role of affect in contemporary leadership research illustrates that leaders are influenced by affective elements. Our current understanding of relational leadership processes can be enhanced by examining affective exchanges between leaders and followers based on processes of emotional contagion, and evaluating the impact of these exchanges on overall leadership effectiveness. In this respect, we provided a brief overview on the social phenomenon of emotional contagion and explained how this tacit expression and mimicry of affective states between two parties has implications for relational leadership processes. Building on recent work on the cyclical nature of emotions in organizations (Dasborough et al., 2009; Hareli & Rafaeli, 2008), we discussed how emotional contagion processes among team members (lateral contagion), from leaders to followers (downward contagion), and from followers to leaders (upward contagion) can all have implications for the quality of leader–follower relationships. Methodologically, and consistent with our methodological arguments, we propose that three specific avenues may be fruitful.

First, we suggest that researchers consider employing mixed-method designs in future studies of relational leadership processes. We argue that quantitative and qualitative research designs are not necessarily incompatible, although we do acknowledge they can be challenging to implement effectively. Nonetheless, researchers and the field of study more generally stand to be richly rewarded from studies that integrate the strengths of these two traditionally distinct research paradigms. The use of multiple research methods benefits the study of relational leadership theory by enhancing methodological rigor via triangulation and by refining the theory itself.

Second, and consistent with our arguments that emotions and in particular emotional contagion plays a central role in developing leader–member relations, we urge researchers in this field to employ some of the newly developed approaches to studying emotions in organizational contexts. While such approaches are not without their problems, as Gooty and her associates (2009) point out, the study of emotions presents a range of exciting new possibilities for improving our understanding of relational leadership.

Finally, and following from our suggestion that researchers should consider the broader contextual factors impacting leader–follower relationships, we also recommend that researchers conceptualize relational leadership processes in multi-level models. Multi-level models are able to capture the hierarchical and multi-layered nature of leader-team interactions more accurately, and to account for meaningful variances that exist in multiple followers' perceptions and affect. Although multi-level research in relational leadership is still in its infancy, with the increasing availability of appropriate statistical software packages to facilitate multi-level data analysis, along with recent publications that conceptualize leader–follower relationships at multiple levels, the study of affect in relational leadership looks set to continue being a worthwhile perspective on understanding the determinants of effective leadership.

REFERENCES

Albrow, M. (1992). *Sine ira et studio*–Or do organizations have feelings? *Organization Studies, 13,* 313–329.

Amabile, T. M., Barsade, S. G., Mueller, J. S., & Staw, B. M. (2005). Affect and creativity at work. *Administrative Science Quarterly, 50,* 367–403.

Anderson, C., Keltner, D., & John, O. P. (2003). Emotional convergence between people over time. *Journal of Personality and Social Psychology, 84,* 1054–1068.

Ashby, F. G., Isen, A. M., & Turken, U. (1999). A neuropsychological theory of positive affect and its influence on cognition. *Psychological Review, 106,* 529–550.

Ashforth, B. E., & Humphrey, R. H. (1993). Emotional labor in service roles: The influence of identity. *Academy of Management Review, 18,* 88–115.

Ashkanasy, N. M. (2003). Emotions in organizations: A multi-level perspective. In F. J. Yammarino, & F. Dansereau (Eds.), *Multi-level issues in organizational behavior and processes. Research in multi-level issues* (Vol. 2, pp. 9–54). Oxford, England: Elsevier.

Ashkanasy, N. M., & Ashton-James, C. E. (2005). Emotion in organizations: A neglected topic in I/O Psychology, but with a bright future. In G. P. Hodgkinson, & J. K. Ford (Eds.), *International review of industrial and organizational psychology* (Vol. 20, pp. 221–268). Chichester, England: John Wiley & Sons.

Ashkanasy, N. M., Härtel, C. E. J., & Daus, C. S. (2002). Diversity and emotion: The new frontiers in organizational behavior research. *Journal of Management, 28,* 307–338.

Ashkanasy, N. M., & Humphrey, R. H. (2011). A multi-level view of leadership and emotions: Leading with emotional labor. In D. Collinson, K. Grint, B. Jackson, & M. Uhl-Bien (Eds.), *Sage handbook of leadership* (pp. 363–377). London, England: Sage Publications.

Ashkanasy, N. M., & Tse, B. (2000). Transformational leadership as management of emotion. In N. M. Ashkanasy, C. E. J. Härtel, & W. Zerbe (Eds.), *Emotions in the workplace: Research, theory, and practice* (pp. 221–235). Westport, CT: Quorum Books.

Ballinger, G. A., Schoorman, F. D., & Lehman, D. W. (2009). Will you trust your new boss? The role of affective reactions to leadership succession. *The Leadership Quarterly, 20,* 219–232.

Barade, S. G. (2002). The ripple effect: Emotional contagion and its influence on group behavior. *Administrative Science Quarterly, 47,* 644–675.

Bartel, C. A., & Saavedra, R. (2000). The collective construction of work group moods. *Administrative Science Quarterly, 45,* 197–231.

Bass, B. M. (1985). *Leadership and performance beyond expectations.* New York, NY: Free Press.

Boies, K., & Howell, J. M. (2006). Leader–member exchange in teams: An examination of the interaction between relationship differentiation and mean LMX in explaining team-level outcomes. *The Leadership Quarterly, 17,* 246–257.

Bolden, R., & Gosling, J. (2006). Leadership competencies: Time to change the tune? *Leadership, 2,* 147–163.

Bono, J. E., & Ilies, R. (2006). Charisma, positive emotions and mood contagion. *The Leadership Quarterly, 17,* 317–334.

Bradbury. H., & Lichtenstein, B. M. B. (2000). Relationality in organizational research: Exploring the space between. *Organization Science, 11,* 551–564.

Brotheridge, C. M., & Grandey, A. A. (2002). Emotional labor and burnout: Comparing two perspectives on 'people work.' *Journal of Vocational Behavior, 60,* 17–39.

Brower, H. H., Schoorman, F. D., & Tan, H. H. (2000). A model of relational leadership: The integration of trust and leader–member exchange. *The Leadership Quarterly, 11,* 227–250.

Butz, D. A., & Plant, E. A. (2006). Perceiving outgroup members as unresponsive: Implications for approach-related emotions, intentions, and behavior. *Journal of Personality and Social Psychology, 91,* 1066–1079.

Chemers, M. M. (2000). Leadership research and theory: A functional integration. *Group Dynamics: Theory, Research, and Practice, 4,* 27–43.

Chen, G., Kirkman, B. L., Kanfer, R., Allen, D., & Rosen, B. (2007). A multilevel study of leadership, empowerment, and performance in teams. *Journal of Applied Psychology, 92,* 331–346.

Conger, J. A., & Kanungo, R. N. (1998). *Charismatic leadership in organizations.* Thousand Oaks, CA: Sage.

Cottrell, C. A., & Neuberg, S. L. (2005). Different emotional reactions to different groups: A sociofunctional threat-based approach to 'prejudice.' *Journal of Personality and Social Psychology, 88,* 770–789.

Creswell, J. W. (1994). *Research design: Qualitative quantitative approaches.* Thousand Oaks, CA: Sage.

Creswell, J, W., & Plano-Clark, V. L. (2007). *Designing and conducting mixed methods research.* Thousand Oaks, CA: Sage.

Dasborough, M. T., & Ashkanasy, N. M. (2002). Emotion and attribution of intentionality in leader–member relationships. *The Leadership Quarterly, 13,* 615–634.

Dasborough, M. T., & Ashkanasy, N. M. (2005). Follower emotional reactions to authentic and inauthentic leadership influence. In W. L. Gardner, B. J. Avolio, & F. O. Walumbwa (Eds.), *Monographs in leadership and management, authentic leadership theory and practice: Origins, effects and development* (Vol. 3, pp. 281–300). Oxford, England: Elsevier/JAI Press.

Dasborough, M. T., Ashkanasy, N. M., Tee, E. Y. J., & Tse, H. H. M. (2009). What goes around comes around: How meso-level negative emotional contagion can ultimately determine organizational attitudes toward leaders. *The Leadership Quarterly, 20,* 571–585.

Dasborough, M. T., Sinclair, M., Russell-Bennett, R., & Tombs, A. (2008). Measuring emotion: Methodological issues and alternatives. In N. M. Ashkanasy, & C. L. Cooper (Eds.), *Research companion to emotions in organizations* (pp 197–210). Cheltenham, England: Edwin Elgar Publishing.

Erez, A., Misangyi, V. F., Johnson, D. E., LePine, M. A., & Halverson, K. C. (2008). Stirring the hearts of followers: Charismatic leadership as the transferal of affect. *Journal of Applied Psychology, 93,* 602–615.

Fineman, S. (2005). Appreciating emotion at work: Paradigm tensions. *International Journal of Work, Organization and Emotion, 1,* 4–19.

Fisher, C. D. (2008). What if we took within-person variation seriously? *Industrial and Organizational Psychology, 1,* 185–189.

George, J. M. (2000). Emotions and leadership: The role of emotional intelligence. *Human Relations, 53,* 1027–1055.

Glasø, L., & Einarsen, S. (2006). Experienced affects in leader-subordinate relationships. *Scandinavian Journal of Management, 22,* 49–73.

Gooty, J., Gavin, M., & Ashkanasy, N. M. (2009). Emotions research in OB: The challenges that lie ahead. *Journal of Organizational Behavior, 30,* 833–838.

Graen, G. B., & Uhl-Bien, M. (1995). Relationship-based approach to leadership: Development of the leader–member exchange (LMX) theory of leadership over 25 years: Applying a multi-level multi-domain perspective. *The Leadership Quarterly, 6,* 219–247.

Grandey, A. A., Dickter, D. N., & Sin, H. (2004). The customer is not always right: Customer aggression and emotion regulation in service employees. *Journal of Organizational Behavior, 25,* 397–418.

Hareli, S., & Rafaeli, A. (2008). Emotion cycles: On the social influence of emotion in organizations. *Research in Organizational Behavior, 28,* 35–59.

Harris, K. J., Wheeler, A. R., & Kacmar, K. M. (2009). Leader–member exchanges and empowerment: Direct and interactive effects on job satisfaction, turnover intentions, and performance. *The Leadership Quarterly, 20,* 371–382.

Hatfield, E., Cacioppo, J. T., & Rapson, R. L. (1994). *Emotional contagion.* New York, NY: Cambridge University Press.

Henderson, D. J., Liden, R. C., Glibkowski, B. C., & Chaudhry, A. (2009). LMX differentiation: A multilevel review and examination of its antecedents and outcomes. *The Leadership Quarterly, 20,* 517–534.

Hofmann, D. A. (1997). An overview of the logic and rationale of hierarchical linear models. *Journal of Management, 23,* 723–744.

Hofmann, D. A., Griffin, M. A., & Gavin, M. B. (2000). The application of hierarchical linear modeling to organizational research. In K. Klein, & S. W. J. Kozlowski (Eds.), *Multi-level theory, research, and methods in organizations* (pp. 467–511). San Francisco, CA: Jossey-Bass.

Hollander, E. P. (1992). Leadership, followership, self and others. *The Leadership Quarterly, 3,* 43–54.

House, R. J., Rousseau, D. M., & Thomas-Hunt, M. (1995). The meso paradigm: A framework for the integration of micro and macro organizational behavior. In L. L. Cummings, & B. M. Staw (Eds.), *Research in organizational behavior* (Vol. 17, pp. 71–114). Greenwich, CT: JAI Press.

Humphrey, R. H. (2002). The many faces of emotional leadership. *The Leadership Quarterly, 13,* 493–504.

Hox, J. (2002). *Multilevel analysis: Techniques and applications.* Mahwah, NJ: Lawrence Erlbaum Associates.

Hsee, C. K., Hatfield, E., Carlson, J. G., & Chemtob, C. (1990). The effect of power on susceptibility to emotional contagion. *Cognition and Emotion, 4,* 327–340.

James, L.R., Choi, C.C., Ko, C.E., McNeil, P.K., Minton, M.K., Wright, M.A, & Kim, K. (2008). Organizational and psychological climate: A review of theory and research. *European Journal of Work and Organizational Psychology, 17,* 5–32.

Johns, G. (2006). The essential impact of context on organizational behavior. *Academy of Management Review, 31,* 386–408.

Johnson, P., & Duberley, J. (2000). *Understanding management research: An introduction to epistemology.* London, England: Sage.

Johnson, S. K. (2008). I second that emotion: Effects of emotional contagion and affect at work on leader and follower outcomes. *The Leadership Quarterly, 19,* 1–19.

Kelly, J. R., & Barsade, S. G. (2001). Mood and emotion in small groups and work teams. *Organizational Behavior and Human Decision Processes. 86,* 99–130.

Klein, K. J., & Kozlowski, S. W. J. (2000). From micro to meso: Critical steps in conceptualizing and conducting multi-level research. *Organizational Research Methods, 3,* 211–236.

Larson, R., & Csikszentmihalyi, M. (1983). The experience sampling method. In H. T. Reis (Ed.), *Naturalistic approaches to studying social interaction. New directions for methodology of social and behavioral science* (Vol. 15, pp. 41–56) San Francisco, CA: Jossey-Bass.

Lord, R. G., & Hall, R. J. (1992). Contemporary views of leadership and individual differences. *The Leadership Quarterly, 3,* 137–157.

Lord, R. G., Brown, D. J., & Freiberg, S. J. (1999). Understanding the dynamics of leadership: The role of follower self-concepts in the leader/follower relationship. *Organizational Behavior and Human Decision Processes, 78,* 167–203.

Luke, D.A. (2004). *Multi-level modeling.* London, England: Sage.

Maitlis, S., & Özçelik, H. (2004). Toxic decision processes: A study of emotion and organizational decision making. *Organization Science, 15,* 375–393.

Meindl, J. R. (1995). The romance of leadership as a follower-centric theory: A social constructionist approach. *The Leadership Quarterly, 6,* 329–341.

Mumford, M. D., Dansereau, F., & Yammarino, F. J. (2000). Followers, motivations, and levels of analysis: The case of individualized leadership. *The Leadership Quarterly, 11,* 313–340.

Nezlek, J. B. (2001). Multi-level random coefficient analyses of event- and interval-contingent data in social and personality psychology research. *Personality and Social Psychology Bulletin, 27,* 771–785.

Prasad, A., & Prasad, P. (2002). The coming age of interpretive organizational research. *Organizational Research Methods, 5,* 4–11.

Pratt, M. G. (2000). The good, the bad, and the ambivalent: Managing identification among Amway distributors. *Administrative Science Quarterly, 45,* 456–493.

Raudenbush, S., & Bryk, A. (2002). *Hierarchical linear models: Applications and data analysis methods* (2nd ed.). Thousand Oaks, CA: Sage.

Robinson, M. D., & Clore, G. L. (2002). Belief and feeling: Evidence for an accessibility model of emotional self-report. *Psychological Bulletin, 128,* 934–960

Schriesheim, C. A., Castro, S. L., & Cogliser, C. C. (1999). Leader–member exchange (LMX) research: A comprehensive review of theory, measurement, and data-analytic practices. *The Leadership Quarterly, 10,* 63–113.

Shamir, B., Pillai, R., Bligh, M., & Uhl-Bien, M. (Eds.). (2007). *Follower-centered perspectives on leadership: A tribute to the memory of James R. Meindl.* Greenwich, CT: Information Age Publishing.

Smith, K. K., & Crandell, S. D. (1984). Exploring collective emotion. *American Behavioral Scientist, 27,* 813–828.

Stamper, C. L., & Masterson, S. S. (2002). Insider or outsider? How employee perceptions of insider status affect their work behavior. *Journal of Organizational Behavior, 23,* 875–894.

Sy, T., Côté, S., & Saavedra, R. (2005). The contagious leader: Impact of the leader's mood on the mood of group members, group affective tone, and group processes. *Journal of Applied Psychology, 90,* 295–305.

Tangirala, S., Green, S. G., & Ramanujam, R. (2007). In the shadow of the boss's boss: Effects of supervisors' upward exchange relationships on employees. *Journal of Applied Psychology, 92,* 309–320.

Tashakkori, A. (1998). Introduction to mixed method and mixed method model studies in the social and behavioral sciences: Paradigm wars and mixed methodologies. In A. Tashakkori, & C. Teddlie (Eds.), *Mixed Methodology: Combining Qualitative and Quantitative Approaches* (pp. 3–19). Thousand Oaks, CA: Sage.

Tee, E. Y. J., & Ashkanasy, N. M. (2007, August). Can followers' mood states influence a leader's performance? A laboratory study of upward contagion. *When Emotion is no Longer (Merely) Feelings: The Social Role of Emotion in Organizations showcase symposium.* Symposium presented at the 67th Academy of Management Conference, Philadelphia, PA.

Tee, E. Y. J., & Ashkanasy, N. M. (2008, August). *Upward emotional contagion and implications for leadership.* Paper presented at the 68th Academy of Management Conference, Anaheim, CA.

Tee, E. Y. J., Ashkanasy, N. M., & Paulsen, N. (2009, June). A qualitative study of upward contagion: How followers influence leaders by expressions of emotions. *Emotions, Leadership and Performance symposium.* Symposium presented at the 8th Industrial and Organizational Psychology Conference, Manly Pacific, Sydney, Australia.

Totterdell, P., & Holman, D. (2003). Emotion regulation in customer service roles: Testing a model of emotional labor. *Journal of Occupational Health Psychology, 8,* 55–73.

Totterdell, P. (2000). Catching moods and hitting runs: Mood linkage and subjective performance in professional sports teams. *Journal of Personality and Social Psychology, 85,* 848–859.

Totterdell, P., Kellett, S., Teuchmann, K., & Briner, R. B. (1998). Evidence of mood linkage in work groups. *Journal of Personality and Social Psychology, 74,* 1504–1515.

Tse, H. H. M., Dasborough, M. T., & Ashkanasy, N. M. (2008). A multi-level analysis of team climate and interpersonal exchange relationships at work. *Leadership Quarterly, 19,* 195–211.

Uhl-Bien, M. (2006). Relational Leadership Theory: Exploring social processes of leadership and organizing. *The Leadership Quarterly, 17,* 654–676.

Uhl-Bien, M., Marion, R., & McKelvey, B. (2007). Complexity leadership theory: Shifting leadership from the industrial age to the knowledge era. *The Leadership Quarterly, 18,* 298–318.

Van Maanen, J., Dabbs, J. M., & Faulkner, R. R. (1982). *Varieties of qualitative research.* Beverly Hills, CA: Sage.

Weierter, S. J. M. (1997). Who wants to play 'follow the leader?' A theory of charismatic relationships based on routinized charisma and follower characteristics. *The Leadership Quarterly, 8,* 171–193.

Weiss, H. M., Nicholas, J. P., & Daus, C. S. (1999). An examination of the joint effects of affective experiences and job beliefs on job satisfaction and variations in affective experiences over time. *Organizational Behavior and Human Decision Processes, 78,* 1–24.

Wolff, S. B., Pescosolido, A. T, & Druskat, V. U. (2002). Emotional intelligence as the basis of leadership emergence in self-managing teams. *The Leadership Quarterly, 13,* 505–522.

Wong, C., & Law, K. S. (2002). The effects of leader and follower emotional intelligence on performance and attitude: An exploratory study. *The Leadership Quarterly, 13,* 243–274.

Yammarino, F.J., & Dansereau, F. (2008). Multi-level nature of and multi-level approaches to leadership. *The Leadership Quarterly, 19,* 135–141.

Yukl, G. (2006). *Leadership in Organizations* (6th ed.). Englewood Cliffs, NJ: Prentice-Hall.

CHAPTER 12

RELATIONAL LEADERSHIP

Creating Effective Leadership with Diverse Staff[1]

Lynn R. Offermann

As our world becomes increasingly interconnected, and as workers from a wide variety of races, ethnicities, genders, and nationalities take their place in the U.S. workforce, relationships between and among leaders and followers of differing demographic backgrounds have become increasingly common. Yet, many of those in positions of leadership are underprepared to face the challenges of working with diverse followers, and all of us, leader or follower, may need to overcome the tendency to gravitate towards those more similar to ourselves. The program of research described in this chapter builds on previous work by extending the examination of leadership relationships into the domain of diversity research. In particular, the studies that follow examine the distinctive challenges and limitations of cross-demographic relationships that occur as the leadership process unfolds in contexts where those engaged in leadership and followership are demographically different from each other. The chapter outlines our research on developing more inclusive leadership relationships and, within organi-

Advancing Relational Leadership Research, pages 361–380
Copyright © 2012 by Information Age Publishing
All rights of reproduction in any form reserved.

zational systems built on numerous such relationships, more inclusive organizational climates that allow individuals from a broad spectrum of society to achieve their full potential in their workplaces to the benefit of their organizations as well.

The study of leadership in the context of diverse interactional dynamics is by its nature the study of relationships. Relationships have always had a place in leadership research although more recent theorists have come to term early work on leader-follower relationships "relationship-based" rather than "relational." Uhl-Bien (2006) suggests that the term "relational" be reserved for work that goes beyond the traditional focus on leader influence or even reciprocal leader-follower influence to examine leadership as a more dynamic and socially-constructed system of interdependent relations in which shared leadership and organizational change can occur. Looked at this way, traditional leadership theories took entity-based perspectives that focused on individuals as they engaged in interpersonal relationships, including leader-follower interactions, whereas some more recent work has taken a more constructionist view, such that "leadership happens when a community develops and uses, over time, shared agreements to create results that have collective value" (Ospina & Sorenson, 2006, p. 188). These constructionist approaches emphasize the importance of empowered "followers" in the work of leadership, where followers develop into leaders, and where context/community matter. In these contexts, leadership may be shared, either with one or more "followers" or among an entire group (Offermann & Scuderi, 2007), rather than vested in the person of a single individual. The work described in the present chapter attempts to incorporate issues of meaning typical of constructionist approaches into the more traditionally entity-based study of relational leadership.

RELATIONSHIP-BASED LEADERSHIP APPROACHES

As noted above, most classic work on leadership took entity-based approaches, typically focusing on the person of the leader or more broadly focusing on leader-follower relationships. These relationships have been well-studied in a number of established leadership theories, notably Leader-Member Exchange theory (LMX) (Dansereau, Graen, & Haga, 1975; Graen & Uhl-Bien, 1995), Hollander's work on leadership as a two-way process of influence between leader and followers (Hollander, 1978, 2009), as well as the study of supportive or considerate leadership that appears in research ranging from the Ohio State University studies of the 1950s (e.g., Fleishman, 1953) to the individualized consideration behavior component of transformational leadership (Bass, 1985, 1996).

Of these relationship-based approaches, more recent approaches have paid more detailed attention to one-on-one relationships between leaders and followers rather than just leader-group interactions. The literature on leader-member exchange theory has been of particular influence within the field of leadership in understanding the value and limitations of studying dyadic leader-follower relationships. LMX theory (Dansereau, Graen, & Haga, 1975; Graen & Uhl-Bien, 1995) suggests that leaders establish different kinds of relationships with different followers, so that those followers with high-quality relationships with their leaders benefit from more latitude in negotiating their work roles and more support from their leaders, but may face higher leader demands and expectations in return. Followers with lower quality relationships with their leaders may labor under lower, more contractually-based leader demands but have concomitantly less freedom or latitude in their work.

Decades of research on leader-member exchange supports the contention that a high-quality relationship between a leader and a follower has a significantly positive impact on follower satisfaction overall, follower satisfaction with the leader, and with follower performance, as well as being associated with less follower intention to quit (Gerstner & Day, 1997). High quality leader-follower relationships have also been associated with enhanced creative production from innovative employees (Tierney, Farmer, & Graen, 1999). Based on these positive outcomes for followers in high-quality relationships with their leaders, Graen and Uhl-Bien (1995) have advocated that leaders try to form such high-quality relationships with as many of their followers as possible.

Another approach to studying the leader-follower relationship in the process of leadership is exemplified by Hollander's work (1978, 2009). Hollander has amassed an impressive amount of evidence of the importance of the follower in leadership, departing from traditional views focusing primarily on the leader's role and making clear that leadership is a process, not a person. In his view, examination of leadership must include both parties in the study of "relationships that can accomplish things for mutual benefit" (Hollander, 2009, p. 3), and needs to include concerns about follower-perceived leader legitimacy, encouraging an active followership, and doing things *with* people rather than *to* people. His most recent work has used critical incidents taken from the follower's point of view to differentiate good and bad leadership, finding that relational qualities such as trustworthiness, communication, and delegation/empowerment make a key difference.

Other theories have emphasized the importance of leader-follower relationships through the constructs of leader consideration and supportive behavior. Although work on transformational leadership as formulated by Bass (1985, 1996) has focused more on how a leader can motivate followers to do more than they expected, rather than directly focusing on the leader-follower relationship, the set of hypothesized transformational leader behaviors have always included as a key component the concept of individualized consideration. Individualized consideration, as posited by Bass, includes leader provision of support, encouragement, and coaching on an individual leader-to-follower (as opposed to leader-to-group) basis. In this respect, his individualized consideration is a modern extension of the work of classic Ohio State University studies which, in the 1950s, highlighted consideration as one of two independent forms of leadership behavior, though that early work typically measured it on a work group level (Fleishman, 1953). The heart of consideration is supportive leadership—leadership that shows concern for the follower and his or her needs. Yukl (2006) summarizes many years of work on supportive leadership by noting its importance in building and maintaining interpersonal relationships, with the body of evidence finding that followers of supportive leaders are usually more satisfied employees.

LEADING THE DEMOGRAPHICALLY DIFFERENT

Just as there is evidence of the positive outcomes for followers engaged in higher-quality and more supportive relationships with their leaders, there is also evidence that leaders establish less satisfactory relationships with followers who are demographically different from them than they do with more similar followers. Support for this contention comes from research in relational demography (Tsui & O'Reilly, 1989), which looks at the demographic differences of individuals in dyads or work groups. Tsui and O'Reilly (1989) defined *relational demography* as "the comparative demographic characteristics of members of dyads or groups who are in a position to engage in regular interactions" (p. 403). Relational demography theory builds on social categorization theory (Turner, 1987), social identity theory (Tajfel & Turner, 1985), and the earlier Similarity/Attraction Paradigm (Byrne, 1971). All of these theoretical perspectives converge in their suggestion that more positive effects are associated with demographic similarities between individuals.

Relational demography theory proposes that it is the comparison of oneself with others in the work unit that can influence attitudes and behavior. Once social categorization has taken place, in-groups and out-groups are determined, and those perceived as being like oneself are perceived more favorably, while unfavorable attitudes and behavior may be displayed towards those perceived to be in an out-group (Alderfer & Sims, 2003). Research on demographic similarity in leader-follower dyads has found that increasing difference between leader and follower demographics is associated with lower leader ratings of follower performance, less attraction toward followers, and the experience of greater follower role ambiguity (Tsui & O'Reilly, 1989). This latter effect is likely to be indicative of less frequent and/or poorer quality communication between leader and follower. Negative relational demography effects are not limited to minority group members; rather, they have sometimes been found to be even more pronounced for Whites than minorities (Riordan & Shore, 1997; Tsui, Egan, & O'Reilly, 1992). For example, a study by Vecchio and Bullis (2001) found that while demographic similarity between supervisor and subordinate was associated with subordinate satisfaction, it was White subordinates working under non-White supervisors who were the least satisfied group. Lest one think that such effects are limited to the U.S., work by Chong and Thomas (1997) with ethnic groups in New Zealand found similar results, namely that higher levels of follower satisfaction were reported when leaders and followers were ethnically similar.

Thus, empirical evidence lends support to the idea that demographic similarity between leaders and followers would lead to more positive organizational outcomes. Researchers have looked at directly observable attributes such as race, gender, and age, as well as less observable attributes, such as job tenure and functional/professional background (Milliken & Martin, 1996). Observable characteristics such as race, gender, or age will most likely influence initial impressions of others, and serve as cues to separate or affiliate one with other people. This categorization of people as similar/dissimilar to oneself can then influence subsequent interactions, making interactions with those deemed similar to oneself more frequent than those deemed dissimilar. For example, Polzer, Milton, and Swann (2002) found that diverse group member appraisals of each other during their first 10 minutes of interaction influenced group outcomes 9 weeks later.

Given that work in LMX theory suggests that determination of the nature of the leader-follower relationship (in-group/out-group status) and their attendant level of quality develops very early in the leader-follower relationship, demographic dissimilarity may well set the relationship off on a less than ideal course that may be resistant to later change. This suggests that members of underrepresented demographic groups may have greater difficulty in securing positive relationships with their leaders that might encourage their own participation in the leadership process, and in turn, may be less likely to be satisfied and more likely to quit. The quality of the leader-follower relationship may be at least a partial explanation for these lower work outcomes (greater dissatisfaction and higher intention to quit) for diverse workers. From a constructionist perspective, dissimilarity may disrupt the process of forming the kind of positive communities and shared agreements that would be most associated with successful leadership. Given our diverse workforce, the challenge of finding ways for those charged with the tasks of leadership to overcome the tendency to work more effectively with those more similar to themselves is a pressing concern, with the goal being the ability to work successfully with both similar and dissimilar others.

Interest in the relational processes of leadership in increasingly diverse organizations presents challenges for both theory and method. On the theoretical side, work in cross-cultural psychology may help frame differing expectations that employees bring with them to their interactions. Those in designated leader and follower roles may differ in their implicit theories of leadership, bringing with them differing expectations of leader and follower roles and appropriate behaviors. Based on cultural background, these differing expectations may cause social interactions to become strained, if indeed followers expect those interactions to occur at all. From an entity perspective, there is evidence that attributes of individuals as they engage in relationships with their leaders can be affected by cultural background. For example, in high power distance cultures, followers do not expect to have engaging relationships with their hierarchical superiors, and attempts by leaders to involve such followers in leadership by empowering them may be perceived as weak leadership rather than as a desirable relationship. Although modern Western leadership theories have been emphasizing the expansion of the traditional follower role into that of a partner in the leadership process with those in traditional leader roles (e.g., Offermann & Scuderi, 2007), non-Western staff may find such expansion inconsistent with their cultural traditions. From a Western leader's perspective, the follower's reluctance to initiate, step forward, and participate in the leadership process may seem like resistance or a desire to maintain a more strictly contractual relationship rather than culturally-appropriate deference to a perceived source of authority. The culturally-unaware leader may then assume that a lesser-quality relationship is the best that can emerge with this follower, and that the follower is not interested in sharing leadership.

In terms of methodology, no single approach is likely to be able to fully capture such complex leadership dynamics. To best examine leader-follower relationships in the context of diverse workforces, we have employed a combination of quantitative and qualitative methods described in detail below. Our team considers this combination of approaches to be the most helpful in providing a full understanding of social processes and relationships. I will describe findings from a three-pronged approach that began with an analysis of the existing literature and an assessment of organizational best practices for leading diversity, followed by a series of quantitative studies to empirically test theoretically-driven hypotheses, followed in turn by qualitative, onsite contact with leaders and followers in one host organization to discern—in their own words—how successful leadership relationships with diverse staff can best be achieved.

Leading Demographically Diverse Followers: Best Practices

At the organizational level, there are many strategies that have been implemented by leaders and organizations hoping to reap the benefits of diversity. Looking at a broad range of organizations that are successfully leading diverse workforces shows a wide variation in the scope and intensity of programs offered, requirements for participation, and opportunities for cross-cultural exchange. However, Offermann and Matos (2007) noted some general commonalities that offer suggestions to leaders for developing competencies in managing in diverse environments. Some of these best practices deal with the organizational level rather than the interpersonal, relational level, for example viewing managing diversity as a business imperative and being out front and visible as champions of diversity. However, a number of the identified best practices are best carried out in a high-quality interpersonal relationship between those designated as leaders and their followers. These relationally-oriented recommendations are:

- *Take a broad view of who could be a high potential employee.* Leaders may unduly limit the domain of acceptable job behavior to what they are culturally familiar with, and attempt to force others into that mold, experiencing predictable difficulties. The true benefit of a diverse workforce is to capitalize on the varied skills and capabilities brought by diverse staff rather than attempt to homogenize them. As leaders develop relationships with those different from them, openness to new ways of accomplishing goals and new styles of interaction can allow for more positive relationships as well as potential innovation. This suggests that leaders adopt more synergistic approaches that allow for a combination of styles or methods without a presumption of inherent superiority of any single way (Miroshnik, 2002).
- *Communicate commitment to fairness both verbally and through behaviors.* Followers observe leader's behaviors in hiring, promoting, and giving choice assignments and will quickly note if those receiving the most desirable opportunities are not from different backgrounds.
- *Share the unwritten rules.* Often leaders inaccurately assume everyone shares their expectations without the need to specify them, an assumption that becomes an impediment for dissimilar staff. For example, cultures differ widely in their views of time, affecting expectations about deadlines and the promptness of meeting start times, with some Non-Westerners being more relaxed about promptness than their Western counterparts. Clearly explaining expectations on

issues like these can yield far better compliance from those whose cultural expectations may differ from one's own and ease potential tensions in the leader–follower relationship.

- *Try different approaches.* As discussed earlier, follower expectations of their leaders may differ significantly based on cultural differences. For example, Schmidt and Yeh (1992) identified common leader influence strategies across Australian, English, Japanese, and Taiwanese managers, but noted that both their relative importance and tactical definition differed by nationality. Although Taiwanese and Japanese leaders combined both hard (assertiveness) and soft (reasoning) tactics, they differed in that Taiwanese endorsed greater use of sanctions, while Japanese emphasized sanctions less and bureaucratic channels more than the Taiwanese. Even cultures that might appear similar, like the U.S. and U.K., can show differences. This same study reported that U.K. leaders emphasized assertiveness and appealing to higher authorities more than U.S. leaders, who emphasized reasoning more. Leaders must be prepared and able to adapt their ways of interacting with diverse staff to accommodate cultural differences and to help their multicultural staff to adapt better.
- *Set high expectations for all staff.* Organizational research on goal setting clearly suggests that challenging goals can motivate superior performance. Leaders who do not expect as much from dissimilar staff are likely to get less, perpetuating a self-fulfilling prophecy that serves no one. Challenging goals within the follower's capability and assurance of leader support as needed provide motivation for goal achievement and participation in leadership.
- *Be inclusive.* Diversity includes everyone, and no one should be excluded or blamed for past societal discrimination. Some organizations have put such emphasis on including previously underrepresented groups that White male employees have felt left out and even attacked. As indicated by LMX theorists and others, leaders should be encouraged to develop high-quality relationships with any and all followers who are interested in such a relationship.
- *Learn from your diverse staff.* Actively listening and watching for potential diversity factors that may be interfering with a follower's ability to perform successfully was a hallmark of those leaders with successful relationships with diverse followers. Leaders should structure time for discussions with staff, both individually and collectively, to discern any problems or concerns they may have and to encourage participation and collective learning.

One of the practical difficulties with implementing the more individualized and relationship-oriented leadership style suggested above are concerns regarding potential fairness issues. Although fairness is one of the more universal ethical premises, it may mean different things in different places. Some leaders interpret fairness as exactly equal treatment without consideration of individual needs or capabilities, such that everyone in a given position should have the same training, the same working conditions, and the same opportunities. Clearly, such "equality" hampers the ability to create environments that provide each staff member with what s/he needs to thrive and will relegate those requiring different treatment to failure. Success comes from matching treatment with optimal conditions for growth, without viewing different needs as inherent inadequacies. Yet, leaders often resist giving certain staff members "special treatment." High-quality relationships do not need to be all the same; allowing followers latitude in negotiating their work situations does not require all to make the same choices. It does require equal commitment to maintaining successful relationships with a variety of people whose strengths and needs will differ, both initially and over time.

Quantitative Research

We have used quantitative methods to draw reasoned conclusions about theoretically-driven hypotheses about the impact of diversity on organizational life across large numbers of individuals. Our data consists of thousands of respondents from over 200 worksite locations of a large service-sector organization, comprising substantial numbers of workers from a variety of racial/ethnic backgrounds and occupational categories, over multiple years. Our work uses information from the company's detailed annual attitude survey in which staff from all levels report their views on the company, their supervisors and senior management, and their benefits and opportunities, as well as their personal satisfaction, commitment, and intent to stay with the company. Since this organization gives staff time off to complete the survey, guarantees anonymity, and uses an outside company for the data analysis, they get response rates from staff in excess of 85% on the surveys we have used for analyses.

The kind of quantitative approach we have used typifies most organizational work on leadership relationships and is consistent with an entity-based orientation. That said, service-sector organizations, such as the one we have been working with, may be particularly well-suited to examinations of processes of shared leadership more consonant with constructionist approaches. Although like most organizations our worksites had identified "leaders" in positions of authority, the success of service organizations largely derives from the actions of those at the point of service to the client, where identified leaders are typically not present. Quality service happens where committed and empowered "followers" engage in leadership behaviors to better serve their clients. Thus, service organizations are likely to be most successful when a committed employee collective exemplifying shared leadership unites around the goal of providing their customers the best possible service. In this respect, we have found our host organization to be a good source for both the quantitative analyses discussed here and for the qualitative analyses that will be discussed later.

Initial quantitative analyses showed that there were significant differences in mean perceptions of both immediate supervisors and senior management between White respondents and either Hispanic, African American, or Asian respondent group, with Whites giving more positive ratings. These non-white groups also reported a lower intention to stay than did Whites. Although we do not have the demographics of the specific senior manager or focal supervisor identified for any respondent, we know that the senior management ranks of the worksites sampled are over 75% White, thus most non-White respondents would have evaluated a cross-race senior manager. The supervisor ranks are more mixed, becoming increasingly White with each jump up the supervisory ranks. These results support the suggestion that racial similarity results in more positive perceptions of those in managerial and supervisory positions, even in an organization that has a reputation as a good place to work for minorities and women.

Of additional interest for future relational research is the finding that the least favorable perceptions of senior management and supervisors came from two other employee "groups." In addition to the four primary racial/ethnic groups (Whites, African Americans, Hispanics, and Asians), the organization's survey had other categories to which respondents could assign themselves. Respondents could identify themselves as being of two or more races, Native American, Pacific Islander, or fill in a line with any other racial/ethnic identification of their choosing. Due to low numbers of these in any single location, we coded these together as "Other." In addition to this group, we also had individuals who completed the survey but did not choose to identify themselves in terms of race/ethnicity, a group we term Demographic Non-respondents. Perceptions of senior management and supervisors were significantly lower for both the Other and the Demographic Non-respondent groups than for any of the four identified racial groups.

These racial group differences in perceptions of senior managers and supervisors were not huge—though significant, effect sizes were in the small to moderate range. This was not surprising since, by and large, we expected that the kind of relational issues associated with preferences for similar others to fall in the category of subtle discrimination rather than overt discrimination, the latter of which we would assume to generate larger effects. Specifically, we have hypothesized cross-demographic relational issues to be the kinds of "slights, snubs, and slurs" that can create distress and a sense of unwelcomeness for minority group members but which are harder for them to prove and seek legal recourse (Offermann, 2009). Although more ambiguous and hard to prove, these subtle forms of discrimination may nonetheless be associated with declines in employee motivation and performance (Graebner et al., 2008). In addition, for a large organization with a diverse employee population, we have found that even small demographic effects can have a significant financial effect on an organization's profitability (Offermann, Matos, & Malamut, 2008). Results derived from an organization with a more checkered reputation for diversity leadership would likely be even larger.

This work has taught us a lot, including the fact that the body of research that typically only compares Whites to non-Whites loses much by assuming that the relational experiences of all non-White subgroups are comparable. Our empirical work suggests that the Hispanic experience in our organization may be more comparable to that of Whites, while both African Americans and Asian groups often report less satisfactory relationships with supervisors than either Hispanics or Whites. In addition, African Americans and Asian groups also report lower levels of commitment and intent to stay than either Whites or Hispanics. Although with correlational data we cannot say that the quality of supervisory relationships actually caused these lower outcomes, as we might with an experimental methodology, the fact that our far larger and more diverse sample shows patterns similar to what more diversity-and-size-restricted experimental samples have shown in previous research suggests that this may well be the case. The greater favorability in Hispanic responses compared to those of African American or Asian staff suggests that research lumping all non-Whites together may be masking demographic effects by combining a more satisfied group with others who are less satisfied. Reasons for the comparable levels of response from White and Hispanic groups are certainly fodder for future empirical work.

A second general finding that is emerging is that the composition of the worksite—an important element of context—can make a difference. African Americans and Asians were most likely to consider leaving employment at their worksites when there were fewer of them at their site, even if they were not dissatisfied with their jobs (Offermann et al., 2007). Similarity drives leaders and followers alike, and it may be that, even if you like your job, you might want to leave if the interpersonal, social environment does not contain at least some people who share your gender, ethnic, or racial background. It is also interesting to note that the two groups who seem to be most negatively affected by being in a numerical minority are from backgrounds that tend to be more collectivistic in world view than the more individualistic White American profile, leading to the speculation that similarity to others in one's workgroup may be more important for those from collectivistic backgrounds. Such context effects may also account for the least favorable perceptions of senior managers and supervisors from employees who do not see themselves as fitting into one of the traditional four racial/ethnic groups (our "Other" category), as they may see themselves as most different from almost everyone around them.

Most importantly, in our perspective, is our evidence that an inclusive climate within worksites can make a significant difference. In a number of our analyses, positive diversity climate—operationalized as one perceived as fair to all, supportive of diversity, with equal opportunity based on merit—moderated the effects of relational demography (Offermann et al., 2007), removing the negative effects of racial/ethnic group membership on intent to stay. Simply put, where inclusiveness is high, people of all backgrounds are more likely to be committed and want to stay. The role of leadership in establishing and maintaining organizational climate is well-established in the organizational literature, and hence we believe that if leaders and followers can create this kind of climate in diverse organizations, the organization will benefit as well as the individual followers. This is consistent with what we found in our examination of best practice organizations, where leaders needed to be at the forefront of maintaining inclusive climates that welcomed a diversity of people and perspectives.

Qualitative Research

To delve deeper into the more dynamic, interactive aspects of leadership in diverse organizational contexts, qualitative methods are likely to be particularly suitable. To expand and follow up on our quantitative findings, my research team and I conducted interviews and focus groups at work sites in three different U.S. states of the same service-sector organization used in our quantitative analyses. We interviewed site leadership and the heads of human resources at each location, as well as conducted 90-minute focus groups at each site separately by racial/ethnic group with a total of 97 non-supervisory employees, representing each of four major race/ethnic groups: Whites, Blacks, Hispanics, and Asians. Structured, predetermined questions were used to provide comparability across sites, but in each case, open-ended follow-up of responses was also employed. Comments were transcribed and content analyzed by three raters: myself and one other team member who participated in the onsite focus groups, and a third team member who had not been onsite and who worked solely from transcripts. For the purpose of this chapter, I will present findings from two cuts at this enormously rich dataset, the first focusing on the issue of language that has clear leadership implications and the second focusing directly on the issue of leadership and how those charged with leadership can work effectively with others who are different from him or herself.

The Challenge of Language

Increasingly, U.S. workforces have become multilingual, as well as multiracial and multiethnic, with many organizations pleased to hire non-English-speaking staff for positions not requiring language proficiency. In our organization, as with many others, the predominant non-English language of choice was Spanish. Although English was not the native tongue of many Asian workers in our sample, the diversity of languages spoken across that vast continent meant smaller pockets of Asian staff speaking any one tongue at any site, and concomitantly more incentive for those Asian staff to learn at least some English. Indeed, almost all Asian staff members in our qualitative sample were quite fluent, if not totally fluent, in English. In contrast, in some of our sites, Hispanics were employed in sufficient numbers to create communities both inside and outside the organization that enabled them to forgo learning much English if they didn't wish to do so.

As a result, in all locations, we offered the opportunity for Hispanic focus groups to be run in Spanish, and all Hispanic groups accepted our offer due to the presence in each group of some workers who were not conversant in English. This choice immediately revealed one potential relational leadership obstacle since, at all sites, the most senior manager was not fluent in Spanish. Although in all cases immediate supervisors who were bilingual were in place, to us the language gap clearly presented a challenge to top site leadership in establishing relationships with all staff beyond a smile and an "Hola." Of particular interest, however, was the fact that these site managers did not seem to see their lack of ability to converse even informally with Hispanic staff as a significant impediment, but rather were comfortable having supervisory-level leaders who were fluent in Spanish as intermediaries who in this context would be those charged with developing high-quality relationships with and among staff members.

Our findings indicated that language barriers created problems on multiple fronts (Offermann, Matos, Basu, & Jayatilake, 2008). For the present discussion, it is relevant to note the difficulties of creating a shared leadership process where participants do not share a common language. Most leader-member exchange work, and indeed most leadership research in general, makes the tacit assumption of common language between supervisors and staff, and among staff members. In our study, establishing effective working relationships between members of different language groups proved to be a significant challenge. For English speaking staff, there was distrust and feelings of rejection and isolation at sites where many coworkers spoke Spanish. Bilingual supervisors who were able to develop positive relationships with Spanish-speaking staff did so at the risk of alienating these English-speaking staff, who sometimes resented supervisors spending time with coworkers speaking in a language they could not understand, feeling that everyone should learn English. Language subgroups harbored suspicions of each other, making it difficult for supervisors with staff from different subgroups to develop relationships with all staff without seeming to favor one group over another. This was particularly true since in this U.S.-based organization, as we suspect in many others, bilingual supervisors were more often native Spanish-speakers who learned English rather than native English-speakers who had become proficient in Spanish. Thus, English-only staff may have perceived themselves as the ones different from their supervisors, rather than the often-assumed picture of the English-speaking leader trying to establish relationships with Spanish-speaking followers. Problems increased when Hispanics were a larger proportion of the staff, where two distinct subgroups emerged, and where Hispanics often had little felt need to learn English. If leadership as a process is to be shared by a community, language differences inherently truncate the network of participants, in our case creating two separate networks or communities connected primarily by the person of the bilingual supervisor.

Consideration of leader-member exchange and the development of high-quality leader-follower relationships need to extend in order to include ways in which leaders can manage across linguistic diversity. Most LMX research understandably examines the leader-follower dyad although, at its inception, LMX theory clearly discussed "in-groups" and "out-groups", and as noted above, language disparity can certainly create in-groups and out-groups. What leadership theory has yet to sufficiently plumb are the responses of in-groups and out-groups to each other—in other words, if leaders establish high-quality relationships with some, what is the reaction of those with lower-quality relationships? Presumably, if leaders offer the opportunity for all interested followers to have high-quality relationships with them as has been recommended, there should be little concern, as those followers remaining in low-quality, contractual-style relationships have chosen that course. But, if leaders develop better quality relationships with some followers based on language similarity, some of those left out may have preferred relationships of higher quality but have had to settle for less.

On the positive side, some bilingual supervisory leaders seemed to have been able to overcome the obstacles of a multi-lingual followership to achieve positive working relationships with most or all followers and to create a more integrated network of staff. Although much more research needs to be undertaken, in the present case, those who were most successful managed to be attentive to all and were very careful about translating what was said to one in one language to others speaking a different tongue to ward off suspicions. For example, exchanges that generate laughter in one group might generate suspicions in another if it were thought that the laughter was at their expense. A quick translation to let everyone in on the joke was reported to help reduce suspicion and let everyone share in the fun and camaraderie. Leader attempts to learn at least rudimentary conversational exchanges in other tongues were also well-received. Along similar lines, being very aware of fairness issues and being seen as open to establishing good relationships with all went a long way toward dousing follower concerns.

The Challenge for Leaders

A final section of our focus group discussions centered directly on what those in positions of leadership did or could do to develop successful relationships with staff members regardless of their demographic background. Content analysis showed seven distinct characteristics of highly successful diversity leaders (Basford, Offermann, & Basu, 2009). Specifically, leaders who were successful with diverse staff showed respect to all, recognized and appreciated staff contributions, rewarded desirable behavior, were perceived as fair, were available to staff, communicated effectively, and set a positive example.

These are not radical concepts, nor are they bad recommendations for a leader working with homogeneous followers who are similar to oneself. What is different here is that, in homogeneous settings, followers who have less satisfying relationships with leaders do not have the explanation of difference to account for their status. In diverse environments, poor quality leader-follower relationships are often assumed—correctly or not, we cannot tell from our data—to be the result of discomfort on the part of leaders with those who do not share their background and style. There is the definite attributional perception of an "in-group," based on similarity to the leader, that is favored, and an "out-group" that struggles for comparable leader time and attention.

In the eyes of followers, unsuccessful diversity leaders are perceived to respect some followers more than others, to recognize the efforts of some while ignoring comparable efforts of dissimilar others, and to differentially reward based on factors other than actual performance. Poor quality relationships are evidenced by leaders who are available to their similar favorites ("in-group") but not equally available to others, and who do not communicate well with those who are different. In contrast, those reputed to have high-quality relationships that span differences set an example by interacting comfortably with those who differ from them as well as those who are similar and rewarding and promoting based on contributions rather than similarity. Talking about the value of diversity isn't enough— these followers based their conclusions on leader behaviors. So, in terms of setting an example, leaders could talk all they wanted about treating people equally and the importance of different perspectives, but if the only perspective they respected was their own, and if followers saw leaders surrounding themselves with similar others, promoting similar others, and interacting primarily with similar others, the conclusions they drew were based on those exclusionary behaviors. As was found in our earlier work on leadership and sexual harassment reporting (Offermann & Malamut, 2002), organizational policies are important, but leadership is required to implement fair policies through day-to-day actions.

Likewise, respondents saw ineffective leaders as sometimes creating schisms between groups of followers as well. Although the literature presents those with high quality relationships as benefitting from those relationships in terms of satisfaction and career progression, in our focus groups those with lesser quality relationships demonstrated some resentment of the leader's "favored children" and noted how it created ill feelings between groups of followers. At one site, respondents noted that leaders sometimes favored one ethnic group over another because they thought they could count on them to do the work reliably and on time. Rather than seeing that reliance as a positive vote of leader confidence evidencing a positive relationship, members of that favored group groused about having to do another ethnic group's work because the other group was too lazy. Leaders need to take care that, in counting on their high-quality-relationship followers, they may actually be burdening them in a way that is not perceived as a benefit and that may distance them from other followers. LMX theory has traditionally viewed expanding the number of higher-quality relationships with individual followers as a strong positive, but if those expansions are limited within certain racioethnic groups, relationship problems between groups might emerge. This is the type of finding that could be explored further with a constructionist approach in order to examine underlying group-on-group stereotypes and how those are constructed.

ISSUES FOR FUTURE RESEARCH: QUESTIONS AND METHODOLOGIES

There is a lot we need to know about how to best foster effective leadership relationships across the bounds of demographic similarity. It is clear from both quantitative and qualitative research that today's workers still perceive that it is an advantage to them to be demographically similar to those in positions of leadership. It is also clear from leaders that they appreciate the necessity of reaching out to those different from them, even as they are perceived as often failing to do so. The power of similarity is magnetic, even as one understands the importance of reducing that alluring pull toward the more familiar. What's tough is to walk the talk.

Still, there are leaders who have established positive leadership relationships with a wide variety of staff. We have tried to identify some of their characteristics as perceived by their hierarchical subordinates, but it would also be instructive at the individual leader level to do a more detailed analysis of the antecedent conditions—personal, attitudinal, and contextual—that influence leader success in diverse organizations. At first blush, it might be tempting to conclude that "color-blindness" or, more generally, "demographic blindness," might be the desired end-state, but data from our focus groups, as well as the psychological literature, suggest otherwise. Our respondents all wanted equally fair treatment, but they were not advocating turning a blind eye to racial differences. Neville (2000) notes that the modern-day conception of color blindness is the idea that "racial differences should not and does not matter" (p. 60), blurring the distinction between "race should not matter" and "race does not matter." Such blurring creates an ideological confusion that can deny the impact of racial and ethnic differences in treatment, at work and elsewhere, that can still exist. A better approach is shown in a recent experiment by Vorauer, Gagnon, and Sasaki (2009), who found that prompting people to take a more multicultural view of out-group members, and focusing on appreciating out-group members' distinctive qualities, led to more positive, other-directed comments to an out-group interaction partner than did prompting people to take a color-blind approach and try to ignore social categories.

People are shaped by their experiences growing up in a particular setting and culture, and to deny difference is, to many people, a denial of themselves. Work in the area of so-called "micro-inequities" (Rowe, 1990), that is, subtle forms of discrimination in organizations that nonetheless create barriers for minorities, suggests that denial of difference can be perceived as invalidating a major part of who a person is (Sue et al., 2007). A more promising approach is to cultivate high quality exchange relationships with and among staff from a variety of backgrounds, using what transformational leadership theory refers to as individual consideration—that is, developing individual leader-follower relationships based on an appreciation of each particular person's needs and aspirations. Periodic examination of one's leadership actions can reveal what others see: Who am I promoting? Giving the most responsibility/latitude? Are they all of the same group(s)? Do they all look like me? Many different eyes follow a leader's actions.

Our work contributes by combining quantitative and qualitative approaches to best flesh out the complexities of leadership relationships with followers from diverse backgrounds. Quantitative work allowed us to systematically examine a wide variety of workers, from many occupational streams, across many geographic locations, and to apply conventional analytic approaches to discovering significant relationships. First-person narrative descriptions and stories served to flesh out with examples the essence of effective relationships and how they develop or derail, as well as to generate additional research questions by surfacing issues and concerns that need further research. The numbers reveal patterns of significance, but the words provided richness and context. Future constructionist studies have the potential to move even further into the depths of how individuals from different backgrounds construct mutual realities in the workplace. As we move forward in trying to help improve leadership for the next generation of diverse workers and organizations, we can clearly benefit from multiple strategies.

NOTE

1. The quantitative and qualitative work reported here was supported by a grant from the National Science Foundation.

REFERENCES

Alderfer, C. P., & Sims, A. D. (2003). Diversity in organizations. In W. C. Borman, D. R. Ilgen, & R. J. Klimoski (Eds.), *Handbook of psychology. (Vol. 12: Industrial and organizational psychology* pp. 595–614). New York, NY: Wiley.

Basford, T.E., Offermann, L.R., & Basu, S. (2009, August). *Creating diversity-inclusive climates: What leaders can do.* Paper presented at the meeting of the American Psychological Association, Toronto, Ontario, Canada.

Bass, B. M. (1985). *Leadership and performance beyond expectations.* New York, NY: Free Press.

Bass, B. M. (1996). *A new paradigm of leadership: An inquiry into transformational leadership.* Alexandria, VA: U.S. Army Research Institute for the Behavioral and Social Sciences.

Byrne, D. (1971). *The attraction paradigm.* New York, NY: Academic Press.

Chong, M. A., & Thomas, D. C. (1997). Leadership perceptions in cross-cultural context. *Leadership Quarterly, 8,* 275–293.

Dansereau, F., Graen, G., & Haga, W. J. (1975). A vertical dyad linking approach to leadership within formal organizations: A longitudinal investigation of the role-making process. *Organizational Behavior and Human Decision Processes, 13,* 46–78.

Fleishman, E. A. (1953). The description of supervisory behavior. *Personnel Psychology, 37,* 1–6.

Gerstner, C. & Day, D. V. (1997). Meta-analytic review of leader-member exchange theory: Correlates and construct issues. *Journal of Applied Psychology, 82,* 827–844.

Graebner, R., Basu, S., Jaffer, S., Offermann, L., & Basford, T. (2009, April). Microaggressions and outcomes: Ambiguity, intention, and employee impact. In L. Offermann (Chair), *Slights, snubs, and slurs: Examining subtle forms of organizational discrimination.* Paper presented at the meeting of the Society for Industrial Organizational Psychology, New Orleans, LA.

Graen, G. B. & Uhl-Bein, M. (1995). Relationship-based approach to leadership: Development of the leader-member (LMX) exchange theory over 25 years. *Leadership Quarterly, 6,* 219–247.

Hollander, E. P. (1978). *Leadership dynamics: A practical guide to effective relationships.* New York, NY: Free Press.

Hollander, E. P. (2009). *Inclusive leadership: The essential leader-follower relationship.* New York, NY: Routledge.

Milliken, F.J. & Martins, L.L. (1996). Searching for common threads: Understanding the multiple effects of diversity in organizational groups. *Academy of Management Review, 21,* 401–433.

Miroshnik, V. (2002). Culture and international management: A review. *Journal of Management Development, 21,* 521–544.

Neville, H. A., Lilly, R. L., Duran, G., Lee, R., & Browne, L. (2000). Construction and validation of the color-blind racial attitudes scale (CoBRAS). *Journal of Counseling Psychology, 47,* 59–70.

Offermann, L.R. (2009, April). *Slights, snubs, and slurs: Examining subtle forms of organizational discrimination.* Symposium presented at the meeting of the Society for Industrial Organizational Psychology, New Orleans, LA.

Offermann, L. R. & Malamut, A. B. (2002). When leaders harass: The impact of target perceptions of organizational leadership and climate on harassment reporting and outcomes. *Journal of Applied Psychology, 87,* 885–893.

Offermann, L. R., Malamut, A. B., Matos, K., Jayatilake, N., & Wirtz, P. W. (2007, April). *Racial/ethnic diversity, satisfaction, and turnover intentions: A relational demography approach.* Paper presented at the meeting of the Society for Industrial and Organizational Psychology, New York, NY.

Offermann, L. R., & Matos, K. (2007). Best practices in leading diverse organizations. In J. A. Conger, & R. E. Riggio (Eds.). *The practice of leadership: Developing the next generation of leaders* (pp. 277–299). San Francisco, CA: Jossey-Bass.

Offermann, L.R., Matos, K., Basu, S., Jayatilake, N. (2008, May). *¿Están hablando de mí?: Language challenges for multilingual organizations.* Paper presented at the 20th Annual Convention of the Association for Psychological Science, Chicago, IL.

Offermann, L. R., Matos, K., & Malamut, A. B. (2008, April). *Diversity's bottom line: Diversity climate and organizational financial performance.* Paper presented at the 23rd Annual Conference of the Society for Industrial and Organizational Psychology, San Francisco, CA.

Offermann, L. R., & Scuderi, N. F. (2007). Sharing leadership: Who, what, when, and why. In B. Shamir, R. Pillai, M. Bligh, & M. Uhl-Bien (Eds.), *Follower-centered perspectives on leadership: A tribute to the memory of James R. Meindl* (pp. 71–91). Greenwich, CT: Information Age Publishing.

Ospina, S., & Sorenson, G. L. J. (2006). A constructionist lens on leadership: Charting new territory. In G. Goethals, & G. Sorenson (Eds.), *The quest for a general theory of leadership* (pp. 188–204). Northampton, MA: Edward Elgar.

Polzer, J.T., Milton, L.P., and Swann, W.B. Jr. (2002). Capitalizing on diversity: Interpersonal congruence in small work groups. *Administrative Science Quarterly, 47,* 293–324.

Riordan, C., & Shore, L. (1997). Demographic diversity and employee attitudes: Examination of relational demography within work units. *Journal of Applied Psychology, 82,* 347–358.

Rowe, M. P. (1990). Barriers to equality: The power of subtle discrimination to maintain unequal opportunity. *Employee Responsibilities and Rights Journal, 3,* 153–163.

Schmidt, S. M., and Yeh, R. (1992). The structure of leader influence: A cross-national comparison. *Journal of Cross-Cultural Psychology, 23,* 251–264.

Sue, D. W., Capodilupo, C. M., Torino, G. C., Bucceri, J. M., Holder, A. M. B., Nadal, K. L., & Esquilin, M. (2007). Racial microaggressions in everyday life: Implications for clinical practice. *American Psychologist, 62,* 271–286.

Tierney, P., Farmer, F. M., & Graen, G. B. (1999). An examination of leadership and employee creativity: The relevance of traits and relationships. *Personnel Psychology, 52,* 591–620.

Tajfel, H., & Turner, J. C. (1986). The social identity theory of intergroup behavior. In S. Worchel, & W. G. Austin (Eds.), *The social psychology of intergroup relations* (pp. 7–24). Chicago, IL: Nelson-Hall.

Tsui, A. S., Egan, T. D., & O'Reilly, C. A. (1992). Being different: Relational demography and organizational attachment. *Administrative Science Quarterly, 37,* 549–579.

Tsui, A. S. & O'Reilly, C. A. (1989). Beyond simple demographic effects: The importance of relational demography in superior-subordinate relationships. *Academy of Management Journal, 32,* 402–423.

Turner, J.C. (1987). *Rediscovering the social group: A self-categorization theory.* Oxford, England: Basil Blackwell.

Uhl-Bien, M. (2006). Relational leadership theory: Exploring the social processes of leadership and organizing. *The Leadership Quarterly, 17*(6), 654–676.

Vecchio, R. P. & Bullis, R. C. (2001). Moderators of the influence of supervisor-subordinate similarity on subordinate outcomes. *Journal of Applied Psychology, 86*(5), 884–896.

Vorauer, J. D., Gagnon, A., & Sasaki, S. J. (2009). Salient intergroup ideology and intergroup interaction. *Psychological Science, 20,* 838–845.

Yukl, G. (2006). *Leadership in organizations.* Upper Saddle River, NJ: Prentice Hall.

CHAPTER 13

POLITICAL SKILL, RELATIONAL CONTROL, AND THE SELF IN RELATIONAL LEADERSHIP PROCESSES

Darren C. Treadway, Jacob W. Breland, Laura A. Williams, Jun Yang, and Lisa Williams

The landscape of leadership research is strewn with conceptualizations of leadership characteristics, exchanges, and styles. Despite an abundance of models, frameworks, and theories, only recently have scholars turned their attention to the most fundamental aspect of the leadership context: the relationship that exists between a leader and follower. This focus on the relationship itself has been broadly termed as *relational leadership* and is understood as "a social influence process through which emergent coordination...and change...are constructed and produced" (Uhl-Bien, 2006, p. 668).

Despite its acknowledgment as a social influence process, no research to date has explicitly integrated aspects of influence and control into the framework of relational leadership. Furthermore, although recognized

Advancing Relational Leadership Research, pages 381–420
Copyright © 2012 by Information Age Publishing
All rights of reproduction in any form reserved.

as primarily a communication process (Dachler, 1992), little work has attempted to depict the mechanisms through which communication processes operate within the relational leadership context. We attempt to expand our understanding of both relational leadership and political skill by more comprehensively articulating the mechanisms that drive healthy leader-member communications. In doing so, the importance of communication in relational leadership is highlighted, as is its recognition as a key linking mechanism between the leadership and organizational politics.

In linking the leadership, politics, and communication literatures, the present paper articulates a model of relational leadership development that is grounded in the understanding of the self as a socially constructed relational entity. Therefore, we implicitly adopt a dramaturgical perspective on the construction of self in social settings (Goffman, 1959), and integrate ideas of relational leadership, political skill, and self within the framework of relational control. In doing so, this paper offers a point of discussion and evaluation for future research.

CONCEPTUALIZATION OF RELATIONAL LEADERSHIP

The proposed conceptualization recognizes relational leadership as a developmental process, and the process model depicted in Figure 13.1 represents an episode in this process. Evident in this depiction is the reciprocal and time-dependent nature of a relational transaction. We begin our discussion of this model by developing our understanding of the theoretical foundations of the model: relational leadership and relational control. Then, we describe political activity as an element of relational control, and argue for the role of the relational self as a critical mechanism in leader-member transactions. Finally, we discuss the temporal implications of our conceptualization.

Relational Leadership

The strongest call for examination of the relationship within leadership research may have come over a decade ago, in Graen and Uhl-Bien's (1995) expansion of the concept of leader member exchange (LMX). In calling for a more explicit representation of the levels of leadership in research models, these scholars suggested that the relationship itself represented a level worthy of analysis, an entity unto itself. As such, research should focus on answering questions of "the proper mix of relational characteristics to promote desired outcomes" (p. 223).

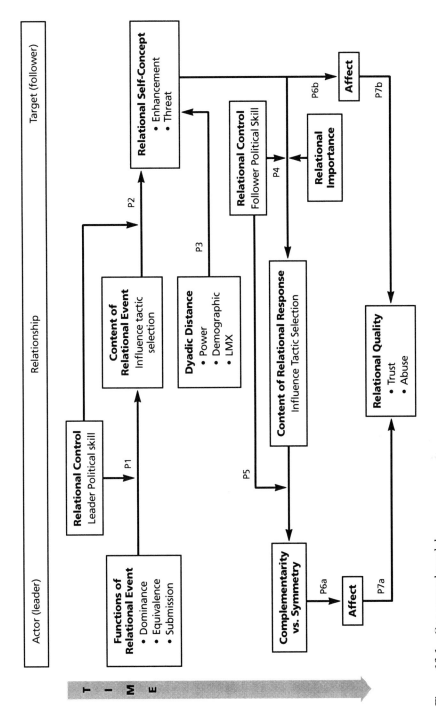

Figure 13.1 Conceptual model.

Building upon Graen and Uhl-Bien's (1995) description of trust and LMX as key aspects of relational leadership, Brower, Schoorman, and Tan (2000) presented the first broad model of relational leadership in organizations. In this model, several characteristics of the leader were positioned as increasing the likelihood of trust development. Specifically, leader's risk propensity and perceptions of subordinates' ability and trustworthiness were seen as positively influencing the likelihood leaders would trust their subordinates. Absent from Brower et al.'s work is the acknowledgment that the relationships themselves are subject to "reciprocal influence between the leaders and followers" (Graen & Uhl-Bien, 1995, p. 223).

Recently, Uhl-Bien (2006) sought to more clearly define the concept of relational leadership and to identify the theories and mechanisms contributing to an integrated view of the phenomenon. In doing so, she described relational leadership perspectives as traditionally representing one of two approaches. The first perspective views relationships as an entity. That is, scholars using this framework assume that individuals not only are the drivers of leadership relations, but also are explicitly aware of their capabilities and able to effectively parcel themselves from the situation and other participants.

Most notable in using the entity perspective are the views of LMX and charismatic leadership (Uhl-Bien, 2006). These theories of leadership are singled out by their reliance on distinguishable aspects of leadership relations; that is, the recognition of leadership traits and processes as precisely measurable and discernible. Whereas it is impossible to refute the impact that LMX and charismatic leadership have demonstrated on our understanding of leadership relations, their inability to fully explain the role of the situation and the organic nature of relations provides ample opportunities for extensions of the entity view of relational leadership.

In sharp contrast to the clearly defined nature of the entity perspective, the relational perspective assumes that "social reality lies in the context of relationships" (Uhl-Bien, 2006, p. 661). From this perspective, the relationship is shifting and dynamic and its characteristics are less extractable from the situation. Key characteristics of this perspective include the temporality of the relationship, the individuals, and the situation. This acknowledgment of relational path dependence forces researchers to consider models that integrate temporal considerations.

Uhl-Bien (2006) has woven an eloquent tale of relational leadership that is both a vivid depiction of the boundaries of the phenomenon, and a "call to arms" for the current generation of leadership researchers. Her arguments lay the foundations of the theoretical development of the relational leadership perspective using several key concepts. Some of these concepts are explicit in her explanation, whereas others represent subtle undertones in the depiction of the relationship.

We identify several foundations within Uhl-Bien's (2006) work that we believe highlight core aspects that any comprehensive model of relational leadership must contain. First, a relational perspective of leadership should acknowledge that the process of leadership is one of communication, which represents a structuring of roles and understandings as participants negotiate their interactions with the environment. Second, the ongoing development of the leadership relation is in part affected by individuals' understanding of their self-concept. Third, relations are social by their very definition, and as such it should be expected that the underlying processes of role negotiation are affected by interpersonal influence.

To that point, the individual differences of participants are critical to defining their self-concept, environmental perceptions, and response patterns. Finally, leadership relations are dynamic and shifting, such that these relations, and their participants, are ever growing, maturing, withering, and dying. Thus, these natural processes cannot be disconnected from the greater understandings that individuals derive from participation in these relationships.

Relational Control

Leadership scholars have asserted that relational leadership is, at its core, an ongoing communication system (e.g., Fairhurst, 1993; Graen, 1976; Kramer, 2004). Expanding these ideas, the present chapter suggests that relational control represents an overarching framework for integrating social influence processes into a comprehensive model of relational leadership. "[R]elational control concerns the interpersonal context in which a given message is delivered rather than merely what is said," and assumes that influence is a defining aspect of social interactions (Heatherington & Freidlander, 1990, p. 261). Relational control appears relevant for the relational leadership context because of its focus on dyadic interactions, communication, influence, and relational negotiation. Indeed, "[t]he emergent relational definition, then, is considered to be a product of a couple's joint interactive behavior, rather than individual actions. Thus, this view entails an emphasis on process and change" (Sabourin, 1995, p. 273). Whereas not explicitly defined as a leadership or political theory, relational control is ultimately concerned with issues of dominance and submission (Zietlow & VanLear, 1991). Indeed, the communication between the actor and target define the boundaries of control within a relationship (Heatherington & Freidlander, 1990).

The concept of relational control is based on the early work of Bateson (1958), who suggested that each message has two levels of meaning. The first level of meaning, content, is focused on what the message actually says.

From the political perspective, we can think of this as the actual political behavior demonstrated by the actor. The second level of meaning, relational, is concerned with how the message is communicated. In our conceptualization, this would focus on the key element of political skill, which represents the ability to effectively convey a message in a medium and in a manner that is appropriate for the target.

Content Level Meaning and Political Behavior

Within each relational communication, there exist several possible functions (Ellis, 1976). First, actors may exhibit the dominance function by demanding compliance, interrupting the target, or offering non-support for the target. Second, actors exhibit structuring through the process of guiding a conversation toward their goals, and extending current topics into areas more closely aligned with their interests. Both dominance and structuring are designed to define a relationship by restricting the behavioral options of the target. A third communication function, equivalence, is focused on demonstrating agreement on the role of the communication. By signifying agreement, the actors and the targets establish the mutually agreed upon boundaries of the relationship. The final function, submission, represents the actor's complete reliance on the target (Tullar, 1989). These functions represent the content level of meaning that is seen by the target. We argue that these functions are reflected in the political behaviors exhibited by the leader.

Political behavior in organizations has long been of interest to organizational researchers. Despite often being considered a negative aspect of organizational life, scholars have argued that political behavior is necessary for effective organizational functioning (e.g., Ferris, Perrewé, & Douglas, 2002; Mintzberg, 1983; Pfeffer, 1981). As such, political behavior in organizations has been defined as "the management of influence to obtain needs not sanctioned by the organization or to obtain sanctioned ends through unsanctioned means" (Mayes & Allen, 1977, p. 675). Therefore, we agree with previous work that has cast impression management, influence tactics, and self-presentation under the umbrella of political behavior (e.g., Ferris et al., 2002; Treadway, Hochwarter, Kacmar, & Ferris, 2005).

Because of this "broad brush" approach to political behavior, it is important to achieve definitional clarity as we move forward with our conceptualization. Initial interest in organizational politics was focused on the behavioral manifestations of power activation. Kipnis, Schmidt, and Wilkinson (1980) were the first to investigate the types of behaviors that individuals used to "get their way" in organizational settings. Subsequent empirical refinement of their ideas has resulted in six stable influence tactic dimensions: ingratiation, rationality, assertiveness, coalitions, upward appeal, and exchange.

Ingratiation is an attempt to place the target in a good mood before asking for compliance with a request. Rationality involves providing evidence to support your request. Assertiveness refers to making demands of the target. Coalitions engage others in their cause before making a request of the other party. Upward appeals are evident when the actor communicates directly to a target's supervisor, and tries to convince him/her to influence the target. Exchange tactics represent this-for-that arrangements in which mutual benefit is achieved.

Toward mapping influence tactic implementation onto the functions and content of relational control, it is conceptually cleaner to use the aggregation of tactics articulated by Kipnis and Schmidt (1988). These authors argued that influence tactics can be grouped into three broad categories: hard tactics, soft tactics, and rational persuasion. Hard influence tactics are those in which the actor relies on his/her authority or position power. Assertiveness, upward appeal, and coalitions are examples of these tactics. In contrast, soft tactics are those that attempt to persuade the target through flattery, or emphasize the need that the actor has for the target. Ingratiation, exchange, and self-handicapping are classified as soft tactics. Rational persuasion strategies rely on logic and facts to persuade individuals, and one might include the use of rationality and logic as rational tactics (Farmer, Maslyn, Fedor, & Goodman, 1997).

We suggest that hard, soft, and rational influence tactics are similar to the original three functions of relational control defined by Bateson (1958). Specifically, hard influence tactics resemble attempts to exert relational dominance in that these tactics include assertive behaviors and those designed to disrupt the target's environment. Rational tactics indicate equivalence in that these tactics demonstrate mutual respect for the individual and procedures within the organization. Lastly, soft influence tactics signal submission in that they demonstrate an observation of, and an acquiescence with, the power structure inherent in the relationship. As such, individuals engaging in soft influence tactics are communicating a message of submission.

Relational Level Meaning and Political Skill

Inherent in the functions and goals of relational communication are the effective selection and execution of social influence behaviors. Burgoon, Johnson, and Koch (1998) explicitly suggested that interpersonal dominance is a "set of communicative acts by which power is exerted and influence achieved" (p. 315). To the degree that the dynamics of power and roles in organizations affect the achievement of relational goals, it would appear useful to integrate these relational aspects with notions of political activity within organizations.

Previous conceptualizations of relational leadership explicitly have acknowledged the role that social abilities may play in the development of high-quality relations. Indeed, "personal relationships do not have a natural tendency to be conducted successfully" (Bradbury, 2002, p. 572). Hosking (1988) argued that leadership, as an act of organizing, is fundamentally successful to the degree that the leader possesses the appropriate social skills. Similarly, Balkundi and Kilduff (2005) alluded to the role that social intelligences may play in relational leadership. These scholars suggest that leadership effectiveness requires both the perceptual accuracy of social relations and the ability to manage the impressions of others.

Whereas Balkundi and Kilduff (2005) pointed to network acuity as critical to leadership relations, Hosking (1988) suggested that networking ability affects the decision-making ability of leaders. We contend that the more expansive construct of political skill better represents the set of competencies needed for individuals to effectively navigate the social contexts of organizations. Indeed, the capacities of politically skilled leaders include the awareness to effectively read network patterns and the ability to leverage those networks for personal gain, and also, political skill more directly acknowledges an understanding of self, others, and the importance of authentic communications that lead to effective decision-making.

Political skill is "the ability to effectively understand others at work, and to use such knowledge to influence others in ways that enhance one's personal and/or organizational objectives" (Ahearn, Ferris, Hochwarter, Douglas, & Ammeter, 2004, p. 311). Politically skilled individuals are capable of accurately assessing the pattern of social networks within an organization and are better able to centrally position themselves within these networks. These networks are built through politically-skilled employees' ability to effectively read the motivations and needs of others (Ferris et al., 2007). Finally, the behaviors of politically-skilled individuals are more likely to be perceived and interpreted as sincere and genuine (Treadway, Ferris, Duke, Adams, & Thatcher, 2007).

Scholars have acknowledged the conceptual overlap that exists between political skill and other social effectiveness constructs, especially those of self-monitoring and emotional intelligence (e.g., Ferris et al., 2002; Ferris et al., 2007). Conceptually, political skill incorporates the chameleon-like elements of self-monitoring, but also explicitly acknowledges the role of perceptual accuracy and perceived genuineness in determining the effectiveness of the actor. Similarly, political skill extends beyond conceptualizations of emotional intelligence in that it incorporates the aspects of network awareness and network development. Empirically, extensive scale validation demonstrated the distinctiveness of political skill from these constructs (Ferris, Treadway et al., 2005), and subsequent research has demonstrated the relative dominance of political skill in the prediction of organizational outcomes compared to other social effectiveness constructs (e.g., Ferris et al., 2005; Jawahar, Meurs, Ferris, & Hochwarter, 2008; Semadar, Robins, & Ferris 2006).

A growing amount of literature is demonstrating support for the preliminary notions of political skill in organizations. Political skill has been shown as a resource for reducing stress in organizations (Harvey, Harris, Harris, & Wheeler, 2007; Perrewé et al., 2004; Perrewé et al., 2005; Treadway et al., 2005). Additionally, several studies have shown that political skill has a favorable impact on performance in organizations (e.g., Harris, Kacmar, Zivnuska, & Shaw, 2007; Jawahar et al., 2008; Semadar et al., 2006; Treadway et al., 2007). Further validating the conceptualization of political skill, other research has demonstrated that political skill predicts performance beyond the contributions of emotional intelligence, self-monitoring, and leadership self-efficacy (Semadar et al., 2006), and that politically skilled individuals achieve higher levels of performance through their ability to manage impressions of intent in the targets of their behavior (Treadway et al., 2007).

Because political skill provides the capacity to strategically navigate and achieve success through the social arena of organizations, it is not surprising that some research has evaluated the role of political skill in leadership processes. Initiating interest in this research is the work of Ammeter and his colleagues (Ammeter, Douglas, Gardner, Hochwarter, & Ferris, 2002). Within the organizational politics framework, Ammeter et al. discussed "organizational leadership as the constructive management of shared meaning" (p. 751). From this perspective, they suggested that a leader's directed efforts can enhance leader, subordinate, and constituent outcomes. Although not articulated as such, their comprehensive model of political leadership can be broadly cast into Graen and Uhl-Bien's (1995) description of the three aspects of leadership relations: leader, relationship, and follower. The present conceptualization builds from their work and parcels out several aspects that subsequent research has shown to be critical to leader success in the context of relational leadership.

Subsequent research has supported the assertion that political skill is an important aspect of leadership relations, and supports Ammeter et al.'s (2002) notions of leadership as a political process. Ahearn et al. (2004) demonstrated that leader political skill was an antecedent to team performance. Other research has indicated that politically skilled leaders may achieve higher performance through their ability to improve trust in their subordinates (Treadway et al., 2004), or by elevating follower perceptions of political skill (Douglas & Ammeter, 2004).

More recently, research has begun to investigate the role of political skill from the relational entity perspective of leader-member exchange. Specifically, Breland, Treadway, Duke, and Adams (2007) found that political skill buffered the negative effect of low quality leader-member exchange on followers' career success. Brouer, Duke, Treadway, and Ferris (2009) found that followers in racially dissimilar dyads were less likely to experience low-quality leader-member exchange if they were highly politically skilled. Whereas this research offers evidence of the potential for political skill to affect relational leadership, it focused exclusively on follower attributes within the leadership process.

Evident in the work of these scholars is that political skill plays an important role in the prediction of leadership effectiveness. Despite the quality of this previous research, no model or study of political skill in the leadership context has demonstrated the reciprocal engagement that exists between leader and follower. Similarly, no model of leader-member political exchange has provided an explicit explanation of the complicated and interactive effects that political skill can demonstrate on the selection and implementation of influence tactics, despite previous research that exhibits evidence for these effects (e.g., Kolodinsky, Treadway, & Ferris, 2007; Treadway et al., 2007). The framework presented in the present chapter attempts to address this oversight. Toward that objective, we suggest that influence tactics represent the content aspect of communication, the implementation of which is designed to achieve the functions of relational communication.

Political Skill and Content Choice

Social norms, organizational roles, and power differences were evident in early research on political behavior. Kipnis and his colleagues (1980) suggested that individuals might utilize different tactics based on the audience they are attempting to influence. Their results indicated that assertiveness, ingratiation, rationality, and sanctions are directed toward targets at all levels. In contrast, upward appeals, sanctions, coalition building, and exchange of benefits are directed at superiors. Implied in these findings is that the effectiveness of a particular influence tactic is dependent on the nature of the goals of the actor and the power nested in the relationship.

In agreement with the socially constrained nature of political behaviors, scholars have argued that politically skilled individuals are more likely to choose political behaviors that are situationally appropriate (e.g., Ferris et al., 2005; Ferris et al., 2007). Some have suggested that within most organizational settings, ingratiation is the least threatening (Kipnis et al., 1980), and therefore, the most appropriate tactic to use (Liden & Mitchell, 1988). However, other research has indicated that this type of soft influence behavior does not reflect stereotypical notions of effective leadership (Falbe & Yukl, 1992), and actors are likely sanctioned for engaging in non-role conforming political behavior (Rudman, Greenwald, Mellott, & McGhee, 1999). Indeed, assertive behaviors have been shown to be effective for managers (Kipnis et al., 1980). This suggests that assertive or equivocal communication would be most consistent with leadership roles, and, as such, should be more likely invoked by politically skilled leaders.

The present chapter argues for the key role of political skill in the selection, activation, and effectiveness of leadership communication. (See Ferris, Davidson, & Perrewé, 2005 for a discussion of leader political skill and effective communication.) Some support for the importance of political skill in the process can be found in the work of Burgoon and Dunbar (2000), who spoke of a contingent social skill in relational communications. They argued that not all dominance behaviors are viewed as aggressive or assertive. Indeed, actors with higher self-rated social skills were perceived as more dominant by targets. Burgoon and Dunbar (2000) concluded that "skillful interaction patterns tend to beget perceptions of dominance, and many dominant behaviors are perceived as socially competent" (p. 99). This suggests that dominant behaviors, which are softened by their delivery and are reinforced by socially appropriate roles, can be effective. Hence,

Proposition 1: *The relationship between the function of the leader's communication and influence tactic usage will be moderated by political skill such that politically skilled leaders will be more likely to use dominance or equivalence rather than submission in communicating with their followers.*

To this point, we have integrated the leadership, communication, and organizational politics literatures to outline the role of political skill and influence tactics in the relational leadership process. In the following section, we consider the effects that the relational leadership process has on the target. The discussion begins with an assessment of the role that the targets' conceptualization of self has on their reaction to leaders' behavior. This discussion extends previous work of leadership scholars who have suggested that the conceptualization of self plays an important role in leadership effectiveness.

Relational Self

Self-concept is seen as a "person's sense of unique identity differentiated from others" (Brewer & Gardner, 1996, p. 83), and it is fundamental to the development of an informed understanding of psychological well-being. Most simply, the self is how individuals understand themselves and their place in the world (van Knippenberg, van Knippenberg, De Cremer, & Hogg, 2004). Individuals' understandings of self are formed in their interpretations of their individual, collective, and relational selves. Of particular interest to leadership researchers is the role that the relational self, as it is formed through the interactions of leaders and followers, affects the self-concept of the dyadic participants.

A person's understanding of their relational self comes from "interpersonal relationships and interdependence with specific others and those that derive from membership in larger, more interpersonal collectivities" (Brewer & Gardner, 1996, p. 83). It represents "the self-concept derived from connections and role relationships with significant others" (Brewer & Gardner, 1996, p. 84) and is maintained by reinforcing role appropriate behaviors. As such, the relational self appears particularly sensitive to social influence behavior.

In their socio-cognitive theory of the relational self, Anderson and Chen (2002) described five theoretical propositions important to our conceptualization. First, the relational self is only active in situations in which the opposite member of the relational dyad holds significant meaning or value for the individual. Second, the transference of relational characteristics is critical to the development of the relational self. Third, each relational self is, at the same time, socially apparent and unique to the individual. Fourth, relational selves interact with elements of individuals' personalities. Finally, relational selves provide affective activation of personality traits. It is within these five elements that we begin to build an understanding of how the follower's relational self is activated by the self-enhancing or -debilitating influence behavior of the leader.

Andersen and Chen (2002) suggested that the relational self is the product of unique relationships with significant others. A significant other is "any individual who is or has been deeply influential in one's life and in whom one is or once was emotionally invested" (p. 619). Each relationship with an emotional other assists in the development of self by defining ourselves and others by transference of memory characteristics from the significant other to self or novel other relations.

The similarities between the conceptualization of relational leadership as an entity and the memory representation of the relational self are evident. Recall that the entity approach to relational leadership assumes that the three components of relational leadership (i.e., leader, follower, and relationship) are seen as distinct and self-aware entities. The representation of the relational self is very similar to entity perspectives (i.e., LMX) of relational leadership in that the selves (followers) understand themselves through the relationships they develop with significant others (leaders). As such, the definition of the self-significant other relationship should be driven by the communication the follower receives from the leader.

As previously discussed, recent representations of relational leadership have depicted leadership as primarily a communication process (Dachler, 1992; Kramer, 2004). Watson (1982) indicated that leadership roles were defined within the reciprocal communication between leader and follower.

Indeed, her work specifically articulates the importance of the relationship itself in defining the roles of followers and leaders. This study found that when a leader engages in dominance as a form of communication, the follower is likely to respond with deferential communication, thus displaying compliance. However, these studies lacked direct evaluations of the impact that leader-directed communication exhibits on the relational self of the follower, and the subsequent influence this has on the reciprocal response from the follower.

Effect of Leader Communication on Follower Relational Self

Much of the work on use of political behavior by supervisors and leaders has focused on how leaders use these behaviors to shape followers' attitudes and behaviors toward the leader. However, absent from the discussion of effectiveness is any consideration of the more hidden, and potentially more detrimental, impact that leader behaviors can demonstrate on the followers' sense of self. To the degree that individuals understand their worth through the interactions with significant others (Mead, 1934), this oversight appears both curious and significant.

Whereas the literature in the organizational sciences has not directly addressed the question of how influence behavior affects the perception of the targets' self, some insights into this relationship can be found in work on supervisor aggression. Burton and Hoobler (2006) evaluated the impact of abusive supervision on the self-esteem of followers. Using vignettes that described supervisors berating respondents for suggesting work improvements, this research found that subjects introduced to the abusive supervision condition were more likely to report reductions in their level of self-esteem.

Adding some merit to the arguments of Burton and Hoobler (2006) is research in child psychology that addresses the impact of authority figure aggression on target self-esteem. Solomon and Serres (1999) found that school children reporting higher levels of parental verbal aggression also reported lower levels of general and task self-esteem. To the extent that parents are leaders to their children and that this category of relationship will transfer to adult leader-subordinate relations, these findings indicate that aggressive behavior of leaders has the potential to negatively affect the self-esteem of subordinates.

Whereas the previous studies provide evidence of the detrimental impact of assertive behaviors on followers' concept of self, other research indicates that supportive or positive evaluations from significant others can produce higher evaluations of self-worth. Harter, Waters, and Whitesell (1998) reported that adolescents that experienced higher levels of self-validation from significant others were more likely to see themselves as more valued in the context of that relationship. This research is in line with reasoning from balance theory (Heider, 1958). The tenets of this theory reason that, if actors provide positive feedback to targets regarding targets' self, targets will align their sentiments toward their relational self with those of actors. This process of alignment is necessary to balance the favorable sentiments followers hold toward leaders, and the sentiments leaders express regarding follower self-worth with follower construal of self.

Although the studies discussed above engage multiple theoretical perspectives, their collective findings point strongly to the impact of leader influence activity on follower conceptualization of self. Specifically, these studies suggest that leaders' use of hard influence tactics (e.g., aggression) should negatively influence the relational self of followers, and thus be more likely interpreted as threatening to their self-concept. Although we accept the strength of these findings, we argue that there is a mechanism that has not been not considered in the leadership context to date: the authenticity with which the communication is delivered.

In this relational context, the quality of a leader's communication is paramount to preserving the vitality of the dyadic relationship. We argue that relational quality is enhanced when leaders are aware of their followers' needs, and are able to demonstrate genuine concern for the well-being of their followers while trying to achieve their own relational objectives. To this point, politically skilled leaders should be more capable of reading the dynamics of social situations, and sensing the motivations and concerns of others (Ferris et al., 2005; Ferris et al., 2007). As such, we would expect politically skilled leaders to be more sensitive to the immediate impact that their influence behaviors potentially can exert on the dyadic relationship, and the long-term repercussions of damaging the self-concept of their followers.

Authenticity in Communication

Tedeschi (1990) was among the first to articulate the importance of authenticity in social influence communication processes. He positioned believability of a communication episode as the key mediating mechanism in determining the effectiveness of an influence attempt. Focusing on a singular episode, Tedeschi recognized that previous events had created reputational cues from which any particular behavior could be interpreted. As such, he contended that actors with a reputation for truthfulness would be more likely to evoke perceptions of trust in the target, and ultimately increased believability of their message.

Within the social influence literature, the concept of believability or authenticity lay relatively dormant until researchers began to discuss the outcomes of political skill in organizations. In their conceptualization of the construct, Ferris and his colleagues (2007) depicted authenticity as a component of politically skilled individuals. We go one step further and suggest that the ability to generate target attributions of authenticity is the most critical element in relation to the effective usage of influence tactics in the leadership context.

The role of authenticity in leadership process is not new, although only recently scholars have argued that authentic leadership is an important aspect of understanding leader-member dynamics based on the tenets of positive psychology. These scholars stress the role of leader self-awareness in aligning their identity with behavior. From this view, leaders are more or less effective to the degree they are able to establish relationships that are transparent, are directed toward functional goals, and focus on the development of their followers (Gardner, Avolio, Luthans, May, & Walumba, 2005).

While we acknowledge the important contributions of authentic leadership scholars, our view decidedly differs from their view in that we focus on the perception of authenticity evoked in the follower by leader behavior. And although it is appealing to present the positive nature of authenticity in communication processes, this positioning does not consider a full range of authentic behaviors. As such, it is important to recognize that individuals can be authentically cruel and genuinely harsh. Furthermore, when perceived as authentic, these leaders are more likely to evoke related sentiments in their followers, whether those sentiments are negative or positive. Indeed, "the more believable a communication, the more likely it is the target will comply" (Tedeschi, 1990, p. 307).

To the degree it can be assumed that perceptions of leader authenticity produce higher quality communications (e.g., openness), we find support for the importance of the content of the relational event. We suggest that the effectiveness of influence tactics will be dictated by the believability or authenticity of that message. Because the communications of politically skilled leaders are more likely to be perceived as authentic by their followers (Treadway et al., 2007), they are more likely to evoke the desired perceptions of self-concept enhancement or threat in their followers. Hence,

Proposition 2: *Leader political skill will moderate the relationship between the content of the relational event and the self-concept of the followers. Specifically, leaders high in political skill will be more likely to generate perceptions of self-concept threat in their subordinates when using hard influence tactics and more likely to generate perceptions of self-concept enhancement when using soft or rational influence tactics.*

Role of Dyadic Distance in the Relational-Self Definition

Whereas the proposed conceptualization ultimately is framed within the role of political behavior in leader-follower relationships, we would be remiss in not acknowledging the impact of dyadic distance on the formation of leader-member relations. The concept of distance has long been studied in supervisor-subordinate relationships (e.g., Ferris & Rowland, 1985; Rothaus,

Morton, & Hanson, 1965; Sundstrom, Burt, & Kamp, 1980). However, much of the research has developed independently of a comprehensive framework, thereby limiting understanding of this area (Napier & Ferris, 1993).

To address this shortcoming, Napier and Ferris (1993) introduced a more comprehensive model of multidimensional distance. They coined the term *dyadic distance*, argued that it is parceled into three aspects that consist of psychological, structural, and functional considerations, and suggested that the composite of these aspects provides the most relevant perspective from which to study distance. Specifically, Napier and Ferris defined dyadic distance as "a multidimensional construct that describes the psychological, structural, and functional separation . . . between a supervisor and a subordinate" (p. 326), and this concept represents psychological, physical, and relational properties of distance. This conceptualization provides the opportunity to consider the hierarchical nature of the supervisor-subordinate dyad in these terms as well.

Napier and Ferris (1993) described psychological distance as referring to the "psychological effects of actual and perceived demographic, cultural, and value differences" (p. 328) perceived in a supervisor-subordinate dyad. It is related to perceptions of similarity and values, (e.g., power distance) (Napier & Ferris, 1993). These individual differences affect the way leaders and followers perceive the hierarchical nature of the supervisor-subordinate dyad. For example, while there may be high formal or hierarchical distance related to a particular dyad, individuals may not perceive this distance because their values are driven by egalitarianism.

While psychological distance addresses psychological dispositions, structural distance focuses on the amount of dyadic interaction allowed by the design of the work spaces of an organization. Specifically, structural distance "encompasses those aspects of distance brought about by the physical structure" of the workplace (Napier & Ferris, 1993, p. 333). Structural distance also includes the concept of propinquity, defined as "nearness in place or time." Other models of distance hypothesize that proximity is positively related to performance ratings and subordinate satisfaction (Byrne, 1961; Homans, 1951; Triandis, 1959, 1960). This dimension of distance in organizations is most closely related to the concept of hierarchical distance based on formal position in the organization through its recognition of span of management and opportunities for contact.

The third factor of dyadic distance is functional distance, which expands on the other dimensions by describing the behavioral manifestations of distance. Specifically, Napier and Ferris defined functional distance as "the degree of closeness and quality of the functional working relationship between [a] supervisor and subordinate" (Napier & Ferris, 1993, p. 337) and is related to affect (e.g., liking, support, and trust), perceptual congruence (e.g., sex role perceptions), latitude (e.g., role discretion), and relationship quality (e.g., supervisor and relationship satisfaction). In addition, Napier and Ferris (1993) assert that functional distance is a mediator of the relationship between psychological and structural distance and outcomes of interest, such as subordinate performance.

High levels of these functional qualities of a supervisor-subordinate dyad indicate closeness between the supervisor and subordinate, but they do not necessarily address the hierarchical nature of the working relationship. For example, a protégé could have a very close functional relationship with her mentor while still recognizing high levels of power (i.e., hierarchical) distance between herself and her mentor. This type of relationship might be described as patriarchal or matriarchal.

Manifestations of the distance framework are abundant within the leadership literature. Tsui and O'Reilly (1989) studied the effects of demographic similarity, a component of psychological distance, on supervisor and subordinate perceptions and reported that demographic dissimilarity was associated with decreased personal attraction by superiors for subordinates, lowered subordinate effectiveness as rated by supervisors, and increased perceptions of subordinate role ambiguity. Demographic similarity also has been associated with subordinate satisfaction with supervisors, and with continued organizational membership (Vecchio & Bullis, 2001).

Liden, Wayne, and Stilwell (1993) examined the factors that contribute to LMX development and determined that supervisor and subordinate liking and perceived similarity predict LMX (a component of functional distance). Employing organizational tenure distance as a moderator, Epitropkai and Martin (1999) found that subordinates who were in the out-group, and were dissimilar, experienced decreased subordinate organizational commitment, job satisfaction, and well-being than those who were just in the out-group.

Based on the conceptualization of distance in organizations, its relationship to leader-follower dyads (i.e., hierarchical relationships) and evidence of its relationships with organizational outcomes such as commitment and satisfaction, it is suggested that distance in organizations is also related to individuals' relational self-concept. Specifically, arguments supporting Proposition 2 assert that specific leader influence tactics result in threats to or enhancement of follower relational self. Distance between the dyad members (dyadic distance) could signal a weak significant-other relationship and so would be inversely related to the relational self. Specifically, if the subordinate views structural or functional distance as discretionary on the part of the leader then the subordinate would develop the belief that the dyadic relationship was weak, unimportant, or low quality. Conversely, low levels of dyadic distance signal the strength, importance, and high quality of the supervisor-subordinate relationship and result in the enhancement of follower relational self. Hence, we propose the following:

Proposition 3a: *Dyadic distance will be negatively related to follower percep-tions of enhancement to relational self.*

Proposition 3b: *Dyadic distance will be positively related to follower percep-tions of threat to relational self.*

Role of Self in Response to Leader Communication

As we have made the case, if an individual's conceptualization of the self is critical to understanding and promoting effective leader-member rela-tions, it is likely that the relationship is influenced by the effect the com-munication has on the relational self. Indeed, one of the most enduring concepts in the psychological literature is that individuals strive to maintain a positive self-image (e.g., Doherty & Schlenker, 1991), and an individual's sense of self-image is acquired through "internalizing the reactions of sig-nificant other persons toward him or her" (Tunnell, 1984, p. 549). To that point, it is likely that individuals' understanding of their self has much to do with the way they interpret others' influence behavior (Kim, Kim, Kam, & Shin, 2003).

There is some support for the role of self in the interpretation of anoth-er's political behavior, and its subsequent effect on the target's definition of self. In particular, three studies offer building blocks for understanding the relationship. First, Kim et al. (2003) found that individuals with indepen-dent self-construals (i.e., those high in cultural individualism) were more likely to interpret positive statements favorably and less likely to interpret negative statements favorably. Second, research suggests that transference of emotions to another individual is likely to be based on attributes of the actor (Anderson & Chen, 2002).

Collectively it would seem that leader communication indicates his or her values to the follower; when that communication mirrors previous neg-atively laden communications received by the follower, the follower might be more likely to experience a detrimental impact on his or her self-worth. Finally, this may be exacerbated by the importance followers place on this relationship, due to an increased desire to act in accordance with self-rein-forcing roles or relational norms (Barreto & Ellemers, 2000). These studies indicate that the protection of a positive self-image is a critical component in assessing the motivations of followers to respond with political activity. Absent from these considerations is an explicit consideration of political theory. Given its grounding in Goffman's (1959) work on self-presentation, it would seem that much could be gained from integrating protective moti-vation and self-presentation in a model of leader-member relations.

Political Behavior as a Response to Perceived Threat

Some research has indicated that leader political behavior can motivate followers' behavior. For example, Sparrowe, Soetjipto, and Kraimer (2006) found that followers in high-quality leader-member relationships perceived that their leaders used exchange influence tactics as helping behavior designed to aid the followers, and so followers also engaged in more helping behaviors. However, if the quality of the leader-member relationships is low, exchange influence tactics used by leaders most likely would be viewed negatively or as of little value. In addition, if leaders in low-quality relationships seek to influence those followers through consultation, the followers may reevaluate their views of the quality of the leader-member relationship.

These results demonstrate the influence of leader political behaviors on follower action, but they do not assess the impact that leader communication has on follower self-concept. As such, these findings may represent more of what has been described as the "how" of influence, and less of the "why" (Ferris, Hochwarter et al., 2002). To better understand the motivations behind follower action, we more directly consider the potential effects that leader communication can exert on follower self-concept.

To this point, we have argued that the protection or enhancement of the relational self is a major impetus for engaging in social interaction in general, and political behavior in particular. Indeed, "all other things being equal, one comes to feel relatively good or bad about the self as a function of how one feels toward the significant other" (Andersen & Chen, 2002, p. 632). Therefore, to the degree that relational leadership is positioned as a communication process, target interpretation is paramount to understanding whether the follower's response to leader communication is that of perceived threat or enhancement to self. We frame this reaction within two views of behavior. First, stress paradigms help us understand how individuals might react to a perceived threat to their relational self. Second, theories of aging offer one demonstration of the manner in which individuals use influence behavior to maintain a positive self-concept.

Conservation of Resources theory (COR) suggests that individuals are likely to perceive an environment as stressful to the degree that they do not possess adequate resources to meet the challenges of the situation and, as such, human beings are driven to obtain and protect valuable resources (Hobfoll, 1989). COR specifies four classes of resources that individuals may possess. Of particular importance for the proposed conceptualization of relational leadership are personal resources, which are characteristics of individuals that assist them in coping with stressful situations. We suggest that a follower's positive self-concept represents one such resource. Indeed, research indicates that self-efficacy and self-esteem are personal resources that act as buffers in stressor-strain relationships (Xanthopoulou, Bakker, Demerouti, & Schaufeli, 2007). Therefore, to the degree that the self is threatened by the communication of the leader, it is more likely that individuals will experience strain and attempt to protect that valued resource.

As a threat to personal resources, a threat to self precedes the activation of other resources to combat this strain. Indeed, "[s]elf-regulatory processes should occur when shifts in the working self-concept pose a threat to the self, such as when these shifts involve an influx of negative self-attributes" (Anderson & Chen, 2002, p. 632). People who are conscious of their public self are aware of themselves as social objects, and concerned about maintaining a positive image of themselves (Doherty & Schlenker, 1991). Accordingly, politically-skilled employees, who by definition have high awareness of how they relate to their social environment, are likely to be aware of attacks on their relational self and so will be more likely to defend such attacks regardless of their personal outcomes.

As a dimension of personal mastery (Hobfoll, 1989), political skill serves as a resource to assist in the replenishment of the relational self. Most broadly, politically-skilled individuals are more competent at embedding themselves within powerful networks, and thus gaining access to valued social and tangible resources (Ferris et al., 2005; Ferris et al., 2007). Indeed, research has positioned political skill within the COR framework (Jawahar, Stone, & Kisamore, 2007) and, in agreement with previous research (Treadway et al., 2005), has shown that political skill reduces the strain of emotional labor.

Whereas this research has recognized political skill as reflecting the potential to operate as a resource in stress contexts, it has not directly accounted for the fact that political skill operates through behaviors. The mere possession of this self-regulatory resource does not ensure individual success. Consistent with previous conceptualizations, we argue that resource depletion activates political skill and, in turn, political behaviors. Furthermore, it is the authenticity and appropriateness of these behaviors that determines the ability of the follower to reclaim or enhance the quality of the leader-follower relationship.

The potential for political activity to operate as a protection mechanism is supported by research. Specifically, research investigated the impact of negative feedback from authority figures on positive self-image and found that a perceived ego threat leads high self-esteem individuals to overcompensate and set impressive, but unattainable, goals (Baumeister, Heatherton, & Tice, 1993; Smith, Norrell, & Saint, 1996). Ultimately, high self-esteem individuals are set up for failure by this behavior. To the degree that goal-setting can be viewed as social influence behavior (e.g., Frink & Ferris, 1998), these results indicate that individuals with initially healthy self-concepts attempt to protect their perception of self by projecting images of confidence and competence. These findings implicitly acknowledge that political behavior represents one possible pathway to the protection of the self.

Similarly, the literature on aging indicates that the protection of a vibrant social identity is important to successful aging (Baltes & Baltes, 1990).

As individuals experience age-related deficiencies in physical or mental capacities, they engage in influence behaviors to optimize their social self and maintain a positive self-image (Abraham & Hansson, 1996). This research indicates that when individuals were faced with stress, perhaps as a result of identity threat, they were likely to engage in political behavior as a compensatory mechanism that protected their identity.

Behavioral Choice of Followers

Relational control suggests that any communication is designed to achieve one of two overarching goals: complementary or symmetrical exchange. A complementary goal is achieved when the actor asserts and the target agrees or complies. In contrast, a symmetrical exchange occurs when the actor's assertion is met with an assertion by the target (Heatherington & Friedlander, 1990). Previous research within the organizational sciences has demonstrated the utility of relational control as a framework for investigation.

For example, Tullar (1989) found that individuals who had successful interviews were more likely to engage in dominance during the interview. Additionally, these successful job applicants were more likely to respond to the interviewers with complementary communications. That is, interviewer dominance was met with submission and interviewer submission was met with dominance. Similarly, Heatherington and Friedlander (1990) found that therapists were less likely than clients to use complementary messages when clients used assertion.

Consistent with relational control theory, our conceptualization recognizes complementarity and symmetry as leader goals when enacting follower-directed political behavior. Moreover, we explicitly acknowledge the role of follower motivations and abilities in crafting a response that will evoke perceptions of role-appropriate symmetry or complementarity. Key to this model is the importance of the relationship quality and the political skill of the follower.

Relational Importance

Most simply, we argue that politically-skilled followers will be better able to read the motivations of their leaders (Ferris et al., 2007), and this ability makes them capable of responding to leader communication with political behaviors that serve to enhance the leader's relational goals. However, this analysis is incomplete in that it assumes that each follower places equal importance on the leader-follower relation. Much literature in parallel disciplines suggests that the various roles that employees play in their leader's lives are not equally important, and do not demonstrate the same effect on individual outcomes (e.g., Parasuraman & Greenhaus, 2002). This suggests that it is important to consider the role that relational importance or salience may have on the response.

In agreement with the role-salience literature, there is evidence that indicates that the importance individuals place on a particular relationship affects their behavioral responses. Harter et al. (1998) argued that an individual's sense of self-worth was directly affected by the relationship in question. As such, they found that some relationships would have a greater impact on self-worth than others. Accordingly, Barreto and Ellemers (2000) distinguished between members with high group identification (high identifiers) and those with low group identification (low identifiers), and they found that low identifiers are more likely to act on self-presentational motives, whereas high identifiers are more likely to act on social identity motives. Specifically, high identifiers are likely to act in accordance with group norms, and low identifiers are likely to act in accordance with group norms if they are likely to be held accountable. These findings imply that if the leader-member relationship is important to followers, then they will be more likely to engage in role appropriate behaviors. However, if the relationship is not important to followers, then they are more likely to use role appropriate behaviors if there is fear of punishment or retribution.

Role of Political Skill in Behavioral Choice

To the degree that the preservation of a vibrant leader-follower relationship is important to followers, they are likely to activate political skill toward the goal of selecting relation-enhancing behaviors. However, if the relationship is not of high importance, we would suggest that political skill would be more likely directed toward protecting or enhancing the follower's self concept. Fundamental to the ability of effectively enacting the appropriate political behavior is the ability to accurately perceive the environment, and then enact behaviors strategically aligned to obtain the greatest benefit for the actor (Ferris, Davidson, & Perrewé, 2005; Ferris et al., 2007). Some scholars have argued that this ability is critical in leadership processes (Blass & Ferris, 2007).

Consistent with the work of Barretto and Ellemers (2000), it could be argued that when perceiving a threat to self, those high in political skill will be more likely to enact rational political behaviors to deny submission to the leader, while not offending the leader with role inappropriate assertive behavior. However, if the relationship is not of high importance to followers, they may respond with symmetrically assertive tactics that ultimately would damage the leader-follower relationship, while defending the follower's concept of self. As such, we see the role of relational importance in motivating the actions of followers.

However appealing it may be to articulate the advantages political skill provides in the protection of self and the maintenance of relationships, it may be even more enlightening to conceptualize the challenges presented to those who lack sufficient political skill. Because some research indicates that individual exclusion from important groups leads to impairment of self-regulatory processes (Baumeister, DeWall, Ciarocco, & Tweenge, 2005), it is likely that individuals low in political skill will be more detrimentally affected by threats to the relational self. Adding to the challenges of being deficient in political skill, the mere enactment of influence behavior has been shown to exhibit a more deleterious effect on personal resources under conditions of challenge or threat (Vohs, Baumeister, & Ciarocco, 2005).

These findings imply that as low political-skill followers respond to self-threat with political behavior, they reduce their personal resource reservoir. Because of their ineffectiveness in enacting these behaviors, they are not likely to acquire additional resources to replace those expended, and so they are more likely to perceive subsequent leader communication as threats (i.e., further resource depletion) and begin the cycle again. Ultimately, the logical conclusion of these findings is that, over time, the political-skill deficits of followers result in a downward spiral of self-defeating political behavior.

Taken together, this suggests a complex hypothesis regarding followers' reactions to threat. We suggest that, when faced with threat, politically-skilled employees will respond with rational tactics, which are most likely role conforming and organizationally sanctioned. However, it could be argued that to the degree the relationship is unimportant to followers, they may be less likely to engage in influence behavior as a response. Similarly, if low politically-skilled followers perceive a threat, but find the relationship important to them, they should be less likely to engage in defensive, assertive behaviors. However, we do not assume that political skill-deficient followers will be able to totally overcome the challenges of self-awareness they face. Hence,

> **Proposition 4a:** *Politically-skilled followers who place high importance on the leader-member relationship will be more likely to engage in role-conforming rational or ingratiatory behaviors than will those who do not perceive the relationship to be important.*

> **Proposition 4b:** *Similarly, politically-skilled followers who do not place high importance on the leader-member relationship will be less likely to respond to threats to self with role-conforming ingratiatory behaviors and be more likely to respond with defensive, assertive behaviors.*

Follower Behavior Effectiveness

Recall that it was argued that politically skilled leaders are more likely to be perceived as authentic in their communications. As such, they are more likely to present images that enhance their message in a way that increases the effectiveness of the communication. Therefore, similar to Proposition 2, we argue that politically-skilled followers are more likely to be perceived as genuine and authentic in their communications with their leader. Hence,

> **Proposition 5:** *Follower political skill will moderate the relationship between the content of the relational response and the leader's perception of complementarity or symmetry. Specifically, highly politically-skilled followers will be more likely to generate perceptions of complementarity when responding to leader hard influence tactics than with soft influence tactics. Similarly, highly politically-skilled followers will be more likely to generate perceptions of symmetry when responding to leader's tactic usage with the same tactic.*

Relational Outcomes

Up to this point, we have discussed the communication processes that determine the dyadic role of a participant's motivation and skills in determining the effectiveness of leader-follower communication episodes. However, the process described above must manifest itself in the change of attitudes and behaviors of both the followers and leaders. We argue that a shift in affect toward the dyadic partner as a result of the communication episode leads to perceptions of relational quality. We draw from several literatures to develop these propositions.

Affect

Interpersonal affect describes either a liking or disliking between a supervisor and subordinate (Zajonc, 1980). Interpersonal affect, consistent with the similarity-attraction paradigm (Byrne, 1971), posits that greater similarity between individuals is related to higher levels of interpersonal attraction. Supporting this proposition, Bauer and Green's (1996) research on LMX found that similarities in personality (i.e., positive affect or negative affect) impact the quality of the relationship in supervisor-subordinate dyads as well as supervisor judgments of subordinates' performance. They suggested that personality similarity may translate into more positive performance judgments of subordinates, higher levels of supervisor trust in a subordinate, and a higher propensity for supervisor delegation to the subordinate.

Additional support for the role of interpersonal affect within dyadic relations in organizations comes from the mentoring literature, where it is often assumed that interpersonal affect is automatic within informal mentoring relationships (Lankau, Riordan, & Thomas, 2005), as individuals naturally make connections in order to initiate and maintain such relationships. Lankau et al. (2005) found that mentors and protégés differed in regard to the roles similarity and liking played in the dyad. For example, demographic similarity was more important for mentors than protégés, whereas deep-level similarity, such as personality, and so forth, was important for both parties. Ragins (1997) suggested demographic similarity may be more important to mentors due to expected stereotypes or interpersonal barriers that may be present regarding performance of the mentoring obligations. On the other hand, protégés simply appreciate the opportunity to be mentored, and are cognizant of the fact they are receiving benefits from the mentoring relationship and are therefore not as concerned with dissimilarity (Lankau et al., 2005).

To the degree we can suggest that communication is a signaling process, there are two events that signal congruence to the dyadic partners. The first event is the follower's interpretation of congruence between their perception of value and the value communicated by their leader's behavior. The second event is the leader's interpretation of the degree to which the function of their relational communication is accepted or rejected by the follower. We argue that to the degree the elements of each communication are not aligned, the target is likely to experience dissonance, and will be less likely to experience interpersonal affect toward the actor. Hence,

> **Proposition 6a:** *Leader perceptions of complementarity will be positively related to feelings of interpersonal affect toward the follower.*

> **Proposition 6b:** *Follower perceptions of self-enhancement will be positively related to feelings of interpersonal affect toward the leader. Similarly, follower perceptions of threat toward self will be inversely related to feelings of interpersonal affect toward the leader.*

Interpersonal Affect and Outcomes

The current study argues that increased levels of interpersonal affect between leaders and followers will lead to higher quality leader-member relations. This assertion is relatively well-established within the leader-member exchange literature. Indeed, Dienesch and Liden (1986) suggested liking was a component of their multi-dimensional conceptualization of leader-member relations. Subsequent research has found that liking is a relatively dominant predictor of relational quality during the formation of leader-member exchanges (Liden, Wayne, & Stillwell, 1993). Additional research has shown that liking, and consequently leader-member exchange, is influenced by political behavior (Wayne & Ferris, 1990). Specifically, this research found that supervisor-focused behaviors were more likely to lead to supervisor perceptions of liking. Hence,

> **Proposition 7a:** *Leader's interpersonal affect toward a follower will be positively related to their perceptions of the quality of leader-member exchange.*

> **Proposition 7b:** *Follower's interpersonal affect toward a leader will be positively related to their perceptions of the quality of leader-member exchange.*

TEMPORAL CONSIDERATIONS

Time, Leadership, Self, and Politics

Evident in conceptualizations of relational leadership is the reliance on temporality in leadership relations. For example, Uhl-Bien (2006) indicated that relational leadership is an ongoing *process* that results in social structuring. Similarly, researchers have investigated the development of leader-member exchanges as a key theoretical underpinning of understanding relations in organizations (Liden et al., 1993).

The notion of time is also prevalent in articulations of the self. For example, Markus and Nurius (1986) discussed an individual's possible selves as being the way individuals conceptualize their future self. The activation of the ideal possible self has been shown to be the product of how individuals perceive and value perceptions of future time (Kivetz & Tyler, 2007). As such, the self can be considered a subjective, evolving understanding of one's self. This evolution provides the backdrop for interpretation and interaction with others and therefore represents a dynamic phenomenon not easily captured in static research models.

Although less prevalent, some research on political activity in organizations suggests that time plays a role in the interpretation and effectiveness of influence behavior. Most intriguing in this line of research is the work of Dulebohn, Murray, and Ferris (2004) who, in addressing the need for longitudinal research on political activity, reported that influence behavior changes over time, events, and conditions. They also indicated that interpersonal affect of both the supervisor and subordinate played an important role in the effectiveness of influence behaviors.

Organizational scientists have rarely acknowledged the role of time in their theory building, and when they have they have struggled to accurately represent this facet of their theory (George & Jones, 2000). Whereas the current model depicts the impact of time on relational leadership development, our conceptualization may not offer enough to address this aspect of the phenomenon. However, we do present four assumptions of the model depicted in the current manuscript, and acknowledge the implicit role of time in the theoretical building blocks of our model.

Assumptions of Time

Several qualifying assumptions are offered with regard to our conceptual model as it relates to the experience of time in organizations and relationships. First, the current model is presented as one episode within the broader context of previous and future interactions. In this manner, it reflects the path dependent and developmental nature of relational leadership. The effects of any particular episode are interpreted within and built upon previous interactions. Therefore, previous threats (or enhancements) to self should make the target more likely to perceive threat (or enhancement) in the future, even when that is not the goal of the actor.

Second, several variables may be changed by their interaction with time. For example, previous research indicates that, as individuals perceive their time in life to be limited, they shift the depth and breadth of social ties to maximize the emotional aspects of these relationships (e.g., Carstensen & Lang, 1996). As such, the importance a follower places on a relationship may shift over the life of the relationship as the individual approaches retirement or death. Similarly, the functions of an event may shift as a follower moves closer to these anticipated endings.

A third consideration of time comes in relating some aspects of dyadic distance. It is not uncommon for diversity researchers to conceptualize tenure diversity as one aspect of distance within organizations (e.g., Epitropaki & Martin, 1999; Tsui, Egan, & O'Reilly, 1992). Over time, the advantages or mutual experiences that members of any dyad share will increase. As such, the understanding that dyadic partners develop concerning one another should increase as well. This implies that the effect of surface-level diversity measures may dissipate over time, but deeper-level diversity may become more of an issue.

DISCUSSION

In their call for a focus on relationships in organizational research, Ragins and Dutton (2007) argued that the field needs to "build bridges across silos of scholarship" (p. 5), "put relationships to the foreground of organizational studies" (p. 5), and "extend our boundaries of knowledge about relationships in organizations" (p. 6). Toward addressing these calls, the current chapter has articulated a comprehensive model of the development of leader-member relations in organizations. This model integrates theories from politics, leadership, communication, and psychology in focusing explicitly on the processes from which leader-member relations emerge. As such, this model extends our knowledge of relationships in organizations and has several theoretical, methodological, and practical implications for leaders and those that study these phenomena.

Theoretical Implications

Unlike other notable models or frameworks of political behavior in organizations (e.g., Wayne & Ferris, 1990; Yukl & Tracey, 1992), the current model attempts to portray political activity as a dynamic, reciprocal process that specifically acknowledges the abilities and motivations of both the actor and target. Too often, research has assessed the effectiveness of a particular influence behavior without consideration of the ability of the target to accurately assess the motivations and behaviors of the actor. Indeed, no research on political skill has assessed the target's capabilities to determine the effectiveness of the political behaviors. If the self is an entity that an actor wishes to enhance or defend, then this oversight appears particularly troublesome. In relation to the self, Swann (2005) suggested that "[n]ot only did perceivers shape the minds of targets, but targets shaped the minds of perceivers" (p.69).

It would seem likely that, in dyads with highly skilled participants, an actor's ability to manipulate the impression of the target would be mitigated by the skill of the target to read the motivations of the actor. What is less clear is the role that this ability will play in the relational aspects of the dyadic partnership. Certainly, it is possible that the ability to detect inauthentic behavior would be fully explained by the model presented in the present chapter. However, it is also possible that a target may appreciate the challenge of participating with a skilled partner, or may recognize the actor as a potential resource for building broader networks in the future. Subsequent research on political skill in leadership dyads would be well-served to consider these aspects in developing more integrated models of dyadic processes in organizations.

Within the organizational sciences, relational leadership is one of the few areas where the relationship itself has been positioned as the key organizing mechanism. Indeed, Graen and Uhl-Bien's (1995) positioning of leader-member exchange as a relation-based approach to leadership could be considered on the forefront of this movement. However, scholars in other disciplines are more rapidly and directly recognizing the utility of focusing on relationships as the basic unit of human interaction. Termed *relationship science* (Berscheid, 1999), the goals of this new field echo calls of prominent organizational behavior scholars. In particular, the relational science's focus on multi-disciplinary research findings and linking science with practice hint of Porter's (1996) suggestions for organizational behavior. In the same vein, Ragins and Dutton (2007) have recently argued that the positive nature of relationships is a vital aspect of the modern work environment.

If the dyad is the most fundamental of relations, then the leadership context provides the most logical and perhaps most important extension of relational science to organizations. A more comprehensive understanding of the relational nature of the leadership dyad should more closely consider the outcomes of relational quality. The present model suggests that interpersonal affect of each dyadic partner should be positively related to perceptions of leader-member exchange. Although there are positive outcomes associated with high-quality LMX relationships (Bauer & Green , 1996; Wayne & Ferris, 1990), recent research has examined the effects of low-quality leader-member relations on performance. This work identified perceived supervisor competence, low politics, and decentralized decision making (Kacmar, Zivnuska, &White, 2007) as antecedents of low-quality relations. However, specific negative outcomes were not identified. Our proposed model provides a framework to synthesize and empirically examine both positive and negative outcomes of relational quality by explicitly acknowledging that negative, even malicious, motivations and outcomes can be associated with the relational exchange between leader and follower.

Fletcher (2007) suggested that embedding relational leadership within the broader context within which it occurs represents an opportunity for relational scientists interested in leadership and power. The current model exploits an opportunity by acknowledging time and interpersonal distance as the context within which the relational transactions occur. Separately, researchers have acknowledged both time (Rousseau & Fried, 2001) and distance (Napier & Ferris, 1993) as important contextual elements or organizational processes. The current chapter is an initial attempt at integrating these topics into a comprehensive model that explicates their effects on a dyadic partner's understanding of self and the role of nesting in these leadership episodes. It would seem helpful to advance these notions into our understanding of diversity within the leadership context.

If, at the most basic level, relationships "do not have a tendency to be conducted successfully" (Duck, 1988, p. 122), then effortful activation of personal resources is required. From this perspective, exploitation and victimization are potential results of an abundance or deficiency in skill-related personal resources, in particular political skill. This implies that opportunities to benefit oneself are only apparent to those with the social awareness to see and the ability to leverage these challenges. Indeed, some research indicates that victimization is more likely to occur when the target does not possess the capabilities to respond (see Aquino & Thau, 2009 for a review). Therefore, an understanding of motivation in the leadership realm seems insufficient if a consideration of resource capacity is not explicitly acknowledged.

One might extend this proposition to suggest that models of leader-member relations, in which the motivations and abilities of each party to the dyad are not considered, are inherently flawed in their reasoning. Although we have pointed to the work of Ammeter et al. (2002) as being an important foundation for the current chapter, these scholars implicitly assumed that the followers of politically-skilled leaders were themselves unskilled and yet motivated by the desire to maximize their self-interests. Similarly, but from the opposite view, Harris et al. (2007) and Treadway et al. (2007) found that politically-skilled subordinates were more likely to achieve higher performance ratings from their supervisors by effectively engaging in political behavior.

These collective findings demonstrate that both sides of the leader-member dyad are engaged in political activity to obtain valued resources and rewards. However, researchers approach the phenomenon as if the target of the behavior is devoid of the ability to detect deception and the motivation to counter such deception. We suggest that future research would be well served to expand upon the model presented in the current chapter and develop models of leader-member relations that are truly dyadic representations of the relationship.

Methodological Implications

Concepts of organizational politics and relational leadership theory have been integrated to better understand the process through which leaders and followers interact with one another, and the outcomes of those interactions. The success that the conceptual model introduced in this chapter will demonstrate in furthering our understanding of the relational aspects of leadership is dependent upon to the degree to which suitable methodology is leveraged to empirically assess the phenomena (Edmondson & McManus, 2007). Studying relational leadership calls for the consideration of several methodological aspects, including network embeddedness, temporal considerations, and multi-level issues.

Views of leadership as human social constructions must include considerations of the interdependencies and connections of organizational members (Bradbury & Lichtenstein, 2000; Hosking, Dachler, & Gergen, 1995; Uhl-Bien, 2006). Indeed, Uhl-Bien argued that relational leadership occurs within relational dynamics that are embedded within the social contexts of those dynamics (Osborn, Hunt, & Jauch, 2002). Also, many scholars note that one's relationship with others is a key aspect of defining oneself (Anderson & Chen, 2002; Brewer & Gardner, 1996; Lord, Brown, & Freiberg, 1999). Given the social context of relational leadership and the degree to which individual's use relationship status (Uhl-Bien, 2006) and "role relationship[s] with significant others" (Brewer & Gardner, 1996, p. 84) to define themselves, the use of social network analysis may be a useful tool for understanding this phenomena.

Social network analysis focuses on structuration and examines the interdependencies between individuals. In a conceptual argument, Balkundi and Kilduff (2005) stated that networks represent an important aspect of leadership. Specifically, they suggested that a leader's network position may either support or contradict his/her actions. In a meta-analysis, Balkundi and Harrison (2006) reported that more centrally-located leaders contribute to increased team performance. These early findings suggest that employing social network methodologies could be potentially fruitful for understanding relational leadership research.

Social network methodologies could be leveraged in a number of ways to better understand relationship leadership phenomena. Social network researchers use techniques to identify and understand the role of relationships as opposed to unique actor characteristics in defining and predicating other relationships. It is not the case that actor characteristics are excluded, but rather that the focus is on the ties between individuals. Such research focuses on how central an actor is to a specific network and how that centrality predicts important outcomes. In the relational leadership context, the potential impact of such focus becomes apparent. Within our conceptual model, specifically, a subordinate's centrality or importance within a work flow network might dictate the content of the relational event and the influence tactic selected. For instance, those individuals who are more central may be more willing to engage in harder tactics, such as assertiveness, while those less central may choose ingratiation, a softer tactic. Social network methodologies can also be used to measure specific variables, such as relational quality. For instance, centrality indices can be calculated regarding how abusive or (un)trustworthy an actor is. That information can be then be used as a potentially more objective assessment with an empirical model.

The use of longitudinal research designs is clearly needed. If relational leadership develops as we have suggested, a longitudinal approach is necessary to understand/discover the variables involved and how they emerge. Indeed, Hosking (2006) argued that relational orientations are built on understanding processes and not individuals. Furthermore, some scholars see leadership as socio-relational in nature (Dachler, 1992), and subject to constant change (e.g., Abell & Simons, 2000; Dachler, 1992). Additionally, whereas social network analysis can be used to obtain a snapshot of individual interdependencies, relationships are formed over time, and research in this area could benefit from understanding how relational leadership aspects and network positioning unfold.

Evaluating our propositions longitudinally is made rather direct given our explicit incorporation of time into the conceptual model. Therefore, the first step in trying to better understand the causal ordering of variables would be to be cognizant of our theoretical arguments for the causal ordering of the relationships shown in Figure 13.1. As with previous empirical research, future empirical work evaluating our model would take small segments of the overall model and expose them to further scientific scrutiny. Such efforts to establish causal ordering would involve at least two distinct time periods of data collection and maybe more, depending upon the research questions. For instance, if the question under inspection regarded

P6b and P7b, the researcher might collect relational self data at Time 1, affect at Time 2, and relational quality at Time 3. These relationships would then be tested statistically according to the demands of one's research.

This model also suggests the presence of multi-level issues. Hunt and Dodge (2000) argued that "[Leadership] is not restricted to a single or even small set of formal or informal leaders; and, in its strongest form, functions as a dynamic system embedding leadership, environmental, and organizational aspects" (p. 448). Similarly, Bradbury and Lichenstein (2000) referred to the interdependencies of individuals and organizations, whereas Balkundi and Harrison (2006) considered the role of leaders and leadership within groups. Given the complex nature of relationships and their formation across multiple levels of analysis (i.e., individuals, groups, and organizations), traditional statistical analyses, such as multiple regression, may be inadequate to parcel out effects, and research may require more advanced methodologies, such as hierarchical linear modeling.

Typically, organizational scientists have viewed hierarchical linear modeling as solely addressing issues of levels. As evidenced above, we agree with this assertion. However, the current model is ultimately concerned with change—change in the participants and in their relationship. Thus, models of relational development such as the current model must recognize the temporally nested nature of individual and dyadic relationships and theorize these as such. Raudenbush and Bryk (2002) recognized the potential of hierarchical linear modeling to address such questions of personal change. In practice, resource constraints are likely to limit researchers to few observation points for the study of relational change. In these situations, the application of a linear growth model would appear most appropriate (Raudenbush & Bryk, 2002). To assess the propositions in the current chapter, the initial quality of a relationship or of an individual's self-concept would be compared with subsequent measures to determine if "growth" or more simply, change, had occurred. If so, the relational events could be modeled as level-2 predictors of subsequent change.

Limitations

Whereas we have attempted to provide a comprehensive model of the communication processes involved in the development of leadership understandings, we certainly have failed to capture all of the potential conditions and characteristics that define these processes. The findings of Lambird and Mann (2006) demonstrated the complexity inherent in understanding leadership processes that limit the generalizability of the current perspective. These authors found that those with high self-esteem are less capable of self-regulation if the threat to self evokes defensiveness. We have proposed that political skill will increase the probability that they will respond with political behavior. For reasons of parsimony, we did not specify the role that defensiveness might play in our model. Therefore, we must acknowledge that future research would benefit from applying multiple theoretical lenses to the dynamics of leader-member communication.

The current model also suffers from cultural biases. Indeed, our model does not explore culture differences in understandings of leadership or self-concept. Many researchers have advocated the importance of cultural difference in the relationship between leaders and members, especially the perception of political skills and the effectiveness of them (e.g., Littrell, 2002; Pillai, Scandura, & Williams, 1999). Accordingly, this western conceptualization may prevent generalizing this model to global organizations. For this reason, future studies employing our framework would benefit from either testing its cultural boundaries or better specifying its cultural limitations.

SUMMARY

In this chapter, we expanded on the framework of relational leadership theory (Uhl-Bien, 2006) by integrating the concepts of influence and control. Specifically, we attempted to depict the mechanisms through which communication processes operate within the relational leadership context to ultimately impact relational quality. The proposed conceptualization is unique in that we introduce the self as a socially constructed relational entity, consider the role of both subordinates and leaders, and chart the communication process over time.

First, we reviewed the literature on relational leadership, especially focusing on the recent work of Uhl-Bien. We then introduced political skill as a mechanism for relational control and argued that the political skills of both subordinates and leaders act as important moderating factors within the relational leadership process. Aspects of dyadic distance and individual affect were also integrated to better understand the development of relational leadership. This chapter concluded with theoretical, methodological, and practical implications that we hope will fuel future research in this evolving area of discovery.

REFERENCES

Abell, E. & Simons, S. (2000). How much can you bend before you break: An experience of using constructionist consulting as a tool for organizational learning in the corporate world. *European Journal of Work and Organizational Psychology, 9,* 159–175.

Abraham, J. D., & Hansson, R. O. (1996). Gender differences in the usefulness of goal-directed coping for middle age and older workers. *Journal of Applied Social Psychology, 26,* 657–669.

Ahearn, K.K., Ferris, G.R., Hochwarter, W.A., Douglas, C., & Ammeter, A.P. (2004). Leader political skill and team performance. *Journal of Management, 30,* 309–327.

Ammeter, A.P., Douglas, C., Gardner, W.L., Hochwarter, W.A., & Ferris, G.R. (2002). Toward a political theory of leadership. *The Leadership Quarterly, 13,* 751–796.

Andersen, S., & Chen, S. (2002). The relational self: An interpersonal social-cognitive theory. *Psychological Review, 4,* 619–645.

Aquino, K. & Thau, S. (2008). Workplace victimization: Aggression from the target's perspective. *Annual Review of Psychology, 60,* 717–741.

Balkundi, P., & Harrison, D.A. (2006). Ties, leaders, and time in teams: Strong inference about network structure's effects on team viability and performance. *Academy of Management Journal, 49,* 49–68.

Balkundi, P., & Kilduff, M. (2005). The ties that lead: A social network approach to leadership. *The Leadership Quarterly, 16,* 941–961.

Baltes, P.B., & Baltes, M. M. (1990). Psychological perspectives on successful aging: The model of selective optimization with compensation. In P.B. Baltes, & M.M. Baltes (Eds.), *Successful aging: Perspectives from the behavioral sciences* (pp. 1–34). New York, NY: Cambridge University Press.

Barreto, M., & Ellemers, N. (2000). You can't always do what you want: Social identity and self-presentational determinants of the choice to work for a low status group. *Personality and Social Psychology Bulletin, 26,* 891–906.

Bateson, G.S. (1958). *Naven.* Palo Alto, CA: Stanford University Press.

Bauer, T. N., & Green, S.G. (1996). Development of leader-member exchange: A longitudinal test. *Academy of Management Journal, 39,* 1538–1567.

Baumeister, R.F., DeWall, C.N., Ciarocco, N.J., & Tweenge, J.M. (2005). Social exclusion impairs self-regulation. *Journal of Personality and Social Psychology, 88,* 589–604.

Baumeister, R.F., Heatherton, T. F., & Tice, D. M. (1993). When ego threats lead to self-regulation failure: Negative consequences of high self-esteem. *Journal of Personality and Social Psychology, 64,* 141–156.

Blass, F.R., & Ferris, G.R. (2007). Leader reputation: The roles of mentoring, political skill, contextual learning, and adaptation. *Human Resource Management, 46,* 5–19.

Berscheid, E. (1999). The greening of relationship science. *American Psychologist, 54,* 260–266.

Bradbury, T.N. (2002). Invited program overview: Research on relationships as a prelude to action. *Journal of Social and Personal Relationships, 19,* 571–599.

Bradbury, H., & Lichtenstein, B. (2000). Relationality in organizational research: Exploring the space between. *Organization Science, 11,* 551–564.

Breland, J.W., Treadway, D.C., Duke, A.B., & Adams, G. L. (2007). The interactive effect of leader-member exchange and political skill on subjective career success. *Journal of Leadership & Organizational Studies, 13,* 1–14.

Brewer, M. B., & Gardner, W. (1996). Who is this 'We'? Levels of collective identity and self representations. *Journal of Personality and Social Psychology, 71,* 83–93.

Brouer, R. L., Duke, A., Treadway, D. C., & Ferris, G. R. (2009). The moderating effect of political skill on the demographic dissimilarity— leader-member exchange quality relationship. *The Leadership Quarterly, 20,* 61–69.

Brower, H. H., Schoorman, F.D., & Tan, H. H., (2000). A model of relational leadership: The integration of trust and leader-member exchange. *The Leadership Quarterly, 11,* 227–250.

Burgoon, J.K., & Dunbar, N.E. (2000). An integrationist perspective on dominance-submission: Interpersonal dominance as a dynamic, situationally contingent social skill. *Communication Monographs, 67,* 96–121.

Burgoon, J. K., Johnson, M. L., & Koch, P. T. (1998). The nature and measurement of interpersonal dominance. *Communication Monographs, 65,* 308–335.

Burton, J. P., & Hoobler, J. M. (2006). Subordinate self-esteem and abusive supervision. *Journal of Managerial Issues, 18,* 340–355.

Byrne, D. (1971). *The attraction paradigm.* New York, NY: Academic Press.

Carstensen, L. L, & Lang, F. R. (1996). *Future time perspective scale.* Unpublished manuscript.

Dachler, H. (1992). Management and leadership as relational phenomena. In M.V. Cranach, W. Doise, & G. Mugny (Eds.), *Social representations and social bases of knowledge* (pp.169–178). Lewiston, NY: Hogrefe and Huber.

Darley, J., & Fazio, R. (1980). Expectancy confirmation processes arising in the social interaction sequence. *American Psychologist, 35,* 867–881.

Dienesch, R.M., & Liden, R.C. (1986). Leader-member exchange model of leadership: A critique and further development. *Academy of Management Review, 11,* 618–634.

Doherty, K., & Schlenker, B. R. (1991). Self-consciousness and strategic self-presentation. *Journal of Personality, 59,* 1–18.

Douglas, C., & Ammeter, A. P. (2004). An examination of leader political skill and its effect on ratings of leader effectiveness. *The Leadership Quarterly, 15,* 537–550.

Duck, S. (1988). *Relating to others.* Chicago, IL: Dorsey.

Dulebohn, J. H., Murray, B., & Ferris, G. R. (2004). The vicious and virtuous cycles of influence tactics and performance evaluation outcomes. *Organizational Analysis, 12,* 53–74.

Edmondson, A. C., & McManus, S. E. (2007). Methodological fit in management field research. *Academy of Management Review, 32,* 1155–1179.

Ellis, D. G. (1976). *An analysis of relational communication in ongoing group systems.* Unpublished doctoral dissertation, University of Utah.

Epitropaki, O., & Martin, R. (1999). The impact of relational demography on the quality of leader-member exchanges (LMX) and employees' work attitudes and well being. *Journal of Occupational and Organizational Psychology, 72,* 237–240.

Fairhurst, G.T. (1993). The leader-member exchange patterns of women leaders in industry: A discourse analysis. *Communication Monographs, 60,* 321–351.

Falbe, C. M., & Yukl, G. (1992). Consequences for managers of using single influence tactics and combinations of tactics. *Academy of Management Journal, 35,* 638–652.

Farmer, S. M., Maslyn, J. M., Fedor, D. E., & Goodman, J. S.(1997). Putting upward influence strategies in context. *Journal of Organizational Behavior, 18,* 17–42.

Ferris, G. R., Davidson, S. L., & Perrewé, P. L. (2005). *Political skill at work: Impact on work effectiveness.* Mountain View, CA: Davies-Black Publishing.

Ferris, G. R., Hochwarter, W. A., Douglas, C., Blass, R., Kolodinsky, R. W., & Treadway, D. C. (2002). Social influence processes in organizations and human resources systems. In G. R. Ferris, & J. J. Martocchio (Eds.), *Research in personnel and human resources management* (Vol. 21, pp. 65–127). Oxford, England, UK: JAI Press/Elsevier Science.

Ferris, G. R., Perrewé, P. L., & Douglas, C. (2002). Social effectiveness in organizations: Construct validity and research directions. *Journal of Leadership and Organizational Studies, 9,* 49–63.

Ferris, G. R., & Rowland, K. M. (1985). Physical design implications for the performance evaluation process. *Nursing Administration Quarterly, 9,* 55–63.

Ferris, G. R., Treadway, D. C., Perrewé, P. L, Brouer, R. L., Douglas, C., & Lux, S. (2007). Political skill in organizations. *Journal of Management, 33,* 290–320.

Ferris, G. R., Treadway, D. C., Kolodinsky, R.W., Hochwarter, W. A., Kacmar, C. J., Douglas, C., & Frink, D. D. (2005). Development and validation of the political skill inventory. *Journal of Management, 31,* 126–152.

Fletcher, J. K. (2007). Leadership, power, and positive relationships. In J. E. Dutton, & B. R. Ragins (Eds.), *Exploring positive relationships at work* (pp. 347–372). Mahwah, NJ: Lawrence Erlbaum.

Frink, D. D., & Ferris, G. R. (1998). Accountability, impression management, and goal setting in the performance evaluation process. *Human Relations, 51,* 1259–1283.

Gardner, W. L., Avolio, B. J., Luthans, F., May, D.R., & Walumba, F. (2005). "Can you see the real me?" A self-based model of authentic leader and follower development. *The Leadership Quarterly, 16,* 343–372.

George, J. M., & Jones, G. R. (2000). The role of time in theory and theory building. *Journal of Management, 26,* 657–684.

Goffman, E. (1959). *The presentation of self in everyday life.* New York, NY: Anchor.

Graen, G. B. (1976). Role making processes within complex organizations. In M.D. Dunnette (Ed.), *Handbook of industrial and organizational psychology* (pp. 1201–1245). Chicago, IL: Rand-McNally.

Graen, G. B., & Uhl-Bien, M. (1995). Relationship-based approach to leadership: Development of leader-member exchange (LMX) theory of leadership over 25 years: Applying a multi-level multi-domain perspective. *The Leadership Quarterly, 6,* 219–247.

Harris, K. J., Kacmar, K. M., Zivnuska, S., & Shaw, J. D. (2007). The impact on political skill on impression management effectiveness. *Journal of Applied Psychology, 92,* 278–285.

Harter, S., Waters, P., & Whitesell, N. R. (1998). Relational self-worth: Differences in perceived worth as a person across interpersonal contexts among adolescents. *Child Development, 69,* 756–766.

Harvey, P., Harris, R. B., Harris, K. J., & Wheeler, A. R. (2007). Attenuating the effects of social stress: The impact of political skill. *Journal of Occupational Health Psychology, 12,* 105–115.

Heider, F. (1958). *The psychology of interpersonal relations.* New York, NY: John Wiley and Sons.

Heatherington, L., & Friedlander, M. L. (1990). Complementarity and symmetry in family therapy communication. *Journal of Counseling Psychology, 37,* 261–268.

Higgins, C. A., Judge, T. A., & Ferris, G. R. (2003). Influence tactics and work outcomes: A meta-analysis. *Journal of Organizational Behavior, 24,* 89–106.

Hobfoll, S. E. (1989). Conservation of resources: A new attempt at conceptualizing stress. *American Psychologist, 44,* 513–524.

Homans, G. (1951). *The human group.* New York, NY: Harcourt/Brace.

Hosking, D. (1988). Organizing, leadership, and skilful processes. *Journal of Management Studies, 25,* 147–166.

Hosking, D. (2006). Not leaders, not followers: A post-modern discourse of leadership processes. In B. Shamir, R. Pillai, M. Bligh, & M. Uhl-Bien (Eds.), *Follower-centered perspectives on leadership: A tribute to the memory of James R. Meindl.* Greenwich, CT: Information Age Publishing.

Hosking, D., Dachler, H., & Gergen, K. (Eds.). (1995). *Management and organization: Relational alternatives to individualism.* Brookfield, England: Avebury.

Hunt, J., & Dodge, G. (2000). Leadership déjà vu all over again. *The Leadership Quarterly, 11,* 435–458.

Jawahar, I. M., Meurs, J. A., Ferris, G. R., & Hochwarter, W. A. (2008). Self-efficacy and political skill as comparative predictors of task and contextual performance: A two-study constructive replication. *Human Performance, 21,* 1–20.

Jawahar, I. M., Stone, T. H., & Kisamore, J. L. (2007). Role conflict and burnout: The direct and moderating effects of political skill and perceived organizational support on burnout dimensions. *International Journal of Stress Management, 14,* 142–159.

Kacmar, K. M., Zivnuska, S., & White, C. D. (2007). Control and exchange: The impact of work environment on the work effort of low relationship quality employees. *The Leadership Quarterly, 18,* 69–84.

Kim, J., Kim, M.-S., Kam, K. Y., & Shin, H. C. (2003). Influence of self-construals on the perception of different self-presentation styles in Korea. *Asian Journal of Social Psychology, 6,* 89–101.

Kipnis, D., & Schmidt, S. M. (1988). Upward-influence styles: Relationship with performance evaluations, salary, and stress. *Administrative Science Quarterly, 33,* 528–542.

Kipnis, D., Schmidt, S. M., & Wilkinson, I. (1980). Intra-organizational influence tactics: Exploration of getting one's way. *Journal of Applied Psychology, 65,* 440–452.

Kivetz, Y., & Tyler, T. R. (2007). Tomorrow I'll be me: The effect of time perspective on the activation of idealistic versus pragmatic selves. *Organizational Behavior and Human Decision Processes, 102,* 193–211.

Kolodinsky, R.W., Treadway, D. C., & Ferris, G. R. (2007). Political skill and influence effectiveness: Testing portions of the expanded Ferris and Judge (1991) model. *Human Relations, 60,* 1747–1777.

Kramer, M.W. (2004). The complexity of communication in leader-member exchanges. In G.B. Graen (Ed.), *New frontiers of leadership* (pp. 167–189). Greenwich, CT: Information Age Publishing.

Lambird, K. H., & Mann, T. (2006). When do ego threats lead to self-regulation failure? Negative consequences of defensive high self-esteem. *Personality and Social Psychology Bulletin, 32,* 1177–1187.

Lankau, M. J., Riordan, C. M., & Thomas, C. H. (2005). The effects of similarity and liking in formal relationships between mentors and protégés. *Journal of Vocational Behavior, 67*, 252–265.

Liden, R. C., & Mitchell, T. R. (1988). Ingratiatory behaviors in organizational settings. *Academy of Management Review, 13*, 572–587.

Liden, R. C., Wayne, S. J., & Stillwell, D. (1993). A longitudinal study on the early development of leader-member exchanges. *Journal of Applied Psychology, 78*, 662–674.

Littrell, R. F. (2002). Desirable leadership behaviours of multi-cultural managers in China. *Journal of Management Development, 21*, 5- 74.

Lord, R., Brown, D., & Freiberg, S. (1999). Understanding the dynamics of leadership: The role of follower self-concepts in the leader/follower relationship. *Organizational Behavior and Human Decision Processes, 78*, 1–37.

Markus, H., & Nurius, P. (1986). Possible selves. *American Psychologist, 41*, 954–969.

Mayes, B. T., & Allen, R. W. (1977). Toward a definition of organizational politics. Academy of Management Review, 2, 672–678.

Mead, G. H. (1934). *Mind, self, and society from the standpoint of a social behaviorist.* Chicago, IL: University of Chicago Press.

Mintzberg, H. (1983). *Power in and around organizations.* Englewood Cliffs, NJ: Prentice Hall.

Napier, B., & Ferris, G. (1993). Distance in organizations. *Human Resource Management Review, 3*, 321–357.

Osborn, R., Hunt, J., & Jauch, L. (2002). Toward a contextual theory of leadership. The *Leadership Quarterly, 13*, 797–837.

Parasuraman, S., & Greenhaus, J. H. (2002). Toward reducing some critical gaps in work-family research. *Human Resource Management Review, 12*, 299–312.

Perrewé, P. L, Zellars, K. L., Rossi, A. M., Ferris, G. R., Kacmar, C .J., Liu, Y., Zinko, R., & Hochwarter, W. A. (2005). Political skill: An antidote in the role overload-strain relationship. *Journal of Organizational and Occupational Health Psychology, 10*, 239–250.

Perrewé, P. L., Zellars, K. L., Ferris, G. R., Rossi, A. M., Kacmar, C. J., & Ralston, D. A. (2004). Neutralizing job stressors: Political skill as an antidote to the dysfunctional consequences of role conflict stressors. *Academy of Management Journal, 47(1)*, 141–152.

Pfeffer, J. (1981). *Power in organizations.* Boston, MA: Pitman.

Pillai, R., Scandura, T. A., & Williams, E. A. (1999). Leadership and organizational justice: Similarities and differences across cultures. *Journal of International Business Studies, 30*, 763–779.

Porter, M. E. (1996). What is strategy? *Harvard Business Review, 74*, 61–81.

Ragins, B. R. (1997). Diversified mentoring relationships in organizations: A power perspective. *Academy of Management Review, 22*, 482–521.

Ragins, B. R., & Dutton, J. E. (2007). Positive relationships at work: An introduction and invitation. In J. E. Dutton & B. R. Ragins (Eds.), *Exploring positive relationships at work: Building a theoretical and research foundation* (pp. 3–25). Mahwah, NJ: Lawrence Erlbaum.

Raudenbush, S. W., & Bryk, A. S. (2002). *Hierarchical linear models: Applications and data analysis methods.* Thousand Oaks, CA: Sage.

Rothaus, P., Morton, R., & Hanson, P. (1965). Performance appraisal and psychological distance. *Journal of Applied Psychology, 49,* 48–54.

Rousseau, D. M., & Fried, Y. (2001). Location, location, location: Contextualizing organizational research. *Journal of Organizational Behavior, 22,* 1–13.

Rudman, L. A., Greenwald, A. G., Mellott, D. S., & McGhee, D. E. (1999). Measuring the automatic components of prejudice: Flexibility and generality of the implicit association test. *Social Cognition, 17,* 437–465.

Sabourin, T. C. (1995). The role of negative reciprocity in spouse abuse: A relational control analysis. *Journal of Applied Communication Research, 23,* 271–283.

Semadar, A., Robins, G., & Ferris, G. R. (2006). Comparing the effects of multiple social effectiveness constructs in prediction of managerial performance. *Journal of Organizational Behavior, 27,* 443–461.

Smith, S. M., Norrell, J. H., & Saint, J. L. (1996). Self-esteem and reactions to ego threat: A (battle) field investigation. *Basic and Applied Social Psychology, 18,* 395–404.

Solomon, C. R., & Serres, S. (1999). Effects of parental verbal aggression on children's self-esteem and school marks. *Child Abuse and Neglect, 23,* 339–351.

Sparrowe, R. T., Soetjipto, B.W., & Kraimer, M.L. (2006). Do leaders' influence tactics relate to members' helping behavior? It depends on the quality of the relationship. *Academy of Management Journal, 49,* 1194–1208.

Sundstrom, E., Burt, R., & Kamp, P. (1980). Privacy at work: Architectural correlates of job satisfaction and job performance. *Academy of Management Journal, 23,* 101–117.

Swann, W. B., Jr. (2005). The self and identity negotiation. *Interaction Studies, 6,* 69–83.

Tedeschi, J. T. (1990). Self-presentation and social influence: An interactionist perspective. In M. J. Cody & M.L. McLaughlin (Eds.), *The psychology of tactical communication* (pp. 301–323). Clevedon, England: Multilingual Matters.

Treadway, D. C., Ferris, G. R., Duke, A. B., Adams, G. A., & Thatcher, J. B. (2007). The moderating role of subordinate political skill on supervisors' impressions of subordinate ingratiation and ratings of subordinate interpersonal facilitation. *Journal of Applied Psychology, 92,* 848–855.

Treadway, D. C., Hochwarter, W. A., Ferris, G. R., Kacmar, C. J., Douglas, C., Ammeter, A. P., & Buckley, M. R. (2004). Leader political skill and employee reactions. *Leadership Quarterly, 15,* 493–513.

Treadway, D. C., Hochwarter, W. A., Kacmar, C. J., & Ferris, G. R. (2005). Political will, political skill, and political behavior. *Journal of Organizational Behavior, 26,* 229–245.

Triandis, H. (1959). Cognitive similarity and interpersonal communication in industry. *Journal of Applied Psychology, 43,* 321–326.

Triandis, H. (1960). Cognitive similarity and communication in a dyad. *Human Relations, 13,* 175–183.

Tsui, A. S., Egan, T. D., & O'Reilly, C. A. (1992). Being relationally different: Relational demography and organizational attachment. *Administrative Science Quarterly, 37,* 549–579.

Tsui, A. S., & O'Reilly, C. A. (1989). Beyond simple demographic effects: The importance of relational demography in superior-subordinate dyads. *Academy of Management Journal, 32,* 402–423.

Tullar, W. L. (1989). Relational control in the employment interview. *Journal of Applied Psychology, 74,* 971–977.

Tunnell, G. (1984). The discrepancy between private and public selves: Public self consciousness and its correlates. *Journal of Personality Assessment, 48,* 549–555.

Turban, D., & Jones, A. Supervisor-subordinate similarity: Types, effects, and mechanisms. *Journal of Applied Psychology, 73,* 228–234.

Uhl-Bien, M. (2006). Relational leadership theory: Exploring the social processes of leadership and organizing. *The Leadership Quarterly, 17,* 654–676.

van Knippenberg, D., van Knippenberg, B., De Cremer, D., & Hogg, M. A. (2004). Leadership, self, and identity: A review and research agenda. *Leadership Quarterly, 15,* 825–856.

Vanlear, C., & Zeitlow, P. (1990). Toward a contingency approach to marital interaction: An empirical investigation of three approaches. *Communication Monographs, 57,* 202–218.

Vecchio, R., & Bullis, R. (2001). Moderators of the influence of supervisor-subordinate similarity on subordinate outcomes. *Journal of Applied Psychology, 86,* 884–896.

Vohs, K. D., Baumeister, R. F., Ciarocco, N. J. (2005). Self-regulation and self-presentation: Regulatory resource depletion impairs impression management and effortful self-presentation depletes regulatory resources. *Journal of Personality and Social Psychology, 88,* 632–657.

Watson, K. M. (1982). An analysis of communication patterns: A method for discriminating leader and subordinate roles. *Academy of Management Journal, 25,* 107–120.

Wayne, S. J., & Ferris, G. R. (1990). Influence tactics, affect, and exchange quality in supervisor-subordinate interactions: A laboratory experiment and field study. *Journal of Applied Psychology, 75,* 487–499.

Xanthopoulou, D., Bakker, A. B., Demerouti, E., & Shaufeli, W.B. (2007). The role of personal resources in the job demands-resources model. *International Journal of Stress Management, 14,* 121–141.

Yukl, G., & Tracey, J. B. (1992). Consequences of influence tactics used with subordinates, peers, and the boss. *Journal of Applied Psychology, 77,* 525–535.

Zajonc, R. B. (1980). Feeling and thinking: Preferences need no inferences. *American Psychologist, 35,* 151–175.

Zietlow, P. H., VanLear, C. A. (1991). Marriage duration and relational control: A study of developmental patterns. *Journal of Marriage and Family, 53,* 773–785.

CHAPTER 14

SHARED LEADERSHIP 2.0

A Glimpse into the State of the Field

Christina L. Wassenaar and Craig L. Pearce

In the past, the primary focal point of the study of leadership has been on single leaders at the top of organizations or teams: Their relationships to their followers, their styles of control, how productive groups are under their guidance, as well as various other individual, group, and organizational outcomes (Bass & Bass, 2008). Lately, there has been a movement away from simply focusing on the leader to an increased interest in understanding those around the leader (Pearce, 2008; Wassenaar, Pearce, Hoch, & Wegge, 2010; Yukl, 2002), the followers (Riggio, Chaleff & Lipman-Blumen, 2008; Uhl-Bien & Pillai, 2007), and how they interact with the leader and each other. This has opened a new avenue for conceptualizing leadership beyond that of a simple hierarchical role. Uhl-Bien (2006) points out that some of the key questions which will become part of the future research in leadership will be: "How are leadership relationships produced?" and just as importantly, "How do people work together to define their relationship?" It is these questions, and others, which will allow a more complete understanding of leadership and how it can continue to be a source of organizational strength and vigor.

Advancing Relational Leadership Research, pages 421–432
Copyright © 2012 by Information Age Publishing
All rights of reproduction in any form reserved.

421

Relational leadership theory articulates a perspective on leadership that is focused on the social processes of leadership (Brower, Schoorman & Tan, 2000; Ospina & Sorenson, 2006; Uhl-Bien, 2006). Uhl-Bien (2006) describes the leader-member exchange theory (LMX) that is perhaps the best known of the relational based approaches to leadership (Gerstner & Day, 1997; Graen, Novak, & Sommerkamp, 1982; Graen & Uhl-Bien, 1995; Liden, Sparrow, & Wayne, 1997). However, even with the value on relationships which LMX offers, it is still only in its infancy when it comes to the empirical research on how relationships are actually formed in organizations (Uhl-Bien, 2006).

Shared leadership is an interactive and dynamic social influence process that individuals on teams or in groups use to influence each other to achieve a stated goal or objective (Pearce & Conger, 2003). Clearly, shared leadership theory and relational leadership theory occupy similar conceptual space. Accordingly, the purpose of this chapter is to review the empirical evidence on shared leadership: The research indicates that shared leadership has generally positive effects on organizational outcomes such as group attitudes, behavior, cognition, and performance. Emerging research is also pointing to several antecedents of shared leadership (Pearce, 2008).

EVIDENCE ON SHARED LEADERSHIP

Recently, there has been an uptick in the study of shared leadership, including its antecedents and outcomes. The research that has been done suggests there are several antecedents that can facilitate the occurrence of shared leadership, as well as several outcome variables that are affected by shared leadership (e.g., Pearce & Sims, 2002) across a wide variety of contextual settings—ranging from nursing to research and development, to blue collar manufacturing, to white collar virtual teams, and even up to the ranks of executive top management teams. Having said that, there is still a large amount of work that needs to be done to further understand the role of shared leadership in organizational systems.

Shared Leadership and its Antecedents

There have been at least 11 studies that have identified 15 potential antecedents of shared leadership. Trust, for instance, has long been thought an important ingredient that facilitates smooth social interaction (Dirks & Ferrin, 2002). Thus, not surprisingly, George et al. (2002) found that trust in the hierarchical leader was related to the development of shared leadership in nursing teams. Similarly, Olsen-Sanders (2006), in a study of 502 members of 51 cross-functional R & D teams, found that vertical leadership was significantly related to the development of shared leadership. While trust in the hierarchical leader seems like an important component for the development of shared leadership, Elloy (2008), in a study of 141 employees of a non-union paper mill, found that providing team training, encouraging team communication, and allowing team members latitude in decision making were also important facilitators of shared leadership.

While the previous three studies were quantitative in nature, several in-depth qualitative studies have also been conducted. For example, building on previous work on psychological flow (Csikszentmihalyi, 1990) at the individual level of analysis, Hooker and Csikszentmihalyi (2003) conducted a qualitative study of flow at the group level of analysis in research and development laboratories. In their study, they concluded that flow and shared leadership were inextricably linked, and they identified six hierarchical leader behaviors positively related to the development of shared leadership: (1) valuing excellence; (2) providing clear goals; (3) giving timely feedback; (4) matching challenges and skills; (5) diminishing distractions; and (6) creating freedom.

As the majority of the studies of shared leadership have been conducted in North America, we need to question whether the phenomenon translates across cultural settings. Pearce (2008) argued that it does, however, he speculated that its enactment would be culturally specific. Partially addressing this issue, Shamir and Lapidot (2003), in a qualitative study of the Israeli Defense Forces, first concluded that alignment between leaders and followers facilitates the development of shared leadership. Similar to George et al. (2002), they also found that trust in, and satisfaction with, hierarchical leaders was positively related to the degree that shared leadership existed in military units.

Executive coaching has recently been receiving considerable attention in the academic literature, as well as the practitioner press (Bono, Purvanova, Towler, & Peterson, 2009; Elmhirst, 2008; Leonard, 2003). It is touted as a prerequisite for both leader and team success; yet, empirical examinations of coaching are scant, particularly when it comes to teams. To address this gap, especially in regards to shared leadership, Carson, Tesluk and Marrone (2007), in a sample of 59 consulting teams, found that coaching was positively related to the display of shared leadership. They also found what they labeled as "internal environment" to be associated with shared leadership.

There is a long line of the examination of similarities and differences between male and female leaders (Paris, Howell, Dorfman, & Hanges, 2009). The majority of this research suggests that female leaders tend to be more nurturing than their male counterparts. As such, we might speculate that female leaders, on average, have an advantage when it comes to the development of shared leadership. In fact, this is exactly what Konu and Viitanen

(2008) found in a study of 433 mid-level Finnish health care managers. Interestingly, they also discovered that shared leadership is more closely linked to the functional area in which the team's activity takes place, rather than a particular professional background.

Religion is another important domain for the study of leadership. For instance, a recent Gallup poll (Gallup, 2008) found that 65% of respondents in North America reported that religion is an important part of their daily life. Additionally, the traditional religious model of leadership entails considerable deference to authority. Because of this historically more vertical model, an important question for consideration is whether shared leadership can occur or be developed in this generally hierarchical context. Wood (2005) addressed this issue in a study of 200 participants in church top management teams and found that the answer is "yes." He found that the development of shared leadership in a team was, to a large extent, dependent on the increased perceptions of empowerment as experienced by the team members.

Much of our world has moved into the virtual realm. As such, virtual teams have become a ubiquitous part of the organizational landscape (Wassenaar et al., 2010). The question, however, remains as to whether and how shared leadership can be developed in such teams. Not surprisingly, and partially addressing this question, Balthazard, Waldman, Howell, and Atwater (2004) found that face-to-face teams were more likely to demonstrate higher levels of shared leadership than were virtual teams.

More recently, Cordery, Soo, Kirkman, Rosen, and Mathieu (2009) found that support structures, both technological and social, were critical to the development of sustained shared leadership in virtual teams. Finally, the question remains as to whether shared leadership can be developed across organizational lines and shared more broadly across stakeholder groups. In this vein, Ropo and Sauer (2003), in a longitudinal qualitative study of orchestras, found relationship longevity to be an important predictor of the development of shared leadership between orchestra leaders, members, sponsors, and other outside constituents. In sum, in research both qualitative and quantitative, across a broad variety of organizational and cultural contexts, it is clear from the initial research that there are identifiable causes, or antecedents, which, solely or combined with other variables, result in the development of shared leadership in groups. Next, we examine the potential outcomes of shared leadership.

Shared Leadership and Outcomes

At least 23 studies have identified at least 32 potential outcome variables of shared leadership. Naturally, some of the 23 studies identified multiple outcome variables, and several studies evaluated similar variables with comparable results.

Attitudes and Cognition

Attitudes and cognition have long been important outcome variables in organizational behavior research in general (e.g., Petty, McGee, & Cavender, 1984; Judge, Piccolo, Podsakoff, Shaw, & Rich, 2010) and in leadership research in particular at both the individual (Bandura, 1986) and group (Gully, Incalcaterra, Joshi, & Beaubien, 2002) levels of analysis. As such, the effect of shared leadership on attitudes and cognition are important areas of consideration. We identified 10 studies that examined 15 potential attitudinal and cognitive outcomes of shared leadership.

Satisfaction is perhaps the most widely researched attitudinal variable in organizational behavior (e.g., Cranny, Smith, & Stone, 1992) and two of the studies specifically examined the effects of shared leadership on satisfaction. First, in a study of undergraduate project teams (Avolio, Jung, Murray, & Sivasubramaniam, 1996), team member satisfaction was found to be strongly related to shared leadership. Second, Shamir and Lapidot (2003), in a study of shared leadership in the context of the Israeli military officer training, found that shared leadership was positively related to satisfaction with, as well as trust in, hierarchical leaders.

Cohesion has also occupied a prominent role in organizational behavior research (e.g., Evans & Dion, 1991). Along this line, Balthazard et al. (2004) found shared leadership to positively predict group cohesion. Confidence at the individual level (e.g., Bandura, 1986; Locke & Latham, 1990) or at the group level (e.g., Guzzo, Yost, Campbell, & Shea, 1993) has also become an important variable of study. For example, Hooker and Csikszentmihalyi (2003) found shared leadership to be positively related to lab members' confidence in ability to perform, as well as their sense of value, understanding of the research context, sense of autonomy, and sense of flow.

Beyond the face-to-face teams Pearce, Yoo and Alavi (2004), in a study of 28 virtual teams, found that, controlling for team size and vertical leadership, shared leadership was positively related to team potency. Concordantly, the Pearce (1997) study on change management teams found that shared leadership was a strong predictor of potency. George et al. (2002) also found on a more micro-level that shared leadership is directly related to follower self-efficacy. As such, shared leadership appears to be predictive of positive group attitudes, as well as cognitive outcomes.

Behavior

While the effect of shared leadership on attitudes and cognition is important, the translation to actual behavior is perhaps more important. As a dramatic example, it is not a crime to think about stealing, but it is indeed a crime to steal. Seven studies shed light on 10 behavioral outcomes of shared leadership. First, Hooker and Csikszentmihalyi (2003) found mimetic effects of shared leadership behavior in R&D laboratories. In other words, as followers learned shared leadership in the original laboratory from the initial lead scientist, they mimicked those behaviors and created favorable conditions for the development of shared leadership in their own laboratories, similar to the "falling dominoes effect" noted by Bass, Waldman, Avolio and Bebb (1987) for transformational leadership. Similarly, Balthazard et al. (2004) also found shared leadership was positively predictive of a constructive interaction style and negatively associated with a defensive interaction style. Moreover, Klein, Zeigert, Knight and Xiao (2006), in a qualitative study measuring shared leadership in an emergency trauma center found that, when vertical leaders shared leadership, the skill development of junior staff was positively affected. Klein et al. (2006), also found shared leadership to be positively related to swift coordination of activities and higher performance reliability.

Another important behavioral variable in organizational behavior research is organizational citizenship behavior (e.g., Organ, 1988), and leadership has been found to be an important predictor (e.g., Pearce & Herbik, 2004). Moving to the shared leadership level of analysis, Pearce (1997) found shared leadership to be predictive of team citizenship behavior and team networking behavior. Similarly, Pearce et al. (2004), found that, controlling for team size and vertical leadership, shared leadership was positively related to social integration. Moreover, Khourey-Bowers, Dinko and Hart (2005), in a study of 216 educators in 17 school districts who were part of a change management plan, found that shared leadership facilitated information exchange among teachers.

Solansky (2008) found that, in a quantitative laboratory study of 20 work teams with an average size of four, teams with shared leadership had higher levels of motivation and cognitive advantage over the teams that used a more traditional vertical leader model. Similarly, Olson-Sanders (2006), in a study of 502 members of 51 cross-functional Research and Development teams, found that shared leadership is positively associated with team performing orientation, as opposed to a learning orientation. Finally, Rodríguez (2005) found, in a study of 32 U.S. and Mexico strategic alliances, that shared leadership can facilitate the development of intercultural fit. As such, shared leadership appears as an important predictor of behavioral outcomes.

Effectiveness

The ultimate outcome in organizational behavior, as well as leadership research, is effectiveness or performance (Luthans, 2001). Nine studies have identified 10 effectiveness outcomes of shared leadership, and the results generally appear positive. For example, Pearce and Sims (2002) found that shared leadership, relative to vertical leadership, was a more useful predictor of team effectiveness in 71 change management teams from the point of view of managers, internal customers, and team members. Similarly, Olson-Sanders (2006) found that shared leadership was positively linked with R&D team effectiveness. In the same vein, Carson et al. (2007) found that shared leadership predicted consulting team performance and Avolio et al. (1996) found shared leadership to be appreciably related to group members' self-ratings of effectiveness.

Moving to the virtual team arena, Carte, Chidambaram, and Becker (2006), in a study of 22 virtual teams, also found shared leadership to be a significant predictor of team performance. Moreover, Pearce et al. (2004) found that, controlling for team size and vertical leadership, shared leadership was positively related to problem-solving quality and an increased perception of task effectiveness.

Perhaps most importantly, one should consider the effects of shared leadership at the organizational level of analysis. Here, three studies help to shed some light. First, O'Toole, Galbraith, and Lawler (2003), in a qualitative study of shared leadership at the top of organizations, concluded that shared leadership has generally positive effects on company performance. Of the 25 firms they studied, 17 experienced positive effects, while eight experienced negative effects.

Even more significantly, Ensley, Hmieleski, and Pearce (2006) conducted a two-sample quantitative study of shared leadership in top management teams. Their first sample was drawn from the Inc. 500—the fastest growing, privately held firms in the United States, as identified by *Inc.* magazine. The second sample was a random national sample of firms drawn from Dun & Bradstreet's market identifiers database. In both samples, they found that, controlling for CEO leader behavior, shared leadership predicted financial performance of firms.

In sum, shared leadership appears to be an important predictor of several outcome variables that span attitudinal, behavioral, cognitive, and effectiveness outcomes. In the following section, we speculate on the future of leadership in organizations.

THE FUTURE OF LEADERSHIP IN ORGANIZATIONS

Developing an environment of true shared leadership is challenging. That said, we believe most people are capable of being both leaders and followers and that relational approaches to leadership, those that foster *relationships*, instead of those that simply are based on dominance, historical hierarchical models, or traditional authority (Ospina & Sorenson, 2006; Uhl-Bien, 2006), are an organizational imperative and are integral to the formation of new leadership approaches for the age of knowledge work (Pearce, 2010). Although there are circumstances where shared leadership approaches might not work, the research demonstrates that shared leadership can positively affect a group's attitudes, cognition, behavior, and effectiveness.

Understanding all of this still doesn't ensure that shared leadership is the correct path for all. For instance, it might not be appropriate for certain tasks. Organizational members need to be open to the idea or concept of sharing leadership if it is to succeed. Some of the resistance to the development of shared leadership can be cultural (Pearce, 2008) or based on industrial norms and values. Or perhaps if, as we have briefly noted, there is a lack of understanding of the merit of relationships and their dynamics, of how certain social interactions build influence, the ability for each group member or leader to contribute value will be lessened and will result in a more traditional, top-down and autocratic dyadic interrelation (Uhl-Bien, 2006). As an example, the individual or societal attribute of power distance can affect how likely group members are to embrace the concept of shared leadership: People who are from cultures high in power distance (Hofstede, 1980) are far more unlikely to be able to easily grasp the notion of shared leadership; yet, this is something that would benefit from future research.

Also, shared leadership will not work if those in the group simply don't know how to do the tasks required of them. This might be the case for various reasons, such as newness to the project, educational level, and even the degree of member motivation. The research has clearly begun to demonstrate that a key component of shared leadership implementation in groups is fostered by trust in peer group members. A major component of the development of trust is the demonstration of expertise and contribution by each member of the group. These are clearly just a few of the possible limitations to the development of shared leadership, and they also demonstrate that this type of leadership, as well as those that are interrelated and complimentary, such as relational and connective theories, require far more research, not only on their outcomes, but also on their antecedents and moderators. As this research continues to expand our knowledge of how people interact and build new forms of influence, the results of these investigations will yield more insights for the organizations of tomorrow.

REFERENCES

Avolio, B. J., Jung, D., Murray, W., & Sivasubramaniam, N. (1996). Building highly developed teams: Focusing on shared leadership process, efficacy, trust, and performance. In M. M. Beyerlein, D. A. Johnson, & S. T. Beyerlein (Eds.), *Advances in interdisciplinary studies of work teams* (pp. 173–209). Greenwich, CT: JAI Press.

Balthazard, P., Waldman, D., Howell, J., & Atwater, L. (2004). Shared leadership and group interaction styles in problem-solving virtual teams. *Proceedings of the annual Hawaii international conference on system sciences.* Conf. 37, (p. 43).

Bandura, A. (1986). *Social foundations of thought and action: A social cognitive theory.* Englewood Cliffs, NJ: Prentice Hall.

Bass, B. M., & Bass, R. (2008). *The Bass handbook of leadership: Theory, research, and managerial applications.* New York, NY: Simon & Schuster, Inc.

Bass, B. M., Waldman, D. A., Avolio, B. J., & Bebb, M. (1987). Transformational leadership and the falling dominos effect. *Group & Organization Studies, 12*(1), 73.

Bono, J., Purvanova, R., Towler, A., & Peterson, D. (2009). A survey of executive coaching practices. *Personnel Psychology, 62*(2), 361–404.

Brower, H. H., Schoorman, F. D., & Tan, H. H. (2000). A model of relational leadership: The integration of trust and leader-member exchange. *Leadership Quarterly, 11*(2), 227–250.

Carson, J., Tesluk, P., & Marrone, J. (2007). Shared leadership in teams: An investigation of antecedent conditions and performance. *Academy of Management Journal, 50*(5), 1217–1234.

Carte, T. A., Chidambaram, L., & Becker, A. (2006). Emergent leadership in self-managed virtual teams: A longitudinal study of concentrated and shared leadership behaviors. *Group Decision and Negotiation, 15*(4), 323–343.

Cordery, J., Soo, C., Kirkman, B., Rosen, B., & Mathieu, J. (2009). Leading parallel global virtual teams: Lessons from Alcoa. *Organizational Dynamics, 38*(3), 204–216.

Cranny, C. J., Smith, P. C., & Stone, E. F. (1992). *Job satisfaction: how people feel about their jobs and how it affects their performance.* Lexington, MA: Lexington Books.

Dirks, K. T., & Ferrin, D. L. (2002). Trust in leadership: Meta-analytic findings and implications for research and practice. *Journal of Applied Psychology, 87*(4), 611–628.

Elloy, D. F. (2008). The relationship between self-leadership behaviors and organization variables in a self-managed work team environment. *Management Research News, 31*(11), 801–810.

Elmhirst, K. (2008). Executive coaching. *Leadership Excellence, 25*(1), 11.

Ensley, M. D., Hmieleski, K. M., & Pearce, C. L. (2006). The importance of vertical and shared leadership within new venture top management teams: Implications for the performance of startups. *Leadership Quarterly, 17*(3), 217–231.

Evans, C.R., & Dion, K. L. (1991). Group cohesion and performance: A meta-analysis. *Small Group Research, 22*(2), 175–186.

Gallup. (2008). *State of the states:* Importance of religion. Retrieved from www.gallup.com/poll/114022/state-states-importance-religion.expx.

George, V., Burke, L. J., Rodgers, B., Duthie, N., Hoffmann, M. L., Koceja, V.... & Gehring, L. L. (2002). Developing staff nurse shared leadership behavior in professional nursing practice. *Nursing Administration Quarterly, 26*(3), 44–59.

Gerstner, C. R., & Day, D. V. (1997). Meta-analytic review of leader-member exchange theory: Correlates and construct issues. *Journal of Applied Psychology, 82*(6), 827–844.

Graen, G. B., Novak, M. A., & Sommerkamp, P. (1982). The effects of leader-member exchange and job design on productivity and satisfaction: Testing a dual attachment model. *Organizational Behavior and Human Performance, 30*(1), 109–131.

Graen, G. B., & Uhl-Bien, M. (1991). Toward a psychology of dyadic organizing. In B. B. Staw, & L. L. Cummings (Eds.), *Research in organizational behavior* (Vol. 9, pp. 175–208). Greenwich, CT: JAI Press.

Gully, S.M., Incalcaterra, K. A., Joshi, A., Beaubien, J. M., (2002). A meta-analysis of team-efficacy, potency, and performance: Interdependence and level of analysis as moderators of observed relationship. *Journal of Applied Psychology, 87*(5), 819–832.

Guzzo, R.A, Yost, P.R. Campbell, R.J., & Shea, G. P. (1993). Potency in groups: Articulating a construct. *British Journal of Social Psychology, 32*(1), 87–106.

Hofstede, G. (1980). *Culture's consequences: International difference in work related values.* Thousand Oaks, CA: Sage.

Hooker, C., & Csikszentmihalyi, M. (2003). Flow, creativity, and shared leadership: Rethinking the motivation and structuring of knowledge work. In C. L. Pearce, & J. A. Conger (Eds.), *Shared leadership: Reframing the hows and whys of leadership* (pp. 217–234). Thousand Oaks, CA: Sage.

Judge, T. A., Piccolo, R. F., Podsakoff, N. P., Shaw, J. C., & Rich, B. L. (2010). The relationship between pay and job satisfaction: A meta-analysis of the literature. *Journal of Vocational Behavior, 77*(2): 157–167.

Khourey-Bowers, C., Dinko, R. L., & Hart, R. G. (2005). Influence of a shared leadership model in creating a school culture of inquiry and collegiality. *Journal of Research in Science Teaching (42)*1, 3–24.

Klein, K. J., Zeigert, J. C., Knight, A. P., & Xiao, Y. (2006). Dynamic delegation: Shared, hierarchical, and deindividualized leadership in extreme action teams. *Administrative Science Quarterly (51)*4, 590.

Konu, A., & Viitanen. E., (2008). Shared leadership in Finnish social and health care. *Leadership in Health Services, 21*(1), 28–40.

Leonard, H. S. (2003). Leadership development as an intervention for organizational transformation. *Consulting Psychology Journal, 55*(1), 58–67.

Liden, R. C., Sparrowe, R. T., & Wayne, S. J. (1997). Leader-member exchange theory: The past and potential for the future. In G. R. Ferris (Ed.), *Research in personnel and human resource management* (pp.). New York, NY: McGraw-Hill.

Locke, E. A., & Latham, G. P. (1990). *A theory of goal-setting and task performance.* Englewood Cliffs, NJ: Prentice Hall.

Olson-Sanders, T. (2006). *Collectivity and influence: The nature of shared leadership and its relationship with team learning orientation, vertical leadership and team effectiveness.* (Ed.D. dissertation). Available from ABI/INFORM Global. (Publication No. AAT 3237041).

Organ, D. W. (1988). *Organizational citizenship behavior: The good soldier syndrome.* Lexington, MA: Lexington Books.

Ospina, S., & Sorenson, G. L. J. (2006). A constructionist lens on leadership: Charting new territory. In G. R. Goethals, & G. L. J. Sorenson (Eds.), *The quest for a general theory of leadership* (pp. 188–204). Cheltenham, England: Edward Elgar Publishing Limited.

O'Toole, J., Galbraith, J., & Lawler, III, E. E. (2003). The promise and pitfalls of shared leadership: When two (or more) heads are better than one. In C. L.

Pearce, & J. A. Conger (Eds.), *Shared leadership: Reframing the hows and whys of leadership* (pp. 217–234). Thousand Oaks, CA: Sage.

Paris, L., Howell, J., Dorfman, P., & Hanges, P. (2009). Preferred leadership prototypes of male and female leaders in 27 countries. *Journal of International Business Studies, 40*(8), 1396–1405.

Pearce, C. L. (1997). *The determinants of change management team (CMT) effectiveness: A longitudinal investigation.* (Unpublished doctoral dissertation). University of Maryland, College Park, MD.

Pearce, C. L. (2008, July 7). Follow the leaders. *The Wall Street Journal,* p. R8.

Pearce, C. L. (2010). Leading knowledge workers: Beyond the era of command and control. In C.L. Pearce, J. A. Maciariello, & H. Yamawaki (Eds.), *The Drucker difference* (pp. 35–46). New York, NY: McGraw-Hill.

Pearce, C. L., & Conger, J. A. (Eds.). (2003). *Shared Leadership: Reframing the hows and whys of leadership.* Thousand Oaks, CA: Sage.

Pearce, C. L., Conger, J. A., Locke, E. (2008). Shared leadership theory. *Leadership Quarterly, 19*(5), 622.

Pearce, C. L., & Herbick, P. A. (2004). Citizenship behavior at the team level of analysis: The role of team leader behavior, team dynamics, the team's environment, and team demography. *Journal of Social Psychology, 144*(3), 293–310.

Pearce, C. L., & Sims, Jr., H. P. (2002). Vertical versus shared leadership as predictors of the effectiveness of change management teams: An examination of aversive, directive, transactional, transformational, and empowering leader behaviors. *Group Dynamics, Theory, Research, and Practice 6*(2002), 172–197.

Pearce, C. L., Yoo, Y., & Alavi, M. (2004). Leadership, social work, and virtual teams: The relative influence of vertical versus shared leadership in the nonprofit sector. In R. E. Riggio, & S. Smith Orr (Eds.), *Improving leadership in nonprofit organizations* (pp. 160–203). San Francisco, CA: Jossey-Bass.

Petty, M.M., McGee, G.W., & Cavender, J.W. (1984). A meta-analysis of the relationships between individual job satisfaction and individual performance. *Academy of Management Review, 9*(4) 712–721.

Riggio, R.E., Chaleff, I., & Lipman-Blumen, J. (Eds.). (2008). *The art of followership: How great followers create great leaders and organizations.* San Francisco, CA: Jossey-Bass.

Rodríguez, C. (2005). Emergence of a third culture: Shared leadership in international strategic alliances. *International Marketing Review, 22*(1), 67–95.

Ropo, A., & Sauer, E. (2003). Partnerships of orchestras: Towards shared leadership. *International Journal of Arts Management, 5*(2), 44–55.

Shamir, B., & Lapidot, Y. (2003). Shared leadership in the management of group boundaries: A study of expulsions from officers' training courses. In C. L. Pearce, & J. A. Conger (Eds.), *Shared leadership: Reframing the hows and whys of leadership* (pp. 235–249). Thousand Oaks, CA: Sage.

Solansky, S. (2008). Leadership style and team processes in self-managed teams. *Journal of Leadership & Organizational Studies, 14*(4), 332.

Uhl-Bien, M. (2006). Relationship leadership theory: Exploring the social processes of leadership and organizing. *Leadership Quarterly, 17*(6), 654.

Uhl-Bien, M., & Pillai, R. (2006). The romance of leadership and the social construction of followership. In B. Shamir, R. Pillai, M. Bligh, & M. Uhl-Bien.

(Eds.), *Follower-centered perspectives on leadership: A tribute to the memory of James R. Meindl* (pp. 187–209). Greenwich, CT: Information Age Publishing.

Wassenaar, C.L., Pearce, C.L., Hoch, J., & Wegge, J. (2010). Shared leadership meets virtual teams: A match made in cyberspace. In P. Yoong (Ed.), *Leadership in the Digital Enterprise: Issues and Challenges* (pp. 15–27). Hersey, PA: IGI Global.

Wood, M. S. (2005). Determinants of shared leadership in management teams. *International Journal of Leadership Studies, 1*(1) 64–85.

Yukl, G. A. (2002). *Leadership in organizations* (5th ed.). Englewood Cliffs, NJ: Prentice Hall.

CHAPTER 15

DIALOGUE

A Research Agenda for Relational Leadership

Gail Fairhurst and John Antonakis

We are happy to have this chance to comment on the book chapters in Part II, as it allows us to further the debate on a topic that is important for the social scientific study of leadership. We decided to reflect these views in a conversational format in which Gail will lead off, and John follows with his comments on the chapters and on Gail's thoughts. After another exchange, the chapter concludes with some joint recommendations.

FAIRHURST'S FIRST LETTER TO ANTONAKIS

Dear John,

To make sense of the chapters that were our assignment, I created Table 15.1. Using Gronn's (2002) distinction between ontological, observational, and analytic units, I classified each of the six chapters accordingly. I also added Mary Uhl-Bien's (2006) *Leadership Quarterly* paper as it was often

Advancing Relational Leadership Research, pages 433–459
Copyright © 2012 by Information Age Publishing
All rights of reproduction in any form reserved.

TABLE 15.1   Analysis of the Empirical Chapters

	Ontological Units	Observational Units	Analytical Units
Uhl-Bien, 2006	Leadership as social reality; a social construction made in ongoing local-cultural processes; leadership as the process of organizing	Communication because "it is the medium in which all social constructions of leadership are continuously created and change"	Recommended: discourse analysis, modeling qualitative data, grounded theory, case studies; participatory methods and action science; intensive ethnographic and interview methods
Ashkanasy, et al.	Followers' and/or leaders' emotion and affect as it impacts the leader-follower relationship	Individuals who report emotional contagion as leaders or followers	Recommended: real-time self reports of emotion through diaries or experience sampling
Crosby & Bryson	Integrative public policy leadership as an outcome of shared meaning; policy making and implementing; and managing conflict	(Heavily) individual policy entrepreneurs (sponsors and champions) who report collaborative practices	Case-generated practices through interviews, archival data, and participant observation
Offerman	Followers' and/or leaders' ethnicity and language as it impacts the leader-follower relationship	Individuals' beliefs, attitudes, and demographics in the service industry	Surveys, interviews, and focus groups; first-person narrative descriptions
Ospina, et al.	Relational leadership as an outcome of shared sense-making, meaning-making, tacit agreements, shared vision and adaptive organizing	Social change work as told through the stories of award recipients in a leadership recognition program of collaborative leadership practices	Case-generated practices through interviews (narrative accounts); ethnography via immersion, interviews, observation; and cooperative inquiry
Treadway, et al.	Relational leadership as a reciprocal communication process of influence and control	Individuals who report influence tactics and relational strategies	Recommended: social network analysis; self-reported ties and influence strategies
Wassenaar & Pearce	Shared leadership as an interactive, social influence process among team or group members in pursuit of a stated goal or objective	None recommended, but research reported tends to assess individuals' self-reports	None recommended, but the assumption is that survey and interview data are acceptable

referenced in the chapters. Here's what this table tells me. *Ontological Units* define the object of study; in this case, it is the leadership relationship (or aspects of it) for all of the chapters and Uhl-Bien (2006). Interestingly, for *Observational Units*, which define who or what an analyst observes, Uhl-Bien (2006) locates communication at the center of understanding relationships "because it is the medium in which all social constructions of leadership are continuously created and change" (p. 665). However, the chapters mainly emphasize self-reports and storytelling by individual leadership actors. *Analytic Units* detail that which is to be deconstructed, measured, or explained, and here we see the panoply of data sources in the third column, in which interviews figure prominently.

If one takes seriously the charge to advance a relational agenda, I see a major disconnect in this table between Uhl-Bien's (2006) charge to place communication at the center of relational study and the chapters' heavy reliance on individuals reporting about communication or some other aspects of the relationship in story or survey form. Please note here that I am not against individual interview or self-report data *per se;* I have used plenty of this kind of data myself. What I object to is the overwhelming dominance of the individual as the observational unit when the ontological unit is relational. This is because people do not relate and then talk; they relate *in* talk (Duncan, 1967; McDermott & Roth, 1978). Recalling Gregory Bateson (1972), the exchange of messages *is* the relationship.

How so? There is a content and relational aspect to each message we formulate (Watzlawick, Beavin, & Jackson, 1967). The content deals with the subject matter at hand; the relational specifies *how* that content is to be taken. So if I said to you, "Gee, John, you're looking good today," and I smiled and looked approvingly, you would likely infer this to be a compliment. However, were I to smirk and speak sarcastically, you might well feel insulted or ridiculed. Note that the content is exactly the same in both messages. But the relational aspect (i.e., how I have defined myself in relation to you) differs when I signal politeness and approval versus sarcasm and ridicule.

While there could be great variety in the content of our communications, relational patterns are thought to operate within a narrower bandwidth and stabilize over time with our every move and countermove (Watzlawick et al., 1967). Here, the key is *not* to understand individual behavior, in this case, how much I compliment or insult you. The key is to understand how you and I act relationally—in Weick's (1979) terminology, not our individual "acts," but our "interacts" and "double interacts" (how you respond to me, how I respond to you responding to me, and so on). Moreover, As Hinde (1979) so beautifully relays in the case of husbands and wives, it makes a relational difference whether partners consistently kiss after they quarrel or quarrel after they kiss—even though the amount of kissing and quarrelling may be the same. In short, relationship definition coheres as a sequence, and the temporal patterns that mark relational systems are always co-defined (Rogers & Escudero, 2004; Rogers, Millar, & Bavelas, 1985).

The implications for a relational leadership agenda are clear (and, I might add, have been for awhile if one will peruse the date of the publications cited above). In addition to the plethora of research currently available on cognition and "what leadership actors mean" when they account for and story their leadership relationships, there must be a greater shift to "how behavior means" or indexing relational patterns (Scheflen, 1974).

Interviews and surveys ask individuals to retrospectively summarize the patterns that mark the relationship typically *from the perspective of only one person in the relationship*, thus implying that a single relational reality can be assumed (Rogers et al., 1985). (For example, this has been fairly standard practice in LMX research because leaders are putatively prone to give socially desirable answers.) However, this is an empirical question that goes to the heart of Uhl-Bien's (2006) recommendation to place communication at the center of relationships. According to Rogers et al. (1985), "The structural web...spun by recurring relational patterns emerging from ongoing message exchanges...(are) redundant, stochastic behavioral sequences" that are constitutive of the relationship and measurable as such (p. 176). These sequences must acquire a greater share of the spotlight in relational leadership research because, whether the system is relational, organizational, or institutional, systems can *only* emerge from repeated interactions that evolve into multi-leveled orders of patterns (Bateson, 1972; Rogers & Escudero, 2004). If "process" is to remain as one the key value commitments of the relational agenda (Uhl-Bien, 2006), then we must find ways of apprehending it beyond the static depictions of relational processes that most leadership scholars currently favor (Fairhurst, 2007).

Admittedly, this is a good news-bad news mandate. The good news is that a small group of social scientists in psychology, communication, and management have been doing this work for some time now. Much of this work requires the development of coding schemes that are applied to talk and action. Relational analyses have been a focus for psychologists in therapy contexts (Watzlawick et al., 1967), among husbands and wives (Bakeman & Gottman, 1986; Gottman, 1982), and in mother-infant interactions (E. Tronick, 2007; E. Z. Tronick et al., 1998). I wrote a recent review of the literature in the organizational sciences (Fairhurst, 2004b), in which coding schemes applied to organizational interactions can be found in the study of group processes (Bales, 1950; DeSanctis & Poole, 1994; Gersick, 1988; Olekalns, Smith, & Walsh, 1996; Poole & DeSanctis, 1992), bargaining and negotiations (Bednar & Currington, 1983; Putnam & Jones, 1982; Weingart, Hyder, & Prietula, 1996), leadership interactions (Courtright, Fairhurst, &

Rogers, 1989; Fairhurst, Green, & Courtright, 1995; Fairhurst, Rogers, & Sarr, 1987; Gioia & Sims, 1986; Watson-Dugan, 1989), police communications (Fairhurst & Cooren, 2004; Glauser & Tullar, 1985), interviewing (Tullar, 1989), and computer mediated interactions (Walther, 1995). Most of these appear in management journals.

The bad news, and I speak from experience here, is that this work is highly labor-intensive (Fairhurst, 2004b). It often requires verbatim transcript preparation, coding scheme development and reliability tests, stochastic analyses, and more. Coding schemes can also fall prey to leader centrism, such as we see with Komaki's (1986, 1998; Komaki & Citera, 1990; Komaki, Zlotnick, & Jensen, 1986) work on performance monitoring, or produce stereotyped superior-subordinate behavior, such as we see with Watson's student sample (1982).

Finally, coding schemes are not always as sensitive as they need to be to capture more nuanced relational dynamics (Fairhurst, 2004a; Firth, 1995; Gronn, 1982). For example, in my work examining how control is enacted relationally in leadership relationships, I focus on how actors' control attempts are met with acceptance or rejection by the other. Each turn at talk is coded as to whether it asserts control, acquiesces or requests control, or neutralizes the control move of the previous utterance. The "interact," or two contiguous control moves, is the basic unit of analysis in the search for relational patterns. However, my relational control coding scheme performs much better in a high reliability organizational context than a high efficiency organizational context because control dynamics are much more explicit in the latter (Fairhurst & Cooren, 2004).

Fortunately, more interpretive and qualitative relational analyses are available, such as with Harré and Langrove's (1999) discursive positioning theory, which focuses on first-, second-, and third-order positioning akin to the double interact, and L. M. Brown and Gilligan's "Listening Guide" (1992), which attends to the polyphonic, nonlinear voices within a narrative (A. D. Brown, 2006). Other forms of discourse analysis such as rhetorical analyses or an ethnomethodology-informed conversation analysis are certainly capable of detecting relational patterns; it's just that it isn't necessarily their focus (Boden, 1994). Importantly, most qualitative analyses sacrifice the ability to gauge the redundant and stochastic nature of relational patterns marking the system for more nuance and detail in the sequencing of *key* relational moves and counter-moves. Depending upon the research question, the trade-off either way can pay dividends.

As I close out my initial recommendation for a relational leadership agenda, let me recap what I have said. First, as I looked over the chapters that we have been given to read, I was bothered by their heavy reliance on the study of individuals to discern relational patterns. Again, I am not objecting to the use of interviews and surveys *per se* to study relational dynamics; I am objecting to their overwhelming dominance.

Second, more process descriptions of the leadership interactions are necessary if we are to move beyond understanding relationships as an entitative state (Hosking, 1988). Those process descriptions are not likely to come from methods that promote summary judgments. The essential argument here is that the *pattern* of leadership interaction itself is its own best explanation of leadership dynamics.

Third, quantitative methods needed to assess the redundant and stochastic patterns that characterize leadership relationships already exist, not just in psychology and communication, but in the organizational sciences and in the study of leadership (Fairhurst, 2004b). However, coding schemes have their own limitations. More qualitative methods to assess key relational moments in more nuanced exchanges exist in the discourse analysis literature; however, we don't have the track record here as we do for coded interaction analyses in organizations. If communication is indeed at the center of understandings relationships, then *both* types of approaches must be taken more seriously by mainstream leadership researchers. John, your thoughts?

Sincerely,

Gail

ANTONAKIS'S FIRST LETTER TO FAIRHURST

Dear Gail,

I enjoyed your first missive, Gail. On the whole I agree with most of your assertions; studying relations means going beyond many of the current research paradigms that are being used. The table you created makes sense and helps to tease out measurement and levels-of-analysis issues. So, I agree that there is an overreliance on individual-level observational units, retrospective ratings, and not enough focus on communication processes that undergird relationships. I guess that what strikes me as odd after having read the chapters and your article (Fairhurst, 2004b), as well as other articles (see later), is that researchers are not leveraging the methodological and technological advances regarding measurement of relationships. There are methods, or at least methods that researchers could extend to suit the purposes of this research stream, that could disentangle the antecedents and consequences of relational leadership.

Before responding to your thoughts, however, I must first admit that after reading the chapters, I am still not very clear about what *relational leadership* actually means and what the implications are for its study. I thought it would be helpful for me, and readers, if I revisited the original ideas behind this research stream. Reading the chapter contributions and comparing their frameworks and research approaches with what Uhl-Bien (2006) proposed made it difficult for me to determine whether the relational leadership research agenda is actually being concretized; perhaps as an "outsider" (i.e., coming from a quantitative and "traditional" leadership perspective focusing on transformational and charismatic leadership), I am missing something.

Uhl-Bien (2006) defined relational leadership it as "a social influence process though which emergent coordination (i.e., evolving social order) and change (e.g., new values, attitudes, approaches, behaviors, and ideologies) are constructed and produced" (p. 655). Later, she defined it as "both *relationships* (interpersonal relationships as outcomes of or as contexts for interactions) and *relational dynamics* (social interactions, social constructions) of leadership. . . . [and] on the *relational processes* by which leadership is produced and enabled" (p. 667). Another definition of *relational leadership* is that it is a "process by which social systems change through the structuring of roles and relationships" (p. 668).

As you noted, too, Uhl-Bien (2006) suggests that "relational perspectives do not seek to identify attributes or behaviors of individual leaders but instead focus on the communication processes (e.g., dialogue, multilogue) through which relational realities are made" (p. 664). Thus, the heart of relationship leadership is, according to its architect, communication. My confusion about the construct stems from several points. For instance, it is unclear to me at which level of analysis the theory operates and the way in which the chapter authors suggest to test the theory is concordant to the theoretical level of operationalization. Communication process occurs between actors: One to one, one to many, many to one, or many to many. It is not clear to me that, with the heavy individual-level emphasis, there is an alignment of the theoretical level with the level at which the authors propose to test their constructs; failure to consider this issue can lead to spurious findings (Schriesheim, Castro, Zhou, & Yammarino, 2001; Yammarino, Dionne, Uk Chun, & Dansereau, 2005). At this time, I agree with you that communication is not at the center of a relational-oriented theory although it should be, as should be the study of "wholes of individuals," which is also possible to do from a quantitative perspective, too (Muthen & Muthen, 2000; Muthen & Shedden, 1999).

So, there is a need to study wholes, communication, and to model the levels correctly. Such a goal is an ambitious one because it is clear that relational leadership is a multilevel theory. As such, the communication processes, their antecedents, and consequences must consider these multilevel effects both in theorizing, observing, and testing. Relational leadership's cousin, LMX, which is a dyadic theory of leadership, fell into the trap of not correctly specifying observations in its empirical tests. I hope that this fate will not befall relational leadership. For example, LMX's unit of analysis is, theoretically, the leader-follower dyad (i.e., the level of analysis at which the phenomenon operates). The following quotation, in a recent article by Schriesheim et al. (2001), highlighted the gravity of not employing the correct level of analysis:

> Although it seems clear that the unit of analysis is the leader-subordinate relationship (Graen & Uhl-Bien, 1995) and that the level of analysis should therefore be the dyad, no LMX research has employed this level (Schriesheim et al., 1999). Instead, data have typically been collected from either just the subordinate or just the boss; when data have been collected from both, they have not been used in any type of dyadic analysis. Consequently, we believe that all the extant research is fundamentally uninformative about the LMX process because it has not studied the exchange at the dyadic level of analysis.... Future research, and paying careful attention to aligning the theory and the level of analysis at which LMX predictions are tested therefore seem urgently needed. (p. 525)

Thus, apart from the levels issue, I think that there is not enough "process theorizing." Going back to the Uhl-Bien (2006) conceptualization of relational leadership, as I understand it, certain antecedent conditions and contextual factors, operating at multiple levels of analysis (e.g., individual followers and leaders, groups, organizational, environmental, time, etc.) engender certain evolving social orders over time, which lead to certain outcomes. This all happens because of multi-way communication processes; these are the core of the theory, whose effects are carried from the independent variables (whether they are individuals, variables, or something else). However, as you have noted, there is not much of such process-oriented theorizing around communication in the chapters and too much of a focus on individuals.

As for specifying antecedent conditions, I am reminded of House and Aditya's (1997) critique of LMX theory where they noted that "The distinguishing feature of LMX theory is the examination of relationships, as opposed to behavior or traits of either followers or leaders" (p. 430). They note further: "While it is almost tautological to say that good or effective leadership consists in part of good relationships between leaders and followers, there are several questions about such relationships to which answers are not intuitively obvious" (p. 431). House and Aditya (1997) note further that, "A specification of the attributes of high-quality LMX—trust, respect, openness, latitude of discretion—is as close as the theory comes to describing or prescribing specific leader behaviors. The theory implies that any leader behavior that has a positive effect on LMX quality will be effective. However, precisely what these behaviors are is not explicitly stated, as the appropriate leader behavior is dependent on anticipated subordinate response" (p. 432).

Thus, from a research point of view, "relations" are endogenous variables—they depend on other factors, and it is important to model these factors completely to better understand the process model that leads to dependent outcomes (Antonakis, Bendahan, Jacquart, & Lalive, 2010). The consequences of the above are really important for correct empirical testing. Briefly, if x is endogenous, then its effect on y cannot be correctly estimated unless the antecedent exogenous conditions of x (e.g., z, q, or what have you, whether they operate on the individual, group, organizational, or another level) are included in the model (Antonakis et al., 2010). By *exogenous*, we mean that the factors vary randomly and do not depend on other factors or omitted variables. That is, the exogenous factors must not correlate with the error terms of the systems of specified equations; if they do, then they have the same problem that the endogenous variables do, which means the effect of x on y cannot be identified. (For those who are interested to learn about this problem, and the remedy, see Antonakis et al., 2010). We discuss this identification problem extensively in a recent review piece, where, unfortunately, we found that much of the leadership literature is stuck with correlating endogenous variables with other endogenous variables. As we show in Antonakis et al. (2010), such descriptive correlations are not useful because they confound the effects of omitted variables. That is, the correlations could be overstated or understated or could be of a different sign from that of the true population correlation. Thus, what is important for me to mention is that using "relations" (in whichever form it is measured) to predict other outcomes is not very useful *per se* and that any coefficient capturing this relation has no inherent statistical meaning.

How can this research stream advance? Apart from the statistical issues I have identified above, there are many exciting contributions being made at the interface of psychology and information sciences that could be useful for researchers measuring communication—particularly real-time, naturally-occurring, and open-ended communication. Many recent advances have been made in open-ended analysis of semantic meanings in text (see Foltz, Kintsch, & Landauer, 1998; Landauer, 1999; Landauer, Foltz, & Laham, 1998; Landauer, Laham, & Derr, 2004; Landauer, Laham, Rehder, & Schreiner, 1997). There are methods that can even code human emotions (Picard, Vyzas, & Healey, 2001; Sorci, Antonini, Cruz, Robin, Bierlaire, & Thiran , 2010) or other social interaction processes (Paradiso et al., 2010;

Pentland, 2010a, 2010b). These new technologies are currently available and can really help to advance research in relational leadership and in other domains and organizational behavior. More importantly, these methods can start to unify disparate research fields and to begin to model and quantify the unquantifiable.

So to recap, I largely agree with you; beyond the "communication problem" though, I think that it would be important to theorize, observe, and test in open-ended and causally-defensible ways so that the relational leadership research agenda can one day be reified.

Sincerely,

John

FAIRHURST'S SECOND LETTER TO ANTONAKIS

Dear John,

John, as I read your response, I flashbacked to my earlier quantitative training. Indeed, had I stayed solely with this view of the world, I might be arguing for the same agenda as you. But something happened on my way to becoming a leadership communication scholar. I not only switched from studying surveys and 7-point scales to the routine work conversations of leadership actors, I switched from a being a quantitative interaction analyst to a more qualitative discourse analyst.

It wasn't consciously planned, and it didn't happen overnight. Ironically, it was my experience with LMX that triggered my shift to a more qualitative and constructionist discourse stance. LMX founder George Graen was at my university for many years, and several of his students invited me to be on their dissertation committees. As a communication analyst, I knew LMX must be negotiated in social interaction (because telepathy has yet to be proven, but unconscious mirroring is a definite possibility as your last group of references suggest), and that retrospective summary judgments of the relationship were a far cry from relationships-as-they-happen.

So, I designed a study in which I would measure LMX conventionally and collect routine work conversations from each participating dyad. As mentioned in my opening remarks, my coding scheme measured the control moves of every turn-at-talk; indeed, it seemed ideally suited to pick up the shared control and mutual influence of high (quality) LMXs and the more restricted control and unidirectional influence of low (quality) LMXs (Graen & Scandura, 1987; Graen & Uhl-Bien, 1995). To my surprise, there was no clear relationship between LMX and the interactional data

(Fairhurst et al., 1987), but there were other findings (Courtright et al., 1989). In a second much larger study, LMX continued to be a no-show (Fairhurst et al., 1995).

However, I had made some modifications to the coding scheme between the first and second study and spent a good deal of one summer checking my coder's treatment of the interaction. It was there I discovered a world largely unknown to me until then. I found relational markers that were small, subtle, varied, and ubiquitous. They were part of the messy details of unadulterated speech that surveys and 7-point scales—and many coding schemes—tend to sweep under the rug like so many particles of dust. It was better to gloss them by folding them into "styles," "types," "patterns," or "qualities" and to view relationships in snap-shots of meaning instead of its ongoing negotiation.

Not only was my coding scheme not sensitive enough to the relational dynamics in play, it became difficult to imagine *any* coding scheme fitting the bill because of their endless combinations. Incidentally, the company I studied was the epitome of corporate America, blue chip in every way. Unlike the aforementioned high reliability organizations where time and safety issues push control out into the open, this is not the case in their high efficiency counterparts where subtlety, strategy, and even sleight-of-hand are the order of the day. This is not because folks are necessarily dishonest but because they carry the weight of multiple, co-occurring communication goals—an identity to manage, relationships to define, and tasks to complete *all at once,* especially in highly charged political environments. The broad strokes that leadership theory paints, and still paints, leave much to be desired in capturing these dynamics. Suffice it to say that in discourse analysis, I found the tools to understand LMX and its relationalities (Fairhurst, 1993; 2007; Fairhurst & Chandler, 1989; Fairhurst & Hamlett, 2003).

So, the bottom line is that, because of my journey and experience with LMX, I only *partly* share your concern for levels of analysis. Deidre Boden (1994) in *The Business of Talk* captures some of my thinking in this regard:

> In the study of organizations especially, scholarship has become highly fragmented by virtue of a near-obsession with so-called 'levels of analysis' . . . Driven almost entirely by considerations that are rooted in methodological constraints rather than empirical evidence, quite a number of talented researchers critique or ignore each other's findings and theories based on essentially socially constructed, if methodologically tidy, distinctions that are features of data sets and statistical convention rather than properties of the real world. These many and separate levels are then treated as 'structure' and assumed to shape the behavior of microscopic human actors. (p. 3)

The alternative that Boden articulates, and that many discourse analysts like me embrace, is to ground structure-in-action and to let *actors* demonstrate how levels of context reflexively interrelate. Let me address both of these points in more detail before I discuss their deliverables for a relational agenda.

Grounding Structure-in-Action

When reading the mainstream literature in leadership, I often get the sense that "relations" are something that befalls leadership actors, rather than being what they do. While this approach follows leadership psychology's emphasis on experience, it under-theorizes agency, making it easier to overlook the negotiated nature of relationships. In addition, as Boden (1994) suggests, "Framed as external, constraining, and *big*, the discrete actions of situated actors are treated as 'effects,' that is, as indicators, expressions or symptoms of social structures such as relationships, informal groups, ... and the like" (p. 12, emphasis original). In short, relationships structure social interaction, which is only half of the story.

What is the alternative? Like Boden, I favor Anthony Giddens' (1979, 1984) "duality of structure," which suggests that social structure is both a medium and outcome of social interaction. Here "structure" is short for, "society," "culture," or "our shared history," which boils down to a set of rules and resources that leadership actors draw from to deal with the matters at hand. As such, these rules and resources are also products of the interaction that actors' either reaffirm or modify depending upon how they have used them. In this way, agency is restored to leadership actors, yet kept within limits, because rules and resources are simultaneously enabling and constraining (e.g., see Fairhurst, Cooren, & Cahill, 2002; Howard & Geist, 1995). Importantly, the study of leadership is grounded in task accomplishment, not "floating ethereally" above, it as is often the case in the literature (Robinson, 2001; see also Gronn, 2002). One key way to advance a relational leadership agenda is to ask about the resource base from which leadership actors draw, a point I will return to below.

Knowledgeable Leadership Actors

Garfinkel (1967), Giddens (1984) and others object to the widespread derogation of the lay actor in the social sciences. This view is based in Garfinkel's ethnomethodological argument that action is organized from within. This means that actors are knowledgeable agents who reflexively monitor the ongoing character of social life as they continuously orient to and position themselves with respect to the contingencies of the moment—looming deadlines, abundant resources, up-against-the-wall constraints, value commitments, role expectancies, and/or other situational features that come into view. Note that what is paradoxical to the researcher may well be reasonable to the actor. Actors' language choices thus become a window on human agency because "actions and the interpretations of their meanings are inseparable and occur simultaneously in the course of their production" (Boden, 1994, p. 47). Moreover, actors can be responsible agents and still not fully comprehend or intend the full nature of unfolding events (Giddens, 1984; Ranson, Hinnings & Greenwood, 1980).

To attribute knowledgeability and reflexivity to leadership actors is to pay attention to how they account for their worlds. These accounts routinely surface in naturally occurring work conversations, but interviews can elicit them as well. Problems, breaches, surprises, or unmet expectations occasion in actors a need to explain, justify, or reconcile the "facts" of their world and their place in it. Such sense-making is the stuff of accounts, and it is here that actors are most likely to indicate, and perhaps even negotiate, exactly which levels of context (and their features) factor into the action. Thus, I am arguing that levels of context need to be made *practically relevant* by the actors involved because the researcher's birds eye view of the world is just that—a removed view of the actors' world given to (sometimes sweeping) generalizations about a host of contingencies (statistical or otherwise) thought to structure the course of events.

But, you might ask, have I not just contradicted myself, given Table 15.1 and my earlier concern for the chapter authors' heavy emphasis on interviews and individuals as the unit of analysis? I would argue "no" because I am looking to study accounting practices in the sequencing of interaction in which levels of context are made *practically relevant*, most often, over multiple turns at talk where text becomes con-text and sense-making is a collective achievement, not solely an individual one (Fairhurst, 2007). Put simply, the reporting of interview data must literally bring researchers into the interaction—treated as another "actor" if you will—to examine the ways in which *they, too,* make certain levels of context more or less salient through the questions asked and answered. Such a view is consistent with extending that which is "relational" to greater reflexivity in the actor and analyst relationship (Bradbury & Lichenstein, 2000; Dachler, 1992; Uhl-Bien, 2006).

With an orientation that grounds structure-in-action and attributes knowledgeability to leadership actors, there are two important ways to advance a relational agenda for leadership study. The first is the "resources" question mentioned above, and it is here that I depart from Boden's (1994) ethnomethodological argument. I prefer instead to focus on a poststructuralist alternative, Foucault's (1980, 1990, 1995) view of Discourse (capitalized to mark its distinctiveness from more standard use) as historically-grounded systems of thought—and its use by discursive psychology as a linguistic resource for communicating actors (Potter, 2003; Potter & Wetherell, 1987;

Wetherell, 1998). Through Discourse, we see how *culture* influences the definition and formation of leadership relationships, and we know this because actors will invoke familiar-sounding terminology, metaphors and stories, habitual forms of argument, and customary categories to name and understand "the relationship here and now" (see also Fairhurst, 2007, 2011). The footprints of culture are in the linguistically familiar, much as Bennis and Thomas (2002) found in their analysis of "geeks" and "geezers." These are two groups of leaders, each marked by their own historical eras, orientations to work relationships, and *ways of talking about their worlds.* The ways in which culture and its Discourses influence the formation and maintenance of leadership relationships have not been a particular focus in the mainstream literature (Fairhurst, 2007); however, its promise is best understood after explaining the second research agenda.

A second research agenda for relational leadership draws again from Giddens (1984) who argues that to put actors in charge of their own affairs in ways marked by both freedom and constraint, they must continuously manage the tension between agency and constraint (structure). Baxter (2011) recasts this argument in terms of the struggle between competing, often contradictory Discourses in her theory of relational dialectics. Drawing from the dialogism of Bakhtin (1981), Baxter (2011) argues that Discourses not only animate talk, but often compete with one another, more or less in zero-sum terms. She says, "(W)hat something means in the moment depends on the interplay of competing (D)iscourses that are circulating in that moment" (p. 3). More to the point, *"relationships* achieve meaning through the active interplay of multiple, competing (D)iscourses" (p. 5, emphasis added).

In practical terms, the interplay of Discourses source dialectical tensions that create simultaneous pulls to fuse with and differentiate from the other. Thus, relational bonding not only implies fusion, closeness, and interdependence, but also separation, distance, and independence (Baxter & Montgomery, 1996). It is the working out of these tensions *through Discourse and in communication* that forge the relationship and directly calls into question the assumption that relationships are generally stable (see also Lee & Jablin, 1995).

In the past, I've used relational dialectics (Baxter & Montgomery, 1996) to write about what those tensions might be for LMX (Fairhurst, 2001). Briefly, they include connection-autonomy, where connection is as central to the LMX as autonomy is to individuals' identities. In openness-closedness, a second tension, the former is a prerequisite for LMX bonding, yet creates vulnerability, necessitating the latter. Predictability-novelty is a third; too much predictability can create rigidity that ultimately necessitates novelty or change. Baxter's point is that the *strategic responses* to these tensions (and others) in communication form the basis for understanding *how* relationships are forged. For example,

> Member latitude in decision making is a form of autonomy that has been reframed as connection in high LMX relationships... However, the management of the autonomy-connection dialectic over the life cycle of the leader-member relationship has rarely been viewed as an ever-evolving negotiated process between opposite poles. (Fairhurst, 2001, p. 420)

Indeed, other LMX actors may favor one pole to the exclusion of the other, alternate between them, or vary their tension management strategies using other contingencies (Seo, Putnam & Bartunek, 2004). Lee and Jablin's (1995) work suggests that even when LMX relationships are in a "maintenance" phase, there is potential volatility to be managed. Relational bonding can escalate or deteriorate, for example, over disagreements or conflicts that impact how open or closed LMX members choose to be in those moments. Finally, the predictability-novelty dialectic may take shape in far fewer scripted episodes and "secret tests" (Graen & Uhl-Bien, 1995) in high LMX relationships than low ones due, in part, to the interactional freedom (and, by implication, the potential for novelty) that trust engenders.

If attention to dialectics tells us more about *how* the LMX relationship is brought off, attention to the Discourses impacting LMX answers the all important "what" question as in, "*What* kind of LMX relationship are we talking about?" (Fairhurst, 2007). While it is hardly news that high LMX leaders and members likely draw from the more collaborative Discourse of teams (in which status differences are suppressed) versus the more authority-based Discourses of low LMX members, the role that gender, ethnicity, age, or education/training Discourses may play in the negotiation of medium LMXs is particularly interesting given that performance issues alone do not always decide LMX quality (Fairhurst, 1993).

The promise of relational dialectics is a more complex understanding of relational bonding, transformation, and disconnecting processes. Moreover, the study of dialectical tension, contradiction, and paradox and their management are growing in popularity in the organizational sciences (Collinson, 2005; Ford and Backoff, 1988; George, 2007; Mumby, 2005; Seo et al., 2004; Trethewey & Ashcraft, 2004; Zoller & Fairhurst, 2009). I believe they offer similar promise for the study of leadership relationships.

John, I worry that I only have touched the surface of what is necessary to explain. But let me conclude by saying that I understand and appreciate that the function of most leadership theorizing has been to predict and causally explain leadership phenomena. Like Baxter (2011) and Boden (1994), I use theories more heuristically to make leadership relationships intelligible and open to insight in ways we would not otherwise have had. Traditional approaches want to answer cause-effect, *why* questions, while my goal is to answer *how* (as in, "How are leadership relationships brought off?") and *what* questions (as in "What kind of leadership relationship are we talking about?").

Sincerely,

Gail

ANTONAKIS'S SECOND LETTER TO FAIRHURST

Dear Gail,

I appreciate your thoughtful comments, Gail. Given that my strengths are in theory-building and testing, I would like, however, to still make the case that studying relationships *per se* should be accompanied by a systems model of theorizing and testing; this approach is what I think will advance LMX research.

I will motivate my argument with an example I use to teach my students about causality. I will call it the *clay-pigeon causality conundrum* (cf. Antonakis, Bendahan, Jacquart, & Lalive, in press). I will go over this example in detail so that I can better explain the problem of "endogeneity" in the hope that researchers will better see why it is a good idea to develop process models that include exogenous variables (so as to truly understand whether relationships matter for organizational outcomes). I will discuss this example because I think the major point I tried to make was missed in my first contribution (because my first explanation was rather short).

I would also like to make it clear that I write purely theoretical pieces (e.g., Antonakis & Atwater, 2002; de Treville & Antonakis, 2006; de Treville, Antonakis, & Edelson, 2005); however, I also do "hard-core" quantitative research to test theories (e.g., Antonakis, Avolio, & Sivasubramaniam, 2003; Antonakis & Dalgas, 2009; Antonakis & Dietz, 2011; Fiori & Antonakis, in press). I see value, too, in gathering qualitative data and have taken doctoral-level coursework in qualitative case-study research; I do qualitative research, too—at this time quantified content analysis (Antonakis, Fenley, & Liechti, 2011). So, I try to practice an inclusive and "ecumenical" scientific view of research though I lean heavily towards quantifying what I observe. As Maxwell—whose pedigree in the qualitative community requires no bruiting about—notes, "there are legitimate and valuable uses of numbers even in purely qualitative research" (2010, p. 476). My only goal is to use the best-available methods for the task at hand to improve our explanation of naturally-occurring phenomena. I am open to any kind of scientific method of inquiry that builds useful theory, which is the ultimate aim of science. I would be fine with any type of research, irrespective of the flag-waving paradigm, that:

1. Has carefully sampled their units to ensure that they are not sampling on the dependent variable;
2. Demonstrates that they have sufficient units of observations to ensure that they understand and accurately model the phenomenon that they are observing;
3. Can document that data were measured or coded and reported in a reliable manner; and
4. Models causal explanations correctly.

I guess that most would agree that the point of science is to build theories; all we should care about is the rigor of the theory-building process and, where relevant, the rigor with which observations are used. It is imperative that I get my point across this time about the problem of endogeneity in a vivid and easy-to-understand way because I think that the viability of the LMX construct (and other constructs, too) depends on researchers understanding the problem of endogeneity. Whether they use a quantitative or qualitative mode of inquiry is irrelevant. I will focus my efforts on explaining the problem of endogeneity and how it relates to LMX because all scientific endeavors are about, or should lead to theory-building; endogeneity, whether in the empirical or theoretical form, is but two sides of a coin, so understanding it from an empirical point-of-view will hopefully make the theoretical problem more salient.

Unfortunately, as a recent review that my colleagues and I undertook demonstrates, most researchers in management and in related areas do not quite realize the insidious effects of endogeneity (Antonakis et al., 2010)—that it threatens theory-building endeavors follows as a direct consequence. Although our review was applicable to quantitative research, qualitative researchers are not immune from the criticism we made and in particular because their ultimate goal should be to build theories, too. As we all know, theories are causal explanations of phenomena, though many researchers shy away from using causal language when providing an account of a phenomenon and prefer to couch their causal language using other suggestive terms. However, they should not (cf. Pearl, 2000; Shipley, 2000), and they should focus on explaining the causal mechanisms behind what they state.

All theoretical explanations have implicit or explicit causal claims by definition. When a researcher states that x is associated with y and goes on to explain *how* (i.e., the mechanism linking x with y), she is making a causal claim. If she does not, the claim that is made cannot help science advance. Associations or patterns do not help science advance, as I will explain in a little while. What I wish to show is that claiming that *x* and *y* are correlated, related, or associated (or to use more qualitative vernacular *co-occur* or *match-up* or what have you) is not very useful to society if this relationship is due to other *unmodeled* causes. Although I think more could be gained by quantifying what we observe, quantification is irrelevant for the point I am making. What I care about most is that the theory we use to explain a phenomenon or a process is accurate; that's all. So, researchers should use LMX in whichever way they wish to, as long as they deal with the endogeneity problem upfront.

Note, also, that it has been claimed that quantitative research is "variance-driven," whereas qualitative research is "process-driven," focusing on "how" and "why" questions (Maxwell, 1996; Yin, 1994); thus, relations between variables are (apparently for some researchers) irrelevant for qualitative research. At the end of the day, however, both qualitative and quantitative researchers make implicit or explicit claims about how variables are *causally related* to one another, whether in a process or a conditioned relationship. Qualitative researchers claim to want to generalize to the theory (and thus avoid using causal language of the quantitative type); however, implicitly, what they state is causal, given the fact that they develop chains of events and patterns of occurrences (cf. Yin, 1994).

For example, if *a* is linked to *b* (and then one goes on to explain the *"how's"* and *"why's"* of this relationship), then there must be some causal process that has engendered the link between *a* and *b*. That is, if researchers claim that they find *b* whenever they find *a*, then *a* and *b* are somehow associated. Indeed, Maxwell (2010) notes explicitly that the point of qualitative research is to uncover "actual causal mechanisms and processes that are involved in particular events and situations" (p. 477). To uncover the causal mechanisms, one must first implicitly or explicitly articulate *what* is causally linked. Only then can the *how* and *why* questions be adequately answered. If I can get qualitative researchers to buy-in to this point (that explanations of chains or processes imply first showing associations), then the arguments I will make below will follow logically. However, it seems to me that this type of causal thinking is not the province of qualitative research, not because qualitative researchers cannot handle causal thinking, but because causal thinking of this kind is has not yet become apparent to qualitative researchers (as it is still not apparent to most quantitative researchers). For instance, here is a typical account of what process theorizing is apparently all about (Maxwell, 2010):

> Process theory... deals with events and the processes that *connect* them; its approach to understanding relies on an analysis of the processes by which some

events *influence* others. It relies much more on a local analysis of particular individuals, events, or settings than on establishing general conclusions and addresses "how" and "why" questions, rather than simply "whether" and "to what extent." (p. 477, italics mine)

What does *connect* or *influence* mean actually above? It seems to me that it means "linked"—a connection can only be a link or an association. If two entities are connected, they are bound somehow; when one is found, so is the other. Ditto for "influence," which is even closer to making a causal claim. (However, we are not concerned about causality at this point but by the fact that process theorizing implies associations or relations.) Also, if *a* influences *b*, then each time *a* is present, *b* will be present; or, each time *a* changes its form or intensity, *b* changes, too. Having established (I trust) that qualitative research is rife with implicit or explicit causal associations, too, I move to the next aspect of my argument: *That associations are not helpful for establishing theories.* I say this explicitly, too, about quantitative research (cf. Antonakis et al., 2010), so please do not take this as critique of qualitative research only.

The Clay-Pigeon Causality Conundrum

Suppose that a philosopher from the ancient times were transported in the flesh and skin by a time machine to the present day. She is brought to a field in the countryside and asked to make observations about a naturally-occurring phenomenon. She has no prior theories or expectations about what she will be observing; she is an objective bystander with no *a priori* theory about what to expect to see and what caused it. Now, on one side of the field is a shooter and on the other side a clay pigeon thrower; however, both are not observable to her because they are hidden behind thickets. Suddenly, the philosopher sees a disc of sorts streaking across the horizon. Then, she hears a deafening "crack" and, instantaneously, the disc disintegrates to smithereens. The process is repeated several times. In fact, almost every time she hears the "crack," the disc shatters. Being the keen observer that she is, the philosopher links the sound (x) to the disc disintegrating (y). Even in the absence of the counterfactual (i.e., what would happen to y if x was not present), she infers that it is highly probably that x must have caused y. She then goes on to build a theory about *how* x probably caused y and *why* this may have occurred. After much thought and insight, she supposes that the sound waves from the loud crack shattered the disk, so she develops a nice theory around that. Based on what she has seen, this is a plausible anecdotal account of what has happened, and it can even be nicely quantified with a chi-square test. The philosopher, however, is wrong.

Now, here is an example of observing an association that is quite clear and appears quite evident (and can even be tested for statistical significance); however, it is a specious association. Does this help us to understand the phenomenon at hand? No, because it is not the sound (x), but the birdshot (z), that caused the disc to shatter (y). Thus, in the absence of modeling the common cause z, it appears that x causes y; however, x and y both simply co-occur as a function of z. In fact, there is no relationship between x and y once the true causal relationship among the variables is accounted for by z. Important to understand here is that x (and of course y, too) is endogenous; x does not vary independent of any unmodeled causes of y (i.e., z, which is the exogenous variable causing z excluded from the model). Accounting for this endogeneity would show that the residual correlation between x and y is naught, *even though* the observed correlation between x and y is not zero. A detailed example with some basic algebra and Monte Carlo simulations explaining this problem is documented in Antonakis et al. (in press). Again, it is irrelevant to me whether the theoretical explanation follows from an inductive or deductive process, and irrelevant, too, whether an association between variables is expressed theoretically, or observed and modeled qualitatively or quantitatively.

Thus, finding associations (in the quantitative or qualitative sense) between endogenous variables is not a useful endeavor *per se*. As with the gunshot noise, LMX is endogenous. It is caused by something. Thus, studying LMX and then "correlating" LMX, whether in the quantitative or qualitative sense, with other dependent variables or explaining processes that rely on correlations or associations is not a useful endeavor unless the "something" that is behind the scenes is better understood. If the philosopher had poked around a bit, she might have discovered the shooter and then realized what was truly going on. Then, her account of the *how* and *why* of the disc disintegration would have been dramatically different, and of course more accurate!

I hope that my point of view regarding the fact that *how* and *why* questions depend on understanding processes and associations between entities or variables is clear. Whether one chooses or not to quantify these associations is not the issue here. To go back to what I said before, the problem that House and Aditya (1997) identified had to do with causes of LMX, as well as the problem of simultaneity (simultaneous causality). I would take the critique further and note that the whole system in which the relations occur need to be modeled. To accomplish such an ambitious goal one has to go beyond the simple 7-point questionnaires or studying the single-sided (leader or follower) views of LMX. That is why I pleaded in my first missive that researchers must take advantage of the technological advances that have been made to reliably gather (and ideally quantify) naturally occurring data that can capture the entities that really matter for understanding LMX.

Sincerely,

John

CONCLUSION

We enjoyed this exchange and found each other's perspectives interesting and useful for advancing relational leadership. So, where does this leave us, given that we come from contrasting views of science? On several points, we have to agree to disagree. However, here's where we do see some agreement for a relational leadership agenda:

1. The chapters we have been asked to respond to are generally marked by an overreliance on individual-level observational units when the ontological unit of study is the leadership relationship. Analysts must do more to match their analytic and observational units with the ontological unit under study.
2. The chapters show a heavy reliance on retrospective ratings and not enough focus on communication processes that undergird leadership relationships. As such, there is not enough process theorizing about relational communication insofar as leading (and managing) are concerned. Analysts are likely going to have to leave their comfort zones in order to do this type of theorizing and research.
3. Coding schemes are one way to capture relational processes; however, they have their own limitations (e.g., they may lack sensitivity to more nuanced relational dynamics) that must be recognized. Furthermore, technological advancements must be harnessed to capture naturally-occurring and dynamic open-ended data.
4. The meanings for the term *relational* are multifarious. Analysts must carefully specify their use of the term and then align their mode of scientific inquiry accordingly.
5. Systems-wide, contextually-relevant data (broadly defined), whether they are qualitative or quantitative, should be gathered to better understand the relational leadership phenomenon.

To conclude, although we have contrasting views of science, we agree that the point of science is to develop good theory. There is also little value in perpetuating a war between quantitative and qualitative methods; each perspective has its advantages and disadvantages. While we may never see a day when researchers will use a unified "post-paradigm-wars" mode of scientific inquiry to study leadership, the drive to understand leadership and its complexities is our common bond.

REFERENCES

Antonakis, J., & Atwater, L. (2002). Leader distance: A review and a proposed theory. *The Leadership Quarterly, 13*, 673–704.

Antonakis, J., Avolio, B. J., & Sivasubramaniam, N. (2003). Context and leadership: An examination of the nine-factor full-range leadership theory using the Multifactor Leadership Questionnaire. *The Leadership Quarterly, 14*(3), 261–295.

Antonakis, J., Bendahan, S., Jacquart, P., & Lalive, R. (2010). On making causal claims: A review and recommendations. *The Leadership Quarterly, 21*(6), 1086–1120.

Antonakis, J., Bendahan, S., Jacquart, P., & Lalive, R. (in press). Causality and endogeneity: Problems and solutions. In D. V. Day (Ed.), *The Oxford Handbook of Leadership and Organizations.*

Antonakis, J., & Dalgas, O. (2009). Predicting Elections: Child's Play! *Science, 323*(5918), 1183.

Antonakis, J., & Dietz, J. (2011). Looking for Validity or Testing It? The Perils of Stepwise Regression, Extreme-Scores Analysis, Heteroscedasticity, and Measurement Error. *Personality and Individual Differences, 50*(3), 409–415.

Antonakis, J., Fenley, M., & Liechti, S. (2011). Can charisma can be taught? Tests of two interventions. *Academy of Management Learning & Education, 10*(3), 374–396.

Bakeman, R., & Gottman, J. M. (1986). *Observing interaction: An introduction to sequential analysis.* Cambridge, England: Cambridge University Press.

Bakhtin, M. M. (1981). Epic and novel. In M. Holquist (Eds.), *The dialogic imagination: Four essays by M.M. Bakhtin* (C. Emerson, & M. Holquist, Trans. pp. 3–40). Austin, TX: University of Texas Press.

Bales, R. F. (1950). *Interaction process analysis.* Cambridge, MA: Addison-Wesley.

Bateson, G. (1972). *Steps to an ecology of the mind.* New York, NY: Ballentine.

Baxter, L. (2011). *Voicing relationships: A dialogic perspective.* Los Angeles, CA: Sage.

Baxter, L., & Montgomery, B. (1996). *Relating: Dialogue and dialectics.* New York, NY: Guilford.

Bednar, D. A., & Currington, W. P. (1983). Interaction analysis: A tool for understanding negotiations. *Industrial and Labor Relatons Review, 36,* 389–401.

Bennis, W. G., & Thomas, R. J. (2002). *Geeks and geezers: How era, values, and defining moments shape leadership.* Boston, MA: Harvard Business School Press.

Boden, D. (1994). *The business of talk: Organizations in action.* Cambridge, England: Polity.

Bradbury, H., & Lichtenstein, B. M. B. (2000). Relationality in organizational research: Exploring *The Space Between. Organization Science, 11,* 551–564.

Brown, A. D. (2006). A narrative approach to collective identities. *Journal of Management Studies, 43,* 731–753.

Brown, L. M., & Gilligan, C. (1992). *Meeting at the crossroads.* New York, NY: Ballantine Books.

Collinson, D. L. (2005). Dialectics of leadership. *Human Relations, 58,* 1419–1442.

Courtright, J. A., Fairhurst, G. T., & Rogers, L. E. (1989). Interaction patterns in organic and mechanistic systems. *Academy of Management Journal, 32,* 773–802.

Dachler, H. P. (1992). Management and leadership as relational phenomena. In M. V. Cranach, W. Doise, & G. Mugny (Eds.), *Social representations and the social bases of knowledge* (169–178). Lewiston, NY: Hogrefe & Huber.

DeSanctis, G., & Poole, M. S. (1994). Capturing the complexity in advanced technology use: Adaptive structuration theory. *Organization Science, 5,* 121–147.

de Treville, S., & Antonakis, J. (2006). Could lean production job design be intrinsically motivating? Contextual, configurational, and levels-of-analysis issues. *Journal of Operations Management, 24*(2), 99–123.

de Treville, S., Antonakis, J., & Edelson, N. M. (2005). Can standard operating procedures be motivating? Reconciling process variability issues and behavioral outcomes. *Total Quality Management and Business Processes, 16*(2), 231–241.

Duncan, H. D. (1967). The search for a social theory of communication in American sociology. In F. E. X. Dance (Ed.), *Human Communication Theory.* New York, NY: Holt, Rinehart and Winston.

Fairhurst, G. T. (1993). The leader-member exchange patterns of women leaders in industry: A discourse analysis. *Communication Monographs, 60,* 321–351.

Fairhurst, G. T. (2004a). Organizational relational control research: Problems and possibilities. In L. E. Rogers, & V. Escudero (Eds.), *Relational communication: An interactional perspective to the study of process and form* (pp. 197–215). Mahwah, NJ: Lawrence Erlbaum.

Fairhurst, G. T. (2004b). Textuality and agency in interaction analysis. *Organization, 11,* 335–354.

Fairhurst, G. T. (2007). *Discursive leadership: In conversation with leadership psychology.* Thousand Oaks, CA: Sage.

Fairhurst, G.T. (2011). *The power of framing: Creating the language of leadership.* San Francisco, CA: Jossey Bass.

Fairhurst, G.T., & Chandler, T.A. (1989). Social structure in leader-member interaction. *Communication Monographs, 60,* 321–351.

Fairhurst, G. T., & Cooren, F. (2004). Organizational language in use: Interaction analysis, conversation analysis, and speech act schematics. In D. Grant, C. Hardy, C. Oswick, N. Phillips & L. Putnam (Eds.), *The Sage handbook of organizational discourse* (pp. 131–152). London, England: Sage.

Fairhurst, G., Cooren, F., & Cahill, D. (2002). Discursiveness, contradiction and unintended consequences in successive downsizings. *Management Communication Quarterly, 15,* 501–540.

Fairhurst, G. T., Green, S. G., & Courtright, J. A. (1995). Inertial forces and the implementation of a sociotechnical systems approach: A communication study. *Organization Science, 6,* 168–185.

Fairhurst, G., & Hamlett, S. R. (2003). The narrative basis of leader-member exchange. In G. B. Graen (Eds.). *Dealing with diversity* (117–144). Greenwich, CT: Information Age Publishing.

Fairhurst, G. T., Rogers, L. E., & Sarr, R. (1987). Manager-subordinate control patterns and judgments about the relationship. In M. McLaughlin (Ed.), *Communication yearbook 10* (pp. 395–415). Beverly Hills, CA: Sage.

Fiori, M., & Antonakis, J. (2011). The ability model of emotional intelligence: Searching for valid measures. *Personality and Individual Differences, 50*(3), 329–334.

Firth, A. (Ed.). (1995). *The discourse of negotiation: Studies of language in the workplace.* Oxford, England: Pergamon.

Foltz, P. W., Kintsch, W., & Landauer, T. K. (1998). The measurement of textual coherence with latent semantic analysis. *Discourse Processes, 25*(2–3), 285–307.

Ford, J. D., & Backoff, R. W. 1988. Organizational change in and out of dualities and paradox. In R. E. Quinn, & K. S. Cameron (Eds.), *Paradox and transformation: Toward a theory of change in organization and management* (81–121). Cambridge, MA: Ballinger.

Foucault, M. (1980). *Power/knowledge: Selected interviews and other writings 1972–1977.* New York, NY: Pantheon.

Foucault, M. (1990). *The history of sexuality: Volume 1.* New York, NY: Vintage/Random House.

Foucault, M. (1995). *Discipline and punish.* New York, NY: Vintage/Random House.

Garfinkel, H. (1967). *Studies in ethnomethodology.* Englewood Cliffs, NJ: Prentice Hall.

George, J. M. (2007). Dialectics of creativity in complex organizations. In T. Davila, M. J. Epstein, & R. Shelton (Eds.), *The creative enterprise: Managing innovative organizations and people* (Vol. 2, pp. 1–15). Westport, CT: Praeger.

Gersick, C. J. G. (1988). Time and transition in work teams: Toward a new model of group development. *Academy of Management Journal, 31,* 9–41.

Giddens, A. (1979). *Central problems in social theory.* Berkeley, CA: University of California Press.

Giddens, A. (1984). *The constitution of society.* Berkeley, CA: University of California Press.

Gioia, D. A., & Sims, H. P., Jr. (1986). Cognition-behavior connections: Attributions and verbal behavior in leader-subordinate interactions. *Organizational Behavior and Human Decision Processes, 27,* 197–229.

Glauser, M. J., & Tullar, W. L. (1985). Citizen satisfaction with police officer-citizen interaction: Implications for changing the role of police organizations. *Journal of Appplied Psychology, 70,* 514–527.

Gottman, J. M. (1982). Temporal form: Toward a new langue for describing relationships. *Journal of Marriage and Family, 44,* 943–962.

Graen, G. B., & Scandura, T. (1987). Toward a psychology of dyadic organizing. In B. M. Staw, & L. L. Cummings (Eds.), *Research in organizational behavior* (Vol. 9, pp. 175–208). Greenwich, CT: JAI Press.

Graen, G. B., & Uhl-Bien, M. (1995). Relationship-based approach to leadership: Development of a leader-member exchange (LMX) theory of leadership over 25 years—Applying a multi-level multi domain perspective. *Leadership Quarterly, 6,* 219–247.

Gronn, P. (1982). Neo-Taylorism in educational administration? *Education Administration Quarterly, 18,* 17–35.

Gronn, P. (2002). Distributed leadership as a unit of analysis. *Leadership Quarterly, 13,* 423–451.

Harre, R. L., & Langenhove, V. (1999). *Positioning theory.* Oxford, England: Blackwell.

Hinde, R. (1979). *Toward understanding relationships.* New York, NY: Academic Press.

Hosking, D. M. (1988). Organizing, leadership, and skilful process. *Journal of Management Studies, 25*(2), 147–166.

House, R. J., & Aditya, R. N. (1997). The social scientific study of leadership: *Quo vadis? Journal of Management, 23*(3), 409–473.

Howard, L. A., & Geist, P. (1995). Ideological positioning in organizational change: The dialectic of control in a merging organization. *Communication Monographs, 62,* 110–131.

Komaki, J. L. (1986). Toward effective supervision: An operant anaysis and comparison of managers at work. *Journal of Applied Psychology, 71,* 270–279.

Komaki, J. L. (1998). *Leadership from an operant perspective.* London, England: Routledge.

Komaki, J. L., & Citera, M. (1990). Beyond effective supervision: Identifying key interactions between superior and subordinate. *Leadership Quarterly, 1,* 91–106.

Komaki, J. L., Zlotnick, S., & Jensen, M. (1986). Developing an operant-based taxonomy and observational index of supervisory behavior. *Journal of Applied Psychology, 71,* 260- 269.

Landauer, T. K. (1999). Latent semantic analysis: A theory of the psychology of language and mind. *Discourse Processes, 27*(3), 303–310.

Landauer, T. K., Foltz, P. W., & Laham, D. (1998). An introduction to latent semantic analysis. *Discourse Processes, 25*(2–3), 259–284.

Landauer, T. K., Laham, D., & Derr, M. (2004). From paragraph to graph: Latent semantic analysis for information visualization. *Proceedings of the National Academy of Sciences of the United States of America, 101,* 5214–5219.

Landauer, T. K., Laham, D., Rehder, B., & Schreiner, M. E. (1997). *How well can passage meaning be derived without using word order? A comparison of latent semantic analysis and humans.* Mahwah, NJ: Lawrence Erlbaum.

Lee, J., & Jablin, F. M. (1995). Maintenance communication in superior-subordinate work relationships. *Human Communication Research, 22,* 220–257.

Maxwell, J. A. (1996). *Qualitative research design: An integrative approach.* Thousand Oaks, CA: Sage Publications.

Maxwell, J. A. (2010). Using Numbers in Qualitative Research. *Qualitative Inquiry, 16*(6), 475–482.

McDermott, R. P., & Roth, D. R. (1978). The social organization of behavior: Interactional approaches. *Annual Review of Anthropology, 7,* 321–345.

Mumby, D. K. (2005). Theorizing resistance in organization studies: A dialectical approach. *Management Communication Quarterly, 19,* 1–26.

Muthen, B., & Muthen, L. K. (2000). Integrating person-centered and variable-centered analyses: Growth mixture modeling with latent trajectory classes. *Alcoholism—Clinical and Experimental Research, 24*(6), 882–891.

Muthen, B., & Shedden, K. (1999). Finite mixture modeling with mixture outcomes using the EM algorithm. *Biometrics, 55*(2), 463–469.

Olekalns, M., Smith, P. L., & Walsh, T. (1996). The process of negotiating: Strategies, timing and outcomes. *Organizational Behavior and Human Decision Processes, 68,* 68–77.

Paradiso, J. A., Gips, J., Laibowitz, M., Sadi, S., Merrill, D., Aylward, R. . . . & Pentland, A. (2010). Identifying and facilitating social interaction with a wearable wireless sensor network. *Personal and Ubiquitous Computing, 14*(2), 137–152.

Pearl, J. (2000). *Causality: Models, reasoning, and inference.* New York, NY: Cambridge University Press.

Pentland, A. (2010a). To Signal Is Human: Real-time data mining unmasks the power of imitation, kith and charisma in our face-to-face social networks. *American Scientist, 98*(3), 204–211.

Pentland, A. (2010b). We Can Measure the Power of Charisma. *Harvard Business Review, 88*(1), 34–35.

Picard, R. W., Vyzas, E., & Healey, J. (2001). Toward machine emotional intelligence: Analysis of affective physiological state. *Ieee Transactions on Pattern Analysis and Machine Intelligence, 23*(10), 1175–1191.

Poole, M. S., & DeSanctis, G. (1992). Microlevel structuration in computer-supported group decision making. *Human Communication Research, 19*, 5–49.

Potter, J. (2003). Discursive psychology: Between method and paradigm. *Discourse & Society, 14*, 783–794.

Potter, J., & Wetherell, M. (1987). *Discourse and social psychology*. London, England: Sage.

Putnam, L. L., & Jones, T. S. (1982). Reciprocity in negotiations: An anlysis of bargaining interaction. *Communication Monographs, 49*, 171–191.

Ranson, S., Hinnings, B., & Greenwood, R. (1980). The structuring of organizational structures. *Administrative Science Quarterly, 25*, 1–17.

Robinson, V. M. J. (2001). Embedding leadership in task performance. In K. Wong, & C. W. Evers (Eds.), *Leadership for quality schooling* (pp. 90–102). London, England: Routledge/Falmer.

Rogers, L. E., & Escudero, V. (2004). *Relational communication: An interactional perspective to the study of process and form*. Mahwah, NJ: Erlbaum.

Rogers, L. E., Millar, F. E., & Bavelas, J. B. (1985). Methods for analyzing marital conflict discourse. *Family Process, 24*, 175–187.

Scheflen, A. E. (1974). *How behavior means*. Garden City, NY: Anchor.

Schriesheim, C. A., Castro, S. L., & Cogliser, C. C. (1999). Leader-member exchange (LMX) research: A comprehensive review of theory, measurement, and data-analytic practices. *The Leadership Quarterly, 10*(1), 63–113.

Schriesheim, C. A., Castro, S. L., Zhou, X., & Yammarino, F. J. (2001). The folly of theorizing "A" but testing "B"—A selective level-of-analysis review of the field and a detailed Leader-Member Exchange illustration. *Leadership Quarterly, 12*(4), 515–551.

Seo, M., Putnam, L. L., & Bartunek, J. M. (2004). Contradictions and tensions of planned organizational change. In M. S. Poole, & A. Van de Ven (Eds.), *Handbook of organizational change and innovation* (pp. 73–107). New York, NY: Oxford University Press.

Shipley, B. (2000). *Cause and correlation in biology: A user's guide to path analysis, structural equations, and causal inference*. Cambridge, England: Cambridge University Press.

Sorci, M., Antonini, G., Cruz, J., Robin, T., Bierlaire, M., & Thiran, J. P. (2010). Modelling human perception of static facial expressions. *Image and Vision Computing, 28*(5), 790–806.

Trethewey, A., & Ashcraft, K. L. (2004). Special issue introduction. Practicing disorganization: The development of applied perspectives on living with tension. *Journal of Applied Communication Research, 32*(2): 81–88

Tronick, E. (2007). *The neurobehavioral and social-emotional development of infants and children.* New York, NY: W.W. Norton & Company.

Tronick, E. Z., Bruschweiler-Stern, N., Harrison, A. M., Lyons-Ruth, K., Morgan, A. C., Nahum, J. P. ... & Stern, D. N. (1998). Dyadically expanded states of consciousness and the process of therapeutic change. *Infant Mental Health Journal, 19,* 290–299.

Tullar, W. L. (1989). Relational control in the employment interview. *Journal of Applied Psychology, 74,* 971–977.

Uhl-Bien, M. (2006). Relational leadership theory: Exploring the social processes of leadership and organizing. *Leadership Quarterly, 17,* 654–676.

Walther, J. B. (1995). Relational aspects of computer-mediated communication: Experimental observations over time. *Organization Science, 6,* 186–203.

Watson, K. M. (1982). An analysis of communication patterns: A method for discriminating leader and subordinate roles. *Academy of Management Journal, 25,* 107–120.

Watson-Dugan, K. M. (1989). Ability and effort attributions: Do they affect how managers communicate performance feedback information? *Academy of Management Journal, 32,* 87–114.

Watzlawick, P., Beavin, J. H., & Jackson, D. D. (1967). *Pragmatics of human communication.* New York, NY: Norton.

Weick, K. (1979). *The social psychology of organizing* (2nd ed.). Reading, MA: Addison-Wesley.

Weingart, L. R., Hyder, E. B., & Prietula, M. J. (1996). Knowledge matters: The effect of tactical descriptions on negotiation behavior and outcome. *Journal of Personality and Social Psychology, 35,* 366–393.

Wetherell, M. (1998). Positioning and interpretative repertoires: Conversation analysis and post structuralism in dialogue. *Discourse & Society, 9,* 387–412.

Yammarino, F. J., Dionne, S. D., Uk Chun, J., & Dansereau, F. (2005). Leadership and levels of analysis: A state-of-the-science review. *The Leadership Quarterly, 16*(6), 879–919.

Yin, R. K. (1994). *Case study research: Design and methods.* Thousand Oaks, CA: Sage.

Zoller, H.Z., & Fairhurst, G.T. (2007). Resistance leadership: The overlooked potential in critical organization and leadership studies. *Human Relations, 60,* 1331–1360.

PART III

A CONVERSATION ACROSS PERSPECTIVES

CHAPTER 16

DIALOGUE

A Dialogue on Entitative and Relational Discourses

Dian Marie Hosking and Boas Shamir

HOSKING'S FIRST LETTER TO SHAMIR

Dear Boas,

As I recall, we were asked to engage in a "dialogue" in the sense of engaging in a conversation with people's views—rather than agreeing or disagreeing—rather than critiquing or debating the truth value of their claims. I should say that the emphasis on "dialogue" resonates very strongly for me, not least because it is central to my theorizing of leadership and transformative change work. In addition, since I do not assume that there needs to be a sharp distinction between the practice I write about and my own practice, I prefer to work in ways that could be described as "dialogical."

This said, of course the term *dialogue* can be used to mean many different things, so I think I should say something about the rather special ways I use the term. This means that I need, first, to say something about social science "discourses" of person and world and their relations. I shall outline

Advancing Relational Leadership Research, pages 463–476

just two: one that I call relational constructionist and the other (contrasting discourse) that I call "entitative." I regard these discourses as framework(s) of premises that are "wider than a theory, less monolithic than a paradigm, and more modest than a worldview" (Hosking, 2008, p. 669). I need to provide this outline because I want to use the term *dialogue* in the context of a discourse of relational processes. I want further to propose that relational processes can construct (some degree of) soft self/other differentiation and that dialogical practices are key to producing such relations.

On Entitative and Relational Discourses

I can outline what I mean by "entitative" and "relational" discourses through reference to my early work on leadership. I was curious about Fiedler's contingency model of leadership effectiveness and the ways it constructed person-world relations. My explorations led me to the following conclusions:

- Selecting and centering one particular person (in this case, "the leader") and focussing on individual characteristics and behaviors gives too much significance to that individual;
- Treating "the leadership context," "world," or "other" as "out there" and independent of the person (in this case, the leader), draws a too sharp and singular boundary between self and not-self;
- Differentiating self and other (person and context or "world') in these ways overemphasizes stable things with stable characteristics and means that relating can only happen within and between things; and
- Differentiating self and other in these ways reduces relating to an instrumental process that is potentially "*value-able*" for self (e.g., as leader) in that it is confined to (a) producing "aboutness" knowledge ("knowledge that," propositional knowledge) and (b) achieving "power over" other (Hosking, 1981, Hosking, 2011).

In "*A social psychology of organizing*," Ian Morley and I referred to the above as an "entitative" approach (Hosking & Morley, 1991). We argued that entitative constructions of self, other, and relations dominated the literatures of Organizational Behavior, Human Resource Management—and leadership. We stated our purpose as being to avoid entitative constructions of person (which we also called the *individualistic fallacy*) and entitative constructions of organization (which we called the *culturalist fallacy*). Later, I came across the work of a North American social psychologist, Edward Sampson (1995), who spoke of these (what we called "entitative') constructions as "monological" and "self celebratory." Using these descriptors allowed him to highlight that they orient around the notion of (i) a singular and rational self, (ii) who is able to know other as other really (or probably) is, (iii) who can speak for and about other (followers, women, other ethnic groups…), and (iv) who can use other in the rational pursuit of (supposedly) rational goals and interests (Sampson, 1995). In sum, these are the premises/constructions that I call "entitative." These assumptions have long dominated work on leadership—both in the (usually implicit) "meta-theoretical" discourse of science—and in the particularities of the scientist's more local theory of leadership.

In developing what I have variously called a "processual," "relational," and "relational constructionist" approach, my intention has been to explore a discourse of self, other, and relations that does *not* make entitative assumptions, that "starts somewhere else" so to speak. So, in my relational discourse and theorizing, I do *not* begin with the assumption of already existing entities that relate through mind and world structuring operations. Rather, I start with the assumption that always ongoing relational processes are the "moving location," so to speak, for person (self) and world (other) making. In other words, I see self, other, and relations as relational realities that co-arise and are co-constituted in relational processes. Further, I see "relational realities" as arising in local and changing networks of relations. The self, viewed as a relational reality, now is discoursed as multiple and local, as contingent, rather than singular/generalized and trans-historical. So, for example, the relational processes that construct a "leader" also construct not-leaders and leader/non-leader relations. Similarly, the processes of doing research necessarily (re)construct researcher-researched identities and relations (Dachler & Hosking, 1995). However, this talk of relating includes not just "other" persons but all that is constructed as "outside" of self–including, for example, other as a machine, other as nature, other as any artifact of human activity (Hosking, 2008, 2011).

The relational-constructionist discourse I have just outlined assumes constitutive relational processes and gives them center stage. Scholars have used many different terms to theorize these processes, including, for example, terms such as *conversation, dialogue, discursive activity, narrative* or *storytelling, interacts* and *text-con-text* or *act-supplement* (e.g., Edwards & Potter, 1992; Gergen, 1994, 1995; Hermans, Kempen, & van Loon, 1992; Hosking & Morley, 1991; Latour, 1987; Sampson, 1995). However, the interested reader must take great care, as often terms such as *conversation* or *dialogue* are used in the context of an entitative discourse—where they mean something else entirely. So, for example, in this relational discourse, talk of narrative or dialogue becomes a reference to ongoing constitutive processes. Narratives, for example, in the form of interview transcripts, become viewed as live, lived-in relational performances and not dead, individual products and possessions. The "scientist"/researcher working from this perspective regards the relational realities made in these performances as local-historical and local-cultural, rather than subjective or objective ways of knowing some singular reality. And, of course, references to dialogue or discursive activity are considered to include—but not to be confined to—conceptual language. Language is now considered a form of action. Further, it is placed on a par with all other forms and not elevated to a representational role; the researcher writes a narrative in the form of a journal article—and does not claim to "tell it how it (probably) is"—but tells one possible story—recognizing that others could also be told.

The above (albeit brief) outline should have made clear some of the important ways in which this relational discourse differs from entitative or "modernist" constructions, for example, of the rational agent, of empirical evaluation, and of language as a means to represent the real (Gergen & Thatchenkerry, 2006). It parts company from post-positivist science and its focus on individual acts and individual (subjective or less than fully objective) knowledge (see, for example, Hosking, 2006, 2011). Instead, language-based relational construction processes are assumed to construct multiple local, relational rationalities. This means that relational processes (a) construct stabilities—often experienced as "entities," as "how things really are"; and (b) they construct changes—changes in the content, so to speak, of particular local relational realities (Hosking, 2004). This view of relational processes invites attention, for example, to repetition and improvisation, to social (dis)certification and mobilization of bias, to dialogue and debate. Interactionist, constructionist, and systemic studies, for example, in social psychology and micro-sociology have helped to elucidate these processes (e.g., Barge, Chapter 4) as has more recent work employing deconstruction (Boje, 1995; Chia, 1995).

The potentially wide significance of this postmodern relational discourse is illustrated in the work of Hermans and his colleagues (Hermans, Kempen & van Loon, 1992), who noted that all persons, in all cultures and at all times, listen to and tell stories and, in these ways, could be said to socially construct particular ways of relating self and world. They drew from writers such as Vico to argue that mind and body should be viewed as inseparable and "in history" while also actively making history. In this context, one could say that knowing and doing are seen as the same (Hermans, Kempen and van Loon, 1992, p. 24). Hermans and his colleagues went on to theorize story telling or narrating (and history making) as a dialogical process. They did so by drawing on the work of Russian literary theorist Mikhail Bakhtin. Bakhtin noted that Dostoevsky—rather than having the narrator's voice dominate and speak for others—gave all of the characters in his novels their own voice. In other words, Dostoevsky's narratives were characterized by a "polyphony" of voices in dialogical relation, rather than by "a multitude of characters within a unified objective world" (Hermans, Kempen and van Loon, 1992, p. 27). In my view, the implications of such a perspective for relational practices that some communities might call "research" or "leadership" are well worth exploring.

I need to say a little more about this talk of a "polyphony of voices in dialogical relation" to further clarify how it differs from the modernist, entitative construction of one independently existing self speaking with one voice. It is vital to appreciate that polyphony is possible because persons can engage in imaginal dialogues. The dialogical self is social or, as I prefer to say, relational, "... in the sense that other people occupy positions in the multi-voiced self" (Hermans, Kempen and van Loon, 1992, p. 29). My students sometimes ask, "Well, what about when someone is alone on a desert island? Then they are not relating," to which I answer, "Well, yes, they are"—the "outside" is "inside" when person is storied as a "relational being" (Gergen, 1994) rather than as a self-existing entity. Remember, I said that the relational view does *not* assume some centralized and singular self attempt to know and to influence some separate and relatively stable other. Of course, as Hermans and his colleagues remarked, the western-cultural "tendency to centralization" may encourage practices that center *one* self in dominance relation with other entified constructions, "thereby reducing the possibility of dialogue that, for its full development, requires a high degree of openness for the exchange and modification of perspectives" (Hermans, Kempen & van Loon, 1992, p. 30). So, a relational view can explore how relational processes might go on, (a) when one narrator speaks for others while claiming a "unified objective world" of separately existing entities, and/or (b) by exploring multiple voices, dialogical practices, and openness to multiple and changing local (relational) realities.

"Subject-object" (S-O) constructions of entities and relations are centered in an "entitative" discourse. The discourse, sometimes tacitly and sometimes implicitly, constructs one entity as Subject—who is assumed to act, to know, and to speak for, form, shape, or structure another entity—constructed as Object (at least, in these relations). The subject (for example, the scientist and/or leader) acts to build "knowledge that" or "aboutness" knowledge (about other) and acts to achieve "power over" other as object (Dachler & Hosking, 1995; Gergen, 1995; Hosking, 1995; Sampson, 1995). We see these assumptions at work, for example, in postpositivist science practices that try to separate the scientist (self as scientist and knowing subject) from that which he wants to know (other as object) so that reasonably objective knowledge can be produced. This "objective" knowledge then is used to claim warrant for the rationality of organizational (re)design and leadership interventions.

In contrast, the postmodern relational discourse gives ontology and prominence to relational processes, views knowing as ongoing—as in action—and sees knowing as intimately interwoven with power. In addition, power (in a rather special sense) is discoursed as key to how self and other can be in ongoing relations. So, for example, the appearance of one voice, of unity and stability or, to put it the other way around, the apparent absence of movement and multiplicity, now are theorized as relational realities made, stabilized, and changed in construction processes and *not* as "how things really are." The relational discourse invites exploration of how realities and relations are made real. So, for example, how does *the appearance* of entities and *the appearance* of subject-object relations get made real? Similarly, how would it be possible to make soft(er) self/other differentiation without fixing, solidifying, and unifying? It is around this latter possibility that I think the relational constructionist discourse has so much to offer. It allows and invites the question: How can relational processes construct "soft" lines of differentiation, for example, in leadership research, theory, and practice? The relational discourse and this question offer a new "voyage of discovery" for leadership researchers, and it is on such a voyage that a certain sort of dialogical practice can have so much potential.

Dialogue and Soft Self-other Differentiation

There are methodologies that could be said to facilitate softer self/other differentiation (Hosking, 2000). These include appreciative inquiry (Cooperrider, 1990), "collaborative consulting" (Anderson, 1997), "participative action research" (Reason & Bradbury, 2001), and various ways of working through dialogue (for example, Chasin, Herzig, Roth, Chasin, & Becker, 1996; Gergen, McNamee, & Barrett, 2001). They share a focus on (a) multiple conversations—rather than single-voiced leadership edicts and the avoidance of talk and discussion; (b) multiple self-other relations—rather than a single hierarchy of knowledge and expertise; (c) working with what is already (potentially) available and with "stuff" that the participants believe relevant—rather than imposing the mono-logical constructions, for example, of leaders and/or outside experts; and (d) inviting and supporting many lines of action—rather than requiring or imposing one consensus. These sorts of processes can facilitate multiple, local, community-based voices and can help multiple communities (as local relational realities) to participate such that other local realities can be "allowed to lie" rather than being questioned, grasped, judged, and fixed by a particular, knowing, and structuring leader or change agent.

The sorts of multi-voiced conversations to which I have just referred are sometimes called *dialogues*. In this context, the term is being used to refer to a rather special kind of conversation, relational process or performance.

Dialogue, in this sense, is theorized as a slow, open, and curious way of relating characterized (a) by a very special sort of listening, questioning, and being present; (b) by a willingness to suspend one's assumptions and certainties; and (c) by reflexive attention to ongoing processes and one's own participation. So, rather than constructing separate, fixed, or closed realities [e.g., of self (other) and one's own (others) position on some issue (which would be an entitative narrative)], dialogical practices open up to relationality, open up to possibilities, and open-up space for self and other to co-emerge and to "go on" in different but equal (not right/wrong or better/worse) relations.

I find myself particularly attracted to the work of David Bohm (2004), an eminent physicist who developed a holistic and ongoing or processual view of reality. He linked dialogue with (in)coherence, arguing that relational processes are incoherent when people position themselves apart from the whole (as separate entities in S-O relation), when they try to understand wholeness through abstract thought, and when they hold on to fixed positions—all of which seem to me to be aspects of what I have called the entitative discourse. He remarked, "incoherence on a large scale (involves) patterns of thinking and acting that separate people from one another and from the larger reality in which they are attempting to live" (Senge as cited in Bohm, 2004, p. x). Bohm suggested that science and western rationalism contribute to incoherence by assuming and orienting towards some unique truth. In contrast, he argued, dialogue is a process that can reveal incoherence in people's thinking; dialogue can support exploration of what hinders communications (ways of relating) for example, between different parts of some organization or between different nations.

According to Bohm, dialogical processes allow participants to "take part in truth." It is taking part that allows the coherence of the whole. But, I should reiterate, "the whole" of which he speaks is not a whole "thing" or entity—he views reality as processual—as always unfolding. Bohm's view could be described as "participative" and is, for example, reflected in Reason and Torbert's talk of practical, participative knowing or participative consciousness in participative action research (Reason, 1994; Reason & Torbert, 2000). Bohm's view has also been called dialogical (see Nichol in Bohm, 2004, p. xv). For Bohm, dialogue allows participants to experience (what I earlier called) "relational realities" as continually unfolding and allows participants to see themselves as contributors. Over time, dialogical practices enable and support (a) nowness—rather than holding on to past solidifications, convictions, and prejudices; (b) emergent possibilities and insights—flow rather than solidification; and (c) collective learning and a sense of participating in wholeness—rather than multiple, separately existing entities.

Dialogical practices can provide a way out of constantly re-constructing some seemingly solid, stable, and singular "I," who can build individual knowledge about and attempt to control other—when other is a person, organization, the environment, and so on. The relational discourse opens up possible ways of relating that are not available when entities and subject-object relations are assumed to be how things really are or how they should be; the relational discourse invites us to explore the ways "things" are made and how things could be. Dialoguing, called by Bohm the "discipline of collective inquiry," can open up and appreciate possibilities. Dialoguing allows appreciation of other constructions—"letting them lie"—rather than subjecting them to debate, critique, and partisan claims to have better access to some universal Truth. This relational, dialogical view invites and enables us to view *all* social science discourses—including our own—and *all* leadership theories—including our own—as constructions that could be otherwise. They are all relative (or as I would prefer to say, relational); none is self-standing; each is to be made sense of in its own terms—in relation to its own local rationality—its own ground of assumptions and interests.

Dian Marie

SHAMIR'S RESPONSE TO HOSKING

Dear Dian Marie,

I spent about three weeks in June in Israel, partly as a home vacation and partly attending to family related matters (most of them enjoyable, like spending time with my six-month-old granddaughter). During this period, however, I've read all the chapters in the book, re-read some related material, such as Mary's *LQ* 2006 article and your chapter in the book on follower-centered perspectives that we co-edited, and started to write my commentary.

Thanks for inviting me to engage in a relational dialogue with you and clarifying what you mean by such a dialogue. I respect you for seeking to apply your relational perspective to your own work, including the contribution to this book, but I am afraid I am the wrong partner for a relational dialogue as you describe it. Several chapters in this book have been inspired directly or indirectly by your approach to relational processes, including relational leadership. I've been challenged and inspired by these chapters and reading them and reflecting on them has given me an opportunity to clarify my thoughts about the social constructionist relational approach. I have some serious reservations about the potential usefulness of some key elements of this perspective for the study of leadership and for advancing knowledge more generally. Engaging in a dialogue of the sort you invite me to would therefore be inconsistent with the critique I want to write. Please allow me to respond to some points included in your invitation document in order to clarify my position (on the relational dialogue, not on leadership and leadership theory, which I hope to do in my contribution).

You characterize the relational dialogue as a non-entitative, fluid, or flowing polyphonic process. Occasionally, I may enjoy such a process socially, but I don't think it is very useful for a purposeful activity. I believe all knowledge, science, and practice is necessarily entitative. In fact, I cannot act in this world without an entitative perspective, which distinguishes between me and you, or even me and my family. More to the point, I cannot study leadership or write about it without distinguishing leadership from non-leadership (which, incidentally, has nothing to do with centering on the leader, in my opinion).

The inevitability of entitative thinking is clearly exemplified in your own document because the characterization (some would say caricaturization) of a certain approach as "entitative" is, of course, an act of entity construction par excellence. Furthermore, your critique and rejection of this approach clearly and necessarily comes from a position of assuming to "know" something the other does not know or recognize, and can be seen as an attempt to persuade or influence (which, for some reason, in your relational perspective is immediately and automatically equated with an attempt to gain power and dominance). So, what exactly is relational about the distinction between the entitative and the relational approaches? Was it achieved through a relational dialogue with representatives of the entitative approach? Incidentally, I am not sure that characterizing potential partners as fixated, dis- heartened, dis-engaged, dis-enchanted, and seeking to dominate and use people for their own instrumental purposes would be a good starting point for such a dialogue. Take this book as another example. Even though it is designed, I think, as an exercise in relational science, it is titled: *Advancing Relational Leadership Theory: A Conversation among Perspectives.* All the words in this title refer to entities. Even the first word "advancing" connotes a distinction between advancing and not advancing, a belief that the book should contribute to advancement, some notion of the editors of what *advancement* means, and an assumption that there is a public out there who will buy and read this book because they share these meanings, at least partially. Does that mean that Sonia and Mary want to dominate us? I don't think so. On the contrary, I believe they want to enlighten us, expand our horizons, and set us free from the confines of conventional leadership theories.

In other words, entitative thinking and talking is part and parcel of any dialogue I can imagine, and critique and debate are often also parts of a useful dialogue. I am all for dialogue, listening, inclusion, open-mindedness, and so forth. I don't want to dominate. I am not even sure I want to persuade. All I want, like you, I presume, is to express my ideas and hopefully contribute to a collective purpose, which in this case, is "advancing leadership theory."

Note, that the last statement, beyond its entitative nature, connotes two other elements, which stand in contrast with the relational approach to dialogue as described in your document. First, it connotes an interest in "producing knowledge about." I see nothing wrong with that, even if the "about" is only about a socially constructed phenomenon. Much of our knowledge—scientific, religious, or astrological—is "knowledge about." The only other type of knowledge I can think of is "knowing how to" which in some cases (e.g., flying an aircraft) is related to knowing about and in other cases (e.g., riding a bicycle) is not. However, I am not sure my work can contribute much to knowing how to do leadership, and I think the social constructionist relational view, with its emphasis on situated and fluid knowledge can do even less than I in this regard.

Second, my statement connotes instrumentality. Not instrumentality in the sense of presuming that my comments will help people to do leadership better, and certainly not instrumentality in the sense of wanting to use the other for my purposes. But, instrumentality in the sense of furthering debate and understanding, together with a group of people who share my interest in a phenomenon, some of the social constructions about its nature, and some view about what would constitute a useful contribution to our collective purpose.

Of course, the fact that my purpose is not only expressive but also instrumental and my use of such terms as *advancement* and *contribution* may be seen as reflecting a commitment to *rationality*, another term your perspective seems to reject. I am not a great fan of behavioral and social theories that explain human behavior from a purely or primarily rational perspective, and I am also aware of the fact that rationality is, in some respects, socially constructed and that many people do not use the Western concept of rationality to guide even their conscious and deliberate decisions. However, I believe this concept, which has been essential for the development of the natural sciences, has also been very useful for advancing both knowledge and practice in the social sciences. If I am not mistaken, the whole idea of the social construction of reality (which, for me, is the most significant contribution of sociology to the social sciences) was advanced on the basis of rational arguments. I therefore cannot imagine a fruitful knowledge creation effort that does not follow some criteria of usefulness and advancement of knowledge and does not use some version of rational analysis in order to determine what counts as a useful contribution and what counts as advancement.

From a perspective that views knowledge creation as a collective effort and is committed to usefulness, the slow, polyphonic, and flowing processes with indeterminate results that you promote may be useful in some parts or phases of knowledge creation. However, at a certain point, to become knowledge, it has to be organized and solidified, it cannot just flow continuously. In other words, for both knowledge creation and social action, there is a need to abandon at a certain point the multiple realities, multiple narratives, multiple voices view of the world, in which all voices are equal, and to create or adopt a shared understanding that is given priority over other voices and other possible understandings. I also beg to disagree with the view that all knowledge, or at least the most important knowledge, is always situated and always moving. Of course, some aspects of knowledge are situated and changing, but I believe the usefulness of knowledge is related to the extent to which it is temporarily stable and can be applied across situations. For instance, I believe your participation in a volume, which is going to be read and used by different people in different situations, and the consistency of your arguments across publications spanning over 20 or 30 years, attest to the fact that even you attempt to produce and present knowledge that has some relatively stable value and is not limited only to the situation in which it was created.

The knowledge creation enterprise called *science* has created mechanisms for creating and solidifying knowledge. These mechanisms include criteria for judging contributions and are therefore hierarchical. It is true that some of these mechanisms have exhausted their usefulness and may be maintained, not because they advance knowledge creation, but because they give certain people and groups a privileged status in the hierarchy. However, without hierarchical standards and norms for recognizing and increasing the quality of contributions, what we will have is chaos that will result in slower and poorer knowledge creation. You and I, of course, enact this hierarchy on a daily basis when we claim the title *professor*, teach students, edit journals, review papers, and research grants, write reference letters, and sit in appointments or promotion committees. We can avoid certain duties and roles, use more relational practices in teaching or research, or work to change some aspects of the hierarchy and minimize the risks it entails, but basically we are in the game. Would we be there if we did not believe in the need for some hierarchy and in the basic logic and criteria behind the scientific hierarchy?

Knowledge, power, and hierarchy are indeed interrelated. A knowledge hierarchy may have negative consequences for science, when it becomes too rigid, excludes ideas, and blocks creativity. It may also have negative social consequences, when it excludes the voices and influence of individuals and groups that could and should participate and have influence, and when it extends beyond the domain in which it is useful and justified into domains unrelated to knowledge creation. We should be aware of these risks and try to minimize them, but to abandon the knowledge hierarchy because of its risks and to accept polyphony of equal status voices is to settle for much poorer knowledge and practice. My experience tells me it is not really possible to operate in the knowledge creation arena without standards and criteria which entail a hierarchy. Even my postmodernist colleagues who adhere to a multiple narratives view, in the end, especially if they do empirical work and not only philosophy, present us with a story for which they explicitly or implicitly claim a privileged status.

I believe that the phenomenon of leadership is to a large extent socially constructed, both at the macro cultural-historical level and at the micro level of particular groups, processes, and relationships. I also agree that all social science perspectives, including all leadership theories and my own modest contributions, are constructions that could be otherwise. I don't pretend to know a truth that is separate from social construction, and I don't assume I'll ever know one. In view of that, and because I'd like to believe I am still able to develop, my current thoughts on the issues discussed here and in the book are probably not my final thoughts.

You have kindly invited me to enter your game and specified the rules of the game. As you understand, I don't feel comfortable with at least some of these rules. I therefore beg for permission to write my contribution as a monologue under my name. I have never written about these issues, and I'd like to make some statements that I believe might be more dialogically useful in this form than if they are diluted in the framework of a relational dialogue of the sort you believe in. This monologue is part of a dialogue because it has been informed and influenced by your work and those of other authors in this volume; because I'll send you a copy, and you are welcome to respond to it, if the editors give you the space; and because, hopefully, other readers will also respond in some way. I have a tentative title for this monologue: "Leadership Research or Post-Leadership Research? Advancing Leadership Theory versus Throwing the Baby out with the Bath Water." I hope this title will convince you that my approach to this dialogue is anything but "dis-engaged, dis-heartened, and dis-enchanted."

I hope to be able to send you and the editors a draft in about a week.

All the best,

Boas

REFERENCES

Anderson, H. (1997). *Conversation, language, and possibilities: A postmodern approach to therapy.* New York, NY: Harper Collins.
Bohm, D. (2004). *On dialogue.* London, England: Routledge.

Boje, D. (1995). Stories of the storytelling organization: A postmodern analysis of Disney As "Tamara-Land." *Academy of Management Journal, 38*(4), 997–1035.

Chasin, R., Herzig, M., Roth, S.A., Chasin, L., & Becker, C. (1996). From diatribe to dialogue on divisive public issues: Approaches drawn from family therapy. *Mediation Quarterly, 13*(4), 323–344.

Chia, R. (1995). From modern to postmodern organizational analysis. *Organization Studies, 16*(4), 579–604.

Cooperrider, D. L. (1990). Positive image, positive action: The affirmative basis of organizing. In S. Srivastva, & D. L. Cooperrider, *Appreciative management and leadership.* San Francisco, CA: Jossey-Bass.

Dachler, H. P., & Hosking, D. M. (1995). The primacy of relations in socially constructing organizational realities. In D. M. Hosking, H. P. Dachler & K. J. Gergen (Eds.), *Management and organization: Relational alternatives to individualism* (pp. 1–29). Aldershot, England: Avebury.

Edwards, D., & Potter, J. (1992). *Discursive psychology.* London, England: Sage.

Gergen, K. J. (1994). *Realities and relationships: soundings in social construction.* Cambridge, MA: Harvard University Press.

Gergen, K. J. (1995). Relational theory and the discourses of power. In D. M. Hosking, H. P. Dachler, & K. J. Gergen (Eds.), *Management and organization: Relational alternatives to individualism* (pp. 29–51). Aldershot, England: Avebury.

Gergen, K. J., & Thatchenkerry, T. (1996). Organization science as social construction: Postmodern potentials. *Journal of Applied Behavioural Science, 32*(4), 356–377.

Gergen, K. J., McNamee, S., & Barrett, F. J. (2001). Toward transformative dialogue. *International Journal of Public Administration, 24*(7/8), 679–707.

Hermans, H., Kempen, H., & Van Loon, R. (1992). The dialogical self. Beyond individualism and rationalism. *American Psychologist, 47*(1), 23–33.

Hosking, D. M. (1981). A critical evaluation of Fiedler's contingency hypothesis. In G. A. Stephenson, & J. M. Davis (Eds.), *Progress in applied social psychology* (Vol. 1, pp. XX–XX). Wiley.

Hosking, D. M. (1995). Constructing power: Entitative and relational approaches. In D. M. Hosking, H. P. Dachler, & K. J. Gergen (Eds.), *Management and organization: Relational alternatives to individualism,* (pp. 51–71). Aldershot, England: Avebury.

Hosking, D. M. (2000). Ecology in mind, mindful practices. *European Journal for Work and Organizational Psychology, 9*(2), 147–158.

Hosking, D. M. (2004) Changeworks: A critical construction. In J. Boonstra (Ed.), *Dynamics of organisational change and learning.* Chichester, England: Wiley.

Hosking, D. M. (2006). Discourses of relations and relational process. In O. Kyriakidou, & M.E. Ozilgin (Eds.), *Relational perspectives in organisation studies* ( ). Cheltenham, England: Elgar.

Hosking, D. M. (2008). Can constructionism be critical? In J. A. Holstein, & J. F. Gubrium (Eds.), *Handbook of constructionist research* (pp. 669–686).

Hosking, D. M. (2011). Telling tales of relations: Appreciating relational constructionism. *Organization Studies, 32*(1), 47–65.

Hosking, D. M., & Morley, I. E. (1991). *A social psychology of organising.* Chichester, England: Harvester Wheatsheaf.

Latour, B. (1987). *Science in action.* Milton Keynes: Open University Press.

Nichol, L. (2004). Foreword. In D. Bohm, *On dialogue.* London, England: Routledge.

Reason, P. (Ed.). (1994). *Participation in human inquiry.* London, England, Sage.

Reason, P., & Bradbury, H. (2001). *Handbook of action research: Participative inquiry and practice.* London, England: Sage

Reason, P. &, Torbert, W. (2001). The action turn. Towards a transformational social science. *Concepts and Transformation, 6*(1), 1–37.

Sampson, E. E. (1995). *Celebrating the other.* London, England: Harvester Wheatsheaf.

Senge, P. (2004). Preface. In D. Bohm, *On dialogue.* London, England: Routledge.

CHAPTER 17

LEADERSHIP RESEARCH OR POST-LEADERSHIP RESEARCH?

Advancing Leadership Theory versus Throwing the Baby Out with the Bath Water

Boas Shamir

This volume contains a set of chapters which, separately and collectively, have considerable potential to make very significant contributions to leadership studies. The editors and authors of this volume share a sense of dissatisfaction with conventional leadership theories, studies, and practices and offer us, under the umbrella term *relational leadership*, a family of alternative approaches to thinking about, studying, and practicing leadership. Most, if not all, authors share a critical stance toward leader-centered, heroic, and romantic views of leadership, the tendency to equate leadership with formal positions or titles, and the tendency to think about leadership in terms of fixed and rigid entities or dichotomies like "leader" and

Advancing Relational Leadership Research, pages 477–500
Copyright © 2012 by Information Age Publishing
All rights of reproduction in any form reserved.

"follower." Collectively, they suggest a shift from focusing on leaders' attributes and behaviors and on what leaders do to followers, to focusing on leadership in terms of relationships, which are co-produced by all the parties involved, regardless of their formal positions or titles. Most of them also view social construction and joint meaning-making activities as lying at the heart of leadership processes, and emphasize that these processes have to be understood as embedded in their cultural, historical, and organizational context. The volume contains a wealth of theoretical ideas, methodological suggestions, examples of research, and suggestions for further research to guide leadership scholars in the future.

However, beyond these common themes, the chapters vary greatly in terms of their conceptualization of relationships, relational processes, and relational theory. They also vary in terms of their ontological and epistemological assumptions and hence their approach to social science. Consequently, they vary in their implications for theoretical and empirical research on leadership. Some chapters represent important yet relatively modest extensions of the currently dominant approach to leadership studies, such as increased attention to the role of affective processes in shaping effective leader-follower relationships (Ashkanasy et al.), the challenges of establishing leadership relationships with demographically diverse followers (Offerman), and the effects of political skills on communication and influence processes between leaders and followers (Treadway, et al). The other chapters adopt, to varying degrees, the social constructionist approach (Ospina & Sorenson, 2006; Uhl-Bien, 2006) to studying and understanding leadership relationships and processes. Some of the latter chapters (particularly those by Alvesson & Svenningson, Barge, and Ospina et al.) represent and advocate a revolutionary shift of paradigm in leadership research and practice on the basis of the social constructionist perspective and related post-modernist ideas (e.g., Hosking, 2007). These chapters echo Drath's (2001) assertion that "nothing less than a revolution of the mind is required, a shift in order of thought, a reformation of how leadership is known" (p. 124).

The chapters that propose a paradigm shift in leadership studies and some of the social constructionist ideas included in other chapters are more intellectually challenging and have more radical implications for the field than those that remain closer to the traditional approach to leadership studies. However, I believe some of these ideas and implications are inconsistent with the term *leadership* even in its broadest definition and dilute it beyond any usefulness. I also believe some of them cannot be followed and are therefore not likely to contribute to the creation of knowledge about leadership. Therefore, I would like to present my stance toward these challenging ideas and suggestions and my reservations about them in the first part of this essay. My critique of the radical constructionist ideas centers on four points:

- The constructionists' rejection of the conventional discourse on leadership is not useful because they cannot offer an alternative way of defining *leadership* and distinguishing it from other social processes.
- The constructionists' emphasis on the uniqueness of every situation and every phase in each situation is less useful than the attempt to create knowledge that has more general value.
- The severance of the link between leadership and collective outcomes, which is suggested by some constructionists, undermines the usefulness of the term *leadership* and the importance of studying leadership.
- The impracticality of the radical constructionist perspective is demonstrated by the fact that even the proponents of this perspective cannot follow it when they address issues of empirical research or practice.

I will try to use the chapters of this volume to exemplify my arguments.

Following my critique, I argue that we need a common notion of *leadership* to advance leadership theory, and that a useful notion has to include the element of differentiation among individuals or groups on the basis of their influence on other actors in their social arena. This element entails certain risks and negative consequences but—I argue—we should deal with these risks within our common discourse, rather than throw the baby out together with the bath water. In the concluding part of this essay, I highlight some directions for future research from a relational perspective that seem to me to be particularly promising.

THE RADICAL SOCIAL CONSTRUCTIONIST CHALLENGE TO THE CONVENTIONAL DISCOURSE ON LEADERSHIP AS A DEAD-END STREET

The radical social constructionist perspective uses the term *relational* to challenge the conventional discourse (sometimes called "Discourse" or big "D" discourse) on leadership, namely the way we conventionally think, talk, practice, teach, theorize, and study leadership. Proponents of this perspective view the conventional discourse as a historically and culturally situated social construction that has become conventional and taken for granted, and they attribute many of the limitations and biases of current leadership theories to the dominance of this discourse, which they claim is based on erroneous assumptions, is no longer useful, and may even be socially harmful (because it represents the interests and views of individual and group power holders and excludes the legitimate and potentially useful views and interests of others). The constructionist perspective challenges not only the conventional distinction between leaders and followers and the association between leadership and formal or informal positions of power, but first and foremost, it challenges the term *leadership* as most of us understand it.

I share the view that leadership is, to considerable extent, a socially constructed phenomenon both at the macro, cultural level and at the more micro, local level of particular groups and social processes. I also accept the claim that, once a discourse becomes conventional and taken for granted, its socially constructed nature should be exposed in order to reveal different possibilities for understanding a phenomenon, which cannot be seen within the confines of the taken for granted discourse (Fairhurst, 2007). I therefore welcome the challenges posed by the social constructionist perspective on relational theory. However, I submit that some of the proponents of this perspective (e.g., Alvesson & Sveningsson, Barge, and Ospina et al., this volume; Hosking, 2007) push their arguments too far, thus excluding them from the realm of even the broadest possible arena of leadership studies. I think it is important to try to identify the points at which their arguments lose their potential usefulness for understanding leadership.

Rejection of the dominant big "D" discourse on leadership leaves the proponents of this position with two possible options. The first is the replacement of this discourse with another big "D" leadership discourse. However, this option is inconsistent with the constructionists' "multiple realities" view of the world and their claim that leadership is (or can be, or should be) differently constructed in every conversation, social interaction, or social process. Therefore, the second option is to leave us without a common leadership discourse. This position is consistent with the "multiple realities" view but is not likely to be useful for advancing leadership studies. In fact, as half-heartedly admitted by Alvesson and Sveningsson (Chapter 7), it amounts to promoting the replacement of the leadership discourse with a post-leadership discourse and a replacement of the focus on leadership processes with a focus on non-leadership and un-led social processes.

There is a fundamental contradiction between the social constructionist emphasis on multiple realities, multiple narratives, multiple voices, and infinite possibilities to construct leadership in each situation, conversation, and relationship, and the advancement of leadership theory. For any concept to be useful, even for common talk and certainly for social scientific purposes, it has to be differentiated from other concepts. Therefore, those who believe that leadership is (or can be, or should be) differently constructed in every social process and yet want to use the term *leadership* and stay within the umbrella of leadership studies, still have to provide an answer to the question: "What counts as leadership?" Barge (Chapter 4) acknowledges the difficulty of defining or recognizing *leadership* within the constructionist perspective:

> This is a difficult question to answer from a systemic constructionist perspective because the meaning of any social practice is viewed as co-created, contextual, and contestable... [and] defining what counts as leadership is made even more difficult and vexing when we consider that situations are dynamic.

However, these difficulties do not deter Barge from trying to offer an answer which is consistent with his constructionist perspective: "This means that determining what counts as leadership can only be accomplished by exploring how people negotiate a working definition of the situation." I submit that this is not a useful answer because, from this perspective, anything can count as leadership, and if this is so, nothing is gained by using the term *leadership*.

In other words, the logical conclusion from the social constructionist critique is not the replacement of the currently dominant leadership discourse with a different leadership discourse. Rather, it is either the replacement of the currently dominant leadership discourse with a non-leadership or post-leadership discourse, a position that can perhaps be justified on theoretical and ideological grounds, but excludes its proponents from the arena of leadership studies or, in consistence with their post-modernist, multiple realties, multiple narratives view of the world, the abolition of any big discourse, a position which is consistent with their emphasis on the complex, ambiguous, fluid, open-ended, and indeterminate nature of social relations. The latter position undermines any potential usefulness of the leadership construct, and therefore, as I will try to show later, is not practical and cannot be followed even by its advocates.

Moreover, in my opinion, the radical social constructionists over-emphasize the uniqueness and freshness of every social interaction and conversation. "Our social constructions of leadership are also fluid and dynamic as shifts in language create fresh understandings for leadership, as well as new patterns of social arrangements" (Barge, Chapter 4). We should note in passing that this position is inconsistent with the large influence attached by the social constructionists to the conventional discourse on leadership in their critique of this discourse. If leadership is freshly constructed in each interaction, why should we worry about the limiting effects of some dominant external discourse? More importantly, I believe this view of the social world is grossly exaggerated and may represent wishful thinking more than a reflection of common experience. I believe common experience tells us that (perhaps unfortunately) with slight variations and very rare dramatic changes, most of our relationships are characterized by regularities and patterns that evolve only slowly and tend to remain relatively stable across interactions and conversations. Therefore, the focus on the unique aspects of each episode and each social construction, while a legitimate choice, is less useful for knowledge creation because it directs our attention to relatively marginal and less consequential aspects of the phenomenon.

To quote Barge (Chapter 4) again:

> The unfolding conversation and conversational moments have the quality of being for the first time, something that has never been experienced before in quite this way. To be sure, there are regularities in communication patterns and frameworks for sense-making and action within any human system; but the unique combination of people, topics, time, place, and context give the conversations and conversational moments a unique flavor.

A "unique flavor," I agree, but not much more than that, certainly not the quality of "being for the first time." In fact, in many of our relationships, including leadership relationships, even the first time doesn't have the quality of being for the first time, as it is being conditioned by norms, expectations, reputations, and experiences with similar others.

It is a matter of choice whether one wants to focus on the regularities and patterns in a relationship or on the unique flavor of each conversation or phase in a conversation, but I submit that the former are more robust and more important than the latter for the creation of knowledge about leadership and for guiding practices that are related to this knowledge. We have limited cognitive capacities, and therefore knowledge creation inevitably involves simplification and some sacrifice of the uniqueness of each case and the variation among manifestation of the same phenomenon. Much potential for knowledge creation lies in exploring variation, but ultimately this variation must be captured in recognition of regularities that cannot do full justice to the unique flavor of each case. Leadership is a complex, varied, and messy phenomenon, and, as a result, our understanding of it is limited. Most probably, we have erred on the side of oversimplification and overgeneralization, but abandoning our attempts to identify patterns and regularities for a program of studies that gives priority to the uniqueness of and fluidity of each conversation is likely to be even less useful for increasing knowledge, in my opinion.

Furthermore, paradoxically, some versions of the social constructionist view even undermine the potential importance of the concept of social construction to leadership studies. Most leadership researchers who recognize the importance of social construction in leadership processes do so because they believe that collective action is guided by shared meanings, and it is therefore important to understand the processes by which shared meanings are constructed and the role of leadership in these processes (e.g., Smircich & Morgan, 1982). For instance, in presenting the relational perspective, Uhl-Bien (1996) defines *leadership* as a social influence process through which emergent coordination and change are produced, and Ospina & Sorensen (2006) assert "leadership happens when a community develops and uses, over time, shared agreements to create results that have collective value" (p. 188). However, the logic of the multiple realities approach leads some radical constructionists to reject even the view that leadership plays a role in achieving shared meanings and in the coordination which results from these meanings.

Thus, Alvesson and Sveningsson (Chapter 7) follow the multiple realities view of the social constructionist approach to its logical conclusion and suggest that *leadership* should be viewed as "a complex set of construction processes, sometimes coalescing, sometimes diverging, and leading to ambiguity and confusion or divergence of meanings around the goals, means, and relations typically characterizing a leadership process." Leadership is indeed a complex phenomenon with varied manifestations, but a notion of leadership that gives an equal status to both the construction of shared meanings and to the creation of ambiguity, confusion, diverse constructions, and incoherent meanings, and does not enable us to link leadership to the achievement of shared meanings, loses its distinctiveness and hence its usefulness for me. If I accept such a notion, I would not know what leadership is, how to study it, and, perhaps most importantly, why I should study it. Therefore, while I share the view implied in many chapters of this volume, that conventional leadership theories have been oversimplified, and I welcome the introduction of more complexity and less determinism to our thinking, these trends should not be carried too far, or we will find ourselves drowning in a sea of complexity and ambiguity in which we will lose the phenomenon we wish to understand.

The impossibility of reconciling the radical "multiple realities" social constructionist perspective with making contributions to leadership theory or practice is demonstrated by several chapters in this volume. Let me give some examples. First, even Barge cannot remain faithful to this perspective and follow his own suggestion for how to determine what counts as leadership, namely by exploring how people negotiate a working definition in each situation. In the conclusion of his chapter, he asserts, "relational leadership's next great challenge . . . is to shift from talking about the way leadership is constructed, to developing practices that help leaders to anticipate how they might act within an unfolding situation and to be present in the situation." Note, first, that this assertion retains the conventional discourse on leadership by focusing on leaders as distinct from others. More importantly, it completely abandons the constructionist perspective on relational leadership by suggesting shifting the focus of this perspective to the development of leaders' practices and skills, namely to what leaders have to do in order to lead. Such a leader-centered focus is, of course, the ultimate focus of the conventional approach to leadership that the constructionists seek to get rid of.

This point is perhaps even better exemplified by the chapter written by Kennedy et al. (Chapter 6), which compares and contrasts two training programs, one based on the conventional approach and the other supposedly on the constructionist approach. This comparison is inconsistent with the social constructionists' rejection of the conventional discourse on leadership. The so-called constructionist training program assembled a group of people in the framework of a leadership training center, and engaged them in a learning process which was presumed to equip them with certain skills or knowledge that would be useful to them in very different situations. By doing so, it differentiated between leaders and others, focused on the leaders' knowledge, and assumed that knowledge attained or constructed by leaders in one situation could (or even should) be used in other situations. In other words, this alternative program may have been different in its contents from the conventional program. However, it stayed very much within the premises of the conventional discourse and violated the basic premises of the constructionist approach, which rejects the distinction between leader and others and the focus on leaders' capabilities, and emphasizes the uniqueness and freshness of every leadership situation or encounter.

Such inconsistencies exist not only in proposals for practice but also in the way empirical research is carried out and reported about. For instance, the Ospina et al. (Chapter 9) impressive program of studies demonstrates two common inconsistencies between the premises of the social constructionist approach and empirical work that follows this approach and the inability to generate useful knowledge without deviating from the constructionist premises. The first manifestation is the inability to retain the commitment to multiple realities and multiple narratives. Even scholars who declare strong philosophical and theoretical allegiance to multiple realities and multiple narratives, when reporting about their empirical work, inevitably present us with a narrative for which they claim a privileged status. This narrative may be different from a currently dominant story, but it is nevertheless based on choices about what to look at, what to look for, and how to interpret the findings. More importantly, the alternative story contains implicit or explicit claims about validity, namely about correspondence between the story and some observed phenomenon, that is between the presented story and some reality. It is simply impossible, if one wants to make a scientific contribution, to treat all narratives equally, avoid composing and presenting a privileged narrative, and refrain from making statements and drawing conclusions about the observed or experienced phenomenon. This is exactly what Ospina et al. do so well when they summarize their findings in terms of certain collective practices and link these practices to the effectiveness of producing social changes.

The second inconsistency has to do with the treatment of context. The central construct in Ospina et al.'s study is that of practice: "a collective construct, the outcome of collective-meaning making, which rests upon shared knowledge that is largely tacit and embodied, *historically and culturally specific*" (my emphasis). This commitment to situated local constructions is also reflected in their quoting of Hosking (1997) to the effect that "leadership cannot be abstracted from the organizational processes of which it is a part." However, the framework developed by Ospina et al. to interpret and present their findings does exactly that. It is a set of generalizations about social practices, which was derived (abstracted) from a study of 60 organizations operating in a wide variety of contexts. This is not a criticism of this exemplary study or the proposed framework or of the grounded approach, which does not start from abstractions but generates them inductively from the findings. It is merely a demonstration that, ultimately, the creation of knowledge, especially useful knowledge, requires abstracting from particular cases and generalizing across particular cases, even if these abstractions and generalizations do not do full justice to the variation among the studied cases. Thus, the radical constructionist lens, which may look convincing in the form of an abstract argument on paper, meets its limitations when it is translated to a program of empirical research.

The conclusion to be drawn from the critique presented above is not that the constructionist perspective has nothing to offer to the field of leadership studies in terms of theoretical ideas; or that useful empirical research cannot be carried out from a constructionist perspective; or that this perspective cannot generate useful practices. It has much to offer in all three arenas, and in the latter part of this chapter, I'll give some examples of potentially useful contributions from this perspective. Rather, the conclusion is that those constructionists who call for a revolution that amounts to complete total rejection of the conventional leadership discourse, and substituting it with an open-ended view according to which leadership is freshly constructed in each situation or is not associated with any shared meanings at all, have very little to offer to those of us who believe that leadership is a distinct social phenomenon which shows some regularities across situations and relationships.

WHAT SHOULD COUNT AS LEADERSHIP?
THE NECESSITY OF DIFFERENTIATION

I therefore suggest that for the purposes of theorizing about leadership and studying leadership in the framework of a collective effort to advance knowledge, we need at least a basic common discourse. In the very least, this discourse should include a shared understanding of what constitutes leadership and how leadership is different from other social processes. If the term *leadership* is to retain some meaning and have some usefulness, not every consequential social process should be called *leadership*. As argued above, a perspective that seeks to remove the currently shared construct of leadership and cannot offer an alternative construct—because such an offer is inconsistent with its basic premises—is a dead-end street from the viewpoint of advancing leadership theory.

I now come to what would probably be the most controversial element in my position, not only from a social constructionist perspective, but also from other recent perspectives, those that promote ideas of shared or distributed leadership. The issue is how to define *leadership* in a useful way. Definitions, of course, are arbitrary. There are no right definitions or wrong definitions. However, there are more useful and less useful definitions. I submit that, in order to distinguish leadership from other social processes so that we can recognize it, focus on it, theorize it, study it, and exchange ideas about it, we cannot view every social process, not even every process that results in shared meanings and coordinated collective action, as leadership. We need to retain a central element of the conventional discourse, and that is the differentiation among individuals, groups, organizations, or other social entities. Leadership may be viewed as a collective phenomenon in the sense of being co-produced or co-constructed by many people, groups or organizations, but if the process of co-production does not include differentiation among the producers, I would not know how to distinguish leadership from other collective processes, and, therefore, would not have a useful construct of leadership.

I therefore suggest that we should reserve the term *leadership*, and use it only for situations and processes in which there is disproportionate or asymmetrical influence in a social arena. At the group level, for the term *leadership* to be useful, some individuals have to be observed as exerting more influence on the group than others, or at least to be recognized or perceived by others as exerting such disproportionate influence. Often these individuals are expected by others and by themselves to exert such influence. Hence, the differentiation in the degree of influence usually entails differentiation on two other dimensions: roles (in the sense of shared expectations, not formal roles) and role identities (see Seers & Chopin, Chapter 2). The same principle of distinction should apply, I believe, to leadership of higher-level actors, such as groups, organizations, or nations. Thus, even when we talk about the leadership of the United States among the nations, we have to mean the disproportionate influence of this country. Otherwise the term *leadership* will be meaningless.

This view does not mean that the differentiation between leaders and others is fixed. It does not require the construction of "leader" and "followers" as fixed entities and does not entail that we should view leadership as embodied in the fixed characteristics of leaders and other participants and that leadership theory or research should center on these characteristics. It certainly does not mean that leadership theory or research should center on the leader. Other participants (perhaps we should start calling them *partners* or *collaborators* because these terms are less fixed and more egalitarian than *followers*) play many active roles in the leadership process and make essential contributions to the construction of the leadership relationships and to the achievement of the collective purposes (Shamir et al., 2007). Leadership can also be rotated and shifted between situations and between various phases of a social process. However, if we accept a notion of leadership that includes differentiation, leadership cannot be fully shared or dispersed. If it is fully shared, I suggest we don't call it *leadership* because that term loses any added value.

Thus, from my perspective, if all members, partners, or collaborators have the same degree of influence, the group or social process of interest has no leadership, even if the group or the processes creates shared meanings and is highly effective in creating a change or achieving some other collective purpose. It is perfectly legitimate and useful to study leaderless social processes and to prefer or advocate such processes in practice, but it is highly confusing, and therefore not useful, to expand the term *leadership* to include such processes. For a phenomenon to be called *leadership*, we have to be able to identify certain actors who, at least in a certain situation and during a specified period of time, exert more influence than others on the group or the process.

My suggestion to retain the differentiation among actors in our shared concept of leadership is not without problems. First, for cognitive and motivational reasons, we tend to exaggerate the extent of differentiation, its importance and its implications (e.g., Meindl, 1995). Second, the inequality of influence, which, in my view, is an essential component of the definition of *leadership* is, of course, closely linked to power differences (some would say even equivalent with power differences). This linkage entails considerable risks, such as the abuse of power, the exclusion of individuals and groups from exerting influence (e.g., Fletcher, Chapter 3), the intensification of inequality, and the spilling over of inequality from the task domain to other dimensions, such as earnings or access to valuable resources. It is perfectly legitimate to view the potential negative consequences of leadership as too common and too large, and therefore to study and promote social processes that do not include differentiation in level of influence. However, I suggest that it would be more useful if the holders of this position present their efforts in terms of a non-leadership, post-leadership, or even anti-leadership approach, rather than as contributions to the advancement of leadership studies.

Those of us who wish to contribute to leadership studies have to acknowledge the potentially negative consequences of this phenomenon, study them, and explore ways to minimize them as an integral part of our leadership studies and practice. More generally, I suggest that it is possible to throw out the bath water (leader centeredness, the fixed entities view, the exaggerated, heroic, and romantic views of leadership, and the negative implications of power differentials) without throwing away the baby, namely the essence of the leadership phenomenon, and leaving us with no useful construct of leadership.

Some of the chapters included in this volume demonstrate this possibility very well, especially those by Seers and Chopin (whose approach is closer to the conventional approach) and by Fletcher (who is mainly a constructionist). Much of Fletcher's work has been devoted to uncovering relational dimensions of good work and competence that were excluded from the dominant discourse (and hence from conceptions of effective organization and effective leadership) because of their association with the feminine. Consequently, some practices were held to be leadership, and some, arguably as important to organizational ends, were not. Fletcher has a *relational ideology* (her term), and her analysis largely follows a constructionist approach. Thus, her practical aim is "helping practitioners strategize ways to interrupt and influence the social construction of leadership such that their relational practices get constructed as leadership rather than as not-leadership." Yet, Fletcher does not abandon the conventional discourse on leadership completely, but rather wishes to expand it to include relational elements that have hitherto been excluded. She clearly links the concept of leadership to collective outcomes when she writes, "the practice of good leadership is increasingly conceptualized as the ability to create conditions under which co-constructed outcomes, such as coordinated action, collective achievement, and shared accountability can be achieved." She explicitly declares that she wishes to retain some elements of what has been called the "entitist" view of leadership (Uhl-Bien, 2006) because of its emphasis on personal agency. Furthermore, at least implicitly, she even retains the notion of differentiation between leaders and followers when she characterizes good leadership practices as "egalitarian, mutual, collaborative and two-directional, with *followers* (my emphasis) playing an integral, agentic role in the leadership process."

I now want to take a further step and argue that the leaderless version of the radical constructionist approach is also not useful because, in certain respects at least at the group level, the differentiation among individuals in degree of influence exists "out there." First, as Seers and Chopin (Chapter 2) show, it can be observed in some non-human groups, so it probably is not fully socially constructed. Second, there is ample evidence from 100 years of experimental leadership research that leadership, in the sense of differentiation of influence, emerges in task groups even when these groups are composed of children, exist only temporarily, and do not operate in an organizational culture that includes norms of differentiation. Furthermore, it tends to emerge even in groups that deliberately try to abolish it, like the Israeli Kibbutzim, which, in the first decades of their existence adhered very strictly to an egalitarian ideology and practice, frequently rotated all formal leadership positions, and sent back former occupants of leadership positions to work in menial laborer roles. Despite these efforts, there are many testimonies that certain members were both expected to and did exert disproportionate influence on their communities.

Third, what social constructionists (e.g., Alvesson & Sveningsson, Chapter 7) call the "contemporary leadership discourse" is not so contemporary and is much less historically and culturally situated than the constructionists argue. The basic element of this construction, namely the attribution of disproportionate influence to some actors, is similar across societies and cultures and has remained stable across historical periods, as evidenced by the texts and teaching of major religions and ancient myths from different historical periods and different parts of the world. If roles, identities and other meanings are indeed only situated and very fluid, and participants can construct their reality in multiple ways, one wonders how we can explain the fact that so many human groups in different locations and different times have constructed leadership in a basically similar way. Wouldn't we expect a much greater variety in the basic construction of leadership? Perhaps the differentiation implied by the term *leadership* is not just an arbitrary social construction? Perhaps its basis is to be found in common biological processes (e.g., the fact that we are all born as helpless babies that need to be guided by adults)? Perhaps it is a result of evolutionary processes that have retained this differentiation as an effective way by which groups deal with their existence and adaptation problems (Van Vugt, Hogan, & Kaiser, 2008)?

So, it may be misleading to suggest that every interaction is original, and every group can construct leadership in a different way and to imply that the conventional discourse on leadership can be changed if we just expose its situated and socially constructed nature. In a very fundamental way, namely in identifying certain individuals as leaders and attributing to them disproportionate influence, the majority of groups tend to construct leadership in a similar way, even when they deliberately attempt not to do so.

It is, of course, possible to argue, as critical thinkers are likely to do, that the reason for the basic similarity and stability of constructions of leadership is that in every human group there have always been individuals and groups (kings, priests, managers) whose interests were served by maintaining the conventional idea of leadership, and these individuals and groups influenced the constructions in a way that served their interests. Note, however, that this is a conventional discourse argument *par excellence* because it attributes the constructed shared meaning to the disproportionate influence of some individuals. Presumably, therefore, the changing of this discourse would also require such influence, namely leadership. This brings us back to square one, namely to the need to acknowledge asymmetric influence as a potentially important aspect of any analysis of social processes and hence the usefulness of defining *leadership* in a way that retains this element.

To exemplify, let me go back to the Ospina et al. (Chapter 9) study. From the perspective of leadership that includes differentiation in levels of influence, this is a study of important collective processes leading to important social changes, but it is not really a study of leadership, at least not at the intraorganizational level. Ospina et al. can argue that their study is a study of leadership at the interorganizational level (because they studied successful social change organizations), but that is not what they focused on empirically. They focused on intraorganizational processes. Essentially, their study is a study of collective meaning-making and the creation of shared practices within social change organizations that does not distinguish between leadership and other processes by which shared agreements are reached and shared practices are created.

From a leadership studies perspective, potentially useful questions would have been: How and when does leadership (in the sense of asymmetric influence) contribute to the creation of shared meanings and practices that result in social change? Is leadership needed at all to produce such shared meanings, practices, and results? A negative answer to the last question would have been a legitimate and important finding from a leadership studies perspective. However, if researchers *a priori* adopt the social constructionist approach that rejects the idea of differential social influence as a mark of leadership (and as a potentially useful practice), they are not likely to look at possible manifestations of leadership, and consequently are not likely to find them. Nor can they find that such manifestations do not exist in the organizations they study. In other words, if the radical social constructionist lens is accepted as the theoretical framework that guides an empirical study, it is unlikely that we will learn something about leadership from this study, even if the study is exemplary in all other respects.

Crosby and Bryson (Chapter 10) are also interested in social changes and social policy changes and how they come about. They share Ospina et al.'s view that leadership is a collective phenomenon and view the leader and follower roles as shifting along the various phases of the collective efforts to reform or transform social policies. However, in contrast with Ospina et al., they attend to and, to some extent, highlight the role of leadership in such efforts. The collective processes and policy reforms they studied had not occurred in non-led collectives. Crosby and Bryson identify the roles that certain individuals play as champions of change, sponsors of change, and creators of structures and forums that enable and facilitate the joint construction of meanings. Policy entrepreneurs were required to initiate these processes, plan and organize various forums, and invest more time and energy than others to push them forward. Crosby and Bryson name these individuals and describe their actions in various stages of the policy reform efforts. It is possible to argue that the difference between the findings of the two study programs derives from differences between the organizational populations they studied. It is more likely in my opinion that this difference derives from the fact that one group of researchers rejected the concept of leadership as differential influence *a priori*, and the other did not.

QUESTIONS AND SUGGESTIONS FOR FUTURE RESEARCH FROM A RELATIONAL PERSPECTIVE

Although I've dedicated most of this essay to a critique of the social constructionist perspective on relational leadership, I acknowledge that some of the arguments of this approach can be empirically tested. If the social constructionists wish to test their claims and convince others of their validity or usefulness, the first thing they need to do, in my opinion, is to re-open for empirical research the whole issue of leadership emergence in task oriented groups. How much variation is there in the way groups construct leadership and other structures and processes they adopt to coordinate their efforts and achieve their results? When does leadership (in the asymmetrical influence sense) emerge? Under what conditions it does not emerge? To what extent does the emergence or non-emergence of leadership depend on the influence of external forces (culture, managers, facilitators, researchers) that dictate or guide the social construction of leadership?

Given the existence of much evidence on the emergence of disproportionate influence in groups, and the emergence of social roles and role identities that accompany this differentiation, we need much more new evidence about the extent and nature of the variation in the way leadership is constructed in groups and the antecedents of this variation in order to accept the multiple realities, multiple options claims of the constructionist perspective. If considerable variation is found in the way leadership is constructed, the next step would be to study the relationships between different constructions of leadership and various outcomes of interest in order to show that the way leadership is constructed matters for members' satisfaction, motivation and commitment, the way work is organized and carried out by the group, the level of coordination in the group, and the achievement of collective goals.

Leadership emergence is also a pressing research topic for those of us who accept that leadership concerns differentiation of roles, identities, and levels of influence, and yet believe that beyond this basic principle, the specific differentiation and specific relationship are constructed locally. The question is, How is this specific differentiation constructed in an arena that includes multiple participants and multiple possibilities for attributing influence to some individuals? In other words, from this perspective, important questions concern the emergence, change, and decline of the differentiation that characterizes a leadership relationship. Traditional research approached this question from a leader-centered approach and focused on the leader's personality, prototypicality, capabilities, and behaviors. However, if the differentiation is socially constructed through interactions among group members, a relational perspective would focus on studying the relational processes from which the differentiation emerges. As Seers & Chopin (Chapter 2) assert: "relational analyses provide us with the opportunity to account for what gives rise to leading and following, how leading and following may persist over time, and the role they play in the achievement of desirable outcomes."

A good example of a theory that represents such a relational approach has been recently offered by DeRue & Ashford (2010). These authors recognize that current leadership theory offers little insight into how individuals influence each other to collectively construct their respective identities as leaders and followers, and the leader-follower relationship. They are interested in the question, what relational and social processes are involved in coming to see oneself, and being seen by others, as a leader or a follower? They present a theory explaining the development of leadership relationships that is comprised of reciprocal and mutually reinforcing influence that occurs when individuals claim and grant leader and follower identities in their social interactions. *Claiming* refers to the actions people take to assert their identity as either a leader or follower; *granting* refers to the actions that a person takes to bestow a leader or follower identity onto another person. Through this claiming- granting (or granting-claiming) process, individuals internalize an identity as leader or follower, and those identities become relationally recognized through reciprocal role adoption and collectively endorsed within the organizational context.

DeRue & Ashford (2010) argue that the development of a leadership relationship can start with either claiming or granting and specify the conditions under which claims are reciprocated by grants, and grants are reciprocated by claims. They also emphasize the dynamic nature of this process and the possibility that interactions among group members, and between them and various contextual factors, can cause leader and follower identities to shift over time and across situations. Thus DeRue & Ashford's theory is a relational theory in its focus on the development of leadership relationships, its adoption of a social construction lens, and its attendance to the mutual and dynamic nature of the process. It nevertheless retains the idea that leadership concerns differentiation between leaders and other members of the group.

But, the leadership relationship is not the only meaning constructed in a group or organization, and from a relational perspective, we want to understand the role of leadership in constructing other meanings as well. One of my favorite definitions of *leadership* is "the guidance and facilitation of the social construction of a reality that enables the group to achieve its goals" (Maier, 2002, p. 186). To coordinate collective action and work towards collective purposes, groups have to agree on many other things, such as perceptions of their environment, perceptions and interpretations of their current performance, definition of the problem or the challenge, definition of their goals, perceptions of their collective efficacy to deal with the challenge, and the structures and processes of social action needed to achieve their goals (e.g., Shamir, 2007). Those of us who believe that shared meanings are the basis of collective action, and that leadership plays a particularly important role in the construction of these meanings, should devote more attention to studying meaning construction processes and the roles that various participants play in these processes.

"Leadership as the management of meanings" is a misleading definition because it is too leader-centered and connotes too much control. Meanings are constructed in arenas that include multiple possibilities for interpretation and sense-making, and the leader is only one actor in these arenas. Yet, according to the notion of leadership offered above, leaders, by definition, are those who have disproportionate influence on the meaning construction process. We don't know how this leadership role is carried out because we have seldom studied meaning-making processes from a leadership perspective. We have analyzed some leaders' inputs to these processes, such as their speeches (e.g., Emrich et al., 2002). We have also studied partners' reactions to leaders' speeches, but not from the perspective of meaning-making. We have never studied the leadership role in meaning-making as a reciprocal process, paying attention to how the various actors act and react to each other, and how this reciprocal process generates a shared meaning.

One meaning that may deserve particular attention is the group's identity—the shared answer to the question "who are we?" This is a particularly pressing issue in a world that witnesses many organizational mergers and an increasing number of intergroup and interorganizational arrangements and collaborations. Traditional leadership theory has treated groups and organizations as bounded entities in which leaders and their collaborators share both membership and identity. It has devoted some attention to how leaders attempt to articulate this identity and raise its salience so it can increase members' contributions to the collective efforts and their collaboration with other group members. However, one of the most important roles of leadership in both the political and the organizational fields is to facilitate collaboration and integration across group and organizational boundaries. This challenge may require meaning-making and identity-making processes beyond those that are employed in order to articulate an already existing group identity and raise its salience (Crosby & Bryson, 2010; Pittinsky, 2009). This is a practical challenge for leaders and a theoretical challenge for leadership scholars. So far, relational leadership theory has focused mainly on meaning-making within groups. Perhaps expanding its focus to include intergroup relationships may provide us with a theoretical basis for examining the issue of intergroup leadership as well.

Regardless of the specific meaning we are interested in, viewing meaning-making as a central leadership activity indicates a needed expansion of the way by which we assess the impact of leadership. We have to include shared meanings in our definitions of *leadership effectiveness* and the ways by which we assess effectiveness. We have to be able to assess whether leadership results in new meanings or modified meanings, and the extent to which these new or modified meanings are shared. Quantitative and qualitative studies of organizational culture, climate, and identity may provide the basis on which such assessment methods can be developed, although the specific contents of the shared meanings are likely to vary in accordance with the nature of the group, its sphere of action, and its goals. When such methods are developed, we will be in a better position to link shared meanings with leadership activities and processes. We will also be able to link shared meanings with group behaviors and practices, the level of intra- and intergroup coordination, and the achievement of collectively valued results.

As several authors have indicated (Fletcher, Chapter 3; Uhl-Bien, 2006), in some respects, the quality of the relationship between leaders and their partners has been at the center of leadership studies for many years. There is still much to be learned on the process of the emergence, development, change, and decline of leadership relationships from a perspective that views these relationship as co-produced by all parties involved and includes the beliefs, thoughts, emotions, actions, and reactions of all parties (Seers & Chopin, Chapter 2). However, because this topic has been central in leadership studies for some time, I don't want to expand on it except to highlight one aspect, which has not received sufficient attention, in my opinion, and is indicated in the work of Fletcher (Chapter 3). In the latter part of her contribution, Fletcher draws a distinction between relational practices in the service of work, and relational practices in the service of relationships. This is an important distinction that has been neglected since most of the leadership theories that include a dimension of consideration, support, or a people-orientation have assumed that these relational aspects serve the accomplishment of the group's goals; that is, they are in the service of the work. By and large, the relational perspective on leadership seems to accept this assumption uncritically.

However, Fletcher's distinction implies that, in some situations, there may be a contradiction or a conflict between serving the work and serving the relationship. There may be situations in which the relationship has to be sacrificed in the service of work and others in which the work has to be sacrificed in the service of the relationship. Leadership may even involve inflicting pain on others (Molinsky & Margolis, 2005). We all know that. Furthermore, the tension between the relational aspect and the task-oriented aspect of leadership is implied, though not fully developed, in several leadership theories, most notably in Fielder's (1967) theory, which posits the relational orientation and the task orientation as two opposing poles of the leader's motivation and style. But, we have not studied this tension or the related tension between the leader's relationships with individual members and his or her relationship with the group. The relational perspective on leadership, even when it does not focus on the quality of the relationship, should not gloss over this tension. A more comprehensive relational perspective would also pay theoretical and empirical attention to the potential conflicts between the emphasis on relationships and the task of leadership.

Relatedly and lastly, I think the relational perspective indicates that we need to re-introduce power into the field of leadership studies. With few exceptions, such as research on the consequences of leaders' power motivation (e.g., House, Spangler & Woycke, 1991) and research on influence tactics used by leaders (e.g., Yukl & Falbe, 1990), the study of power relations and the study of leadership relations have been separated for several decades. Perhaps this separation exists because the leadership literature wanted to dissociate itself from the "command and control" connotations of power. Thus, it has emphasized that leadership does not necessarily have to be associated with positional power, and distinguished between influence by leadership, which connotes volition on the part of the influenced, and influence by power, which is not associated with volition. However, the exercise of leadership inevitably entails the accumulation and use of power, even if it is only referent power or "soft" power, and many of the negative consequences associated with leadership derive from the power inequality that leadership implies.

Power has always been a central topic in sociology and political science and has become a more central topic in social psychology in recent decades (for reviews see Fiske & Berdahl, 2007; Magee & Galinsky, 2008). The social psychological studies may be particularly relevant to relational leadership as they explore the manifestations of power in social interactions, their antecedents, and consequences. The implications of these studies are relevant from both a social constructionist perspective that seeks to remove, as much as possible, the element of power from leadership relationships, and a perspective which accepts that leadership inevitably entails power inequality and wishes to explore ways to contain this inequality and minimize its potentially negative consequences. The social psychological studies demonstrate very clearly that power (which is a relational construct because one's level of power can only be assessed and manifested in relation to other actors) is a very powerful phenomenon. They imply that power is likely to affect the behaviors of leaders and others in a leadership relationship, the dynamics of the interactions between them, and nature of the relationship and its consequences. However, in contrast with the social psychological literature, which views power as something that certain individuals have and bring to their relationships and interactions, a relational perspective would view power as something that is also socially constructed in interactions and relationships as participants negotiate the power distribution, and take and give power to themselves and to each other.

All my suggestions have several common and interrelated implications. Perhaps the most important implication of this volume, which I think is shared by all authors, is that, in order to study leadership from a relational perspective, we need to devote more time and effort to studying leadership relations and processes "in action," as opposed to studying relationships between variables that summarize ratings of personality characteristics, actors' attitudes and behaviors, and the quality of relationships. Leadership occurs in interactions, and we should study these interactions. Such studies may include detailed analyses of single conversations or episodes, but I think more importantly, they should focus on processes over longer periods and multiple interactions. This is because, with successive interactions, the leadership relationship evolves over time and may spiral up or down, or change in other ways as a result of what happens in the interactions, the intervention of external factors or events, or the mere passage of time.

We tend to pay lip service to the need to study dynamic processes, but the best we do is carry out longitudinal studies with 2–3 measurements spanning over a time period that sometimes include variables which are hypothesized to mediate the relationship between some leadership input and some leadership output. Such studies seldom tell us anything about reciprocal relational processes and dynamics. Even multi-wave longitudinal studies are at best a series of time-spaced sequential snapshots, which do not tell us much about *how* the process of leadership unfolds. Similarly, qualitative studies of leadership which are carried out over lengthy periods often do not provide a better understanding of leadership processes because such an understanding is not an automatic result of spending a long time in the field and collecting many interviews and observations (e.g., Maitlis & Lawrence, 2007). It requires deliberate attention to the dynamic, mutual, and reciprocal aspects of leadership relations. Therefore, the implication of the relational perspective is not a blanket call for more longitudinal or more qualitative studies.

Leadership theories and studies have largely been a-temporal. In a recent paper, Bluedorn & Jaussi (2008) write: "because relationships between followers and leaders occur over time, it is difficult, if not impossible, to consider leadership without time playing a role...Yet, our review of the literature suggests that the formal use of temporal variables in leadership research has been scarce and scattered" p. 657). In other words, we have tended to ignore the obvious fact that leadership takes time (Shamir, 2011). Not only have leadership theories been a-temporal, but our dominant research methods have limited our ability to study processes over time, and we need to expand the range of our methodological tools. Due to the lack of sufficient guidance from existing theories and methods about how to study and understand leadership processes over time, primarily what we need at this stage is to adopt a more inductive approach. We need more studies that follow, observe, and describe the evolution of leadership relationships and processes and their consequences in real time.

Some of these studies may adopt a quantitative approach and employ recently developed digital technologies of experience sampling to follow participants and obtain relationally relevant data on a weekly or daily basis or even several times a day (e.g., Bono et al., 2007). Others are likely to provide qualitatively based narratives of collective meaning-making and the development of leadership relations. Hopefully, such studies will eventually identify patterns, and the identification of such patterns will lead to the development of "grounded" (Strauss & Corbin, 1990) relational theories. The chapters of Crosby and Bryson and Ospina et al. in this volume give good examples of such an approach, and the chapter by Seers and Chopin (Chapter 2) cites useful sources that can be consulted when carrying out process studies of leadership. Regardless of the specific method used, it is primarily by following and describing leadership relationships as they evolve over time that we are likely to increase our understanding of relational processes and the role of time in these processes, and eventually develop time-sensitive "process theories" of leadership (Shamir, 2011). (Also see Langley, 1999, on translating process studies from descriptions to theories).

SUMMARY

The field of leadership studies is in strong need of new perspectives because, at least in the last 20 years, and possibly for a longer period, we have mainly made relatively modest modifications and refinements to existing knowledge and because, despite our hundreds of studies and hundreds or thousands of publications, many of us feel that there is still a considerable gap between the importance of the phenomenon we study and our understanding of this phenomenon. In an introduction to a recent special issue of the *American Psychologist* devoted to leadership, Warren Bennis (2007), one of the most prominent leadership scholars of our time writes: "After studying leadership for six decades, I am struck by how small is the body of knowledge of which I am sure." In view of such a declaration, it is tempting to seek refuge in the social constructionist, postmodern view that, because leadership is always situated and freshly constructed, we will never have a general body of knowledge of which we'll be sure. However, such an approach would undermine our individual and collective efforts to create useful knowledge for science or for practice. We therefore need new approaches, perhaps even radically different approaches to the study of leadership, because continuing to do "more of the same" with some extensions, refinements, and modifications is not likely to have a significant enough effect on our understanding of the phenomenon.

The relational perspectives presented in this volume offer new and promising directions for studying leadership and increasing our understanding. They suggest shifting the focus from individuals to relationships, from leaders to all participants in the leadership process, and from the relationships between leaders' characteristics and the effects of leaders on followers, to the joint social construction of leadership relations and collectively shared meanings. The relational perspectives also imply greater openness to the variety in how leadership is constructed and enacted by different groups in different situations and the introduction of more complexity and less determinism to our theories.

Many of the chapters in this volume rely to varying degrees on the social constructionist perspective on social relations and social science. Some of them present a version of this perspective that calls for a radical paradigm shift in leadership studies and a total rejection of the construct of leadership that has guided our efforts so far. This call deserves serious attention. I have therefore given it such attention, devoted the first and largest part of this essay to examining its implications, and concluded that the paradigm shift suggested by this version of social constructionism, if accepted, is not likely to advance the field of leadership studies but rather to dilute it out of existence. I have argued that for many reasons, only some of which could be covered here, what the radical social constructionist perspective offers to the field is a series of dead-end alleys and a post-leadership and post-leadership-studies scenario.

In the second part of this essay, I have argued that if we wish to retain the distinctiveness and usefulness of the construct of leadership, we need to reserve its use to social processes in which asymmetric influence can be recognized. This entails differentiation among individuals or other social actors, which, in turn, entails potentially negative consequences. But, I argued, these risks should be studied as part of our leadership studies program, rather than dealt with by treating asymmetric influence (and therefore leadership) as a phenomenon that doesn't exist or shouldn't exist.

In the third part of the essay, I have attempted to demonstrate that the relational perspective contains many promising directions for theory development and empirical research, even if we don't accept some of the premises of the radical social constructionist perspective. Out of the many possible research directions suggested by the chapters of this book, I have selected to highlight some topics and research questions that seem to me particularly important and promising.

My comments, criticisms, and suggestions are offered in the spirit of a relational dialogue and in the framework of an exercise in relational science. Hopefully, this book will get from the community of leadership scholars the attention it deserves and will serve as a catalyst for joint meaning-making efforts to define or redefine our field and our collective identity and to find new ways of understanding leadership.

REFERENCES

Bennis, W. (2007). The challenge of leadership in the modern world. *American Psychologist, 62*(1), 2–5.

Bluedorn, A. C., & Jaussi, K. S. (2008). Leaders, followers, and time. *The Leadership Quarterly, 19,* 654–668.

Bono, J. E., Foldes, H. J., Vinson, G., & Muros, J. P. (2007). Workplace emotions: The role of supervision and leadership. *Journal of Applied Psychology, 92,* 1357–1367.

Crosby, B. C., & Bryson, J. M. (2010). Integrative leadership and the creation and maintenance of cross-sector collaborations. *The Leadership Quarterly, 21,* 211–230.

DeRue, S., & Ashford, S. J. (2010). Who will lead and who will follow? A social process of leadership identity construction in organizations. *Academy of Management Review, 35,* 1–21.

Drath, W. (2001). *The deep blue sea: Rethinking the source of leadership.* San Francisco, CA: Jossey-Bass.

Emrich, C. G., Brower, H. H., Feldman, J. M., & Garland, M. G. (2001). Images in words: Presidential rhetoric, charisma, and greatness. *Administrative Science Quarterly, 46,* 527–557.

Fairhusrt, G. (2007). *Discursive leadership: In conversation with leadership psychology.* Thousand Oaks, CA: Sage.

Fiedler, F. (1967). *A theory of leadership effectiveness.* New York, NY: McGraw-Hill.

Fiske, S. T., & Berdahl, J. L. (2007). Social power. In E. T. Higgins, & A. W. Kruglanski (Eds.), *Social psychology: Handbook of basic principles.* New York, NY: Oxford University Press.

Hosking, D. M. (1997). Organizing, leadership, and skillful processes. In K. Grint (Ed.), *Leadership: Classical, contemporary and critical approaches* (pp. 293–318). Oxford, England: Oxford University Press.

Hosking. D. M. (2007). Not leaders, not followers: A post-modern discourse on leadership processes. In B. Shamir, R. Pillai, M. Bligh, & M. Uhl-Bien (Eds.), *Follower-centered perspectives on leadership: A tribute to J. R. Meindl* (pp. 167–186). Greenwich, CT: Information Age Publishing.

House, R. J., Spangler, W. D., & Woycke, J. (1991). Personality and charisma in the U.S. presidency: A psychological theory of leadership effectiveness. *Administrative Science Quarterly, 36,* 364–396.

Langley, A. (1999). Strategies for theorizing from process data. *Academy of Management Review, 24,* 691–710.

Magee, J. C., & Galinsky, A. D. (2008). Social hierarchy: The self-reinforcing nature of power and status. *Academy of Management Annals, 2,* 351–398.

Maier, C. (2002). *Leading Diversity.* St. Gallen, Switzerland: University of St. Gallen IFPM, Schriftenreihe, Band 3.

Maitlis, S., & Lawrence, T. B. (2007). Triggers and enablers of sensegiving in organizations. *Academy of Management Journal, 50,* 57–84.

Molinsky, A., & Margolis, J. D. (2005). Necessary Evils and interpersonal sensitivity in organizations. *Academy of Management Review, 30,* 245–268.

Meindl, J. (1995). The romance of leadership as a follower-centric theory: A social construction approach. *The Leadership Quarterly, 6,* 329–341.

Ospina, S., & Sorensen. G. (2006). A constructionist lens on leadership: Charting new territory. In G. Goethals, & G. Sorensen (Eds.), *In quest of a general theory of leadership.* Cheltenham, England: Edward Elgar Publishers.

Pittinksy, T. L. (Ed.). (2009). *Crossing the divide: Intergroup leadership in a world of difference.* Cambridge, MA: Harvard Business School Publishing.

Smircich, L., & Morgan, G. (1982). Leadership: The management of meanings. *Journal of Applied Behavioral Science, 18,* 257–273.

Shamir, B. (2007). Strategic leadership as management of meanings. In R. Hooijberg, J. Hunt, J. Antonakis, & K. Boal (Eds.), *Being there even if you are not: Leading through strategy, structures, and systems* (pp. 105–125). Elsevier,

Shamir, B. (2011). Leadership takes time: Some consequences of (not) taking time seriously in leadership research. *The Leadership Quarterly, 22*(2), 307–315.

Shamir, B., Pillai, R., Bligh, M., & Uhl-Bien, M. (2007). *Follower-centered perspectives on leadership: A tribute to J. R. Meindl.* Stamford, CT: Information Age Publishing.

Strauss, A., & Corbin, J. (1990). *Basics of qualitative research: Grounded theory procedures and techniques.* Newbury Park, CA: Sage.

Uhl-Bien, M. (2006). Relational leadership theory: Exploring the social process of leadership and organizing. *The Leadership Quarterly, 17,* 654–676.

Van Vugt, M., Hogan, R., & Kaiser, R. B. (2008). Leadership, followership, and evolution. *American Psychologist, 63*(3), 182–186.

Yukl. G., & Falbe, C. M. (1990). Influence tactics and objectives in upward, downward, and lateral influence attempts. *Journal of Applied Psychology, 75,* 132–140.

CHAPTER 18

EXPLORING THE PROSPECTS FOR DIALOGUE ACROSS PERSPECTIVES

Dian Marie Hosking, Boas Shamir, Sonia M. Ospina, and Mary Uhl-Bien

At a particular moment during the conversation between Hosking and Shamir, editors Uhl-Bien and Ospina were invited to join. Meanwhile, the dialogue between Hosking and Shamir continued to expand after he shared his essay (included as Chapter 17 of this volume). The present chapter is structured in three sections to document these exchanges among four scholars voicing differing discourses of relational and entitative perspectives. The first section includes an exchange between Uhl-Bien and Shamir. Another between Ospina and Shamir follows, based on her response to his drafted essay. The final section returns to the dialogue between Hosking and Shamir. As Hosking joins the conversation again, she comments on the previous exchanges, and zeros-in on Shamir's essay. Shamir's response to her, in turn, is followed by Hosking's final reflections on the overall conversation.

Advancing Relational Leadership Research, pages 501–535
Copyright © 2012 by Information Age Publishing
All rights of reproduction in any form reserved.

ON POTENTIAL CONTRIBUTIONS OF THE DIALOGUES: EXPLORING ALTERNATIVE PATHS TOWARD A SHARED VISION

Letter from Uhl-Bien to Shamir, Following First Hosking–Shamir Exchange (cc: Hosking & Ospina)

Hi Boas,

I haven't seen a reply to your email yet, so thought I would respond. It is certainly up to you and Dian Marie how you want to handle this, but I am ok with you writing a paper as you suggest, and then Dian Marie responding to it in whatever form she likes. Is that OK with you Dian Marie?

I can relate to what you are saying, Boas, as I struggle with similar issues. Sonia and I have talked about it as well and are trying to write about it in our sections of the book. I think I can summarize the main point you make as: The challenge for entity scholars is to buy an argument where there isn't an entity construction. The problem is, we know we have stuff in our heads and that we interact with the world with a consciousness and in our heads, so trying to understand a perspective that denies(?) this is a "non-starter." I think this is the reason the dialogue doesn't advance. Entity scholars (using that term for convenience of a label here only) can't get past this (and the other issues you raise) and don't know what to do with it, so we ignore it. In fact, many "entity" researchers have told me they loved the Uhl-Bien 2006 *LQ* article, but they don't "get" it. They don't know what to do with it in a practical sense. They don't know what they should, or how they can, do things differently.

So, what I am wondering is if we can push ourselves to get beyond esoteric discussions (e.g., the paradigm wars of the past) and instead really talk to one another about how we could do our research in different ways if we considered both perspectives. It is the "thinking space" Dian Marie talks about, and what I hear in Dian Marie's writing is an openness to dialogue, which means a willingness to not take a hard-line stand *per se* and instead really talk about how we could enrich research overall with a multi-theoretical, multi-paradigmatic lens. To me, that is what this book needs to do if we are to make any progress on this front. I see it as needing to lay out a multi-theoretical research agenda with real practical value for researchers wanting to do this work. The authors couldn't do that necessarily in their chapters, so this is why we need the dialogue scholars. They can look deeper into the issues to enhance understanding but also identify a way forward. What we are looking for you to do is help us see if there is a way forward and provide direction regarding how to get there.

I have not seen in print any dialogue from scholars representing each perspective with respect to relational leadership, and I think the two of you are perfectly positioned to help us get this dialogue in print because: a) you are both tremendous scholars in your fields, and b) you are intellectually curious. You are interested in learning and open to, and effective at, dialoguing with other perspectives. You engage in the spirit of advancing knowledge— not to simply defend or attack. I see real intellectual curiosity in each of you. What we want to do is capture that and see if we can get this down on paper so others can benefit from it. This can help people who "don't get it" gain more insight.

Sorry this got long, but hope it was helpful.

Mary

Shamir's Reply to Uhl-Bien while Writing His Essay (cc: Hosking & Ospina)

Mary,

Thanks for reading and responding. I think you and I share a feeling of dissatisfaction with traditional conventional leadership theories and studies. I greatly respect you for looking for new sources of intellectual challenge that have a potential to guide our thinking and research, so that we don't just continue to do more of the same. I am in a sort of transition period in my life, and I eagerly look for new inputs to my thinking. In this regard, I believe you and Sonia make a very important contribution by importing and highlighting the relational approach both through this book and other related writings. I've found this book and some of the related readings the most intellectually challenging and rewarding work on leadership I've read for a long time. I've spent many hours during the last few weeks thinking about the chapters and the challenges they raise.

The last thing I want to do is to ignore the social constructionist approach. I think it deserves very serious consideration because it is a truly different way of thinking, has far reaching implications, and is presented by serious scholars. However, it is because I believe this approach deserves serious consideration that I think its implications should not be glossed over in the frame of a multi-theory, multi-paradigm approach that gives equal weight to all voices and ignores their radically different implications. The postmodern version of the social constructionist view (Hosking, Alvesson and Sveningsson, and Barge chapters in this volume, and Ospina, in her theoretical arguments, though not necessarily in her empirical work) calls for a paradigm shift. It is very much about the "what" and not only about the "how." This is where the potential promise of this perspective is claimed to lie, and therefore, while it is useful to assemble different perspectives under the same umbrella in an edited book or a review paper, doing it from an "all my sons (daughters)" perspective without examining the challenges and their implications does not do full justice to the social constructionists and amounts to ignoring their most serious arguments.

Therefore, I'll have to disappoint you. My contribution will be largely polemic in its first and longer part because I believe the social constructionists lead us into a series of dead-end streets, and I think it is a more important contribution to try to substantiate this argument than to dilute it. "Making progress" and advancing leadership theory requires the separation of open-ended streets from dead-end streets. I don't want to start a paradigm war or engage in one, but sometimes one has to take a stand to make a contribution. Incidentally, I've been around for a while, and I am not aware that the "paradigm wars of the past" have ever reached the field of leadership studies, and perhaps the field could benefit from some discussion about paradigms. Note that the constructionists' writing when they attack the conventional discourse on leadership is very polemic, so if I am accused of starting a paradigm war (or re-opening an old one), I can always use the kindergarten claim that "the other side started it."

I don't think I don't "get" the constructionist view. I think I now (after clearing my way through the fog of jargon and abstract philosophical arguments) get it very well, including its implications for research and practice. I believe in the social construction of reality and think there is much to be gained in leadership studies by focusing on social construction processes. I also believe there is much to be gained by focusing on relationships in leadership studies, and that the gain primarily lies not in focusing on the quality of relationships but on relational processes, studying them as they evolve, describing them, and trying to identify patterns. But, I cannot support some of the more fundamental, far-reaching claims of the constructionist approach because they are not likely to be useful for leadership studies—not because they are necessarily wrong, but because what they offer is an alternative to leadership (which is perfectly legitimate), not an alternative view of leadership.

I am not an "entity" person in the sense of seeing leaders and followers as fixed entities or seeing leadership as embodied in leaders and followers, but I am an entity person in the sense that I think a distinction between the entity *leadership* and *non-leadership* is essential for any useful theory of leadership, and I therefore see risks in blurring this distinction. I am also an entity person in the sense of believing that no one, not even the constructionists, can contribute to leadership studies without being "entitative." See how even Sonia, in reporting about her very impressive program of studies, does so by cutting the world and highlighting entities she calls "leadership practices" and other entities. Notice how she brilliantly generalizes across 60 studies in different contexts despite declaring allegiance to Dian Marie's assertion that "leadership cannot be abstracted from its context." This is not a criticism of Sonia or her studies; it is a criticism of the illusion that knowledge creation can be non-entitative.

There is a certain temptation in the social constructionist approach because it is intellectually invigorating; it introduces more complexity to an over-simplified field, and supposedly offers an inclusive and egalitarian view of leadership. I think we should follow these temptations up to a point, but those of us who wish to remain focused on leadership processes rather than other collective processes, should know where to stop and why.

I will also point out what I view as the most promising potential contributions of the relational approach to advancement of leadership theories and studies, so I hope my contribution will not only be defensive, but also constructive. At least it would be another voice in a polyphonic relational dialogue. All the best, Boas

Uhl-Bien's Response to Shamir (cc: Hosking & Ospina)

Hi Boas,

I am very much enjoying the "dialogue" even though I am blurring the line between my role as editor versus dialogue scholar. Oh well, I never was one much for following rules!

You raise a very important point that I had definitely not considered: that by glossing over the differences between the two, it ignores the radically different voices. Yes, I need to think about that. (I am wondering what Dian Marie thinks of that, and Sonia as well.) On the other hand, when I hear Dian Marie say we need a multi-paradigmatic perspective and a thinking space, I hear her saying that we are willing to engage in conversation that does not take a hard-line stand. It does not have to be one way or the other—can't it be both? That is the approach I have taken in thinking about these issues. What can we each learn from the other, and where can we open up to alternative perspectives and approaches?

So, if I think about relational leadership theory as Fairhurst and Putnam (2004) quoting Deetz said: "The function of theory, as Deetz (1992, p. 74) purported, is conception not definition. In other words, theory should direct attention and focus rather than characterize the intrinsic nature of stable objects or mirror fixed attributes among them." Can't relational leadership theory direct attention in both realms? It could be a research program in which we work together to see what the two perspectives have to offer in helping us learn about relationships and relational processes. Constructionist researchers would pursue it using their paradigms and methodologies, and we could pursue it using ours, but the difference is, we talk to each other and inform each other's work (with a caveat which I discuss in the next paragraph). We work together to explore common kinds of questions. I think what this calls for is a modified agenda (and discussion) on both parties—I could imagine entity researchers engaging in more mixed methods kinds of studies that would let us better get at relationality; I could see constructionist researchers pursuing questions about relationships and relationship development that they may not have considered otherwise. I could see communications scholars offering rich depth into the communication processes, which we as psychology-based scholars have ignored. So, it would truly be a multi-paradigmatic and interdisciplinary effort. Given how important relationships and relationality are, I think it would be worth the effort. Moreover, given the technologies and methods available, I think we could do this in ways that weren't possible previously. (I am a dreamer, so I am sure there are holes in my argumentation.)

The caveat is your "don't throw out baby with the bathwater" point. I think a key part of your reaction, and I share it, is with Mats Alvesson's paper on postleadership, or the idea that all collective action is leadership. The issue is, how far do we take it, and when does it become "not" leadership? I think a lot about that and haven't gotten far enough in my thinking to find yet an answer I am satisfied with. For me, the jury is still out. I had long discussions with Mats last year about this, and he and I plan to continue the conversation when I visit Lund this fall. I am not willing to go as far as he is in throwing out the term *leadership* altogether, but I am intrigued by the discussion. I will also say, however, and I said this to him: I think his conception of *leadership* has been too much associated with management. I think he has equated *leadership* as *management* and hadn't been thinking of the kind of leadership that occurs beyond management, so while I think the points are interesting, I am not in agreement with his conclusion (throw out leadership). I think that gets us nowhere, except out of the conversation altogether!

From my own standpoint, I believe I am where you are. I agree that social reality is constructed, but I also see that we are entities. I see both. I don't think they need to be as incompatible as our discussions make them sound. I had never quite been able to figure out what that meant or what I "am" until I recently read Ralph Stacey (2001), and his complex responsive processing. I am still processing on it, but it is the closest thing I have seen yet in terms of how it can be both. Here, I may be glossing over important issues, however, so I think Dian Marie and Sonia could help out with their reactions.

All of that said, I don't want to cut off your thoughts or your proposed discussion. I very much agree with your concerns and am happy you are voicing them. If we can then engage more dialogue around them, I think we have opened up the thinking space we are working toward. I look forward to reading your paper and to seeing what Dian Marie has to say about these issues. I honestly do think it will be the first time this type of discussion will be in print (unless you all know of something written that I have not seen on this), and there is great value in that. I am excited to see engagement around this very important topic. Thanks! Mary

Shamir's Response to Uhl-Bien (cc: Hosking & Ospina)

Mary, I, too, enjoy the dialogue. In fact, I have already received my intrinsic rewards from participating in this project: from reading the material, my earlier exchange with Dian Marie, and now the exchange with you, which is particularly useful because we both dance between open-mindedness and the need to accept challenges on the one hand, and on the other hand the question of boundaries: Do we need them? Where shall we put them? Three brief comments:

1. The idea of "working together to see what the two perspectives have to offer in helping us to learn about relationships and relational processes" is a noble idea, but note that there is no leadership in this goal. Is your project now to understand relationship and relational processes rather than leadership?
2. I agree that methods should be expanded and the constructionists have good ideas in this regard that should be adopted. Also, as I wrote in a very brief comment on Fairhust's (2007) book, there is absolutely no contradiction between leadership psychology and communication studies and methods in the sense of studying the *little "d"* discourse. The problems lie with the *big "D"* discourse.
3. I respect Alvesson's position and find it more useful than the position that tries to hold the stick at both sides: rejection of leadership on the one side, and claiming to contribute to leadership theory on the other. Alvesson's position is consistent with his epistemological and ontological assumptions and with his ideological beliefs. I would have respected his position even more if he called it "An alternative to leadership." Incidentally, for similar reasons, I also respect Dian Marie for including the term *postmodern* in the title and text of her chapter in our 2007 book. As far as I could ascertain, none of the authors in the current book openly uses this term.

Really respectfully, Boas

ON THE (SOCIAL) SCIENTIFIC NATURE OF CONSTRUCTIONISM AND ITS POTENTIAL TO ADVANCE RELATIONAL LEADERSHIP THEORY

Ospina's Response to Shamir (cc: Hosking & Uhl-Bien)

Dear Boas (and Dian Marie and Mary),

Thanks for sharing this and your previous letter to Dian Marie where you announce that you will write your piece alone. I had not entered the conversation before because I was traveling and had not had a chance to read your piece. Now I have.

Unfortunately, I did not read Dian Marie's original invitation to you (no reason to receive it as the dialogue was intended to be between the two of you), but now that I read your piece, I do appreciate the opportunity to engage with you (and Dian Marie and Mary) in the conversation, given both your comments on my chapter and your general discussion of constructionism. So, I thank Mary for inviting me to join, even though this is not what we originally had in mind when we designed the book's logic around dialogue between the two of you.

Because I have had the opportunity to develop a good relationship with you, Boas, and I know there is mutual appreciation, I have taken the risk of just writing comments in your document that react to points you make in your chapter (see below), without necessarily trying to find ways of being too diplomatic. With this as a starting point, I have two other reasons to take that approach: First, I want to send this quickly, and second, I want to respond to your straightforward and transparent style with a similar one, given your invitation to not dodge controversy.

Of course, you are welcome to completely ignore my comments at the end, but I felt I needed to make them, at the risk of sounding defensive. Also, if you want, I am also happy to engage in conversation about any specific comment, or about the general point I make—that your argument sort of falls flat on its face once you dismiss the possibility of doing empirical constructionist work. Such a bold statement ignores work of that perspective which has helped to illuminate many aspects of the social world, and, in doing so, has contributed to create the foundations of contemporary social science in other fields outside of leadership. I invite you to rethink some of the assertions you make that seem to dismiss the power of this approach just because it does not correspond to your definition of *leadership*, and I humbly hope that my comments help you to see something else that you were not seeing before.

I am actually excited about this meta-dialogue that has generated and also would hope to hear about Dian Marie's response both to your chapter and to Mary's and my comments. Best, Sonia

OSPINA'S COMMENTS TO SHAMIR'S FIRST DRAFT

(edited, reordered, and numbered for clarity and flow)

1. You correctly indicate that social constructionists do not all fully agree about the value of "the concept of social construction to leadership studies." You contrast Alvesson's (Chapter 7) call for replacing the concept of leadership altogether with others who still find value in the concept—including Smircich & Morgan's (1982) exploration of the role of leadership in the construction of shared meanings; Uhl-Bien's (2006) efforts to link leadership as a social influence process to the production of emergent coordination and change; and Ospina & Sorenson's (2006) view of *leadership* as shared agreements helping to create results with collective value. But, why are you collapsing these various perspectives into a single constructionist blanket theory in your comments? I see a big difference between saying that leadership can be studied by looking at shared agreements of what a community values as the results they want, from saying that leadership should be replaced by something else. You use arguments from the most extreme case to characterize constructionism as a whole.

   And yet, your comment does point to the importance of distinguishing between the various constructionist approaches when making a critique. It may be that it is still not possible to make blanket statements about a constructionist perspective to the study of leadership. Like Dian Marie well notes, there is a distance between the more postmodernist approaches of Alvesson and Hosking (and even between the two of them), and approaches like those of Fairhurst, Barge, or Ospina et al. I actually think that the differences among scholars using constructionist assumptions offer richness to the present conversation, despite the potential for confusion. Without trying to speak for other constructionists, I offer my version of it, which I have developed precisely in the context of trying to push the envelope of constructionist theoretical underpinnings to do rigorous social science empirical research.

2. You claim that the social constructionist challenge to the conventional discourse on leadership is a "dead-end street," and see a fundamental contradiction between advancing leadership theory and the constructionist emphasis on multiple realities and possibilities to

construct leadership. Referring to Barge's claim of *leadership* as something that is differently constructed in each situation ("co-created, contextual, and contestable" in his terms), you suggest that having to constantly determine "what counts as leadership" reduces the power of the term. This conclusion, I believe, relies on an approach to research that assumes that only "social facts" that are observable can be studied. A contrasting approach to research, one in line with Weber's (1978) sociological perspective, for example, which emphasizes the relevance of the meanings people give to those social facts for really understanding what is going on.

This is what is meant by the value of understanding the meanings that people give, in the situation, *to their experience of leadership* and to their relationship to the "other," whether the "other" is formally defined as *leader* or *follower*. Constructionists are proposing a different—equally legitimate—way to *enter* the social phenomenon, one that assumes the need for researchers to pay attention, not only to what they see, but also to what those involved—in what researchers see—experience, think, and feel about it. In an early and brilliant article contrasting inquiry modes to enter organizations, Evered and Louis (1981) call this approach *inquiry from the inside* (in contrast to *inquiry from the outside*).

3. You also point to inconsistencies in the context of a constructionist research practice. For example, you argue that the way Ospina et al. carry out and report their empirical research deviates from constructionism by not retaining a "commitment to multiple realities and multiple narratives," and instead reporting "with a narrative for which they claim a privileged status." A scientific contribution, you argue, cannot treat all narratives equally and must draw conclusions privileging the researchers' voice. So, you continue, when constructionists do exactly this—making choices, reporting in their own voice and making claims about validity or the "correspondence between the story and the observed phenomena"—they ultimately deviate from their own premises.

Again, there is a misconception here about what it means to do constructionist social science . . . this is really an epistemological issue with practical implications for methodology. The Weberian approach to social science invites approaching people's experience, seeing things from their perspective, and taking into consideration the multiplicity of voices and perspectives of different actors (or even of a single actor), to then use what we learn to theorize, with a different voice—an analyst voice—about a particular phenomenon, in this case leadership. Suggesting that constructionism cannot be translated into science seems to ignore the excellent accumulated knowledge that has come out of using this social science approach over centuries of building social theory and research. In reference to the issue of validity as a correspondence between story and observed phenomenon, constructionists understand that the account offered is but a partial representation of reality, not the whole reality, and as such, it is an interpretation of the experience of others once their perspective has been considered as the starting point!

You summarize the argument by saying that "a perspective that seeks to remove the currently shared construct of leadership and cannot offer an alternative construct because such an offer is inconsistent with its basic premises is a dead-end street from the viewpoint of advancing leadership theory." Sorry to say, Boas, that your argument had a basic flaw in the way it built constructionism as something that cannot be used to develop social science...

You do acknowledge that a constructionist approach can be empirically tested, arguing that to do this well, it would be necessary to "re-open for empirical research the whole issue of leadership emergence in task oriented groups." You propose questions such as, "How much variation is there in the way groups construct leadership and other structures and processes they adopt to coordinate their efforts and achieve their results?" However, constructionists are less interested in variations and more interested in mechanisms and processes. You cannot impose your variance questions on them. You also call for "new evidence about extent and nature of the variation in the way leadership is constructed in groups and the antecedents of this variation in order to accept the multiple realities, multiple options claims of the constructionist perspective." So, basically, you are asking constructionists to take the approach and methods of positivism as the only possible ways in which you would accept their (our) empirical tests? This does not seem to be that helpful...

4. You compare a search for "the regularities and patterns in a relationship" (which you attribute to traditional leadership studies) to a focus on "the unique flavor of each conversation or phrase in a conversation" (which you attribute to constructionist studies). The first is a more robust way of creating knowledge and guiding practice, you indicate, arguing that scientific knowledge requires sacrificing uniqueness, because the need to explore variation and regularities cannot "do full justice to the unique flavor of each case." The solution to the traditional literature's tendency "to err on the side of simplification and overgeneralization" cannot consist, you conclude, in replacing the goal of pattern finding with "a program of studies that gives priority to the uniqueness of and fluidity of each conversation."

I contend that if we use the assumptions of the research approach discussed above, focusing on the uniqueness of the moment in the research practice is not mutually exclusive with trying to find regularities and patterns. The focus on the uniqueness allows us to understand what is going on for people (social actors), from their perspective, which will help understand what is going on in the situation. As analysts, we consider this and then try to find patterns and regularities, but the generalizations that we make are not to the populations studied (like with statistical generalization), but to the concepts or theories explored (analytical generalizations). *Inquiry from the inside* is premised on the following assumption: What is unique in one context can in fact help us learn something that is universal about the human condition if we are able to find in what is unique to a particular context the elements that illuminate what is common to human experience.

Using the same logic as above, you also suggest that by creating a "framework" that generalizes "about social practices derived from the study of organizations operating in a variety of contexts," the Ospina et al. study contradicts the constructionist "commitment to situated local constructions." Yet, the point missed is that the "framework" is the result of doing research that respects and zeros-in on uniqueness, not to stay in that uniqueness, but to understand it deeply and in ways that precisely allow us to find something about the nature of human experience in that particular situation. The goal is to move up in the analytical level of abstraction, just as in any other approach to empirical research that claims to be based on social science.

The notion that "leadership cannot be abstracted from its context" means (at least to me), first of all, entering its study with the commitment *to understand what is going on* in all its complexity, in the here and now. Once we understand this well (precisely by considering the historically and culturally specific circumstances, to put it in elegant social science terms), it is possible to use analytical techniques, including the method of comparisons across situations, to identify differences and commonalities, and to find patterns about the phenomenon under study, despite the unique features of the context. If taking context into account meant not being able to abstract afterward, we would not be doing social science. What is different between this way of doing it and other ways, such as *inquiry from the outside*, is that in the latter, the analyst tries to simplify as much as possible, and one way of doing it is by "holding context constant," that is, putting all those details aside from the very start.

You suggest that you are not criticizing the study or the framework, merely pointing to the contradiction as demonstration of the futility of constructionist research, because in research you will always abstract and generalize "across particular cases even if these abstractions and generalizations do not do full justice to the studied phenomenon." And, of course, I agree with you that abstractions do not do full justice to the phenomenon—if by this you mean that they do not reflect fully the particularities of the context where it was studied—because they are abstractions! This has nothing to do with constructionism, but with the nature of good research, independent of epistemological stance. The key point is that, as you are learning about the phenomenon, you do not ignore or set aside what is unique, but integrate it fully into the inquiry to have a sense of what's going on. What you do with what you learn, if you are practicing social science (and not poetry or fiction or other non-scientific forms of representation), is to theorize, which *always* requires going one level of abstraction up. There is no contradiction between the constructionist lens and the goal of building theory within a framework of social science.

5. You cite other chapters in this volume as examples of the futility of trying to build theory or practice from "the radical 'multiple realities' social constructionist perspective." For example, you find fault in Barge's assertion that it is challenging to "shift from talking about the way leadership is constructed, to developing practices that help leaders to anticipate how they might act within an unfolding situation and to be present in the situation." You say that this is contradictory and reverts to a conventional discourse by identifying leaders as distinct from others and because of the focus on practices and skills (which, you argue, reflects the conventional approach rejected by constructionism). You also use Kennedy et al.'s article to point out that they also "revert to conventional discourse" and "violate [its] basic premises" when they focus on leadership training, where the goal is to build skills or knowledge generalizable to different situations.

Yet, it seems to me that these assertions are based on the same confusion about constructionism: Like any other theoretical lens, when used appropriately, constructionism can help to "see things with fresh eyes," and therefore can be helpful in finding practical applications of use in the real world. Calling contradictory this interest in making practical applications or in supporting people's desire to enhance their skills, including those in formal positions of leadership, reflects an abrupt shift in your critique from an analytical to a practical level, as if they were on the same plane. Constructionism offers a way of looking at the world, not a negation of the constructed reality or of the practical consequences of the existence of (constructed and reified) institutions and systems. For example, I believe that constructionism does not negate the factual point that people take up leadership roles, it just does not see these roles as those assigned formally in a hierarchy, but assumes that there are other contexts where other people can also take up leadership roles. Similarly, it does not deny the fact that, in today's practice, those in positions of authority are called *leaders,* nor that people can enhance their leadership capabilities. Thinking about and doing leadership development is *not* inconsistent with a constructionist lens, what changes is what you focus on when helping people who want to take up (formal or informal) leadership roles in their practice: For example, as Kennedy et al. suggest, the shift may go from an emphasis on personal skills and growth to one on the relational aspects of the individual's work.

6. Accepting a notion of leadership that includes differentiation implies, you argue, that fully shared or dispersed leadership should not be called *leadership.* You say: "...from my perspective, if all members, partners, or collaborators have the same degree of influence, the group or social process of interest has no leadership, even if the group or the processes creates shared meanings and is highly effective in creating a change or achieving some other collective purpose." While finding it legitimate to study (and prefer) leaderless social processes, you find it confusing to include them in the term *leadership.* You conclude: "For a phenomenon to be called *leadership,* we have to be able to identify certain individuals who, at least in a certain situation and during a specified period of time, exert more influence than others on the group or the process."

   It seems to me, Boas, that you do not want to give up a version of leadership that is not just about differentiation, but about vertical differentiation. What I have thought about this point is that the form that leadership takes, from individual to collective, from hierarchical to more participative, from concentrated in a single actor to more distributed, is itself an empirical question that needs to be explored in every instance in which we want to explore leadership, rather than taking the notion of vertical differentiation as the starting point. You seem to imply that leadership can only take one possible form, one where two actors enter in relation, with one influencing another. Yet, taking the approach that leadership is what happens when a group achieves what it wanted to do by working together—leadership as collective achievement, a la Drath—precisely opens up new vistas to exploring different ways in which leadership can emerge and manifest itself.

Furthermore, to make your case, you argue that your definition of *leadership* as "the attribution of disproportionate influence to some actors" can be evidenced across societies and cultures. You argue that leadership is a universal way to deal with adaptation in human groups. You conclude that it

> may be misleading to suggest that every interaction is original and every group can construct leadership in a different way and to imply that the conventional discourse on leadership can be changed if we just expose its situated and socially constructed nature.

What Berger and Luckman (and their ancestors, as well as those who followed them) nicely show is that, over time, people's negotiations result in agreements that become fixed and immutable in appearance, but in fact can be changed by having people stop agreeing to see things the way they did. Drath puts it very nicely when he talks about the broad sets of shared agreements that have resulted in three different ways of defining leadership over time—they all seemed like permanent agreements around what was leadership to those who experienced them, but over time, as organizations have changed, so have the ways people agree to see leadership!

Citing yet again the Ospina et al. study, you argue that it is a good study but *not* a leadership study: It is essentially a study of collective meaning-making and the creation of shared practices in social change organizations that, you say, does not distinguish between leadership and other processes by which shared agreements are reached and shared practices are created. Indeed, there was a decision from the start to not study again how one person influences another or a group (although I presume this could also be done with a constructionist lens, but since it has been done already over time, it seemed futile). So instead of focusing on leader (individual) to follower (individual) influence, we focused on group to outcome influence, thus making a decision to downplay (not reject) the individual dimensions of leadership and highlight its collective dimensions, given previous bias in the other direction. I think the two choices represent different approaches and a decision to work at different levels of analysis, each one equally legitimate, to learn something about leadership. I do not deny that there may be asymmetrical influences in the organizations we studied; we did see traditional "leaders" in some of them, but we were not interested in just observing what they personally did. Of course, if the only way in which you think the analyst can enter the phenomenon of leadership is through individual leaders, then, yes, we did not study leadership.

You argue that more useful questions would have included: How and when does leadership (in the sense of asymmetric influence) contribute to the creation of shared meanings and practices that result in social change? Is leadership needed at all to produce such shared meanings, practices, and results? I ask whether these questions are not equivalent to asking how and when does a leader contribute . . . ?; and is a leader needed . . . ? If so, I agree, we did not do it. And, I must comment that we ourselves have come to the conclusion that maybe, to highlight the collective dimension, we underplayed too much the individual dimension. If I had to do it again, I would pay more attention to the role of leaders and try to link it to the broader processes we were looking at—but I would not start there . . .

You then argue that rejecting *a priori* differential influence as a mark of leadership prevented the study from seeing any manifestations of leadership. You conclude: "In other words, if the social constructionist lens is accepted as the theoretical framework that guides an empirical study, it is unlikely that we will learn something about leadership from this study, even if the study is exemplary in all other respects." Again, this statement negates the long tradition of empirical work that has been done with a constructionist lens and from which all social scientists have benefited. You have built your argument that it is impossible to truly study leadership using constructionism in a way that leads one to believe that it is just impossible to truly study anything empirically using constructionism . . . this is quite a problematic statement, worth re-considering!

Finally, you contrast this study with that of Crosby and Bryson (Chapter 10), who also view the leader and follower roles as shifting along situational contexts but explicitly identify the leadership role of certain individuals, name them, and describe their actions in various stages of the policy reform efforts studied. You argue that maybe the difference between the findings of the two study programs derives from "the fact that one group of researchers rejected the concept of leadership as differential influence *a priori*, and the other did not." Another interpretation is that the two studies had different goals. Ospina et al.'s was to illuminate the shared agreements that allowed participants in the organizations *to make things happen to produce change* and then identify the ways these agreements manifested in how people did the work and the strategic choices they made. Crosby and Bryson wanted to contextualize the leadership work of the policy entrepreneurs and see how their actions influenced the policy reform process. So, there was no way we could find similar things because we were not looking for the same things. They focused on *the work of the leaders*—individual actions in context—we focused on *the work of leadership*—practices that reflect shared agreements about a shared desired end and that result in patterned, deliberate actions over time toward a concrete outcome that is viewed as a collective achievement (which makes them leadership related).

Shamir's Response to Ospina (cc: Uhl-Bien & Hosking)

Dear Sonia (Mary, Dian Marie), Thanks for reviewing my contribution and commenting on it. Indeed, there is mutual appreciation both personally and professionally. I highly respect you and your work, as well as the work of other constructionist colleagues included in the book. I am also grateful to you for adopting a straightforward manner. For me, as an Israeli, your style was very polite and gentle. If you wrote in an even more polite style, I would have probably failed to understand you.

Your comments made me think, and I will certainly review my contribution and examine whether there are things I want to take back or re-phrase. There are certain things I'll have to clarify. As a first step towards such clarification, I include my responses to some of your comments here.

For me, perhaps the main difference between our approaches lies in your following comment: "You seem to imply that leadership can only take one possible form, one where two actors enter in relation with one influencing another. Yet, taking the approach that leadership is what happens when a group achieves what it wanted to do by working together—leadership as collective achievement, a la Drath—precisely opens up new vistas to exploring different ways in which leadership can emerge and manifest itself."

What I have tried to suggest is that "taking the approach that leadership is what happens when a group achieves what it wanted to do by working together" is not useful because it is too broad. Many things happen when groups work together, and lumping all of them under the term *leadership* negates the usefulness of this term. For a term or a construct to be useful, it has to so be distinguished from other constructs. Leadership is only one of the things that can happen when people work together or achieve common goals. It may not be the most common, most important, or most useful mechanism for achieving collective purposes. I simply think that we should retain the distinctive usefulness of the term. I fail to understand what is the value of lumping together all the things that happen when groups work toward collective goals under one umbrella and calling this umbrella *leadership*, which is very confusing. Wouldn't it be clearer, more useful, and more consistent with your stance toward *leadership* as conventionally defined to demonstrate that collective work and collective achievements can be achieved by other influence processes which are not characterized by asymmetry?

So, I agree with you with you when you say in your comments that "leadership can be studied by looking at shared agreements of what a community values as the results they want," and I see it as a useful contribution, but I don't see as a useful contribution your suggestion that leadership is what happens when a group engages in collective action. Similarly, your assertion that "leadership is essentially about meaning making in communities of practice" (citing Drath & Palus, 1994 in Ospina & Sorenson, 2006) is a potentially useful contribution. But the assertion (definition?) "leadership happens when a community develops and uses, over time, shared agreements to create results that have collective value" (same place) is too broad, in my opinion. To retain the distinctiveness of the construct, I would have said "leadership happens when certain individuals or groups exert disproportionate influence over time on the shared agreements that a community develops and uses to create results that have collective value." Of course, the community may develop and use these shared agreements without leadership.

Paradoxically, by clinging to the term *leadership* and broadening it to include many other aspects of collective action, the constructionist approach may demonstrate an attachment to the conventional discourse in a manner that is not less fundamental than the aspects of that discourse that are rejected by the constructionists. The conventional discourse not only distinguishes between leaders and followers, it also attaches a positive connotation to the term *leadership*. Hence, the current tendency (within the conventional discourse) is to broaden the term *leadership* to include everything under the sun. For instance, a course that I currently teach at a business school is called "Leadership in Organizations." It is basically the core course in general management for MBAs, which until 3 years ago was called "Management of Organizations." The school changed the title, but most of the contents have remained the same (strategy, structure, environment, culture, power, etc.). The only reason I can think of for changing the name of the course without changing its content is the social desirability of the term *leadership* relative to the term *management*. Is it possible that the constructionists, too, perhaps not consciously, cling to the term *leadership* for the same reason?

Because this point is fundamental to me, let me give a couple of other examples, which I hope will clarify my point. I hope they will also clarify that my attachment to the principle of differential influence as a defining characteristic of *leadership* is not ideological. In fact, while I believe leadership is a useful coordinating and integrating mechanism in some cases, I share many of your concerns about hierarchy.

The first example is taken from your chapter in this book. You very strongly argue against the treatment of context as background. I am not sure I fully understood your reasons for that. Maybe part of it is that context is also socially constructed (a position which I partially accept). However, that is beside the point. My point is rather that, even if context is fully socially constructed, surely it is constructed in terms that differentiate between the group or the event and the circumstances that surround them. If not, and here is the parallel between this example and leadership, there is no need for the term *context*, and it loses its usefulness. This means that the term *context* is useful only if the distinction between background and foreground is retained. In fact, your other argument about context, which is that leadership should be understood in terms of its historical and cultural local context, follows this distinction. Now, you could argue that my stance toward leadership is conservative, old-guard, even fundamentalist because of my age, my career stage, and my long-term investment in studying leadership from a conventional stance, but believe me, I have no attachment whatsoever and no investment whatsoever in the term *context*, and yet I would make the same argument about *context* as I make about *leadership*—to be useful, its essence has to be retained.

The second example is the term *constructionist*. Would you call me a constructionist? Probably not, because I do not accept some of the fundamental elements of *constructionism* as you define or describe it. Calling me a constructionist would probably dilute the very essence of the constructionist approach in your view and would blur the distinction between constructionists and people like me, for whom you created a straw (and utterly wrong, in my case) term—*entitist*. Now, believe it or not, I could call myself a constructionist. As I said in one of my previous letters, I view the social construction of reality as the most important contribution of sociology to the social sciences, I believe in knowledge as social construction, and I think leadership is largely a social construction, which also operates to a great extent through its influence on other social constructions. But, since this is not a specialty of mine and not a defining element of my identity, if the group of people who identify themselves as constructionists and developed the approach find that including me under this term would blur the distinctive value of this term, I accept it because I understand that a construct may lose it distinctiveness if it is broadened too much.

Now, you may say, "I merely raise the phenomenon from the individual level to the collective level." Of course, leadership is a collective phenomenon in several respects, and of course, it is perfectly legitimate to focus on the leadership of groups or organizations. These groups may or may not have intragroup or intraorganizational leadership. But, if the focus is on a group or organizational level of analysis, the principle of asymmetric influence should still be retained, in my opinion. In other words, for a group or organization to lead, it will have to exert disproportionate influence on the other groups or organizations. Contrary to the way you characterize me, I do not think the principle of differential influence applies only to individuals, and I don't think that "the only way in which the analyst can enter the phenomenon of leadership is through individual leaders." Differential influence can apply to groups, organization, or nations. Even if we talk about the leadership of the United States among the nations, we have to mean the disproportionate influence of this country. Otherwise, the term *leadership* will be meaningless.

If a certain social movement led a certain social change, then to me it means that this movement exerted more influence than other actors. So, even if personally I have not focused so far on the study of leadership at higher levels, the difference between you and me is not in the level of analysis, but in the question, "How do you define and recognize this collective leadership you want to focus on?" I will have to clarify this point in my contribution. From this perspective, the program of studies described in your chapter is clearly relevant to leadership, but it has focused, as far as I could see, on intraorganizational meanings and practices. Your focus was not on *collective leadership*, as I understand this term, because you have not attended to the other actors influenced by the organizations you studied, nor to the manner in which they were influenced.

I did not mean to suggest that constructionism cannot contribute to social science or to imply that it hasn't made important contributions to social science. I am sorry this is the impression you received, and I'll try to correct it. I certainly did not mean to dismiss the possibility of doing empirical work from a constructionist approach. I admire your own work, for instance. Yet, I do believe that the extreme postmodernist version of constructionism contains some inconsistencies and encounters some problems, so that when it does excellent empirical work, it necessarily violates some of the premises it declares allegiance to. I tried to exemplify this in my contribution.

I also don't think that useful practical work cannot be done from the constructionist perspective, but it seems to me there are two options here in order for the practical work to be consistent with the theoretical framework: Either you target your practices at helping specific groups with their relational processes in specific contexts, or you (I don't mean you, personally) develop and teach relational leadership in the same way you develop and teach other leadership practices, even though you focus on different practices and/or teaching methods. If one chooses the latter option, one must tone down the assertions about the uniqueness of each situation and the unlimited degrees of freedoms groups have to construct their reality because the practice of assembling a group of leaders or aspiring leaders from different organizations and developing them in isolated workshops is inconsistent with such assertions.

I have no problem with both options. I would have, of course, preferred the extreme constructionists to present their arguments (and believe it themselves) in a less extreme form. Indeed, my own view is that some of the differences between you and me are a matter of degree and stem from the fact that some of the postmodernist arguments have been taken too far. If phrased in more modest terms, I could easily agree with some of the constructionist arguments, and other arguments I could accept as potentially valuable contributions even if I did not agree with them. What I find difficult to accept is, for instance, the view that every situation is totally freshly constructed, that all aspects of identity are always situated and freshly constructed in each relationship or each conversation, that all voices or narratives have equal value, that leadership can never or should never be abstracted from the situation, and so forth.

If these arguments were presented differently, so that our attention would be drawn to the socially constructed nature of the relationship, to degrees of freedom in constructing meanings, to the fact that there is value in both abstracting from situations and locally situated understating, and so forth, I would have no problem with these arguments. For instance, if constructionism were only what you say about it in the following sentence, I could not agree more: "constructionism does not negate the factual point that people take up leadership roles, it just does not see these roles as those assigned formally in a hierarchy but assumes that there are other contexts where other people can also take up leadership roles." Unfortunately, as evidenced in some of the chapters of this book, including your own chapter, the postmodern constructionist perspective argues much more than that.

I do not understand what generalizations to concepts or theories mean. If what you mean is using an inductive, grounded approach to construct concepts and theories, fine, I support that. But, what is the point of suggesting a concept or a theory if it is not meant to apply more generally to other cases? I have never encountered a theory that does not imply that it applies to more than a single case. To the extent that you move beyond description and analysis of the single case, you are by implication generalizing across cases, even if you don't want to frame your generalization in statistical probabilities. I agree, however, with your statement, "what is unique in one context can in fact help us learn something that is universal about the human condition, if we are able to find in what is unique to a particular context the elements that illuminate what is common to human experience." I have spent my entire academic career (excluding my time as a student) in a department of sociology and anthropology, so I have gathered some understanding and appreciation of the emic approach and of ethnographic case studies. I think I can appreciate both the values of the positivist approach and the value of the nonpositivist approaches. (I also think both are fundamentally and seriously limited, which is the main problem of the social sciences, but that is beside the point.)

One of the values of the approach you represent is captured very well in your comments about context and abstraction. However, it is one thing to argue against the removal of context by holding it constant and for first understanding a phenomenon in its context, and only then abstracting to a higher level. It is another thing to argue strongly about the utmost importance of the uniqueness and freshness of each situation and the futility or impossibility of abstracting from context. If the arguments in the constructionist chapters were phrased the way you phrase them in your last comments, they would not differ from general arguments about inductive theory development and ethnographic studies, and I would have no ground to claim there is a contradiction between the constructionists' premises and the practice of empirical research following that approach. Unfortunately, they are not presented in this way, but in a way that does make it very difficult to reconcile them with an empirically based contribution to science.

I couldn't agree more with your following statement "the form that leadership takes, from individual to collective, from hierarchical to more participative, from concentrated in a single actor to more distributed, is itself an empirical question that needs to be explored in every instance that we want to explore leadership, rather than taking the notion of vertical differentiation as the starting point."

One of the main issues behind our debate is, of course, the issue of hierarchy. I cannot deny that the notion of differentiated influence, which I see as the essence of a useful leadership construct, connotes a hierarchy or produces a hierarchy. I do deny, however, the fact that it has to be associated with a formal hierarchy. So, here is the difference between us, or between me and some other colleagues. I accept the hierarchy as part of the phenomenon. I don't like it, but for me, almost by definition, *leadership* involves some hierarchy, and this has all sorts of ethical, social, and practical implications. I may be wrong here, but I believe one of the engines that fuel the work of many constructionists is your strong reservations about a hierarchical order and its implications. I can sympathize with that. But for reasons specified above, I believe it would be more useful for people who don't want to see hierarchy in social relations to present their approach as an (more socially just, more humane, more beneficial) alternative to leadership, rather than as a different approach to leadership. If your project is to change the way people see leadership, why don't you focus on showing the problems with leadership, its shortcoming, and its negative implications, and demonstrate the feasibility and the benefits of the alternatives. Wouldn't that be a more direct way of introducing the desired change than saying to people "leadership is not what you've always thought (agreed) it is. Anything you do to create shared meanings and act collectively is leadership."

You say: "I must comment that we ourselves have come to the conclusion that maybe to highlight the collective dimensionm we underplayed too much the individual dimension. If I had to do it again, I would pay more attention to the role of leaders and try to link it to the broader processes we were looking at . . . but I would not start there. . . ." There could be two reasons to attend to the role of leaders: One is to demonstrate that they may not be needed or when they may not be needed. The other, as Joyce Fletcher says in her chapter, is to retain the possibility of individual agency. I believe this possibility should be retained for both practical and ideological reasons.

To summarize: I do not think that it is impossible to study leadership from a constructionist perspective. In fact, I think it is very important to study leadership from a constructionist perspective. However, if the constructionist perspective is the version that takes the multiple realities idea too far, so that it dilutes the notion of leadership, I don't think it is useful. I also don't think the constructionists should adopt positivist methods (though I value these methods as well). In fact, I call for process studies that are likely to be mostly qualitative and inductive, provided that such studies are not based on a perspective that rejects the phenomenon of leadership *a priori* on meta-theoretical or ideological grounds, and that the aim of such studies is to identify patterns (call them *mechanisms* if you like) that have some general potential values beyond the understanding of a specific relationship or group. (I wouldn't go as far as you did in one of your comments and talk about universal value.)

Thanks again for your comments, and please don't feel obliged to respond to mine.

Boas

PART 2 OF HOSKING AND SHAMIR'S DIALOGUE: ON ENTITATIVE THINKING, THE POTENTIAL FOR INTEGRATING ENTITATIVE AND RELATIONAL APPROACHES, AND IMPLICATIONS FOR UNDERSTANDING LEADERSHIP

Hosking's Response to Shamir (cc: Uhl-Bien & Ospina)

Dear Boas, Mary, and Sonia,

I am now able to give more time to my part in this project. . . . I find myself unsure about how best to proceed following Boas' first response to my "dialogue invitation" and subsequent exchanges between all of you. I feel some tensions, differences, and confusions in these exchanges; I hear questions being raised about some issues that I think are really important; I feel drawn to join the dance. However, (a) I cannot and do not want to try speak for or about all relational or entitative approaches; (b) I do not want to claim to speak for the other book contributors whose work I have read; and (c) many important issues have been raised, and there is not space to work with them all. So, instead, I shall try again to dance the entitative-relational duality as this might be discoursed from what I call a "postmodern relational" perspective. I have taken from the last exchanges three issues that might be of most general significance and interest. They concern the use of the term "entitative," and the possible "inevitability" of entitative constructions; relations between entitative and relational approaches; and the potential value of the postmodern relational discourse for leadership—including the role of empirical work.

The Term "Entitative," and the Inevitability of "Entitative" Thinking
Working in this area has helped me further to appreciate the delicacy of conceptual language and taught me much about disciplined use of words and their meaning in complex webs of intertextuality. In our email exchanges, I understood Boas and Mary (in their email exchange) to suggest that linguistic reifications are evidence of entitative thinking. As I understood them, to speak of a "relational approach" or to speak of an "entitative discourse" IS indicative of entitative thinking— and this means that (in his view) entitative thinking is inevitable. In response, I would say that, of course, the relational and the entitative discourses are expressed in conceptual language, and these discourses embrace abstract constructs such as *person, world, leadership*; and, of course, conceptual language is a differentiating device. So, relating expressed in the form of conceptual language does indeed involve some degree of reification—particularly when the language has a subject, verb, object form (see e.g., Fenellosa, 1969). However, linguistic reification is not, in itself, evidence of what I have set out as an entitative discourse.

When I refer to an "entitative discourse," I refer to a bundle of interrelated "discursive features" (Alvesson & Deetz, 2000, p. 32), including assumptions and related practices. This is why I always take care to set out at some length what I mean by *entitative* and *relational*—providing the more detailed description of the interrelated themes—and acknowledging that there are other constructions of these terms. The "bundle" of discursive features to which I have given the name *entitative* includes: treating abstracted reifications as what IS the case, and so, asking "what is it"-type questions; assuming that IT stays still long enough to be studied; assuming that IT has a sufficiently robust existence independently of your attempts to know it that it can be studied as if it had its own independent existence; assuming that (one's own version of) science is not "with philosophy" (Bentz & Shapiro, 1998, p. 6); requiring (as far as is possible) that the researcher relate to their research subject as an object; treating processes as what goes on within and between already formed/pre-existing entities, and so on. (See my chapter; see Hosking, 2011 for a recent and more detailed discussion.)

In my first letter to you, Boas, (see Chapter 16) I outlined a discourse of relational processes. I argued that relational processes can (and often do) *construct* the hard self/other differentiation characteristic of the entitative discourse. I further suggested that relational processes *could* construct soft self/other relations—and here is where I lingered—to pursue my interest in exploring the practices that might enable such constructions.

Thinking further on your comments, Boas, has led me to think that I should say something more about my interest in what I have summarized as my "relational constructionist" discourse. In response to some of your reflections in our exchanges, I should say that I am *not* interested in "characterizing" or trying to "pin down" any text, for example, as *either* entitative *or* relational. Furthermore, I do not want to be read as discoursing two, and only two, discreet and stable entities in "either/or" relation. Nor do I wish to claim to know what *is* or to know what is *right.* Such claims are, as you suggest, inconsistent with my relational view, and these are some of the reasons why I am not interested in critique (at least, as it is usually understood, see Hosking, 2011).

Rather, I was and am interested in articulating lines of arguments about processes, about construction, about person/world relations, about leadership... *that differ from those that dominate,* for example, the leadership literatures. I want(ed) to open up new possibilities—often lamented as lacking from leadership work. It was *not* that I wanted to critique the entitative discourse, and it was not that I wanted to critique other people's work as "entitative." Rather, my interest was in opening-up other possibilities, other views about processes, construction, leadership... I wanted these other views to be understood as different, as coming out of a different discourse, and for them not be distorted by being made sense of and critiqued in relation to assumptions I did not share (see Brown & Hosking, 1986; Dachler & Hosking, 1995).

The bundle of interrelated themes that together I call(ed) "entitative" emerged in contrasting relation to what I came to call a "relational" discourse. Speaking from the latter standpoint, I am led to re-emphasize that neither relational nor entitative *exists* independently of the other; this is one example of the self-other relations that my relational perspective brings to the foreground. The construction of what I came to call an "entitative" perspective gradually emerged as I struggled to put into words what I did *not* want to assume (e.g., about persons, person-context relations, language, hierarchy...) and what I did *not* mean when I used terms like *process* or *relational*. The summary term was used as a convenience—to bundle interrelated themes that emerged as I tried to clarify, for example, what I meant by the term *process*. At that time (the 1970s), there were (a few) writings that theorized leadership as a process—but they all viewed processes as what happened within and between self-existing individuals (see discussion by Hosking & Morley, 1988). So, this entitative-relational construction emerged in a struggle for voice—the voice of a different discourse. (We do not have to think of it as "my" voice.) The dynamic seems closely related to what Joyce Fletcher (Chapter 3) spoke of as "the disappearing acts—that acted on relational constructs to render them invisible." I wanted the entitative-relational construction to make space for and to explore the latter—and not to linger on and critique the former.

In sum, I want(ed) to open-up the articulation of relational work that "begins with" the assumption of relationality (e.g., Fletcher, Chapter 3). I should add that, following on from the above, I have *not* been interested in differentiating important and nuanced differences within the discourse that I called "entitative." I do believe that, depending on which literatures you look at, there is a great deal of work that is nuanced, complex, and not easily or helpfully categorized as "entitative." Further articulating nuances can only be helpful—especially when explicitly connected with wider philosophical assumptions; but I am on another journey.

Entitative and Relational Discourses: Neither Integration nor Rejection

In this section, I will try to say a little more about what I wanted when I borrowed from Sandra Harding to call for a "new thinking space" (Harding, 1998; Hosking, 2007). I would like to link this to the suggestion by Boas (in earlier referenced email exchanges) that I present a "critique and rejection" of the entitative approach and to Mary's own attempts to integrate entitative and relational, along with her wondering about how I see their relations. Let me begin by saying very clearly that I see the discourses as incommensurate. For me, that was the whole point of making the distinction. They are incommensurate in that (a) each makes totally different assumptions about self-other relations and how science can play a part in this; (b) each means different things by the same words (*relation, relating, process,* etc); and (c) each invites very different questions in relation to different practical interests (e.g., Gergen, 1994; Hosking, 2011).

Second, I also do not "aim to reject the entitative approach"—as Boas suggests in a number of places. The relational perspective I have outlined provides no secure foundations for rejection—nor for any other universalizing right/wrong construction (Gergen, 1994). Indeed, wanting to reject the entitative discourse would be more consistent with modernist assumptions and the entitative discourse (again, as Boas has recognized). Further, given the relational discourse, it makes little sense to "reject" the entitative discourse— they are co-emergent, relational constructions—each implied and defined in relation to Other. And last, but not least, when considered from a relational perspective, the entitative discourse (assumptions, practices, and interests) is seen as a construction—just as the relational discourse is a construction. A researcher whose orientation is relational constructionist may on occasion decide that particular issues and relevancies call for a postpositivist methodology, oriented towards producing (relatively) objective knowledge. In sum, the relational discourse means that it makes no sense to see relational and entitative as independently existing discourses; to see them as being in "either/ or" relation; or to treat them as the only available possibilities.

I called for "a thinking space" (Bouwen & Hosking, 2000; Hosking, 2007) for exploring different social science discourses because I would like space for multiple discourses. While this has happened in the literatures of Organization Studies, it has been slower to occur in the leadership literatures (see also Bryman, 1996; Dachler & Hosking, 1995; Morley & Hosking, 2003; Uhl-Bien, 2006). In my view, this "space" would not be made in debating the relative merits of "entitative" and "relational" discourses. Rather, it would come about through being "mindful" and explicit about the "philosophy" we put to work in our research (Bentz & Shapiro, 1998) and put to work in our e-valuations of the work of others. Being mindful in this way would require recognizing that there is no one "God's eye view from nowhere," but rather many possible social science discourses, assumptions, and interests (e.g., Hosking, 2011). Space for such multiplicity would also be facilitated by a form and style of writing that views different "bundles of assumptions" as potentially useful, and that explores the particular possibilities that they open up. Space for multiplicity is created by relating in ways that allow "different but equal," rather than imposing one ordering of value and so constructing difference as unequal (and usually, less good). I am reminded of Alvesson and Deetz's (2000) discussion of "alternative social science research perspectives," where they caution against using conceptualizations (such as *entitative*) as "devices for division and classification" and instead recommended seeing them as "interesting ways to call attention to similarities and differences that matter" (p. 25).

The Potential Value of a Postmodern Relational Approach to Leadership

There are two more "differences that matter" on which I want to finish. The first concerns empirical work and the link (made by Boas) between empirical work and the practicality, or rather "impracticality of the radical constructionist perspective." In a dialogue with Mary, he stated, "The impracticality of the radical constructionist perspective is demonstrated by the fact that even the proponents of this perspective cannot follow it when they address issues of empirical research or practice" (Shamir, Chapter 18). Boas goes on to talk about empirical testing and the possibility that constructionists may wish to test their claims and may wish to "convince" others of their validity or usefulness. I have to begin by voicing partial agreement—but only in the case of "constructionists" or rather of constructionist work—that unreflexively retains modernist assumptions. As I outlined earlier (borrowing from Gergen & Thatchenkerry, 1996), modernist approaches distinguish between theory and method, see empirical methods (particularly observation, experiments, and the hypothetico-deductive method) as ways to produce data, view data as the means by which to evaluate theory, and see language as the means to re-present findings about the world. In contrast, postmodern practices (a) do *not* distinguish theory, method, and "data"; (b) do *not* valorize empirical findings as the way to decide between theories; and (c) are not oriented around an interest in deciding between theories or persuading others of the relative superiority of their own.

So, my postmodern relational discourse takes a very different view of empirical work—viewing "empirical" broadly speaking, as "experiential" or "based on experience" (Bentz & Shapiro, 1998, p. 122). For example, by centering "the how" of relating—as a process of construction—the discourse invites researchers to regard their inquiry process as itself an (ongoing) product (Pearce, 1992, p. 151). In this view, inquiry does not discover what (probably) IS in order to provide the basis for some subsequent ("evidence based") intervention. Rather, the objects of inquiry are the inquiry processes themselves: as they (re)make identities and relations, as they construct and stabilize or "freeze" particular patterns—perhaps including leadership. In this relational constructionist perspective, empirical (inquiry) processes are viewed, not as "finding out," but as *constitutive*— as constituting particular "language games" and "forms of life" (Wittgenstein, 1953). And, as I set out in my first letter to you, Boas, these "language games" and "forms of life" are viewed as local rationalities. So, in this view, multiple, ongoing, local-cultural, and local-historical rationalities replace the view of rationality as singular, universal, and transhistorical.

The relational constructionist discourse could be thought of as *an orientation to practice*—one that gives the inquirer the possibility to explore "a changed aesthetic" of soft self/other differentiation, rather than striving for subject-object separation. So, for example, should the inquirer wish to lean towards "research," there is now the possibility to orient towards doing this "with" rather than "on" other (Pearce, 1992). This may mean working in ways that minimize *a priori* assumptions about local rationalities and their (hierarchical or otherwise) relations, and that avoid centering scientific rationality above others, for example, in a postmodern variant of participative or collaborative inquiry (Friere, 1982; Reason & Bradbury, 2008). But, since "empirical practices" are seen as construction work, the relational discourse also offers the possibility to orient more towards change work (both inquiry and intervention) with (rather than "on') other. Either way, "The practical point of doing constructionist studies has very often been to promote a better way of thinking and, more important, living..." (Weinberg, 2008, p. 15). So, returning to your critique, Boas, I do not see the radical constructionist perspective as "impractical," but rather intensely practical—but not in the way you define it.

This brings me to the second "difference that matters" concerning the potential value of a postmodern relational constructionist approach to leadership. Boas, you criticized the "radical" relational approach on the grounds that leadership "disappears." Again, I have to say "well, yes and no." Leadership disappears in the sense that this relational discourse does not "start" with some science community's "elite, *a priori*" definition of leadership (Alvesson & Deetz, 2000). Rather, it "starts" with relational processes and explores what relational realities and relations—including perhaps leadership—unfold. One or more of the local "forms of life" might discourse "leadership" as part of "what's going on." But, the relational constructionist perspective "comes to this," so to speak, as a "local, emergent" reality (Alvesson & Deetz, 2000).

Another way of saying the above is that the postmodern relational constructionist approach (e.g., to leadership) is "light" on content, focusing instead on *how* (e.g., leadership) identities and relations are constructed *in a particular case.* In my view, this approach has considerable potential. In particular, it invites us to "foreground" and make "figure" that which is usually left as background or ground, namely relational processes. Rather than "disappearing," I could equally well suggest that space is opened-up for leadership to appear, to manifest, in process. And, its "appearances" could now include ways, for example, that do not necessarily reflect sharply differentiated and "stabilized" identities and relations, that can "go on" in ways other than through "power over" (Gergen, 1995; Hosking 1995), and that can embrace multiple local- cultural valuations of value (im/practicality).

As I indicated in my first letter to Boas, my own particular interest is in relational processes as they might construct soft (rather than hard) self/ other differentiation. This leads to an interest in leadership as it might be constructed in processes of "soft" (rather than "hard') self/other differentiation. So, perhaps I can say a little about the possible practicalities of leadership in relation to three, analytically distinguished, process themes.

(1) *Dialogue and relationally-engaged practices.* There are now many relational approaches that give prominence to a dialogical view of person and use dialogical practices to facilitate a "better way of think-

ing and . . . living" [sic]. Approaches of this sort (a) work through multiple dialogues rather than through top-down leadership edicts and the avoidance of dialogue; (b) work with many different self-other relations rather than a single hierarchy of knowledge and expertise; (c) work with what is already (potentially) available and with what participants believe to be relevant, rather than imposing mono-logical constructions of leaders or outside experts; and (d) invite and support many lines of action, rather than requiring or imposing consensus. Dialogical processes can enable multiple "forms of life" to participate in different but equal relations. Dialogical ways of working can open up "power to," rather than close down through "power over," and can construct and support distributed leadership (Brown & Hosking, 1986).

(2) *Leadership and light structuring.* Light structuring is an important aspect of dialoguing. Often, those who are invited to participate in a dialogue are invited to agree to certain rules of engagement that help them to learn—while practicing—the "collective discipline" of dialogue (e.g., Chasin, Herzig, Roth, Chasin, Becker, & Stains, 1996). Such minimal or light structures can help to block or interrupt already solidified patterns and, in this way, help to open up new possibilities and softer (non subject-object) ways of relating. The idea is to provide enough, but not too much, structure—to provide a container, so to speak, that invites and supports the gradual emergence of slow, open, coherent, in-the-present-moment performances. Structuring can be thought of as *light* when it "goes on" in multiple, temporary, and variable forms rather than in one singular, stable form, such as a formalized hierarchy. For example, temporary groups might emerge to perform particular projects and, like a sand or flower *mandala,* be allowed to dissolve as the project is completed. Last, structuring can be thought of as *light* when "empty" of pre-specified content—as in the present construction of leadership. In light structuring, leadership is not provided by one individual and does not fix and separate. Rather, it is a relational practice ongoing in, and supportive of, dialogues, emergent processes, relational responsiveness, multiplicity, and appreciation (Hosking & Kleisterlee, 2009).

(3) *Sound leadership and heart-felt listening.* Implicit in my discussion of dialogue and light structuring were two important themes that now need repetition and slower development. One is the theme of being in the present (rather than already knowing); we could call this "being in the now rather than the know." The other, interrelated theme, is listening. In the entitative discourse, the knowing and influencing subject is assumed to be largely closed to other: to other as other possible selves, to "other" as body and not mind, to "other" as other

people and "other" sentient and non-sentient *things*. But, listening shifts into a very different context without these familiar "hard differentiations." When part of soft self-other differentiation, listening or *legein*—what Corradi Fiumara (1990) called "the other side of language"—gains prominence, relative to talk as *logos*. In this context, listening becomes understood as embodied, heart-felt participation in relational processes characterized by dialoguing and light structures. Listening, rather than for producing *aboutness knowledge*, can now be understood as key to participatory knowing/action. Listening—in the sense of *legein*—allows space for what is; rather than molding or structuring other, listening allows *both* multiplicity *and* wholeness.

In Conclusion

What I have been outlining looks very different from "leadership" as we have been able to know it in the context of hard self-other differentiation—as possessed by, or the action of, a bounded individual—in relation to other bounded entities that can be known and influenced. This "relationally engaged" or heart-felt construction could provide the leadership needed for current times. It seems to me that the postmodern relational perspective invites increased attention to the practical-philosophical question of "how to live a good life" when self and other are co-arising. Maybe relationally engaged leadership practices offer just what we need, now.

Shamir's Message to Hosking (cc: Uhl-Bien & Ospina)

Dear Dian Marie,

I read your last contribution. I then re-read it trying to practice what you call heart-felt listening, which you define as "embodied, heart-felt participation in relational processes characterized by dialoguing and light structure." I certainly agree with your desire to see "space for multiple perspectives." I also agree that eventually we should let go of the *entitist* and *constructionist* labels. Having read the book, I think some aspects of the two perspectives can perhaps be integrated if both sides relax their premises a little. For instance, I've found some interesting ideas in the Seers and Chopin chapter which, from a constructionist perspective, would probably be seen as mainly entitist and conservative, and also in the Fletcher chapter, which is mainly constructionist but still attempts to retain some entitist elements. However, I certainly agree that some central aspects of these discourses cannot be integrated as they contain incommensurable propositions.

Perhaps because of my *entitistic entity*, I've found myself particularly sym-
pathizing with your frank description of the emergence of the dichotomy
from your struggle to find and express your voice. You've certainly succeeded in that. I think that it is a very important achievement for a scholar
(perhaps for everyone) and a crucial achievement for both individual and
collective leaders. If I may be personal for a minute, I think Mary found her
voice when she moved from the LMX domain (George Graen's voice?) to
complexity theory and relational theory, and Sonia, whose work I know for
fewer years, has certainly clarified her voice in the years I have followed her
work. Note, however, that voice is an entitistic construction, like personality
or self-concept. Furthermore, I think that finding your voice and expressing it, which I believe is beneficial not only to you but also to your relational
partners, necessitates that, at a certain point, you lower the volume of other
external and internal voices, and move from heart-felt listening to heart-felt
expression. Polyphony is incommensurable with finding a voice.

I have not yet found my voice with respect to the entitist-constructionist
tension. I have used my contribution to this book as a step in my attempt to
clarify it, but I realize it is still not fully clear. As I expected in my response
to your first letter, I have not found a way to relate directly to your contribution in my own contribution, perhaps because I am (still?) entrenched in
the old discourse. Meanwhile, I think we should be grateful to Mary and
Sonia for providing us with a "space for multiple discourses."

Best,

Boas

Hosking's Response to Shamir (cc: Uhl-Bien & Ospina)

(edited and numbered to avoid paragraph repetitions from Shamir's message)

1. In reference to Boas' point about the possibility of integrating "some
   aspects of the two perspectives . . . if both sides relax their premises
   a little," and to his agreement with her "that some central aspects of
   these discourses cannot be integrated as they contain incommensurable propositions," Dian Marie says:

   > . . . maybe it's helpful to make a distinction between (a) the different
   > social science perspective/discourses—in themselves so to speak; and
   > (b) particular pieces of (empirical/theoretical) work. In the case of (a),
   > I would say that their premises are different... they construct different
   > territories... and each territory provides a different vantage point for
   > looking at the other. So, for example, when viewing from the relational

constructionist viewpoint, I see e.g., the post-positivist discourse as one possible discourse with its own coherence and project...

In the case of (b), I would not talk about possibilities of "integration"—rather I would say that the narrative of that particular piece of work is messy and that to try to say *it is this* or *it is that,* is bound to do violence to the complexities of the piece *and* would, in itself, be a modernist move (inconsistent with the premises of my perspective).

2. In reference to Boas' comments about scholars' struggles to find and express their voice and his assertion that doing so eventually "necessitates that at a certain point you lower the volume of other external and internal voices, and move from heart-felt listening to heart-felt expression. Polyphony is incommensurate with finding a voice," Dian Marie says:

> Mmmm—a number of points come up for me here. First, I do not share your view that "voice is an entitistic construction, like personality or self-concept"...I do not see that voice IS this or that...rather I take the view that there is *both* an entitative narrative of voice *and* a relational narrative..."mine" is the latter—and I tried to outline it in my draft using Sampson, Bakhtin and others to set out the dialogical, relational view—which they see (as do I) as very different from the entitative view. So, when I speak about finding my voice, I am talking about a lengthy and ongoing relational process and using the metaphor of finding my voice to speak about an emerging and very relational-contextual voice...of course, other ongoing relations involve other identities and voices...
>
> Second, I do not share your view that "Polyphony is incommensurate with finding a voice."...the key issue here is that different voices are sounded and heard. I do not privilege an already in place *me*/identity or ego that I want to express, hold on to, and drown out other voices...I have written about holding all metaphors lightly/not grasping, etc....I am interested in the voice play, the play of voices, the playing with possibilities...

3. In reference to Boas' last paragraph (and his comment of being grateful to the editors for providing the "space for multiple discourses"), Dian Marie ends:

> Thank you, too, Boas—I am enjoying this play....

REFERENCES

Alvesson, M., & Deetz, S. (2000). *Doing critical management research.* London, England: Sage Publications.

Bentz, V. M., & Shapiro, J. J. (1998). *Mindful inquiry in social research.* Thousand Oaks, CA: Sage.

Bouwen, R., & Hosking, D. M. (2000). Reflections on relational readings of organizational learning. *European Journal of Work and Organizational Psychology, 9*(2), 267–274.

Brown, M. H., & Hosking, D.M. (1986). Distributed leadership and skilled performance as successful organisation in social movements. *Human Relations, 39* (1), 65–79.

Bryman, A. (1996). Leadership in organizations. In: S. R. Clegg, C. Hardy, & W.R. Nord (Eds.), *Handbook of organization studies* (pp. 276–293). London, England: Sage.

Chasin, R., Herzig, M., Roth, S. A., Chasin, L., & Becker, C. (1996). From diatribe to dialogue on divisive public issues: Approaches drawn from family therapy. *Mediation Quarterly, 13*(4), 323–344.

Corradi Fiumara, G. (1990). *The other side of language: A philosophy of listening.* London, England: Routeledge.

Dachler, H. P., & Hosking, D. M. (1995). The primacy of relations in socially constructing organizational realities. In D. M. Hosking, H. P. Dachler, & K. J. Gergen (Eds.), *Management and organization: Relational alternatives to individualism* (pp. 1–29). Aldershot, England: Avebury.

Drath, W. H., & Palus, C. J. (1994). *Making common sense: Leadership as meaning-making in a community of practice.* Greensboro, NC: Center for Creative Leadership.

Evered, R., & Louis, M.R. (1981). Alternative perspectives in the organizational sciences: "Inquiry from the inside" and "Inquiry from the outside." *The Academy of Management Review, 6*(3), 385–395.

Fairhurst, G. (2007). *Discursive leadership: In conversation with leadership psychology.* Thousand Oaks, CA: Sage.

Fairhurst, G. T., & Putnam, L. L. (2004). Organizations as discursive constructions. Communication Theory, 14, 5–26.

Fennollosa, E. (1969). The Chinese written character as a medium for poetry. In *Instigations of Ezra Pound.* Freeport, NY: Books for Libraries Press.

Friere, P. (1982). Creating alternative research methods: Learning to do it by doing it. In B. Hall, A. Gillete, & R.Tandon (Eds), *Creating knowledge: A monopoly? Participatory research in development.* New Delhi, India: Society for Participatory Research in India.

Gergen, K. J. (1994). *Realities and relationships: Soundings in social construction.* Cambridge, MA: Harvard University Press.

Gergen, K. J. (1995). Relational theory and the discourses of power. In D. M. Hosking, H. P. Dachler, & K. J. Gergen (Eds.), *Management and organization: Relational*

Gergen, K. J. & Thatchenkerry, T. (1996). Organization science as social construction: Postmodern potentials. *Journal of Applied Behavioural Science, 32*(4), 356–377.

Harding, S. (1998). *Is science multicultural?* Bloomington, IN: Indiana University Press.

Hosking, D. M. (1995). Constructing power: Entitative and relational approaches. In D. M. Hosking, H. P. Dachler, & K. J. Gergen (Eds.), *Management and or-*

ganization: Relational alternatives to individualism (pp. 51–71). Aldershot, England: Avebury.

Hosking, D.M. (2007). Sound constructs: a relational discourse. *Revue Sciences de Gestion, 55,* 55–75.

Hosking, D.M. (2011). Telling tales of relations: Appreciating relational constructionism. *Organization Studies, 32*(1), 47–65.

Hosking, D.M., & Kleisterlee, E. (2009). *Centering the path.* Paper presented at the Critical Management Studies Conference, University of Warwick, England. (Also available at www.relationalconstructionism.org.)

Hosking, D.M., & Morley, I.e., (1988). The skills of leadership. In J. G. Hunt, R. Baliga, H.P. Dachler, & C. Schriesheim (Eds), *Emerging leadership vistas.* Lexington, MA: Lexington Press.

Morley, I.e., & Hosking, D.M. (2003). Leadership, learning and negotiation in a social psychology of organising. In N. Bennett, & L. Anderson (Eds.), *Rethinking educational leadership* (pp. 43–60). London, England: Sage.

Ospina, S., & Sorensen, G. (2006). A constructionist lens on leadership: Charting new territory. In G. Goethals, & G. Sorenson (Eds.), *Quest for a general theory of leadership* (pp. 188–204). Cheltenham, England: Edward Elgar Publishers.

Pearce, W. B. (1992). A "camper's" guide to constructionisms. *Human Systems: The Journal of Systemic Consultation & Management, 3,* 139–161.

Reason, P., & Bradbury, H. (2008). *Handbook of action research: Participative inquiry and practice,* (2nd ed.). London, England: Sage.

Smircich, L., & Morgan, G. (1982). Leadership: The management of meanings. *Journal of Applied Behavioral Science, 18,* 257–273.

Stacey, R. (2001). What can it mean to say that the individual is social through and through? *Group Analysis, 34*(4), 457–471.

Uhl-Bien, M. (2006). Relational leadership theory: Exploring the social process of leadership and organizing. *The Leadership Quarterly, 17,* 654–676.

Weber, M. (1978). The definition of sociology and of social action. In G. Roth, & C. Wittich (Eds.), *Max Weber: Economy and society: An outline of interpretive sociology* (Vol. 1 pp. 4–24). Berkeley, CA: University of California Press.

Weinberg, D. (2008). The philosophical foundations of constructionist research. In J. A. Holstein, & J. F.Gubrium (Eds.), *Handbook of constructionist research.* New York, NY: The Guildford Press

Wittgenstein, L. (1953). *Philosophical Investigations* (G. E. M. Anscombe., Trans.). Oxford, England: Blackwell.

CONCLUSION

PARADIGM INTERPLAY IN RELATIONAL LEADERSHIP

A Way Forward

Mary Uhl-Bien and Sonia M. Ospina

This book was motivated by a lofty vision: The desire to advance under-standing among relational leadership scholars crossing multiple research paradigms, with the ultimate goal of identifying new ways to approach re-lational leadership research and practice. As described in the introductory chapters, we knew that paradigmatic issues were going to be important and play a key role in the discussion. We also knew that researchers would bring a variety of views and perspectives to the discussion.

What we did not know was how far this would stretch us, both intellectu-ally and personally. And what an amazing journey it has been! Perhaps the biggest surprise was the sheer difficulty of engaging dialogue across per-spectives. As a result, what began as a somewhat naïve belief that we would obtain common understandings among leadership scholars has evolved into recognition of the rich differences, and deep diversity of perspectives, that a conversation about relational leadership brings.

Advancing Relational Leadership Research, pages 537–580
Copyright © 2012 by Information Age Publishing
All rights of reproduction in any form reserved.

In this final chapter we bring the conversation full circle by returning to the issues of paradigmatic perspectives we raised in the introductory chapters. We now see the primary challenge as one of interplay among the paradigms (Romani, Primecz, & Topcu, 2011). We agree with Romani et al. (2011) that multiple paradigms offer diverse views and research methods that can complement one another and lead to new insights and creative thinking. Therefore, the issue is not about compromise but about paradigm interplay: a "respectful interaction between different paradigmatic analyses" (Romani et al., 2011, p. 436) that maintains distinctions, while acknowledging connections, among research paradigms (Romani et al., 2011; Schultz & Hatch, 1996). The goal of paradigm interplay is to build more accommodating understandings by juxtaposing and linking ideas across perspectives (Romani et al., 2011).

Through paradigm interplay, we focus first on the problem—*enhancing understanding of relational perspectives of leadership*—and then engage the heterogeneous perspectives represented in this book to generate new knowledge regarding relational leadership. We see the start of this in the dialogues inspired by, and reflective of, the chapters. We need to go further, however. As identified by Dave Day in his dialogue (Chapter 8):

> ... [T]his is an ideal opportunity to walk our talk as a scholarly community with regard to dialogue. Collectively, we have to transcend dominance and influence approaches in this philosophical and scientific turf battle. It is not a matter of which approach is better. The limits of those leadership principles in this debate have been reached.

Here, we take up this challenge. In this chapter, we work to advance a field-level understanding of relational leadership by using an approach of openness and a focus on learning, rather than defending a theory or method, to generate deeper, richer insights than are possible from any one of the perspectives alone.

We begin by describing what is meant by "paradigm interplay," and why we see it as valuable, and *necessary*, for relational leadership research. We then present three paradigm interplays based on the materials presented by authors in this book (i.e., leadership as co-constructed, leadership as a relational process, and leadership can and should be developed). Following this, we identify our learnings and summarize the take-aways from the interplays. We conclude by challenging leadership scholars to acknowledge the limitations of predominant approaches for studying leadership, and to begin to take seriously issues of relationality in leadership research.

A MULTI-PARADIGMATIC VIEW OF RELATIONAL LEADERSHIP

As has become clear in this book, our paradigms—our ontological and epistemological worldviews—pervade our theories and research studies.

We may not always recognize them, but we cannot avoid them. They are evidenced in the rich intellectual diversity, deep emotion, and closely held assumptions brought to the chapters and dialogues in this volume.

Paradigmatic discussions can take a variety of forms (Romani et al., 2011). One form is an isolationist/protectionist approach, in which paradigms are seen as competing, and the goal is to preserve and perpetuate one's paradigm. Another form is an integrationist approach, seeking ontological and epistemological consensus. A third form is a multi-paradigmatic approach. This approach urges the use of multiple paradigms, and the variety of ontological and epistemological standpoints they bring, to enrich a construct of interest. It grants paradigms their separate academic worldviews, seeing each as legitimate in its own terms, and argues that the partial understandings each paradigm can gain from the other leads to richer knowledge generation (e.g., Hassard & Kelemen, 2002; Lewis & Kelemen, 2002).

We opt for this third approach. We believe multi-paradigmatic theory building is essential for tackling the complex challenges presented when adopting a relational lens on leadership. As described in the introduction to this book, "relationality" has emerged as a key concept in leadership research. Independent of leadership school or approach, the notion that leadership is relational is a starting point of most inquiry. Yet, for the different paradigmatic perspectives, it carries a variety of meanings. From a postpositive lens, it means relationships and relational interactions between leaders and followers as they work together to produce outcomes. From a constructionist lens, it means the processes through which meaning and understandings of what constitutes leadership come to be attributed or emerge within a social system. These meanings reflect significant differences that cannot, and should not, be discounted.

A multi-paradigmatic approach to theory building does not get bogged down in differences, but instead frames the issue at a higher level: advancing theoretical and practical understanding of relational leadership. We enter this discussion with the assumption that there are benefits and learning available from each paradigmatic perspective. As described by Kennedy et al. (Chapter 6):

> ...what is underdeveloped in the entity/constructivist perspective ("the collective group," "what's in the moment"), is precisely what is strongest in the social construction perspective... [and] what is underdeveloped in terms of social construction ("the 'I' story, past personal history") is precisely what an entity/constructivist perspective brings to the development picture.

Therefore, we use the concept of paradigm interplay to help us identify the areas of connects, disconnects, tensions, and new insights across the chapters and dialogues. We compile and analyze these to see what they reveal with respect to moving the dialogue on relational leadership forward.

PARADIGM INTERPLAY

To achieve paradigm interplay (Romani et al., 2011), we draw from two main perspectives represented by the chapters and dialogues in this book: postpositivism and interpretivism. We also capitalize on perspectives informed by critical theory (see Chapter 1 for an explanation of these paradigms). Critical theory, with its goal of unmasking domination, offers an interesting perspective on the relational by bringing to light operations of power in ways that other paradigms may not consider.

We identify *relational leadership* as views that recognize leadership, not as a trait or behavior of an individual leader, but as a phenomenon generated in the interactions and relationships among people—a "collective capacity" (Day, 2000; Drath, 2001). Relational leadership may occur in formal, managerial contexts (e.g., manager and subordinate) or in leadership roles and processes that do not involve formal authority (e.g., informal and collective leadership processes). Relational leadership processes are those that "generally enable groups of people to work together in meaningful ways" (Day, 2000, p. 582; see also Hosking & Morley, 1991; Ospina & Foldy, 2010).

The objective of our paradigm interplay is enhancement of overall understanding of relational leadership. This enhancement occurs when scholars learn to build upon and use alternative or critical views to enrich the work in their own paradigm. It comes from learning about other perspectives. As described by Romani et al. (2011), paradigm interplay can be likened to a bilingual conversation and its possible outcome:

> A francophone and an Anglophone talk about management in their respective mother tongues, well known to their interlocutor (Step 1 of the interplay). In light of each other, the words reveal differences and connections between their semantic fields. For example, the interlocutors realize that the French "gérer" is strongly associated with the verbs direct and administrate, while the English "manage" is related to the idea of being in charge and successful despite obstacles. Yet, both "gérer" and "manage" contain the idea of organizing. From their conversation (Step 2 of the interplay), they may start seeing management as a control of a situation by organizing it. For example, the control is about "administrating" or being "successfully in charge." The interlocutors open a new angle to their conversation (the interplay control). (p. 437)

In other words, paradigm interplay involves (a) understanding the different languages (and perspectives), (b) engaging in respectful and inquiring conversation, and (c) identifying and capturing new insights gained without giving up one's paradigm. Romani et al. (2011) emphasize that interplay is *not* about creating a new language or a new word that would merge both meanings, nor is it about restricting the use of the words to what they have in common. Instead, it is about increasing awareness of the semantic meanings attached to words to achieve a level of "multilingualism" that will allow for dialogue that generates larger understandings (cf. Deetz, 1996, p. 204). The goal is to enrich our own views and advance broader knowledge.

To demonstrate this process, in the sections below we engage in three paradigm interplays on relational leadership drawing from the chapters and dialogues in this book. In these interplays, we first identify a general topic addressed by all the authors. We then describe the varying perspectives on the topic, noting tensions associated with the different paradigmatic approaches and meanings brought by the multiple perspectives. From these different meanings, we summarize new insights gained through the interplay.

Interplay #1: Leadership is Co-Constructed

We begin with paradigm interplay at the broadest level. One key area we can identify among relational leadership scholars is: Leadership is co-constructed. All the perspectives in this book share a view that leadership is co-created in relational interactions between people, and that relational leadership is dynamic, developing, and changing over time. This can be summarized as:

- Leadership is co-created in relational interactions between people.
- Relational leadership is dynamic, developing and changing over time.

Comparison of Views

The authors in this book bring a variety of definitions and assumptions to the study of leadership. They all, however, share a basic view of leadership as a relational phenomenon.

Several of the chapters (Ashkanasy et al., Chapter 11; Offermann, Chapter 12; Treadway et al., Chapter 13) approach relational leadership from a postpositive view of the leader-follower relationship (Graen & Uhl-Bien, 1995; Hollander, 1978; 2009). These approaches emphasize individuals' perceptions of relationships and relational processes (e.g., LMX). This perspective theorizes that leadership is generated in high quality leader-member exchange (LMX) relationships, and the co-constructed nature of leadership occurs in the dyadic relationship-building process between leaders and followers. This happens over time, as leaders and followers engage in social exchange processes that come to define and provide context for the nature of their work relationships.

For example, building from LMX theory, Treadway et al. (Chapter 13) describe leadership from the perspective of a reciprocal communication process. They add to existing views a construct of relational control, based on political behavior and political skill. In their chapter, context is a relational context, involving perceptions of relational self, dyadic distance, and affect generated in the relational interactions.

Ashkanasy et al. (Chapter 11) similarly focus on affect, and propose that examination of affective processes in the development of leadership relationships can add to understanding of relational leadership. They go beyond the dyadic approach, however, to describe a process in which followers and leaders collectively shape leadership outcomes through emotional contagion—a social process, occurring in relational interactions over time, that involves the tacit expression and mimicry of affective states among team (i.e., work unit) members.

Offermann (Chapter 12) describes a research program combining quantitative and qualitative approaches to best flesh out the complexities of leaders' relationships with followers from diverse backgrounds. She draws from both LMX theory and Hollander's (1978, 2009) view that leadership is a process, not a person. As she describes in her chapter, in Hollander's view, "examination of leadership must include both parties in the study of 'relationships that can accomplish things for mutual benefit'" (Hollander, 2009, p. 3), and needs to include concerns about follower-perceived leader legitimacy, encouraging an active followership, and doing things *with* people rather than *to* people."

Barge (Chapter 4), like Treadway et al., sees leadership as a communication process. Barge brings a new angle to the role of communication in the leadership process with his systemic constructionism, rather than LMX, lens. He describes leadership as a "co-created, performative, contextual, and attributional process where the ideas articulated in talk or action are recognized by others as progressing tasks that are important to them." From this perspective, leadership is co-constructed in linguistic interaction, attributions, and meaning-making. Systemic constructionism considers "how individuals draw on historical and cultural knowledge to co-create particular patterns of coordination and meaning-making with other people in conversation by using linguistic material." Barge focuses us on thinking about leadership from the standpoint of language—how language invites, creates, and sustains particular patterns of coordination and discourages others.

Ospina et al. (Chapter 9) also pay attention to narrative as a reflection of socially constructed experience. But, in contrast to Barge, who focuses on the specific moments of linguistic interaction that help to negotiate and constitute everyday life between leaders and followers at the most micro level of interaction, Ospina et al. consider leadership from the standpoint of relatively enduring agreements over time, as reflected in the recurrent social practices participants engage in as they try to move the work forward in a context where power cannot be ignored. Social practices emerge from negotiated meaning over time at the group level, not from single dyadic interactions. Drawing from practice theory, they argue that: "Practice is a collective construct. It is the outcome of collective meaning-making, and rests upon shared knowledge that is largely tacit and embodied, historically and culturally specific, and transcends the innate mental faculty of individuals (Orlikowski, 2002; Wenger, 1998)." Their view of leadership is as a collective dynamic, co-constructed in context. This is evidenced in their conclusion that: "A focus on practice helps us to tap into the construction of leadership by helping identify the recurrent assumptions, actions, and interactions that document how leadership emerges as a collective achievement from the organizing demands for social change."

Crosby and Bryson (Chapter 10) do not view themselves as constructionists, but acknowledge the importance of the dynamics of social construction for understanding leadership. They define *leadership* as the inspiration and mobilization of others to undertake collective action in pursuit of the common good. In their framework, leadership aimed at tackling complex public challenges is necessarily a shared and collective phenomenon, but "at the same time, we have found that the characteristics, strengths, and weaknesses of particular individuals, who act as formal and informal leaders, significantly affect the outcome of this leadership work." Therefore, Crosby and Bryson see leadership as a combination of both individual and collective acts.

Similarly, Wassenaar and Pearce (Chapter 14) identify shared leadership as an interactive and dynamic social influence process that individuals on teams or in groups use to influence each other to achieve a stated goal or objective (Pearce & Conger, 2003). From this perspective, leadership is a collective process generated through individual influence behaviors.

Fletcher (Chapter 3) adopts a multi-paradigmatic approach in her view of co-created leadership, explicitly espousing a feminist genre of relational theory (Ross, 2002) that allows her to embrace elements of both entity and constructionist perspectives. She identifies the relational interactions that typify good leadership as egalitarian, mutual, collaborative, and two-directional, with followers playing an integral, agentic role in the leadership process. The entity perspective in her approach focuses on a particular set of leadership skills and competencies that are relational and interactional in nature. The constructionist dimensions of her approach highlight the way a particular set of (relational) leadership practices is perceived, co-created and "acted upon" by larger organizational and societal systems, including systems of sense-making and cognition, as well as systems of power and privilege.

Drawing from a different genre of relational theorizing, Fitzsimons (Chapter 5) adds tension to the paradigm interplay by bringing to the discussion a view that has not been considered before: a psychodynamic perspective. He describes this perspective as offering a lens for relational leadership that complements both entity and constructionist views. According to psychodynamic theory, an individual's feelings, thoughts, and actions are not seen as functions of an individual psychology, but of systemic group processes that are often unconscious. The most influential psychodynamic theory, object relations, emphasizes *relatedness*, proposing that the object of human drives is connection with others. From this relational genre, the basic unit of study is not the individual entity, but the "interactional field within which the individual arises and struggles to make contact and articulate himself." In order to understand leadership behavior, Fitzsimons purports that exploring the relational dynamics between individuals requires paying attention to unconscious relational dynamics *within* individuals—that is, between different aspects of the psyche of individuals—as well as the linkages of individuals to collectives.

Returning to LMX-based approaches, Seers and Chopin (Chapter 2) explore how constructionist perspectives can inform the study of relational leadership from an LMX perspective. Their paradigm interplay generates a framework they call *relational organizing*—in which leadership is seen as a socially produced dynamic. They see their view as paralleling constructionist thinking more than entity thinking. It differs, however, from the constructionist premise in two key ways: Its realist ontology and its rejection of the assumption that narrative meaning-making is essential to leadership. Regarding the latter, they explain: "narrative elaborates, sophisticates, and complicates leadership, but leadership can be produced before it is cognitively constituted." To emphasize the distinction in their approach from constructionism, Seers and Chopin refer to their framework as the "social production, and not construction, of reality." Social production focuses on the functional operation of organizing. They argue that what's essential to leadership is action—"leaders leading, with followers following." They see leadership as a "natural" asymmetry: "supervisors have higher role status... the leader expects to use information to direct the follower, and the follower expects that direction."

This asymmetrical view is consistent with Shamir (Chapter 17), who calls for reserving the term *leadership* for situations where there is disproportionate or asymmetrical influence in a social arena. For the term *leadership* to be useful, he argues, some individuals have to be observed as exerting more influence on the group than others, or at least to be recognized or perceived by others as exerting such disproportionate influence. Hence, both Shamir and Seers and Chopin see asymmetry as a key element of the definition of *leadership*, while acknowledging that there is plenty of room for mutual influence (i.e., the co-creation of leadership) despite this asymmetry. This is also implied by the other authors, many of whom recognize leader (and follower) roles.

Hosking (Chapter 16, Chapter 18) also sees leadership as asymmetrical (Hosking & Morley, 1988). According to Hosking, leadership should be studied as it emerges in the moment—as the broader organizing processes that constitute the social reality within which individuals experience organizational life as its develops and evolves over time. Here the co-construction of leadership is less about mutual influence among individuals in differentiated roles, and more about the ongoing processes of negotiation of order. She suggests that where we will find the clues to understanding the emergence of leadership is in "skillful organizing."

Drath (Chapter 8) is consistent with this, but defines negotiation of order a bit more precisely. In Drath's view, the group's meaning-making processes produce a set of outcomes—direction, alignment, and commitment—that support cooperation, and in doing so, call forth leadership (Drath, McCauley, Palus, Van Velsor, O'Connor, & McGuire, 2008).

Finally, other authors approach their chapters in ways that reflect more directly a standpoint of paradigm interplay. Kennedy et al. (Chapter 6), for example, provide an excellent illustration of the tensions evoked by paradigm interplay on relational leadership. Since their chapter focuses primarily on leadership development, we discuss their work more fully in Interplay #3.

Discussion

We can see in this interplay a general agreement among leadership scholars that leadership is relational: It is co-constructed in interactions that occur in a social context. Because of the relational leadership lens, all of the authors in this book recognize leadership as involving elements associated with both individuals (e.g., those who engage in leadership) and relational processes (e.g., co-creation of leadership).

The authors differ in how they identify what leadership is and where it is located (and therefore where to look for it when doing research). Those coming from a postpositivist, LMX perspective locate leadership in the skills and abilities of individuals for developing effective leader-follower relationships. Those coming from a constructionist perspective locate it in relational processes, considering social constructions of leadership generated through communication, negotiation, sense-making, and meaning-making. From this perspective, leadership emerges as a collective phenomenon embedded in context, in which individuals may (or may not) have a clear, identifiable leader/follower role. Some offer a mix of the two, seeing roles of both individual leaders/followers and collective, contextual processes.

Therefore, although the authors share a basic view of leadership as a relational phenomenon (i.e., something that is co-constructed), the ontological and epistemological assumptions they bring to their work vary quite a bit. As a result, the pace and rhythm of the views of co-construction vary significantly from one perspective to the other. Co-construction is an unfolding process of reality negotiation for constructionists, while it is most likely a developmental stage, something that happens early in the relationship through attribution processes, for postpositivists. These differences are in part a function of the disciplines from which authors approach their research. Authors coming from a more psychologically-based view look for leadership in perceptions about interactions between a leader and a follower acting in a relational context. Authors coming from a communications view look for leadership as generated in language constructions. Authors coming from a sociologically-based view look for leadership in negotiation and organizing processes.

Some of these differences can also be seen relative to the analytical distinction between *leaders* and *leadership* as separate, relational phenomena (Rost, 1991; Ospina & Sorenson, 2006). Drath describes this in his dialogue with Dave Day when he argues that leadership "is not leader-ship (the act of the leader), but is a shared social activity (the act of a collective) that can be freed from a dependence on leaders." As he explains, "leaders (and their followers) are not the only agents of leadership. Under some conditions—such as on the project team described above—people can achieve vital leadership outcomes as peers without leaders." This is a significant difference from perspectives that see leadership as involving behaviors of individuals acting as leaders (and followers).

From this interplay we can clearly see that relational processes are a key element of relational leadership. Therefore, we turn next to a paradigm interplay addressing leadership as a relational process. What we will see in this next interplay is that this discussion draws out the differences in ontological and epistemological assumptions—and the accompanying tensions and emotions—that authors bring to the study of relational leadership.

Interplay #2: Leadership is a Relational Process

A second key area we can identify for our paradigm interplay is: Leadership is a relational (social) process. It is a distinct and pervasive social phenomenon that has important outcomes in society (both good and bad). Moreover, because it is a *social* process, it occurs in context. Therefore, to learn more about relational leadership, we need to consider process and context in the study of leadership. This can be summarized as:

- Leadership is a relational (social) process; it is a pervasive phenomenon that has important outcomes in society.
- It occurs in a social context.

- Therefore, process and context must be considered in the study of leadership.

While the authors view leadership as an important relational process, they vary significantly in the meanings they attach to "relational" and the approaches they use to study leadership process and context. Some authors approach the study of process and context from a more variance perspective. These authors presume fixed entities with variable attributes, and investigate process as co-variation patterns across hypothesized cause-effect relationships among the attributes of interest (Mohr, 1982). They use a situational/contingency lens to context, meaning they see context as a variable that interacts with leadership (cf. Liden & Antonakis, 2009).

Other authors approach the study of process and context more from a process perspective. These authors presume that participant narratives of their experience of relationships inform us of the unfolding and co-evolving nature of intersubjective realities. These perspectives use a contextual lens, seeing leadership as necessarily embedded in context (cf. Fairhurst, 2009; Osborn, Hunt & Jauch, 2002). The core assumption of a contextual view is that leadership emerges from process and context. This constructionist perspective does not introduce context and process to the study of leadership; instead it studies leadership *through* process and context.

As we will see below, these differences are the source of some of the most heated debate, strongest tensions, and perhaps greatest misunderstandings demonstrated in this book.

Comparison of Views

The leader-member relationship based approaches presented in this book (Ashkanasy et al., Chapter 11; Offermann, Ch. 12; Treadway et al., Chapter 13) theorize about and study leadership from the assumption of dyadic leader-follower relationships as the key unit of analysis and antecedent of leadership effectiveness. The distinct social process of leadership from this perspective can be seen in Ashkanasy et al.'s description of the assumptions of LMX theory: "Leadership outcomes are seen not to be solely reliant on leader-related elements, but also depend on the interplay of leader and follower cognitions, behaviors, and affect."

In these approaches, leadership is identified as interactions among leaders and followers (i.e., managers and subordinates). The relational process in this approach is the interaction of leader and follower cognitions, behaviors, and affect. The approach to context is a situational (contingency) view. Process and context are operationalized as variables that are antecedent to leadership relationships; context can also moderate the relationship between leadership relationships and outcomes. Typically context is handled as a dyadic interpersonal context (e.g., Treadway et al., Chapter 13), though in the case of Ashkanasy et al. (Chapter 11), context is elevated to the group level. In Ashkanasy et al.'s case, the process of emotional contagion happens in a group relational context. In Offermann (Chapter 12), societal context is also implied in the discussion of the descriptions of societal norms and assumptions regarding issues of diversity.

Shared leadership (Wassenaar & Pearce, Chapter 14) is identified as a distinct social process occurring in a team context. It is defined as an interactive, social influence process among team or group members. Despite this, it is studied as reports (perceptions) of individual behaviors (rather than as process). Like LMX, shared leadership is generally operationalized using survey methods gathering individualized self-reports. These surveys are adapted from measures of full-range leadership theory that focus on leader behaviors (e.g., transformational leadership, transactional leadership, *laissez-faire*). It, too, represents a "situational" (contingency) approach to context. The context of shared leadership is the work unit, and when it is operationalized, contextual variables are typically examined as antecedents to shared leadership or moderators of the shared leadership to outcome relationship (see Chapter 14).

Leadership from a systemic constructionism perspective, as defined by Barge (Chapter 4), offers a contextual, rather than situational, view. In this view, leadership is a social process that can be found in the overt conversational behavior of participants. Leadership is described as "performative," meaning that it is always performed in relation to tasks. It is a distinct social process in which patterns of meaning-making and action are created that move people forward together (i.e., performance). Leadership occurs when it is linguistically constructed and made ontologically real by the participants through an attribution process, in which people attribute actions as "leadership" and people as "leaders." In this approach, outcomes are not variables but "performance," defined as forward movement on tasks. Leadership is contextual in that "our understanding of what counts as leadership or a leader depends on the unique combination of people, task, context, time, and place" (Barge, Chapter 4).

Seers and Chopin (Chapter 2) describe a process similar to that of Barge, but from the standpoint of role theory—that is, they see role behavior (i.e., role enactments) rather than language as the source of leadership. Their relational organizing framework conceptualizes leadership as the organizing of behavior, and leadership processes are described as occurring in relational interactions that reinforce the individual actor's identity as leader or follower within that particular relationship. Therefore, advancing understanding of relational leadership dynamics can be achieved by studying the causes underlying the repetitive behavior patterns that trigger interpretation, meaning-making, and sense-making negotiations. Again, varying from Barge, they say: "it is action, not narrative, that is the primary point of leverage in social relationships." Context in this approach is the dyadic interpersonal relationship, and outcomes are leader/follower relationships. In this view, *relational* means dyadic relationships within a broader context, and these relationships play multiple roles: as *both* outcomes of interest and mechanisms of production.

Fletcher (Chapter 3) identifies leadership from the standpoint of practice. Leadership practice is the ability to create conditions under which co-constructed outcomes—such as coordinated action, collective achievement, and shared accountability—can be realized. These outcomes are achieved through relational leadership processes (described in the next paragraph). Her outcome of interest is multi-level learning. These multi-level learning outcomes include dyadic learning, when the relationship is between individuals; group learning, when considering teams and communities of practice; and, ultimately, organizational learning that results in positive action, when considering organizational levels. Hers is a contextual view: Leadership is relational, embedded in broader organizational and social contexts. (She cautions against simply identifying relational constructs and adding them to traditional leadership criteria uncritically.)

In Fletcher's view, understanding of leadership processes can be obtained by: (1) unpacking and identifying specific micro-processes between actors that operationalize two-directional concepts, such as egalitarianism or mutuality, in a stratified leadership context (i.e., where there are status differences due to identity, position, or organizational level); (2) explicating the process by which outcomes achieved at the dyadic level link to broader leadership goals, such as organizational learning and adaptability (note that this is similar to Seers and Chopin's view of levels); and (3) understanding the motivating set of beliefs or "logic of effectiveness" (Fletcher, 1999, 2004) that prompt someone to use relational skills to enact mutuality and two-directionality in a context that traditionally has had neither.

Like Fletcher, Ospina et al. (Chapter 9) consider collective processes and outcomes as they relate to leadership. Using Drath's (2001) constructionist framework and Heifetz's notion of leadership as work (1994), they investigate leadership as the type of work that helps a group achieve collective action toward an articulated vision of change. They study social change leadership by identifying practices that manifest the constructed shared agreements about the envisioned social change results and what needs to be done in the organization to produce them. Ospina et al. emphasize process and interpretation, rather than variance and explanation, in their methodologies. They elicit stakeholder stories (i.e., narratives) about collective work that emerged from participants' efforts to produce the negotiated desired change. While interested in studying leadership as an outcome itself—achieving collective capacity—the authors also view it as the purposive work to produce concrete long-term community benefits. Therefore, similar to Seers and Chopin's relational organizing approach, leadership is both an outcome (it happens in a situated community through members' joint meaning-making), and a process (as it happens, it creates the conditions for the community to leverage its power and produce the desired change). This is a contextual approach, where narrative and action are not viewed as separate constructs, but represent interconnected manifestations of the same socially constructed reality—in this case leadership work that emerges in historically specific contexts.

Crosby and Bryson (Chapter 10) study leadership by examining behaviors of individual policy entrepreneurs (sponsors and champions) who report collaborative practices that relate to outcomes associated with public good (e.g., public value; first-, second-, and third-order effects; resilience; and reassessment) and accountabilities (e.g., tracking systems, results management systems, relationships with constituencies). While behaviors are individual, the outcomes are generated in relational (e.g., constructionist) processes that also influence those involved in the process. Both behaviors and processes are accessed in their research using qualitative, case-based research. This view is at the same time situational and contextual in that it focuses on "understanding the social, political, economic, technological, and ecological 'givens' as well as potentialities" (Crosby & Bryson, Chapter 10) while also identifying the contingencies (constraints and opportunities) that help explain individual behavior.

The psychodynamic approach described by Fitzsimons (Chapter 5) is also contextual in that it is concerned with the social, political, and cultural milieu in which leadership takes place. In this approach, leadership processes occur in a complex field of systemic forces that are psychological (individual) as well as social (contextual) in origin. Leadership processes are understood by paying attention to how the emotional needs of individuals and groups influence the processes, structures, and cultures in which leadership emerges and is sustained in organizations, and how these leadership processes, structures, and cultures in turn shape the emotional experiences of individuals and groups—without privileging one above the other. Using an action research framework based on pragmatic theory and the Tavistock Institute's group relations model, leadership research is carried out in the context of consulting to organizations, and leadership is accessed by engaging organizational members fully to be able to experience and observe how psychological and social dynamics interact to influence both leaders and followers. To conduct this work, it is critical that consultant-researchers develop, over a number of years, a familiarity with the way their own personal history may be influenced by, as well as influence, the organizational and leadership dynamics of which they are a part.

Hosking (Chapter 16, Chapter 18) also uses an action-oriented research approach reflected in methodologies like appreciative inquiry, collaborative consulting, and participative action as she embraces fully the notion of relationality as the core of leadership. Rather than explicitly drawing from a particular genre of relational theory, like Fitzsimons and Fletcher, her goal is to do relational theorizing by embodying relationality in her approach to research and in her "dialogue" for this volume. For Hosking, leadership is a relational reality arising in local and changing networks of relations. The relational processes that construct a "leader" also construct not-leaders and leader/non-leader relations. (Similarly, the processes of doing research necessarily construct researcher-researched identities and relations.) Because reality is processual (i.e., always unfolding), leadership theories are constructions that "could be otherwise," meaning that leadership discourses are all relative. This approach is characterized by its multivoice "dialogic" emphasis that highlights interdependence and connectedness. A dialogic view involves listening and self-reflection, and assumes a willingness to suspend one's assumptions and certainties and reflexively pay attention to ongoing processes and one's own participation.

Consistent with Barge and Fairhurst, Hosking sees dialogue as the way in which leadership can be accessed. Through dialogic processes, participants experience relational realities, including leadership, as continually unfolding, with themselves as contributors. Similar to Fletcher, Hosking focuses on collective relational processes (i.e., dialogical practices) that, over time, enable and support now-ness, emergent possibilities and insights, collective learning, and a sense of participating "in wholeness—rather than multiple, separately existing entities." Leadership is clearly contextual in this view, as leadership and context cannot be separated. Instead, leadership is emergent and unfolding in discourses and actions, and these emerge in relation to "local" rationality that has its own grounding of assumptions and interests.

Shamir (Chapter 17) agrees that leadership is a relational process and a socially constructed phenomenon. He views this process, however, as something that must be defined as unique to, and indicative of, leadership. In reaction to Alvesson and Sveningsson and other constructionist approaches that "unbound" leadership in social processes, he argues that if leadership theory is to advance, we must have a basic common discourse. He proposes *asymmetrical relational influence* as the basis for this discourse. In Shamir's view, leadership processes involve the guidance and facilitation of the social construction of a reality that enables a group to achieve its goals. Shared meanings are the basis of collective action, and leaders play a particularly important role in the construction of these meanings.

According to Shamir, the study of leadership should devote more attention to studying meaning construction processes and the roles that various participants play in these processes. He argues that leaders, by definition, are those who have disproportionate influence on the meaning construction process. This differentiation is not fixed—leadership does not have to be seen as embodied in the fixed characteristics of leaders and other participants, and leadership research does not have to be leader-centric. For a social phenomenon to be called *leadership*, however, we have to be able to identify certain actors who, at least in a certain situation and during a specified period of time, exert more influence than others on the group or the process.

Discussion

In this interplay, we see that the authors agree that leadership is a relational (social) process, but they disagree on what that means. To help us discuss these differences, we roughly associate them with the distinction between variance and process approaches to research, which resonates with the distinct metaphors of the "window" and the "lantern" described in Chapter 1. The former (i.e., variance) approach assumes fixed entities with variable attributes, and a focus on process as co-variation patterns across hypothesized cause-effect relationships among the attributes of interest. Variance approaches address context as a variable in line with a "situational," or contingency, view (i.e., context is represented as a variable in a model that is tested statistically). This view sees clear boundaries and separations between leaders and followers as well as between leadership and context. In the latter (i.e., process approaches) participant narratives are used to uncover unfolding and co-evolving intersubjective realities that emerge in relation. This is a "contextual" view that sees leadership as *necessarily* embedded in context—"socially constructed in and from a context" (Osborn et al., 2002, p. 798).

The differences among perspectives create tensions in the paradigm interplay, which can be clearly seen in the dialogues in this volume. For example, Shamir and Hosking (Chapter 16, Chapter 18) engage around definitional and boundary issues in leadership. In reacting to Hosking and other constructionist views, Shamir (Chapter 17) suggests that we have to be careful when opening up leadership to broader social processes and expanded views of context, so as not to lose focus on what is the essence of leadership. Hosking, arguing from a constructionist perspective, however, denies the idea that leadership has an essence in and of itself. A constructionist relational ontology suggests that leadership is defined contextually, and how people view its essence will vary considerably. This is also at the core of Drath's discussion of three different ways of thinking about leadership that have dominated different time periods, from leadership as personal dominance, to leadership as interpersonal influence, to leadership as relational dialogue (Drath, 2001).

From a critical lens, the reaction to a search for the essence of leadership is even stronger. Alvesson and Sveningsson in Chapter 7 describe the focus in academic psychology on natural science ideals such as finding law-like patterns, correlations between variables, and measuring leadership as discounting the inherently subjective nature of leadership. According to Alvesson and Sveningsson, efforts to use abstract definitions and turn leadership phenomena into "variables, objects for the control and dissection of neo-positivism" results in there being very little feeling for "what goes on." As a result, appreciation of how subjects involved construct their realities in social interaction is missed.

Fairhurst and Antonakis (Chapter 15) engage around issues of how relationality (with its emphasis on process) is studied in leadership research. One of the key issues we see in this interplay is what Fairhurst identifies as the disconnect between ontological level and epistemological assumptions in theorizing about relational leadership (see Fairhurst's Table 15.1). Fairhurst identifies the problem as "the overwhelming dominance of the individual as the observational unit when the ontological unit is relational." For example, LMX approaches theorize about dyadic relational realities, but test individual relational realities (e.g., ontological unit of reciprocal communication but observational unit of individually reported influence tactics and relational strategies). Shared leadership theorizes about social influence processes but tests individual perceptions of leader behavior. Fairhurst argues that to address these problems, we need two things (at least): (1) ontological levels that match observational and analytical units, and (2) more focus on process (and communication).

Fairhurst's first point is that, if authors theorize a certain ontological level, their observational and analytical units should match that level. Both she and Antonakis agree on this point. Extending their point, we could say that there are two ways to address this: First, authors who theorize relational leadership *change their observational and analytical units* to study process, or authors who use observational and analytical units that study individuals *revise their ontological level* to indicate that it is individual and not relational.

For example, in the case of LMX theory, the recognition must be made that it has not been a theory that studies relational processes, but rather a theory that studies individuals' perceptions of a relational partner (predominantly a subordinate's perception of a manager). In shared leadership, we should recognize that—despite its definition—it has not studied shared social influence processes, but instead has investigated individuals' perceptions of team members' (and vertical leaders') leadership behaviors. There is value in studying these phenomena, *so we are not disparaging the approaches or the need to study these topics.* Moreover, they have played a critical role in leading us to the recognition of the importance of relationality and process in leadership research. The problem is that their observational and analytical units at the individual behavior level do not allow us to advance understanding of leadership *processes* (e.g., relationship-building in LMX; dynamic, social influence processes in shared leadership). For leadership research to advance, *we must recognize and prioritize the study of relational (social) processes in leadership research.*

In the spirit of interplay, we recognize the different ontologies brought by the varying perspectives. This means that consistency between ontological and methodological choices around level of analysis will result in entity and constructionist scholars accessing "process" in quite different ways, as they should. We explore the assumptions that lead to this statement in the book's introductory chapter, around the idea of "indication of method." Further discussions by Fairhust (Chapter 15) and Ospina et al. (Chapter 9) in this volume, and the comparisons developed in the interplay above make this distinction even more relevant for sharing insights across paradigms in the context of multi-paradigmatic theory-building. The point here is that, independent of perspective, we need to make explicit design choices that consistently align ontological, epistemological, and methodological assumptions around relationality if we are to produce research results about relational leadership that can help advance the field.

To extend this point further, we can interpret Fairhurst and Antonakis (Chapter 15) to be saying that we must not tolerate "overclaims" in our research. The reason is that *when we claim we are studying process but we are really studying individual perceptions of another individual (and analyzing it inappropriately), process gets lost,* and the consequence is where we are now: a dearth in understanding of the essential "relational" aspects that are core to the co-production of leadership.

This relates to Fairhurst's second key point: We need more process descriptions of leadership interactions, and these process descriptions are not likely to come from methods that collect data from individuals using summary judgments. She says: "The essential argument here is that the *pattern* of leadership interaction itself is its own best explanation of leadership dynamics" (Chapter 15). On this point, Antonakis takes a different approach. He argues that the problem is not summary judgments of individuals, but rather mis-specifying levels of analysis (i.e., saying we are testing dyad level when we are really testing individual level) and handling of endogenous variables in our statistical modeling. On the latter point, Antonakis argues that:

> From a research point of view, "relations" are endogenous variables—they depend on other factors, and it is important to model these factors completely to better understand the process model that leads to dependent outcomes.... [I]f x is endogenous, then its effect on y cannot be correctly estimated unless the antecedent exogenous conditions of x (e.g., z, q, or what have you, whether they operate on the individual, group, organizational, or another level) are included in the model.... [T]he exogenous factors must not correlate with the error terms of the systems of specified equations; if they do, then they have the same problem that the endogenous variables do, which means the effect of x on y cannot be identified.... [W]e found that much of the lead-

ership literature is stuck with correlating endogenous variables with other endogenous variables. . . . such descriptive correlations are not useful because they confound the effects of omitted variables. . . . Thus, what is important for me to mention is that using "relations" (in whichever form it is measured) to predict other outcomes is not very useful *per se* and that any coefficient capturing this relation has no inherent statistical meaning. (Antonakis, Ch. 15)

This goes to another issue at the core of this interplay—the meaning of relationality. Underlying the Fairhurst/Antonakis dialogue is a paradigmatic difference around relationality. Antonakis (Chapter 15) sees relationality more from a *variance* lens, focusing on beginning to "model and quantify the unquantifiable" and then identifying statistical analyses that can test at the appropriate level (e.g., dyadic level for interpersonal relationships; multilevel when group contexts are considered; appropriately handling endogeneity). Fairhurst sees relationality more from a *process* lens, focusing on quantitative *and* qualitative methods that can assess key moments in relational discourse. She argues that it isn't a matter of statistics, but a matter of authors not matching their observational and analytical level to the ontological level, and a consequent failure to capture relational process.

Ospina et al. make the same argument (Chapter 9). Contrary to Treadway et al. (Chapter 13) and Ashkanasy et al. (Chapter 11), who describe the need to move to more sophisticated variance models that incorporate issues like context, timing, and levels of analysis, Ospina et al. suggest (Chapter 9) the issue is not as simple as choosing a different methodology. It is more a matter of "reframing" the way we think about how to enter the reality of leadership. Using process models is a first step, but it is not enough because such models still rest on assumptions that partition realities in ways not reflecting the interconnections and reciprocal dynamics of micro-interactions embedded in broader systems of relations. According to constructionists, a shift to methodologies that help view reality as fluid is not a luxury, but the only way to go. For example, Ospina et al. (Chaper 9) argue that if narrative and language are key, if the experience of meaning-making is at the core of leadership, then interpretive methodologies, such as phenomenology and hermeneutics, might be as helpful or more helpful than hierarchical linear or linear growth models proposed by Treadway et al. (Chapter 13), and so forth.

Fairhurst also points to the importance of narrative, arguing for the need to place communication at the center of relational study: "This is because people do not relate and then talk, they relate *in* talk . . . the exchange of messages *is* the relationship" (Fairhurst, Chapter 15). Studying relational patterns in communication refocuses us. As she says, the key is not to understand individual behavior, but to understand how people act relationally—in Weick's (1979) terminology, not our individual "acts," but our "interacts" and "double interacts." She elaborates that if process is to remain one of the key value commitments of the relational agenda, then we must find ways of apprehending it beyond the static (and individual-level) depictions of relational processes that most leadership scholars currently favor:

> Interviews and surveys ask individuals to retrospectively summarize the patterns that mark the relationship typically *from the perspective of only one person in the relationship*, thus implying that a single relational reality can be assumed (Rogers et al., 1985)....According to Rogers et al. (1985), "The structural web...spun by recurring relational patterns emerging from ongoing message exchanges... (are) redundant, stochastic behavioral sequences" that are constitutive of the relationship and measurable as such (p. 176). These sequences must acquire a greater share of the spotlight in relational leadership research because, whether the system is relational, organizational, or institutional, systems can *only* emerge from repeated interactions that evolve into multi-leveled orders of patterns (Bateson, 1972; Rogers & Escudero, 2004). (Fairhurst, Ch. 15)

Part of the difference here goes to the heart of the issue as identified by Fitzsimons (Chapter 5) that the most central debate the RLT model elicits is how the self is construed (and, therefore, how the individual is handled): "From this stems all subsequent theorizing about the nature of relationship and relational dynamics with respect to the link between individuals, the collectives to which they belong, and their wider social, political, and cultural contexts." Independent of whether they take a sociological or a psychological approach, authors who explicitly draw from a relational theory (like Fletcher and Fitzsimons) or who approach research with a constructionist "relationality" lens (like Barge, Hosking and Ospina et al.) consider individuals always in relation to the systemic forces that surround them. As discussed in Chapter 1, this perspective draws from a *relational theory of self* (Emirbayer, 1997; Miller, 1976; Patton, 2007; Slife, 2004), defined as *something that develops only in relation and in contexts of interdependence.* It contrasts significantly with perspectives drawing from *psychological theories of the self* (Gailliot, Mead, & Baumeister, 2008; Robins, Tracy, & Trzesniewski, 2008), *which consider autonomy and independence as the developmental source of the self.*

These contrasting definitions of self and the consequent distinct views of relational leadership (and its study) have generated tensions that are evident in the dialogue between Antonakis and Fairhurst. Antonakis's focus on statistics implies that relationality can be studied when the data and statistical tests are modeled at the right level and appropriate statistical and methodological assumptions are made. Fairhurst's focus on communication patterns and discourse analysis says that relationality can only be accessed in relational data (i.e., it is not a matter of using relational analyses of individual-level data, it is a matter of having relational data in the first place). She does not deny the importance of statistics and analyses, but argues that we cannot unpack relationality from a single relational reality (e.g., individual-level summary reports).

The tension on the handling of the individual (i.e., self) can also be seen in the dialogue between Day and Drath (Chapter 8). At the core of this dialogue is a questioning about the role of the individual in relational leadership. Day agrees that leadership is not just a solitary leader—he recognizes leadership as "embedded in interactions and social relations." What he does not agree with is his perception (from the descriptions of some of the authors) that there is no individual. His frustration is shown in this statement: "Perhaps that is the point of the social constructionists, *which neatly dispenses with any sense of individual merit or differential human abilities*" (emphasis in original). For Day, this is a non-starter to dialogue and an indication that relational leadership does not add value to leadership research.

The basis of the issue here is whether a relational approach to leadership has room for the individual. In this dialogue, Day reacts to his sense from reading the chapters that "postmodernists" disparage postpositivism and its methods, and oversimplify entity and constructionist distinctions—which he sees as not mutually exclusive, but rather, on a continuum. (We provide such a continuum in the introductory chapter.) He questions whether reality is only constructed such that it means there is no room for the individual. His greatest discomfort is his take-away from the authors that: (a) there is no individual cognition and (b) there is no role for the individual (leader), only the collective.

Drath replies by laying out the difference between modernist and postmodernist assumptions, and emphasizing the "relational" (social) in leadership. He tries to clarify the assumptions brought by the relational perspective and indicate why it is needed and what it adds to the conversation:

> The point is not to make entity thinking the "bad old way," but to recognize its limitations. For example, taking an entity approach to understanding leadership has not been particularly helpful in trying to understand how to make shared leadership or leadership across significant differences more effective. I think a relational perspective can help with these needs for leadership by pointing to the generative capacity of the spaces in between where people share or where they meet difference. Those spaces aren't just barriers; they can be productive of new ideas that integrate old ideas. *But only if the people doing shared leadership or leadership across boundaries see leadership in new ways that go beyond concepts of leadership effectiveness based on leader behavior* [emphasis added]. (Drath, Chapter 8)

In this way, Drath agrees with Fairhurst that there is a problem in trying to learn about relational (social) processes by looking only at individual behavior. What is not made clear in this dialogue is that Drath is not dismissing the individual—he recognizes that individuals are a part of leadership

(Drath, 2001); he just *doesn't give precedent* to them. He approaches relational leadership *from a different starting point*: that of a collective achievement. He argues this achievement cannot be adequately seen through [only] an individual lens.

What we see here is a common problem in multi-paradigmatic discussions of relational leadership: the problem of trying to achieve "multilingual" understanding. In the process of conveying meaning, contrasts are created to try to distinguish the perspectives so that each "side" understands the other. (We had to do this ourselves in the introductory chapters of this book.) In the process, labeling, categorization, and quite often, *false dichotomies* are created. In relational leadership, this happens around the individual, and the effect is devastating to dialogue: It leads to a breakdown in communication that results in paradigmatic conversations reflecting isolationism/ protectionism rather than paradigm interplay. To get out of this hole, *we need to refocus this conversation to paradigm interplay.*

From the perspective of paradigm interplay, what can we conclude regarding the issue of the handling of the individual from the chapters represented in this book? The answer is this: Relational leadership acknowledges that leadership processes involve *both* individual and collective elements. *All the authors* in the book, even those termed by Shamir as "radical constructionists" (e.g., Barge, Alvesson and Sveningsson, Ospina et al., Hosking), acknowledge individuals as part of the leadership process. They also recognize leadership as co-constructed in relational (collective) processes. The difference among the authors is *the extent to which they "privilege" the individual or the collective*—that is, the difference is in their starting points (as described in Chapter 1). Some authors approach relational leadership from the standpoint of the individual engaging in collective leadership processes. Other authors try to bring about and balance considerations of both the individual and collective processes. Still others approach relational leadership from the standpoint of collective processes, and may or may not describe the individual in these processes (e.g., Barge does while Ospina et al. chose not to).

What we can also conclude from this interplay is that relational leadership must include *some element* of collective (e.g., dyadic, group, social) to be considered relational—it is *not* an individual-only level phenomenon. At the core of relational leadership are assumptions of co-construction, relational processes, and social contexts—this is what distinguishes it from leader-centric views. A focus on only individual, without adequate investigation of relational/social process or context, would be part of the *leader-centric* or *follower-centric*, rather than the *relational*, leadership paradigm.

This issue plays out again in the dialogue between Hosking and Shamir (Part III of this volume), which is largely influenced by Shamir's reaction to the language used by those he refers to as the "radical constructionists."

Shamir identifies some of the same issues that bothered Day. For example, he, too, sees the constructionist characterization of conventional (entity) discourse on leadership as problematic. He also questions the usefulness of the constructionist approach, arguing that constructionists don't offer a viable alternative for defining *leadership* and distinguishing it from other social processes, and that their emphasis on the uniqueness of every situation runs counter to our ability to create broad (generalizable) understandings.

In this dialogue, Shamir reacts to Alvesson and Sveningsson's critical analysis that leadership research has been too "LERO"-based: leader-centric, entitistic, romantic, objectivist. Taking this to its "logical" conclusion, Alvesson and Sveningsson propose instead that leadership research go to the opposite extreme. Leadership should be *redefined*, with leadership being seen as:

> [A] local variation of the organizational and cultural frameworks and templates for structuring and producing meaning around authority and, to some extent, systematic relations between actors or groups involved in and/or producing a-symmetrical relations. These constructions are, to various degrees, broadly shared, diverse, fragmented, and conflictual, making any agreement (co-construction) of the leader(ship) relation potentially fragile and contested. The actors and groups are typically trying to produce some degree of consensus and compromise around authority and influencing around work—means, relations, and objectives—while driven by sectional interests around rewards (broadly defined) and increasing autonomy (implying a degree of control over others, minimally reducing their impact), thereby acting in politically conscious ways. These actor interests contribute to diversity of constructions. Effective political action involves the use of power, best accomplished through making sectional interests appear as the shared interest of the group and organization (Alvesson & Deetz, 2000). Both people emerging as leaders (active/dominant subjects) and as non-leaders (or less salient in leadership) positions may be involved here, busy constructing relations around leadership in, for them, not too unfavorable ways. These would always be framed and constrained by ideologies, discourses, and institutions putting flexible structuring imprints on local interactions. Efforts in a more or less contested setting to make one's own construction influential and stick in formation and revisions of the self-, other-, and relation-construction work would be a key element in leadership, then seen as an expression of, as well as driver of, power relations.

To some extent, Alvesson and Sveningsson are inviting leadership researchers to think about the potential role that ideology plays in their research. For example, by using researcher-imposed definitions to study leadership, they suggest that researchers fall into a dangerous trap of the results merely reflecting back ideas of the researcher, that in turn, reflect ideas that are part of dominant discourses in society. Reacting against modernist

perspectives of science that impose "neutral" and decontextualized definitions, Alvesson and Sveningsson propose that researchers see how broader
social forces of a stratified system affect people's narratives and behaviors of
leadership. Their broadened perspective of leadership is offered as a way to
break the cycle in which dominant ideology maintains existing power relations and pursues particular interests in the name of universal truths. This
view of redefinition aligns with other constructionist authors, like Fairhurst,
Hosking, Drath, Barge, and Ospina et al., who want the definition of *leadership* to *inductively* come from the data—from the experience and narratives
of the research participants—rather than from the researcher. They may or
may not take the emergent definition at face value, but they use this information as data to better understand relational processes and dynamics associated with leadership. This contrasts with *deductive* approaches, where the
researcher is encouraged to start with a definition, often taking for granted
its universality, rather than seeing it as context specific.

Shamir would likely not disagree with the inductive approach, but he
argues that we need to have at least some shared understanding as a research community around the meaning of *leadership,* or the term is not useful (i.e., we should not broaden it so much that it loses any sense of meaning). For example, Shamir reacts to Alvesson and Sveningsson's proposed
redefinition by saying that such views as presented in radical constructionist
perspectives are inconsistent with the term *leadership*—even in its broadest
definition—and the consequence of adopting such views is the dilution of
the term *leadership* beyond any usefulness. This is somewhat recognized by
Alvesson and Sveningsson, as their use of the term *"post-leadership"* reflects
their ambiguity as to whether this is leadership or not. Shamir picks up on
this, and argues that the perspective presented by Alvesson and Sveningsson (and other radical constructionists) goes too far:

> The conclusion is that those constructionists who call for a revolution that
> amounts to complete total rejection of the conventional leadership discourse,
> and substituting it with an open-ended view according to which leadership
> is freshly constructed in each situation or is not associated with any shared
> meanings at all, have very little to offer to those of us who believe that leader-
> ship is a distinct social phenomenon which shows some regularities across
> situations and relationships. . . . I therefore suggest that for the purposes of
> theorizing about leadership and studying leadership in the framework of
> a collective effort to advance knowledge, we need at least a basic common
> discourse. In the very least, this discourse should include a shared under-
> standing of what constitutes leadership and how leadership is different from
> other social processes. If the term *leadership* is to retain some meaning and
> have some usefulness, not every consequential social process should be called
> leadership. As argued above, a perspective that seeks to remove the currently
> shared construct of leadership and cannot offer an alternative construct—be-

cause such an offer is inconsistent with its basic premises—is a dead-end street from the viewpoint of advancing leadership theory.

Shamir offers his own perspective. He argues that in order to recognize, focus, theorize, study, and exchange ideas about relational leadership, we need to retain a central element of the conventional discourse—and that element is the differentiation among individuals, groups, organizations, or social entities. This differentiation points to the disproportionate or asymmetrical influence in a social arena. What this means is that, for a phenomenon to be labeled and studied as leadership, some individuals have to be observed as exerting more influence on the group than others, or at least to be recognized or perceived by others as exerting such disproportionate influence. This differentiation in the degree of influence is usually associated with roles and role identities (i.e., leaders and followers).

Perhaps ironically, when we look at this, it is the same thing Alvesson and Sveningsson (Chapter 7) are saying, but with different language and coming from a very different perspective: "systematic relations between actors or groups involved in and/or producing a-symmetrical relations" (see quote above). The difference in the approaches is in *how far they are willing to go* in describing the context and elements involved in generating these relations. Alvesson and Sveningsson are willing to put broad processes and locally defined meanings around these constructions. Shamir is uncomfortable with this redefinition for two reasons.

First, he is concerned that the essence of leadership will get lost: "We cannot view every social process, not even every process that results in shared meanings and coordinated collective action, as leadership." Second, he does not see a clear link between leadership and collective outcomes. He identifies the search for this link as a key agenda of leadership research, acknowledging that leadership may also produce outcomes with negative consequences. Shamir's focus on outcomes is associated with his view of the co-production of leadership (Shamir, 2007). This term differs from co-construction, in that *co-construction* refers to the ways in which individuals co-construct leadership, that is, leadership is the outcome; whereas *co-production* refers to how leaders and followers work to co-produce outcomes, that is, the focus of interest is the outcomes produced by leadership.

We now bring the conversation full circle by showing how the ontological and epistemological assumptions authors bring to their work play out very differently, not only in their views of research, but also in their views of leadership development. We do this with our third paradigm interplay, which is a focus on how leadership scholars approach their work from the standpoint of influencing leadership practice.

Interplay #3: Leadership Can and Should be Developed

The discussion above naturally flows into our third paradigm interplay: Leadership can and should be developed. Given that leadership is a pervasive social phenomenon associated with important outcomes, and that it involves individual (leader) and collective (leadership) roles and practices, it is important to explore how the individual and collective dimensions of leadership can be developed. Therefore, this interplay examines leadership development from a relational leadership lens. We can summarize this interplay as:

- Relational leadership views leadership development in the context of a collective, social process.
- In so doing, it extends the focus on leader development (building a person's capacity to be effective in leadership roles and processes) to include a focus on leadership development (building a collective's capacity to produce leadership).

Comparison of Views

This interplay revolves around the difference between leader development and leadership development. McCauley, Van Velsor, and Ruderman (2010) define *leader development* as the expansion of a *person's* capacity to be effective in leadership roles and processes, and *leadership development* as the expansion of a *collective's* capacity to produce direction, alignment, and commitment (McCauley et al., 2010). The former focuses on developing the individual, while the latter is focused on developing a collective.

These distinctions are associated with differing ontological and epistemological assumptions. In Kennedy et al. (Chapter 6), we see how differences in ontological and epistemological assumptions play out in their varying approaches to leadership development. At the core of the tensions in Kennedy et al. is the difference between "realist" and "constructionist" ontologies. They use the terms "constructivism" and "constructionism" (for more about this, see Chapter 1) to represent these distinctions:

> Constructivism is concerned with the sense-making activity of individuals. The location of sense-making then is *within individual minds* and is concerned with an individual's perceptions and cognition. Social constructionism locates meaning-making in the spaces between people. Ideas, concepts, and memories are seen as arising out of social interchange and mediated through language. "All knowledge . . . evolves in the space between people, in the realm of the common world or the common dance" (Hoffman, 1992, p. 6). Thus, both constructivism and social constructionism take issue with the "modernist idea that a real world exists and can be known with objective certainty" (p. 6). However, the differences in where meaning-making is located are consequen-

tial. Accordingly, constructivism has been associated with an "entity" perspective, and social constructionism with a relational perspective (Uhl-Bien, 2006). The former perspective is associated with a realist ontology, viewing "individuals as separate, independent bounded entities" (p. 665). This paper is in part a reminder that a realist ontology is not inherent to constructivism, and we draw attention to the difficulties of holding that distinction in the field of leadership development.

In Kennedy et al. (Chapter 6), "Rachel" represents the constructivist view. According to this view, "relating is . . . an individual act (Uhl-Bien, 2006, p. 665). Therefore, from this perspective leadership development involves the development of individual *selves.*" Consistent with this perspective, self-examination and self-development serve as the foundation for developing leadership. This work is located as internal to individuals: "As Rachel puts it, participants in leadership development are 'exploring what they had in their heads.'" The focus is on tools, methods, models, and technologies, drawing from the belief that knowledge can be identified and codified, and that truth and reality are "unproblematic" and attainable. This approach assumes there is a separation between self and environment, "supporting the possibility that individuals can step *outside* their environment in order to firstly know it and then act upon it" (Chapter 6). The trainer is "outside" this dynamic ("holding her own unique history separate from those of her participants").

On the other side is the constructionist view that the self is always in relationship to others, and therefore leadership development is concerned with "*inviting different selves and realities out of hidden places*" through a wide array of discursive resources. Here, we see clearly the idea of multivocality in action (see Chapter 1). From this, perspective reality is constructed between people in the moment, and the premise of development is to make these processes visible. Because the assumption is that the learning can only happen in relation, in the process of co-creating meaning, the focus here is an emergent view of leadership development. Facilitators work without templates that bring a sense of order and predictability to their development work; instead they use of metaphor, imagery, and symbols to engage with others in the face of unpredictability and to produce generative spaces where collective learning will take place. This approach assumes that self and environment cannot be separated. Therefore, the facilitator adopts a position of interdependence with the rest of the facilitation team and the participants. "Meg is 'in there' just like everybody else, discovering and complicating things, making mistakes as she goes along" (Kennedy et al., Chapter 6).

Similar tensions between entity and constructionist perspectives play out in the dialogue between Day and Drath (Chapter 8). As defined by Day, leader development focuses on developing individual human capital skills, for example, enhancing one's *intrapersonal* competence base through self-awareness, self-regulation, and self-motivation. Leadership development focuses on developing interpersonal relations in the form of *social capital skills*, for example, building and accessing social resources embedded in work relationships. According to Day, "leader development must always precede leadership development...Intrapersonal competence is needed as a foundation on which interpersonal competence and social capital can develop."

In dialogue with Drath, Day says, "I think we are pretty much on the same page about leader development and leadership development." Drath offers a very different view of leadership development, however. In contrast to Day's focus, which remains ultimately on leadership development as an *individual skill* (i.e., an individual's "social capital skills," "interpersonal competence"), Drath and his colleagues McCauley et al. (2010) focus on leadership development as a *collective capacity* (i.e., the development of the collective capacity to produce leadership outcomes of direction, alignment, and commitment). Drath communicates this to Day using, as he says, "strong relational theory." Day interprets this, however, as having no individual, which Drath responds to with:

> OK, so the strong [relational] theory is a bit much to swallow. However, I do believe the strong version of relational theory is important as a counterweight to the individualism juggernaut that Western culture has created. It is important to offer an alternative to the idea that "at bottom" human beings are essentially separate, independent, and capable of private self-generation. Considering the extent to which we humans are social creatures, depending for our very survival on our ability to create sustaining cultures, this [overly] individualist view seems a bit romantic, even nostalgic. The strong theory is just another way to point out that there isn't anything "essential" about human beings since we are products of ongoing and ever-changing relations; we are embedded social creatures who transform as societies and cultures transform.

According to Drath (Chapter 8), in our approaches to leader and leadership development, we must bring in *all* of the "entities" associated with the co-production of leadership (e.g., individual leaders, follower development, peer development, colleague development, professional development, and organization development). Drath does not dismiss the individual skilled component—he "relationalizes" it. In response to Day's query about the positioning of leader and leadership development, Drath says: While leader development usually matters, leadership development *always* matters. He explains: "The 'individual skilled component' is itself already relational, so it can't be something essentially non-relational waiting at the bottom to make relations more effective." Drath's perspective is that the collective (i.e., leadership development) *necessarily* brings in the individual (e.g., collective action is based on combinations of individual actions), but the reverse is not true: The individual (i.e., leader development) does not necessarily bring in the collective. Drath makes this point to emphasize that *it is in this collective component* where relational leadership adds value to leadership research.

Like Drath, Fletcher (Chapter 3) recognizes the value relational leadership brings in, adding the collective component to leadership development while retaining the leader development focus on individual competencies. Consistent with Kennedy et al., Fletcher also sees the tensions created when entity and constructionist perspectives are used conjointly in development work:

> One of the critiques of critical management studies and other perspectives that focus on the social construction of reality is that they so often leave practitioners feeling powerless, with few options to engage personal agency. Indeed, I have found that discussions of the constructionist dimensions of my work have sometimes had the effect of making practitioners feel powerless, as if these social processes are beyond the reach of individuals to influence. Practitioners who are faced, on the one hand with entity perspectives of relational leadership that tout it as a new model more appropriate to today's global context, and on the other with constructionist perspectives that detail the social processes by which leadership is constructed, need help in reconciling these two perspectives at the level of individual action. (Fletcher, Chapter 3)

According to Fletcher, one of the key challenges of constructionist perspectives is helping individuals understand and strategize ways to interrupt and influence social constructions of leadership that result in their relational practices getting constructed as "not leadership," rather than leadership. She resolves this by focusing on how she can help individuals understand and reflect on ways in which they can resist social processes—and their own approaches to discourse—that "perhaps unwittingly" reinforce the very dynamic they seek to interrupt. Using a gender lens, she lays out key differences between relational practice and relational *mal*practice that can help distinguish internalized stereotypical (gender-linked) notions of caring behavior (i.e., *mal*practice) from effective "relational practice" (i.e., creating high quality, growth-in-connection relational interactions in the service of the work).

As described previously, Barge (Chapter 4) approaches leadership from a "first-person" systemic constructionist lens. Barge's approach to leader development can be summarized as:

> If we think of conversations as unfolding, then leaders need to be able to position themselves in three ways: (a) they need to be able to develop anticipations of what might happen that help guide their subsequent actions;

(b) they need to be present in the situation connecting to what is unfolding in the here and now; and (c) they need to develop the ability to look back on the conversation and reflect on what has transpired and what they have learned from the process.

Barge's communication lens identifies a new set of challenges for constructionist views of leader development: The need to shift the focus from discussing how leadership is constructed to identifying practices that help leaders anticipate how they might act and be present within an unfolding situation. Using a framework of sense-making, positioning, and play, Barge articulates a broad array of discursive practices that facilitate ways of working with meaning-making and developing contexts. According to Barge (Chapter 4), "If we can develop ways of working that assist leaders in developing their linguistic capacity to anticipate, to be present, and to reflect on their conversational experience, then we will have begun to fulfill the promise of relational leadership."

Discussion

In this interplay we see paradigmatic differences fully played out. For example, in Kennedy et al.'s struggle with issues of objectivism and instrumentalism in the design and delivery of leadership development programs, we are immersed once again in the tensions from Interplay #2 arising from alternative meanings attached to *relationality*. These tensions, according to Kennedy et al., are central in relational leadership:

> We propose that such objectivism and instrumentalism challenge the relationality so core to relational leadership theory to the extent that entity/constructivism and social construction struggle to even be in dialogue together. (Kennedy et al., Chapter 6)

In Day and Drath's dialogue (Chapter 8), we are witness to this struggle. Here, we see the not-at-all-trivial challenge of trying to advance an understanding beyond the individual. Although Drath's definition is fully relational (i.e., strong relational theory), Day's remains entity. What we see is the "creeping back in" of entity thinking (as described in Kennedy et al., (Chapter 6) in Day's definition of *leadership development* that makes it difficult for him and Drath to connect.

The tension here isn't that Day wants to focus on the individual; it is that his *leadership development* definition is not the same as Drath's. Day's is about how the individual operates in the context of the collective; Drath's is fully about the collective. So what we can see from the interplay is that we actually have *three* definitions: (1) leader development focused on a *person's* capacity to be effective in leadership roles and processes. (Day; Drath; and McCauley et al. 2010 are consistent in this definition.) (2) leadership development focused on developing interpersonal relations in the form of *social capital skills* and *interpersonal competence* (Day's version, Chapter 8), and (3) "relational leadership" development focused on the expansion of a *collective's* capacity to produce direction, alignment, and commitment (Drath, Chapter 8, and McCauley et al.'s 2010 version).

The insights revealed from this interplay are therefore quite interesting: What it shows is the multi-faceted nature of relational leadership. In relational leadership, constructionism plays out in a variety of ways. For example, in Fletcher (Chapter 3) and Barge (Chapter 4), we see that constructionism does not mean a disregard for the individual. In these chapters, constructionist lenses are used to focus on developing the individual, consistent with the constructionist idea that intrapersonal competence can be gained through developing one's interpersonal competence (e.g., Hosking's notion of "skillful organizing" (Chapters 16 and 18). In Fletcher, we see constructionism applied through a focus on how individuals can interrupt and influence social constructions of leadership, with the objective of engaging in strong relational practice. In Barge, we see a similar focus, but this time from the perspective of how individuals can be trained in discursive practices that can help them more effectively produce leadership constructions. These perspectives are consistent with Smircich and Morgan's (1982) early constructionist view that leadership has to do with the management of meaning; by extension, leadership development is about equipping leaders with this capability.

Hence, constructionism does not reflect "abandonment" of the individual—clearly we see in Fletcher and Barge (and other constructionist scholars) a focus on the individual. The difference is in the *contextualization* of leadership development. From a constructionist view, relational leadership development is about training leaders in context, meaning, in Drath's case, in the context of the collective processes through which leadership work is performed. It does not mean training skills as if they were isolated from a context. From this perspective, leadership development is about working with a collective and engaging developmental interventions around the actual work that is done in the organization.

The insights from this interplay are revealing in the larger context of relational leadership: *A consideration of collective and contextual issues in leadership is where relational leadership can offer some of the greatest advances.* Reiterating a point made in the discussion of Interplay #2, relational leadership does not dismiss the individual; it adds a consideration of the collective and the context. In other words, Drath does not disregard leader development; he adds leadership development: Relational leadership can include *both* leader and leadership development. However, unless we begin to also use Drath and McCauley et al.'s definition of *leadership development* as a *collective's* capacity to produce leadership, the full promise of relational leadership will not be achieved.

This all has strong implications for leader and leadership development. Specifically, we can summarize our learnings from this interplay as:

1. We can examine relational leadership in the context of *leader* development, but this would be Day's version of *leadership* development. In other words, Day's *leadership development* definition as interpersonal competence and social capital skills would be *relational leader development*. There is real benefit to be gained from applying a relational lens to leader development, as seen in Day (Chapter 8), Barge (Chapter 4) and Fletcher (Chapter 3), and it is an area that needs more work. Therefore, future research and practice in leader development should more fully flesh out what can be gained from a focus on relational leader development.
2. We need much more attention to *relational leadership development*, which is Drath's (Chapter 8) and McCauley et al.'s (2010) definition of *leadership development* as enhancing a collective's capacity to produce leadership. Ospina, et al's (Chapter 9) findings offer a glimpse of the promise of a focus on leadership development as collective capacity: The leadership practices they uncover in social change organizations represent ways in which collective capacity is built in these organizations. But, we have barely scratched the surface in this area, and there are huge opportunities for advancing understanding and practice of leadership from this perspective. As Drath says:

   > Current providers of leader development better gear up their developmental curricula to include development of leadership, which means developing the beliefs and practices by which the whole of a collective produces leadership, even when those beliefs and practices do not include individuals known as leaders. (Drath, Chapter 8)

3. Relational leadership opens us up to perspectives from multiple fields that can enrich our thinking about leadership and its development. In this interplay, we see how the feminist perspective brought by Fletcher (Chapter 3) and the communication perspective brought by Barge (Chapter 4) can help us think about leadership development in different, and exciting, new ways. Therefore, the study and practice of leader and leadership development from a relational perspective should draw from a variety of fields and disciplines.

The issues, tensions and emotions revealed in this interplay illustrate the deep challenges of trying to be "in" paradigm interplay. These include the challenge to: (a) achieve multilinguality on the issues—to figure out how to explain them to the "other side" without making them overly "pizzled" (see Day, Chapter 8); (b) still respect the other side when our views are so vastly different; (c) not get frustrated in the process and quit (see Chapter 6); and (d) move beyond a focus on "technical challenges" to engage in the hard work of "adaptive challenges" (Heifetz, 1994), which is where the most significant advancements, and the greatest insights, can be achieved. Kennedy et al. (Chapter 6) describe these challenges—and the rich rewards—associated with paradigm interplay:

> This chapter is the result of numerous research, design, and planning conversations which sought to build shared thinking with respect to leadership development and how to "know" and explore the leadership terrain. Many of those conversations have not been entirely comfortable. They have often been contentious and contested, and have always (ultimately) led to surprises in insight, connection, and action...

> Through these stories, we suggest that a "broad church" that is home to both constructivist *and* social constructionist assumptions presents problems for the design and facilitation of leadership programs. While an overarching framework of Relational Leadership Theory (Uhl-Bien, 2006, p. 1) is a useful construct, we suggest that in practice, working with fundamentally different orientations to relationships is a very tall order. At the very least, it requires a community of practice where differences and their implications can be articulated and where members have the rhetorical skills (Bouwen & Hosking, 2000) and commitments to address these differences.

> The sense of an overarching framework that is shared has given our team the courage to keep pushing questions about where we are different and what it means for our relationships, our leadership development practice, and our research. Indeed, we have been reassured by the proposition of a common framework when our differences have felt particularly threatening. Beyond this, we need as a discipline to address the creeping objectivism that can beset both the construction and ongoing development of theories, such as this, that seek to bring perspectives into what is both a greatly needed, but undeniably uncomfortable, dialogue.

RELATIONAL LEADERSHIP: THE ROAD AHEAD

What we can see from this paradigm interplay is that, despite the multitude of perspectives represented in the book, there are strong areas of potential agreement. This agreement occurs around the relational nature of leadership. At a minimum, as Seers and Chopin (Chapter 2) say, "all approaches to relational leadership recognize that relationships matter greatly." Shamir reiterates this:

Collectively [the authors]...suggest a shift from focusing on leaders' attributes and behaviors and on what leaders do to followers, to focusing on leadership in terms of relationships, which are co-produced by all the parties involved, regardless of their formal positions or titles. Most of them also view social construction and joint meaning-making activities as lying at the heart of leadership processes, and emphasize that these processes have to be understood as embedded in their cultural, historical, and organizational context. (Shamir, Chapter 17)

Yet, we see clear differences as well. These represent differences in philosophical perspectives, ontological and epistemological assumptions, and disciplinary approaches. Broadly speaking, the greatest differences are around (a) meaning of relationality (e.g., objective or intersubjective reality; relational or individual theory of self), (b) handling of process (e.g., variance or process models; linear or reciprocal causality), (c) handling of context (situational or contextual), (d) theoretical and analytical level (individual or collective), and (e) underlying disciplinary approach (psychology, communication, sociology, public policy, or critical management studies).

By engaging in paradigm interplay, we have uncovered rich new insights regarding relational approaches to leadership that help advance understanding across the paradigmatic differences. We now summarize what we have learned.

What is Relational Leadership?

Relational leadership is a view that sees leadership as emerging from social processes and relationships among people. A key assumption of relational leadership is that leadership is co-constructed in social/historical context: Leadership is co-created in relational interactions between people—in social processes that "generally enable groups of people to work together in meaningful ways" (Day, 2000, p. 582; see also Drath, 2001; Hosking & Morley, 1988; Ospina & Foldy, 2010; Uhl-Bien, 2006).

Therefore, a primary concern of relational leadership is advancing understanding of the relational processes and contexts through which leadership is constructed and produces outcomes. Focusing exclusively on the relationship, or incorporating attention to relational constructs like meaning-making or language, however, do not alone produce a relational understanding of leadership. Relational leadership calls instead for scholars to push the envelope: *to deconstruct and make more evident the underlying assumptions of their own paradigm to see whether it reflects relationality, and to build models and constructs with the insights of such deconstruction* (see Chapter 1).

Relational leadership considers leadership to be a collective capacity (e.g., dyads, groups, teams, networks, social movements), and recognizes that leadership occurs not only in formal, managerial contexts (e.g., manager, subordinate) but also in contexts that do not involve formal authority (e.g., informal and collective leadership processes). It includes elements associated with both individuals (e.g., those who engage in leadership) and collective processes (e.g., social constructions, patterned interactions and behaviors, and discourses of leadership). That said, scholars who study relational leadership often vary in the extent to which they "privilege" the individual or the collective in their study of leadership.

Relational leadership sees leadership as dynamic—developing and changing over time. In so doing, it brings a new lens to many issues that have been overlooked in leadership research to date. In going beyond concepts of leadership effectiveness based on behavior, or relationship quality, to leadership as a collective capacity, it allows us to view issues of shared and collective leadership in new ways. It also allows us to explore more thoroughly the emergent nature of leadership and to see its interconnections and embeddedness in social contexts. It fosters paying equal attention to the potential role of the various actors involved, and not just the visible leader or followers.

Relational leadership also brings a new focus on processes and constructions of leadership. One of the benefits of this is that it allows us to study *actual leadership processes, rather than equating leadership with holding a formal (e.g., managerial) position.* The tradition in organization studies of defining leaders as managerial position-holders is what Bedeian calls the lack of "truth-in-advertising" in leadership research (Bedeian & Hunt, 2006). According to Bedeian:

> Indeed, if truth-in-advertising laws were applied to the leadership literature, it is my belief that the field would be found guilty on multiple counts of false promotion. To wit, in some studies, leaders are defined by formal position and, by extension, followers are taken to be individuals who directly report to them.... Leading is thus treated as synonymous with holding a supervisory or managerial position. In other studies, leadership is a word used to mean the possession of certain personal qualities... draw[ing] upon the notion that leadership springs from a dispositional source. Finally, in some studies, leadership is a word used to describe a category of behavior in which an individual acts in a certain manner, thereby influencing others to follow.... [T]his tendency gives me pause, especially in instances where leadership is defined by formal position. (Bedeian & Hunt, p. 191)

By studying the co-construction of leadership *and* non-leadership (e.g., see Fletcher, Barge, Hosking), relational leadership may offer a way through this problem. Rather than assuming that managers are leaders and subordinates are followers, we can examine relational interactions, look for patterned behaviors, find particular types of practices, and identify role enactments that signify actual leading and following. Moreover, techniques like discourse analysis help us understand how subordinates' interactions with managers construct non-leadership as well as leadership (Fairhurst, 2007).

With its privileging of relationality and co-construction, relational leadership brings new light to the role of followers in leadership processes (see Seers & Chopin, Chapter 2; Shamir, Chapter 17). A relational leadership lens differs from follower-centric views in that it sees followership as a relational concept, addressing how followers interact with leaders to produce leadership and its outcomes. This changes the focus from followers as those who are subordinates of managers, to followers as those whose behaviors help construct leadership, independent of a hierarchical relationship. We could say that *it is in following that leadership is constructed* (i.e., when following occurs, leaders are made).

Moreover, a relational approach can help us move beyond thinking of co-construction in terms of cognitive attribution. From this perspective, it is not just about followers accepting the leader as leader, but about the outcomes of interactions among social actors doing meaning-making and organizing work together. Leadership is thus about the ways actors engage, interact, and negotiate with each other in to influence organizational understandings and produce outcomes.

Finally, relational leadership offers new ways to view leadership development. *Relational leader development* considers how interpersonal competence and social capital skills (e.g., see Day, Chapter 8; Barge, Chapter 4; Fletcher, Chapter 3) contribute to effective relational leadership processes and constructions. *Relational leadership development* helps us identify the beliefs and practices and other conditions by which the whole of a collective produces leadership at the level of the system, even when those beliefs and practices do not include individuals known as leaders (e.g., see Drath, Chapter 8).

The Road Ahead

The findings from our paradigm interplay also offer some important and interesting insights for the field of relational leadership as it moves forward. We present these as take-aways. While these are the key take-aways in the context of the interplays we developed here, there are many more to be found in the book. We offer the set below only as a broad roadmap to get us started. Our hope is that more take-aways will be advanced as researchers begin to build on the intriguing ideas and rich insights provided by the scholars in this book.

Take-Away #1: Relational Leadership Calls for Interdisciplinary Study

Perhaps one of the greatest contributions relational leadership offers is its ability to engage scholars from across disciplines and perspectives in the study of leadership. To be able to benefit from these varied perspectives, however, we must view relational leadership through an interdisciplinary lens. We propose that *relational leadership* serve as an "umbrella" term for research that studies leadership as generated in social processes and relationships among people. We are not suggesting the disciplines work together in collaborations (although that might be good), or that there must be only *one* way to do research; in fact, it is in the rich diversity of approaches and perspectives where we have the most to gain. It does mean that we need to recognize and pay attention to one another—to listen for advances being made in other fields that can enrich our own thinking and produce broader understandings. This can only occur if we open ourselves to learning about what is happening in fields beyond our own. *We suggest the* relational leadership *umbrella term can help us locate one another as we engage in these searches.*

The objective of relational leadership research should be to learn more about and enhance relational leadership such that we can generate broader understandings of leadership. Relational leadership can serve as the "thinking space" called for by Hosking (Bouwen & Hosking, 2000; Hosking, 2007) to allow for exploring different social science discourses. As Hosking (Chapter 18) says:

> While this [space for multiple discourses] has happened in the literatures of Organization Studies, it has been slower to occur in the leadership literatures (see also Bryman, 1996; Dachler and Hosking, 1995; Morley and Hosking, 2003; Uhl-Bien, 2006). In my view, this "space" would not be made in debating the relative merits of "entitative" and "relational" discourses. Rather, it would come about through being "mindful" and explicit about the "philosophy" we put to work in our research (Bentz and Shapiro, 1998) and put to work in our e-valuations of the work of others. Being mindful in this way would require recognizing that there is no one "God's eye view from nowhere," but rather many possible social science discourses, assumptions, and interests (e.g., Hosking, 2011). Space for such multiplicity would also be facilitated by a form and style of writing that views different "bundles of assumptions" as potentially useful and that explores the particular possibilities that they open up. Space for multiplicity is created by relating in ways that allow "different but equal," rather than imposing one ordering of value and so constructing difference as unequal (and usually, less good). I am reminded of Alvesson and Deetz's discussion of "alternative social science research perspectives," where they caution against using conceptualizations (such as entitative) as "devices for division and classification," and instead recommended seeing them as "interesting ways to call attention to similarities and differences that matter." (Alvesson and Deetz, 2000, p. 25)

This will require not so much using the same constructs and language, as recognizing what others mean and the assumptions they hold when they use certain constructs and language within the context of their discipline. Like when learning a language, we need not give up our own meanings and signifiers, but we must be aware and distinguish how, when, and why we use one language or the other. This requires educating ourselves to be able to appreciate and understand the differences.

Take-Away #2: Relational Leadership Research Requires Paradigm Interplay

To achieve a "thinking space," we need to be able to engage in paradigm interplay. Paradigm interplay requires scholars to engage in respectful "multilingual" conversation. Without multilingualism, we cannot engage in dialogue, as individuals struggle in misunderstandings. In paradigm interplay, we don't have to agree, but we do have to understand one another. We recognize, however, the caution of Deetz regarding multilinguality (Deetz, 1996):

> I, like many others, sometimes wish we were all multilingual, that we could move across orientations with grace and ease, but this type of Teflon-coated multiperspectival cosmopolitan envisioned by Morgan (1986) or Hassard (1991) is often both illusionary and weak (see Parker and McHugh 1991). Good scholars have deep commitments. Multiperspectivialism often leads to shallow readings and uses of alternative orientations since unexamined basic assumptions have unexpected hidden qualities. Some scholars are more multilingual than others, but doing good work within an orientation still must be prized first. A tenuous balance between tentativeness and commitment is probably a sign of maturity of any scholar. Struggling with understandings and having arguments across programs of work are important, but the outcome is well conceived in neither synthetic (integrative) nor additive (pluralistic, supplementary) terms. Complementarity of forms of research questions and procedures is probably better (see Apel 1979, Albert et al. 1988). Not everyone needs to do each, but each has to be fostered both by giving space and taking their concerns and arguments seriously, seriously enough and with enough understanding to debate and make demands on all groups for justification and clarity of purpose. (p. 204)

This quote also reminds us of Deetz's allusion—quoted in our Introduction —to tensions and competitions among more and less dominant paradigms in a field. A multi-paradigmatic conversation will require creating the conditions for equal footing of postpositivist and constructionist perspectives on leadership. This means an acceptance of the legitimacy of different approaches to social science. For example, incorporation of the interpretive tradition of research into the U.S. training curriculum of leadership scholars would help level the playing field. Likewise, the judgment of the work's quality—independent of the paradigm—ought to include as a key criterion its internal consistency (between ontological and analytical level) as discussed in Chapter 1, Fairhurst (Chapter 15), Ospina et al. (Chapter 9), and in our earlier Interplay #2.

Take-Away #3: At the Core of Relational Leadership Research Is a Focus on Relationality

Relationality is the key distinguishing feature provided by relational leadership. It is in relationality that we move beyond leader-centric and follower-centric approaches to view leadership as a phenomenon generated in the space between people (Bradbury & Lichtenstein, 2000). Relationality draws us to consider issues of process, context, and relational interacts in ways that have been overlooked in the cognitive and behavioral approaches that have predominated leadership theory.

Because the meanings for the term *relational* are multifarious, analysts must be careful to specify their use of the term. Once the term is specified, the mode of scientific inquiry must be aligned accordingly (Ospina & Uhl-Bien, Chapter 1; Fairhurst & Antonakis, Chapter 15; Ospina et al. Chapter 9). Moreover, considering the present tendency described in the book's introductory chapters of postpositivist scholars to downplay philosophical considerations of their work and of constructionist scholars to downplay methodological considerations, a commitment to relationality as a common anchor for interplay may require an effort from both groups to be more explicit and transparent in their handling of relationality.

The difficulty of studying relationality is not to be underestimated. This is perhaps the greatest challenge of relational leadership. For many of us, it means we must push ourselves to engage in different ways of doing research: "Analysts are likely going to have to leave their comfort zones in order to do this type of theorizing and research" (Fairhurst & Antonakis, Chapter 15). For example, it is important to incorporate methods beyond linear regressions, and to consider issues of data collection, process, time, and analytical level. Moreover, we must not dismiss as less legitimate approaches from paradigms other than our own. While it would be unrealistic to expect scholars to master both types, they should be sufficiently familiar with the differences to ensure making choices or judgments from knowledgeable, rather than uninformed, positions.

Take-Away #4: A Focus on Relationality Means We Must Do a Better Job of Incorporating Social Context into Leadership Research

The focus on relational leadership brings to the fore an issue that has been long talked about, but greatly under-considered, in leadership research: context. The relational approaches in this volume all consider context as a key element of leadership. Reflecting the different perspectives, however, in some cases context is viewed as background, and in others as foreground, to leadership (Ospina & Hittleman, 2011).

When context is viewed as background, leadership is isolated, and contextual variables or qualitative narratives of context are added to complement understanding or add richness and detail to the view of leadership. While this might be sufficient to explore qualities of leaders and followers in a leader- or follower-centric approach, when the focus is on actors viewed as intersections of multiple relationships, as in relational leadership, this technique falls short because it does not sufficiently capture issues of embeddedness and dynamic processes. Postpositivist scholars have tried to expand their tools to address this challenge (see Treadway et al. in Chapter 13). While much is to be gained by following this path, such methods do not question key assumptions that may be limiting in the entity perspective, and therefore may not push the envelope sufficiently.

In shifting from individual to relational views, the notion of context as foreground offers new insights. Intepretivist scholars have been thinking about this for a while, as this is their point of departure. In viewing context as foreground, it is understood that leadership and context cannot be separated. Alvesson & Sveningsson (Chapter 7) highlight the complexities associated with this interdependence: Leadership includes "multi-level phenomena." A key source of leadership is the cultural context, so "meanings, understandings, ideals, and norms...are intimately intertwined with it." This context "is not just given, but presumably interpreted by those involved—and possibly in different ways." In a sense, then, "the context not only forms an outside scene for the influencing process, but guides, frames, and actually produces the dispositions, attributions, and so forth." It is the job of the researcher to disentangle analytically what appears in reality as a unified experience for social actors. In so doing, analytical tools are used that do not contradict the assumption of relationality.

This holistic view might be hard to operationalize, but seriously considering it may offer new insights for finding innovative ways to approach context in the study of relational leadership. It is not a matter of advocating this over the "background" approach to context. The point is the importance of understanding the differences between the foreground and background approaches, and being aware of the limits and possibilities offered by each. In doing so, scholars can focus on trying to invent innovative and creative ways to address context in relational leadership.

CONCLUSION

This book represents a journey, for us personally, and for the field of leadership. Like most journeys, it has come with its own unique set of challenges and rewards. The biggest challenge occurred for us when we realized the objective we set for ourselves was much more "messy" than we had originally anticipated. Little did we know when we started this process the huge can of worms that was about to be unleashed. And, like all cans of worms, after it was opened, the challenge was what to do with the mess.

The issues became more complicated when our own strong paradigmatic assumptions and biases would draw us down into the tensions, limiting our ability to see the issues from a higher level. When this happened, we had to help each other climb out. It was in those climbs that we recognized the true power and potential of paradigm interplay. Paradigm interplay, both with each other and with the content provided by the authors, was the key tool that allowed us to proceed.

By training ourselves to become multilingual, and then engaging in respectful dialogue with one another, we were able to work our way through the interplays you see here. What paradigm interplay allowed us to do was take an analytical perspective on the issues and use the chapters as "empirical material" that provided the content for the analysis. Like all good analytical techniques, paradigm interplay brought with it new discoveries and insights. In every case, the interplay revealed something we hadn't seen from our own reading.

While we tried to represent the major issues, we were amazed and, at times, overwhelmed by the sheer magnitude of information and new ideas provided by the authors. Clearly, there is much more to be discovered. What we offer here is a start. Our hope is that others will continue this process by enriching their own work from the insights provided throughout this book.

We believe the dialogue undertaken in the chapters represents a significant step forward for leadership research. It brings to the forefront a tension that has been bubbling under the radar in leadership research for decades, but that has not been well recognized or understood (particularly in the U.S.): that of different paradigmatic perspectives on the meaning of relationality in leadership research. The voices heard throughout this volume, and the points they raise, are surprisingly clear: *It is time we take seriously the issues of relationality in leadership.*

Addressing relationality means that we must begin by acknowledging the co-constructed and contextual nature of leadership. We must no longer assume away issues of process and context in leadership research. And, we should no longer be satisfied with studies of *only* individuals as sufficient to inform us more generally about leadership; leadership involves both individual *and* collective elements. It is in taking seriously issues of relationality where we have the greatest opportunities to attain a deeper understanding of the social processes at the heart of this phenomenon we call *leadership*.

REFERENCES

Alvesson, M., & Deetz, S. (2000). *Doing critical management research.* London, England: Sage Publications.

Bedeian, A. G., & Hunt, J. G. (2006). Academic amnesia and vestigial assumptions of our forefathers. *The Leadership Quarterly, 17*(2), 190–205.

Bouwen, R. & Hosking, D. M. (2000). Reflections on relational readings of organizational learning. *European Journal of Work and Organizational Psychology, 9*(2), 267–274.

Bradbury, H., & Lichtenstein, B. (2000). Relationality in organizational research: Exploring the "space between." *Organization Science, 11*(5), 551–564.

Day, D. V. (2000). Leadership development: A review in context. *The Leadership Quarterly, 11,* 581–613.

Deetz, S. (1996). Describing differences in approaches to organization science: Rethinking Burrell and Morgan and their Legacy. *Organization Science, 7*(2), 191–207.

Drath, W. (2001). *The deep blue sea: Rethinking the source of leadership.* San Francisco, CA: Jossey-Bass.

Drath, W. H., McCauley, C. D., Palus, C. J., Van Velsor, E., O'Connor, P. M. G., & McGuire, J. B. (2008). Direction, alignment, commitment: Toward a more integrative ontology of leadership. *The Leadership Quarterly, 19*(6), 635–653.

Emirbayer, M. (1997). Manifesto for a relational sociology. *American Journal of Sociology, 103*(2), 281–317.

Fairhurst, G. (2007). *Discursive leadership: In conversation with leadership psychology.* Thousand Oaks, CA: Sage.

Fairhurst, G. (2009). Considering context in discursive leadership research. *Human relations, 62*(11), 1607–1633.

Fletcher, J. K. (1999). *Disappearing acts: Gender, power and relational practice at work.* Cambridge, MA: MIT Press.

Fletcher, J. K. (2004). The paradox of post heroic leadership: An essay on gender, power and transformational change. *The Leadership Quarterly, 15,* 647–661.

Gailliot, M. T., Mead, N. L. & Baumeister, R. F. (2008). Self-regulation. In O. P. John, R. W. Robins, & L. A. Pervin (Eds.), *Handbook of Personality: Theory and Research* (3rd ed., pp. 472–491). New York, NY: The Guilford Press.

Graen, G., & Uhl-Bien, M. (1995). Relationship-based approach to leadership: Development of leader-member exchange (LMX) theory of leadership over 25 years: Applying a multi-level multi-domain perspective. *The Leadership Quarterly, 6*(2), 219–247.

Hassard, J., & Kelemen, M. (2002). Production and consumption in organizational knowledge: The case of the 'paradigms debate.' *Organization, 9,* 331–355.

Heifetz, R. (1994) Leadership without easy answers. Cambridge, MA: Harvard University Press.

Hollander, E. P. (1978). *Leadership dynamics: A practical guide to effective relationships.* New York, NY: Free Press.

Hollander, E. P. (2009). *Inclusive leadership: The essential leader-follower relationship.* New York, NY: Routledge.

Hosking, D. M. (2007). Sound constructs: a relational discourse. *Revue Sciences de Gestion, 55,* 55–75.

Hosking, D. M., & Morley, I. E. (1988). The skills of leadership. In J. G. Hunt, B. R. Baliga, H. P. Dachler, & C. A. Schriesheim (Eds.), *Emerging leadership vistas* (pp. 80–106). Lexington, MA: Lexington Books/D. C. Heath and Co.

Hosking, D. M., & Morley, I. E. (1991). *A social psychology of organising.* Chichester, England: Harvester Wheatsheaf.

Lewis, M. W., & Kelemen, M. L. (2002). Multi-paradigm inquiry: Exploring organizational pluralism and paradox. *Human Relations, 55,* 251–275.

Liden, R. & Antonakis, J. (2009). Considering context in psychological leadership research. *Human relations, 62*(11), 1587–1605.

Miller, J. B. (1976). *Toward a new psychology of women.* Boston, MA: Beacon Press.

McCauley, C. D., Van Velsor, E., & Ruderman, M. N. (2010). Introduction: Our view of leadership development. In E. Van Velsor, C. D. McCauley, & M. N. Ruderman (Eds.), *The Center for Creative Leadership handbook of leadership development* (3rd ed., pp. 1–26). San Francisco, CA: Jossey-Bass.

Mohr, L. B. (1982). *Explaining organizational behavior.* San Francisco, CA: Jossey-Bass.

Orlikowski, W. J. (2002). Knowing in practice: Enacting a collective capability in distributed organizing. *Organization Science, 13*(4), 249–273.

Osborn, R. N., Hunt, J. G., & Jauch, L. R. (2002). Toward a contextual theory of leadership. *The Leadership Quarterly, 13,* 797–837.

Ospina, S.M., & Hittleman, M. (2011). "Thinking sociologically about leadership." In M. Harvey, & R. Riggio (Eds.), *Leadership studies: The dialogue of disciplines* (pp. 89–100). Cheltenham, England: Edward Elgar.

Ospina, S., & Foldy, E. (2010). Building bridges from the margins: The work of leadership in social change organizations. *The Leadership Quarterly, 21*(2), 292–307.

Ospina, S., & Sorensen, G. (2006). A constructionist lens on leadership: Charting new territory. In G. Goethals, & G. Sorenson (Eds.), *In quest of a general theory of leadership* (pp. 188–204). Cheltenham, England: Edward Elgar Publishers.

Patton, W. (2007). Connecting relational theory and the systems theory framework: Individuals and their systems. *Australian Journal of Career Development, 16*(3), 38–46.

Pearce, C. L., & Conger, J. A. (2003). *Shared leadership: Reframing the hows and whys of leadership.* Thousand Oaks, CA: Sage.

Robins, R. W., Tracy, J. L., & Trzesniewski, K. H. (2008). Naturalizing the self. In O. P. John, R. W. Robins, & L. A. Pervin (Eds.), *Handbook of personality: Theory and research* (3rd ed., pp. 421–447). New York, NY: The Guilford Press.

Romani, L. Primecz, H. & Topcu, K. (2011). Paradigm interplay for theory development: A methodological example with the Kulturstandard method. *Organizational Research Methods, 14,* 432–455.

Ross, H. (2002). The space between us: The relevance of relational theories to comparative and international education. *Comparative Education Review, 46*(4), 407–432.

Rost, J. C. (1991). *Leadership for the twenty-first century.* New York, NY: Praeger.

Schultz, M., & Hatch, M. J. (1996). Living with multiple paradigms: The case of paradigm interplay in organizational culture studies. *Academy of Management Review, 21,* 529–557.

Shamir, B. (2007). From passive recipients to active co-producers: Followers' roles in the leadership process. In B. Shamir, R., Pillai, M., Bligh, & M. Uhl-Bien (Eds), *Follower-centered perspectives on leadership: A tribute to J. R. Meindl* (pp. ix–xxxix). Greenwich, CT: Information Age Publishing.

Slife, B. D. (2004). Taking practice seriously: Toward a relational ontology. *Journal of Theoretical and Philosophical Psychology, 24*(2), 157–178.

Smircich, L., & Morgan, G. (1982). Leadership: The management of meaning. *Journal of Applied Behavioral Studies, 18,* 257–273.

Uhl-Bien, M. (2006). Relational leadership theory: Exploring the social processes of leadership and organizing. *The Leadership Quarterly, 17,* 654–676.

Weick, K. (1979). *The social psychology of organizing (2nd ed.).* Reading, MA: Addison-Wesley.

Wenger, E. (1998). *Communities of practice: Learning, meaning, and identity.* Cambridge, England: Cambridge University Press.

ABOUT THE CONTRIBUTORS

Mats Alvesson is Professor of Business Administration at the University of Lund, Sweden and at University of Queensland Business School, Australia. He is Honorary Professor at University of St. Andrews, and Visiting Professor at Exeter University. Research interests include critical theory, gender, power, management of professional service (knowledge intensive) organizations, leadership, identity, organizational image, organizational culture and symbolism, qualitative methods, and philosophy of science. Recent books include *Interpreting Interviews* (Sage, 2011), *Metaphors We Lead By: Understanding Leadership in the Real World* (Routledge, 2011, edited with Andre Spicer), *Oxford Handbook of Critical Management Studies* (Oxford University Press, edited with Todd Bridgman and Hugh Willmott), *Understanding Gender and Organizations* (Sage, 2009, 2nd edition, with Yvonne Billing), *Reflexive Methodology* (Sage, 2009, 2nd edition, with Kaj Skoldberg), *Changing Organizational Culture* (Routledge 2008, with Stefan Sveningsson), and *Knowledge Work and Knowledge-Intensive Firms* (Oxford University Press, 2004).

John Antonakis is Professor of Organizational Behavior in the Faculty of Business and Economics of the University of Lausanne, Switzerland. His research is currently focused on leadership measurement and development and research methods. He has published over 35 book chapters and articles in journals such as *Science, The Leadership Quarterly, Journal of Operations Management*, and *Human Relations, Personality and Individual Differences*, among others. He is co-editor of *The Nature of Leadership*, and *Being There Even When You Are Not*. Antonakis is Associate Editor of *The Leadership Quarterly*, and he is on the editorial boards of the *Academy of Management Review* and other top journals.

Advancing Relational Leadership Research, pages 581–589
Copyright © 2012 by Information Age Publishing
All rights of reproduction in any form reserved.

Neal M. Ashkanasy is Professor of Management in the UQ Business School at the University of Queensland. He earned his PhD in social and organizational psychology from the same university. His research focuses on the role of emotion in organizational life, as well as leadership, culture, and ethics. He has published his work in the *Academy of Management Journal*, the *Academy of Management Review*, and the *Journal of Management*. Professor Ashkanasy is Editor-in-Chief of the *Journal of Organizational Behavior*, Associate Editor for the *Academy of Management Review* and *Emotion Review*, and series editor for *Research on Emotion in Organizations*.

J. Kevin Barge is a Professor in the Department of Communication, Texas A&M University. His major research interests center on developing a communication approach to management and leadership, as well as exploring the relationship between discourse and public deliberation, specifically practices that facilitate communities working through polarized and polarizing issues. His research has been published in *The Academy of Management Review, Human Relations, Management Communication Quarterly, Communication Theory, Journal of Applied Communication Research*, and *Communication Monographs*.

Jacob W. Breland is an Assistant Professor of Management at Youngstown State University. He received his Ph.D. from the University of Mississippi and his MBA from the University of Southern Mississippi. His research interests include organizational politics and power, individual differences, organizational fit, and social networks. His research has been published in journals such as the *Journal of Management, Journal of Leadership and Organizational Studies, Journal of Management History*, and *Career Development International*.

John M. Bryson is McKnight Presidential Professor of Planning and Public Affairs at the Hubert H. Humphrey School of Public Affairs at the University of Minnesota. He works in the areas of leadership and strategic management. He wrote *Strategic Planning for Public and Nonprofit Organizations, 4th Edition* (Jossey-Bass, 2011), and co-wrote with Barbara C. Crosby *Leadership for the Common Good, 2nd Edition* (Jossey-Bass, 2005). Dr. Bryson is a Fellow of the National Academy of Public Administration and received the 2011 Dwight Waldo Award from the American Society for Public Administration for outstanding contributions to the professional literature of public administration over an extended scholarly career.

Suzette M. Chopin is a doctoral student in counseling psychology at Virginia Commonwealth University. She has an MA in English from George Washington University, an MBA from the University of New Orleans, and an MS in psychology from Virginia Commonwealth University. Her master's thesis was on the relationship between mentoring and both leadership self-efficacy and political skill.

Barbara C. Crosby is Associate Professor at the Humphrey School of Public Affairs, University of Minnesota, and a member of the school's Public and Nonprofit Leadership Center. Dr. Crosby has taught and written extensively about leadership and public policy, women in leadership, and strategic planning. She is the author of *Leadership for Global Citizenship* and co-author with John M. Bryson of *Leadership for the Common Good*. She formerly was academic co-director of the University of Minnesota's Center for Integrative Leadership and has conducted training for senior managers of nonprofit, business, and government organizations in the U.S., U.K., Poland, and Ukraine.

David V. Day is the Woodside Professor of Leadership and Management at the University of Western Australia Business School. Professor Day has core research interests in leadership and leadership development. He is the lead author on *An Integrative Approach to Leader Development: Connecting Adult Development, Identity and Expertise* (Routledge, 2009) and is the editor of *The Oxford Handbook of Leadership and Organizations* (2012). Professor Day serves as an Associate Editor for the *Journal of Applied Psychology* and serves as a Consulting Editor on several other journals. He is a Fellow of the American Psychological Association and the Society for Industrial and Organizational Psychology.

Jennifer Dodge is an Assistant Professor of Public Administration and Policy, Rockefeller College, SUNY Albany. Dr. Dodge is a Fellow of the Research Center for Leadership in Action at the Wagner School at New York University. Her research focuses on public and social change leadership; nonprofit organizations in public deliberation and democratic governance; and environmental politics. She has published articles in *Policy & Society, Public Administration Review, Critical Policy Studies,* and *Handbook of Action Research;* and has supported social change work in various organizations, including the Edna McConnell Clark Foundation, the U.S. State Department, and the NYC Research and Organizing Initiative.

Bill Drath is a retired Senior Fellow at the Center for Creative Leadership in Greensboro, NC. In his thirty years at CCL, Bill established the publications function, founded the periodical now known as *Leadership in Action,* helped develop the original version of the Looking Glass Experience program, and participated in developing the theory of leadership as a relational achievement. He has written numerous articles and book chapters and *The deep blue sea: Rethinking the source of leadership* (2001, Jossey-Bass). Bill has an A.B.

in literature from the University of Georgia and attended graduate school at the University of North Carolina.

Waad El Hadidy's work as a senior associate for the Research Center for Leadership in Action at New York University Robert F. Wagner Graduate School of Public Service, helps expand possibilities for understanding leadership. She has co-authored various book chapters and peer-reviewed articles. Prior to joining NYU, she lived in Egypt and worked as a practitioner in international development. She has held posts at the Near East Foundation, the European Delegation, and Booz-Allen & Hamilton. Waad holds an M.Phil. in Social Anthropology from the University of Cambridge in England and an MBA from Georgia State University. One of her emerging interests is how design can improve our lives and particularly how physical spaces can engender social relations.

Gail T. Fairhurst is a professor of communication at the University of Cincinnati, USA. Her research and writing interests are in organizational communication, leadership, organizational discourse analysis, framing, and identity. She has published over 60 chapters and articles in management and communication journals. She is the author of three books, including *The power of framing: Creating the language of leadership* (Jossey-Bass, 2011) and *Discursive leadership: In conversation with leadership psychology* (Sage, 2007). Her work has received numerous awards. She is also a Fellow of the International Communication Association, a Fulbright Scholar, and an Associate Editor for *Human Relations*.

Declan Fitzsimons is Adjunct Professor in Organizational Behaviour at IN-SEAD, France. He specializes in experiential Leadership Development and is an Organizational Development consultant based in London, UK. His teaching, consulting, and research focus on distributed leadership, unconscious processes in groups and organizations, experiential and action learning, and organizational change. During 10 years working in Eastern Europe and Russia, he developed expertise in the design and implementation of leadership development programs that integrate leadership and strategy in complex multi-stakeholder environments. He has contributed to open and in-company Leadership Development programs including the full time MBA programs at the Copenhagen Business School in Denmark, and at IMD in Switzerland.

Joyce K. Fletcher is a Distinguished Research Scholar, Center for Gender in Organizations, Simmons School of Management, Boston, Massachusetts. Professor Fletcher uses relational theory to study a wide range of workplace issues including leadership, organizational learning, and gender dynamics. She is a frequent speaker at national and international conferences on the topic of women, power, and leadership and is the co-author of a widely read *Harvard Business Review* article entitled: "A modest manifesto for shattering the glass ceiling." She is author of *Disappearing acts: Gender, power and relational practice at work* (MIT Press), a book that explores the subtle dynamics that often disappear women's leadership behavior at work, and co-author of *Beyond work family balance: Advancing gender equity and workplace performance* (Jossey Bass), a book about how to lead organizational change efforts to achieve the dual outcomes of equity and effectiveness.

Erica Gabrielle Foldy is an Associate Professor of Public and Nonprofit Management at the Robert F. Wagner Graduate School of Public Service at New York University and affiliated faculty with the Research Center for Leadership in Action and with the Center for Gender in Organizations at the Simmons School of Management in Boston. She received her Ph.D. in Organization Studies from Boston College. Published in a variety of journals and edited books, her research explores what enables and inhibits joint work and collective learning across potential divisions such as race, gender, and differences of opinion.

Amparo Hofmann-Pinilla is the deputy director of the Research Center for Leadership in Action (RCLA) at New York University's Robert F. Wagner Graduate School of Public Service. At RCLA, Amparo directs national and international research and evaluation projects which use action research as a tool for research and leadership development. Currently, Amparo is leading the Social Change Leadership Network, a program which offers leadership development and action research opportunities to social change leaders and organizations. She has co-authored various book chapters and peer-reviewed articles on social change leadership; the use of Participatory Action Research; and the role of universities in supporting social transformation. Amparo earned a LLB in Law from Universidad Externado de Colombia (Colombia, SA) and an MA and M. Phil. in Sociology from New York University.

Dian Marie Hosking, Ph.D., is a Professor in Relational Processes at Utrecht University School of Governance, Utrecht University, The Netherlands. She has published on the social psychology of leadership and organizing, critical relational constructionism, development and change; the Turku School of Economics awarded her an honorary DSc (Econ) for her constructionist work on leadership and organization theory. Her current interests focus on relations between relational constructionism, Buddhism, and the management and organization of end-of-life care. She is a member of the board, and advisor to, the Hospice de Liefde in Rotterdam.

Lynn Offermann is Professor of Industrial and Organizational Psychology in the Department of Organizational Sciences and Communication, and the Department of Management, George Washington University. Her research focuses on leadership and followership, teams, organizational processes and influence, and diversity issues. Dr. Offermann is a Fellow of the Society for Industrial and Organizational Psychology, the American Psychological Association, and the Association for Psychological Science, and her work has appeared in the *Journal of Applied Psychology, American Psychologist, Academy of Management Journal, Leadership Quarterly, Harvard Business Review, Journal of Cross Cultural Psychology, Human Performance, Journal of Applied Social Psychology,* and the *Journal of Occupational Health Psychology,* among other outlets.

Sonia M. Ospina is Professor of Public Management and Policy, New York University Robert F. Wagner Graduate School of Public Service and Faculty Director of the Research Center for Leadership in Action (RCLA). A sociologist by training, she applies organization and management theories to public problem solving and governance, both in the United States and Latin America. Her recent scholarly publications focus on leadership and social transformation, change in public management systems, and engaged scholarship. She is Co-editor of the *Journal of Public Administration Research and Theory,* and Book Review Co-editor of *Public Administration Review,* as well as a member of several journals' editorial boards, including some in Brazil, Colombia and Chile.

Neil Paulsen is Senior Lecturer in Management, UQ Business School, University of Queensland, Australia. Dr. Paulsen's research includes intergroup perspectives in organizational behavior, leadership, and innovation. Current projects explore the role of leadership and professional identity in organizational culture change, team identification in clinical networks, and innovation in teams. He serves on the editorial board of *Journal of Organizational Behavior,* and has published his work in journals including *Personality & Social Psychology Bulletin, Human Relations, Management Communication Quarterly,* and *Journal of Applied Communication Research.* He is co-editor with Professor Tor Hernes of *Managing Boundaries in Organizations: Multiple Perspectives* (Palgrave MacMillan).

Craig L. Pearce, Ph.D., is Dean of the School of Business and Entrepreneurship at the American University of Nigeria. He has pioneered the development of shared leadership theory and practice. His work is widely cited and has been featured in the *Wall Street Journal.* His book, *Shared leadership,* is published by Sage Publications. His most recent book, *The Drucker difference,* is published by McGraw-Hill and is translated into 10 languages. His forthcoming book, *Share the lead*, will be published by Stanford University Press. He is an active keynote speaker and consultant to organizations.

Anson Seers is Professor of Management at Virginia Commonwealth University. He has published widely cited research on topics pertaining to work roles and working relationships, including team-member exchange, leader-member exchange, emergent leadership, as well as role conflict and role ambiguity. Dr. Seers is an elected member of the Society for Organizational Behavior, and is a Fellow and former President of the Southern Management Association. He has served on several journal editorial boards and is an active member of the Academy of Management, the American Psychological Association, and the Society for Industrial and Organizational Psychology.

Boas Shamir is Professor in the Department of Sociology and Anthropology, Hebrew University of Jerusalem, and Visiting Professor, Stern School of Business, New York University. He received his Ph.D. in social psychology from the London School of Economics and Political Sciences. He is a member of the editorial boards of the *Academy of Management Review, The Leadership Quarterly,* and *Leadership* and has published numerous articles on leadership in these journals and others. His current research interests include leaders' life stories, leadership and the management of meanings, leadership and power, and the role of followers in the leadership process.

Celina Su is Associate Professor of Political Science at Brooklyn College, City University of New York. Her work looks at civic engagement, civil society, and the cultural politics of education and health policy. She is the author of *Streetwise for book smarts: Grassroots organizing and education policy in the Bronx* (Cornell University Press) and co-author of *Our schools suck: Young people talk back to a segregated nation on the failure of urban education* (NYU Press). She is the co-founding Program Officer for the Burmese Refugee Project, an organization focused on participatory community development among Shan refugees living in Thailand.

Stefan Sveningsson is Associate Professor of Business Administration at the School of Economics and Management, Lund University, Sweden. Research interests include leadership, identity, strategic and organizational change, as well as management of knowledge intensive firms. He has published about leadership in several international journals including *Human Relations, Leadership Quarterly, Organization Studies, International Studies of Management and Organization,* and *Leadership*. Recent books include *Changing Organizational Culture* (Routledge 2008, with M. Alvesson) and *Leadership* (Liber, 2010 with M. Alvesson).

Eugene (Yu Jin) Tee completed his Ph.D. at the University of Queensland, Business School in 2010 in the field of Management. He is presently lecturer at the Department of Psychology at HELP University College, Kuala Lumpur, Malaysia. Eugene's research interests revolve around emotions and their impact on both team and leadership contexts, and the role of emotions in social identity theory. His research focuses specifically on the role of emotional contagion processes and its influences across organizational levels. Email: teeyj@help.edu.my

The New Zealand Leadership Institute (NZLI) is a research and development center within The University of Auckland Business School. Its primary purpose is to advance critical thinking and understanding of leadership and leadership development through its programs. A feature of our work is empirical data that are generated through the development process. The NZLI faculty are both researchers and facilitators of the leadership development programs. **Brigid Carroll** is Principal Researcher at NZLI and a senior lecturer in Management and International Business at the University of Auckland. **Joline Francoeur** is Director of Leadership Programs and foundation faculty of NZLI. **Fiona Kennedy** is a leadership facilitator and researcher at NZLI. **Brad Jackson** is the Fletcher Building Employee Education Trust Chair in Leadership.

Darren C. Treadway is an Associate Professor of Organization and Human Resources at the State University of New York at Buffalo. He received a Ph.D. from Florida State University (2003) and an MBA from Virginia Tech (1996). Dr. Treadway's research interests include social influence processes in organizations, with particular reference to organizational politics, political skill, and leadership.

Mary Uhl-Bien is Professor and Howard Hawks Chair in Business Ethics and Leadership at the University of Nebraska. Her current research interests include complexity leadership, relational leadership, and followership. She is senior editor of the Leadership Horizons series for Information Age Publishers, and has served on the editorial boards of the *Academy of Management Journal, Academy of Management Review, The Leadership Quarterly, Leadership,* and *International Journal of* Complexity *in Leadership and Management.* Her recent books include *The Sage handbook of leadership* (Sage, 2011), *Complexity leadership* (Information Age, 2008) and *Follower-centered perspectives on leadership: A tribute to the memory of James R. Meindl* (Information Age, 2007).

Christina L. Wassenaar is a Ph.D. candidate at the Peter F. Drucker and Masatoshi Ito Graduate School of Management, Claremont Graduate University, and a Lecturer at the American University of Nigeria. Her research and writing include publications on the topics of shared leadership, virtual groups, and management/leadership history. She served as the Academic Director and Director of Executive Programs at the Drucker School, and her professional career outside of academia includes 11 years of experience in the consumer packaged goods and entertainment industries. She has held various positions in Marketing, Market Research/Category Management, Business Development, and Project Management, and has worked or consulted for Johnson & Johnson, MGM, Con Agra, Pacific Bell (now Verizon), and ACNielsen. She is also actively consulting in the private sector in various industries, as well as for several academic institutions in the areas of strategic planning, accreditation, marketing/branding, and organizational change.

Laura A. Williams is an Assistant Professor of Management at Lipscomb University in Nashville, TN. She earned her Ph.D. in Organizational Behavior at the University of Mississippi. Her research focuses on the antecedents and consequences of occupational stress, work-family conflict, and proactive employee behaviors. Her work has appeared in the *Journal of Applied Social Psychology, Social Networks, Journal of Applied Management and Entrepreneurship*, and in Graen and Graen's LMX Leadership book series, *Knowledge-driven corporation: A discontinuous model.*

Lisa V. Williams is an Assistant Professor of Management at Niagara University. She received a Ph.D. from The State University of New York at Buffalo School of Management. Dr. Williams' research addresses the development of interpersonal trust in organizations from several perspectives: individual differences (e.g., intelligence, political skill, self-monitoring) that affect interpersonal dyadic trust, and situational factors such as emotion and incentives that affect anonymous interpersonal trust decisions.

Jun Yang is a Ph.D. candidate in Organization and Human Resource at the State University of New York at Buffalo. Jun's research addresses social influence and social identity processes in interpersonal relationships, with particular reference to political skill, stress, justice, and culture. A key focus of her research is to understand how employees' social standing and relational capital interact with their political skill in affecting performance-rated outcomes. In addition, her interest in social influence process has focused on workplace stress and how political skill impacts employees' coping strategies. These stressful work environments range from work-family conflict, to victimization at work, to bullying behaviors. Further, she has co-authored research that investigated the role of national culture on justice in the workplace and the impact of justice on employee stress.

CPSIA information can be obtained at www.ICGtesting.com
Printed in the USA
BVOW041651041012

302193BV00002B/2/P